VBA Developer's Handbook

VBA Developer's Handbook™

Ken Getz
Mike Gilbert

SYBEX

San Francisco • Paris • Düsseldorf • Soest

Associate Publisher: Amy Romanoff
Acquisitions Manager: Kristine Plachy
Acquisitions & Developmental Editor: Melanie Spiller
Editor: Dusty Bernard
Project Editor: Shelby Zimmerman
Technical Editor: David Shank
Book Designer: Patrick Dintino, Catalin Dulfu
Graphic Illustrator: Inbar Berman
Electronic Publishing Specialist: Debi Bevilacqua
Production Coordinator: Amy Eoff
Indexer: Matthew Spence
Cover Designer: Design Site
Cover Photographer: Color Photograph: The Image Bank

Library of Congress Card Number: 97-65126
ISBN: 0-7821-1951-4

Manufactured in the United States of America

10 9 8 7 6 5 4 3 2 1

Software License Agreement:
Terms and Conditions

The media and/or any online materials accompanying this book that are available now or in the future contain programs and/or text files (the "Software") to be used in connection with the book. SYBEX hereby grants to you a license to use the Software, subject to the terms that follow. Your purchase, acceptance, or use of the Software will constitute your acceptance of such terms.

The Software compilation is the property of SYBEX unless otherwise indicated and is protected by copyright to SYBEX or other copyright owner(s) as indicated in the media files (the "Owner(s)"). You are hereby granted a single-user license to use the Software for your personal, noncommercial use only. You may not reproduce, sell, distribute, publish, circulate, or commercially exploit the Software, or any portion thereof, without the written consent of SYBEX and the specific copyright owner(s) of any component software included on this media.

In the event that the Software or components include specific license requirements or end-user agreements, statements of condition, disclaimers, limitations or warranties ("End-User License"), those End-User Licenses supersede the terms and conditions herein as to that particular Software component. Your purchase, acceptance, or use of the Software will constitute your acceptance of such End-User Licenses.

By purchase, use or acceptance of the Software you further agree to comply with all export laws and regulations of the United States as such laws and regulations may exist from time to time.

Software Support

Components of the supplemental Software and any offers associated with them may be supported by the specific Owner(s) of that material but they are not supported by SYBEX. Information regarding any available support may be obtained from the Owner(s) using the information provided in the appropriate read.me files or listed elsewhere on the media.

Should the manufacturer(s) or other Owner(s) cease to offer support or decline to honor any offer, SYBEX bears no responsibility. This notice concerning support for the Software is provided for your information only. SYBEX is not the agent or principal of the Owner(s), and SYBEX is in no way responsible for providing any support for the Software, nor is it liable or responsible for any support provided, or not provided, by the Owner(s).

Warranty

SYBEX warrants the enclosed media to be free of physical defects for a period of ninety (90) days after purchase. The Software is not available from SYBEX in any other form or media than that enclosed herein or posted to *www.sybex.com*. If you discover a defect in the media during this warranty period, you may obtain a replacement of identical format at no charge by sending the defective media, postage prepaid, with proof of purchase to:

SYBEX Inc.
Customer Service Department
1151 Marina Village Parkway
Alameda, CA 94501
(510) 523-8233
Fax: (510) 523-2373
e-mail: info@sybex.com
WEB: HTTP://WWW.SYBEX.COM

After the 90-day period, you can obtain replacement media of identical format by sending us the defective disk, proof of purchase, and a check or money order for $10, payable to SYBEX.

Disclaimer

SYBEX makes no warranty or representation, either expressed or implied, with respect to the Software or its contents, quality, performance, merchantability, or fitness for a particular purpose. In no event will SYBEX, its distributors, or dealers be liable to you or any other party for direct, indirect, special, incidental, consequential, or other damages arising out of the use of or inability to use the Software or its contents even if advised of the possibility of such damage. In the event that the Software includes an online update feature, SYBEX further disclaims any obligation to provide this feature for any specific duration other than the initial posting.

The exclusion of implied warranties is not permitted by some states. Therefore, the above exclusion may not apply to you. This warranty provides you with specific legal rights; there may be other rights that you may have that vary from state to state. The pricing of the book with the Software by SYBEX reflects the allocation of risk and limitations on liability contained in this agreement of Terms and Conditions.

Shareware Distribution

This Software may contain various programs that are distributed as shareware. Copyright laws apply to both shareware and ordinary commercial software, and the copyright Owner(s) retains all rights. If you try a shareware program and continue using it, you are expected to register it. Individual programs differ on details of trial periods, registration, and payment. Please observe the requirements stated in appropriate files.

Copy Protection

The Software in whole or in part may or may not be copy-protected or encrypted. However, in all cases, reselling or redistributing these files without authorization is expressly forbidden except as specifically provided for by the Owner(s) therein.

To Drs. Paul Bamberg and Harry Leitner, of Harvard University's Extension program, who started me off on this amusing chapter of my life. Also, to Joan Weinstein, one of my first students, who (if nothing else) made sure I really knew what I was talking about.
—K.N.G.

To my parents, Robert and Donna Johnson, who provided me with the most important development tools—those for life. Also, to Robert and Rick Sterrett, for being the role models every young man needs.
—M.T.G.

ACKNOWLEDGMENTS

As with any book, this one wouldn't have been possible without the contributions of many people besides the authors. First of all, we'd like to thank our tireless editor, Dusty Bernard, who, even on the third pass through the material, can pinpoint details to make our words appear as though we actually know how to write. Along with other books we've written, Dusty has now plowed through greater than 5000 pages of our writing, and she deserves some kind of award for just getting through all that writing, not to mention for making it readable!

We'd also like to pay special tribute to our technical editor, David Shank. His eye for detail is unsurpassed, and in the course of reviewing this book, he provided innumerable comments that measurably improved the content and examples. This is our second book with David (he also worked his way through *Access 97 Developer's Handbook*) and, given the choice, we'd work with him on any and every future project. David currently works on developer documentation at Microsoft, contributed to the Access 97 documentation, and worked on the Access 95 and 97 sample applications.

Of course, no book can make it to the shelves without the publisher. At Sybex, Shelby Zimmerman, our production editor, did extraordinary work managing our ever-changing schedule. We'd also like to acknowledge the work of our developmental editor, Melanie Spiller. Melanie's job was to keep us happy, inspired, producing, and on schedule. She's been a friend, a confidant, and a teacher, all rolled into one. Certainly, this book could never have happened without her involvement.

Thanks to Dan Haught, of FMS, Inc., who originally prepared an outline for a book similar to this one and then decided to go a different route: his company created the *Total Access SourceBook*, a source code library for Microsoft Access, which includes material that parallels the topics covered in this book. Dan kindly provided us with his detailed outline, from which we began the process of writing the book. (For more information on FMS, Inc., and their products, visit their Web site at www.fmsinc.com.) Thanks also to Luke Chung, of FMS, Inc., who provided us with documentation and examples, involving numeric rounding and calculation errors, that were helpful in the creation of Chapter 3.

We'd also like to thank Mary Chipman, a senior consultant with MCW Technologies, and Andy Baron, president of Key Data Systems. They both dug through the VBA issues surrounding numeric operations and provided most of the material in Chapter 3 of the book.

Michael Kaplan, of Trigeminal Software, Inc., crafted Chapter 11 for us. This chapter, covering the issues involved in working with networks programmatically, was greatly enhanced by Michael's contributions, based on his research and experience with networks and network management.

We'd also like to thank those experts who provided us with suggestions, ideas for chapter topics, and code review, including Jim Ferguson, Mike Gunderloy, and Brian Randell. Malcolm Stewart, of Microsoft's Access support group, provided the NEATCODE.MDB sample database, from which we began much of our research into the various programming topics. In addition, we'd like to thank the entire Internet Platform & Tools Marketing group at Microsoft, including Michael Risse, David Lazar, Scott Horn, Robert Green, and of course, Neil Charney, who wrote the foreword for this book. These folks were instrumental in our getting the information and contacts we needed to write this book. We'd like to thank Craig Symonds, Visual Basic Group Program Manager at Microsoft, who graciously provided us with the interview included in the book's Introduction. Finally, Greg Reddick and Paul Litwin deserve special thanks. Paul not only provided ideas and spiritual and moral support, he also graciously granted permission for us to use some of the work he did for our sister book, *Access 97 Developer's Handbook*. Greg laboriously updated his naming conventions for Office 97 and VBA, and we've included this document as Appendix A.

Special thanks also go to Mickey Friedman and the staff at Pinnacle Publishing, for graciously allowing us to excerpt and revise specific code examples, and some text, that we had previously published in *Smart Access* (the newsletter from Pinnacle Publishing, written for developers creating solutions using Microsoft Access).

Kudos are also in order for the crew of the Parkside Starbucks in Richmond, Virginia, where a good portion of this book was written. These folks unknowingly played a key role in this book's development by providing a never-ending supply of coffee and lattes along with hours of rent-free counter space. (Now, if we can just persuade them to install an electrical outlet....)

Most of all, we'd like to thank Karen Jaskolka and Peter Mason, without whom this (or any of our other books) wouldn't have been possible. Their unending support, good nature, and willingness to entertain themselves on their own has made our writing, and this book, possible.

ABOUT THE AUTHORS

Ken Getz

Ken Getz is a senior consultant with MCW Technologies, focusing on the Microsoft suite of products. He has received Microsoft's MVP award (for providing technical support on CompuServe) for the years 1993 through 1996 and has co-written several books on developing applications using Microsoft Access, including the best-selling *Microsoft Access 2 Developer's Handbook* and the Access 95 and 97 editions of that book. Ken is also a contributing editor to *Smart Access* and a frequent contributor to other developer publications. Currently, Ken spends a great deal of time traveling around the country for Application Developer's Training Company, presenting training classes for Access and Visual Basic developers. He also speaks at many conferences and shows throughout the world, including Tech*Ed, Advisor Publication's DevCon, Windows Solutions, and Access and VB Teach. When taking a break from the computer, he turns the chair around and handles another keyboard: the grand piano that fills the other half of his office. You can reach Ken on the Internet at keng@mcwtech.com.

Mike Gilbert

Mike Gilbert is a senior consultant with MCW Technologies, specializing in application development using Microsoft Access, Visual Basic, SQL Server, and Microsoft Office. He has worked with Microsoft on numerous ventures, including the Workgroup Templates, Office Developer's Kit, and DevCast. He writes for several periodicals and is a contributing editor to *Smart Access* and *Access/Visual Basic Advisor*. Mike was co-author of *Microsoft Access 95 Developer's Handbook* and *Access 97 Developer's Handbook*. He is a trainer with Application Developer's Training Company and a regular speaker at conferences such as Tech*Ed, Advisor Publication's DevCon, and VB Teach. He spends what spare time he has enjoying the quiet, Southern life in Richmond, Virginia, with his wife Karen and their two cats, Chicago and Cairo. You can reach Mike on the Internet at mikeg2@mcwtech.com.

CONTENTS AT A GLANCE

TABLE OF CONTENTS

Chapter 6: Creating Dynamic Data Structures Using Class Modules

Appendix B: Accessing DLLs and the Windows API   845

FOREWORD

Immature artists imitate. Mature artists steal.

—Lionel Trilling

Good development starts with stolen code. Okay, so it's not really about stealing—it's about "leveraging" solid code, allowing you to develop powerful solutions quickly. That's part of the reason Microsoft Office has become one of the most popular development platforms in the world: you can leverage any of the over 500 prebuilt, pretested objects exposed by Microsoft Office 97.

As a developer, I don't want to have to write a charting application from the ground up. And with Microsoft Excel, I don't have to. Need a corporate calendar or contact management system? You can customize Microsoft Outlook and reuse the scheduling, contact management, and task management functionality built right into the product.

Luckily, it isn't very difficult to appropriate the functionality of Microsoft Office into your custom applications; you can do so by taking advantage of the Office programming language, Visual Basic for Applications (VBA). VBA is now available throughout Microsoft Office, and it's the same VBA found in Visual Basic 5.0. Now that Microsoft licenses Visual Basic for Applications, the same routines you develop for (or leverage from) one solution can now be applied to hundreds of third-party applications that license the VBA technology.

So, prebuilt objects are everywhere, and you've got a consistent development environment and a single cross-application programming language; life for the developer is pretty good. Well, this book makes life even better. Code reuse doesn't apply simply to complete applications, it applies to routines written in VBA. In this book, Ken Getz and Mike Gilbert provide well written, highly professional, and exceedingly applicable routines that are immediately reusable in any VBA application.

Need a bulletproof error handler? Looking for an elegant routine for manipulating and converting date and time values? Searching for the perfect string manipulation routine? Sure, you could continue to create those yourself. (And really, don't we all just love writing and rewriting those routines?) I'm happy to tell you that you no longer have to build these essential building blocks of any application from scratch. By purchasing this book, you can ensure that the applications you create will be built on the most solid of foundations.

What Ken Getz and Mike Gilbert have delivered in this book is what I consider to be the "Office" of VBA resources—a rich set of fully tested prebuilt tools and methodologies that you can immediately reuse in your own custom applications. Best of all, the code and tips from this book will work not only in all the Microsoft Office applications, but also in any of the applications hosting Visual Basic for Applications. So, if you're a Visual Basic developer, an Office Developer, a Visio developer, or an AutoDesk developer, you're a VBA developer, and you want this book. (My only concern is that with Office 97, VBA licensing, and the prebuilt code found in this book and on the accompanying CD, developers will have too much time on their hands. This could possibly lead to packs of developers roaming loose, just looking for trouble.)

Of course, just because prebuilt objects and code make the development process *easier,* that doesn't make you a good developer. For that, this handbook is essential. It provides the methodology and approach to writing professional code that, in addition to enabling you to create your solutions faster, will ensure that you've also used the most effective, efficient, and solid code.

By building on the routines and development principles found in this book, you can be sure you're leveraging from two of the finest developers I've ever had the pleasure of working with. And the greatest thing about it is that they don't even seem to mind that you'll be "leveraging" their code!

—Neil Charney

Product Manager

Office 97, Developer Edition

INTRODUCTION

Visual Basic for Applications (VBA) started its life as a tool that would allow Excel, and then other Microsoft Office applications, to control their own environment programmatically and that would work with other applications using OLE Automation. In 1996, the VBA world exploded when Microsoft allowed other vendors to license the VBA language engine and environment for their own products. At the time of this writing, over 40 vendors have licensed this exciting technology, making it possible for users of many products to control their applications, and any Automation server, using VBA.

The best part about all this for the VBA developer is that the skills you learn in one product will carry directly to any other VBA host. The programming environment is the same, the debugging tools are the same, and the language is the same. Finally, Basic programmers (after all, VBA is still a variant on the original BASIC language) are getting some respect: using tools that end-users can appreciate and work with, you can write applications that they can live with, modify, and extend.

About the Book

VBA has become the glue that ties together the various pieces of multiplatform solutions, and many new programmers are being tossed into situations in which they need programming help. In this book, you'll find creative solutions to many programming problems, including (but certainly not limited to):

- Parsing a string (Chapter 1)
- Reading a value from the Registry (Chapter 10)
- Sorting an array (Chapter 4)
- Finding out what kind of processor your computer includes (Chapter 9)
- Creating a new network share (Chapter 11)
- Playing a movie from within an application (Chapter 13)
- Trapping and handling application errors (Chapter 7)

- Calculating the greatest common factor between two numbers (Chapter 3)

- Writing code that can modify existing code (Chapter 8)

Is this book a replacement for the VBA programmer's reference manuals? Not even close! Nor does it intend to provide you with a complete reference. This book is about ideas, about solutions, and about learning. We've taken our combined years of Basic programming, come up with a list of topics that we think are interesting and that provide challenges to many developers, and created a book that, we hope, collates all the information in useful and interesting ways.

First and foremost, this book is *not* product specific. That is, whether you're using Microsoft Office 97 or any other product that hosts VBA 5.0 or later, you'll be able to take advantage of the code in this book. Because we've provided the code in three formats (as Microsoft Access 97 databases, Microsoft Excel 97 workbooks, and as separate text files), anyone who has a CD-ROM reader can immediately make use of this code. We'll say it again: although we used Office 97 in developing this book, *the code provided here should work in any product that hosts VBA.*

For these reasons, we've focused on code, not the user interface, so you'll find very few examples in the book that actually *look* like anything much. For the most part, the examples involve calling code from the Immediate window. Don't expect lots of pretty examples, with forms you can dig into—that wasn't our goal at all. We've provided the tools; now *you* provide the spiffy interface!

NOTE What about Visual Basic 5.0, you ask? VB5 uses a variant of VBA that includes more features than any other VBA host. To make the code in this book usable for the masses of programmers using the version of VBA that's in Office 97 and that has been licensed to many outside vendors, we pay only lip service to the new version of Visual Basic. That is, if there's a limitation in VBA 5.0 that's been lifted for VB5, we mention it in the text. Otherwise, all the code presented here works fine in VB5, although there may be a more expeditious way to solve the same problem using the new features in VB5.

Our goal in writing this book was both to provide useful code and to explain that code so you can modify and extend it if you need to add more or different functionality. We've covered a broad range of topics but haven't even made an attempt to be the absolute final word on these, or any topic. Doing so would require a book ten times the size of this one; no, this book is meant as a starting place for explorations into new topics, in addition to providing a ton of useful code.

Is This Book for You?

This book is aimed squarely at the legions of developers, both new to and experienced with VBA development, who need help with specific coding situations. But if you're looking for a description of how the If...Then construct works or for someone to hold your hand while you write your first VBA procedure, then perhaps this isn't the right book for you. On the other hand, if you want to work through a great deal of code, copy and paste code and complete modules from our samples directly into your applications, and work through the code line by line, you've come to the right place.

This book will appeal to three separate audiences:

- **VBA beginner to intermediate:** You've written a few procedures and are trying to put together an application. You need help writing specific procedures; stopping to figure out the code on your own would be an insurmountable task. You can copy and paste code from the book right into your modules, skip the boring part where we describe how the code works, and get back to working on your application.

- **VBA advanced:** You've written a lot of code and are facing more and greater coding challenges. You need specific procedures written and could do it yourself, but there are other pressing needs (like getting the application finished yesterday). You can take the routines from this book, modify them to exactly meet your needs, and work through the explanations provided here to add to your working knowledge about the usage of VBA.

- **VBA expert:** Even if you're among the most experienced of VBA programmers, there are some procedures you'll need and just haven't written yourself. You can take the code provided here as a starting point and embellish and fine-tune to your heart's content. Of course, you may find a better way to rewrite the code we've provided, and if so, we'd love to hear from you!

If you find yourself in any one of these three categories, have we got some code for you!

What You Need to Know

To make it possible to stuff as much code as possible into this book, we've had to dispense with material specifically geared for beginners. If you're not sure, in VBA, where to put the code, how to create a module, or even what the different variable types are, perhaps you'd do best to put this book aside for a week or so and study the reference materials provided with the VBA host you're working with. Make sure you have a good grasp of the following topics before jumping into this book:

- Creating modules
- Creating procedures
- Variables and their datatypes
- VBA syntax (including If…Then, For…Next, and other control structures)

If you take the time to review these concepts before delving into this book, you'll get a great deal more out of the material here.

Conventions Used in the Book

Having worked on a number of projects together, we've found that a consistent style and defined conventions make it much simpler for multiple programmers to work together on a project. To make it easier for you to understand our code (and for us to understand each other's), we've adopted a naming standard, which we've stuck to both throughout this book and in all our professional work.

We've used version 4.0 of the Reddick VBA (RVBA) naming conventions for the naming of objects, which have been accepted by many Access and VBA developers as the naming standard to follow. Greg Reddick, a noted Access and Visual Basic developer and trainer, developed the standard, which bears his name. Even if you don't subscribe to the RVBA standard, you'll likely appreciate the fact that it has been consistently used throughout this book. These conventions, which were first published in *Smart Access*, are included in their entirety in Appendix A.

In addition to following the RVBA standard, we've prefaced all public functions, subroutines, and user-defined types that you may wish to use for your own code with the "dh" prefix (which stands for *Developer's Handbook*), aliased all public Windows API declarations using a "dh_api" prefix, and prefixed all global constants with "dhc". These conventions should avoid naming conflicts with any existing code in your applications. If, however, you import multiple modules from various chapters' samples into a single application, you may find naming conflicts as a result of our using consistent naming throughout the chapters. In that case, you'll need to comment out any conflicting API declarations or user-defined types.

A note about error handling: when writing utility procedures, such as those found in this book, it's always a toss-up whether to include extensive error handling. We decided, both for the sake of simplicity and because we both hate using service routines that display error messages, to include very little error handling, except in cases where the procedures need it for their own use. This means that your code, calling our procedures, will need to trap and handle errors that bubble up from the code provided here. Of course, if you'd rather, you can simply add your own error handling to the procedures you import. (For more information on using error handling, see Chapter 7.)

Chapter Descriptions

This book is divided into three informal sections, as described below. Every chapter includes many examples, all of which (except the most trivial) are included in the samples for the chapter on the CD-ROM that accompanies this book.

Using the Built-In VBA Functionality

Chapters 1 through 4 each touch on one area of the built-in VBA functionality. Each chapter starts out discussing the built-in features of VBA and then expands on these with custom VBA procedures. Chapter 1 focuses on string manipulation, including string parsing. Chapter 2 discusses everything you ever wanted to know about dates (except how to get one). Chapter 3 covers the numeric data types, working with data conversions, and other numerical analyses. Chapter 4, finally, gives the array structure a real workout, covering searching and sorting in great detail.

Advanced Usage of VBA

The second section of the book focuses on more advanced VBA topics. Chapter 5 introduces class modules and their use in VBA solutions. We hope that, once you've worked through this chapter, you'll be convinced (as we are) that class modules are the key to writing solid, reusable VBA code. Chapter 6 takes a side road into the VBA fringes, discussing the usage of class modules to create data structures most VBA programmers assumed were impossible—linked lists, binary trees, stacks, and queues. Chapter 7 focuses on writing bulletproof, well-tuned VBA applications, including handling errors, creating event logs, and the creation of a procedure-tracking stack for your applications. Finally, Chapter 8 exposes one of VBA's most exciting features (next to the inclusion of class modules, of course): its ability to function as an Automation server. Using the material presented in this chapter, you'll be able to create and modify code, write add-ins, and investigate and document your code.

Using the Windows API to Extend VBA

The final third of the book discusses many ways to use the Windows API to accomplish tasks that VBA itself can't handle. Chapter 9 provides a series of nine class modules (a complete coincidence) that provide, and often allow you to set, information about the current software and hardware environment. Chapter 10 digs deep into the System Registry, providing a series of class modules that wrap up all the gory details involved in writing the code yourself. Chapter 11 provides information on working with a network: creating shares, choosing devices, and working with users. Chapter 12 digs into the API functions that handle disks and drives and provides a series of functions that allow you to work with, and investigate, your computer's file system. Finally, Chapter 13 rounds out the book by investigating multimedia, including the use of sound, movies, and bitmaps in your applications.

Using the Chapter Samples

Each of the chapters in the book corresponds to a folder on the included CD-ROM. In each folder, you'll find all the example files used in the book. We've provided each chapter's examples in at least three formats. First, each chapter's folder includes a Microsoft Excel 97 workbook containing all the modules discussed in the chapter, ready for you to experiment with. In addition, we've provided each module as a separate BAS or CLS file, so you can import these into your projects, in whatever VBA host you're using. Finally, to make it simpler for Microsoft Access developers, we've created one database file for each of the chapters, with all the modules imported for you.

In addition to the chapter samples, we're in the process of gathering useful demos and tools to include on the CD as well. Look for the file README.TXT in the CD's root directory for late-breaking information on the final contents of the CD.

TIP

> Because of the way CD-ROM software creates the CD, all the files on the CD are marked with a read-only flag. When you copy files to your hard disk, depending on the manner in which you copy them, you may need to use Windows Explorer (or any other method you like) to remove the read-only attribute. To do this in Explorer, right-click the file or files, choose Properties from the drop-down menu, and then deselect the Read Only attribute.

How to Use This Book

We can think of two ways in which you might want to use this book. You may just want to start at the beginning and plow straight through until you've reached the other side. That's fine, but keep some sticky notes near at hand so you can mark interesting code as it goes by. Otherwise, you'll never remember where all the fun stuff was.

More likely, however, you'll peruse this Introduction, browse through a few chapters, and then use the book as a reference when you need it. That's fine, too. Just do us two favors:

- If you're not comfortable with class modules, work your way through Chapter 5, at least, to find out how they work and what they bring to the VBA "party."

- If you've never used Windows API calls, be sure to visit Appendix B. This appendix introduces ways in which the Windows API can contribute to your programming efforts and explains how to use this valuable technique.

Both of these topics are crucial to a complete understanding of much of the rest of the book, and attempting to work through the remaining chapters without an understanding of at least these prerequisites will make for a steep climb.

The remainder of this Introduction consists of an interview between co-author Ken Getz and Craig Symonds, currently Visual Basic Group Product Manager at Microsoft. This conversation gives some insight into the history of VBA, where it's going from here, and some of the details buried in the implementation.

What Is This VBA Thing, Anyway? (An Interview with Someone Who Knows)

During the summer of 1996, Ken contacted Craig Symonds at Microsoft, and they arranged to meet for a short interview. The following is an edited transcript of their meeting, which delves into some of the history, future, and present details of Visual Basic for Applications (VBA).

Ken: This is Ken Getz, sitting with Craig Symonds, in his office in rainy Redmond. Craig, what exactly is your title?

Craig: I am the Group Program Manager for the Visual Basic group, which includes VB, VBA, and Visual Basic Scripting.

Ken: And how long have you been with this group?

Craig: Five years, same group.

VBA's Past

Ken: Let's start out easy: What's the history of VBA? How did we get where we are?

Craig: It started several years ago. There was a precursor product to VBA, called Embedded Basic, which was used in the first and second versions of Access and in the first three versions of Visual Basic. It actually had ties to the DOS versions of Basic. We took some of the implementations of the DOS versions of Basic and converted them to Windows.

Ken: So was code shared between Access and VB at any point?

Craig: Yes, the entire language engine was completely shared. There were some extensions to the Embedded Basic product for Access, and one of the things that we took on for the development of VBA was to make sure we had a single, shared technology that wasn't special-cased. In 1990, we started a project called Object Basic, which was the original name for Visual Basic for Applications. We started a small team to put together the next version of Basic, a somewhat object-oriented version of Basic. Its primary goals would be to have fast execution speed, to be portable to multiple platforms, and to modernize the technology that it was built upon. And in 1993, we shipped the first version, as part of Excel 5.

Ken: So what happened to the rumors that VBA, or some Basic-based scripting, would be part of the operating system itself?

Craig: In every version, we look at the feasibility of making VBA a part of the operating system. We look at the costs of feature requests, versioning issues, et cetera, but up until now, we have had to spend our time satisfying Visual Basic and the Applications groups. We still look at it; it's still a compelling opportunity for us. We need to satisfy these primary clients; then we'll work on pushing it out everywhere else.

Ken: It seems like you almost have that now, anyway. The standard version of VB is so inexpensive that almost everybody could have it.

Craig: That's true, and in fact, in some countries, it is actually given away with some book deals.

Ken: Actually there are book deals here where they give it away too. Since 1993, you've shipped with all of the Office products.

Craig: Access, Excel, VB, and Project already have it, and PowerPoint uses it for its internal Wizard development. Word and PowerPoint both will have it in the Office 97 release.

Language Features and Integration with Office

Ken: I didn't see major language feature changes between VBA 93 and VBA 94 (the version that shipped with Office 95). Can you comment about the changes made between those versions, and about planned features for future versions?

Craig: In answer to the first comment you had, about the difference between VBA 93 and 94, the biggest difference comes in performance and capacity. There were some fairly major changes internally to support vtable binding as opposed to just using the IDispatch interface for binding objects. Many capacity restrictions were removed. The execution performance was improved across the board, and there were some language additions to support being fully backward compatible with VB3 when VBA became the language technology in VB4. So most of our effort in that release was spent making sure we were 100 percent backward compatible with VB3.

In the future, as I mentioned, we are going to continue to improve the object orientation of the language and continue to improve its performance. We will add the necessary language features and architecture that enable it to be a very good player on the Internet scene and continue to improve our interaction with the underlying COM object model. We are pretty good in 94 in that we can access COM interfaces directly, we can handle most of the data types that are supported by COM, and we will continue to improve that in the future.

Ken: Does the VBA group drive the changes to VBA, or the product groups who use VBA making change requests?

Craig: It is a very symbiotic relationship, and to a large extent, we drive the language definition in cases where it's an architectural change to the language. In all cases, however, we go through a process to understand the users of each of the application groups and to make sure we are experts in programmability in any of the applications. That means working with their users, working with the programmability Program Managers in those groups to understand what their requirements are and follow through on those requirements. It's a tough decision because, as we get more and more clients of the VBA technology, we get spread thinner and thinner. We have to be very careful to make sure we collate all the requirements and try to push them together and come up with general solutions that solve groups of requirements in a clean way, as opposed to solving every requirement one off.

Ken: But you don't special-case any of the products?

Craig: In general, that's right. VBA directly exposes some functionality for Access in order to store the code into a database. These interfaces are not available through the VBA3 environment. Since Access doesn't use this component, it wasn't necessary to do this work.

Ken: So when Excel adds its ton of financial functions, that is completely out of the realm of VBA? You never see or hear about that?

Craig: Yes, one of the ways we handle multiple clients is that VBA is a very extensible architecture. Our entire run-time is built by an extensibility mechanism. In fact, you can see this in the product. Our run-time functions, like Sin and Cos, are really just DLL entry points that are described by a type library. The compiler just looks at our own type library and figures out how to bind to it. Very few of our run-time functions are built into our compiler. Our run-time works the same way as any other DLL—anyone can take a DLL and expose some functions and create a type library for it, and it becomes an integral part of the language. You cannot tell that these aren't intrinsic functions. That way, it's highly extensible, and any application hosting VBA can add its own DLL functions or COM objects any way it wants. The host object models are added via this mechanism, and add-on technologies like the Data Access Objects are added via this mechanism. It gives us an enormous degree of flexibility.

Ken: The COM interfaces are two-way? You're talking to the applications that way, and they respond using COM interfaces as well?

Craig: Yes, COM objects can fire events that VBA can sink. VBA can then call back to the method and properties of these COM objects. VBA itself can also expose COM interfaces that it can hand to other objects to let them call back to VBA on.

Ken: But aren't all the VBA hosts sharing the same expression evaluator? In Access, when there is a simple function call in a query, aren't they going to call into VBA to resolve the expression?

Craig: The Jet language engine exposes the expression evaluator that uses VBA's expression evaluator. That is the only technology that does use it. When Access uses expressions in fields, it's really a Jet expression. Then Jet turns around and calls back into us, but that's the only technology that uses our expression evaluator.

Ken: So, Excel does all its own expression evaluation?

Craig: That's right. They need to do it for performance reasons. There are special things they can optimize for that we can't.

Ken: I forgot to mention one of my favorite features of the language that was new in Office 95: labels no longer have to be unique within a module! I don't know when or how that snuck in, but I found it one day, and I never saw it documented anywhere.

Craig: When we designed Object Basic (now Visual Basic for Applications), we designed it in such a way that the language is very orthogonal, across the entire language. A lot of the nuances or tricks and hacks that people learned in the first three versions of Visual Basic or the first two versions of Access aren't necessary anymore. There are a lot of little things, like you couldn't have variable-length arrays in structures, and there was a whole series of implementation restrictions that have all gone away, some of them silently. Some new problems have occurred because of new technology, but most of the language limitations went away with the new version. And it helps alot. I went back and wrote a program in various versions of Visual Basic, and I was running into limitations left, right, and center—it was like "Oh yeah, I can't do this or that; you have to code around this." Things like being able to call user-defined methods of forms. That is an incredible limitation. I just can't imagine how people lived without the ability to do it.

Ken: The tricks you had to go through in Access 2 to call a private method of a form were amazing! Having that feature available now is very nice.

I did mean to ask about stack space. Recursion was a real problem in earlier products. Is the stack space much larger in the 32-bit versions?

Craig: Yes, stack space is defined by the operating system, so in 32-bit versions of the operating system, it's limited by system memory. It can actually grow dynamically. The application can set an upper bound to the stack space (and I believe we set the limit at a meg or something like that), but the operating system only allocates the memory as needed. As the stack grows, the OS will actually page-fault the stack and allocate more memory for the stack as we request it.

Ken: So, although recursion under VB3 and Access 2 was rather limited, at this point it seems as long as you control the recursion, you should be able to use it without artificial limits.

Craig: That is true.

Communication between Office and VBA

Ken: How does VBA hook into Office apps?

Craig: There are two issues here. One issue is the Office apps calling us to get things like the list of macros, and hooking our UI. We provide an interface that enables them to do all of that.

The other issue is VBA calling back into the object models provided by the Office applications; I mentioned before that this is done via Automation. They expose their objects as COM objects, and we just call back onto them using COM mechanisms. We reference the type library that they create for their object model, and the objects then become first-class objects in the language that we can access directly. It works exactly the same way whether we are running VBA inside the application or whether it's some other version of VBA running in another application. In either case, you can reference their type library and call it exactly the same way in-process, out-of-process, cross-machine; it doesn't matter. You get exactly the same functionality regardless of where you are. As long as you reference the type library, COM handles all the location transparencies.

Ken: What's new in VBA for Office for 97?

Craig: The primary focus of this version of VBA was to bring the VB program-mability model to Office. We added the VBA language to Excel 5, and some of the comments we got from it were, "This is great that you added the language here, but it doesn't feel like VB." It was just the language and editor there. So we took that and said, "Let's take the entire VB programmability model, and let's add it to Office." That includes all the programmability features. You can put controls on documents, and there's a code module "behind" the document. You can double-click on the control and it brings up a code module, and all the object and proce-dure drop-downs are populated with the events fired by the document and the controls on the document. You can build the event procedures, you can write code in the event procedures, you can write code like "Me.BackColor = 255" and Me refers to the document—we are explicitly bound to the document. You can access the members of the document without qualifications. That is, you can just write "BackColor = 255". We support classes inside Office now so that you can actually build private classes to encapsulate your functionality. The mode model is similar to VB, but a little looser; it doesn't quite make as much sense for there to be a design and run mode and a break mode—explicit states in a document as opposed to a WYSIWYG language. We support a forms package similar to what is in VB as well.

Ken: All the Office products are to get this except Access. Access inherits only the language changes, not the editor changes, right?

Craig: We added a component called Visual Basic Environment (VBE) Access; for reasons of timing and schedule, we decided not to pick up the environment and only pick up the traditional VBA technology. Because of that, it is getting all the technology VBA provides, but it is not getting the environment; it's providing its own environment. What you lose is some of the docking capabilities in the environment, and some of the menu mechanisms. They will pick up all the editor enhancements: the drop-down lists, the indicator bar, and all the auto-completion technology, which I'm sure you have seen. They will actually get all the enhanced debugging capabilities as well, including the Locals pane in the Debug window.

Ken: What about compatibility? Will Office and VB share the same exact VBA functionality?

Craig: There will be some differences between the release of the Office version of the language engine and the VB5 version of the language engine. There are some additions to the language in VB5.

Ken: I keep thinking about poor Excel 95, with its odd drop of VBA that doesn't match anybody else's. In Office 97, all the Office products are the same drop?

Craig: That's correct, all of Office will have the same exact version of VBA, and VB5 is just a little bit beyond Office in terms of capabilities.

Ken: That makes sense. As it should be!

Craig: We will switch more to a model in which Visual Basic will lead the changes. It'll be the first product that integrates the new changes to VBA and will, to some extent, drive the language extensions. Office will then pick up the previous release of VBA. However, there are a lot of cases where Office isn't just a strict subset of VB; we may have to add extensions just for Office.

Ken: Does someone sit down with the Pascal language reference, for example, and see what features of Pascal would be useful to VBA users?

Craig: Very much so, actually. We do look at languages like PERL, for string handling. We look at other Basic implementations in competitive products to see the innovative features that are being added there. We do look at Pascal and try to understand the scenarios that cause certain features to be added to make sure we understand the scenarios.

Ken: Are there differences between the version of VBA found in Office 97 and the one in VB5?

Craig: There are additional language features in the VB version not in the Office version. In the Office release, most of the work we did was to expose the overall VB model to a document-based application. We also added some language features, like the ability to sync events.

Ken: But Access 97 doesn't get that either, right?

Craig: Remember, the form module *is* a class module. VBA has one concept of a class, and whether it derives from a form or whether it derives from a very simple base class is irrelevant to VBA. That's the other reason we do this derivation from the host-provided object even for what you call "classes." It's because we have one class, and in some cases the host passes us a form-based class, and sometimes it passes another class. For VB5, there are a few language features that we are doing to improve the encapsulation story of OLE automation servers—particularly, adding the ability to have members that are public within a project scope but not exposed externally. Also, being able to provide enumerations that are exposed for your class. You won't see constants exposed, but you will see enumerations exposed.

Ken: What if you do want to provide enumerated constants?

Craig: You can provide your own type library that exposes the constants. If you want to write ODL that generates constants, you can do that.

Ken: Great idea!

Craig: Just write your own type library that lists your constants and reference it from Basic. Unfortunately, you cannot do it in an encapsulated way inside Basic itself.

Ken: But that's a good work-around, and I haven't seen anyone suggest that anywhere. It makes perfect sense. Of course, playing with ODL is a nightmare all its own.

Craig: There are some tools that will be released this year that will help generate ODL more visually. That should help more inexperienced users to be able to generate type libraries.

Ken: Well, count me among them. I spent two hours one day looking at syntax that seemed to be completely arbitrary and random!

What is it you deliver to the Office products? Is it a set of DLLs and an interface spec?

Craig: That's right, we provide a complete SDK for integrating VBA. It includes a DLL that has a header file associated with it that describes our interfaces. That allows the products to integrate the UI we provide, provide menu items and other things they need to enable our product. We also include information on how to record macros, call functions, handle toolbar button interactions, iterate over and figure out what all the macros are, and other tricks like that.

Compilation and What It Means to VBA

Ken: What does compilation mean to VBA? I'll back up a bit: people think of compilation as creating a native executable.

Craig: That's not right. Our answer when people ask, "When are you are going to provide compilation for VBA?" is that they had it back in Version 1.

Ken: Right! It's been there all along. But how do you explain what compilation really is, then?

Craig: Compilation means taking source and doing syntactical and semantic analysis on it, intentionally doing optimizations on the generated code, and then generating output code for it. Whether you generate X86 instructions, MIPS instructions, PowerPC instructions, or what we call ex-codes, it is all code. How the interpreter, whether that's the chip's interpreter or a software interpreter, executes the code is irrelevant to the compilation process. People tie together compilation and native code, which is these instructions that are generated that the chip knows how to execute, as the same thing. But it really isn't. They are two orthogonal issues. VBA does do all of those things that I described as compilation—we do a syntactical analysis of the code, we do a semantic analysis of the code, and in some cases we do some minor optimizations of the generated code. We actually do things like internally generating compilation trees and then emitting the trees for generating the actual, what we call the ex-codes, or p-code, depending on the situation. In Visual Basic, we actually serialize these p-codes into Windows code segments. We generate a true portable executable format (PE Exe), and we use the Windows loader to load our p-code into code segments. That way, Windows is doing all the swapping in and out of the p-code, just as it would do for native code.

Ken: The point is that it just doesn't matter.

Craig: In terms of whether or not VBA has a "compiler," it just doesn't matter. It is compilation in all senses of the word. The only difference is that the resulting code that is generated is not directly understood by the X86 chip set. It is understood by an *interpreter* that runs on any of these file types.

Ken: So do you do any optimizations of control structures? I mean collapsing down Select Case statements or removing dead code.

Craig: Not yet, we don't. We may do some of these things in the future. We do things like constant folding, where if you have a constant expression, we will actually evaluate the expression and put the value inline. We do things like optimize local allocations, so if you have a large allocation as a local variable, we will actually do a heap allocation for that thing on entry to the procedure instead of using a stack space for this. But if it's below a certain threshold, we will do a stack allocation for it. We reuse temps in the compilation phase. There is a series of fairly simple optimizations we go through to make sure the code size is as small as possible and the performance meets the requirements.

Ken: Obviously, some optimizations require a two-pass compiler. How does that apply to VBA?

Craig: We actually do multiple passes across the code. It's not really the same process as the passes you'll see in a traditional compilation sense. At the time you enter the code, we actually parse it as soon as you enter it.

Ken: That's how you do grammar checking at the time we leave the line.

Craig: That's right. We parse the text you typed and put it into a form we call op-codes, which is really a parsed version of the p-code. We take out all the names, and we add them to a name table. We identify all the keywords and put that into the op-code stream, and we can list back the op-code stream very fast. As soon as you enter your line, the source as you entered it has gone away, and it's replaced with this binary representation, regenerated for you on the fly.

Ken: So if I type a line of code with it and include in it a bunch of spaces, perhaps to format the line the way I want it, the text I typed is gone. It's replaced with your understanding of that line of code?

Craig: That's right. It's gone to a canonical binary format. That's why some of the spacing changes when you enter the line and we list it back. In some cases, we'll retain the spacing you entered (in Dim statements, for example), but we'll remember that spacing as an explicit part of the op-code—we don't store the spaces themselves. If you enter a number of spaces in a line…

Ken: …you just insert an op-code for those spaces in the binary format?

Craig: Well, no. There's actually a parameter for certain op-codes that specifies the number of spaces you entered. But back to the parsing phase: once we've converted your text into op-codes, we actually take multiple steps to get to the compilation phase. We know all the module-level declare statements, constant declarations, and module-level variables. We also know all the procedures you define in your modules, so we can pick all of those out without going and compiling the whole thing. That is how we can do things like populate the drop-downs, and how the Object Browser can show the members of your project without actually compiling it, and those sorts of things. Even if there are syntax errors or compilation errors in the body of a procedure, we can still pick out all of these module members. Then we go through a couple of other stages where we can figure out all the variables that are declared—even local variables. We then go through a binding phase. And the final phase is where we actually emit the generated code.

Ken: And that's on demand, or when someone asks you to compile the code?

Craig: In the VB 4.0/Access 95 version of VBA, it's done in one of two ways, selected by a user option. One way is that we generate all the code for all your modules as soon as you run any procedure. We go and generate all the code for the entire project at that point. Or, if you have the Compile On demand Switch turned on, we will actually generate the ex-codes on the fly at run time. As the call into the procedure occurs, we will generate the ex-codes at that point. The reason it is an option is that you can no longer tell, in that case, if your code will execute or even compile correctly until you physically run the code.

Ken: It's a very scary feature. Best to leave that one turned off!

Craig: Actually, in the next version, we will add a Compile All menu item to force a full compilation, if you want it to happen. (Of course, Access has had that all along!)

VBA Storage

Ken: What is actually in the VBA storage? You said you are not storing what the user types—that gets thrown away.

Craig: That's right. There are two main things that are in the storage. One is the op-code stream I talked about. That's the parsed representation of the source, which contains pointers into a name table (which contains all the names you've supplied).

The second major thing is the actual compiled code. We serialize the compiled code into the storage in addition to the source code, if the code's compiled. This is the ex-code stream I talked about earlier.

In addition, we store any run-time structures necessary to load and run the ex-code stream. We serialize a resource descriptor table for handling construction and destruction of complex datatypes like objects or structures. There is a table for public entry points that we serialize so that we can answer questions that the host asks us, like, "Can you give me a list of all the public procedures?" We serialize fix-ups that we do at load times, so, depending on where we get loaded, we need to fix up the jump addresses. We actually use native code entry points for all our procedures. Calling a Basic procedure, even though it is p-code, we generate a native code stub that we call into, and this stub turns around and calls the engine, passing the pointer to the p-code.

Ken: At least with some of the products, we have a choice of whether or not to store the compiled code. In Access we can just change some code, and it throws away the compiled status.

Craig: That's right. When we compile is dependent on what you call—when you call it. There is an option in Access to do a "compile all" and force everything to a compilation state before you save it. But in general, when VBA is used as a macro language, novice users really don't want to know or care that we are compiling anything at any time. Record the macro, record the code, and execute it—that's all many users want.

Ken: The problem is that the speed differences in compiling on the fly or compiling and then running the compiled code are so enormous, at least in the Office 95 version of the products, and certainly in Access. If you don't precompile, the code runs much slower because it's compiling as it goes.

Craig: In the Office 97 products, the demand compile has improved significantly. Also, compilation only happens the first time you use the function. What you said is true, but you've got to understand that it's only beyond a certain threshold where that makes any difference. If there are only 100 lines of code, we can compile that so fast that it's irrelevant whether or not it is precompiled.

Ken: But for large solutions, written in many thousands of lines of VBA code....

Craig: For complete solutions written in Access, it does matter. And hence we provide the Compile All and Save All Modules menu items to enable the sophisticated developers that are writing the solutions to save the optimized code.

Ken: The point is that they don't have to do that if they don't want to: it'll always compile when needed.

Craig: That's correct. We also store some intermediate-state information for our compilation so that if you partially decompile something, we don't have to go right back to the op-codes to recompile it. We can go from one of our intermediate compilation states back up to being fully compiled. We actually do fairly intelligent decompilation. Whenever a user edits a certain function, we look at the type of edits they make and sometimes won't decompile anything—we just in-place modify the line, or we may just delete the ex-codes for the procedure but not have to drop out of what we call the "declared state," where all the variables are declared. We can go very quickly and regenerate the ex-codes for the procedure and continue executing. If the edit is what we call a "rude edit" (modification of a public global, for instance), that will cause us to decompile the module completely because we have to regenerate what all the public members are, and that means we have to drop out before the declared state.

Ken: Where is the VBA code stored?

Craig: It depends on the host. The host passes an OLE IStorage interface, and we write to the Istorage. In VB, we use a similar interface that allows VBA to serialize to PE EXE format when we are generating an executable. In Office, we serialize into the document file.

Ken: Whichever document the user is storing?

Craig: That's right; it's all done by the OLE IStorage interface.

VBA and Native Executables

Ken: Could VBA create native compiled code for Office apps? That is, could we create an Excel executable to ship?

Craig: Hypothetically, yes. It's only code. It's feasible that it could happen in future versions of the Office products. I really can't comment one way or the other as to whether it'll ever happen, but it's not happening in the Office 97 release of the product. It's a huge cost, with lots of issues regarding how to package the code with the particular Office document that the code is customizing. It ends up being a matter of where we focus our resources. Do we focus on providing better technology within Office applications for production solutions? Do we focus on new object-oriented and encapsulation features, faster performance for accessing objects? Creating native code doesn't help for these issues.

Ken: That's true, but people seem to always ask, "Why can't we create an Access native executable?" And my response is always, "Why would you want to? What does that get you?"

Craig: We did some experimentation in the last year of the amount of time that is actually spent in executing the p-code. We instrumented our p-code engine to count the amount of time inside the little executables that execute every p-code…

Ken: …which is the only thing that could be translated to native code.

Craig: Even our own run-time is written in C, so it is already native code. So anytime you call Sin, for instance, you're not executing p-code, you're executing native code. The only thing that would help is translating these ex-codes into native code. That way, you could just execute the native code without jumping to this p-code engine.

We found that in the average case, only around 5 percent of the time was spent inside the p-code! Even in what you would consider fairly high-performance cases, for example, sitting in the loop doing string concatenations, we spent just under 50 percent of the time in the p-code. The other part of the time was calling into the Windows subsystem for allocations or calling into Automation to do string manipulation. And all that's written in native code already.

Ken: And in the normal case, people spend most of the time just mucking around with the interface, clicking buttons or typing text in, or something.

Craig: That's right. And this 5 percent figure represents 5 percent of the time *not* in the idle loop. So in the standard case, something like 95 percent of the time is spent in calling the Data Access Objects, calling the form objects, calling the Windows APIs, retrieving properties. So forget about the idle loop issue (where you spend most of the your time), and you are actually using the processor in executing p-code only 5 percent of the time that you're actually executing code. So, let's assume that native code could make the execution performance of p-code go to 0 (which is hypothetical—obviously it can't do that); you just improved the performance of your application by 5 percent, at most. That's not to say that native code isn't important. There are definitely snippets of any solution where the code is computationally bound, like sorting an array or doing some computational operation that could benefit from the performance of the native code, but in end-to-end scenarios, it provides a less dramatic improvement than you might think.

You can see this in some of the comparisons between VB4 and Delphi. Contrary to what you might imagine, VB4 has actually won some of the performance reviews. The outcome depends on whether the review is a real-world application, perhaps a client-server program, or whether it is running a processor-intensive algorithm, like doing nothing but executing the Sieve. There have been a couple of comparisons where the reviewers compared a client-server application they wrote and, because our data access technology was faster for those scenarios, it turned out that VB was faster than Delphi. In some cases we lose and in some we win, depending on the scenario. All these cases have less to do with p-code or native execution engine and more to do with how fast the forms package is or how fast the data access technology is.

Specific Features, and How Features Come to Be

Ken: Can you provide any details on VBA's string handling? Common knowledge has it that you're going through a conversion from ANSI to Unicode and then back again, under Windows 95, every time you make a function call that uses a string.

Craig: We went through a huge process, when developing the 32-bit version of VBA, to figure out how to do strings. We were caught between a rock and a hard place. That is, we have two technologies at Microsoft, one being the existing Windows API and the other up-and-coming technology called COM. And for very good reasons, the designers of COM chose to use the Unicode character set for all strings. Particularly, they had the foresight to look at cross-machine transport of calls and strings in what we now call DCOM and interoperability between different systems and different language versions of the same operating system. For COM, they chose Unicode, because it makes interoperability between different language versions of the operating system possible. When you want to send a message from the U.S. to a Japanese machine, for instance, in the old ANSI character-set world or double-byte character-set world, you have major problems because there are different code pages being used. They chose to use only the Unicode character set as the standard. If they had supported both, they would have ended up with interoperability and conversion problems when sending a string from an ANSI U.S. application to a Unicode Japan application, or vice versa. They would have had to add tons of complexities to the remoting code within the operating system to support this conversion. Then the operating system would run into problems similar to those that VB is in now with the conversion.

Our situation is complex because we need to support calling the Windows API directly from within Basic as we have in the past, and we need to be able to call the COM objects. In the first 32-bit version of VBA (VBA 93), strings were ANSI, and we had a layer that was used to convert all the strings to Unicode when calling an object. This layer added a ton of complexity and performance degradation to the product when calling objects. Some of the technical issues were very difficult to solve. We had to convert entire interface pointers between ANSI and Unicode and wrap the entire COM objects, provide our own proxies and stubs to ANSI versions of the proxies that then call the Unicode version of the proxies. Then we had to clean it all up on the way out the other side. This was a tremendous amount of overhead. In the development of what we call VBA 94, which is the version that went into VB4, we saw that this conversion at the COM layer was providing *major* problems in accessing objects, from both a performance and a technical standpoint. Yet it made it easy to call the Windows APIs.

If you look at typical VB programs, although most of them call Windows APIs at one point or another, much more of their time is spent talking to COM objects, whether ActiveX controls, automation servers, calling the form itself, calling the Data Access Object layer, all of these sorts of things. Much more code is written to call these objects. We decided to change the internal representation of strings in the VBA language to be Unicode so we could remove all the conversion layers between the language and the objects. That way, Unicode is native for all these things, and we just pass the strings around without any conversion. The problem this causes is that now our strings are Unicode, and we need to convert when passing them to a DLL. So, as I said, we were caught between a rock and a hard place, between these two calling conventions that we needed to support. I believe that we chose the right one: if you think about it and think about the Unicode-to-ANSI conversions going on between ActiveX controls, the Data Access Object, any OLE automation server, and other external processes, the problems would be significantly worse than calling the Windows APIs.

Ken: It sure seemed that string handling was much slower in VB4 than in VB3. Everyone I know had assumed this was related to character-set conversion issues.

Craig: That has nothing to do with the ANSI-to-Unicode issue. It is the number of allocations you do that affects the performance, not necessarily the size of the allocation. It does have some impact on the performance, but the cost of the allocation is so insignificant compared to what is going on in the string function that it actually becomes irrelevant.

Ken: So how can people optimize their use of strings in VBA?

Craig: In the version of VBA in Office 97, the string performance is significantly faster. The main reason it's faster is that we have done some optimizations on the allocator to do suballocations, so we don't actually go to the system allocator nearly as often as we used to.

Ken: So you go grab big chunks and break them up as you need them?

Craig: We grab big chunks, and anytime somebody frees the string, we don't actually free it in the system; we hold onto it and just hand it back out the next time somebody does an allocation that fits in that allocation size that we have held onto. We have this series of these allocations that we hold onto, a table of them of different sizes that we can handle. This work is actually done in OLE automation, so if you get an updated version of OLE automation on the system and use it with the old versions of the VBA language engine, your string performance should improve quite dramatically, even without your ever upgrading the language engine.

Ken: That is great. Is garbage collection an issue with strings? Say you have these big chunks of strings and they're no longer used in the application. What happens to that memory?

Craig: Strings in VBA can never have more than one owner; the compiler ensures this. So when you release the pointer to the string or when you release the string itself, we will actually release the memory. Well, we release it as far as calling OLE automation to release it. What OLE automation does with its caching algorithm is independent of the VBA engine. For objects, VBA uses COM's reference-counting mechanism, and it does the correct AddRef and Release calls when the object is created or the pointer is assigned.

Ken: As soon as that pointer goes out of scope, we've lost touch with what actually happens, right?

Craig: That's right. We guarantee that we don't leak memory with strings or objects. There are some cases where you can get into circular references with objects that you have to be aware of, but when we shut down the process, we do track those objects and clean them up and release them.

Ken: How about array handling? VBA seems to be designed not to make arrays friendly. The fact that we have to write VBA code to sort an array seems odd to me. There is no way to copy data from one array to another without walking the elements one by one.

Craig: We are looking at solving some of these areas for future versions. In every version, we look at enhancing our run-time functions to provide more interesting functionality. It's sort of a trade-off: we don't want to bloat the core engine, but in general, we need to take a look at what's common across all the applications—like array handling. If, in 90 percent of solutions, you need a certain function, then we should add that function to the core run-time. Otherwise, if it's a specific function, like a financial function or something that only Excel would use, then Excel will add that to its object model, and it will be available within Excel and not part of the core technology.

Ken: What about Registry-wrapper functions? The ones that are in VBA now are so limited that programmers must use Windows API calls to do anything useful.

Craig: There are two ways we could have handled this. One was to provide a wrapper on the Windows APIs that exposes all the functionality of the Windows API and all its complexity. But the Windows APIs are very easily callable from within Basic. The other was to do what we did: provide a simple way for any programmer to save and restore application-specific information.

We figured that people who want to manipulate the Registry, if they know *how* to manipulate the Registry using the Windows API, can make the three calls to get the key, et cetera. Hence, we attempted to make it very easy for people who are just trying to store and retrieve application information. And anybody who wants to manipulate the Registry in more complicated ways than that should be able to call the Windows APIs.

Ken: It just seems that if you take the SaveSetting procedure and add one more parameter, the full path, so you have complete control of where you get or set the value, that one thing would make this much more useful.

Craig: Would you prefer us to do that, or would you prefer us to add functionality to the language that you *can't* work around using the Windows API?

Ken: Oh, the latter, absolutely. We can always solve the Registry problems ourselves.

Craig: Right. That's the point. The more sophisticated user can use the Windows API. We need to solve problems for the novice user who doesn't even know anything about the Windows APIs. And for the most part, all they want to do is save and restore application settings.

Ken: And there is the issue that most people don't understand: Microsoft may be a force to be reckoned with, but they still have limited resources. Microsoft doesn't have infinite numbers of programmers to put on this product.

Craig: That's right!

Ken: You have to decide which problem can possibly be solved by advanced users.

Craig: One of our arguments is, when we look at features to add to the product, we ask, "Should we spend our time doing this, or should we rely on our very powerful third-party community to provide this technology for us?" And it is a tough trade-off. We do have to ship a very compelling product with which you can build complete solutions straight out of the box. Yet we really love to leverage our third-party community to make our product even more powerful. So it is a tough trade-off, whether we add it to the box or let the third-party community handle the technology. In a lot of cases, they do it better than we can because they are trying to solve a particular problem, and we need to provide a more generic solution for general-purpose work. And sometimes the general solution is not exactly what you want—you need a particular solution—so the third-party community is a huge advantage for VBA, and we really appreciate the advantage it does give us.

VBA's Collections

Ken: I'm interested in VBA's internal collection object. How are you storing these, internally? My guess is a doubly-linked list or something like that, but I'm only guessing, of course.

Craig: It is actually a fairly complex structure. It's two structures in one; we link the nodes together in two different ways. We do use a doubly-linked list, but we use a balanced binary search tree, too.

Ken: The balanced tree makes it so that when I ask for an item by name, VBA can find it quickly, and the linked list makes it possible to walk forward and backward by index?

Craig: That's right. We added these optimizations to improve the performance of the structure in specific cases. You can see this in some of the performance characteristics, I think. After a certain number of elements, inserts start slowing down. That's because we are maintaining these two different structures.

Ken: And you keep the tree balanced?

Craig: That's right. That way, the search capability is fairly fast, regardless of the size. The search time doesn't visibly grow with the size.

Ken: Right, because it is balanced. Given that, how about this one: you have a collection and have added 100 items, and you now want to start over with a fresh one. But there is no way to empty a collection. I've counted on reference counts to work in my favor and have used

```
Set col = New Collection
```

Is this doing what I'm hoping it does?

Craig: Sure! VBA will destruct the previous collection. Because a collection is just an object, we are setting its reference count to 0 and hence we will destruct it.

Ken: Great! I was hoping for that behavior.

Craig: Regardless of what's in it, we'll destruct all the elements. Even if the collection contains complex elements, such as a collection of arrays where each element of the array has an object in it, or whatever.

Ken: Because the only reference to that head object is gone, the whole thing gets destroyed.

Craig: Yes.

Ken: Well that's good; that was crucial for me because I had code that counted on this behavior, and I wanted to make sure it works as expected.

In the last week I have spent a lot of time mucking with dynamic data structures using class models, making binary trees and linked lists, and it seems to work. Is this really a reasonable solution to that problem?

Craig: Sure, absolutely. I mean, one of the main reasons we added classes as a generic type was to support abstract data structures. Another reason was to be able to provide automation servers and class hierarchies of entire object models. But they are great for creating encapsulated data structures.

Code Optimization

Ken: Can you give any hints on what VBA programmers can do to optimize their code?

Craig: Use types wherever possible. Declare your variables explicitly, including object pointers. Unless you need to, don't declare a variable like this:

```
Dim X As Object
```

Instead, use code like this:

```
Dim X As SomeSpecificObject
```

using an explicit object type.

Ken: Looks like we're just talking about early binding here as the big issue.

Craig: That is right—it's a big issue and makes a measurable impact on performance. Use early binding wherever you can. The best way to find out is the White Paper on the Web for optimizing Basic code. It's actually a VB paper, but it's true for most incarnations of VBA.

Ken: What do you think about the use of variants?

Craig: Variants are very useful datatypes. They are a tagged union of all the available intrinsic datatypes we have. Since it's a tagged union and at run-time the tag can change, the compiler can't do anything to optimize the code that is generated from manipulating them. So all the manipulation happens at run time. Any VBA built-in function that takes variants and, for example, adds them together has to check the tags of the two variants before it does the add. Then it jumps through a Switch statement that then says, "Okay, you have two integers, so do use the internal integer add routines." The performance penalty this causes has to be weighed against the benefit of using a tagged union structure like the Variant. It provides a lot of advantages in terms of being able to return a string or an error value or an integer at some time from a single function. Sometimes you may want to take two different datatypes as parameters, so Variants enable you to do a simple case of parameter overloading. But all this flexibility comes at a cost. Therefore, we provide you with the benefits of both strongly typed datatypes and Variants.

It is exactly the same thing for the Object type as well. In a lot of cases, you want to do late binding because you want to be polymorphic across certain interfaces or certain functions. Sometimes there are other situations where you want to use the late binding because some members may be available only at run time; they are not part of the early-bound interface. And in those cases, you have to use late binding. The ability to use early or late binding provides a lot of benefits, but you should always use early binding, if possible.

VBScript

Ken: Let's finish with VBScript. Is the same product team working on both VBA and VBScript?

Craig: Yes, VBScript is actually produced by the VB team. VBScript is a simplified version of the Basic language. The design goals were twofold: very fast compilation speed and very small footprint. To that end, we met and exceeded our design goals in a lot of cases by keeping the language simple. There are no datatypes (it's all Variants). We removed a lot of the hard-coded constructs like file I/O, so really what is left is control flow and variants. And it makes the compilation speed extremely fast. The interpreter itself is about 20K, and the entire DLL is around 200K, including the engine, compiler, run-time, and hosting interfaces.

Ken: The interpreter lives in the browser?

Craig: It's a DLL that we provide, and the browser loads the DLL whenever it sees the "Script" tag in the HTML stream.

VBScript is effectively the entry level of the VB family, and it has a huge role to play in small footprint scenarios or scenarios where you want to download source and very quickly execute the source. Downloading binary information has its problems, in terms of security. Java does a lot of work to try to prove that its binary representation is actually secure, and people are finding limitations in that. When you download source, you don't have to worry about that sort of problem. You don't have to worry about somebody spoofing the binary representation.

Ken: Do you get a lot of people complaining because we can't protect VBScript code by any means?

Craig: There are several folks who are looking into a solution to this problem with the W3C.

Ken: How about a wrapper somehow? Putting it inside something?

Craig: Well, one solution would be to create your application in a VB-created DLL and then download the DLL, but that gets back to the binary representation issue. In fact, that has the same binary problems that Java has, in terms of somebody being able to spoof the binary representation. But that's one way to do it. Actually, using source, but encrypted some way, seems a better solution.

Ken: That seems like a good answer—all you do is turn that source into something that is unreadable, but it is just as understandable as the original source to your interpreter. What a great idea!

Craig: VBScript's primary goals well into the future will be extremely fast compilation and very small footprint and high portability. It is source licensable.

Ken: People can download the source?

Craig: You can contact Microsoft to get the source. There is a free license that restricts, in certain ways, what you can do with the source. But we are working with some companies that want to port it to different platforms, and we'd like to see it running everywhere.

Ken: Do you expect that the people who license it will add features to it?

Craig: The source license allows you to add run-time functions to it but not modify the language.

Ken: I hope so, because otherwise you will have all these bastard variants of this language.

Craig: That is right; our goal is to make sure we can maintain a consistent core language so that you know your code is going to run regardless of what is running or whose implementation you are using.

Ken: Is there a design goal that VBScript code will always run in Visual Basic? Are they trying to make it upward compatible all the time?

Craig: Yes. That is a primary goal of VBScript—it is a strict subset of the VBA language. One of the restrictions for version 1 of VBScript is that it supports only ByVal calling conventions. Even though the default calling convention in VBA is ByRef, VBScript only uses ByVal. For this first version, all parameters will be passed by value, and that's different from the way VBA works. Version 2 of VBScript solves this problem, but in order to stay compatible, you have to type the ByVal keyword in your VBScript code.

Ken: Do you want to make a comment on why we can't use constants in VBScript? What is it about constants that makes them unpleasant for VBScript?

Craig: Why did you pick constants, of all the language features we had to drop?

Ken: Just trying to figure it out—constants just seem so easy. I can see why VBScript doesn't include CreateObject or file I/O; they're not secure functions. But constants?

Craig: Most of the reasons for dropping language constructs were either that they were not mainstream constructs or that they would slow down compilation performance significantly, or for platform independence.

Ken: That is what I was guessing; maybe the constants would require two passes through, once to analyze them and another time to replace them.

Craig: No, VBA actually doesn't do multiple passes for constants. We do the multiple passes, but not for that reason. Constants are just one of the things that didn't make the cut.

The Future of VBA

Ken: Can you comment about what you see for the future of VBA, and where will it end up?

Craig: Our goal for the future of VBA is definitely ubiquity across Microsoft applications. In 1987 or 1988, Bill mentioned that we would have a common scripting language. Well, this is it. It has taken us a while to get here, but eventually we will be available in all applications and, as you mentioned, potentially the operating system at some point. The future? We are working on the technology, to continue to bring it into the future, to continue to improve the language, both in the sense of usability of the language and in providing object-oriented techniques to the language. We'll add object-oriented techniques in innovative ways, as we have in the past. Similar to the way we invented the event model as an object-oriented approach, we will continue to add object-oriented mechanisms to the language in innovative ways. We will continue to improve the technology, from a performance standpoint, and add technologies that enable it to be usable in future technologies like the Internet, similar to the way VBScript has become a very compelling solution for the Internet.

Ken: So what about the Mac?

Craig: VBA runs on the Mac and has since 1993. It runs on both 68K and Power Macs.

Ken: Therefore, code you write, unless you use some odd, obscure features, should run on both platforms.

Craig: That's correct. It's source-level platform independent. As long as you are not calling Windows APIs or other functionality that's limited to the Windows platform. All our run-time functions are supported on both platforms. In some cases, they have minor differences in semantics in order for the product to be compelling on the given platform.

Ken: Do you see other platforms, or can you talk about other platforms at this point?

Craig: We run on all the NT RISC platforms as well.

Ken: Do you run in native mode or in emulation mode?

Craig: Native mode.

Ken: This is true for current products?

Craig: Yes, Excel 93 was ported to all the NT RISC platforms. And so VBA runs on all the Windows platforms we run on, plus the Mac OS—68K and Power Mac. If other decisions are made in the future, then we are capable of porting to other platforms. One thing that is interesting with this is that we are very closely tied to the COM object model, and VBA on a platform without COM is fairly difficult to do and not all that compelling, because all our object access technology, including accessing objects inside of host applications, is done through the COM object model.

Ken: Craig, thank you. We do appreciate your taking the time to fill us in on some of the details about VBA, and I'm sure it'll be a useful addition to the book.

CHAPTER

ONE

1

Manipulating Strings

- Understanding how string values are stored and used in VBA

- Using the built-in VBA string-handling functions

- Searching for and replacing text

- Gathering information about strings

- Converting strings

- Working with substrings

Almost any VBA application will need to handle string (text) data at one point or another. VBA itself provides a useful set of string-handling functions, but the functionality of the functions as a whole is not nearly as full-featured as that provided by other, more text-centric programming languages. This chapter first makes a quick pass through the existing functions and then provides many useful routines to add to your string-handling "bag of tricks." Surely, no chapter on this topic could cover every possible combination of useful functions, but the ones we've provided here should give you a good start in writing your own VBA solutions.

These sample files you'll find on the CD-ROM that accompanies this book are listed in Table 1.1:

TABLE 1.1   String-handling Functions

File Name	Description
STRINGS.XLS	Excel 97 file with sample functions
STRINGS.MDB	Access 97 database with sample functions
STRINGS.BAS	Text file with sample functions
TESTSTR.BAS	Text file with text procedures
PROPER.MDB	Samples for dhProperLookup
PROPER.TXT	Text version of sample for dhProperLookup

How Does VBA Store Strings?

A VBA string is simply a collection of bytes. To make it easier for VBA to work with strings, each string also maintains its own information about its length. In addition, unlike other programming languages, VBA takes care of creating, destroying, and resizing string buffers. You needn't worry about how VBA finds strings in memory, whether they're contiguous in memory, or how or when VBA reclaims the memory the string used once you're done with it.

VBA provides two types of strings: fixed-length and dynamic. Fixed-length strings are those you declare with a fixed size, like this:

```
Dim strFixed As String * 100
```

In this case, strFixed will always contain exactly 100 characters, no matter how many characters you've placed into it. That is, if you attempt to retrieve the length of the string, the output will always be 100:

```
Debug.Print Len(strFixed)
```

VBA fills the extra positions with spaces, and you'll need to use the Trim function in order to use the string in any other expression (see the section "Working with Portions of a String" later in this chapter for more information). Fixed-length strings can be no longer than 65,526 characters.

Dynamic strings, on the other hand, have no fixed size. As you add or remove characters from these objects, VBA takes care of locating memory in which to place the text and allocates and deallocates memory as necessary for your text. To declare a dynamic string, you use a declaration like this:

```
Dim strDynamic As String
```

In this case, if you retrieve the length of the string, the result will accurately reflect the amount of text you've placed into the variable. Dynamic strings can contain up to around 2 billion characters.

How do you decide which type of string to use? Dynamic strings require a bit more processing effort from VBA and are, accordingly, a bit slower to use. On the other hand, you make up the time by not needing to use the Trim function to remove excess space every time you use the string. As you'll see by working through the examples in this chapter, we use fixed-length strings only when it's necessary. When working with a single character at a time, using a fixed-length string, declared to contain a single character, makes sense; because you know you'll always have only a single character in the string, you'll never need to trim off excess space. You get the benefits of a fixed-length string without the extra overhead.

Unicode versus ANSI

The 32-bit Windows "universe" supports two character storage mechanisms: ANSI and Unicode. The ANSI storage standard uses a single byte for every character, with only 256 different characters allowed in any ANSI character set. Windows 95 uses this approach for compatibility with previous versions of Windows. The Unicode standard allows for 65,536 characters, each taking up two bytes. The Unicode character set includes just about all the known written characters and ideograms in a single entity. In this way, an application that embraces the Unicode standard can support (once its text has been translated) just about any written language. Windows NT supports the Unicode standard.

No matter what operating system you're using, VBA stores strings internally in Unicode format. That is, every character takes up two bytes of space. When VBA needs to communicate with Windows 95 (when you include Windows API calls in your code, for example), it must first convert strings to ANSI format. This happens automatically when you use the ANSI version of a Windows API call that involves strings. The only other time you'll care about how VBA stores strings is when you want to convert a string into an array of bytes—a useful technique that we'll take advantage of a few times in this chapter. In this case, a string containing 5 characters becomes an array of bytes containing ten bytes. For example, a string containing the text "Hello" would contain the following ten bytes, once converted to a byte array:

```
72   0   101   0   108   0   108   0   111   0
```

Each pair of bytes (72 and 0 for the *H*, for example) represents the Unicode storage for a single character. If you were running Microsoft Excel in Korea, however, and were entering text in your native language, the second byte wouldn't be 0. Instead, it would be a value that combined with the first byte to represent the character you'd typed.

Using Strings and Byte Arrays

Because it's often faster and simpler to work with arrays of bytes than to work with individual characters in a string (and you'll find some examples in this chapter that use this technique), VBA provides a simple way to convert strings into byte arrays and back. Simply assigning a string to a byte array variable causes VBA to copy the data into the array. When you're done working with the array, you can assign it right back into the string variable. For example, the following code fragment copies data from a string into a byte array, performs processing on the array, and then copies the array back into the string:

```
Sub StringToByteArray()
    Dim strText As String
    Dim aByt() As Byte
    Dim intI As Integer
```

```
        strText = "Hello"
        ' VBA allows you to assign a string into
        ' a byte array and then back again.
        aByt() = strText
        For intI = LBound(aByt) To UBound(aByt)
            Debug.Print aByt(intI);
        Next intI
        Debug.Print
        strText = aByt()
        Debug.Print strText
End Sub
```

Although you won't use this technique often, if you need to process each byte of a string, it's the best solution.

WARNING In previous versions of Basic, many programmers used string variables to contain binary data (that is, nontextual data, such as bitmaps, sound files, and so on). In VBA, this isn't necessary, nor is it advisable. Instead, use arrays of bytes for nontextual data. Because VBA performs ANSI-to-Unicode conversions on the fly, you're almost guaranteed that your non-text data will be ruined once you place it into a string variable.

Using Built-In String Functions

VBA provides a large number of string-handling functions. This section introduces many of those functions, broken down by the area of functionality, and discusses the most useful of the built-in functions. The remainder of the chapter provides techniques that combine the built-in functions to perform tasks for which you would otherwise need to write custom code.

Comparing Strings

VBA provides three ways for you to compare the contents of one string with another: comparison operators (such as =, <, and so on), the Like operator, and the StrComp function. In addition, you can specify the method of comparison for each module using the Option Compare statement in the declarations area.

Option Compare

The Option Compare statement, if it's used at all, must appear in each module before any procedures, and it tells VBA how you want to make string comparisons within the module. The choices are as follows:

- **Option Compare Binary:** Comparisons are made based on the internal sort order of the characters, using their binary representation. In this situation, characters are treated case sensitively (that is, *A* isn't the same as *a*).

- **Option Compare Text:** Comparisons are made based on the text sort order of the current locale. Characters are treated, at least in English, case insensitively.

- **Option Compare Database:** (Available only in Microsoft Access) Comparisons are made based on the locale ID of the current database.

> **TIP**
>
> If you don't specify an Option Compare setting, VBA uses Option Compare Binary. In that case, if you attempt to perform a simple comparison between *A* and *a*, you'll get a False return value. If you're working with strings and performing comparisons, make sure you're aware of the Option Compare setting for the module.

Comparison Operators

You can use the simple logical operators to compare two strings, like this:

```
If strText1 < strText2 Then...
```

In this case, VBA performs a character-by-character comparison according to the Option Compare setting in force in the current module. The result of the comparison will most likely change, based on that setting. You can use the set of simple comparison operators shown in the following table.

Operator	Description
<	Less than
< =	Less than or equal to
>	Greater than

Operator	Description
> =	Greater than or equal to
=	Equal to
< >	Not equal to

In addition, VBA supplies the Like operator for comparing two strings. This operator allows you to specify wildcards, character lists, and character ranges in the comparison string, not just fixed characters. The following table lists all the options for the comparison string using the Like operator:

Characters in Pattern	Matches in String
?	Any single character
*	Zero or more characters
#	Any single digit (0–9)
[charlist]	Any single character in *charlist*
[!charlist]	Any single character not in *charlist*

TIP

The string containing the wildcard information must be on the right-hand side of the Like operator. That is, unlike many mathematical operators, this one is not commutative: the order of the operands is significant.

For example, the following code fragment would compare a string with a template that checks for valid Canadian Postal codes:

```
strTemp = "W1F 8G7"
If strTemp Like "[A-Z]#[A-Z] #[A-Z]#" Then
    ' You know strTemp is a valid Canadian Postal Code
End If
```

To check whether the single character in strTemp was a vowel, you could use the expression:

```
If strTemp Like "[AEIOUaeiou]" Then
    ' You know the character in strTemp is a vowel
End If
```

If you want to see whether the word stored in strTemp doesn't start with a vowel, you could use an expression like this:

```
If strTemp Like "[!AEIOUaeiou]*" Then
    ' You know the word in strTemp doesn't start with a vowel
End If
```

You'll find the Like operator to be invaluable when you need to validate input. Rather than parse the string yourself, you can use wildcards to allow various ranges of characters.

NOTE   The behavior of the Like operator depends on the Option Compare setting. Unless you specify otherwise, each module uses Option Compare Binary (case-sensitive comparisons).

TIP   There are a number of issues you need to be aware of when using the Like operator (sorting, order of the characters within the range, and so on). Be sure to check out the online help for this topic for more information.

Using the StrComp Function

The StrComp function provides a way for you to override the Option Compare statement within a given module. To use StrComp, you specify the two strings and a comparison method (binary, text, or database), and the function returns a value indicating how the two strings compared. In general, you call StrComp like this:

```
intRetVal = StrComp(strText1, strText2, intCompareOption)
```

The two text strings can be any string expressions, and the intCompareOption value should be one of the items from Table 1.2 or a locale ID integer that specifies a local sort order for comparisons. Depending on the parameters, StrComp returns one of the values from Table 1.3.

TIP

The intCompareOption parameter for StrComp is optional. If you omit it, VBA uses the option selected by the Option Compare setting for the module. If you omit the Option Compare, of course, VBA will use binary comparisons (vbBinaryCompare).

TABLE 1.2 Compare Options for StrComp

Constant	Option Compare Equivalent
vbBinaryCompare	Option Compare Binary
vbDatabaseCompare	Option Compare Database
vbTextCompare	Option Compare Text

TABLE 1.3 Return Values for StrComp

If	StrComp returns
strText1 is less than strText	2–1
strText1 is equal to strText	0
strText1 is greater than strText2	1

Using the StrComp function, even if you normally perform case-sensitive comparisons, you can override that requirement for one comparison:

```
If StrComp(strText1, strText2, vbTextCompare) = 0 Then
    ' You know that strText1 and strText2 are the same, as far
    ' as the text comparison goes.
End If
```

Converting Strings

Rather than provide individual functions to convert strings from one format to another, VBA includes the single StrConv function. This function allows you to specify a string, as well as a conversion parameter indicating the conversion you'd like to make. In general, you call the function like this:

strOutput = StrConv(*strInput*, *intConversion*)

where *strInput* is the string to be converted and *intConversion* is a value from the following table. The converted string is the return value from StrConv.

Constant	Description
vbUpperCase	Converts the string to uppercase characters
vbLowerCase	Converts the string to lowercase characters
vbProperCase	Converts the first letter of every word in the string to uppercase
vbUnicode	Converts the string to Unicode using the default code page of the system
vbFromUnicode	Converts the string from Unicode to the default code page of the system

As you can see, the StrConv function performs two basic tasks: converting the case (upper, lower, proper) of strings and converting strings from ANSI to Unicode and back.

TIP If you're working in a Japanese or other Far East locale, you'll want to check out the options for StrConv that are available only in those locales. See the VBA online help for more information.

Creating Strings: The Space and String Functions

VBA provides two functions that make it easy for you to create specific strings. The Space function lets you create a string consisting only of spaces; you indicate the number of spaces, and VBA does the rest. The general syntax looks like this:

strOut = Space(*intSpaces*)

Although this function has many uses, we've used it most often in two particular situations:

- Creating string buffers when calling external DLLs (the Windows API, in particular)

- Padding strings so they're left or right justified within a buffer of a particular size

You can use an expression like this to create a ten-character string of spaces:

```
strTemp = Space(10)
```

If you need more flexibility, you can use the String function to create a string of any number of a specified character. For this function, you specify the number of characters you need and the specific character or ANSI value to repeat:

```
strOut = String(intChars, strCharToRepeat)
' or
strOut = String(intChars, intCharToRepeat)
```

For example, either of the following fragments will return a string containing ten occurrences of the letter *a*. (The ANSI value for *a* is 97.)

```
strOut = String(10, "a")
strOut = String(10, 97)
```

Although you're unlikely to need this particular string, the following code fragment creates a string consisting of one *A*, two *B*'s, three *C*'s, and so on.

```
Dim intI As Integer
Dim strOut As String
For intI = 1 To 26
    strOut = strOut & String(intI, Asc("A") + intI - 1)
Next intI
```

Calculating the Length of a String

Simple yet crucial, the Len function allows you to determine the length of any string or string expression. To use the function, pass it a string or string expression:

```
lngCharCount = Len(strIn)
```

Certainly, you'll often need to find the length of a string expression. But the Len function also has an extra benefit: it's very fast! VBA stores strings with a long integer preceding the string that contains the length of the string. It's very simple for VBA to retrieve that information at run time. For example, what if you need to know whether a particular string currently contains no characters? Many programmers write code like this to check for an empty string:

```
If strTemp = "" Then
    ' You know strTemp is empty
End If
```

Because VBA can calculate string lengths so quickly, you're better off using code like this to find out if a string is empty:

```
If Len(strTemp) = 0 Then
    ' You know strTemp is empty
End if
```

Performing one nonoptimized comparison isn't going to make any difference in the speed of your application, but if you check for empty strings often, consider using the Len function instead.

Formatting a String

VBA allows you to format the output display of a string using placeholders that represent single characters from the input string. In addition, you can use the Format function to convert an input string to upper- or lowercase. The placeholders and conversion characters shown in Table 1.4 allow you to reformat an input string.

TABLE 1.4 Placeholders and Conversion Characters for the Format function

Character	Description
@	Character placeholder for a character or a space. If the input string has a character in the position where the at symbol (@) appears in the format string, display it; otherwise, display a space in that position
&	Character placeholder for a character or nothing. If the input string has a character in the position where the ampersand (&) appears, display it; otherwise, display nothing
<	Displays all characters in lowercase format
>	Displays all characters in uppercase format
!	Forces left to right fill of placeholders. The default is to fill placeholders from right to left. The character can be placed anywhere in the format string

For example, if strTemp contains the string "8364928", the following fragment returns "(   )836-4928":

```
strOut = Format("8364928", "(@@@)&&&-&&&&")
```

This fragment returns "()836-4928":

```
strOut = Format("8364928", "(&&&)&&&-&&&&")
```

In addition, the Format function allows you to format normal strings one way and empty or null strings another. Every character following the symbol will be converted. For example, you may want to indicate an empty value differently from a value with data. To do this, use two sections in the placeholder string separated with a semicolon (;). The first section will apply to non-empty strings, and the second will apply to empty strings. That is:

```
strOut = Format(strIn, "(@@@)&&&-&&&&;No phone")
```

returns a formatted phone number if strIn contains a non-empty string and "No phone" if strIn is empty.

To convert text to upper- or lowercase as it's formatted, add the > or < character to the format string. Every character following the symbol will be converted. For example, the following fragment converts the input text to uppercase and inserts a space between letters:

```
Format("hello there", ">@ @ @ @ @ @ @ @ @ @ @")
```

TIP   Although it's beyond the scope of this chapter, the Format function can also provide user-defined formatting for dates and numeric values. Check out Chapters 2 and 3 for more information.

VBA also supplies two simple functions, UCase and LCase, that you can use to convert your functions to upper- and lowercase. Pass the function the string you want converted, and its output will be the converted string. The following example places the word *HELLO* into strOut:

```
strOut = UCase("hello")
```

TIP

This chapter presents three ways to convert text to upper- or lowercase: the UCase/LCase functions, the > and < characters in the Format function, and the vbUpperCase and vbLowerCase constants with the StrConv function. Use the technique that's most comfortable for you.

Justifying a String

VBA provides two statements, LSet and RSet (note that these aren't functions) that allow you to justify a string within the space taken up by another. These statements are seldom used in this context but may come in handy. In addition, LSet gives you powerful flexibility when working with user-defined datatypes, as shown later in this section.

LSet and RSet allow you to stuff a new piece of text at either the beginning or end of an existing string. The leftover positions are filled with spaces, and any text in the new string that won't fit into the old string is truncated.

For example, after running the following fragment, the string strOut1 contains the string "Hello   " ("Hello" and three trailing spaces) and strOut2 contains "   Hello" (three leading spaces and then "Hello").

```
strOut1 = "ABCDEFG"
strOut2 = "ABCDEFG"
LSet strOut1 = "Hello"
RSet strOut2 = "Hello"
```

TIP

Let's face it: most programmers don't really take much advantage of LSet and RSet with strings. They're somewhat confusing, and you can use other string functions to achieve the same result. Using LSet with user-defined types, however, is key to moving data between different variable types and is discussed in the following paragraphs.

LSet also supplies a second usage: it allows you to overlay data from one user-defined type with data from another. Although the VBA help file recommends against doing this, it's a powerful technique when you need it. Simply put, LSet allows you to take all the bytes from one data structure and place them on top of another, not taking into account how the various pieces of the data structures are laid out.

Imagine that you're reading fixed-width data from a text file. That is, each of the columns in the text file contains a known number of characters. You need to move the columns into a user-defined data structure, with one field corresponding to each column in the text file. For this simple example, the text file has columns as described in the following list.

Column Name	Width
FirstName	10
LastName	10
ZipCode	5

To work with the data from the text file, you've created a user-defined data structure:

```
Type TextData
    FirstName As String * 10
    LastName As String * 10
    ZipCode As String * 5
End Type
```

You've used the various file-handling functions (see Chapter 5 for class modules to help work with text files) to retrieve a line of text from the file, and a String variable named strTemp now contains the following text:

```
"Peter     Mason     90064"
```

How do you get the various pieces from strTemp into a TextData data structure? You could parse the characters out using other string-handling functions, but you needn't—LSet can do the work for you.

The only limitation of this technique is that you cannot use LSet to move data between a simple datatype and a user-defined datatype. It works only with two simple data elements (the technique shown earlier in this section) and with two user-defined datatypes. Attempting to write code like the following will fail:

```
Dim typText As TextData
' This won't work
LSet typText = strTemp
```

To cause LSet to coerce data from one type to another, you'll need to copy your text data into yet another user-defined type. All this takes, however, is a datatype with a single fixed-length string, like this:

```
Type TextTemp
    strText As String * 25
End Type
```

Given that datatype, it takes just one extra step to perform the conversion. You must copy the text into the strText member of the TextTemp datatype. With the text there, you can use LSet to copy the bytes from the temporary data structure on top of the real data structure.

```
Dim typTest As TextData
Dim typTemp As TextTemp

' Copy the data into the temporary data structure,
' and from there into the real data structure.
typTemp.strText = strText
LSet typTest = typTemp
' Test the data and see if it arrived OK.
Debug.Print typTest.FirstName
Debug.Print typTest.LastName
Debug.Print typTest.ZipCode
```

As you can see, LSet provides a very specific usage, but it can save you many lines of code if you've got to move a large number of fields from a text string into a data structure.

WARNING We've just barely scratched the surface of all the interesting, and potentially dangerous, tricks you can play with LSet. Beware that VBA does no checking for you when you use LSet to move data from one data structure to another.

Searching for a String

In many of the solutions presented later in this chapter, procedures will need to search a string for the inclusion of another string. The InStr function can determine whether one string contains another, and it can start looking at a specified location in the string. In addition, you can optionally specify whether the search should be case sensitive.

In general, the syntax for the InStr function looks like this:

intLocation = InStr([*intStart*,] *strSearched*, *strSought*[, *intCompare*])

Table 1.5 explains the parameters and their return values.

TABLE 1.5   Parameters for the InStr function

Part	Description
intStart	Optional. Sets the starting position for each search. If omitted, the search begins at the first character position. The intStart argument is required if you specify the intCompare argument
strSearched	Required. String expression being searched
strSought	Required. String expression sought
intCompare	Optional. Specifies the type of string comparison. The compare argument can be omitted, or it can be one of the values from Table 1.2. If compare is omitted, the Option Compare setting for the module determines the type of comparison
Return value	0 if strSought is not found in strSearched; character position where the first occurrence of strSought begins (1 through the length of strSearched) if strSought is found; intStart (or 1, if intStart is omitted) if strSought is zero-length

For example, the following example returns 3:

```
intPos = InStr("This is a test", "is")
```

This example, which starts looking later in the string, returns 6:

```
intPos = InStr(4, "This is a test", "is")
```

TIP

Although it's documented, it's easy to miss: if you specify the intCompare parameter for InStr, you need to supply a specific value for the intStart parameter. However, you won't often use the intCompare parameter; normally you'll use InStr, supplying neither parameter, since they're both optional.

Working with Portions of a String

Many string operations involve extracting a chunk of a string, and VBA makes this task simple by providing a series of functions that let you retrieve any portion of a string. Combined with the InStr function (see the previous section), you'll be able to find substrings and then extract them as necessary.

VBA supplies three simple functions for working with substrings: Left, Mid, and Right. The Left function allows you to extract the left portion of a string:

Left(*strIn*, *intChars*)

returns the first *intChars* characters from *strIn*. For example, this fragment returns the first two letters of the specified string:

```
strLeft2 = Left("This is a test", 2)
```

The following fragment returns the first word from strIn:

```
' This code fails pretty miserably if there's no space in strIn.
' You can't ask Left for the first -1 characters in a string!
strWord = Left(strIn, InStr(strIn, " ") - 1)
```

The Right function performs the same trick, but taking characters from the right side of the string instead. The following fragment appends a backslash (\) to the file name stored in strFileName, if it's not already there:

```
If Right(strFileName, 1) <> "\" Then
    strFileName = strFileName & "\"
End If
```

The Mid function is a bit more complex because it does more. It allows you to retrieve any specified piece of a string. You supply the string, the starting location, and (optionally) the number of characters to retrieve, and VBA does the rest. If you don't specify the number of characters to retrieve, you get the rest of the characters. The formal syntax for Mid looks like this:

strOut = Mid(*strIn*, *intStart*[, *intLen*])

For example, after running the following line of code:

```
strOut = Mid("This is a test", 6, 2)
```

strOut will contain the text "is". The following example places all the text of strIn, after the first word, into strRest:

```
strRest = Mid(strIn, InStr(strIn, " ") + 1)
```

TIP

Don't ever do what we've done in these examples! That is, never pass an unchecked value to Left, Right, or Mid unless you've included error handling in your procedure. In the examples that retrieved the first word, or all text after the first word, it's quite possible that the variable didn't actually contain a space, and InStr will return 0. In that case, you'll be passing –1 to the Left or Mid, and the functions won't take kindly to that. Make sure you've checked the value returned from InStr, in cases like this, before you call Left or Mid. For more information on slicing a word from a multi-word string, see the section "Working with Substrings" later in this chapter.

One common use of the Mid function is to loop through a string, one character at a time, working with each character. For example, the following loop prints each character in a string:

```
Dim strTest As String
Dim intI as Integer
strTest = "Look at each character"
For intI = 1 To Len(strTest)
    Debug.Print Mid(strTest, intI, 1)
Next intI
```

In addition to using the Left, Mid, and Right functions to extract portions of a string, you may need to remove leading or trailing white space from an existing string. VBA provides the LTrim, RTrim, and Trim functions to take care of these tasks. Each of these simple functions does one thing: LTrim removes leading spaces, RTrim removes trailing spaces, and Trim removes both leading and trailing spaces. The following fragment demonstrates the usage and results of these functions:

```
Dim strTest As String
strTest = "    This is a test    "

strTest = RTrim(strTest)
' strTest is now "    This is a test"

strTest = LTrim(strTest)
' strTest is now "This is a test"

strTest = "    This is a test    "
strTest = Trim(strTest)
' strTest is now "This is a test"
```

```
' You could use LTrim(RTrim(strTest))
' to replace the call to Trim, if you have the urge!
```

Replacing Portions of a String

Although you'll find several routines later in this chapter that make it easy to replace various portions of a string with other text, VBA includes a single statement that implements much of the functionality you'll need. The Mid statement (yes, it has the same name and parameters as the Mid function) allows you to replace text within a string with text supplied by another string.

To replace a substring within a string, use the Mid statement *on the left-hand side* of a line of code. The syntax for the Mid statement is as follows:

Mid(*strText*, *intStart*[, *intLength*]) = *strReplace*

The *intStart* value indicates where in *strText* to start replacing. The *intLength* value indicates how many characters from *strReplace* to place in *strText* at *intStart*.

For example, after calling the following code:

```
Dim strText As String
strText = "That car is fast."
Mid(strText, 6, 3) = "dog"
```

the variable strText will contain the text "That dog is fast". Although the Mid statement has its uses, it's rather limited because you can't control how much of the original string is replaced. You can control only how much of the replacement string is used. That is, if you try the following code:

```
Dim strText As String
strText = "That car is fast."
Mid(strText, 6, 4) = "fish"
```

there's no way to tell VBA to replace the word *car* with the word *fish*. Because the words are of differing lengths, you'll end up with "That fishis fast". Functions presented in the section "Searching for and Replacing Text" later in this chapter make it possible to replace whole words with other words.

ANSI Values

It's the job of the operating system's character set to map numbers representing text characters to those characters. When using the ANSI character set, Windows maps the values 0 through 255 to the 256 different characters that are available in each Windows code page. (When using Unicode, Windows NT does the same mapping, with values from 0 to 65535.) Each individual character represents a value between 0 and 255, and VBA provides two functions, Asc and Chr, to convert back and forth between the values and the characters themselves. These functions are inverses of each other—that is, using both functions on a value returns the original value.

The Asc function returns the character code corresponding to the first character of the string expression you pass it. The Chr function returns a character corresponding to the numeric value you pass it. For example, the following code fragment demonstrates the use of these two functions:

```
Dim intCh as Integer
Dim strCh as String * 1

intCh = Asc("This is a test")
' intCh now contains 84, the value corresponding to
' the "T" character.
strCh = Chr(intCh)
' strCh now contains "T", the letter corresponding to
' the value 84.
```

Speed Considerations with the Asc and Chr Functions

The following two logical expressions are equivalent:

```
If Asc(strChar) = intANSIValue Then
' and
If strChar = Chr(intANSIValue) Then
```

You'll want to use the first construct, however, because it's actually quite a bit more efficient to perform the Asc calculation than to call the Chr function. If you're comparing a large number of characters to specific ANSI values, make sure you convert the character to ANSI rather than convert the ANSI value into a character. This optimization can save you considerable processor time if you use it often.

Working with Bytes

In addition to all the functions VBA provides for working with standard strings, you'll find a set of functions for working with bytes within the strings and a set for working directly with the characters in Unicode strings.

If you want to work with the bytes that make up a string, you can use the LeftB, RightB, MidB, LenB, AscB, InStrB, and ChrB functions. Each of these functions does what its normal relative does, but each works on bytes instead of characters, as shown in Figure 1.1. For example, for a ten-character string, Len returns 10, but LenB returns 20 (each character takes two bytes). The first fragment in Listing 1.1 loops through all the characters in a string, printing each to the Debug window. The second loop in the fragment works through all the *bytes* in the string and lists each one. In this case, the output will include a 0 between bytes because the alternate bytes are 0 for English characters.

Listing 1.1: Loop through Characters and Bytes

```
Sub DumpBytes()
    ' Dump the characters, and then bytes, of
    ' the text "Hello" to the Debug window.
    Dim intI As Integer
    Dim strTest As String
    strTest = "Hello"
    For intI = 1 To Len(strTest)
        Debug.Print Asc(Mid(strTest, intI, 1));
    Next intI
    Debug.Print
    For intI = 1 To LenB(strTest)
        Debug.Print AscB(MidB(strTest, intI, 1));
    Next intI
    Debug.Print
End Sub
```

> **TIP** Generally, you won't write code using MidB like that shown in Listing 1.1. Instead, you'll convert the string into a byte array and work with each element of the byte array. The other byte functions are necessary, however, in order to extract just the bytes you need from the string.

FIGURE 1.1

Looping through
bytes as opposed
to characters

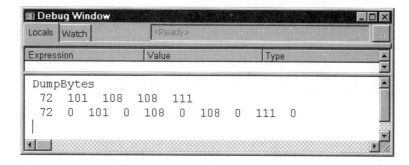

About the Functions Ending in $

VBA supplies all the functions that return strings in two formats—one with a dollar sign ($) at the end and one without. Why did they bother? The versions without $'s return Variants, and the ones with $'s return strings. The variant versions are able to propagate a null value through an expression; the string functions cannot. That is, if the input value is a variant containing Null, the variant functions return Null, and the string functions trigger a run-time error. The string functions, on the other hand, are faster; because they don't need to perform any datatype conversions, they can do their work faster.

How do you decide which version to use? If you're concerned about wringing the best performance out of your application and you can ensure that you won't be sending null values to these functions, then by all means use the string-specific version of any function you can.

Putting the Functions Together

Now that you've seen all the basic string-handling functions, you can start to put them together in various combinations to tackle more complex situations. The remainder of this chapter which provides a number of techniques for use in real-world situations, built up from our personal function libraries, is broken into four sections:

- Searching for and Replacing Text
- Gathering Information about Strings
- Converting Strings
- Working with Substrings

Using Optional Parameters

Many of the procedures in the following sections accept one or more optional parameters. In each case, if you don't specify the parameter in your function call, the receiving function assigns that parameter a value.

When you use optional parameters, you have two basic choices:

- Use a Variant parameter and check for the parameter using the IsMissing function.
- Use a strongly typed parameter and assign a default value in the formal declaration.

We've opted for the second alternative because this allows for type-checking when calling the procedure. On the other hand, it also removes the possibility of using the IsMissing function to check for the omission of the parameter. For example, you'll see declarations like this:

```
Function dhCountIn(strText As String, strFind As String, _
  Optional fCaseSensitive As Boolean = False) As Integer
```

We've assumed that you'll most often want to call this procedure in its case-insensitive mode, so we've chosen that as the default. If you don't specify a value for the third parameter to this function, it will assume you meant to pass False.

Searching for and Replacing Text

In this section you'll find techniques for finding and replacing text within strings. Although these procedures require more code than almost any other procedures in the chapter, they're used by many of the later solutions, so it makes sense to present them first.

In particular, this section includes solutions to performing the following tasks:

- Replacing any character in a specified list with a single other character
- Removing all white space, leaving one space between words
- Removing trailing Null and padding from string
- Replacing one substring with another
- Replacing tokens within a string (by position in an array passed in)

Replacing Any Character in a List with another Character

Editing text often involves replacing any one of a list of characters with another single character. For example, if you want to count the number of words in a sentence, you may need to take the input sentence, replace all the punctuation characters with spaces, and then count the spaces. Or you may want to just remove all extraneous characters; for example, you might want to convert a phone number in the format "(213)555-1212" into the format "2135551212". The function provided in this section, dhTranslate, makes both these tasks simple. (See Listing 1.2 for the entire function.)

Using dhTranslate, you could replace all punctuation characters with spaces, like this:

```
strText = dhTranslate(strText, " ,.!:;<>?", " ")
```

To remove extraneous characters, you could call dhTranslate like this:

```
strText = dhTranslate("(213)555-1212", "()-", "")
```

But dhTranslate does more than that: if you specify a mapping between the set of search characters and the set of match characters, it will replace characters in a one-to-one correspondence. That is, imagine you want to replace letters in a phone number with the corresponding digit. You know, someone says to call l-800-CALLKEN, but you really want to store just the digits to be dialed. You can use dhTranslate to map specific characters to digits, like this:

```
strPhone = dhTranslate("1-800-CALLKEN", _
 "ABCDEFGHIJKLMNOPRSTUVWXY", _
 "22233344455566677788899")
```

That function call will replace each letter with its appropriate digit.

If the replacement string is shorter than the search string, dhTranslate pads it to make it the same width as the search string. That is, when you call dhTranslate with a short replacement string:

```
strText = dhTranslate(strText, " ,.!:;<>?", " ")
```

the function converts the third parameter into a string with the same number of characters as the second parameter, internally, so it's as though you'd called the function like this:

```
strText = dhTranslate(strText, " ,.!:;<>?", "          ")
```

That way, each character in the second string has been mapped to a space for its replacement character.

To call dhTranslate yourself, pass three required parameters and one optional parameter, like this:

strText = dhTranslate(*strIn*, *strMapIn*, *strMapOut*[, *fCaseSensitive*])

The parameters for dhTranslate are as follows:

- *strIn* is the string to be modified.

- *strMapIn* is the string containing characters to find.

- *strMapOut* is the string containing 0 or more characters to replace the corresponding characters from strMapIn. If this string is shorter than strMapIn, the function pads the string with its final character to match the length of *strMapIn*.

- *fCaseSensitive* is optional. Set to True to force the search to be case sensitive. Set to False (the default value) to allow matches independent of the case.

The function's return value is a copy of the original string (strIn) with the requested modifications.

Listing 1.2: Translate One Set of Characters to another Set

```
Function dhTranslate(ByVal strIn As String, _
 ByVal strMapIn As String, ByVal strMapOut As String, _
 Optional fCaseSensitive As Boolean = True) As String
    ' Take a list of characters in strMapIn, match them
    ' one-to-one in strMapOut, and perform a character
    ' replacement in strIn.
    Dim intI As Integer
    Dim intPos As Integer
    Dim strChar As String * 1
    Dim strOut As String
    Dim intMode As Integer

    ' If there's no list of characters
    ' to replace, there's no point going on
    ' with the work in this function.
    If Len(strMapIn) > 0 Then
        ' Set up the comparison mode.
        If fCaseSensitive Then
            intMode = vbBinaryCompare
        Else
            intMode = vbTextCompare
        End If
        ' Right-fill the strMapOut set.
        If Len(strMapOut) > 0 Then
            strMapOut = Left$(strMapOut & String(Len(strMapIn), _
                Right$(strMapOut, 1)), Len(strMapIn))
        End If
        For intI = 1 To Len(strIn)
            strChar = Mid$(strIn, intI, 1)
            intPos = InStr(1, strMapIn, strChar, intMode)
            If intPos > 0 Then
                ' If strMapOut is empty, this doesn't fail,
                ' because Mid handles empty strings gracefully.
                strOut = strOut & Mid$(strMapOut, intPos, 1)
            Else
                strOut = strOut & strChar
            End If
        Next intI
    End If
    dhTranslate = strOut
End Function
```

Before it does any other work, dhTranslate checks to make sure strMapIn actually contains some text. If not, there's no work to do, and the function quickly exits.

Like many other functions in this chapter, the first real step dhTranslate takes is to set up a variable that will indicate how to perform the InStr search. The intMode variable will contain either of the two flags vbBinaryCompare or vbTextCompare, depending on the value of the fCaseSensitive parameter. You'll see this code scattered throughout the rest of this chapter:

```
If fCaseSensitive Then
    intMode = vbBinaryCompare
Else
    intMode = vbTextCompare
End If
```

Next, dhTranslate ensures that the strMapOut parameter contains as many characters as strMapIn. To do that, it takes the right-most character of strMapOut, creates a string of that character as wide as strMapIn, appends it to strMapOut, and then truncates the string to the same width as strMapIn:

```
' Right-fill the strMapOut set.
If Len(strMapOut) > 0 Then
    strMapOut = Left$(strMapOut & String(Len(strMapIn), _
      Right$(strMapOut, 1)), Len(strMapIn))
End If
```

For example, if strMapIn is "1234567890" and strMapOut is "ABCDE", the code creates a string of *E*'s ten characters long (the same length as strMapIn), appends it to the end of strMapOut (so it becomes "ABCDEEEEEEEEEE"), and then truncates the entire string to the length of strMapIn (ten characters, or "ABCDEEEEEE"). This mechanism makes it possible to replace a series of characters, supplied in strMapIn, with a single character, supplied in strMapOut.

Finally, dhTranslate performs the replacements, using brute force. For each character in the input string, dhTranslate attempts to find that character in strMapIn:

```
For intI = 1 To Len(strIn)
    strChar = Mid$(strIn, intI, 1)
    intPos = InStr(1, strMapIn, strChar, intMode)
    ' the code continues...
Next intI
```

If the InStr search found a match, intPos will be greater than 0. dhTranslate finds the appropriate matching character in strMapOut and appends that character to the end of the output string. If InStr failed to find a match, dhTranslate simply appends the character from the original string back to the end of the output string.

```
If intPos > 0 Then
    ' If strMapOut is empty, this doesn't fail,
    ' because Mid handles empty strings gracefully.
    strOut = strOut & Mid$(strMapOut, intPos, 1)
Else
    strOut = strOut & strChar
End If
```

In this way, one character at a time, dhTranslate either copies the character from the input string or uses its replacement from strMapOut. Either way, it returns strOut as its return value.

Many other functions within this chapter count on dhTranslate to do their work for them. You'll surely find many uses for it in your own applications as well.

Removing All Extra White Space

If you need to remove all extraneous white space from a string (and certainly, the dhCountWords function later in this chapter that counts the number of words in a string has reason to need this functionality), the dhTrimAll function will help. This function traverses a string and makes a new output string, copying over only a single space every time it finds one or more spaces inside the string. You can optionally request dhTrimAll to remove tabs as well.

For example, the following function call:

```
strOut = dhTrimAll("   This is     a test" & _
    "    of how   this works")
```

places "This is a test of how this works" into strOut. By default, the function removes tabs as well as spaces. If you want the function to disregard tabs and remove only spaces, send a False value for the second parameter. Listing 1.3 shows the entire dhTrimAll function.

Listing 1.3: Remove All White Space from a String

```
Function dhTrimAll(ByVal strText As String, _
  Optional fRemoveTabs As Boolean = True) As String
    ' Remove leading and trailing white space, and
    ' reduce any amount of internal white space (including tab
```

```
' characters) to a single space.
Dim strTemp As String
Dim strOut As String
Dim intI As Integer
Dim strCh As String * 1

' Trim off white space from the front and back.
' If requested, first convert all tabs into spaces,
' or RTrim and LTrim will miss them.
If fRemoveTabs Then
    strText = dhTranslate(strText, vbTab, " ")
End If
strTemp = Trim(strText)
For intI = 1 To Len(strTemp)
    ' Look at each character, in turn.
    strCh = Mid$(strTemp, intI, 1)

    ' If this character is a space, and the previous
    ' added character was a space, ignore it;
    ' otherwise, add it on.
    If Not (strCh = " " And Right$(strOut, 1) = " ") Then
        strOut = strOut & strCh
    End If
Next intI
dhTrimAll = strOut
End Function
```

How does dhTrimAll do its work? It starts out by converting all the tabs to spaces, if necessary, using the dhTranslate function:

```
If fRemoveTabs Then
    strText = dhTranslate(strText, vbTab, " ")
End If
```

Once the tabs are gone, the next step is to use the Trim function to remove leading and trailing spaces. This takes care of all the spaces before and after your string:

```
strTemp = Trim(strText)
```

The final step is the big one: the following loop works its way through all the characters. For each character, as long as it's not true that the current character is a space and the previous character added to the output string was also a space, the code just adds the character to the output string. Otherwise, if the current character is a space and the previous character was a space, it disregards the current character. This way, the output string is guaranteed never to have more than one space in a row.

```
For intI = 1 To Len(strTemp)
    ' Look at each character in turn.
    strCh = Mid$(strTemp, intI, 1)

    ' If this character is a space, and the previous
    ' added character was a space, ignore it;
    ' otherwise, add it on.
    If Not (strCh = " " And Right$(strOut, 1) = " ") Then
        strOut = strOut & strCh
    End If
Next intI
```

Removing Trailing Null and Padding from a String

Although you'll probably need the dhTrimNull function only if you're working with the Windows API, it's invaluable when you do. API functions don't know what the source of the string is, and they tend to place null-terminated strings into the buffers you send them. Unfortunately, VBA needs to have the length of the string set explicitly, so you need to find the first null character (Chr$(0), or vbNullChar) in the string and truncate the string there using the Left function. Examples in later chapters will use this function, and it's important to have it ready to go when you need it.

The dhTrimNull function, in Listing 1.4, accepts a single string and returns the same string, truncated at the first null character.

Listing 1.4: Trim Strings at the First Null Character

```
Function dhTrimNull(ByVal strValue As String) As String
    ' Find the first vbNullChar in a string, and return
    ' everything prior to that character. Extremely
    ' useful when combined with the Windows API function calls.
    Dim intPos As Integer
    intPos = InStr(strValue, vbNullChar)
    Select Case intPos
        Case 0
            ' Not found at all, so just
            ' return the original value.
            dhTrimNull = strValue
        Case 1
            ' Found at the first position, so return
            ' an empty string.
```

```
            dhTrimNull = ""
        Case Is > 1
            ' Found in the string, so return the portion
            ' up to the null character.
            dhTrimNull = Left$(strValue, intPos - 1)
    End Select
End Function
```

To do its work, dhTrimNull calls the InStr function, passing it the original string to search in and the constant vbNullChar to search for. Depending on the return value of InStr (stored in intPos), the function does one of three things:

- If intPos is 0, the function returns the original string. There weren't any null characters in the string to begin with.

- If intPos is 1, the first character was Null, so the function returns an empty string.

- If intPos is greater than 1, the function uses the Left function to pull out the part up to, but not including, the null character.

Using all three cases removes any possibility that you'll attempt to pass an illegal starting position to the Left function.

Replacing One Substring with Another

You need a routine that will replace all occurrences of ? with ! in a string. Or perhaps you need to replace all quote marks with apostrophes. You could write, over and over, the few lines of code this requires, or you could use a function that's set up to do any sort of generalized replacement. The dhReplaceAll function was written to make it easy to perform almost any text replacement job.

Besides performing simple replacements, dhReplaceAll allows you to specify at which occurrence of the search string to start replacing and how many replacements to make. The following list describes the parameters you can send to dhReplaceAll (the first three are required) and the return value:

- *strText* is the text in which to search.

- *strFind* is the text for which to search.

- *strReplace* is the text with which to replace *strFind*.

- *intFirst* (optional) is an integer indicating the first found occurrence to replace. If larger than the number of occurrences, replace nothing. If −1, replace the final occurrence. If −2, replace the next-to-last occurrence, and so on. The default value is 1, so unless you specify otherwise, the code will make replacements starting at the first match.

- *intCount* (optional) is an integer indicating the number of replacements to make. If larger than the number of occurrences, replace them all. If 0 or less, replace none. The default is dhcNoLimit (−1), so unless you specify otherwise, the function will replace all occurrences.

- *fCaseSensitive* (optional) indicates whether the search is to be case sensitive. The default value is False, so unless you specify otherwise, searches will be case insensitive.

- The return value is a copy of the original string in *strText*, with the requested replacements made.

To make the possible methods of calling dhReplaceAll a bit clearer, Table 1.6 demonstrates a few sample uses of the function. In each case, the first three parameters are the same, allowing you to see how the final three parameters affect the search. Listing 1.5 shows the entire, somewhat complex procedure.

TABLE 1.6   Examples Calling dhReplaceAll

Example	Returns	Comment
dhReplaceAll("This IS a test", "is", "X")	"ThX X a test"	Replaces all occurrences
dhReplaceAll("This IS) a test", "is", "X", 2	"This X a test"	Starts replacing at the second occurrence
dhReplaceAll("This IS a test", "is", "X", -1)	"This X a test"	Starts replacing at the last occurrence
dhReplaceAll("This IS a test", "is", "X", 1, 1)	"ThX IS a test" and makes one replacement	Starts replacing at the first occurrence
dhReplaceAll("This IS a test", "is", "X", fCaseSensitive:=True)	"ThX IS a test"	Search is case sensitive

Listing 1.5: Replace All Occurrences of a Substring

```
Function dhReplaceAll( _
 ByVal strText As String, _
 ByVal strFind As String, _
 ByVal strReplace As String, _
 Optional ByVal intFirst As Integer = 1, _
 Optional ByVal intCount As Integer = dhcNoLimit, _
 Optional ByVal fCaseSensitive As Boolean = False) As String

    ' Replace all instances of strFind with strReplace
    ' in strText.
    Dim intLenFind As Integer
    Dim intLenReplace As Integer
    Dim intPos As Integer
    Dim intStart As Integer
    Dim intI As Integer
    Dim intFound As Integer
    Dim intLast As Integer
    Dim intMode As Integer

    On Error GoTo HandleErr
    ' If anything's wrong in the various parameters,
    ' just exit. Unorthodox method, but it works here.
    If Len(strText) = 0 Then GoTo ExitHere
    If Len(strFind) = 0 Then GoTo ExitHere
    If intFirst = 0 Then GoTo ExitHere
    If intCount = 0 Then GoTo ExitHere

    ' The parameters must be reasonable if you've gotten this far.
    ' Handle the three optional parameters.
    If intFirst < 0 Then
        ' -1 == start at the last match.
        ' -2 == start at the next to the last match, etc.
        intFound = dhCountIn(strText, strFind)
        intFirst = intFound + intFirst + 1
        If intFirst < 1 Then intFirst = 1
    End If
    If intCount > dhcNoLimit Then
        intLast = intFirst + intCount
    End If
    If fCaseSensitive Then
        intMode = vbBinaryCompare
    Else
```

```
        intMode = vbTextCompare
    End If
    ' Store away the length of the find and replace
    ' text, to speed things up later on.
    intLenFind = Len(strFind)
    intLenReplace = Len(strReplace)

    intPos = 1
    intI = 1
    Do
        intPos = InStr(intPos, strText, strFind, intMode)
        If intPos > 0 Then
            ' Did you find a match? If so, check the other
            ' issues (starting replacement and number
            ' of replacements)
            If (intI >= intFirst) And _
              ((intCount = dhcNoLimit) Or (intI < intLast)) Then
                ' If the current item is greater than or equal
                ' to the first item the caller has requested
                ' to be replaced,
                ' and...
                ' If either you don't care about the number of
                ' replacements or this one is less than the
                ' final one you want to make, then do it.
                ' Perform the replacement.
                strText = Left$(strText, intPos - 1) & _
                  strReplace & Mid$(strText, intPos + intLenFind)
                ' Skip over the new text.
                intPos = intPos + intLenReplace
            Else
                ' Just skip over the search string.
                intPos = intPos + intLenFind
            End If
            intI = intI + 1
            ' If you know there are no more replacements, no
            ' need to continue looping. Just get on out!
            If (intCount <> dhcNoLimit And intI >= intLast) Then
                Exit Do
            End If
        End If
    Loop Until intPos = 0
ExitHere:
    dhReplaceAll = strText
```

```
    Exit Function
HandleErr:
    ' If any error occurs, just return the text as it
    ' currently is.
    Select Case Err.Number
        Case Else
            ' MsgBox "Error: " & Err.Description & _
            '  " (" & Err.Number & ")"
    End Select
    Resume ExitHere
End Function
```

This function, one of the longest in this chapter, isn't terribly complicated once you break it down into its functional steps. Although, as you'll see, the procedure seems awfully complex, it's so useful that it's worth the extra complexity. Many of the other procedures in this chapter depend on this procedure as well, so you'll see it pop up in several other explanations. The following list outlines the steps the code needs to take.

1. Validate the parameters.

2. Handle the three optional parameters.

3. Perform the search.

4. Determine whether to make the replacement.

5. Perform the replacement, if necessary.

6. Jump out of the loop.

The sections that follow give you the details of this procedure.

Validate the Parameters

Although the approach given here is somewhat unusual, it works in this situation. That is, any one of several situations can cause the function to terminate. If the string to search is empty, if the string to find is empty, if you tell the function to start replacing at occurrence 0, or if you tell the function to replace 0 occurrences, there's nothing to be done, and the code jumps to a common exit point:

```
If Len(strText) = 0 Then GoTo ExitHere
If Len(strFind) = 0 Then GoTo ExitHere
If intFirst = 0 Then GoTo ExitHere
If intCount = 0 Then GoTo ExitHere
```

Handle the Three Optional Parameters

If you tell the function to start replacing at a negative occurrence, the function knows to start replacing at an occurrence counting backward from the final one. (−1 means to start at the final occurrence, −2 starts at the next to last, and so on). The code uses the dhCountIn function (see the section "Counting the Number of Times a Substring Appears" later in this chapter) to count the number of occurrences in total, adds the value of intFirst, and uses that as the new value of the first occurrence to match. Of course, if that value is less than 1, the code must start at the first occurrence:

```
If intFirst < 0 Then
    ' -1 == start at the last match.
    ' -2 == start at the next to the last match, etc.
    intFound = dhCountIn(strText, strFind)
    intFirst = intFound + intFirst + 1
    If intFirst < 1 Then intFirst = 1
End If
```

If you've specified a number of replacements in the intCount parameter, calculate the final replacement:

```
If intCount > dhcNoLimit Then
    intLast = intFirst + intCount
End If
```

As in many other examples, calculate the value of the local intMode variable, to be used by the InStr function:

```
If fCaseSensitive Then
    intMode = vbBinaryCompare
Else
    intMode = vbTextCompare
End If
```

Determine Whether to Make the Replacement

Once the code has determined that it's found a match, it also has to determine whether it ought to replace the text. It does the deed only if the current match is greater than or equal to the first match (intI >= intFirst), and either it's all the occurrences (intCount = dhcNoLimit) or, if the current match is less than the final match, to (intI < intLast). Once it's made the replacement (see the next section), the code moves the starting search position to the end of the replacement—there's no point searching for another match in the string it just replaced! If it didn't make the replacement, it just moves the starting search position to the end of the search string. Finally, the code increments the count of matches found:

```
' Did you find a match? If so, check the other
' issues (starting replacement, and number
' of replacements)
If (intI >= intFirst) And _
 ((intCount = dhcNoLimit) Or (intI < intLast)) Then
    ' (Code removed) Make the replacement in here
    intPos = intPos + intLenReplace
Else
    ' Just skip over the search string.
    intPos = intPos + intLenFind
End If
intI = intI + 1
' (Code removed)
End If
```

Perform the Replacement, If Necessary   This step's the simplest. Just take the portion of the text before the match, add in the replacement string, and then tack on the portion of the original string after the match and put it back into the search text:

```
strText = Left$(strText, intPos - 1) & _
 strReplace & Mid$(strText, intPos + intLenFind)
```

Jump Out of the Loop   This simple optimization causes the code to exit from the loop prematurely if there are no more matches requested. That is, if you've specified the number of matches to replace and you've made that many replacements, it's time to get out of there!

```
If (intCount <> dhcNoLimit And intI >= intLast) Then
    Exit Do
End If
```

Replacing Numbered Tokens within a String

If you're creating text resources that need to be translated to local languages, or if you just need to replace a series of tokens in a string with a series of text strings, the function shown in Listing 1.6 will help you out. This function allows you to pass in a list of text strings to replace numbered tokens (%1, %2, and so on) in a larger text string.

If you separate the text for your application from the application's user interface, it's far easier to prepare the application for international use. It's inevitable, however, that some of your strings will need to contain replaceable parameters. Using dhTokenReplace makes it simple to perform those replacements at run time. For example, running the following fragment:

```
strText = dhTokenReplace("Unable to add file %1 to %2", _
 "C:\AUTOEXEC.BAT", "C:\FOO.ZIP")
```

would place the text "Unable to add the file C:\AUTOEXEC.BAT to C:\FOO .ZIP" into strText. (The assumption here is that the resource string, "Unable to add…", is coming from a table, a resource file, or some other source external to your application and is translated for use in countries besides your own.) But what if, in a particular language, the correct phrasing would be (translated back into English) "C:\FOO.ZIP is unable to contain C:\AUTOEXEC.BAT"? In that case, the translator could modify the resource to be "%2 is unable to contain %1", and your code would still function correctly.

Even if you're not producing internationalized applications, dhTokenReplace will make your work simpler. Being able to replace multiple substrings in one pass can make your applications run faster and certainly will make them code faster.

Using ParamArray to Pass an Array of Parameters

Although the ParamArray construct has been available in the past few versions of VBA, few programmers have run across it. It's not used often, but when you need it, it's totally indispensable. In this case, being able to pass a virtually unlimited number of parameters to a function makes it possible to write one function that can handle unlimited situations.

To use this feature, you declare your function to accept a ParamArray parameter, like this:

```
Public Function dhTokenReplace(ByVal strIn As String, _
 ParamArray varItems() As Variant) As String
```

Then, when you call the function, you can pass as many items as you like after the required parameter(s), and VBA will convert them into an array and pass them to the procedure. Your procedure receives the array in the parameter you declared as ParamArray, and you can use any array-handling techniques to work with the parameters.

The rules? The ParamArray parameter must be

- The final parameter
- Not mixed with the Optional, ByVal, or ByRef keyword
- Declared as an array of Variants

Listing 1.6: Replace Numbered Tokens in a String

```
Public Function dhTokenReplace(ByVal strIn As String, _
 ParamArray varItems() As Variant) As String
    ' Replace %1, %2, %3, etc., with the values passed in varItems.
    On Error GoTo HandleErr
    Dim intPos As Integer
    Dim strReplace As String
    Dim intI As Integer

    For intI = LBound(varItems) To UBound(varItems)
        strReplace = "%" & (intI + 1)
        intPos = InStr(1, strIn, strReplace)
        If intPos > 0 Then
            strIn = Left$(strIn, intPos - 1) & _
            varItems(intI) & Mid$(strIn, intPos +_
            Len(strReplace))
        End If
    Next intI
ExitHere:
    dhTokenReplace = strIn
    Exit Function
HandleErr:
    ' If any error occurs, just return the
```

```
    ' string as it currently exists.
    Select Case Err.Number
        Case Else
            ' MsgBox "Error: " & Err.Description & _
            '    " (" & Err.Number & ")"
    End Select
    Resume ExitHere
End Function
```

The dhTokenReplace function is quite similar to the dhReplaceAll function and is actually somewhat simpler. There's no need to check parameters (if there's nothing in the varItems array, the loop will drop out immediately and just return to the caller), and you don't need to loop to replace all the occurrences of a string—you're guaranteed there's at most one replacement to be made for each string in the input array.

To do its work, dhTokenReplace loops through all the elements of the input array, from the lower bound to the upper bound:

```
For intI = LBound(varItems) To UBound(varItems)
    ' (Code removed)
Next intI
```

For each item in the array, the code builds a new item number (such as "%1", "%2", and so on) and then searches for the string within the text:

```
strReplace = "%" & (intI + 1)
intPos = InStr(1, strIn, strReplace)
```

If InStr found a match (that is, intPos is greater than 0), dhTokenReplace modifies the input string to contain all the text before the match, then the replacement text, and then all the text after the match:

```
If intPos > 0 Then
    strIn = Left$(strIn, intPos - 1) & _
        varItems(intI) & Mid$(strIn, intPos + Len(strReplace))
End If
```

That's it! Repeating the steps for each item in the input array ends up with all the tokens replaced with text.

Gathering Information about Strings

In this section, you'll find techniques for retrieving information about an existing string, including:

- Determining whether a character is alphanumeric

- Determining whether a character is alphabetic

- Determining whether a character is numeric

- Counting the number of times a substring appears in a string

- Counting the number of tokens in a delimited string

- Counting the number of words in a string

Determining the Characteristics of a Character

When validating text, you may want to check the contents of each individual character in a string. You may want to know whether any specific character is alphabetic (A–Z, in English), alphanumeric (A–Z, 0–9 in English), or just numeric (0–9). The first two tests are most quickly accomplished using API calls, and the final one can be accomplished a few different ways.

> **NOTE** Although the examples in this section focus only on the ANSI character set, the examples on disk also take into account the Unicode character set. See the sidebar "Working with Wide Character Sets"" later in this chapter for more information.

Is This Character Alphabetic?

Should you need to verify that a given character is alphabetic (and not numeric, punctuation, a symbol, and so on), you might be tempted to just check the character and see whether it's in the range of A–Z or a–z. This would be a mistake for two reasons:

- If you want your application to be able to be localized for countries besides your own, this code is almost guaranteed to break in any other language.

- Using VBA to handle this task is almost certainly the slowest way possible.

A better bet is to let Windows handle this task for you. Using the IsCharAlpha API function, you can allow Windows to decide whether the selected character is alphabetic. That way, the test runs faster, and you needn't worry about internationalization issues—Windows will know, for the local environment, whether a given character is alphabetic.

To use the API function, you must first declare the function. (This declaration is included in the sample code for this chapter.)

```
Private Declare Function IsCharAlphaA Lib "USER32" _
 (ByVal bytChar As Byte) As Long
```

To use the IsCharAlphaA API function, you can call the dhIsCharAlpha function:

```
Function dhIsCharAlpha(strText As String) As Boolean
    ' Is the first character of strText an alphabetic character?
    dhIsCharAlpha = CBool(IsCharAlphaA(Asc(strText)))
End Function
```

This simple wrapper function converts the first letter of the text you pass to a numeric value (using the Asc function), calls IsCharAlphaA, and converts the result to a Boolean value.

To verify that the first letter of a value a user supplies is alphabetic, you might use dhIsCharAlpha like this:

```
If dhIsCharAlpha(strText) Then
    ' You know the first letter of strText is alphabetic.
End If
```

Is This Character Alphanumeric?

Expanding on the previous function, if you need to know whether a character is either alphabetic or numeric, Windows provides a simple function for this test as well. You can use the IsCharAlphaNumericA API function, declared like this:

```
Private Declare Function IsCharAlphaNumericA Lib "USER32" _
 (ByVal byChar As Byte) As Long
```

Just as before, we've provided a simple wrapper function for the API function, making it easier to call:

```
Function dhIsCharAlphaNumeric(strText As String) As Boolean
    ' Is the first character of strText an alphanumeric character?
    dhIsCharAlphaNumeric = CBool(IsCharAlphaNumericA(Asc(strText)))
End Function
```

This function will return True if the first character of the value you pass it is either a letter or a digit.

Is This Character Numeric?

Although the task of determining whether a character is numeric could be quite simple, finding the best approach took a few iterations. We ended up with two techniques that are almost identical in their performance, and you'll need to choose one based on your own preferences.

The first technique uses the two previous solutions—that is, a character is numeric if it's alphanumeric but not alphabetic. Therefore, dhIsCharNumeric performs the first determination:

```
Function dhIsCharNumeric(strText As String) As Boolean
    ' Is the first character of strText a numeric character?
    dhIsCharNumeric = dhIsCharAlphaNumeric(strText) _
     And Not dhIsCharAlpha(strText)
End Function
```

An alternative technique is to use the Like operator, discussed in the section "Comparison Operators" earlier in this chapter. If you're checking only to see whether a character is numeric, this is the best solution; it involves no API calls and no declarations. If you're already using the other two API-reliant functions, you might as well use them here as well. This alternative checks the first character of the string you send it, comparing it to "[0–9]*":

```
Function dhIsCharNumeric1(strText As String) As Boolean
    ' Is the first character numeric?
    ' Almost identical in speed to calling the two API functions.
    dhIsCharNumeric1 = (strText Like "[0-9]*")
End Function
```

Working with Wide Character Sets

The two techniques provided here that call the Windows API will fail, unfortunately, if your version of Windows uses wide (2-byte) characters or if you want your solutions to run on machines that use wide characters. In these cases, you'll need to take extra steps.

The simplest solution is to determine the maximum character width in the selected character set and choose the correct API function to call based on that determination. (The code examples on the disk do take these extra steps.) The 32-bit Windows API specification includes two versions of most functions that involve strings: one for the ANSI environment and one for DBCS and Unicode environments. In the examples shown here, we've used the ANSI solution because that solution works for English text.

To determine whether you need to use the alternate API calls, you can use the dhIsCharsetWide function. Once you've got the return value from that function, you can decide whether to call the ANSI or the Unicode version of the API functions, like this:

```
Function dhIsCharAlphaNumeric(strText As String) As Boolean
    If dhIsCharsetWide() Then
        dhIsCharAlphaNumeric = _
        CBool(IsCharAlphaNumericW(AscW(strText)))
    Else
        dhIsCharAlphaNumeric = _
        CBool(IsCharAlphaNumericA(Asc(strText)))
    End If
End Function
```

Note that you must also call the AscW function when working with the "wide" versions of the API functions.

Counting the Number of Times a Substring Appears

The InStr built-in VBA function can tell you whether a particular string appears within another string (InStr returns a position within the string if the substring is there and 0 if it's not), but it can't tell you how many times the substring appears. If you want to count occurrences (and several of the other functions in this chapter will need to do this), you can use the dhCountIn function, shown in Listing 1.7.

Listing 1.7: Find the Number of Occurrences of a Substring

```
Function dhCountIn(strText As String, strFind As String, _
 Optional fCaseSensitive As Boolean = False) As Integer
    ' Determine the number of times strFind appears in strText
    Dim intCount As Integer
    Dim intPos As Integer
    Dim intMode As Integer

    ' If there's nothing to find, there surely can't be any
    ' found, so return 0.
    If Len(strFind) > 0 Then
        ' Set up the comparison mode.
        If fCaseSensitive Then
            intMode = vbBinaryCompare
        Else
            intMode = vbTextCompare
        End If
        intPos = 1
        Do
            intPos = InStr(intPos, strText, strFind, intMode)
            If intPos > 0 Then
                intCount = intCount + 1
                intPos = intPos + Len(strFind)
            End If
        Loop While intPos > 0
    Else
        intCount = 0
    End If
    dhCountIn = intCount
```

```
End Function
```

Of course, if there's nothing to find, the function just returns 0:

```
If Len(strFind) > 0 Then
    ' the real code goes here
Else
    intCount = 0
End If
```

Like many other functions in this chapter, the first real step dhCountIn takes is to set up a variable that will indicate how to perform the InStr search. The intMode variable will contain either vbBinaryCompare or vbTextCompare, depending on the value of the fCaseSensitive parameter:

```
If fCaseSensitive Then
    intMode = vbBinaryCompare
Else
    intMode = vbTextCompare
End If
```

Finally, it's time to perform the search. The code loops through the input text, looking for the string, until it no longer finds any matches (that is, until the return value from InStr is 0). Along the way, if it finds a match, it increments the value of intCount and moves the start position to the character after the end of the sought string in the input text. This not only speeds up the search (why look for the text at the very next character after you just found it if the text you're looking for is, say, four characters long?), it avoids finding overlapping matches. Here's the code fragment that does the major portion of the work:

```
intPos = 1
Do
    intPos = InStr(intPos, strText, strFind, intMode)
    If intPos > 0 Then
        intCount = intCount + 1
        intPos = intPos + Len(strFind)
    End If
Loop While intPos > 0
```

To find the number of vowels in a string, you might write code like this:

```
intVowels = dhCountIn(strText, "A") + dhCountIn(strText, "E") + _
  dhCountIn(strText, "I") + dhCountIn(strText, "O") + _
  dhCountIn(strText, "U")
```

Counting the Number of Tokens in a Delimited String

The dhCountTokens function, shown in Listing 1.8, is a general-purpose function that allows you to find out how many "chunks" of text there are in a string, given text delimiters that you supply. The function interprets any one of the characters in your list of delimiters as a token separator, so

```
dhCountTokens("This is a test", " ")
```

returns 4, as does

```
dhCountTokens("This:is!a test", ": !")
```

Because every delimiter character must delimit a token, the following example returns 10:

```
dhCountTokens("This:!:is:!:a:!:test", ": !")
```

You'll have to look carefully to see them, but the individual tokens are

```
This, "", "", is, "", "", a, "", "", test
```

Listing 1.8: Count the Number of Tokens in a String

```
Function dhCountTokens(ByVal strText As String, _
 ByVal strDelimiter As String) As Integer
    ' Return the number of tokens, given a set of delimiters,
    ' in a string
    Dim strChar As String * 1
    ' If there's no search text, there can't be any tokens.
    If Len(strText) = 0 Then
        dhCountTokens = 0
    Else
        strChar = Left$(strDelimiter, 1)
        ' Flatten all the delimiters to just the first one in
        ' the list.
        If Len(strDelimiter) > 1 Then
            strText = dhTranslate(strText, strDelimiter, strChar)
        End If
        ' Count the tokens.
        dhCountTokens = dhCountIn(strText, strChar) + 1
    End If
End Function
```

The dhCountTokens function is somewhat tricky—it uses the dhCountIn function, which can count the occurrence of only a single item. Rather than call dhCountIn multiple times, once for each different delimiter, dhCountTokens "flattens" the delimiters in the input text. That is, it first calls the dhTranslate function to map all the different delimiters to the first character in your list of delimiters:

```
strChar = Left$(strDelimiter, 1)
' Flatten all the delimiters to just the first one in
' the list.
If Len(strDelimiter) > 1 Then
    strText = dhTranslate(strText, strDelimiter, strChar)
End If
```

That is, if you called dhCountTokens as

```
dhCountTokens("This:!:is:!:a:!:test", ": !")
```

after this step, strText would contain

```
"This:::is:::a:::test"
```

Now, it's just a matter of counting the number of times the first delimiter appears in the string and adding 1. (If there are four delimiters, there must be five tokens.)

```
dhCountTokens = dhCountIn(strText, strChar) + 1
```

That's all there is to it. The next section shows a typical reason to call dhCountTokens.

Counting the Number of Words in a String

Although the dhCountTokens function provides you with total flexibility, you're more often going to want to count specific types of delimited objects. Counting words is a typical task, and dhCountWords uses techniques similar to those used in dhCountTokens to make the task simple. The code, shown in Listing 1.9, takes the following steps:

1. Checks the length of the input text. If it's 0, there's not much point in continuing.

2. Calls dhTranslate to convert all the delimiters to spaces. The function uses a standard set of delimiters, declared as follows:

```
Const dhcDelimiters As String = " ,.!:;<>?"
```

3. Calls dhTrimAll to remove leading and trailing spaces and converts all groups of spaces to a single space within the text.

4. Calls dhCountIn to count the spaces in the string and adds 1 to the result.

For example, calling dhCountWords like this:

```
dhCountWords("Hi there, my name is Cleo, what's yours?")
```

returns 8, the number of words in the string.

Listing 1.9: Count the Number of Words in a String

```
Function dhCountWords(ByVal strText As String) As Integer
    ' Return the number of words in a string.
    If Len(strText) = 0 Then
        dhCountWords = 0
    Else
        ' Get rid of any extraneous stuff, including delimiters
        ' and spaces. First convert delimiters to spaces, and
        ' then remove all extraneous spaces.
        strText = dhTrimAll( _
         dhTranslate(strText, dhcDelimiters, " "))
        ' If there are three spaces, there are
        ' four words, right?
        dhCountWords = dhCountIn(strText, " ") + 1
    End If
End Function
```

Converting Strings

This section presents a series of techniques for performing common tasks involving the conversion of a string from one form to another. The section includes the following topics:

- Converting a number into a string with the correct ordinal suffix
- Reversing a string
- Converting a number to roman numerals

- Performing a "smart" proper case conversion
- Encrypting/decrypting text using XOR password encryption
- Returning a string left-padded or right-padded to a specified width
- Using Soundex to compare strings

Converting a Number into a String with the Correct Ordinal Suffix

If you want to be able to represent a numeric value as its ordinal position in a set, you'll need to write a function that, when provided with an integer, returns a string containing the value and its suffix as a string. The simple dhOrdinal function, shown in Listing 1.10, does what you need; it takes in a numeric value and returns a string containing the ordinal representation of that value. For example:

```
dhOrdinal(34)
```

returns "34th", and

```
dhOrdinal(1)
```

returns "1st".

The dhOrdinal function counts on standard rules to calculate the suffix (once it's removed all but the final two digits, using the Mod operator):

- All values between 11 and 19, inclusive, use "th".

Otherwise:

- Numbers that end in 1 use "st".
- Numbers that end in 2 use "nd".
- Numbers that end in 3 use "rd".
- All numbers that haven't yet been claimed use "th".

Listing 1.10: Convert a Value to Its Ordinal Suffix

```
Function dhOrdinal(intItem As Integer) As String
    ' Given an integer, return a string
    ' representing the ordinal value.

    Dim intDigit As Integer
    Dim strOut As String * 2
    Select Case intItem Mod 100
```

```
        Case 11 To 19
            ' All teens use "th"
            strOut = "th"
        Case Else
            ' Get that final digit
            intDigit = intItem Mod 10
            Select Case intDigit
                Case 1
                    strOut = "st"
                Case 2
                    strOut = "nd"
                Case 3
                    strOut = "rd"
                Case Else
                    strOut = "th"
            End Select
    End Select
    dhOrdinal = intItem & strOut
End Function
```

The code first checks for values between 11 and 19 because they all use the "th" suffix. For other values, the code looks at the "ones" digit because that's all it takes to determine which suffix to use. To find the digit that ends each number, the code uses the Mod operator, which returns the remainder when you divide by the second operand. For example:

```
41 Mod 10
```

returns 1, the remainder you get when you divide 41 by 10.

TIP

The dhOrdinal function would need to be completely overhauled for any language besides English; it's not clear that the ordinal suffixes would even group the same way in any other language. If you intend to distribute applications globally, be sure to allot time for rewriting this function for each localized language.

Reversing a String

Yes, it's true—you may not often need to reverse a string. But when you do, it's nice to have a function written to do it.

Actually, the RInstr function, described in the section "Returning a Specific Word, by Index, from a String" later in this chapter, does require this function to do its work. Since we had to write it for that function, it seemed worth the effort of exposing it publicly as well.

In addition, writing this function presented an opportunity to try out working with byte arrays. Later in the section, you'll see a first, simple attempt at writing this function. The final, more complex version we present does its work approximately 100 percent faster than does the original attempt.

The dhReverse function, in Listing 1.11, accepts a single string and returns that string with the characters reversed. For example:

```
dhReverse("This is a test")
```

returns "tset a si sihT".

Listing 1.11: Reverse a String Using a Byte Array

```
Function dhReverse(ByVal strIn As String) As String
    ' Reverse a string, character by character.
    Dim abytIn() As Byte
    Dim strTemp As String
    Dim intI As Integer
    Dim intMax As Integer
    Dim bytTemp As Byte
    Dim intNew As Integer

    If Len(strIn) = 0 Then
        dhReverse = strIn
    Else
        abytIn = strIn
        ' Now reverse all the characters.
        intMax = UBound(abytIn)
        For intI = LBound(abytIn) To (intMax \ 2) Step 2
            intNew = intMax - intI
            ' Swap the first bytes.
            bytTemp = abytIn(intI)
```

```
                    abytIn(intI) = abytIn(intNew - 1)
                    abytIn(intNew - 1) = bytTemp

                    ' Swap the second bytes.
                    bytTemp = abytIn(intI + 1)
                    abytIn(intI + 1) = abytIn(intNew)
                    abytIn(intNew) = bytTemp
                Next intI
                dhReverse = abytIn
            End If
        End Function
```

As mentioned in the sidebar "Using Strings and Byte Arrays" earlier in this chapter, it is sometimes advantageous to copy a string into a byte array, do the processing there, and then copy the result back into a string. Copying the string into the byte array is trivial:

```
abytIn = strIn
```

Once you've got the text into the byte array, it looks something like the representation for the word *Hello* in Figure 1.2. As you can see, the array consists of ten bytes, numbered 0 through 9, with each letter of the original word occupying a pair of bytes.

To reverse the string, dhReverse makes its way through that array, working with two bytes at a time:

```
For intI = LBound(abytIn) To (intMax \ 2) Step 2
    ' (Code removed)
Next intI
```

FIGURE 1.2:

The string "Hello", converted to a byte array

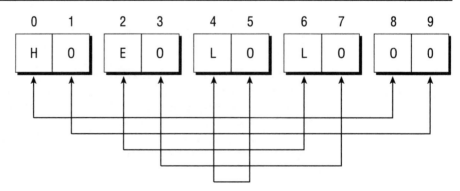

In this case, the loop will go from 0 to 4, in increments of 2 (intMax is 9, so intMax \ 2 is 4). As you can see in Figure 1.2, the code swaps bytes 0 and 8 and then bytes 1 and 9. In the next step, it swaps bytes 2 and 6 and then bytes 3 and 7. Finally, it swaps bytes 4 and 5 and then bytes 5 and 4 (redundant, yes, but faster than skipping this step in the special case of odd-length strings).

TIP Swapping two items programmatically is always a three-step process. You must copy the first item to a temporary location, copy the second item to the first item, and then copy the first item (in its temporary location) into the second item. This isn't an algorithm particular to VBA—it's been in use forever. If you've never run across this, however, it may take some getting used to.

When you first approach a task such as reversing a string, you might write a simple function like the one shown in Listing 1.12. Although significantly shorter than the dhReverse function, it actually executes much slower. Why? String functions in VBA are quite expensive, in terms of time. Working with byte arrays is, on the other hand, quick. In this case, because the code was able to work with each byte individually, it made sense to use a byte array rather than pull off a character at a time using the Mid function. When you write data-handling functions, you'll need to decide whether you can work with the data one byte at a time, using a byte array, or whether you must work one character at a time, using the slower string functions.

Listing 1.12: A Slower, Simpler Version of the Function

```
Function SlowReverse(strIn As String) As String
    Dim strOut As String
    Dim intI As Integer

    For intI = Len(strIn) To 1 Step -1
        strOut = strOut & Mid$(strIn, intI, 1)
    Next intI
    SlowReverse = strOut
End Function
```

Besides the need for reversed strings in the RInstr function described later in this chapter, how else might you use dhReverse? If you want to check a string to see whether it's a palindrome (another terribly common programming activity, of course, or perhaps not), you might write an expression like this:

```
If dhTranslate(strText, " ", "") = _
  dhReverse(dhTranslate(strText, " ", "")) Then
    ' You know strText is a palindrome
End If
```

Converting a Number into Roman Numerals

If you're creating legal documents programmatically, or if your job involves copyright notifications (well, it is somewhat difficult coming up with compelling scenarios for this one), you're likely to require the capability to convert integers into roman numerals. Although this need may not come up often, when it does, it's tricky enough that you'll want to avoid having to write the code yourself.

The dhRoman function, in Listing 1.13, can accept an integer between 1 and 3999 (the Romans didn't have a concept of 0), and it returns the value converted into roman numerals. For example:

```
dhRoman(1997)
```

returns "MCMXCVII", and

```
dhRoman(3999)
```

returns "MMMCMXCIX".

Listing 1.13: Convert Numbers to Roman Numerals

```
Function dhRoman(ByVal intValue As Integer) As String
    ' Convert a decimal number between 1 and 3999
    ' into a roman number.
    Dim varDigits As Variant
    Dim intPos As Integer
    Dim IntDigit As Integer
    Dim strTemp As String

    ' Build up the array of roman digits
    varDigits = Array("I", "V", "X", "L", "C", "D", "M")
    intPos = Lbound(varDigits)
    strTemp = ""
    Do While intValue > 0
        intDigit = intValue Mod 10
```

```
            intValue = intValue \ 10
            Select Case intDigit
                Case 1
                    strTemp = varDigits(intPos) & strTemp
                Case 2
                    strTemp = varDigits(intPos) & _
                      varDigits(intPos) & strTemp
                Case 3
                    strTemp = varDigits(intPos) & _
                      varDigits(intPos) & varDigits(intPos) & strTemp
                Case 4
                    strTemp = varDigits(intPos) & _
                      varDigits(intPos + 1) & strTemp
                Case 5
                    strTemp = varDigits(intPos + 1) & strTemp
                Case 6
                    strTemp = varDigits(intPos + 1) & _
                      varDigits(intPos) & strTemp
                Case 7
                    strTemp = varDigits(intPos + 1) & _
                      varDigits(intPos) & varDigits(intPos) & strTemp
                Case 8
                    strTemp = varDigits(intPos + 1) & _
                      varDigits(intPos) & varDigits(intPos) & _
                      varDigits(intPos) & strTemp
                Case 9
                    strTemp = varDigits(intPos) & _
                      varDigits(intPos + 2) & strTemp
            End Select
            intPos = intPos + 2
        Loop
        dhRoman = strTemp
End Function
```

How does dhRoman do its work? As you probably know, all numbers built in roman numerals between 1 and 3999 consist of the seven digits I, V, X, L, C, D, and M. The I, X, C, and M digits represent 1, 10, 100, and 1000; V, L, and D represent 50, 50, and 500, respectively. The code loops through all the digits of your input value from right to left, using the Mod operator to strip them off one by one:

```
Do While intValue > 0
    intDigit = intValue Mod 10
```

```
    intValue = intValue \ 10
    ' (Code removed)
    intPos = intPos + 2
Loop
```

At each point in the loop, intDigit contains the right-most digit of the value, and intValue keeps getting smaller, one digit at a time. For example, the following table shows the values of the two variables while dhRoman tackles the value 1234:

intValue	intDigit	intPos	Character
123	4	0	I
12	3	2	X
1	2	4	C
0	1	6	M

In addition, intPos indicates which array element to use in building the string as the code moves through the ones, tens, hundreds, and thousands places in the value.

Based on the value in intDigit, the code uses a Select Case construct to choose the characters to prepend to the output string. (That's right—prepend. dhRoman constructs the output string from right to left, adding items to the left of the string as it works.) For example, for the value 1234, dhRoman finds the digit 4 when intPos is 0. The code says to use

```
strTemp = varDigits(intPos) & _
  varDigits(intPos + 1) & strTemp
```

in this case. Since intPos is 0, the output is "IV" (varDigits(0) & varDigits(1)). If the 4 had been in the hundreds place (imagine you're converting 421 to roman numerals), then intPos would be 2, the expression would say to use varDigits(4) & varDigits(5), and the output would be "CD" for this digit.

You won't use this function every day. When you do need to convert a value to roman numerals, however, it will be waiting.

Performing a "Smart" Proper Case Conversion

Although VBA provides the built-in StrConv function to convert words to proper case, it does just what a brute-force hand-coded solution would do: it converts the first letter of every word to uppercase and forces the rest of each word to lowercase. This doesn't help much for articles (*a, the,* and so on) or prepositions (*of, for,* and so on) or for handling proper names like "MacDonald" or "Port of Oakland". Writing code to handle all the special cases would be prohibitively difficult, but if a "smart" proper-casing routine were to look up the exceptions to the rules in a table, the routine might work a bit better than through code alone.

One possible solution, dhProperLookup (in Listing 1.14), walks through the text you pass it, building up "words" of alphabetic characters. As soon as it finds a nonalphabetic character, it checks out the most current word it's collected and looks it up in a table. If it's there, it uses the text it finds in the table. If not, it performs a direct conversion of the word to proper case. The code then continues the process with the rest of the text. Once it hits the end of the string, it handles the final word and returns the result.

Listing 1.14: A "Smart" Proper Case Function

```
Function dhProperLookup(ByVal strIn As String, _
  Optional fForceToLower As Boolean = True, _
  Optional rst As Recordset = Nothing, _
  Optional strField As String = "") As Variant

    ' Convert a word to proper case, using optional
    ' lookup table for word spellings."
    Dim strOut As String
    Dim strWord As String
    Dim intI As Integer
    Dim strC As String * 1

    On Error GoTo HandleErr
    strOut = ""
    strWord = ""

    If fForceToLower Then
        strIn = LCase(strIn)
    End If
    For intI = 1 To Len(strIn)
        strC = Mid$(strIn, intI, 1)
        If dhIsCharAlphaNumeric(strC) Or strC = "'" Then
            strWord = strWord & strC
        Else
            strOut = strOut & _
              dhFixWord(strWord, rst, strField) & strC
```

```
                    ' Reset strWord for the next word.
                    strWord = ""
            End If
NextChar:
    Next intI
    ' Process the final word.
    strOut = strOut & dhFixWord(strWord, rst, strField)
ExitHere:
    dhProperLookup = strOut
    Exit Function

HandleErr:
    ' If there's an error, just go on to the next character.
    ' This may mean the output word is missing characters,
    ' of course. If this bothers you, just change the Resume
    ' statement to resume at "ExitHere."
    Select Case Err
        Case Else
            ' MsgBox "Error: " & Err.Description & _
            '   " (" & Err.Number & ")"
    End Select
    Resume NextChar

End Function
```

To call dhProperLookup, you can pass the following set of parameters:

- *strIn* (required) is the text to be converted.

- *fForceToLower* (optional; default = True) causes the function to convert all the text to lowercase before performing the proper case conversion. If you set the parameter to False, dhProperLookup won't affect any characters except the first character of each word.

- *rst* (optional; default = Nothing) is an open dynaset or snapshot-type DAO recordset, containing the list of special cases.

- *strField* (optional; default = "") is a string expression containing the name of the field to be used for lookups in the recordset referred to by rst. If you specify rst, you must also specify this field name.

For example, suppose you have a database named PROPER.MDB containing a table named tblSpecialCase. In that table, a field named Lookup contains special cases for spelling. The sample code shown in Listing 1.15 opens the database, creates a recordset, and calls the dhProperLookup function.

Listing 1.15: Test the dhProperLookup Function

```
Sub TestProper()
    Dim db As Database
    Dim rst As Recordset

    Set db = DBEngine.OpenDatabase("C:\VBADH\PROPER.MDB")
    Set rst = db.OpenRecordset("tblSpecialCase", dbOpenDynaset)
    Debug.Print dhProperLookup( _
     "headline: cruella de ville and old macdonald _
      eat a dog's food", _
     True, rst, "Lookup")
End Sub
```

If tblLookup contains at least the words "a", "and", "de", and "MacDonald", the output from the call to dhProperLookup would be:

```
Headline: Cruella de Ville and Old MacDonald Eat a Dog's Food
```

If you don't supply recordset and field name parameters for dhProperLookup, it performs the same task as would a call to StrConv, although it does its work somewhat less efficiently than the built-in function. (In other words, unless you intend to supply the recordset, you're probably better off calling the built-in function.) To do its work, dhProperLookup starts by checking the fForceToLower parameter and converting the entire input string to lowercase if the parameter's value is True:

```
If fForceToLower Then
    strIn = LCase(strIn)
End If
```

To work its way through the input string, dhProperLookup performs a loop, visiting each character in turn:

```
For intI = 1 To Len(strIn)
    strC = Mid$(strIn, intI, 1)
    ' (Code removed)
Next intI
```

The code examines each character. If the character is alphanumeric or an apostrophe, it's appended to strWord. If not, the loop has reached the end of a word, so the code calls dhFixWord to perform the conversion and then tacks the word and the current (non-word) character onto the end of the output string.

```
If dhIsCharAlphaNumeric(strC) Or strC = "'" Then
    strWord = strWord & strC
Else
    strOut = strOut & dhFixWord(strWord, rst, strField) & strC
    ' Reset strWord for the next word.
    strWord = ""
End If
```

Once the loop has concluded, one final step is necessary: unless the text ends with a character that's not part of a word, the code will never process the final word. To make sure that last word ends up in the output string, dhProperLookup calls dhFixWord one last time, with the final word:

```
' Process the final word.
strOut = strOut & dhFixWord(strWord, rst, strField)
```

The dhFixWord function, in Listing 1.16, does its work using a recordset containing the special cases for specific words' spellings, passed in from dhProperLookup. Supplying that information is up to you, and the function presented here counts on your having created a DAO recordset object filled with the rows of special names. If you've not supplied the recordset and field name, dhFixWord simply capitalizes the first letter of the word you've sent it and then returns.

Listing 1.16: dhFixWord Converts a Single Word to Proper Case

```
Private Function dhFixWord(ByVal strWord As String, _
 Optional rst As Recordset = Nothing, _
 Optional strField As String = "") As String

    ' "Properize" a single word
    Const conQuote = """"

    Dim strOut As String
    On Error GoTo HandleErr
    ' Many things can go wrong. Just assume you want the
    ' standard properized version unless you hear otherwise.
    strOut = UCase(Left$(strWord, 1)) & Mid$(strWord, 2)
    If Len(strWord) > 0 Then
        If Not rst Is Nothing Then
            If Len(strField) > 0 Then
```

```
                If Left$(strField, 1) <> "[" Then
                    strField = "[" & strField & "]"
                End If
                rst.FindFirst strField & " = " & _
                 conQuote & strWord & conQuote
                If Not rst.NoMatch Then
                    strOut = rst(strField)
                End If
            End If
        End If
    End If
ExitHere:
    dhFixWord = strOut
    Exit Function

HandleErr:
    ' If anything goes wrong, anything, just get out.
    Select Case Err.Number
        Case Else
            ' MsgBox "Error: " & Err.Description & _
            '   " (" & Err.Number & ")"
    End Select
    Resume ExitHere
End Function
```

The dhFixWord function does the bulk of its work in four simple lines of code:

```
rst.FindFirst strField & " = " & _
 conQuote & strWord & conQuote
If Not rst.NoMatch Then
    strOut = rst(strField)
End If
```

It uses the recordset's FindFirst method to look up a string in the format

```
'[Lookup] = "macdonald"'
```

If it finds a match in the table, it replaces the output string with the word it found. In this case, it would replace the value of strOut with the text "MacDonald". (The rest of the code in dhFixWord simply validates input and prepares the lookup string.)

What's missing from this solution? First of all, it's not terribly smart. It can work only with the specific words you've added to the list. If you've added

"McGregor" but not "MacGregor", there's no way for the code to know how to handle the word that's not there. It's not possible to work with proper names that contain spaces (such as *de Long*, for example), although you could add many of the proper name "prefixes" to the lookup table to avoid their being capitalized incorrectly. The code checks only for alphabetic characters and apostrophes as legal characters in words. You may find you need to add to the list of acceptable characters. In that case, you may want to create a list of acceptable characters as a constant and use the InStr function to see whether strC is in the list. For example, to treat apostrophes and hyphens as valid word characters, you could declare a constant:

```
Const conWordChars = "'-"
```

and modify the check for characters like this:

```
If dhIsCharAlphaNumeric(strC) Or _
  (InStr(conWordChars, strC) > 0) Then
```

Encrypting/Decrypting Text Using XOR Encryption

If you need a simple way to encrypt text in an application, the function provided in this section may do just what you need. The dhXORText function, in Listing 1.17, includes code that performs both the encryption and decryption of text strings. That's right—it takes just one routine to perform both tasks.

To encrypt text, pass dhXORText the text to encrypt and a password that supplies the encryption code. To decrypt the text, pass dhXORText the exact same parameters again. For example:

```
dhXORText(dhXORText("This is a test", "Password"), "Password")
```

returns "This is a test", the same text encrypted and then decrypted.

Listing 1.17: Use the XOR Operator to Encrypt Text

```
Function dhXORText(strText As String, strPWD As String) As String
    ' Encrypt or decrypt a string using the XOR operator.
    Dim abytText() As Byte
    Dim abytPWD() As Byte

    Dim intPWDPos As Integer
    Dim intPWDLen As Integer
```

```
Dim intChar As Integer
abytText = strText
abytPWD = strPWD

intPWDLen = LenB(strPWD)
For intChar = 0 To LenB(strText) - 1
    ' Get the next number between 0 and intPWDLen - 1
    intPWDPos = (intChar Mod intPWDLen)
    abytText(intChar) = abytText(intChar) Xor _
    abytPWD(intPWDPos)
Next intChar
dhXORText = abytText
End Function
```

The dhXORText function counts on the XOR operator to do its work. This built-in operator compares each bit in the two expressions and uses the following rules to calculate the result for each bit:

If Bit1 is	And Bit2 is	The result is
1	1	0
1	0	1
0	1	1
0	0	0

Why XOR? Using this operator has the very important side effect that if you XOR two values and then XOR the result with either of the original values, you get back the other original value. That's what makes it possible for dhXORText to do its work. To try this, imagine that the first byte of your text is 74 and the first byte of the password is 110.

```
74 XOR 110
```

returns 36, which becomes the encrypted byte. Now, to get back the original text,

```
36 XOR 110
```

returns 74 back. Repeat that for all the bytes in the text, and you've encrypted and decrypted your text.

To perform its work, dhXORText copies both the input string and the password text into byte arrays. (For another example of using byte arrays, see the section

"Reversing a String" earlier in the chapter.) Once there, it's just a matter of looping through all the bytes in the input strings array, repeating the password over and over until you run out of input text. For each byte, XOR the byte from the input string and the byte from the password to form the byte for the output string.

Figure 1.3 shows a tiny example, using "Hello Tom" as the input text and "ab" as the password. Each byte in the input string will be XOR'd with a byte from the password, with the password repeating until it has run out of characters from the input string.

FIGURE 1.3

XOR each byte from the input string and the password, repeated.

Original text:

H	0	e	0	l	0	l	0	o	0		0	T	0	o	0	m	0
72	0	101	0	108	0	108	0	111	0	32	0	84	0	111	0	109	0

Password (repeated):

a	0	b	0	a	0	b	0	a	0	b	0	a	0	b	0	a	0
97	0	98	0	97	0	98	0	97	0	98	0	97	0	98	0	97	0

Output:

41	0	7	0	13	0	14	0	14	0	66	0	53	0	13	0	12	0

- The code loops through each character of the input string—that's easy!

```
For intChar = 0 To LenB(strText) - 1
    ' (Code removed)
Next intChar
```

The hard part is to find the correct byte from the password to XOR with the selected byte in the input string: the code uses the Mod operator to find the correct character. The Mod operator returns the remainder, when you divide the first operand by the second, which is guaranteed to be a number between 0 and one less than the second operand. In short, that corresponds to rotating through the bytes of the password, as shown in Table 1.7 (disregarding the null bytes). If the password were five bytes long, the "Position Mod 2" ("Position Mod 5", in that case) column would contain the values 0 through 4, repeated as many times as necessary.

```
' Get the next number between 0 and intPWDLen - 1
intPWDPos = (intChar Mod intPWDLen)
abytText(intChar) = abytText(intChar) Xor abytPWD(intPWDPos)
```

TABLE 1.7 Steps in the Encryption of the Sample Text

Char from Input	Position	Position Mod 2	Char from Password	XOR
H (72)	0	0	a (97)	41
e (101)	1	1	b (98)	7
l (108)	2	0	a (97)	13
l (108)	3	1	b (98)	14
o (111)	4	0	a (97)	14
(32)	5	1	b (98)	66
T (84)	6	0	a (97)	53
o (111)	7	1	b (98)	13
m (109)	8	0	a (97)	12

TIP

As you can probably imagine, passwords used with dhXORText are case sensitive, and you can't change that fact. Warn users that passwords in your application will need to be entered exactly, taking upper- and lowercase letters into account.

WARNING

Although no XOR-based algorithm for encryption is totally safe, the longer your password, the better chance you have that a decryption expert won't be able to crack the code. The example above, using "ab" as the password, was only for demonstration purposes. Make sure your passwords are at least four or five characters long—the longer, the better.

Returning a String Left-Padded or Right-Padded to a Specified Width

If you're creating a phone-book listing, you may need to left-pad a phone number with dots so it looks like this:

```
............(310) 123-4567
..................555-1212
```

Or you may want to left-pad a part number field with 0's so "1234" becomes "001234" and all part numbers take up exactly six digits. You may want to create a fixed-width data stream, with spaces padding the fields. In all of these cases, you need a function that can pad a string, to the left or to the right, with the character of your choosing. The two simple functions dhPadLeft and dhPadRight, in Listing 1.18, perform the work for you.

To call either function, pass a string containing the input text, an integer indicating the width for the output string, and, optionally, a pad character. (The functions will use a space character if you don't provide one.)

For example:

```
dhPadLeft("Name", 10, ".")
```

returns " Name" (the word "Name" preceded by six spaces).

```
dhPadRight("Hello", 10)
```

returns "Hello " ("Hello" followed by five spaces).

> **NOTE** Neither dhPadLeft nor dhPadRight will truncate your input string. If the original string is longer than you indicate you want the output string, the code will just return the input string, with no changes.

Listing 1.18: Pad with Characters to the Left or to the Right

```
Function dhPadLeft(strText As String, intWidth As Integer, _
  Optional strPad As String = " ") As String
    ' Pad strText on the left, so the whole output is
    ' at least intWidth characters.
    ' If strText is longer than intWidth, just return strText.
    ' If strPad is wider than one character, this code only takes
```

```
'   the first character for padding.
If Len(strText) > intWidth Then
    dhPadLeft = strText
Else
    dhPadLeft = Right$(String(intWidth, strPad) & _
      strText, intWidth)
End If
End Function
Function dhPadRight(strText As String, intWidth As Integer, _
  Optional strPad As String = " ") As String
    ' Pad strText on the right, so the whole output is
    ' at least intWidth characters.
    ' If strText is longer than intWidth, just return strText.
    ' If strPad is wider than one character, this code only takes
    '   the first character for padding.
    If Len(strText) > intWidth Then
        dhPadRight = strText
    Else
        dhPadRight = Left$(strText & _
          String(intWidth, strPad), intWidth)
    End If
End Function
```

Both functions use the same technique to pad their input strings: they create a string consisting of as many of the pad characters as needed to fill the entire output string, append or prepend that string to the original string, and then use the Left$ or Right$ function to truncate the output string to the correct width. For example, if you call dhPadLeft like this:

```
dhPadLeft("123.45", 10, "$")
```

the code creates a string of ten dollar signs and prepends that to the input string. Then it uses the Right$ function to truncate:

```
Right$("$$$$$$$$$$123.45", 10)
' returns "$$$$123.45"
```

Using Soundex to Compare Strings

Long before the advent of computers, people working with names knew it was very difficult to spell surnames correctly and that they needed some way to group names by their phonetic spelling rather than by grammatical spelling. The algorithm demonstrated in this section is based on the Russell Soundex algorithm, a standard technique used in many database applications.

WARNING The Soundex algorithm was designed for, and works reliably with, surnames only. You can use it with any type of string, but its effectiveness diminishes as the text grows longer. It was intended to make it possible to match various spellings of last names, and its discriminating power is greatest in short words with three or more consonants.

The Soundex algorithm is based on these assumptions:

- Many English consonants sound alike.

- Vowels don't affect the overall "sound" of the name as much as the consonants do.

- The first letter of the name is most significant.

- A four-character representation is optimal for comparing two names.

For example, all three of the following examples return "P252":

```
dhSoundex("Paszinslo")
dhSoundex("Pacinslo")
dhSoundex("Pejinslo")
```

All three provide very distinct spellings of the difficult name, yet all three return the same Soundex string. As long as the first letters match, you have a good chance of finding a match, using the Soundex conversion.

The concept, then, is that when attempting to locate a name, you'd ask the user for the name, convert it to its Soundex representation, and compare it to the Soundex representations of the names in your database. You'd present a list of the possible matches to the user, who could then choose the correct one.

The Soundex algorithm follows these steps:

1. Use the first letter of the string, as is.

2. Code the remaining characters, using the information in Table 1.8.

3. Skip repeated values (that is, characters that map to the same value) unless they're separated by one or more separator characters (characters with a value of 0).

4. Once the Soundex string contains four characters, stop looking.

5. If the Soundex string contains fewer than four characters, pad the end with zeros.

The full code for dhSoundex, in Listing 1.19, follows these steps in creating the Soundex representation of the input string.

TABLE 1.8   Values for Characters in a Soundex String

Letter	Value	Comment
W,H		Ignored
A,E,I,O,U,Y	0	Although removed from the output string, these letters act as separators between significant consonants
B,P,F,V	1	
C,G,J,K,Q,S,X,Z	2	
D,T	3	
L	4	
M,N	5	
R	6	

Listing 1.19: Convert Strings to Their Soundex Equivalent

```
Const dhcLen = 4
Function dhSoundex(ByVal strIn As String) As String
    ' Create a Soundex lookup string for the
    ' input text.

    Dim strOut As String
    Dim intI As Integer
    Dim intPrev As Integer
    Dim strChar As String * 1
    Dim intChar As Integer
    Dim fPrevSeparator As Boolean

    strOut = ""
    strIn = UCase(strIn)
    fPrevSeparator = True
```

```
    strOut = Left$(strIn, 1)
    For intI = 2 To Len(strIn)
        ' If the output string is full, quit now.
        If Len(strOut) >= dhcLen Then
            Exit For
        End If
        ' Get each character, in turn. If the
        ' character's a letter, handle it.
        strChar = Mid$(strIn, intI, 1)
        If dhIsCharAlpha(strChar) Then
            ' Convert the character to its code.
            intChar = CharCode(strChar)
            ' If the character's not empty, and if it's not
            ' the same as the previous character, tack it
            ' onto the end of the string.
            If (intChar > 0) Then
                If fPrevSeparator Or (intChar <> intPrev) Then
                    strOut = strOut & intChar
                    intPrev = intChar
                End If
            End If
            fPrevSeparator = (intChar = 0)
        End If
    Next intI
    ' Return the string, right-padded with 0's.
    dhSoundex = dhPadRight(strOut, dhcLen, "0")
End Function

Private Function CharCode(strChar As String) As Integer
    Select Case strChar
        Case "A", "E", "I", "O", "U", "Y"
            CharCode = 0
        Case "C", "G", "J", "K", "Q", "S", "X", "Z"
            CharCode = 2
        Case "D", "T"
            CharCode = 3
        Case "M", "N"
            CharCode = 5
        Case "B", "F", "P", "V"
            CharCode = 1
        Case "L"
            CharCode = 4
```

```
        Case "R"
            CharCode = 6
        Case Else
            CharCode = -1
    End Select
End Function
```

Now that you've found the Soundex string corresponding to a given surname, what can you do with it? You may want to provide a graduated scale of matches. That is, perhaps you don't require an exact match but would like to know how well one name matches another. A common method for calculating this level of matching is to use a function such as dhSoundsLike, in Listing 1.20. To use this function, you supply two strings, not yet converted to their Soundex equivalents, and dhSoundsLike returns a number between 0 and 4 (4 being the best match) indicating how alike the two strings are. (If you'd rather, you can pass in two Soundex strings, and dhSoundsLike won't perform the conversion to Soundex strings for you. In that case, set the optional fIsSoundex parameter to True.)

Listing 1.20: Use dhSoundsLike to Compare Two Soundex Strings

```
Function dhSoundsLike(ByVal strItem1 As String, _
 ByVal strItem2 As String, _
 Optional fIsSoundex As Boolean = False) As Integer
    ' Return a number between 0 and 4 (4 being the best)
    ' indicating the similarity between the Soundex
    ' representation for two strings.
    Dim intI As Integer
    If Not fIsSoundex Then
        strItem1 = dhSoundex(strItem1)
        strItem2 = dhSoundex(strItem2)
    End If
    For intI = 1 To dhcLen
        If Mid$(strItem1, intI, 1) <> _
         Mid$(strItem2, intI, 1) Then
            Exit For
        End If
    Next intI
    dhSoundsLike = (intI - 1)
End Function
```

It's hard to imagine a lower-tech technique for performing this task. dhSounds-Like simply loops through all four characters in each Soundex string. As long as it finds a match, it keeps going. Like a tiny game of "musical chairs," as soon as it finds two characters that don't match, it jumps out of the loop and returns the number of characters it found that matched; the more characters that match, the better the rating.

To test out dhSoundsLike, you could try

```
dhSoundsLike("Smith", "Smitch")
```

which returns 3, or

```
dhSoundsLike("S125", "S123", True)
```

which returns 3 as well. Of course, you're not likely to call dhSoundsLike with string literals. More likely, you'd call it passing in two string variables and compare their contents.

NOTE   There are variants of this algorithm floating around that aren't as effective as the one used here. Those (admittedly simpler) algorithms don't notice repeated consonants that are separated by a vowel and therefore oversimplify the creation of the Soundex string for a given name. The algorithm presented here is more complex but yields more reliable results, and it matches the output from the Soundex function used by Microsoft's SQL Server.

Working with Substrings

To finish off the chapter, this section provides a few techniques for parsing and extracting substrings from a longer string. Specifically, you'll find out how to perform these tasks:

- Retrieving the first or last word in a string
- Finding the last occurrence of a substring within a string
- Converting a delimited string into a collection of tokens
- Returning a specific word, by index, from a string

Returning a Specific Word, by Index, from a String

Of all the functions in this chapter, the function in this section, dhExtractString, has received the most use in our own applications. It allows you to retrieve a "chunk" of a string, given a delimiter (or multiple delimiters), by the position within the string. Rather than write laborious code to parse a string yourself, you can use dhExtractString to pull out just the piece you need. For example, if you need to take the following string (pulled from some hypothetical INI file):

```
ItemsToBuy=Milk,Bread,Peas
```

and retrieve the item names individually, you could either write the code to parse the string or call dhExtractString in a loop:

```
Function TestExtract(strIniText As String)
    Dim intI As Integer
    Dim strText As String
    Dim strIniText As String

    intI = 2
    Do While True
        strText = dhExtractString(strIniText, intI, "=,")
        If Len(strText) = 0 Then
            Exit Do
        End If
        Debug.Print strText
        intI = intI + 1
    Loop
End Function
```

You can be creative with dhExtractString: You can call it once with one set of delimiters and then again with a different set. For example, you might have tackled the previous problem by first parsing the text to the right of the equal sign as a single chunk:

```
strVals = dhExtractString(strIniText, 2, "=")
```

Then you could pull the various comma-delimited pieces out of strVals:

```
strItem1 = dhExtractString(strVals, 1, ",")    ' Returns "Milk"
strItem2 = dhExtractString(strVals, 2, ",")    ' Returns "Bread"
strItem3 = dhExtractString(strVals, 3, ",")    ' Returns "Peas"
```

As you can see, you can supply a single delimiter character or a list of them.

You'll find the full listing for dhExtractString in Listing 1.21.

WARNING   The return value from dhExtractString can be somewhat misleading. If the input string contains two contiguous delimiter characters, dhExtractString sees that as an empty string delimited by those two characters. This means that you cannot loop, calling dhExtractString until it returns an empty string (unless you're sure the string contains no contiguous delimiters). You'll need to call dhCountIn first, find out how many substrings there are, and then iterate through the string that many times. See the section "Converting a Delimited String into a Collection of Tokens" later in this chapter for an example of using this technique.

TIP   If you don't supply dhExtractString with a delimiter or a list of delimiters, it will default to using the standard text delimiters in the dhcDelimiters constant. You can, of course, change those default values simply by modifying the constant in the code.

Listing 1.21: Extract a Specified Substring

```
Function dhExtractString(ByVal strIn As String, _
 ByVal intPiece As Integer, _
 Optional ByVal strDelimiter As String = dhcDelimiters) As String
    ' Pull tokens out of a delimited list. strIn is the
    ' list, and intPiece tells which chunk to pull out.
    Dim intPos As Integer
    Dim intLastPos As Integer
    Dim intLoop As Integer
    Dim intPos1 As Integer

    intPos = 0
    intLastPos = 0
    intLoop = intPiece

    ' If there's more than one delimiter, map them
    ' all to the first one.
    If Len(strDelimiter) > 1 Then
        strIn = dhTranslate(strIn, strDelimiter, _
        Left$(strDelimiter, 1))
    End If
    Do While intLoop > 0
        intLastPos = intPos
```

```
            intPos1 = InStr(intPos + 1, strIn, _
             Left$(strDelimiter, 1))
            If intPos1 > 0 Then
                intPos = intPos1
                intLoop = intLoop - 1
            Else
                intPos = Len(strIn) + 1
                Exit Do
            End If
    Loop
    ' If the string wasn't found, and this wasn't
    ' the first pass through (intLoop would equal intPiece
    ' in that case) and intLoop > 1, then you've run
    ' out of chunks before you've found the chunk you
    ' want. That is, the chunk number was too large.
    ' Return "" in that case.
    If (intPos1 = 0) And (intLoop <> intPiece) And _
     (intLoop > 1) Then
        dhExtractString = ""
    Else
        dhExtractString = Mid$(strIn, intLastPos + 1, _
         intPos - intLastPos - 1)
    End If
End Function
```

The first thing dhExtractString does is to "flatten" multiple delimiters down to the first item in the list. That is, if you pass a group of delimiters, such as a comma, a space, and a hyphen, the function first replaces all of these with a comma character (,) in the input string:

```
If Len(strDelimiter) > 1 Then
    strIn = dhTranslate(strIn, strDelimiter, _
     Left$(strDelimiter, 1))
End If
```

Next, dhExtractString loops through the string until it's found the delimiter it needs. If you've asked for the fourth token from the input string, it will loop until it finds the fourth instance of the delimiter. It also keeps track of the last position at which it found a delimiter (intLastPos) and the position of the delimiter it's just found (intPos). If the current search for a delimiter using InStr fails (it returns 0), the loop indicates that the current position is one character past the end of the input string and just exits the loop:

```
Do While intLoop > 0
    intLastPos = intPos
    intPos1 = InStr(intPos + 1, strIn, Left$(strDelimiter, 1))
    If intPos1 > 0 Then
        intPos = intPos1
        intLoop = intLoop - 1
    Else
        intPos = Len(strIn) + 1
        Exit Do
    End If
Loop
```

The logic for determining whether to return an empty string or a chunk of the input string is complex (perhaps too complex). There are three conditions that must all be met in order for dhExtractString to return an empty string:

- **intPos1 = 0:** This indicates that the input string ran out of delimiters before it stopped looking for tokens. This could happen, of course, if you requested the final token from a string—there wouldn't be a delimiter after that token, so intPos1 would be 0.

- **intLoop <> intPiece:** The intLoop variable counts down, starting at the value of intPiece, as it loops through the delimiters in the input string. If intLoop is the same as intPiece, that indicates there was only one token to begin with, and no delimiters at all. In that case, dhExtractString returns the entire input string, not an empty string.

- **intLoop > 1:** If intLoop is 0, it indicates that the loop progressed through all the delimiters in the string, and you may have selected the final token in the input string. It also may indicate that you asked for a token past the number of tokens in the string. (That is, perhaps you asked for the sixth word in a sentence that contains only four words; in that case, the function should return an empty string, and it will, because the other two conditions will also be true.)

Unless all three of these conditions are met, the code extracts the string starting at intLastPos + 1 and takes intPos – intLastPos – 1 characters:

```
If (intPos1 = 0) And (intLoop <> intPiece) And (intLoop > 1) Then
    dhExtractString = ""
```

```
Else
    dhExtractString = Mid$(strIn, intLastPos + 1, _
    intPos - intLastPos - 1)
End If
```

> **TIP**
>
> Remember that dhExtractString treats consecutive delimiters as though there were an empty token between them. Requesting the second token from "This;;is;a;test", using ";" as the delimiter, you'll receive an empty string as the return value.

You'll see that several of the other functions in this section use dhExtractString to do their work. We're sure you'll find this extremely useful parsing function invaluable in any code you need to write that extracts portions of text strings.

Retrieving the First or Last Word in a String

Each of the two functions presented in this section, dhFirstWord and dhLastWord, breaks its input string into two pieces: the selected word, and, optionally, the rest of the string. Calling dhFirstWord (see Listing 1.22) returns the first word of the input string and fills an optional parameter with the rest of the string. Calling dhLastWord (see Listing 1.23) returns the final word of the input string and fills an optional parameter with the first portion of the string. For example:

```
Dim strRest As String
dhFirstWord("First words are mighty important", strRest)
```

returns "First" and places " words are mighty important" (note the leading space) into strRest. On the other hand:

```
Dim strRest As String
dhLastWord("First words are mighty important", strRest)
```

returns "important" and places "First words are mighty " (note the trailing space) into strRest.

Listing 1.22: Return the First Word from a String

```
Function dhFirstWord(ByVal strText As String, _
  Optional ByRef strRest As String = "") As String
```

```
' Retrieve the first word of a string
' Fill strRest with the rest of the string
Dim strTemp As String
' This is easy!
' Get the first word.
strTemp = dhExtractString(strText, 1)

' Extract everything after the first word,
' and put that into strRest.
strRest = Mid$(strText, Len(strTemp) + 1)
' Return the first word.
dhFirstWord = strTemp
End Function
```

Listing 1.23: Return the Final Word from a String

```
Function dhLastWord(ByVal strText As String, _
 Optional ByRef strRest As String = "") As String
    ' Retrieve the last word of a string
    ' Fill strRest with the rest of the string
    Dim intCount As Integer
    Dim strTemp As String

    ' This is not quite so easy.
    ' Find the number of words, and then
    ' extract the final word.
    intCount = dhCountWords(strText)
    strTemp = dhExtractString(strText, intCount)

    ' Extract everything before the last word,
    ' and put that into strRest.
    strRest = Left$(strText, Len(strText) - Len(strTemp))
    dhLastWord = strTemp
End Function
```

The dhFirstWord function is simple because it can use the dhExtractString function discussed earlier in this chapter. It first pulls out the first word:

```
strTemp = dhExtractString(strText, 1)
```

Then it places the rest of the string into strRest:

```
strRest = Mid$(strText, Len(strTemp) + 1)
```

The dhFirstWord and dhLastWord functions needn't make any explicit check to see whether you've passed in a variable for the strRest parameter. If you haven't specified the parameter, VBA uses only the local copy of the value and just doesn't pass anything back. No harm done, and it saves adding logic to check the status of that parameter.

The dhLastWord function is a bit more complex because the code must first find the number of words in the string and then extract the correct one:

```
intCount = dhCountWords(strText)
strTemp = dhExtractString(strText, intCount)
```

Once it has the final word, it can extract the previous portion of the string and place it into strRest:

```
strRest = Left$(strText, Len(strText) - Len(strTemp))
```

Of course, once you have as many string functions under your belt as you do by now, you can probably create several alternatives to either of these tasks. You may find it interesting to pursue other methods, and perhaps your solutions will be even more efficient!

Finding the Last Occurrence of a Substring within a String

VBA provides the InStr function to help you find the first occurrence of a substring within a string. This doesn't help, however, when you want to find the *last* occurrence of a substring. The function in this section, dhRInstr, provides that functionality for you.

For example, if you're trying to parse file names, you will need to be able to find the final occurrence of "\" in the string, and you can use dhRInstr to find that final occurrence. If you've declared a variable named strFileName that contains a full path, "C:\WINNT\SYSTEM32\OTHER\ETC\LMHOSTS",

```
dhRInstr(strFileName, "\")
```

returns 28, the position of the final \ in the string.

You can also supply a value for the last position in the string that you want searched. For example, if you want to find the occurrence of \ before the final one in the previous example, you could change the expression to take that into account:

```
dhRInstr(strFileName, "\", 27)
```

returns 24, the position of the next-to-last "\" in the string.

The dhRInstr function, shown in Listing 1.24, accepts up to four parameters:

- *strSearch* is the string to search in.

- *strSought* is the string to search for.

- *intEndAt* (optional; default = 0) is the final position at which to search. If you don't specify a value (or specify 0), the search will include the entire string.

- *fCaseSensitive* (optional, default = False) indicates whether the search should be case sensitive.

Listing 1.24: Find the Final Occurrence of a Substring

```
Function dhRInstr(ByVal strSearch As String, _
 ByVal strSought As String, _
 Optional intEndAt As Integer = 0, _
 Optional fCaseSensitive As Boolean = False) As Integer

    ' The backwards version of InStr:
    ' Return the position, within strSearch, where the
    ' last occurrence of strSought occurs. If intEndAt
    ' is greater than zero, the value indicates the
    ' last valid position in the string at which to look.
    Dim intMode As Integer
    Dim intPos As Integer

    ' Get the compare mode set.
    If fCaseSensitive Then
        intMode = vbBinaryCompare
    Else
        intMode = vbTextCompare
    End If
    ' If caller specified an end location,
    ' truncate the input string now.
    If intEndAt > 0 Then
        strSearch = Left$(strSearch, intEndAt)
```

```
      End If
      ' Reverse both strings.
      strSearch = dhReverse(strSearch)
      strSought = dhReverse(strSought)

      ' Search in the reversed search string for the
      ' reversed sought string.
      intPos = InStr(1, strSearch, strSought, intMode)
      ' If the text was found, the position is off by one
      If intPos > 0 Then
          intPos = Len(strSearch) - intPos + 1
      End If
      dhRInstr = intPos
End Function
```

Although the code in dhRInstr is somewhat unusual, it's not terribly difficult. First, dhRInstr sets up the comparison mode, as you saw in several functions earlier in this chapter:

```
If fCaseSensitive Then
    intMode = vbBinaryCompare
Else
    intMode = vbTextCompare
End If
```

Next, the function truncates the search string if you've specified a value for the intEndAt parameter:

```
If intEndAt > 0 Then
    strSearch = Left$(strSearch, intEndAt)
End If
```

To perform the search, dhRInstr reverses both of the strings. Yes, it's an odd solution, but since you've already got the dhReverse function available, it provides a simple way to take advantage of the built-in InStr function—if both strings are reversed, you can use InStr to search for the reverse of the search string in the reverse of the larger string. The first occurrence in the reversed string corresponds to the final occurrence in the original string:

```
strSearch = dhReverse(strSearch)
strSought = dhReverse(strSought)

intPos = InStr(1, strSearch, strSought, intMode)
```

Once you've found the position of the match, if it's greater than 0, you must "turn it around." That is, to get its offset from the other end of the string, subtract the position at which you found the match from the full length of the string:

```
' If the text was found, the position is off by one
If intPos > 0 Then
    intPos = Len(strSearch) - intPos + 1
End If
```

Certainly an unusual solution to the problem, but reversing the strings makes it possible to use the built-in functions wherever possible. This is an idea worth exploring; no matter how efficiently you write your own VBA code, the built-in functions will run faster. Let's face it—they're written in C++ and your code isn't. Take as much advantage as you can of the built-in VBA functions, and you're almost guaranteed that your applications will execute faster.

Converting a Delimited String into a Collection of Tokens

VBA provides support for easy-to-use, variable-sized Collection objects, and you may want to parse a string into a collection of words. The function in this section, dhExtractCollection, lets you specify input text and, optionally, the delimiters to use in parsing the text. It returns a collection of strings, filled in from your input text.

For example, the following code parses a text string and then prints each word to the Debug window:

```
Function TestExtractCollection()
    Dim varText As Variant
    Dim colText As Collection

    Set colText = dhExtractCollection( _
     "This string contains a bunch of words")
    For Each varText In colText
        Debug.Print varText
    Next varText
    TestExtractCollection = colText.Count
End Function
```

The collection returned from dhExtractCollection has all the properties and methods of any other collection in VBA. The example routine uses a simple For…Next loop to visit each item in the returned collection, and the Count property to inspect the number of items in the collection. Listing 1.25 includes the full listing of dhExtractCollection.

Listing 1.25: Return a Collection Filled with Substrings

```
Function dhExtractCollection(ByVal strText As String, _
 Optional ByVal strDelimiter As String = dhcDelimiters) _
 As Collection
    ' Return a collection containing all the tokens contained
    ' in a string, using the supplied delimiters.
    Dim colWords As New Collection
    Dim intI As Integer
    Dim strTemp As String
    Dim intCount As Integer
    Dim strChar As String * 1

    ' If there's more than one delimiter, map them
    ' all to the first one.
    strChar = Left$(strDelimiter, 1)
    If Len(strDelimiter) > 1 Then
        strText = dhTranslate(strText, strDelimiter, strChar)
    End If
    ' Now, just use the single character as the delimiter
    ' from now on. Find out how many tokens there are
    ' in the input string.
    intCount = dhCountIn(strText, strChar)
    ' Loop through all the tokens, adding them to the
    ' output collection.
    For intI = 1 To intCount + 1
        strTemp = dhExtractString(strText, intI, strChar)
        colWords.Add strTemp
    Next intI
    ' Return the output collection.
    Set dhExtractCollection = colWords
End Function
```

Given the rest of the routines in this chapter, dhExtractCollection is simple. Its first step, after declaring a local collection object to contain all the strings, is to "flatten" the list of delimiters to a single delimiter character so dhCountIn can count the number of occurrences of that delimiter:

```
Dim colWords As New Collection
' (Code removed)
```

```
strChar = Left$(strDelimiter, 1)
If Len(strDelimiter) > 1 Then
    strText = dhTranslate(strText, strDelimiter, strChar)
End If
intCount = dhCountIn(strText, strChar)
```

Next, the function loops through the number of words in the input string, using the number of delimiters plus 1 as the number of words to extract. For each word it finds, it adds the word to a local collection:

```
For intI = 1 To intCount + 1
    strTemp = dhExtractString(strText, intI, strChar)
    colWords.Add strTemp
Next intI
```

Finally, the function sets its return value to the local collection, returning that collection to the function's caller:

```
Set dhExtractCollection = colWords
```

Note that there's no reason not to use dhExtractCollection to find a particular word in a string, if that's what you need. For example, either of

```
dhExtractCollection("This is a test").Item(2)
```

or

```
dhExtractCollection("This is a test")(2)
```

will return the word "is". You'll get the same result calling

```
dhExtractString("This is a test", 2)
```

and dhExtractString is a bit more efficient, but there's no reason besides speed not to call dhExtractCollection, and you may find its syntax easier to use.

Summary

VBA programs seem unable to avoid working with strings as part of each and every application, and this chapter has provided an overview of the built-in VBA functions and a long laundry list of additional procedures that provide additional functionality. Specifically, this chapter covered

- How VBA stores and uses strings

- Many of the built-in string functions and options for:
  - Comparing strings
  - Converting strings
  - Creating strings
  - Calculating the length of a string
  - Formatting a string
  - Justifying a string
  - Searching for a string
  - Working with and replacing portions of a string
  - Using ANSI values and bytes
- Additional functions for:
  - Searching and replacing text
  - Gathering information about strings
  - Converting strings
  - Working with substrings

For similar chapters covering dates and numbers, see Chapters 2 and 3, respectively.

CHAPTER
TWO

2

Working with Dates and Times

- Understanding how date/time values are stored in VBA

- Using the built-in VBA date/time functions

- Extending the built-in functions with new generalized procedures

This chapter is devoted to providing solutions to common problems involving date and time values, including manipulating date values, finding a particular date, and working with elapsed times. Although VBA supplies a rich set of functions that help you work with date/time values, their use can be confusing, and there are many programmatic questions that need to be answered that require functions other than those supplied by the built-in VBA date-handling functions.

Table 2.1 lists the sample files you'll find on the accompanying CD-ROM.

TABLE 2.1   Sample Files

File Name	Description
DATETIME.XLS	Excel 97 file with sample functions
DATETIME.MDB	Access 97 database with sample functions
DATETIME.BAS	Text file with sample functions
HOLIDAYS.MDB	Access 97 database containing tblHolidays
HOLIDAYS.TXT	Exported text version of tblHolidays

What Is a Date, and How Did It Get There?

All other definitions aside, to VBA, a date is an 8-byte floating-point value that can contain information indicating a specific point in time. In particular, the integer portion of the value contains a number of days since December 30, 1899. The fractional portion of the date value represents the portion of the day stored in the value. For example, if the current date is 5/22/97 at 3:00 P.M., VBA stores the value internally as 35572.625. That is, the current date is 35572 days after 12/30/1899, and 3:00 P.M. is 625/1000 of a full day. In general, you don't have to care about the storage mechanism; VBA handles the conversions gracefully to and from the internal floating-point format and the external date display.

An Added Benefit

Because VBA stores dates internally as serial values, you get the added benefit of being able to treat dates as numeric values in expressions if you want. Although VBA supplies the DateAdd function, covered in more detail in the section "Performing Simple Calculations" later in this chapter, you needn't use it if you're adding a number of days to a given date value. For example, to get tomorrow's date, you could just add 1 to today's date, like this:

```
dtmTomorrow = Date() + 1
```

Date is a built-in VBA function that returns the date portion (the integer part) of the current date and time retrieved from Windows. Adding 1 to that value returns a date that represents the next day.

The same mechanism works for subtracting two dates. Although VBA supplies the DateDiff function for finding the interval spanned by two date/time values, if you just need to know the number of days between the two dates, you can simply subtract one from the other. For example, to find the number of days between 5/22/97 and 1/10/97, you could use an expression like this:

```
intDays = #5/22/97# - #1/10/97#
```

Afterward, intDays will contain the value 132, the number of days between May 22 and January 10.

Supplying Date Values

Like some weird date-munching omnivore, VBA's expression engine can "eat" dates in any of several formats. As long as you enclose date literals within number signs (#) and format the literal in some reasonable, unambiguous way, VBA should be able to understand what you mean.

VBA understands any of the following formats (if you're running a VBA host in the United States, that is):

```
#January 1, 1998#
#Jan 1 1998#
#1-Jan-98#
#1 Jan 1998#
#1 1 98#
```

TIP VBA uses your Windows international settings to determine how to parse the value you've entered. This does, of course, cause trouble with dates entered with nothing differentiating days and months. (How is VBA supposed to know, unless you tell it otherwise, that #5/1/98# represents May 1 and not January 5?) To be completely unambiguous, especially in cases in which your application must run in various localized VBA hosts, you might consider abandoning date literals in code altogether and using the DateSerial function instead. This function, discussed in the section "Putting the Pieces Together" later in this chapter, takes three distinct values representing the year, month, and day portions of a date and returns a date value representing the selected date. Using this mechanism, you'll never have any issues with localized versions of your code parsing date literals differently than you'd expected.

When converting from other datatypes into dates, VBA stores the portion to the left of the decimal point (the whole number part) as the date and the portion to the right of the decimal point as the time. For example, if you were to write code like this:

```
Dim dbl As Double
Dim dtm As Date
dbl = 3005 / 12.6
dtm = dbl
Debug.Print dbl
Debug.Print dtm
```

the output would be

```
238.492063492063
8/25/1900 11:48:34 AM
```

Judging from the results, it looks like 8/25/1900 is 238 days after 12/30/1899, and .4920634... is about 11:48:34 A.M.

The Built-In VBA Date Functions

Although VBA provides a large number of built-in functions, there aren't many logical groups as tightly entwined as the VBA functions handling date and time manipulations. The next few sections provide details and examples of using the intrinsic functions to solve simple problems. The remainder of the chapter provides more complex solutions that, in each case, use these basic building blocks.

Exactly When Is It?

VBA provides three functions enabling you to determine the current date and time set in your computer's hardware. These functions—Now, Date, and Time—check your system clock and return all or part of the current setting. None of these functions require any parameters, and they can be summarized simply:

Function	Return Value
Now	Returns the current date and time
Date	Returns the date portion of the current date and time
Time	Returns the time portion of the current date and time

Although these functions seem somewhat redundant, they do each have their purpose. For example, if you want to display only the current time without the date portion, it's simpler to call the Time function than to call the Now function and remove the date portion.

TIP

You can use the Date and Time statements to set the current date and time as well. Placing either keyword on the left-hand side of an equal sign allows you to assign a new value to the system date and time.

For example, the following fragment checks the current time, and if it's past 1:00 P.M., executes some code.

```
If Time > #1:00 PM# Then
    ' Only execute this code if it's after 1 PM.
End if
```

On the other hand, the following comparison wouldn't make any sense in this context because the value in Now (a value like 34565.2345) is guaranteed to be greater than #1:00 PM# (the value 0.5416666667):

```
If Now > #1:00 PM# Then
     ' Only execute this code if it's after 1 PM.
End if
```

> **NOTE** Unlike other functions, Now, Date, and Time don't require trailing parentheses. In fact, if you enter the parentheses, VBA often politely removes them for you.

What If You Just Want the Time Portion?

To retrieve just the *date* portion of a date/time value, use the built-in DateValue function. This function, discussed in the section "Converting Text to Date/Time Format" later in this chapter, takes in either a string or a date value and returns only the date portion. Using DateValue, you can compare the date portion of a Date variable to a specific date value, like this:

```
If DateValue(dtmSomeDate) = #5/14/70# Then
    ' You know the date portion of dtmSomeDate is 5/14/70
End If
```

On the other hand, if you need just the *time* portion of a date variable, you can use the TimeValue function. Using this function, you could write code that checks the time portion of a date variable against a particular time, like this:

```
If TimeValue(dtmSomeDate) > #1:00 PM# Then
    ' You know the date variable contained a date portion
    ' with a time after 1:00 PM.
End If
```

Pulling the Pieces Apart

Of course, if you're working with dates, you're also working with years, months, days, hours, minutes, and seconds. You might also like to work with a date in terms of its placement within the year, or which quarter it's in, or which day of the week it is. VBA provides simple and useful functions for retrieving all this information, and more.

Retrieving Just the Part You Need

To start with, you'll find the functions listed in Table 2.2 to be helpful in extracting simple information from a date value. Each of these functions accepts a date parameter and returns an integer containing the requested piece of information. (You can also use the DatePart function, described in the section "One Function Does It All" later in this chapter, to retrieve any of these values. It's simpler to call the functions in Table 2.2 if you just need one of the values listed.)

TABLE 2.2   Simple Date/Time Functions

Function	Return Value
Year	Year portion of the date
Month	Month portion of the date
Day	Day portion of the date
Hour	Hour portion of the date
Minute	Minute portion of the date
Second	Seconds portion of the date

You can use any of these functions to retrieve a portion of a date value. For example, the following fragment displays the current year value:

```
MsgBox "The current year is " & Year(Now)
```

and the following fragment displays the month and day:

```
MsgBox "Month: " & Month(Now) & " Day: " & Day(Now)
```

The following fragment checks the current time and allows you to take an action at 1:12 P.M.:

```
If Hour(Time) = 13 And Minute(Time) = 12 Then
    ' You know it's 1:12 PM
End If
```

WARNING Don't try sending the Date function to functions that return time portions of a date/time value. Because the return value from the Date function doesn't include any time information (its fractional portion is 0), the Hour, Minute, and Second functions will all return 0. The same warning applies to the Day, Month, and Year functions: don't send them the Time function, because the return value from that function doesn't include any date information.

What Day of the Week Is This?

In addition to working with months and days, you may need to know the day of the week represented by a date value. Of course, you could calculate this yourself (there are published algorithms for calculating the day of a week, given a date), but why bother? VBA knows the answer and can give it to you easily, using the built-in WeekDay function. (You can also use the DatePart function, discussed in the next section, to retrieve the same information.)

To determine the day of the week represented by any date value, use the WeekDay function. Supply it with a date value, and it will return the day of the week on which that date falls. For example,

```
Debug.Print WeekDay(#5/16/56#)
```

returns 4, indicating that May 16 fell on a Wednesday in 1956.

Sunday Isn't Always the First Day of the Week

Online help indicates that you can pass a second parameter to WeekDay, indicating the first day of the week. In many countries, Monday is considered the first day of the week, so most of the VBA date functions allow you to specify what you consider to be the first day of the week. If you don't specify a value, VBA uses the Windows setting for your local country. If you specify a constant (vbSunday through vbSaturday) for this parameter, VBA treats that day as the first day of the week and offsets the return value accordingly.

For example, the following lines represent a sample session in the Immediate window (run in the United States, where Sunday is the first day of the week):

```
? WeekDay(#5/1/98#)
6
? WeekDay(#5/1/98#, vbUseSystemDayOfWeek)
6
? WeekDay(#5/1/98#, vbMonday)
5
```

Note that as you change the value of the FirstDayOfWeek parameter, the return value changes as well. You need to be aware that WeekDay (and the corresponding functionality in the DatePart function) doesn't return a fixed value, but rather, a value relative to the local first day of the week.

Of course, if you want a fixed value, no matter where your code runs, simply specify the first day of the week. The following example returns 6 no matter where you run it:

```
? WeekDay(#5/1/98#, vbSunday)
```

One Function Does It All

In addition to the functions described in the previous sections, VBA supplies the DatePart function. This function allows you to retrieve any portion of a date/time value and also performs some simple calculations for you. (It can retrieve the quarter of the year containing your date value, as well as all the other, simpler information.)

To call DatePart, pass to it a string indicating which information you want returned and a date value. The function returns the requested piece of information from the date value you send it. Table 2.3 lists the possible values for the DatePart function's Interval argument.

TABLE 2.3 Values for the Interval Argument of the DatePart Function

Setting	Description
yyyy	Year
q	Quarter
m	Month
y	Day of year
d	Day
w	Weekday
ww	Week
h	Hour
n	Minute
s	Second

For example, the following two lines of code are equivalent:

```
Debug.Print Day(Date)
Debug.Print DatePart("d", Date)
```

But these two lines have no equivalent alternatives:

```
' Return the ordinal position of the current day within the year.
Debug.Print DatePart("y", Date)
```

```
' Return the quarter (1, 2, 3, or 4) containing today's date.
Debug.Print DatePart("q", Date)
```

DatePart allows you to optionally specify the first day of the week (just as you can do with the WeekDay function) in its third parameter. It also allows you to optionally specify the first week of the year in its fourth parameter. (Some countries treat the week in which January 1st falls as the first week of the year, as does the United States. Other countries treat the first four-day week as the first week, and still others wait for the first full week in the year and call that the first week.)

Performing Simple Calculations

VBA supplies two functions, DateAdd and DateDiff, that allow you to add and subtract date and time intervals. Of course, as mentioned above, if you're just working with days, you don't need these functions—you can just add and subtract the date values themselves. The following sections describe each of these important functions in detail.

Adding Intervals to a Date

The DateAdd function allows you to add any number of intervals of any size to a date/time value. For example, you can calculate the date 100 days from now or the time 35 minutes ago. The function accepts three required parameters, as shown in Table 2.4. Table 2.5 lists the possible values for the Interval parameter.

TABLE 2.4 Parameters for the DateAdd Function

Parameter	Description
Interval	A string expression indicating the interval of time to add
Number	Number of intervals to add. It can be positive (to get dates in the future) or negative (to get dates in the past)
Date	Date to which the interval is added

TABLE 2.5 Possible Interval Settings for DateAdd

Setting	Description
yyyy	Year
q	Quarter
m	Month
y	Day of year
d	Day
w	Weekday

TABLE 2.5 Possible Interval Settings for DateAdd (continued)

Setting	Description
ww	Week
h	Hour
n	Minute
s	Second

For example, to find the date one year from the current date, you could use an expression like this:

```
DateAdd("yyyy", 1, Date)
```

rather than add 365 days to the current date (a common, although incorrect, solution). What about calculating the time two hours from now? That's easy, too:

```
DateAdd("h", 2, Now)
```

DateAdd will never return an invalid date, but if you try to add a value that would cause the return date to be before 1/1/100 or after 12/31/9999, VBA triggers a run-time error.

 WARNING   Watch out! The abbreviation for adding minutes to a date/time value is "n", not "m", as you might guess. (VBA uses "m" for months.) Many VBA developers have used "m" inadvertently and not noticed until the program was in use.

Subtracting Dates

If you need to find the number of intervals between two dates (where the interval can be any item from Table 2.5), use the DateDiff function. Table 2.6 lists the parameters for this function.

TABLE 2.6 Parameters for the DateDiff Function

Parameter	Required?	Datatype	Description
Interval	Yes	String	Interval of time used to calculate the difference between Date1 and Date2
Date1, Date2	Yes	Date	The two dates used in the calculation
FirstDayOfWeek	No	Integer constant	The first day of the week. If not specified, Sunday is assumed
FirstWeekOfYear	No	Integer constant	The first week of the year. If not specified, the first week is assumed to be the week in which January 1 occurs

For example, to calculate the number of hours that occurred between two date variables, dtmValue1 and dtmValue2, you could write an expression like this:

```
DateDiff("h", dtmValue1, dtmValue2)
```

DateDiff's return value can be confusing. In general, it performs no rounding at all, but the meaning of the difference varies for different interval types. For example,

```
DateDiff("h", #10:00#, #12:59:59#)
```

returns 2 because only two full hours have elapsed between the two times.

When working with months or years, DateDiff returns the number of month or year borders that have been crossed between the dates. For example, you might expect the following expression to return 0 (no full months have been traversed), yet the function returns 1 because a single month border has been crossed:

```
DateDiff("m", #11/15/97#, #12/1/97#)
```

The same goes for the following expression, which returns 1 even though only a single day has transpired:

```
DateDiff("yyyy", #12/31/97#, #1/1/98#)
```

When working with weeks, DateDiff becomes, well, strange. VBA treats the "w" (weekday) and "ww" (week) intervals differently, but both return (in some sense) the number of weeks between the two dates. If you use "w" for the interval, VBA counts the number of the day on which Date1 falls until it hits Date2. It counts Date2 but not Date1. (This explanation requires visual aids, so consult Figure 2.1 for an example to work with.) For example,

```
DateDiff("w", #11/5/97#, #11/18/97#)
```

returns 1 because there's only one Wednesday following 11/5/97 before stopping at 11/18. On the other hand,

```
DateDiff("w", #11/5/97#, #11/19/97#)
```

returns 2 because there are two Wednesdays (11/12 and 11/19) in the range.

Using "ww" for the range, DateDiff counts calendar weeks. (That is, every time it hits a Sunday, it bumps the count.) Therefore, the previous two examples both return 2, using the "ww" interval; in both cases, there are two Sundays between the two dates. Just as with the "w" interval, VBA counts the end date if it falls on a Sunday, but it never includes the starting date, even if it is a Sunday. Given that caveat, DateDiff should return the same answer for either the "w" or "ww" interval if Date1 is a Sunday.

FIGURE 2.1

A visual aid for DateDiff calculations

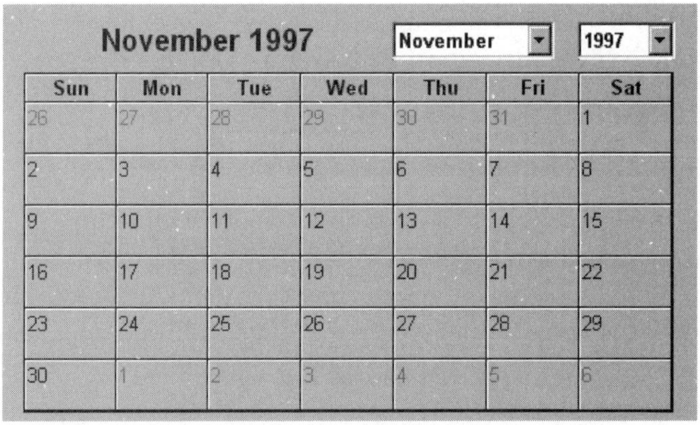

Sun	Mon	Tue	Wed	Thu	Fri	Sat
26	27	28	29	30	31	1
2	3	4	5	6	7	8
9	10	11	12	13	14	15
16	17	18	19	20	21	22
23	24	25	26	27	28	29
30	1	2	3	4	5	6

November 1997 — November 1997

TIP

If you use date literal values (like #5/1/97#), VBA uses the exact date in its calculations. If, on the other hand, you use a string that contains only the month and date (like "5/1"), VBA inserts the current year when it runs the code. This allows you to write code that works no matter what the year. Of course, this makes it difficult to compare dates from two different years because there's no way to indicate any year except the current one. But if you need to perform a calculation comparing dates within the current year, this technique can save you time.

Converting Text to Date/Time Format

Sometimes your code needs to work with date values that are stored as strings. Perhaps you've received data from some outside source and need to convert it to date format, or perhaps the user has entered a value somewhere and you now need to work with it as a date. VBA provides three functions to help you make the necessary conversions: DateValue, TimeValue, and CDate. Each of these functions accomplishes a slightly different task, and their differences aren't apparent from the online help.

DateValue and TimeValue each accept a single argument (usually a string expression) and convert that value into either a date or a time. (As mentioned earlier in this chapter, you can also use these functions to extract just the time or date portion of a combined date/time value.) DateValue can convert any string that matches the internal date formats and any recognizable text month names as well. If the value you send it includes a time portion, DateValue just removes that information from the output value.

For example, all of the following expressions return the same value (assuming the variable intDate contains the value 30):

```
DateValue("12 30 97")
DateValue("December 30 1997")
DateValue("December " & intDate & " 1997")
DateValue("12/30/97 5:00 PM")
DateValue("30/12/97")
```

The final example returns December 30 no matter where you are, of course, only because the date is unambiguous. Try that with a date like "12/1/97", and you'll get the date as defined in your international settings (December 1 in the United States, January 12 in most of the rest of the world).

The TimeValue function works similarly to the DateValue function. You can send it a string containing any valid expression, and it returns a time value. If you send TimeValue a string containing date information, it disregards that information as it creates the output value.

For example, all of the following return the same time value:

```
TimeValue("5:15 PM")
TimeValue("17:15")
TimeValue("12/30/97 5:15 PM")
```

The CDate function coerces any value it can get its hands on into a date/time value, if it can. Unlike the TimeValue and DateValue functions, it returns a full date/time value, with all the information it was sent intact. In addition, it can convert numeric values into dates. For example, all of the following examples return the same value. (The last example is redundant, of course, but it works.)

```
CDate("12/30/97 5:15 PM")
CDate(35794.71875)
CDate(#12/30/97 5:15 PM#)
```

Most often, you'll use CDate to convert text into a full date/time value, and you'll use DateValue and TimeValue to convert text into a date or a time value only.

Putting the Pieces Together

What if, rather than text, you've got the pieces of a date or a time as individual numeric values? In that case, although you could use any of the functions in the previous section to perform the conversion (building up a complex string expression and then calling the function), you're better off using the DateSerial and TimeSerial functions in this case. Each of these functions accepts three values—DateSerial takes year, month, and day, in that order; TimeSerial takes hour, minutes, and seconds, in that order—and returns a date or a time value, much like the DateValue and TimeValue functions did a single expression as input. Many of the functions presented in the remainder of this chapter use the DateSerial or TimeSerial function to create a date from the three required pieces.

For example, what if you need to know the first day of the current month? The simplest solution is to write a function that uses an expression like this:

```
dhFirstDayInMonth = DateSerial(Year(dtmDate), Month(dtmDate), 1)
```

As you'll see, this is exactly the technique the dhFirstDayInMonth function, discussed later in this chapter, uses. By creating a new date that takes the year portion of the current date, the month portion of the current date, and a day value of 1, the function returns a new date that corresponds to the first day in the current month.

The TimeSerial function works just the same way. You pass it hour, minutes, and seconds values, and it creates the appropriate time value for you. You'll use both functions together to build a full date/time value if you've got six values containing the year, month, day, hour, minutes, and seconds. That is, you might find yourself with an expression like this:

```
DateSerial(intYear, intMonth, intDay) + _
  TimeSerial(intHour, intMinutes, intSeconds)
```

Because a date/time value is simply the sum of a whole number representing days and a fraction representing time, you can use both functions together to create a full date/time value.

One useful feature of VBA's built-in date functions is that they never return an invalid date. For example, asking for DateSerial(1997, 2, 35), which certainly describes a date that doesn't exist, politely returns 3/7/97. We'll actually use this feature to our benefit, as you'll see in the section "Is This a Leap Year?" later in this chapter.

Displaying Values the Way You Want

In your applications, you most likely will want to display dates in a variety of formats. VBA supplies the Format function, which you can use to format date values just the way you need. (You can also use the Format function to format numeric values, and string values as well. See the VBA online help for more information.)

When you use the Format function, you supply an expression to be formatted (a date/time value, in this case) and a string expression containing a format specifier. Optionally, you can also supply both a constant representing the first day of the week you want to use and a constant representing the manner in which you want to calculate the first week of the year. (For more information on these two parameters, see Table 2.6 earlier in this chapter.)

The format specifier can be either a built-in, supplied string or one you make up yourself. Table 2.7 lists the built-in date/time formats.

TABLE 2.7 Named Date/Time formats for the Format Function

Format Name	Description	Use Local Settings
General Date	Displays a date and/or time, depending on the value in the first parameter, using your system's Short Date style and the system's Long Time style	Yes
Long Date	Displays a date (no time portion) according to your system's Long Date format	Yes
Medium Date	Displays a date (no time portion) using the Medium Date format appropriate for the language version of the host application	No

TABLE 2.7: Named Date/Time formats for the Format Function (continued)

Format Name	Description	Use Local Settings
Short Date	Displays a date (no time portion) using your system's Short Date format	Yes
Long Time	Displays a time (no date portion) using your system's Long Time format; includes hours, minutes, seconds	Yes
Medium Time	Displays time (no date portion) in 12-hour format using hours and minutes and the AM/PM designator	Yes
Short Time	Displays a time (no date portion) using the 24-hour format; for example, 17:45	Yes

To test out these formats, we took a field trip to a fictional country. The region's time settings for Windows are displayed in Figure 2.2, and their date settings are shown in Figure 2.3. The screen in Figure 2.4 shows some tests, using the Format function, with the various date and time formats.

FIGURE 2.2

Regional settings for times in a fictitious environment

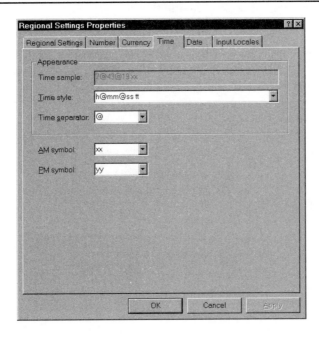

FIGURE 2.3

Regional settings for dates in the same fictitious environment

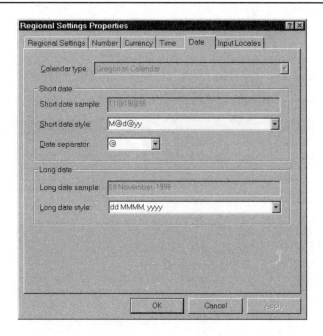

FIGURE 2.4

Test of regional date formats in the Microsoft Access Debug window

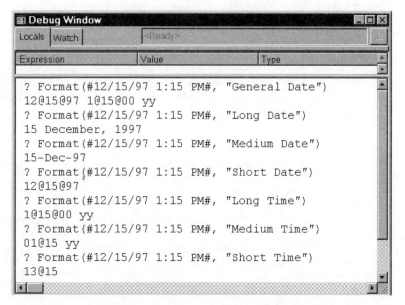

If you're feeling creative, or hampered by the limitations of the named time and date formats, you can create your own formats using the options shown in Table 2.8. If you build a string containing combinations of these characters, you can format a date/time value any way you like. Figure 2.5 demonstrates a few of the formats you can create yourself, using the characters listed in Table 2.8.

FIGURE 2.5

Use the Format function with user-defined formats for complete control.

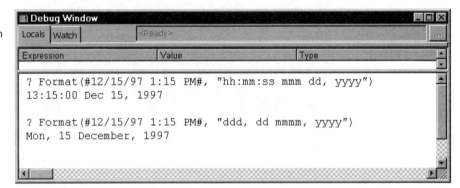

TABLE 2.8   User-Defined Time/Date Formats for the Format Function

Character	Description	Use Regional Settings?	Comments
(:)	Time separator. Separates hours, minutes, and seconds when time values are formatted	Yes	In some locales, this character may have been translated and may not be a colon (:). Output value is determined by local settings
(/)	Date separator. Separates the day, month, and year when date values are formatted	Yes	In some locales, this character may have been translated and may not be a slash (/). Output value is determined by local settings
c	Displays the date as ddddd and displays the time as ttttt, in that order	Yes	Same as the named General Date format
d	Displays the day as a number without a leading 0 (1–31)	No	

TABLE 2.8 User-Defined Time/Date Formats for the Format Function (continued)

Character	Description	Use Regional Settings?	Comments
dd	Displays the day as a number with a leading 0 (01–31)	No	
ddd	Displays the day as an abbreviation (Sun–Sat)	Yes	
dddd	Displays the day as a full name (Sunday–Saturday)	Yes	
ddddd	Displays the date as a complete date (including day, month, and year)	Yes	Same as the named Short Date format
dddddd	Displays a date as a complete date (including day, month, and year)	Yes	Same as the named Long Date format
w	Displays the day of the week as a number (1 for Sunday through 7 for Saturday)	No	Output depends on the setting of the FirstDayOf-Week parameter
ww	Displays the week of the year as a number (1–54)	No	Output depends on the FirstWeekOfYear parameter
m	Displays the month as a number without a leading 0 (1–12)	No	If "m" follows "h" or "hh", displays minutes instead
mm	Displays the month as a number with a leading 0 (01–12)	No	If "mm" follows "h" or "hh", displays minutes instead
mmm	Displays the month as an abbreviation (Jan–Dec)	Yes	
mmmm	Displays the month as a full month name (January–December)	Yes	
q	Displays the quarter of the year as a number (1–4)	No	
y	Displays the day of the year as a number (1–366)	No	
yy	Displays the year as a two-digit number (00–99)	No	

TABLE 2.8 User-Defined Time/Date Formats for the Format Function (continued)

Character	Description	Use Regional Settings?	Comments
yyyy	Displays the full year (100–9999)	No	
h	Displays the hour as a number without leading zeros (0–23)	No	
hh	Displays the hour as a number with leading zeros (00–23)	No	
n	Displays the minute as a number without leading zeros (0–59)	No	
nn	Displays the minute as a number with leading zeros (00–59)	No	
s	Displays the second as a number without leading zeros (0–59)	No	
ss	Displays the second as a number with leading zeros (00–59)	No	
ttttt	Displays a time as a complete time (including hour, minute, and second)	Yes	Same as the named Long Time format
AM/PM	Uses the 12-hour clock	No	Use "AM" for times before noon and "PM" for times between noon and 11:59 P.M.
am/pm	Uses the 12-hour clock	No	Use "am" for times before noon and "pm" for times between noon and 11:59 P.M.
A/P	Uses the 12-hour clock	No	Use "a" for times before noon and "p" for times between noon and 11:59 P.M.
a/p	Uses the 12-hour clock	No	Use "A" for times before noon and "P" for times between noon and 11:59 P.M.
AMPM	Uses the 12-hour clock and displays the AM/PM string literal as defined by your system	Yes	The case of the AM/PM string is determined by system settings

If you want to include literal text in your format string, you have two choices. You can do either of the following:

- Precede each character with a backslash (\).

- Enclose the block of text within quotes inside the string.

The first method becomes quite tedious and difficult to read if you have more than a few characters. The second method requires you to embed a quote inside a quoted string, and that takes some doing on its own.

For example, if you want to display a date/time value like this:

```
May 22, 1997 at 12:01 AM
```

you have two choices. With the first method, you could use a format string including \ characters:

```
Format(#5/22/97 12:01 AM#, "mmm dd, yyyy \a\t h:mm AM/PM")
```

Using the second method, you must embed quotes enclosing the word "at" into the format string. To do that, you must use two quotes where you want one in the output. VBA sees the two embedded quotes as a single literal quote character and does the right thing:

```
Format(#5/22/97 12:01 AM#, "mmm dd, yyyy ""at"" h:mm AM/PM")
```

Either way, the output is identical.

The Turn of the Century Approacheth

How does VBA handle the year 2000 issue? Actually, quite gracefully. Normally, users are accustomed to entering two-digit year values, and this, of course, is what has caused the great, late 20th century computer controversy. VBA interprets two-digit years in a somewhat rational manner: if you enter a date value with a two-digit year between 1/1/00 and 12/31/29, VBA interprets that as a date in the 21st century. If you enter a date with a two-digit year between 1/1/30 and 12/31/99, VBA interprets that as being a date in the 20th century. Although it would be nice if the interpretation had a user-configurable component, this fixed solution is much better than nothing at all.

The following list summarizes how VBA treats date values entered with a two-digit year value:

- **Date range 1/1/00 through 12/31/29:** Treated as 1/1/2000 through 12/31/2029

- **Date range 1/1/30 through 12/31/99:** Treated as 1/1/1930 through 12/31/1999

Beyond the Basics

Once you get the built-in date-handling functions under your belt, you'll find innumerable other tasks you need to solve involving dates and times. The remainder of this chapter presents a series of solutions to common problem that require stand-alone procedures, grouped by their functionality. The three sections deal with three types of date/time issues:

- Finding a specific date

- Manipulating dates and times

- Working with elapsed time

Finding a Specific Date

In this section, you'll find solutions to many simple problems that involve locating a date. Specifically, the routines include

- Returning the first or last day of a specified month

- Returning the first or last day of the week, given a date

- Returning the first or last day of the year, given a date

- Returning the first or last day of the quarter, given a date

- Returning the next or previous specific weekday, given a date

- Finding the next anniversary date

- Returning the date of the nth particular weekday (Monday, Tuesday, and so on) of a month

- Returning the next or previous working day, given a date
- Returning the first or last working day of a specified month

Using Optional Parameters

Many of the procedures in the following sections accept one or more optional parameters. In each case, if you don't specify the parameter in your function call, the receiving function assigns that parameter a value. In most cases, this allows you to omit the date parameter, and the function assumes the current date when it runs.

When you use optional parameters, you have two basic choices:

- Use a Variant parameter, and check for the parameter using the IsMissing function.
- Use a strongly typed parameter, and assign a default value in the formal declaration.

We've opted for the second alternative because this allows for type checking when calling the procedure. On the other hand, this technique also removes the possibility of using the IsMissing function to check for the omission of the parameter. Because the value you assign to the parameter in the formal declaration can only be a constant, not a function value, our solution when working with dates was to use the value 0 to indicate that you'd omitted the date parameter. For example, you'll see declarations like this:

```
Function dhFirstDayInMonth( Optional dtmDate As Date = 0) _
    As Date
```

This requires the procedure to check for the 0 value and replace it with the current date:

```
If dtmDate = 0 Then
    ' Did the caller pass in a date? If not, use
    ' the current date.
    dtmDate = Date
End If
```

> We assumed you would be very unlikely to ever actually use the date 0 (12/30/1899) as a parameter to one of these procedures. If you do attempt to send 12/30/1899 to any of the procedures that accept an optional date parameter, the procedure will treat your input as though you'd entered the current date. If you must allow that date as input, you'll need to either remove the optional parameter or find some other workaround.

Finding the Beginning or End of a Month

Finding the first day in a specific month is easy: use the DateSerial function, breaking out the year and month portions of the specified date, asking for the day value 1. The dhFirstDayInMonth function, in Listing 2.1, performs this function call after first checking the incoming parameter and converting it to the current date if necessary. Calling the function as

```
dhFirstDayInMonth(#5/7/70#)
```

returns 5/1/70, of course.

Determining the last day in the month requires using an obscure, but documented, detail of the DateSerial function. It turns out that any (or all) of the three parameters to the DateSerial function can be numeric expressions. Because VBA will never return an invalid date, you can request the day before the first day of a month by incrementing the month value by 1 and decrementing the day by 1. The dhLastDayInMonth function in Listing 2.1 does just that. Using this expression:

```
DateSerial(Year(dtmDate), Month(dtmDate) + 1, 0)
```

it finds the 0th day of the following month, which is, of course, the final day of the requested month.

Listing 2.1: Find the First or Last Day in a Month

```
Function dhFirstDayInMonth(Optional dtmDate As Date = 0) As Date
    ' Return the first day in the specified month.

    If dtmDate = 0 Then
        ' Did the caller pass in a date? If not, use
        ' the current date.
```

```
        dtmDate = Date
    End If
    dhFirstDayInMonth = DateSerial(Year(dtmDate), _
     Month(dtmDate), 1)
End Function

Function dhLastDayInMonth(Optional dtmDate As Date = 0) As Date
    ' Return the last day in the specified month.

    If dtmDate = 0 Then
        ' Did the caller pass in a date? If not, use
        ' the current date.
        dtmDate = Date
    End If
    dhLastDayInMonth = DateSerial(Year(dtmDate), _
     Month(dtmDate) + 1, 0)
End Function
```

Finding the Beginning or End of a Week

Finding the first or last day in a week counts on the fact that you can subtract integers from a date value and end up with another date value. If the specified date was a Sunday, to find the first day of the week (assuming Sunday was the first day of the week), you'd subtract 0 from the date. If the date was a Monday, you'd subtract 1, if Tuesday, you'd subtract 2, and so on. Because the WeekDay function returns a number between 1 and 7, all you need to do is subtract the WeekDay return value from the date and then add 1. The dhFirstDayInWeek function, in Listing 2.2, does this work for you.

NOTE To be completely correct, the dhFirstDayInWeek and dhLastDayInWeek functions specify the first day of the week for the WeekDay function, using the vbUseSystem constant. This way, the first and last days in the week correspond to the local settings. If you were to omit this constant, the code would treat Sunday as the first day of the week and Saturday as the final day, no matter what the local settings.

The dhLastDayInWeek function in Listing 2.2 uses the same concepts. This time, however, you want to add 6 to the first day of the week. That is (assuming you're in the United States), if the date in question is a Wednesday, you subtract the Weekday return value (4), which takes you to Saturday. Adding 1 takes you to the first day of the week, and adding 6 more takes you to the last day of the week.

Listing 2.2: Find the First or Last Day in a Week

```
Function dhFirstDayInWeek(Optional dtmDate As Date = 0) As Date
    ' Returns the first day in the week specified
    ' by the date in dtmDate.
    ' Uses localized settings for the first day of the week.

    If dtmDate = 0 Then
        ' Did the caller pass in a date? If not, use
        ' the current date.
        dtmDate = Date
    End If
    dhFirstDayInWeek = dtmDate - WeekDay(dtmDate, _
     vbUseSystem) + 1
End Function

Function dhLastDayInWeek(Optional dtmDate As Date = 0) As Date
    ' Returns the last day in the week specified by
    ' the date in dtmDate.
    ' Uses localized settings for the first day of the week.

    If dtmDate = 0 Then
        ' Did the caller pass in a date? If not, use
        ' the current date.
        dtmDate = Date
    End If
    dhLastDayInWeek = dtmDate - WeekDay(dtmDate, vbUseSystem) + 7
End Function
```

To call dhFirstDayInWeek and dhLastDayInWeek, pass a date value to specify a date, or pass no parameter to use the current date. For example, the following code calculates the first and last day in two different weeks:

```
Debug.Print "First day in the current week: " _
 & dhFirstDayInWeek()
Debug.Print "Last day in the current week: " & dhLastDayInWeek()
Debug.Print _
 "First day in the week of 1/1/98: " & dhFirstDayInWeek(#1/1/98#)
Debug.Print _
 "Last day in the week of 1/1/98: " & dhLastDayInWeek(#1/1/98#)
```

Finding the Beginning or End of a Year

Finding the first or last day in a year is simple, compared to the other functions in this section. Once you understand the DateSerial function, it's just a matter of building up a date value that's January 1 or December 31 in the specified year. Because those dates are fixed as the first and last days in the year, no more calculation is necessary. The dhFirstDayInYear and dhLastDayInYear functions, in Listing 2.3, show all that's necessary.

Listing 2.3: Find the First or Last Day in a Year

```
Function dhFirstDayInYear(Optional dtmDate As Date = 0) As Date
    ' Return the first day in the specified year.

    If dtmDate = 0 Then
        ' Did the caller pass in a date? If not, use
        ' the current date.
        dtmDate = Date
    End If
    dhFirstDayInYear = DateSerial(Year(dtmDate), 1, 1)
End Function

Function dhLastDayInYear(Optional dtmDate As Date = 0) As Date
    ' Return the last day in the specified year.

    If dtmDate = 0 Then
        ' Did the caller pass in a date? If not, use
        ' the current date.
        dtmDate = Date
    End If
    dhLastDayInYear = DateSerial(Year(dtmDate), 12, 31)
End Function
```

To call either of these functions, either pass no value (to work with the current year) or pass a date value indicating the year. The functions will each return the requested date. For example, the following code fragment calculates the first and last days in two ways:

```
Debug.Print "First day in the current year: " & _
 dhFirstDayInYear()
Debug.Print "Last day in the current year: " & dhLastDayInYear()
Debug.Print _
 "First day in the next year: " & _
 dhFirstDayInYear(DateAdd("yyyy", 1, Date))
```

```
Debug.Print _
 "Last day in the previous year: " & _
 dhLastDayInYear(DateAdd("yyyy", -1, Date))
```

Finding the Beginning or End of a Quarter

Finding the beginning or end of a quarter takes a bit more effort than do the other functions in this section because there's little support for working with quarters (January though March, April through June, July through September, October through December) in the VBA function library. Listing 2.4 shows the functions that solve this problem, dhFirstDayInQuarter and dhLastDayInQuarter.

Listing 2.4: Find the First and Last Day in a Quarter

```
Function dhFirstDayInQuarter( _
 Optional dtmDate As Date = 0) As Date
    ' Returns the first day in the quarter specified
    ' by the date in dtmDate.

    Const dhcMonthsInQuarter As Integer = 3

    If dtmDate = 0 Then
        ' Did the caller pass in a date? If not, use
        ' the current date.
        dtmDate = Date
    End If
    dhFirstDayInQuarter = DateSerial( _
     Year(dtmDate), _
     Int((Month(dtmDate) - 1) / dhcMonthsInQuarter) * _
     dhcMonthsInQuarter + 1, _
     1)
End Function

Function dhLastDayInQuarter(Optional dtmDate As Date = 0) As Date
    ' Returns the last day in the quarter specified
    ' by the date in dtmDate.

    Const dhcMonthsInQuarter As Integer = 3

    If dtmDate = 0 Then
        ' Did the caller pass in a date? If not, use
        ' the current date.
```

```
        dtmDate = Date
    End If
    dhLastDayInQuarter = DateSerial( _
     Year(dtmDate), _
     Int((Month(dtmDate) - 1) / dhcMonthsInQuarter) _
      * dhcMonthsInQuarter + (dhcMonthsInQuarter + 1), _
     0)
End Function
```

Certainly, once you know how to find the first day in the quarter, you know how to find the last; that's just a matter of adding three months and subtracting one day. But how do you find the first day in the quarter containing a specified date? You know the year portion of the date (it's the same as the date you've specified) and the day portion (which has to be 1), but what month do you use? You could, of course, use the brute-force technique, with a Select Case statement like this:

```
Select Case Month(dtmDate)
    Case 1, 2, 3
        intMonth = 1
    Case 4, 5, 6
        intMonth = 4
    ' etc.
End Select
```

But you just *know* there has to be a better way! This is one situation in which it's worth pulling out some paper and thinking through what's really going on. You may find it useful to create a table listing the input and output of a proposed calculation, in this case, to convert from any month to the first month in that quarter:

Month	First Month of Quarter
1	1
2	1
3	1
4	4
5	4
6	4
7	7
8	7

Month	First Month of Quarter
9	7
10	10
11	10
12	10

Remember, you're looking for a mathematical relationship between the two columns. (Reminds you of high school algebra, right?) It looks as though each output "step" is a multiple of 3, plus 1. After much scribbling, you might come up with the following algebraic relation between the two columns, which turns out to be the exact solution dhFirstDayInQuarter uses:

```
First Month of Quarter = Int((Month - 1) / 3) * 3 + 1
```

This expression finds, for each month value, the largest multiple of 3 less than or equal to the number, multiplies the result by 3, and then adds 1. This calculation, based on the value in the first column, returns the value in the second column in every case. Therefore, rather than asking VBA to perform a lookup and a jump for each call to the function, it performs a moderately simple calculation.

Once dhFirstDayInQuarter has found the first month in the quarter, finding the first day is simple: the function calls DateSerial, building a date from the supplied year, the calculated month, and the day value 1. To find the last day in the quarter, dhLastDayInQuarter repeats the calculation from dhFirstDayInQuarter, adds 1 to the month it calculated to move to the next month, and then uses 0 for the day value. As discussed in the section "Finding the Beginning or End of a Month" earlier in this chapter, supplying 0 for the Day parameter to DateSerial returns the final day of the previous month, which is exactly what you want in this context.

Finding the Next or Previous Weekday

In many financial calculations, you'll need to know the next specific weekday after a given date. For example, you might need to know the date of the Friday immediately following April 29, 1997, or the Monday immediately preceding the same date. As when finding the first or last day in a week, calculating these dates counts on the fact that you can subtract an integer from a date value and end up with another date value.

In this case, it seems simplest to just calculate the beginning of the week containing the specified date and then add on enough days to get to the requested date. That code, from the procedures in Listing 2.5, looks like this:

```
intTemp = WeekDay(dtmDate)
dhPreviousDOW = dtmDate - intTemp + intDOW
```

Say you're looking for the Thursday before 10/7/97 (a Tuesday). In this case, intTemp will be 3 (Tuesday's day of the week) and intDOW will contain 5 (Thursday's day of the week). The expression

```
dtmDate - intTemp + intDOW
' the same as:
' #10/7/97# - 3 + 5
```

will return the date 10/9/97. This, clearly, is not the Thursday before 10/7/97, but the Thursday after. The final step of the calculation, then, is to subtract one week, if necessary. The entire expression looks like this:

```
dhPreviousDOW = dtmDate - intTemp + intDOW - _
 IIf(intTemp > intDOW, 0, 7)
```

When would you not need to subtract 7 to move to the previous week? Reverse the dates in the example. If you're looking for the Tuesday before 10/9/97, the expression would be

```
dtmDate - intTemp + intDOW
' the same as:
' #10/9/97# - 5 + 3
```

which returns #10/7/97#, the correct answer. There's no need to subtract 7 to move to the previous week. The same logic applies to calculating the following weekday, but reversed. In this case, you may need to add 7 to move to the next week if the day you were looking for has already occurred in the current week.

Listing 2.5: Find the Previous or Next Specific Weekday

```
Function dhPreviousDOW(intDOW As Integer, _
 Optional dtmDate As Date = 0) As Date
    ' Find the previous specified day of the week
    ' before the specified date.

    Dim intTemp As Integer
    If dtmDate = 0 Then
        ' Did the caller pass in a date? If not, use
```

```
           ' the current date.
           dtmDate = Date
        End If
        intTemp = WeekDay(dtmDate)
        dhPreviousDOW = dtmDate - intTemp + intDOW - _
         IIf(intTemp > intDOW, 0, 7)
End Function

Function dhNextDOW(intDOW As Integer, _
 Optional dtmDate As Date = 0) As Date
        ' Find the next specified day of the week
        ' after the specified date.

        Dim intTemp As Integer
        If dtmDate = 0 Then
            ' Did the caller pass in a date? If not, use
            ' the current date.
            dtmDate = Date
        End If
        intTemp = WeekDay(dtmDate)
        dhNextDOW = dtmDate - intTemp + intDOW + _
         IIf(intTemp < intDOW, 0, 7)
End Function
```

The following examples demonstrate calling the two functions:

```
Debug.Print "The Monday before 12/25/97 is " & _
 dhPreviousDOW(vbMonday, #12/25/97#)

Debug.Print "The Friday after 12/25/97 is " & _
 dhNextDOW(vbFriday, #12/25/97#)

Debug.Print "It's " & Date & _
 ". The next Monday is " & dhNextDOW(vbMonday)
```

Finding the Next Anniversary

Often, when working with dates, you have stored away a birthday or a wedding date and need to find out the next occurrence of the anniversary of that date. The function in this section, dhNextAnniversary (Listing 2.6), will do that chore for you. Given a date, it finds the next anniversary of that date, taking into account the current date.

Listing 2.6: Find the Next Anniversary of a Date

```
Function dhNextAnniversary(dtmDate As Date) As Date
    ' Given a date, find the next anniversary of that date.

    Dim dtmThisYear As Date

    ' What's the corresponding date in the current year?
    dtmThisYear = DateSerial(Year(Now), Month(dtmDate), _
     Day(dtmDate))

    ' If the anniversary has already occurred, then add 1
    ' to the year.
    If dtmThisYear < Date Then
        dtmThisYear = DateAdd("yyyy", 1, dtmThisYear)
    End If
    dhNextAnniversary = dtmThisYear
End Function
```

This one's actually quite easy. The code follows these steps:

1. Finds the date corresponding to the anniversary in the current year

2. If the date has already passed in the current year, adds one year to the date

To find the anniversary date in the current year, the code uses this expression:

```
dtmThisYear = DateSerial(Year(Now), Month(dtmDate), Day(dtmDate))
```

To correct the result if the date has already passed in the current year, the function uses this fragment:

```
If dtmThisYear < Date Then
    dtmThisYear = DateAdd("yyyy", 1, dtmThisYear)
End If
```

Either way, dtmThisYear contains the next occurrence of the anniversary.

To try out the procedure, you might use code like the following fragment. Given that the current date is 11/12/97,

```
dhNextAnniversary(#5/16/56#)
```

returns 5/16/98 because that date has already passed in 1997.

Finding the nth Particular Weekday in a Month

Perhaps your application needs to find the third Tuesday in November, 1997. The function presented here, dhNthWeekday, in Listing 2.7, solves this puzzle for you. The function accepts three parameters:

- A date specifying the month and year to start in

- An integer greater than 1 that specifies the offset into the month

- An integer specifying the day of week to retrieve (Use the vbSunday...vbSaturday constants.)

and returns a date representing the *n*th specific weekday in the month. If you pass an invalid day of week value or an invalid offset, the function returns the date you passed it.

Listing 2.7: Find the nth Specific Weekday in a Month

```
Function dhNthWeekday(dtmDate As Date, intN As Integer, _
 intDOW As Integer) As Date
    ' Find the date of the specified day within the month. For
    ' example, retrieve the 3rd Tuesday's date.

    Dim dtmTemp As Date

    If (intDOW < vbSunday Or intDOW > vbSaturday) _
    Or (intN < 1) Then
        ' Invalid parameter values. Just
        ' return the passed-in date.
        dhNthWeekday = dtmDate
        Exit Function
    End If

    ' Get the first of the month.
    dtmTemp = DateSerial(Year(dtmDate), Month(dtmDate), 1)
    ' Get to the first intDOW in the month.
    Do While WeekDay(dtmTemp) <> intDOW
        dtmTemp = dtmTemp + 1
    Loop
    ' Now you've found the first intDOW in the month.
    ' Just add 7 for each intN after that.
    dhNthWeekday = dtmTemp + ((intN - 1) * 7)
End Function
```

The function is moderately simple. To do its work, it must:

1. Verify the parameters

2. Find the first day of the specified month

3. Move to the first specified weekday in the month

4. Add enough weeks to find the *n*th occurrence of the specified weekday

It's important to verify the parameters in this case because later, the code loops until it finds the correct day of the week. If the day of the week parameter is invalid, it's possible that the code will look forever. In addition, you must verify that the offset into the month is positive. If either value is invalid, the function returns the passed-in starting date. The code that handles the verification looks like this:

```
If (intDOW < vbSunday Or intDOW > vbSaturday) _
 Or (intN < 1) Then
    ' Invalid parameter values. Just
    ' return the passed-in date.
    dhNthWeekday = dtmDate
    Exit Function
End If
```

Finding the first day of the specified month is, as you know by now, simple. It takes one line of code:

```
dtmTemp = DateSerial(Year(dtmDate), Month(dtmDate), 1)
```

Moving to the first specified weekday requires a bit more work. Although you could use the code shown in the section "Finding the Next or Previous Weekday" earlier in this chapter, that's more work than necessary, because you're already at the first day of the month. In this case, you can just "walk" forward until you hit the day you need:

```
Do While WeekDay(dtmTemp) <> intDOW
    dtmTemp = dtmTemp + 1
Loop
```

Finally, to move to the *n*th occurrence of the weekday, you just need to add the correct multiple of 7 to the date:

```
dhNthWeekday = dtmTemp + ((intN - 1) * 7)
```

For example, to find the date of the third Tuesday in March, 1998, you could call the function like this:

```
dtm = dhNthWeekday(#3/98#, 3, vbTuesday)
```

The return value will be the date #3/17/98#, the third Tuesday in March, 1998.

Working with Workdays

Many calculations involve the five typical workdays (Monday through Friday), but VBA doesn't provide any support for this subset of dates. The functions in this section provide information about the next and previous workday and finding the first and last workday in a month. Skipping weekend days is simple and not worthy of much explanation. The hard part is dealing with the other factor affecting these calculations: holidays. VBA is blissfully unaware of the real world and knows nothing of national and religious holidays. Supplying that information is up to you, and the functions presented here count on your having created a DAO recordset object filled with the rows of information about holidays. You needn't supply a recordset if you don't need this functionality; the recordset parameter to the functions shown here is optional. If you do supply a reference to an open recordset, you must also pass in the name of the field containing holiday date information so the code knows the field in which to search.

Because all the functions in this section count on the same support routines, it makes sense to explain these underlying procedures first. The first routine, IsWeekend, shown in Listing 2.8, accepts a date parameter and returns True if the date falls on a weekend and False otherwise.

Listing 2.8: Indicate Whether a Date Falls on a Weekend

```
Private Function IsWeekend(dtmTemp As Date) As Boolean
    ' If your weekends aren't Saturday (day 7)
    ' and Sunday (day 1), change this routine
    ' to return True for whatever days
    ' you DO treat as weekend days.

    Select Case WeekDay(dtmTemp)
        Case vbSaturday, vbSunday
            IsWeekend = True
        Case Else
            IsWeekend = False
    End Select
End Function
```

The second support function, SkipHolidays (shown in Listing 2.9), takes a reference to a recordset, a field to search in, a date value, and the number of days to skip (normally +1 or –1). It skips over weekend days and holidays until it finds a date that is neither a weekend nor a holiday. It skips past increments of the parameter passed in, so the same code can be used to skip forward or backward.

Listing 2.9: Move a Date Value over Holidays and Weekends

```
Private Function SkipHolidays(rst As Recordset, _
 strField As String, dtmTemp As Date, intIncrement As Integer) _
As Date
    ' Skip weekend days, and holidays in the
    ' recordset referred to by rst.

    Dim strCriteria As String
    On Error GoTo HandleErr

    ' Move up to the first Monday/last Friday if the first/last
    ' of the month was a weekend date. Then skip holidays.
    ' Repeat this entire process until you get to a weekday.
    ' Unless rst contains a row for every day in the year (!)
    ' this should finally converge on a weekday.
    Do
        Do While IsWeekend(dtmTemp)
            dtmTemp = dtmTemp + intIncrement
        Loop
        If Not rst Is Nothing Then
            If Len(strField) > 0 Then
                If Left(strField, 1) <> "[" Then
                    strField = "[" & strField & "]"
                End If
                Do
                    strCriteria = strField & _
                     " = #" & Format(dtmTemp, "mm/dd/yy") & "#"
                    rst.FindFirst strCriteria
                    If Not rst.NoMatch Then
                        dtmTemp = dtmTemp + intIncrement
                    End If
                Loop Until rst.NoMatch
            End If
        End If
    Loop Until Not IsWeekend(dtmTemp)
```

```
ExitHere:
    SkipHolidays = dtmTemp
    Exit Function

HandleErr:
    ' No matter what the error, just
    ' return without complaining.
    ' The worst that could happen is that the code
    ' includes a holiday as a real day, even if
    ' it's in the table.
    Resume ExitHere
End Function
```

The code starts out by skipping over any weekend days. If you send it a date that falls on a weekend, this first bit of code will loop until it lands on a non-weekend date:

```
Do While IsWeekend(dtmTemp)
    dtmTemp = dtmTemp + intIncrement
Loop
```

Its next task is to ensure that the recordset variable is instantiated, that it points to something, and that the field name has been supplied. Once that happens, if the field name doesn't include a leading [character, the code adds leading and trailing brackets. This guards against problems that can occur if the field name includes spaces.

```
If Not rst Is Nothing Then
    If Len(strField) > 0 Then
        If Left(strField, 1) <> "[" Then
            strField = "[" & strField & "]"
        End If
```

Finally, the code enters the loop shown below, checking for a match in the recordset against the current value of dtmTemp. If the code finds a match in the table, it moves to the next day and tries again. It continues in this way until it no longer finds a match in the table. Most of the time, however, this code will execute only once. (There are very few, if any, occurrences of consecutive holidays.) Normally, there won't be any match, and the code will drop right out. If a match is found in the table, there's rarely more than one. Unless you add a row to the table for each day of the year, this code should be extremely fast.

```
Do
    strCriteria = strField & _
```

```
    " = #" & Format(dtmTemp, "mm/dd/yy") & "#"
    rst.FindFirst strCriteria
    If Not rst.NoMatch Then
        dtmTemp = dtmTemp + intIncrement
    End If
Loop Until rst.NoMatch
```

Because this step could drop you off on a weekend date, the entire process repeats until you run out of holidays and don't end up on a weekend date. Of course, the outer loop most likely is never going to be used, but it takes care of an important problem.

NOTE   The code in this example won't do you any good if the Jet database engine is not available to you. If you don't have this database engine (although anyone using Microsoft Office most likely does), you can either rewrite the code to use whatever database engine you do have or just not pass anything for the optional recordset parameter. In that case, you won't be able to skip holidays, but the code will still correctly skip weekend dates.

Finding the Next, Previous, First, or Last Workday in the Month

Once you've got the routines to skip holidays, the rest is simple. If you need to find the previous or next workday, it's just a matter of skipping weekends and holidays until you find another workday. For example, the procedures in Listing 2.10 find the next or previous workday simply by calling the SkipHolidays function. In each case, the functions accepts three optional parameters:

- A date, indicating the month in which to search. If this parameter is omitted, the code uses the current date.

- An open recordset, containing holiday information. If this parameter is omitted, the code skips just weekends, not holidays. If it is supplied, you must supply the field name in the next parameter.

- A string containing the name of a field to be searched in the open recordset. This parameter is used only if the recordset parameter isn't omitted, and it is required if you supply the recordset.

As you can see from the code in Listing 2.10, there's not much to these routines, given the workhorse procedure, SkipHolidays.

Listing 2.10: Find the Next or Previous Workday

```
Function dhNextWorkday(Optional dtmDate As Date = 0, _
 Optional rst As Recordset = Nothing, _
 Optional strField As String = "") As Date
    ' Return the next working day after the specified date.

    Dim dtmTemp As Date
    Dim strCriteria As String

    If dtmDate = 0 Then
        ' Did the caller pass in a date? If not, use
        ' the current date.
        dtmDate = Date
    End If
    dhNextWorkday = SkipHolidays(rst, strField, dtmDate + 1, 1)
End Function

Function dhPreviousWorkday(Optional dtmDate As Date = 0, _
 Optional rst As Recordset = Nothing, _
 Optional strField As String = "") As Date

    Dim dtmTemp As Date
    Dim strCriteria As String

    If dtmDate = 0 Then
        ' Did the caller pass in a date? If not, use
        ' the current date.
        dtmDate = Date
    End If
    dhPreviousWorkday = SkipHolidays(rst, strField, _
     dtmDate - 1, -1)
End Function
```

If you want to find the first or last workday in a given month, all you need to do is maneuver to the first or last day in the month and then skip holidays forward or backward. For example, the dhFirstWorkdayInMonth function, shown in Listing 2.11, handles this for you. The function accepts the same three optional parameters as the previous examples.

The dhFirstWorkdayInMonth function first finds the first day in the month, using the same code as in other procedures in this chapter. Once it gets to the first day, it calls SkipHolidays, passing the recordset, the field name, the starting date, and the increment (1, in this case). The date returned from SkipHolidays will be the first working day in the month.

Listing 2.11: Find the First Workday in a Given Month

```
Function dhFirstWorkdayInMonth(Optional dtmDate As Date = 0, _
 Optional rst As Recordset = Nothing, _
 Optional strField As String = "") As Date
    ' Return the first working day in the month specified.

    Dim dtmTemp As Date
    Dim strCriteria As String

    If dtmDate = 0 Then
        ' Did the caller pass in a date? If not, use
        ' the current date.
        dtmDate = Date
    End If
    dtmTemp = DateSerial(Year(dtmDate), Month(dtmDate), 1)
    dhFirstWorkdayInMonth = SkipHolidays(rst, strField, _
      dtmTemp, 1)
End Function
```

Finding the last workday in the month is very similar. In dhLastWorkdayInMonth, shown in Listing 2.12, the code first finds the final day of the month, using code discussed earlier in this chapter, and then calls the SkipHolidays function to move backward through the month until it finds a day that is neither a weekend nor a holiday.

Listing 2.12: Find the Last Workday in a Given Month

```
Function dhLastWorkdayInMonth(Optional dtmDate As Date = 0, _
 Optional rst As Recordset = Nothing, _
 Optional strField As String = "") As Date
    ' Return the last working day in the month specified.

    Dim dtmTemp As Date
    Dim strCriteria As String

    If dtmDate = 0 Then
        ' Did the caller pass in a date? If not, use
```

```
        ' the current date.
        dtmDate = Date
    End If
    dtmTemp = DateSerial(Year(dtmDate), Month(dtmDate) + 1, 0)
    dhLastWorkdayInMonth = SkipHolidays(rst, strField, _
     dtmTemp, -1)
End Function
```

To work with these procedures, you might write a test routine like the one shown in Listing 2.13. This procedure assumes the following:

- You have Jet and DAO installed on your machine.

- You have a reference set to the DAO type library in your project.

- You have a database named HOLIDAYS.MDB available (and you've modified the code to point to the actual location of HOLIDAYS.MDB).

- HOLIDAYS.MDB includes a table named tblHolidays.

- tblHolidays includes a date/time field named Date, containing one row for each holiday you want tracked.

Listing 2.13: Test Routine for the SkipHolidays Function

```
Sub TestSkipHolidays()
    Dim rst As DAO.Recordset
    Dim db As DAO.Database
    Set db = DAO.DBEngine.OpenDatabase("Holidays.MDB")
    Set rst = db.OpenRecordset("tblHolidays", _
     DAO.dbOpenDynaset)

    Debug.Print dhFirstWorkdayInMonth(#1/1/97#, rst, "Date")
    Debug.Print dhLastWorkdayInMonth(#12/31/97#, rst, "Date")
    Debug.Print dhNextWorkday(#5/23/97#, rst, "Date")
    Debug.Print dhNextWorkday(#5/27/97#, rst, "Date")
    Debug.Print dhPreviousWorkday(#5/27/97#, rst, "Date")
    Debug.Print dhPreviousWorkday(#5/23/97#, rst, "Date")
End Sub
```

If you don't have Jet and DAO or you just don't care about holidays, you could also call these routines like this:

```
Debug.Print dhFirstWorkdayInMonth(#1/1/97#)
' or
Debug.Print dhLastWorkdayInMonth(#12/31/97#)
```

In this case, the procedure calls would just skip weekend days, if necessary, to return the first and last workday, respectively.

> **TIP**
>
> The sample CD with this book includes HOLIDAYS.MDB (which contains tblHolidays), which you can use as a start for preparing your list of holidays. If you have any product that can work with Access databases, you're ready to start filling in your own list of holidays for use with these routines. If not, we've included HOLIDAYS.TXT, a text file you can import into your own database program for use with these samples. Of course, if you're not using Jet as your database engine, you'll need to modify the code in the samples accordingly.

Manipulating Dates and Times

This section provides solutions to five common date manipulation issues:

- Finding the number of days in a specified month
- Counting the number of iterations of a specific weekday in a month
- Determining whether a specified year is a leap year
- Rounding time to a specified increment
- Converting numbers or strings to dates, given an input format specification

In each case, we've provided a VBA function or two, as well as some examples showing the usage of the function, to help get you started.

How Many Days in That Month?

Although there's no built-in function to determine the number of days in a specified month, it's not a difficult task. There are many ways to accomplish this task. You could create a Select Case statement and, knowing the month and the year, look up the length of the month. This requires, of course, knowing the year, because leap years affect February's length.

An alternative (and it's the correct alternative, we believe) is to let VBA do as much of any calculation as possible. Because you can subtract one date value from another to determine the number of days between the dates, you can use the DateSerial function to find the first day in the specified month and the first day in the next month and then subtract the first value from the second.

The dhDaysInMonth function, in Listing 2.14, performs the necessary calculations. You send it a date, and it calculates the number of days in the month represented by that date. In this function, as in many others, if you don't pass a date at all, the function assumes you want to use the current date and finds the number of days in the current month.

Listing 2.14: Calculate the Days in a Given Month

```
Function dhDaysInMonth(Optional dtmDate As Date = 0) As Integer
    ' Return the number of days in the specified month.

    If dtmDate = 0 Then
        ' Did the caller pass in a date? If not, use
        ' the current date.
        dtmDate = Date
    End If
    dhDaysInMonth = DateSerial(Year(dtmDate), _
     Month(dtmDate) + 1, 1) - _
     DateSerial(Year(dtmDate), Month(dtmDate), 1)
End Function
```

TIP Although this tip applies to many functions in this chapter, it is key to this particular function. VBA accepts dates in many formats, as you've seen. One that we haven't mentioned is the #mm/yy# format. That is, you can pass just a month and year as a date, and VBA will assume you mean the first of that month. With the dhDaysInMonth function, it's useful to be able to just send in the month and year portion if you don't care to handle the day portion as well.

How Many Mondays in June?

If your application needs to know how many occurrences there are of a particular weekday in a given month, the dhCountDOWInMonth function is for you. This function, shown in Listing 2.15, allows you to specify a date and, optionally, a specific day of the week. It returns the number of times the specified day of the week occurs in the month containing the date. If you don't pass a day of the week value, the function counts the number of times the day indicated by the date parameter occurs within its own month.

Listing 2.15: Count the Number of Specific Weekdays in a Month

```
Function dhCountDOWInMonth(ByVal dtmDate As Date, _
 Optional intDOW As Integer = 0)
    ' Calculate the number of specified days in
    ' the specified month.

    Dim dtmFirst As Date
    Dim intCount As Integer
    Dim intMonth As Integer

    If (intDOW < vbSunday Or intDOW > vbSaturday) Then
        ' Caller must not have specified DOW, or it
        ' was an invalid number.
        intDOW = WeekDay(dtmDate)
    End If
    intMonth = Month(dtmDate)

    ' Find the first day of the month
    dtmFirst = DateSerial(Year(dtmDate), intMonth, 1)

    ' Move dtmFirst forward until it hits the
    ' matching day number.
    Do While WeekDay(dtmFirst) <> intDOW
        dtmFirst = dtmFirst + 1
    Loop

    ' Now, dtmFirst is sitting on the first day
    ' of the requested number in the month. Just count
    ' how many of that day type there are in the month.
    intCount = 0
    Do While Month(dtmFirst) = intMonth
        intCount = intCount + 1
        dtmFirst = dtmFirst + 7
    Loop
    dhCountDOWInMonth = intCount
End Function
```

The dhCountDOWInMonth function takes four simple steps to do its work. It must

1. Verify the parameters

2. Find the first day of the specified month

3. Move forward within the month until it hits the first day matching the day of week you're interested in

4. Count the days, adding increments of seven days, until the day is no longer in the same month

To verify the parameters, the code checks the intDOW parameter, making sure the value is between vbSunday and vbSaturday. If not, it overrides the value and uses the day of the week represented by the dtmDate parameter:

```
If (intDOW < vbSunday Or intDOW > vbSaturday) Then
    ' Caller must not have specified DOW, or it
    ' was an invalid number.
    intDOW = WeekDay(dtmDate)
End If
```

Finding the first day of the month requires yet another call to the DateSerial function:

```
intMonth = Month(dtmDate)
dtmFirst = DateSerial(Year(dtmDate), intMonth, 1)
```

Moving through the days until the code finds a day matching the required day of the week takes just a few lines:

```
' Move dtmFirst forward until it hits the
' matching day number.
Do While WeekDay(dtmFirst) <> intDOW
    dtmFirst = dtmFirst + 1
Loop
```

Finally, counting the number of matching days requires looping, adding seven days at a time, until the date falls out of the specified month:

```
' Now, dtmFirst is sitting on the first day
' of the requested number in the month. Just count
' how many of that day type there are in the month.
intCount = 0
Do While Month(dtmFirst) = intMonth
    intCount = intCount + 1
```

```
    dtmFirst = dtmFirst + 7
Loop
```

To test this function, you might write code like this:

```
If dhCountDOWInMonth(#3/98#, vbFriday) > 4 Then
    MsgBox "There are more than 4 Fridays in March 1998!"
End If
```

Is This a Leap Year?

Although VBA provides very rich date and time support, it includes no built-in function that will tell you whether a given year is a leap year. Calculating this answer is actually more complex than checking to see whether the year is evenly divisible by four. If that's all it took, you could just check like this:

```
' (Assuming that intYear holds the year in question)
' MOD returns the remainder when you divide, so
' the following expression will return True if
' intYear is evenly divisible by 4.
If intYear MOD 4 = 0 Then
```

But that's not all there is. The year is defined as the length of time it takes to pass from one vernal equinox to another. If the calendar gains or loses days, the date for the equinox shifts. Because the physical year isn't exactly 365.25 days in length (as the calendar says it should be), the current calendar supplies three too many leap years every 385 years. To make up for that, years divisible by 100 aren't leap years unless they're a multiple of 400. Got all that? (In case you're concerned, this schedule will result in an error of only three days in 10,000 years. Not to worry....) This means that 1700, 1800, and 1900 weren't leap years, but 2000 will be.

Yes, you could write the code to handle this yourself, and it's not all that difficult. But why do it? VBA is already handling the algorithm internally. It knows that the day after February 28 (in all but a leap year) is March 1 but in a leap year it's February 29. To take advantage of this fact, dhIsLeapYear (shown in Listing 2.16) calculates the answer for you.

Listing 2.16: Is the Specified Year a Leap Year?

```
Function dhIsLeapYear(Optional varDate As Variant) As Boolean
    ' Is the supplied year a leap year?
    ' Check the day number of the day
    ' after Feb 28 to find out.
```

```
' Missing? Use the current year.
If IsMissing(varDate) Then
    varDate = Year(Now)

' Is it a date? Then use that year.
ElseIf VarType(varDate) = vbDate Then
    varDate = Year(varDate)

' Is it an integer? Use that value, if it's OK.
' Otherwise, use the current year.
ElseIf VarType(varDate) = vbInteger Then
    ' Only years 100 through 9999 are allowed.
    If varDate < 100 Or varDate > 9999 Then
        varDate = Year(Now)
    End If

' If it's not a date or an integer, just use the
' current year.
Else
    varDate = Year(Now)
End If
dhIsLeapYear = (Day(DateSerial(varDate, 2, 28) + 1) = 29)
End Function
```

Most of the code in dhIsLeapYear handles the "optional" parameter; because you can pass either a date or an integer representing a year, you need a larger amount of error-checking code than normal. If you pass nothing at all, the code uses the current year:

```
If IsMissing(varDate) Then
    varDate = Year(Now)
```

If you pass a date, the function uses the year portion of the date:

```
' Is it a date? Then use that year.
ElseIf VarType(varDate) = vbDate Then
    varDate = Year(varDate)
```

If you pass an integer, the code treats that integer as the year to check. Because VBA can only process years between 100 and 9999, it verifies that your integer falls in that range. If you pass a value that's neither a date nor an integer, it uses the current year:

```
ElseIf VarType(varDate) = vbInteger Then
    ' Only years 100 through 9999 are allowed.
    If varDate < 100 Or varDate > 9999 Then
        varDate = Year(Now)
```

```
    End If

' If it's not a date or an integer, just use the
' current year.
Else
    varDate = Year(Now)
End If
```

For example, you might try calling the procedure in any of these three ways:

```
If dhIsLeapYear() Then
    ' You know the current year is a leap year.

If dhIsLeapYear(1956) Then
    ' You know 1956 was a leap year.

If dhIsLeapYear(#12/1/92#) Then
    ' You know 1992 was a leap year.
```

This function compares the date of the day following February 28 to the value 29. If it is 29, the function returns True. Otherwise, it must not be a leap year, and it returns False.

The moral of this story (if there is one) is to let VBA do as much work as possible for you. Although you could have written the dhIsLeapYear function to take into account the algorithm used by the Gregorian calendar, what's the point? The VBA developers have done that work already. You'll get better performance (and fewer bugs) by taking advantage of the work that's already been done.

Rounding Times to the Nearest Increment

If you're writing a scheduling application, you may need to round a time to a specified number of minutes. For example, you may need to find the nearest 5-, 10-, 15-, 20-, or 30-minute interval. The solution isn't trivial, and the code shown in Listing 2.17 takes care of this problem.

To call dhRoundTime(), pass it a date/time value and an interval to round to. (You must use any divisor of 60, but you'll most likely use 5, 10, 15, 20, 30, or 60.) For example:

```
? dhRoundTime(#12:32:15#, 5)
```

returns

```
12:30:00 PM
```

and

```
? dhRoundTime(#12:32:35#, 5)
```

returns

```
12:35:00 PM
```

If you pass dhRoundTime a full date and time value, it will preserve the date portion and just modify the time part.

Listing 2.17: Round Time Values to the Nearest Interval

```
Function dhRoundTime(dtmTime As Date, intInterval As Integer) _
 As Date
    ' Round the time value in varTime to the nearest minute
    ' interval in intInterval

    Dim intTime As Integer
    Dim sglTime As Single
    Dim intHour As Integer
    Dim intMinute As Integer
    Dim lngdate As Long

    ' Get the date portion of the date/time value
    lngdate = DateValue(dtmTime)

    ' Get the time portion as a number like 11.5 for 11:30.
    sglTime = TimeValue(dtmTime) * 24

    ' Get the hour and store it away. Int truncates,
    ' CInt rounds, so use Int.
    intHour = Int(sglTime)

    ' Get the number of minutes, and then round to the nearest
    ' occurrence of the interval specified.
    intMinute = CInt((sglTime - intHour) * 60)
    intMinute = CInt(intMinute / intInterval) * intInterval

    ' Build back up the original date/time value,
    ' rounded to the nearest interval.
    dhRoundTime = CDate(lngdate + _
      ((intHour + intMinute / 60) / 24))
End Function
```

This procedure is probably the most complex in this chapter, at least in terms of the calculations it performs. Its first step is to store away the date portion of the original date/time value so it can preserve the value, which will never be altered by the function:

```
' Get the date portion of the date/time value
lngdate = DateValue(dtmTime)
```

Next, the procedure retrieves the time portion of the parameter and converts it into a decimal number, multiplying the value by 24:

```
' Get the time portion as a number like 11.5 for 11:30.
sglTime = TimeValue(dtmTime) * 24
```

Because the time portion of a date/time value is the fraction of a full day represented by the time, taking a value representing 12:32:15 P.M. (0.522395833333333) and multiplying it by 24 will result in the value 12.5375. Once you have the time in a format like that, you can round it as needed.

Once the function knows the time, it can tuck away the hour portion, because that value will also never change.

```
' Get the hour and store it away. Int truncates,
' CInt rounds, so use Int.
intHour = Int(sglTime)
```

The next step is to pull off just the fractional portion (representing the minutes) and multiply by 60 to find the number of minutes involved. Using the example of 12.5375, multiplying the fractional part by 60 and converting to an integer would return 32, which is the number of minutes involved:

```
intMinute = CInt((sglTime - intHour) * 60)
```

The crucial step involves rounding the number of minutes to the correct interval:

```
intMinute = CInt(intMinute / intInterval) * intInterval
```

Once you've rounded the value, the final step is to reconstruct the full date/time value. The following line of code adds the hour portion to the minute portion divided by 60, divides the entire time portion by 24 to convert to the appropriate fraction, adds the result to the preserved date value, and returns the entire value:

```
dhRoundTime = CDate(lngdate + ((intHour + intMinute / 60) / 24))
```

You may find it useful to single-step through this procedure, checking the value of various variables as it runs. Try calling dhRoundTime from the Immediate window, passing in various times and divisors of 60 as intervals. Once you get the hang of what dhRoundTime is doing, you'll find it useful in many applications that involve time and scheduling.

Converting Strings or Numbers to Real Dates

The world of data isn't perfect, that's for sure, and data can come to your application in many formats. Dates are particularly troublesome because there are so many ways to display and format them. If you routinely need to gather information from outside sources, you'll appreciate the two functions in this section. The first, dhCNumDate (Listing 2.18), attempts to convert dates stored in numeric values into true Date format. The second function, dhCStrDate (Listing 2.19), performs the same sort of task, but with formatted strings as input.

Some computer systems, for example, store dates as integers such as 19971231 (representing #12/31/1997#) or 52259 (representing #5/22/1959#). The code in dhCNumDate can convert those values into real VBA date/time format, as long as you tell it the layout of the number coming in. For example, to perform the first conversion, you might use

```
dtmBirthday = dhCNumDate(19971231, "YYYYMMDD")
```

The function, knowing how the date number was laid out, could pull out the various pieces.

The dhCStrDate function does similar work, but with string values as its input. For example, if all the dates coming in from your mainframe computer were in the format "MMDDYYYY", you could use

```
' strOldDate contains "05221959"
dtmNewDate = dhCStrDate(strOldDate, "MMDDYYYY")
```

to convert the string into a real date.

Listing 2.18: Convert Formatted Numbers to Real Dates

```
Function dhCNumdate(ByVal lngdate As Long, _
 ByVal strFormat As String) As Variant
    ' Convert numbers to dates, depending on the specified format
    ' and the incoming number. In this case, the number and the
    ' format must match, or the output will be useless.
```

```
       Dim intYear As Integer
       Dim intMonth As Integer
       Dim intDay As Integer
       Dim fOK As Boolean

       fOK = True
       Select Case strFormat
           Case "MMDDYY"
               intYear = lngdate Mod 100
               intMonth = lngdate \ 10000
               intDay = (lngdate \ 100) Mod 100

           Case "MMDDYYYY"
               intYear = lngdate Mod 10000
               intMonth = lngdate \ 1000000
               intDay = (lngdate \ 10000) Mod 100

           Case "DDMMYY"
               intYear = lngdate Mod 100
               intMonth = (lngdate \ 100) Mod 100
               intDay = lngdate \ 10000

           Case "DDMMYYYY"
               intYear = lngdate Mod 10000
               intMonth = (lngdate \ 10000) Mod 100
               intDay = lngdate \ 1000000

           Case "YYMMDD", "YYYYMMDD"
               intYear = lngdate \ 10000
               intMonth = (lngdate \ 100) Mod 100
               intDay = lngdate Mod 100

           Case Else
               fOK = False
       End Select
       If fOK Then
           dhCNumdate = DateSerial(intYear, intMonth, intDay)
       Else
           dhCNumdate = Null
       End If
End Function
```

TIP

You'll find an interesting code technique in dhCNumDate. Given a number like 220459 (#4/22/59# in date format), retrieving the month portion requires some effort. The code accomplishes this by first using integer division (the \ operator), resulting in 2204. Then, to retrieve just the month portion, the code uses the Mod operator to find the remainder you get when you divide 2204 by 100. You'll find the integer division and the Mod operator useful if you want to retrieve specific digits from a number, as we did in dhCNumDate.

Listing 2.19: Convert Formatted Strings to Real Dates

```
Function dhCStrdate(strDate As String, Optional _
 strFormat As String = "") As Date
    ' Given a string containing a date value, and a format
    ' string describing the information in the date string,
    ' convert the string into a real date value.

    Dim strYear As String
    Dim strMonth As String
    Dim strDay As String
    Dim fDone As Boolean

    Select Case strFormat
        Case "MMDDYY", "MMDDYYYY"
            strYear = Mid(strDate, 5)
            strMonth = Left(strDate, 2)
            strDay = Mid(strDate, 3, 2)

        Case "DDMMYY", "DDMMYYYY"
            strYear = Mid(strDate, 5)
            strMonth = Mid(strDate, 3, 2)
            strDay = Left(strDate, 2)

        Case "YYMMDD"
            strYear = Left(strDate, 2)
            strMonth = Mid(strDate, 3, 2)
            strDay = Right(strDate, 2)

        Case "YYYYMMDD"
            strYear = Left(strDate, 4)
            strMonth = Mid(strDate, 5, 2)
            strDay = Right(strDate, 2)
```

```
        Case "DD/MM/YY", "DD/MM/YYYY"
            strYear = Mid(strDate, 7)
            strMonth = Mid(strDate, 4, 2)
            strDay = Left(strDate, 2)

        Case "YY/MM/DD"
            strYear = Left(strDate, 2)
            strMonth = Mid(strDate, 4, 2)
            strDay = Right(strDate, 2)

        Case "YYYY/MM/DD"
            strYear = Left(strDate, 4)
            strMonth = Mid(strDate, 6, 2)
            strDay = Right(strDate, 2)

        Case Else
            ' If none of the other formats were matched,
            ' just count on Cdate to do the conversion. It may fail,
            ' but we can't help out here.
            dhCStrdate = CDate(strDate)
            fDone = True
    End Select
    If Not fDone Then
        dhCStrdate = DateSerial(Val(strYear), Val(strMonth), _
        Val(strDay))
    End If
End Function
```

There's no doubt about it—the code in both these functions relies on brute force. Given the examples already in the functions, you should find it to easy add your own new formats, should the need arise. In each case, it's just a matter of using the correct mathematical or string functions to perform the necessary conversions.

Working with Elapsed Time

No matter how much you'd like VBA date/time values to be able to track elapsed time, they're not built that way. As designed, VBA date/time values store a particular point in time, not a span of time, and there's no way to store more than 24 hours in a given date/time variable. If you want to work with elapsed times, you'll generally have to do some conversion work, storing the elapsed times in a numeric datatype and converting them back to a formatted output for display. Other elapsed time issues simply return an integer value indicating the number of elapsed units (year, days, months) between two dates.

This section covers several standard issues when dealing with elapsed times, including these topics:

- Finding the number of workdays between two dates
- Returning a person's age, in years, given the birth date
- Formatting elapsed time using a format specification string
- Formatting cumulative times

Finding Workdays between Two Dates

Many applications require you to calculate the number of days between two dates (and you can simply use DateDiff or subtract the first date value from the second, if that's all you need). In addition, many business applications need to know the number of workdays between two dates, and that's a bit more complex. The function in this section, dhCountWorkdays, uses the code presented previously (see the section "Working with Workdays") to skip holidays and weekends. Listing 2.20 shows the entire function.

Listing 2.20: Count the Number of Workdays between Two Dates

```
Function dhCountWorkdays(ByVal dtmStart As Date, _
 ByVal dtmEnd As Date, _
 Optional rst As Recordset = Nothing, _
 Optional strField As String = "") _
 As Integer

    Dim intDays As Integer
    Dim dtmTemp As Date
    Dim intSubtract As Integer

    ' Swap the dates if necessary.
    If dtmEnd < dtmStart Then
        dtmTemp = dtmStart
        dtmStart = dtmEnd
        dtmEnd = dtmTemp
    End If
```

```
    ' Get the start and end dates to be weekdays.
    dtmStart = SkipHolidays(rst, strField, dtmStart, 1)
    dtmEnd = SkipHolidays(rst, strField, dtmEnd, -1)
    If dtmStart > dtmEnd Then
        ' Sorry, no workdays to be had. Just return 0.
        dhCountWorkDays = 0
    Else
        intDays = dtmEnd - dtmStart + 1

        ' Subtract off weekend days. Do this by figuring out
        ' how many calendar weeks there are between the dates
        ' and multiplying the difference by two (since there
        ' are two weekend days for each week). That is, if the
        ' difference is 0, the two days are in the same week.
        ' If the difference is 1, then you have two weekend days.
        intSubtract = (DateDiff("ww", dtmStart, dtmEnd) * 2)

        ' The answer, finally, is all the weekdays, minus any
        ' holidays found in the table.
        ' If rst is Nothing, this call won't subtract any dates.
        intSubtract = intSubtract + CountHolidays(rst, _
         strField, dtmStart, dtmEnd)
        dhCountWorkdays = intDays - intSubtract
    End If
End Function
```

To call dhCountWorkdays, pass it two dates (the starting and ending dates). In addition, if you want to take holidays into account, pass it a reference to an open recordset and the name of the field within the recordset containing the holiday date information. For more information on working with this type of function, see the section "Working with Workdays" earlier in this chapter. Unlike the functions presented there, however, this one requires a bit of effort to find the right answer.

There are, of course, many ways to solve this problem. The solution we came up with takes these steps:

1. Move the starting date forward, skipping weekend and holiday dates, until it finds a workday:

   ```
   dtmStart = SkipHolidays(rst, strField, dtmStart, 1)
   ```

2. Take the same step with the ending date, moving backward.

   ```
   dtmEnd = SkipHolidays(rst, strField, dtmEnd, -1)
   ```

3.   If the starting date is now past the ending date, there are no workdays in the interval, so just return 0:

```
If dtmStart > dtmEnd Then
    ' Sorry, no workdays to be had. Just return 0.
    dhCountWorkdays = 0
```

4.   Calculate the difference between the dates, so far:

```
intDays = dtmEnd - dtmStart + 1
```

Now for the tricky part, the final three steps:

5.   Subtract the number of weekend days. DateDiff, using the "ww" interval specifier, gives you the number of weeks, and there are two weekend days per weekend:

```
intSubtract = (DateDiff("ww", dtmStart, dtmEnd) * 2)
```

6.   Subtract the number of holiday days. If you've not supplied a recordset variable, the CountHolidays function returns immediately, reporting no holidays in the interval:

```
intSubtract = intSubtract + CountHolidays(rst, strField, _
 dtmStart, dtmEnd)
```

7.   Finally, return the total number of workdays in the interval:

```
dhCountWorkdays = intDays - intSubtract
```

To work with these procedures, you might write a test routine like the one shown in Listing 2.21. This procedure makes these assumptions:

- You have Jet and DAO installed on your machine.

- You have a reference set to the DAO type library in your project.

- You have a database named HOLIDAYS.MDB available (and you've modified the code to point to the actual location of HOLIDAYS.MDB).

- HOLIDAYS.MDB includes a table named tblHolidays.

- tblHolidays includes a date/time field named Date, containing one row for each holiday you want tracked.

Listing 2.21: Test Procedure for dhCountWorkdays

```
Sub TestCountWorkdays()
    Dim rst As DAO.Recordset
    Dim db As DAO.Database
    Set db = DAO.DBEngine.OpenDatabase("Holidays.MDB")
    Set rst = db.OpenRecordset("tblHolidays", _
     DAO.dbOpenDynaset)

    Debug.Print dhCountWorkdays(#12/27/96#, #1/2/97#, _
     rst, "Date")
    Debug.Print dhCountWorkdays(#12/27/96#, #1/2/97#)
End Sub
```

Calculating Age

Calculating someone's age, given that person's birth date, is a commonplace need in data manipulation. Unfortuntaely, VBA doesn't give a complete and correct method for calculating a person's age.

You might be tempted to use this formula:

```
Age = DateDiff("yyyy", Birthdate, Date)
```

to calculate age, but this doesn't quite work. If the birth date hasn't yet occurred this year, the Age value will be off by 1. For example, imagine your birthday is December 31, and you were born in 1950. If today is October 1, 1997, subtracting the year portions of the two dates (1997 – 1950) would indicate that you were 47 years old. In reality, by the standard way of figuring such things, you're still only 46.

To handle this discrepancy, the dhAge function in Listing 2.22 not only subtracts one Year portion of the dates from the other, it checks whether the birth date has already occurred this year. If it hasn't, the function subtracts 1 from the calculation, returning the correct age.

In addition, dhAge allows you to pass an optional second date: the date on which to calculate the age. If you pass nothing for the second parameter, the code assumes you want to use the current date as the ending date. That is, if you use a call like this:

```
intAge = dhAge(#5/22/59#)
```

you'll find the current age of someone born on May 22, 1959. If you call the function like this:

```
intAge = dhAge(#5/22/59#, #1/1/2000#)
```

you'll find out how old the same person will be on the first day of 2000.

Listing 2.22: One Solution for Calculating Age

```
Function dhAge(dtmBD As Date, Optional dtmDate As Date = 0) _
 As Integer
    ' This procedure is stored as dhAgeUnused in the sample
    ' module.

    Dim intAge As Integer

    If dtmDate = 0 Then
        ' Did the caller pass in a date? If not, use
        ' the current date.
        dtmDate = Date
    End If
    intAge = DateDiff("yyyy", dtmBD, dtmDate)
    If dtmDate < DateSerial(Year(dtmDate), Month(dtmBD), _
     Day(dtmBD)) Then
        intAge = intAge - 1
    End If
    dhAge = intAge
End Function
```

> **TIP**
>
> You might also be tempted to solve this problem by dividing the difference between the two dates, in days, by 365.25. This works for some combinations of dates, but not for all. It's just not worth the margin of error. The functions presented here are simple enough that they're a reasonable replacement for the simple division that otherwise seems intuitive.

If you're looking for the smallest possible solution, perhaps at the expense of readability, you could use the version in Listing 2.23 instead. It relies on the fact that a true expression is equal to the value –1 and a false expression is equal to 0. The function adds –1 or 0 to the year difference, depending on whether the specified birth date has passed.

Listing 2.23: A Second Solution for Calculating Age

```
Function dhAge(dtmBD As Date, Optional dtmDate As Date = 0) _
 As Integer
    ' Calculate a person's age, given the person's birth date and
    ' an optional "current" date.

    If dtmDate = 0 Then
        ' Did the caller pass in a date? If not, use
        ' the current date.
        dtmDate = Date
    End If
    dhAge = DateDiff("yyyy", dtmBD, dtmDate) + _
      (dtmDate < DateSerial(Year(dtmDate), Month(dtmBD), _
      Day(dtmBD)))
End Function
```

Formatting Elapsed Time

VBA provides no support for elapsed times or for displaying formatted elapsed times. You'll have to take steps on your own if you want to take two dates, find the difference between them, and display the difference formatted the way you want it. The function in this section, dhFormatInterval, in Listing 2.24 (certainly the longest procedure in this chapter), allows you to specify two dates and an optional format specifier and returns a string representing the difference. As the function is currently written, you can use any of the format specifiers listed in Table 2.9. You are invited, of course, to add your own specifiers to the list by modifying the source code. (For information on retrieving the time delimiter programmatically, see the section "Formatting Cumulative Times" later in this chapter.)

TABLE 2.9   Available Format Specifications for dhFormatInterval

Format	Example
D H	3 Days 3 Hours
D H M	3 Days 2 Hours 46 Minutes
D H M S	3 Days 2 Hours 45 Minutes 45 Seconds
D H:MM	3 Days 2:46

TABLE 2.9 Available Format Specifications for dhFormatInterval (continued)

Format	Example
D HH:MM	3 Days 02:46
D HH:MM:SS	3 Days 02:45:45
H M	74 Hours 46 Minutes
H:MM	74:46 (leading 0 on minutes, if necessary)
H:MM:SS	74:45:45
M S	4485 Minutes 45 Seconds
M:SS	4485:45 (leading 0 on seconds, if necessary)

Listing 2.24: Format the Interval between Two Dates

```
Function dhFormatInterval(dtmStart As Date, datend As Date, _
 Optional strFormat As String = "H:MM:SS") As String
    ' Return the difference between two times,
    ' formatted as specified in strFormat.

    Dim lngSeconds As Long
    Dim sngMinutes As Single
    Dim sngHours As Single
    Dim sngDays As Single

    Dim intSeconds As Integer
    Dim intMinutes As Integer
    Dim intHours As Integer

    Dim intRoundedHours As Integer
    Dim intRoundedMinutes As Integer

    Dim strDay As String
    Dim strHour As String
    Dim strMinute As String
    Dim strSecond As String
    Dim strOut As String

    Dim lngFullDays As Long
```

```
Dim lngFullHours As Long
Dim lngFullMinutes As Long

Dim strDelim As String

' If you don't want to use the local delimiter,
' but a specific one, replace the next line with
' this:
' strDelim = ":"
strDelim = GetTimeDelimiter()

' Calculate the full number of seconds in the interval.
' This limits the calculation to 2 billion seconds
' (68 years or so), but that's not too bad. Then calculate
' the difference in minutes, hours, and days, as well.
lngSeconds = DateDiff("s", dtmStart, datend)
sngMinutes = lngSeconds / 60
sngHours = sngMinutes / 60
sngDays = sngHours / 24

' Get the full hours and minutes, for later display.
lngFullDays = Int(sngDays)
lngFullHours = Int(sngHours)
lngFullMinutes = Int(sngMinutes)

' Get the incremental amount of each unit.
intHours = Int((sngDays - lngFullDays) * 24)
intMinutes = Int((sngHours - lngFullHours) * 60)
intSeconds = CInt((sngMinutes - lngFullMinutes) * 60)
' In some instances, time values must be rounded.
' The next two lines depend on the fact that a true statement
' has a value of -1 and a false statement has a value of 0.
' The code needs to add 1 to the value if the following
' expression is true, and 0 if not.
intRoundedHours = intHours - (intMinutes > 30)
intRoundedMinutes = intMinutes - (intSeconds > 30)

strDay = "Days"
strHour = "Hours"
strMinute = "Minutes"
strSecond = "Seconds"

If lngFullDays = 1 Then strDay = "Day"
Select Case strFormat
    Case "D H"
```

```
            If intRoundedHours = 1 Then strHour = "Hour"
            strOut = lngFullDays & " " & strDay & " " & _
             intRoundedHours & " " & strHour
        Case "D H M"
            If intHours = 1 Then strHour = "Hour"
            If intRoundedMinutes = 1 Then strMinute = "Minute"
            strOut = lngFullDays & " " & strDay & " " & _
             intHours & " " & strHour & " " & _
             intRoundedMinutes & " " & strMinute
        Case "D H M S"
            If intHours = 1 Then strHour = "Hour"
            If intMinutes = 1 Then strMinute = "Minute"
            If intSeconds = 1 Then strSecond = "Second"
            strOut = lngFullDays & " " & strDay & " " & _
             intHours & " " & strHour & " " & _
             intMinutes & " " & strMinute & " " & _
             intSeconds & " " & strSecond

        Case "D H:MM"        ' 3 Days 2:46"
            strOut = lngFullDays & " " & strDay & " " & _
             intHours & strDelim & Format(intRoundedMinutes, "00")
        Case "D HH:MM"       ' 3 Days 02:46"
            strOut = lngFullDays & " " & strDay & " " & _
             Format(intHours, "00") & strDelim & _
             Format(intRoundedMinutes, "00")
        Case "D HH:MM:SS"  ' 3 Days 02:45:45"
            strOut = lngFullDays & " " & strDay & " " & _
             Format(intHours, "00") & strDelim & _
             Format(intMinutes, "00") & strDelim & _
             Format(intSeconds, "00")

        Case "H M"           ' 74 Hours 46 Minutes"
            If lngFullHours = 1 Then strHour = "Hour"
            If intRoundedMinutes = 1 Then strMinute = "Minute"
            strOut = lngFullHours & " " & strHour & " " & _
             intRoundedMinutes & " " & strMinute
        Case "H:MM"          ' 74:46
            strOut = lngFullHours & strDelim & _
             Format(intRoundedMinutes, "00")
        Case "H:MM:SS"       ' 74:45:45
            strOut = lngFullHours & strDelim & _
             Format(intMinutes, "00") & strDelim & _
             Format(intSeconds, "00")
```

```
        Case "M S"            ' 4485 Minutes 45 Seconds
            If lngFullMinutes = 1 Then strMinute = "Minute"
            If intSeconds = 1 Then strSecond = "Second"
            strOut = lngFullMinutes & " " & strMinute & " " & _
             intSeconds & " " & strSecond
        Case "M:SS"           ' 4485:45
            strOut = lngFullMinutes & strDelim & _
             Format(intSeconds, "00")

        Case Else
            strOut = ""
    End Select
    dhFormatInterval = strOut
End Function
```

For example, to test out the function, you might write a test routine like the sample shown in Listing 2.25. This sample exercises all the predefined format specifiers.

Listing 2.25: Test Routine for dhFormatInterval

```
Sub TestInterval()
    Dim dtmStart As Date
    Dim dtmEnd As Date

    dtmStart = #1/1/97 12:00:00 PM#
    dtmEnd = #1/4/97 2:45:45 PM#

    Debug.Print dhFormatInterval(dtmStart, dtmEnd, "D H")
    Debug.Print dhFormatInterval(dtmStart, dtmEnd, "D H M")
    Debug.Print dhFormatInterval(dtmStart, dtmEnd, "D H M S")
    Debug.Print dhFormatInterval(dtmStart, dtmEnd, "D H:MM")
    Debug.Print dhFormatInterval(dtmStart, dtmEnd, "D HH:MM")
    Debug.Print dhFormatInterval(dtmStart, dtmEnd, "D HH:MM:SS")

    Debug.Print dhFormatInterval(dtmStart, dtmEnd, "H M")
    Debug.Print dhFormatInterval(dtmStart, dtmEnd, "H:MM")
    Debug.Print dhFormatInterval(dtmStart, dtmEnd, "H:MM:SS")

    Debug.Print dhFormatInterval(dtmStart, dtmEnd, "M S")
    Debug.Print dhFormatInterval(dtmStart, dtmEnd, "M:SS")

End Sub
```

Let's face it: the dhFormatInterval function defines the term *brute force*. Although we attempted to make this routine as simple as possible, it requires several steps to provide all this flexibility.

How does it work? The function first calculates the difference between the two dates in seconds and then calculates the total number of days, hours, minutes, and seconds. In addition, it calculates the number of leftover hours, minutes, and seconds so it can display those, too. Finally, it also calculates rounded values for hours and minutes. That way, if you choose not to display seconds, the minutes value will be rounded accordingly. The same goes for hours: if you decide not to display minutes, the hours value must be rounded to the nearest full hour. Once the routine has those values, it uses a large Select Case statement to determine which type of output string to create and takes the steps to create the correct result.

WARNING Because dhFormatInterval calculates the difference between the two dates in seconds and places that value in a long integer, you're limited to around 68 years between the two dates. Most likely that won't be a terrible limitation, but you should be aware of it before using this function in a production application.

Formatting Cumulative Times

As we've already stated, VBA has no way of storing, or measuring, elapsed times in its date/time fields. When you enter 8:30, you may *think* you're entering the number of hours someone worked, but you're actually entering a specific time: 8:30 A.M. on the date you entered the value. VBA has no qualms about performing aggregate calculations on date/time fields—they're stored internally as floating-point values, so there's no problem performing the calculation—but the result will not be what you had in mind.

The task, then, is to allow you to enter time values as you've become accustomed. You'll need to convert them to some simple value for calculations and then format the output as a standard time value for display. To make all this happen, you'll need the two functions included here, dhCMinutes and dhCTimeStr. dhCMinutes accepts a date/time value as a parameter and returns the time portion, converted to the corresponding number of minutes. Given that value, you can easily sum up a series of time values. Then, when you're ready to display your sum, you'll need the dhCTimeStr function. This one, given a number of minutes, returns a string representing the total, in hh:mm format.

For example, imagine you need to find the sum of 8:30, 12:30, and 13:25 (in each case, a span of time). To sum the three time values and convert that sum back into a time format, you could use an expression like this:

```
dhCTimeStr(dhCMinutes(#8:30#) + dhCMinutes(#12:30#) + _
  dhCMinutes(#13:25#))
```

The result of that expression would be the string "34:25".

Each of the functions consists of just a few lines of code. The dhCMinutes function, shown in Listing 2.26, uses the TimeValue function to extract the time portion of the date, and multiplies the resulting fraction by 24*60, resulting in the number of minutes represented by the fractional portion.

Listing 2.26: Convert a Date/Time Value into Elapsed Minutes

```
Function dhCMinutes (dtmTime As Date) As Long
    ' Convert a date/time value to the number of
    ' minutes since midnight (that is, remove the date
    ' portion, and just work with the time part). The
    ' return value can be used to calculate sums of
    ' elapsed time.

    ' Convert from a fraction of a day to minutes.
    dhCMinutes = TimeValue(dtmTime) * 24 * 60
End Function
```

The function that converts the number of minutes back to a string formatted as a time value, dhCTimeStr (Listing 2.27), is just as simple. It takes the number of minutes and performs an integer division (using the \ operator) to get the number of hours. Then it uses the Mod operator to find the number of minutes (the remainder when you divide by 60). The function formats each of those values and concatenates them as a string return value.

Listing 2.27: Convert Elapsed Minutes into a Formatted String

```
Function dhCTimeStr (lngMinutes As Long) As String
    ' Convert from a number of minutes to a string
    ' that looks like a time value.
    '
```

```
    CTimeStr = Format(plngMinutes \ 60, "0") & _
      GetTimeDelimiter() & Format(lngMinutes Mod 60, "00")
End Function
```

There's just one small wrinkle here: not everyone uses the same time delimiter character. The built-in VBA formatting specifiers take that into account, but in this case, you're supplying your own formatting. The solution is to ask Windows for the local time delimiter, of course. The problem is that there's no simple way to retrieve this information, even in 32-bit versions of Windows. The simplest method is just to pull the information from WIN.INI, as you might have done in Windows 3.1! Although you can retrieve the information directly from the Registry, that requires much more work. You can also request the information using the Windows API, but that, too, requires many more steps.

Therefore, the function GetTimeDelimiter (Listing 2.28) digs into WIN.INI using the GetProfileString API call. This function retrieves the sTime setting in the [intl] section of the file, so any function needing to format time values can use the native delimiter.

Listing 2.28: Retrieve the Local Time Delimiter

```
Private Function GetTimeDelimiter() As String
    ' Retrieve the time delimiter from, believe it or not,
    ' WIN.INI. This is the only reasonable solution
    ' to this problem, even in this day and age!

    Const conMaxSize = 10
    Dim strBuffer As String
    Dim intLen As Integer

    strBuffer = Space(conMaxSize)
    intLen = GetProfileString("intl", "sTime", "", strBuffer, _
      conMaxSize)
    GetTimeDelimiter = Left(strBuffer, intLen)
End Function
```

> **NOTE** What? Using WIN.INI to retrieve values that ought to be in the Registry? Yes, it's true. The problem is that the Registry doesn't provide a one-step way to retrieve this information. You must first determine the locale ID and then find the necessary information. Because Windows guarantees that it maintains this information in WIN.INI (or in the associated Registry keys, under Windows NT), there's no reason not to do this the simple way, using GetProfileString.

Summary

Almost any VBA application will sooner or later need to work with date values, and this chapter has provided solid coverage of the built-in date functions, as well as many procedures that use those functions to provide more general functionality. Specifically, we covered these topics:

- How dates are represented in VBA
- All the built-in date functions:
  - Date, Time, Now
  - DatePart, WeekDay, Year, Month, Day, Hour, Minute, Second
  - DateAdd, DateDiff
  - DateValue, TimeValue, CDate
  - DateSerial, TimeSerial
  - Format
- Additional extended functions, for:
  - Finding a specific date
  - Manipulating dates and times
  - Working with elapsed time

Given the functions presented in this chapter and the information about writing your own additional functions, you should be ready to handle any date/time challenge facing you in your own applications. For similar chapters covering text and numbers, see Chapters 1 and 3, respectively.

CHAPTER

THREE

3

Working with Numbers

- Understanding how numeric values are stored in VBA

- Using the built-in VBA numeric functions

- Generating random numbers

- Using custom numeric functions

At some point in the development process of your application, you're most likely going to need to work with numbers. You'll be faced with choosing how to store the numeric values you're working with, and you'll probably want to use some of the built-in numeric functions. You may find that you need to create your own functions to expand the functionality VBA provides.

This chapter explains how VBA stores and computes numbers and takes a look at the built-in numeric functions. The remainder of the chapter provides and explains several advanced functions using mathematical algorithms.

The sample files you'll find on the CD-ROM that accompanies this book are listed in Table 3.1.

TABLE 3.1   Sample Files

File name	Description
NUMBERS.XLS	Excel 97 workbook containing sample code
NUMBERS.MDB	Access 97 database containing sample code
NUMBERS.BAS	Numeric functions listed in this chapter
TEST.BAS	Test functions listed in this chapter

How Does VBA Store Numeric Values?

As human beings, we count things in base 10, mainly because we have ten fingers. The earliest mathematicians found that fingers made handy counting tools, and it was easier to group larger numbers of items in groups of ten than in groups of eight, two, or any other arbitrary number. However, your computer, not having ten fingers, does not group things by tens; it uses a base 2, or binary, representation of numbers to store and track information. Because a base 2 system requires only two digits, 0 and 1, it's convenient for mapping numbers to electronic circuits, where open and closed switches can represent 1's and 0's.

Just as each position in a decimal number can contain any digit from 0 to 9, each position in a binary number, called a bit, can contain only a 0 or a 1. Bits are usually grouped in packages of 8, called bytes. One byte can hold 256 combinations of 0's or 1's and can therefore be used to represent only 256 different numbers. To represent larger ranges of numbers, more bytes are required.

You need to take two factors into account when considering numbers you want to store in a variable in VBA. First, how big do the numbers need to be? If you're counting stars in the universe, you need to be able to store larger numbers than if you are counting legs on a pig. The second factor is precision. When counting stars in the universe, you may accept being off by a few million, but your leg count needs to be exactly right. The question of precision becomes especially tricky when you're dealing with very large numbers and numbers that include fractions; the fact that you're counting in base 10 and your computer uses base 2 for storage can create pitfalls for the unwary.

VBA supports several datatypes for storing numeric values in variables. Which one you choose for a particular variable will depend on how large the numbers you're working with can become and on how much precision is needed.

The general rule of thumb when choosing a variable's datatype is to choose the smallest possible one that will fit the task and, if possible, avoid the floating-point datatypes (Single and Double). For example, if you're counting bovine appendages, which rarely exceed four per animal, use a Byte variable. (It can hold values up to 255.) If you need fractions only because you're working with money, use the Currency datatype. If you use a Double just to be on the safe side (because it seems to cover the largest possible range and precision), you could run into unanticipated complications when your base 2 computer tries to store or manipulate floating-point numbers.

The available datatypes are summarized in Table 3.2.

TABLE 3.2   VBA Numeric Datatypes

Datatype	Storage size	Range
Byte	1 byte	0 to 255
Integer	2 bytes	−32,768 to 32,767
Long (long integer)	4 bytes	−2,147,483,648 to 2,147,483,647

TABLE 3.2   VBA Numeric Datatypes (continued)

Datatype	Storage size	Range
Single (single-precision floating-point)	4 bytes	−3.402823E38 to −1.401298E−45 for negative values; 1.401298E−45 to 3.402823E38 for positive values
Double (double-precision floating-point)	8 bytes	−1.79769313486232E308 to −4.94065645841247E−324 for negative values; 4.94065645841247E−324 to 1.79769313486232E308 for positive values
Currency (scaled integer)	8 bytes	−922,337,203,685,477.5808 to 922,337,203,685,477.5807
Decimal (currently available only within variants)	14 bytes	+/−79,228,162,514,264,337,593,543,950,335 with no decimal point; +/−7.9228162514264337593543950335 with 28 places to the right of the decimal; smallest nonzero number is +/−0.0000000000000000000000000001
Variant (with numbers)	16 bytes	Any numeric value up to the range of a Double

The datatypes summarized in Table 3.2 and the ranges they support are examined in detail in the following sections. They can be divided into three groups: those that can hold only whole numbers, those that can hold fractions using floating-point mathematics, and a hybrid group, called *scaled integers*, that use whole numbers to store fractions.

NOTE   You can use the Variant datatype to store values of any of the other datatypes. VBA provides a function, TypeName, that returns the datatype of any value or variable that is passed to it. If a Variant is passed to TypeName, the subtype of the variant is returned. The use of TypeName is demonstrated in the section "Floating-Point Numbers and the Errors They Can Cause" later in this chapter.

Whole Numbers

The Byte datatype is the most straightforward, and the most limited, of the numeric datatypes. It is simply stored as an 8-bit binary number. For example, the number 10 would be stored as 00001010, which represents 1 times 2 to the first power (2), plus 1 times 2 to the third power (8). No negative numbers can be stored in a Byte, and the largest number that can be stored is binary 11111111, or 255.

To understand the ranges of the other datatypes, you need to know about another important difference between decimal and binary numbers. In addition to the digits 0 through 9, the decimal system uses two special symbols that are essential for representing certain values: the decimal point and the minus sign. Since binary numbers are so useful precisely because numeric values can be represented using only 0's and 1's, ways have been developed to represent fractions and negative numbers without the use of any special symbols.

For example, the Integer datatype, which uses 16 bits of storage, employs one of these bits to indicate the sign, positive or negative. This leaves 15 bits to represent the absolute value of the number. The largest number that can be represented with 15 bits is $2^{15} - 1$, or 32,767. The reason it's $2^{15} - 1$ and not simply 2^{15} is that one number is needed to represent 0. Because there's no need for a negative 0, one extra negative number can be represented, which is why the range starts at –32,768.

The Long datatype stores only whole numbers, just as the Byte and Integer datatypes do. With the storage size increased to 4 bytes (32 bits), the largest possible number becomes $2^{31} - 1$ (approximately 2 billion), and the lowest possible negative number is -2^{31}.

TIP

The only differences among the three available whole number datatypes—Byte, Integer, and Long—are the ranges they support. To use computer memory most efficiently, always choose the smallest one that will handle all the values you may need to store in a particular variable. The only time you should consider one of the floating-point datatypes to store whole numbers is when the numbers you are working with could exceed 2 billion. In the section "The New Decimal Datatype" later in this chapter, you'll learn how to use this new datatype to store very large numbers more safely.

Floating-Point Numbers and the Errors They Can Cause

The two floating-point datatypes that cause developers headaches are the Single and the Double. To understand why those headaches come about, you need to know a little about how the floating-point datatypes use binary digits to store potentially very large numbers and fractions.

The Single datatype uses the same number of bytes as the Long datatype (4 bytes), but it uses these 32 binary digits in a completely different way. The method used for both Single and Double datatypes is an industry standard that was developed by the Institute of Electrical and Electronics Engineers (IEEE). This method uses a type of mathematics called floating-point mathematics. A full explanation of this topic is beyond the scope of this book, but the basic strategy behind it is quite simple.

Floating-point numbers are similar to scientific notation in that they express a number as the product of two other numbers. For example, the decimal number 1500 can be expressed in scientific notation as $1.5 * 10^3$, or 1.5E3, and the number .0015 can be expressed as $1.5 * 10^{-3}$, or 1.5E–3. This way of expressing numbers consists of two parts. The first part is a multiplier, called the *mantissa*. The second part is an *exponent*. Positive exponents are used for whole numbers and negative exponents for fractions. The number of digits allowed in the mantissa determines the level of precision, and the maximum size of the exponent determines the range.

In binary floating-point numbers, the bits that are available get divided between those that represent the mantissa and those that represent the exponent. For example, a Double uses 1 bit for the sign (positive or negative), 11 bits for the exponent, and 52 bits for the mantissa.

As you can see in Table 3.2, Single and Double datatypes can hold some really huge positive and negative numbers and some really tiny fractions. However, unlike the Integer and Long datatypes, the floating-point datatypes cannot store every possible number within their ranges. Some of the numbers within that range, including some very large whole numbers, cannot be represented exactly, so they get rounded to the nearest available value. Since there's an infinite number of possible fractional values within any given range, there will always be an infinite number of very precise fractions that will also have to be rounded.

Another reason floating-point numbers get rounded is that not all fractions can be represented exactly by binary (base 2) numbers. Of course, decimal numbers are also unable to exactly represent certain fractions. For example, the fraction ⅓ cannot be exactly represented by any combination of powers of 10. The decimal representation of ⅓, .3333333, does not exactly equal ⅓, and no matter how many more 3s are added on after the decimal point, it never will. Similarly, some fractional numbers that can be exactly represented in decimal notation, like 0.0001, can never be precisely stored as binary values. There is just no exact combination of powers of 2 that can accomplish the task. This rounding that sometimes occurs with floating-point numbers can cause errors, as you can see in the procedure shown in Listing 3.1.

Listing 3.1: Demonstrating Floating-Point Errors

```
Sub TestFloatingPoints()

    Dim intI As Integer
    Dim sngSum As Single
    Dim dblSum As Double

    For intI = 1 To 10000
        sngSum = sngSum + 0.0001
    Next intI
    Debug.Print TypeName(sngSum) & ":"; sngSum
    'This prints "Single: 1.000054"

    For intI = 1 To 10000
        dblSum = dblSum + 0.0001
    Next intI
    Debug.Print TypeName(dblSum) & ":"; dblSum
    'This prints "Double: .999999999999906"
End Sub
```

The TestFloatingPoints procedure in Listing 3.1 demonstrates two ways errors can occur. The first problem is that rounding can cause mathematical operations to produce incorrect results. The second problem is that the same operation can produce different results depending on the floating-point datatype that is used. Not only did the use of Single and Double datatypes both produce wrong numbers, but the wrong numbers were not even the same wrong numbers! This means that if you compare a Single number to a Double number and test for equality, the test may fail even if the numbers look like they should be equal.

To make this situation even more maddening, some floating-point rounding errors can remain completely hidden when the numbers are displayed, and some equality test results can defy the laws of logic. For example, in the code shown in Listing 3.2, dbl1 equals sng1, sng1 equals sng2, sng2 equals dbl2, but dbl1 does not equal dbl2!

Listing 3.2: Rounding Errors Cause Erroneous Inequality

```
Sub TestEquality()
    Dim sng1 As Single
    Dim sng2 As Single
    Dim dbl1 As Double
    Dim dbl2 As Double

    sng1 = 69.82
    sng2 = 69.2 + 0.62
    dbl1 = 69.82
    dbl2 = 69.2 + 0.62

    Debug.Print "sng1 = " & sng1 & ", sng2 = " & sng2
    'This prints "sng1 = 69.82, sng2 = 69.82"

    Debug.Print "dbl1 = " & dbl1 & ", dbl2 = " & dbl2
    'This prints "dbl1 = 69.82, dbl2 = 69.82"

    Debug.Print "dbl1 = sng1: "; (dbl1 = sng1)
    'This prints "dbl1 = sng1: True"

    Debug.Print "sng1 = sng2: "; (sng1 = sng2)
    'This prints "sng1 = sng2: True"

    Debug.Print "sng2 = dbl2: "; (sng2 = dbl2)
    'This prints "sng2 = dbl2: True"

    Debug.Print "dbl1 = dbl2: "; (dbl1 = dbl2)
    'This prints "dbl1 = dbl2: False" !!!

End Sub
```

In the section "Rounding Numbers" later in this chapter, you'll find algorithms you can use to round floating-point numbers to the level of precision you need. By using these functions, you can avoid the hidden rounding errors that were discussed in this section. Another way to avoid these errors is to use the scaled integer datatypes whenever possible, as described in the next section.

Scaled Integers

Rounding errors can occur when you're working with decimal fractions that don't have exact binary equivalents. The Currency and Decimal datatypes use a method called *integer scaling* to avoid these errors. This method relies on the fact that all decimal whole numbers do indeed have exact binary equivalents. Any decimal integer can be exactly represented as some combination of powers of 2. Scaled integers convert decimal fractions to whole numbers before storing them in binary form, by multiplying them by a number large enough to eliminate the decimal point.

You can use the Currency datatype to store any number that falls within its range and has no more than four decimal places. The number is multiplied by 10,000, thereby eliminating the need for the decimal point, and then stored internally in binary form as an integer. This prevents the rounding errors that can occur when decimal fractions are stored as binary floating-point numbers. The procedure shown in Listing 3.3 demonstrates how using the Currency datatype can solve problems with floating-point datatypes.

Listing 3.3: Solve Rounding Errors with the Currency Datatype

```
Sub TestCurrency()

    Dim intI As Integer
    Dim dblSum As Double
    Dim curSum As Currency

    For intI = 1 To 10000
        dblSum = dblSum + 0.0001
    Next intI
    Debug.Print TypeName(dblSum) & ":"; dblSum
    'This prints "Double: .999999999999906"

    For intI = 1 To 10000
        curSum = curSum + 0.0001
    Next intI
    Debug.Print TypeName(curSum) & ":"; curSum
    'This prints "Currency: 1"

End Sub
```

The New Decimal Datatype

The Decimal datatype was introduced in version 5.0 of VBA. Using 12 bytes, this new datatype extends the advantages of the Currency datatype to numbers that can be much larger and much more precise than Currency values. The range of values you can store using the Decimal datatype is variable and depends on the number of decimal places of precision you need. As more decimal places are required, the available range gets smaller. At one extreme, you can store a number with 28 decimal places, but the number would have to fall within the very narrow range between approximately –8 and 8. At the other extreme, if you're working with whole numbers that require no decimal places, huge positive and negative values can be stored. At this time, you can use the Decimal datatype only with variables that are declared as Variants, which can hold anything you care to stuff into them. It's not now possible to directly declare a variable as Decimal. The procedure shown in Listing 3.4 illustrates how you can use the CDec function to create a Decimal Variant and avoid floating-point errors.

Listing 3.4: Use the New Decimal Variant Subtype

```
Sub TestDecimal()

    Dim intI As Integer
    Dim dblSum As Double
    Dim varDblSum As Variant
    Dim varDecSum As Variant

    For intI = 1 To 10000
        dblSum = dblSum + 0.0001
    Next intI
    Debug.Print TypeName(dblSum) & ":"; dblSum
    'This prints "Double: .999999999999906"

    For intI = 1 To 10000
        varDblSum = varDblSum + 0.0001
    Next intI
    Debug.Print "Variant " & TypeName(varDblSum) & ":"; varDblSum
    'This prints "Variant Double: 0.999999999999906"

    For intI = 1 To 10000
        varDecSum = varDecSum + CDec(0.0001)
    Next intI
    Debug.Print "Variant " & TypeName(varDecSum) & ":"; varDecSum
    'This prints "Variant Decimal: 1"
End Sub
```

TIP Because of the hidden errors floating-point datatypes can introduce, you should always use the scaled integer datatypes when you can. They are slightly less efficient in their use of memory since they need more bytes of storage, but your code will be much more efficient if you avoid the need to use special code to handle rounding.

Using Built-In Numeric Functions

VBA provides a large variety of built-in numeric functions. This section presents these functions, broken into several categories. The remainder of the chapter provides techniques and algorithms for performing more complex computations and a few tasks that are not covered by the built-in functions.

Mathematical and Trigonometric Functions

Table 3.3 lists the built-in VBA mathematical and trigonometric functions. Each of these takes an argument, called *number* in the table, which can be any valid numeric expression.

TABLE 3.3   Mathematical and Trigonometric Functions in VBA

Function	Description	Syntax
Atn	Returns a Double specifying the angle that is the arctangent of a number in radians	Atn(*number*), where number is the ratio between two sides of a right triangle
Cos	Returns a Double specifying the ratio that is the cosine of an angle	Cos(*number*), where *number* is an angle in radians
Sin	Returns a Double specifying the ratio that is the sine of an angle	Sin(*number*), where *number* is an angle in radians
Tan	Returns a Double specifying the ratio that is the tangent of an angle	Tan(*number*), where *number* is an angle in radians

TABLE 3.3 Mathematical and Trigonometric Functions in VBA (continued)

Function	Description	Syntax
Exp	Returns a Double specifying e (the base of natural logarithms) raised to a power, sometimes referred to as the antilogarithm	Exp(*number*). If the value of *number* exceeds 709.782712893, an error occurs
Log	Returns a Double specifying the natural logarithm of a number	Log(*number*), where *number* is any valid expression greater than 0
Sqr	Returns a Double specifying the square root of a number	Sqr(*number*), where *number* is any valid expression greater than or equal to 0
Sgn	Returns a Variant (integer) indicating the sign of a number	Sgn(*number*), where *number* is any valid numeric expression

Trigonometry is the mathematics of right triangles. It allows you to calculate angles by knowing the ratio between the lengths of two sides of a right triangle or to calculate the ratios by knowing the angles. VBA uses radians as the unit of measure for angles. Since 180 degrees equal *pi* radians (pi being roughly 3.14159265358979), you can convert degrees to radians by multiplying degrees by pi/180, and you can convert radians to degrees by multiplying radians by 180/pi. The functions we created to handle these conversions are shown in Listing 3.5.

Listing 3.5: Radian-to-Degree Conversion Functions

```
Function dhConvertDegreesToRadians(dblDegrees As Double) _
 As Double
    ' Converts degrees to radians
    Const PI = 3.14159265358979
    dhConvertDegreesToRadians = (dblDegrees / 180) * PI
End Function

Function dhConvertRadiansToDegrees(dblRadians As Double) _
 As Double
     ' Converts radians to degrees
    Const PI = 3.14159265358979
    dhConvertRadiansToDegrees = (dblRadians / PI) * 180
End Function
```

Logarithmic Functions

VBA's logarithmic functions use natural logarithms. The natural logarithm is the logarithm to the base e, where the constant e is approximately 2.718282. You can calculate base–n logarithms for any number x by dividing the natural logarithm of x by the natural logarithm of n as follows:

```
Log_n(x) = Log(x) / Log(n)
```

The following example illustrates our custom function for calculating base 10 logarithms:

```
Function dhConvertLog10(dblDecimal As Double) As Double
    ' Converts a decimal number to Log Base 10
    dhConvertLog10 = Log(dblDecimal) / Log(10)
End Function
```

This logarithmic conversion can be generalized to handle any base (base N) as follows:

```
Function dhConvertLogN(dblDecimal As Double, _
 dblLogBase As Double) As Double
    ' Converts a decimal number to a Log Base
    ' specified by the variable dblLogBase
    dhConvertLogN = Log(dblDecimal) / Log(dblLogBase)
End Function
```

Determining Sign

The Sgn function returns an integer that tells you whether a number is positive, negative, or 0. It can return 1, –1, or 0. For example, Sgn(3) returns 1, Sgn(–3) returns –1, and Sgn(3–3) returns 0. As with any of the mathematical functions that take numeric expressions as arguments, if you pass Sgn a null value, you'll get back a run-time error (error 94, "Invalid use of Null").

Derived Trigonometric Functions

You can combine the built-in trigonometric functions to create more complex functions. Table 3.4 shows the formulas you can use to derive these more complex functions from the ones VBA provides.

TABLE 3.4   Derived Trigonometric Functions

Function	Derived equivalents
Secant	Sec(X) = 1 / Cos(X)
Cosecant	Cosec(X) = 1 / Sin(X)
Cotangent	Cotan(X) = 1 / Tan(X)
Inverse Sine	Arcsin(X) = Atn(X / Sqr(–X * X + 1))
Inverse Cosine	Arccos(X) = Atn(–X / Sqr(–X * X + 1)) + 2 * Atn(1)
Inverse Secant	Arcsec(X) = Atn(X / Sqr(X * X – 1)) + Sgn((X) –1) * (2 * Atn(1))
Inverse Cosecant	Arccosec(X) = Atn(X / Sqr(X * X – 1)) + (Sgn(X) – 1) * (2 * Atn(1))
Inverse Cotangent	Arccotan(X) = Atn(X) + 2 * Atn(1)
Hyperbolic Sine	HSin(X) = (Exp(X) – Exp(–X)) / 2
Hyperbolic Cosine	HCos(X) = (Exp(X) + Exp(–X)) / 2
Hyperbolic Tangent	HTan(X) = (Exp(X) – Exp(–X)) / (Exp(X) + Exp(–X))
Hyperbolic Secant	HSec(X) = 2 / (Exp(X) + Exp(–X))
Hyperbolic Cosecant	HCosec(X) = 2 / (Exp(X) – Exp(–X))
Hyperbolic Cotangent	HCotan(X) = (Exp(X) + Exp(–X)) / (Exp(X) – Exp(–X))
Inverse Hyperbolic Sine	HArcsin(X) = Log(X + Sqr(X * X + 1))
Inverse Hyperbolic Cosine	HArccos(X) = Log(X + Sqr(X * X – 1))
Inverse Hyperbolic Tangent	HArctan(X) = Log((1 + X) / (1 – X)) / 2
Inverse Hyperbolic Secant	HArcsec(X) = Log((Sqr(–X * X + 1) + 1) / X)
Inverse Hyperbolic Cosecant	HArccosec(X) = Log((Sgn(X) * Sqr(X * X + 1) +1) / X)
Inverse Hyperbolic Cotangent	HArccotan(X) = Log((X + 1) / (X – 1)) / 2

Here's an example of how you can use the formulas in Table 3.4 to create your own custom trigonometric functions:

```
Function dhHyperbolicSine(ByVal dblNumber As Double) As Double
    ' Calculates hyperbolic sine using the Exp function
    dhHyperbolicSine = (Exp(dblNumber) - Exp(-dblNumber)) / 2
End Function
```

Numeric Conversions and Rounding

As mentioned earlier in this chapter, the various numeric datatypes differ in the levels of precision they support. Therefore, rounding often occurs automatically when you convert a number from one datatype to another. Sometimes that's the reason you want to convert to a different datatype—to round the number. However, there are other ways of rounding, and sometimes you'll want to use them without having to resort to converting the number to a different datatype. This section describes the built-in numeric conversion functions VBA provides, how you can use them for rounding, and how you'll sometimes need other rounding algorithms to get the results you want.

Conversion Functions

Table 3.5 lists the VBA functions that perform numeric conversions from one datatype to another. Decimal to hexadecimal and decimal to octal conversions are discussed in the section "Base Conversions" later in this chapter.

TABLE 3.5 Numeric Conversion Functions

Function	Returns	Rounding
CByte(*expression*)	Byte (range 0–255)	To whole number; .5 rounded to an even number
CInt(*expression*)	Integer	To whole number; .5 rounded to an even number
CLng(*expression*)	Long Integer	To whole number; .5 rounded to an even number
CCur(*expression*)	Currency	To four decimal places; rounding to five decimal places is undocumented
CDec(*expression*)	Decimal Variant	To a variable number of decimal places depending on the size of the number

TABLE 3.5   Numeric Conversion Functions (continued)

Function	Returns	Rounding
CSng(*expression*)	Single	To the nearest floating-point number in the range
CDbl(*expression*)	Double	To the nearest floating-point number in the range
CVar(*expression*)	Variant Double if numeric; Variant Date/Time if delimited by #; Variant String otherwise	Same as Double for numeric values

The *expression* argument that's passed to any of the numeric conversion functions can be any valid numeric or string expression. If *expression* doesn't fall within the acceptable range for that datatype, a run-time error occurs (error 13, "Type mismatch," or error 6, "Overflow").

WARNING   You can also use another VBA function, Val, to convert expressions to numbers. However, there's an important disadvantage to using Val for this purpose. Unlike the conversion functions in Table 3.5, Val does not provide internationally aware conversions. Different decimal separators, thousands separators, and currency options will be correctly recognized by the conversion functions according to the *locale* setting of your computer. However, Val doesn't have the ability to use the computer's *locale* setting and therefore may not recognize numbers that were typed using standards from outside the United States.

Rounding Numbers

The CInt and CLng functions, used to convert to the Integer and Long Integer datatypes, round fractions to whole numbers. They'll sometimes round up and sometimes round down when passed numbers ending in .5. The rounding in these cases will always result in an even number. For example, CInt(1.5) evaluates to 2, and CInt(2.5) also evaluates to 2.

The CCur function, which converts a number to the Currency datatype, rounds numbers to four decimal places of precision. Unfortunately, Microsoft hasn't documented the rule used in rounding Currency values that have five digits to the right of the decimal place where the fifth digit is a 5. Sometime these numbers are rounded up, and sometimes they're rounded down. The examples in Table 3.6 demonstrate that there is no clear pattern to this undocumented rounding behavior:

T A B L E   3 . 6   Unpredictable Currency Rounding

Type in Immediate Window	Result
?CCur(.00005)	0.0001
?CCur(.00015)	0.0001
?CCur(.00025)	0.0003
?CCur(.00035)	0.0003
?CCur(.00045)	0.0004
?CCur(.00095)	0.0009
?CCur(.00995)	0.01
?CCur(.00895)	0.0089
?CCur(.01895)	0.019

Because such seemingly random rounding behavior might not be reliable enough for your computations, you may want to round numbers yourself to a specified number of decimal places instead of letting VBA do it with the CCur function. A little later in this section, you'll see the dhRound custom function, which you can use to round values predictably to a specified number of decimal places.

Two VBA functions, Int(*number*) and Fix(*number*), remove the fractional part of a number. They don't round the number; they just chop off the part to the right of the decimal place. Both functions return an Integer if the result falls within the Integer range (–32,768 to 32,767) and a Long if the result is outside the Integer range but within the Long range (–2,147,483,648 to 2,147,483,647). It doesn't matter which of these functions you use for positive numbers, but for negative numbers, you have to remember that Int returns the first negative Integer less than or equal to *number,* whereas Fix returns the first negative Integer greater than or equal to *number.* Table 3.7 shows the output of Int and Fix in the Immediate window.

TABLE 3.7   Using Int and Fix

Type in Immediate Window	Result
? Int(–9.4)	–10
? Fix(–9.4)	–9
? Int(9.6)	9
? Fix(9.6)	9

NOTE   Fix(*number*) is equivalent to Sgn(*number*) * Int(Abs(*number*))

Beware of using Int with expressions. Doing so will sometimes yield unanticipated results. For example, Int((1.55*10)+.5) evaluates to 16, as you would expect. However, Int((2.55*10)+.5) evaluates to 25, even though you would expect it to evaluate to 26. For this reason, it's best to set your expression equal to a variable first and then pass the variable to Int, as the procedure shown in Listing 3.6 illustrates.

Listing 3.6: Use a Variable to Control the Int Function

```
Sub TestInt()
    Dim dblNumber As Double

    Debug.Print Int((2.55 * 10) + 0.5)
    'Prints "25"

    dblNumber = (2.55 * 10) + 0.5
    Debug.Print Int(dblNumber)
    'Prints "26"
End Sub
```

As discussed earlier in this chapter, rounding often presents problems with floating-point numbers because some decimal numbers are rounded unpredictably when converted to floating-point binary numbers. Surprisingly, VBA doesn't have a built-in Round function; you have to write your own. Listing 3.7 shows a very common rounding algorithm that allows you to specify the number of decimal places to round to. This function always rounds up numbers ending in 5 after the desired level of precision. For example, 1.25 is rounded to 1.3 if you specify one decimal place of precision.

Listing 3.7: A Generic Rounding Function

```
Function dhRound(dblNumber As Double, _
  intDecimals As Integer) As Double
    ' Rounds a number to a specified number of decimal
    ' places. 0.5 is rounded up
    Dim dblFactor As Double
    Dim dblTemp As Double

    dblFactor = 10 ^ intDecimals
    dblTemp = dblNumber * dblFactor + 0.5
    dhRound = Int(dblTemp) / dblFactor
End Function
```

TIP   You can round numbers to whole digit places (for example, round 1234 to 1200) by specifying a negative value for the number of places. That is, specifying 0 for intDecimals rounds to the ones place, −1 rounds to tens, −2 rounds to hundreds, and −3 rounds to thousands.

Subtracting Floating-Point Numbers While Maintaining Precision

You might assume that VBA wouldn't have problems with simple subtraction, since the result of subtraction can't have more decimal places than either of the two numbers involved, but you would be wrong. Table 3.8 shows some of the surprising results in the Immediate window for subtracting various decimal values, all of which look like they all ought to result in 0.1. To avoid errors in subtraction, you need to first be sure to round any numbers to the required number of decimal places.

TABLE 3.8 Errors in Floating-Point Subtraction

Type in Immediate Window	Result
? 100.8–100.7	9.99999999999943E–02
? 10.8–10.7	0.100000000000001
? 1.8–1.7	0.1

You can subtract one floating-point value from another by figuring out the maximum number of decimals involved because the difference between the two numbers can't have more decimals than either of the two numbers involved in the computation. We created a subtraction function, shown in Listing 3.8, that overcomes the rounding error.

Listing 3.8: Overcome Errors in Subtraction

```
Function dhSubtract(dblVal1 As Double, _
 dblVal2 As Double) As Double
    ' Returns the difference between dblVal2 and dblVal1
    ' while avoiding inaccuracies
    Dim dblResult As Double
    Dim intDecimals1 As Integer
    Dim intDecimals2 As Integer
    Dim intMaxDecimals As Integer
    Dim dblTemp As Double

    dblResult = dblVal1 - dblVal2

    ' Find number of decimals in value 1
    If InStr(dblVal1, ".") = 0 Then
      intDecimals1 = 0
    Else
      intDecimals1 = Len(dblVal1 & "") - InStr(dblVal1, ".")
    End If

    ' Find number of decimals in value 2
    If InStr(dblVal2, ".") = 0 Then
      intDecimals2 = 0
    Else
      intDecimals2 = Len(dblVal2 & "") - InStr(dblVal2, ".")
    End If
```

```
      If intDecimals1 + intDecimals2 > 0 Then
        ' Round values to the maximum number of decimals
        intMaxDecimals = IIf(intDecimals1 > intDecimals2, _
          intDecimals1, intDecimals2)
        dblTemp = dblResult * 10 ^ intMaxDecimals + 0.5
        dblResult = Int(dblTemp) / (10 ^ intMaxDecimals)
      End If
      dhSubtract = dblResult
End Function
```

You can also use the new Decimal datatype introduced earlier in this chapter, which supports a large range of numbers and a high level of precision, to fix floating-point subtraction. The function we've provided in Listing 3.9 uses Decimal Variants to perform accurate floating-point subtraction.

Listing 3.9: Use Decimal Variants for Subtraction

```
Function dhSubtractDec(dblVal1 As Double, _
  dblVal2 As Double) As Double
      ' Uses Decimal Variants to return
      ' the difference between dblVal2 and dblVal1
      ' while avoiding inaccuracies

      Dim varDecVal1 As Variant
      Dim varDecVal2 As Variant

      varDecVal1 = CDec(dblVal1)
      varDecVal2 = CDec(dblVal2)
      dhSubtractDec = varDecVal1 - varDecVal2
End Function
```

Random Numbers

The subject of generating random numbers often causes confusion. First, there's the Randomize statement:

> Randomize [*number*]

Then there's Rnd function:

> Rnd[(*number*)]

VBA generates random numbers by starting with a seed value and then running that seed through a proprietary algorithm that creates a number greater than or equal to 0 and less than 1. Starting with a particular seed will always result in exactly the same "random" number. The VBA Randomize statement initializes the Rnd function by creating a new seed value. If you don't use the optional argument for Randomize, the new seed value is based on the system timer.

If you elect not to use Randomize at all and just call the Rnd function with no arguments, Rnd always uses the same number as a seed the first time it's called. Each subsequent time Rnd is called during that session, it uses the number that was generated by the last call as its new seed. So, unless you use Randomize or supply an argument to Rnd, you'll always get the same sequence of numbers. The *number* argument passed to Rnd affects the value that's returned, as summarized in Table 3.9.

TABLE 3.9 Pass an Argument to Rnd

Rnd Argument	Number Generated by Rnd
< 0	The same number every time, depending on the negative argument used
> 0	Next random number in the sequence, regardless of the positive argument used
= 0	Repeats the most recently generated number
Not supplied	Next random number in the sequence (same as with a positive argument)

The number returned by Rnd is a Single value that's greater than or equal to 0 and less than 1. If you want to create random integers within a certain range of values, you can use the following formula:

$$i = \text{Int}((\textit{<high number>} - \textit{<low number>} + 1) * \text{Rnd}) + \textit{<low number>}$$

For example, if you want to create a series of random numbers between 1 and 10, the expression would look like this:

```
i = Int((10 - 1 + 1) * Rnd) + 1
```

Using 10 as the upper bound won't give you a very wide range of numbers, and after running this procedure a few times, you'll run into duplicates. There's a misconception that using the Randomize function in front of Rnd will eliminate duplicates, but this is not true. Randomize will only reset the random number generator so that it starts at a different place in the set of numbers it generates; nothing keeps it from returning duplicates in a given sequence. The following procedure generates a set of random numbers:

```
Dim i As Integer
Randomize
For i = 1 To 10
    Debug.Print Int(Rnd * 10) + 1;
Next i
```

The output from the Immediate window when run five times might return results like these:

```
2   7   1   2   10  4   1   10  5   7
6   2   8   1   8   5   2   2   8   7
6   9   7   2   3   10  6   10  4   2
5   9   6   8   5   4   4   10  1   6
9   5   9   3   3   7   2   9   5   6
```

What this means is that if you want to avoid duplicates in a list of integers, you have to keep track of them yourself. We've provided the procedure shown in Listing 3.10 to shuffle numbers from 1 to 10, producing a random list of the ten integers with no duplicates.

Listing 3.10: Generate Random Numbers with No Duplicates

```
Sub dhRandomShuffle()
    ' Shuffles ten random numbers

    Dim aintValues(1 To 10) As Integer
    Dim intI As Integer
    Dim intPos As Integer

    ' Fill in the original values.
    For intI = 1 To 10
        aintValues(intI) = intI
    Next intI
    ' Loop through all the items except the last one.
    ' Once you get to the last item, there's no point
    ' using Rnd; just get it.
    For intI = 10 To 2 Step -1
        ' Get a random number between 1 and intI
        intPos = Int(Rnd * intI) + 1
        Debug.Print aintValues(intPos)
```

```
            aintValues(intPos) = aintValues(intI)
        Next intI
        ' Get the last one.
        Debug.Print aintValues(1)
    End Sub
```

Financial Functions

VBA provides a number of built-in functions you can use for performing financial calculations. These are divided into three basic groups: depreciation functions, annuity functions, and cash-flow functions, as described in the following sections.

Depreciation

The depreciation functions are used in accounting to calculate the amount of monetary value a fixed asset loses over a period of time. For example, a business that owns a truck needs to calculate the amount the truck depreciates each year to determine the current value of the truck at any point in time. Because depreciation affects taxes, governments often mandate the depreciation formulas that can be used. For example, the double-declining method of depreciation uses the following formula:

Depreciation over period = ((cost − salvage) * 2) / life

Table 3.10 summarizes the VBA depreciation functions and their arguments, and Table 3.11 describes the arguments used in depreciation functions.

TABLE 3.10 Depreciation Functions

Function	Description
DDB(*cost, salvage, life, period[, factor]*)	Returns a Double specifying the depreciation of an asset for a specific time period using the declining balance method
SLN(*cost, salvage, life*)	Returns a Double specifying the straight-line depreciation of an asset for a single period
SYD(*cost, salvage, life, period*)	Returns a Double specifying the sum-of-years' digits depreciation of an asset for a specified period

TABLE 3.11 Arguments Used in Depreciation Functions

Argument	Description
Cost	Initial cost of the asset
Salvage	Value of the asset at the end of its useful life
Life	Length of the useful life of the asset; must be in the same unit of measure as *Period*
Period	Period for which asset depreciation is calculated
[Factor]	Optional rate at which the balance declines; if omitted, 2 (double-declining method) is assumed

Annuities

An annuity is a series of payments that represents either the return on an investment or the amortization of a loan. Negative numbers represent monies paid out, like contributions to savings or loan payments. Positive numbers represent monies received, like dividends. Tables 3.12 and 3.13 summarize the VBA annuity functions and their arguments.

TABLE 3.12 Annuity Functions

Function	Description
FV(*rate, nper, pmt[, pv[, type]]*)	Returns a Double specifying the future value of an annuity based on periodic fixed payments and a fixed interest rate
Rate(*nper, pmt, pv[, fv[, type[, guess]]]*)	Returns a Double specifying the interest rate per period for an annuity
NPer(*rate, pmt, pv[, fv[, type]]*)	Returns a Double specifying the number of periods for an annuity
IPmt(*rate, per, nper, pv[, fv[, type]]*)	Returns a Double specifying the interest payment for a given period of an annuity
Pmt(*rate, nper, pv[, fv[, type]]*)	Returns a Double specifying the payment for an annuity

TABLE 3.12 Annuity Functions (continued)

Function	Description
PPmt(*rate, per, nper, pv*[, *fv*[, *type*]])	Returns a Double specifying the principal payment for a given period of an annuity
PV(*rate, nper, pmt*[, *fv*[, *type*]])	Returns a Double specifying the present value of an annuity based on periodic fixed payments to be paid in the future at a fixed interest rate

TABLE 3.13 Arguments Used in Annuity Functions

Argument	Description
Rate	Interest rate per period; must use the same unit for *period* as used for Nper
Nper	Total number of payment periods in the annuity
Pmt	Payment to be made each period
Pv	Present value (or lump sum) that a series of payments to be paid in the future is worth now
[*Fv*]	Optional value of the annuity after the final payment has been made (if omitted, 0 is assumed, which is the usual future value of a loan)
[*Type*]	Optional number indicating when payments are due: 0 if payments are due at the end of the payment period and 1 if payments are due at the beginning of the period; if omitted, 0 is assumed

We created a procedure, shown in Listing 3.11, that uses the Pmt function to calculate the monthly payment on a loan.

Listing 3.11: Calculate the Payment on a Loan

```
Function dhCalcPayment(ByVal dblRate As Double, ByVal intNoPmts _
  As Integer, ByVal curPresentValue As Currency, Optional _
  varFutureVal As Variant = 0, Optional varWhenDue As _
  Variant = 0) As Double
```

```
' Calculates payments using Pmt function
If varWhenDue <> 0 Then
    ' set to only other possible value
    ' of 1 indicating payment to occur
    ' at beginning of period
    varWhenDue = 1
End If

dhCalcPayment = Pmt((dblRate / 12), intNoPmts, _
 -CDbl(curPresentValue), varFutureVal, varWhenDue)
End Function
```

Cash-Flow Functions

The cash-flow functions perform financial calculations based on a series of periodic payments and receipts. As with the annuity functions, negative numbers represent payments and positive numbers represent receipts. However, unlike the annuity functions, the cash-flow functions allow you to list varying amounts for the payments or receipts over the course of the loan or investment. Payments and receipts can even be mixed up within the cash-flow series.

Tables 3.14 and 3.15 summarize the VBA cash flow functions and their arguments.

TABLE 3.14 Cash-Flow Functions

Function	Description
IRR(*values*()[, *guess*])	Returns a Double specifying the internal rate of return for a series of periodic cash flows
MIRR(*values*(), *finance_rate*, *reinvest_rate*)	Returns a Double specifying the modified internal rate of return for a series of periodic cash flows
NPV(*rate*, *values*())	Returns a Double specifying the net present value of an investment based on a series of periodic cash flows and a discount rate

TABLE 3.15 Arguments Used in Cash-Flow Functions

Argument	Description
Values()	Array of cash-flow values; the array must contain at least one negative value (a payment) and one positive value (a receipt)
Rate	Discount rate over the length of the period, expressed as a decimal
Finance_rate	Interest rate paid as the cost of financing
Reinvest_rate	Interest rate received on gains from cash reinvestment
[Guess]	Optional value you estimate will be returned; if omitted, *guess* is 0.1 (10 percent)

An array is used to hold the series of cash-flow amounts. See Chapter 4 for more information on working with arrays.

The IRR cash-flow function uses multiple iterations to arrive at its final return value. It starts with the value, *Guess,* and continues running calculations until it achieves a result that's accurate to within 0.00001 percent. If a satisfactory result hasn't been reached after 20 attempts, the function fails.

The function we've provided in Listing 3.12 illustrates how you can use the NPV function to calculate the net present value of a business investment.

Listing 3.12: Calculate the Net Present Value of an Investment

```
Function dhNetPresentValue(ByVal dblRate As Double, _
 ParamArray varCashFlows()) As Double
    ' Calculates net present value

    Dim varElement As Variant
    Dim i As Integer
    Dim lngUBound As Long
    Static dblValues() As Double

    ' get upper bound of ParamArray
    lngUBound = UBound(varCashFlows)
    ' size array to ParamArray
```

```
    ReDim dblValues(lngUBound)
    i = 0
    ' place elements of ParamArray into Array
    For Each varElement In varCashFlows
        dblValues(i) = varElement
        i = i + 1
    Next
    dhNetPresentValue = NPV(dblRate, dblValues())
End Function
```

Base Conversions

For base 16 (hexadecimal), base 8 (octal), and base 10 (decimal) conversions, the simplest way is to use the built-in functions Hex, Oct, and Val, which are summarized in Table 3.16.

TABLE 3.16 Base Conversion Functions

Function	Description
Hex(*number*)	Returns a String representing the hexadecimal value of a number
Oct(*number*)	Returns a Variant representing the octal value of a number, up to 11 octal characters. Returns Null if the number is Null, 0 if the number is Empty (Only a Variant that has not been initialized is Empty.)
Val(*string*)	Returns Double numeric values that are contained in a string, including Hexadecimal and Octal values that use the radix prefixes, &H and &O

Hexadecimal and Octal Conversion

The Hex and Oct functions return a string with the hexadecimal or octal value in it. However, the radix prefixes, &H and &O, are not added to the string. For example, Hex(255) returns "FF", not "&HFF", which is how you would represent the number in code. If you ever want to convert to hexadecimal or octal and then back to decimal, be sure to add the prefix that a VBA conversion function like CLng will need to recognize the number, as illustrated in Table 3.17.

TABLE 3.17 Converting to Hex and Back to Decimal

Type in Immediate Window	Result
?Hex(255)	FF
?CLng(Hex(255))	Error 13 (type mismatch)
?CLng("&H" & Hex(255))	255

NOTE

The Hex function rounds fractions to the nearest whole number before performing the conversion. For example, Hex(256) returns 100, and Hex(256.4) also returns 100. While it's possible to represent fractional data in hexadecimal format (see the dhDecToHex function in the sample), there's no practical reason to do so. VBA conversion functions like CLng recognize only whole hexadecimal numbers.

Binary Conversions

VBA doesn't include any built-in binary conversion functions. The custom functions shown in Listing 3.13 can be used to convert hexadecimal numbers to binary (base 2) numbers, to convert binary to hexadecimal, and to convert decimal numbers to binary.

Listing 3.13: Binary Conversion Functions

```
Function dhBinaryToDec(ByVal strNumber As String) As Long
    dhBinaryToDec = Val("&H" & dhBinarytoHex(strNumber))
End Function

Function dhBinarytoHex(ByVal strNumber As String) As String
    Dim strTemp As String
    Dim intI As Integer
    Dim intLen As Integer
    Dim strOut As String

    ' First, pad the value to the left, with "0".
    ' To do this, find the length of the string
    ' rounded to the next highest multiple of 4.
    intLen = Len(strNumber)
```

```
' Find the next higher multiple of 4:
intLen = Int(intLen / 4 + 1) * 4
strNumber = Right$(String(intLen, "0") & strNumber, intLen)

' Now walk through each group of 4 digits, converting each
' to hex.
For intI = 1 To intLen Step 4
    Select Case Mid(strNumber, intI, 4)
        Case "0000"
            strTemp = "0"
        Case "0001"
            strTemp = "1"
        Case "0010"
            strTemp = "2"
        Case "0011"
            strTemp = "3"
        Case "0100"
            strTemp = "4"
        Case "0101"
            strTemp = "5"
        Case "0110"
            strTemp = "6"
        Case "0111"
            strTemp = "7"
        Case "1000"
            strTemp = "8"
        Case "1001"
            strTemp = "9"
        Case "1010"
            strTemp = "A"
        Case "1011"
            strTemp = "B"
        Case "1100"
            strTemp = "C"
        Case "1101"
            strTemp = "D"
        Case "1110"
            strTemp = "E"
        Case "1111"
            strTemp = "F"
    End Select
    strOut = strOut & strTemp
```

```
        Next intI
        dhBinarytoHex = strOut
    End Function

    Function dhDecToBinary(ByVal lngNumber As Long) As String
        Dim strTemp As String
        Dim intI As Integer

        strTemp = Hex(lngNumber)
        strTemp = dhHexToBinary(strTemp)
        ' Rip off leading 0s.
        Do While Left(strTemp, 1) = "0"
            strTemp = Mid(strTemp, 2)
        Loop
        dhDecToBinary = strTemp
    End Function

    Function dhHexToBinary(strNumber As String) As String
        Dim strTemp As String
        Dim strOut As String
        Dim i As Integer

        For i = 1 To Len(strNumber)
            Select Case Mid(strNumber, i, 1)
                Case "0"
                    strTemp = "0000"
                Case "1"
                    strTemp = "0001"
                Case "2"
                    strTemp = "0010"
                Case "3"
                    strTemp = "0011"
                Case "4"
                    strTemp = "0100"
                Case "5"
                    strTemp = "0101"
                Case "6"
                    strTemp = "0110"
                Case "7"
                    strTemp = "0111"
                Case "8"
                    strTemp = "1000"
```

```
            Case "9"
                strTemp = "1001"
            Case "A"
                strTemp = "1010"
            Case "B"
                strTemp = "1011"
            Case "C"
                strTemp = "1100"
            Case "D"
                strTemp = "1101"
            Case "E"
                strTemp = "1110"
            Case "F"
                strTemp = "1111"
            Case Else
                ' This can't happen, right?
                strTemp = ""
        End Select
        strOut = strOut & strTemp
    Next i
    dhHexToBinary = strOut
End Function
```

Custom Math and Numeric Functions

In this section we've provided several handy custom functions that perform basic mathematical and statistical calculations. You'll also find a function that converts numbers to text. These functions will save you time if you ever need the calculations they perform, but the programming techniques employed are pretty straightforward, so the functions are presented with little additional comment.

Mathematical Functions

Several mathematical functions have already been presented in this chapter. These were mostly built-in VBA functions and combinations thereof. Here are a few more that you can use in specialized situations.

Finding the Greatest Common Factor (GCF) of Two Integers

The *greatest common factor* (GCF) of two numbers is the largest number that will evenly divide into each. The function shown in Listing 3.14 accepts two arguments and computes their GCF.

Listing 3.14: Compute the Greatest Common Factor of Two Numbers

```
Function dhGreatestCommonFactor(ByVal lngX As Long, _
 ByVal lngY As Long) As Long
    ' Returns the largest number that will evenly
    ' divide into both lngX and lngY
    ' comments

    Dim lngTemp As Long

    lngX = Abs(lngX)
    lngY = Abs(lngY)
    lngTemp = lngX Mod lngY
    Do While lngTemp > 0
        lngX = lngY
        lngY = lngTemp
        lngTemp = lngX Mod lngY
    Loop
    dhGreatestCommonFactor = lngY
End Function
```

Finding the Lowest Common Multiple (LCM) of Two Integers

A similar numeric relationship between two numbers is the *lowest common multiple* (LCM). The LCM of two numbers is the smallest number of which the two numbers are factors. Listing 3.15 shows a function that computes this.

Listing 3.15: Compute Two Numbers' Lowest Common Multiple

```
Function dhLowestCommonMultiple(ByVal intX As Integer, _
    ByVal intY As Integer) As Long
    ' Returns the smallest number of which both
```

```
        ' intX and intY are factors
    intX = Abs(intX)
    intY = Abs(intY)
    dhLowestCommonMultiple = intY * (intX \ _
        dhGreatestCommonFactor(intX, intY))
End Function
```

Is This Number Prime?

Prime numbers can be divided evenly only by themselves and by 1. There are many algorithms for figuring out whether a number is prime. Listing 3.16 illustrates a function that employs one of the more commonly used methods. It uses several If statements to eliminate common cases like 0, 1, 2, and other even numbers. It then uses a For...Next loop to determine the "primeness" of other numbers. Be aware that for large numbers, this function can take a bit of time to run.

Listing 3.16: Determine Whether a Number Is Prime

```
Function dhIsPrime(ByVal lngX As Long) As Boolean
    Dim intI As Integer
    Dim dblTemp As Double
    dhIsPrime = True
    lngX = Abs(lngX)

    If lngX = 0 Or lngX = 1 Then
        dhIsPrime = False
    ElseIf lngX = 2 Then
        ' dhIsPrime is already set to True.
    ElseIf (lngX And 1) = 0 Then
        dhIsPrime = False
    Else
        For intI = 3 To Int(Sqr(lngX)) Step 2
            dblTemp = lngX / intI
            If dblTemp = lngX \ intI Then
                dhIsPrime = False
                Exit Function
            End If
        Next intI
    End If
End Function
```

Geometric Calculations

There's a whole host of problems involving geometry that you can solve using VBA (computing the surface area of a sphere, for instance). If you paid attention during junior high geometry class, you probably already know how to write the required VBA code. If, on the other hand, that's just a distant memory, we've provided you with some code that will do the trick. Listing 3.17 shows these functions.

Listing 3.17: Miscellaneous Geometry Functions

```
Const PI = 3.14159265358979

Function dhAreaofCircle(ByVal dblRadius As Double) As Double

    ' Return the area of a circle
    dhAreaofCircle = PI * dblRadius ^ 2
End Function

Function dhAreaOfSphere(ByVal dblRadius As Double) As Double

    ' Return the area of a sphere
    dhAreaOfSphere = 4 * PI * dblRadius ^ 2
End Function

Function dhAreaOfRectangle(ByVal dblLength As Double, _
 ByVal dblWidth As Double) As Double

    ' Return the area of a rectangle
    dhAreaOfRectangle = dblLength * dblWidth
End Function

Function dhAreaOfTrapezoid(ByVal dblHeight As Double, _
 ByVal dblSide1 As Double, _
 ByVal dblSide2 As Double) As Double

    ' Return the area of a trapezoid
    dhAreaOfTrapezoid = dblHeight * (dblSide1 + dblSide2) / 2
End Function

Function dhVolOfPyramid(ByVal dblHeight As Double, _
 ByVal dblBaseArea As Double) As Double

    ' Return the volume of a pyramid
    dhVolOfPyramid = dblHeight * dblBaseArea / 3
End Function
```

```
Function dhVolOfSphere(ByVal dblRadius As Double) As Double
    ' Return the volume of a sphere
    dhVolOfSphere = PI * (dblRadius ^ 3) * 4 / 3
End Function
```

Converting Currency Numbers to Text

If you're programming an application that writes checks, you may need to translate numbers to a textual description. For example, the value $149.56 would be translated as "one hundred forty-nine and fifty-six hundredths." The dhNumToStr function shown in Listing 3.18 demonstrates how to do this by using some of the built-in numeric functions, as well as some string functions, which were discussed in Chapter 1. Listing 3.18 also shows the dhHandleGroup, which dhNumToStr calls.

> **NOTE** The dhNumToStr function uses zero-based arrays. For it to work properly, make sure you haven't included the Option Base 1 statement in the module where it is declared.

Listing 3.18: Convert a Number to Descriptive Text

```
Function dhNumToStr(ByVal varValue As Variant) As String

    On Error GoTo HandleErrors

    Dim intTemp As Integer
    Dim varNames As Variant
    Dim lngDollars As Long
    Dim intCents As Integer
    Dim strOut As String
    Dim strTemp As String
    Dim intI As Integer

    If Not IsNumeric(varValue) Then Exit Function

    ' 999,999,999.99 is the largest possible value.
    If varValue > 999999999.99 Then Exit Function
    varNames = Array("", "Thousand", "Million")
```

```
      varValue = Abs(varValue)
      lngDollars = Int(varValue)
      intCents = (varValue - lngDollars) * 100

      If lngDollars > 0 Then
          ' Loop through each set of three digits,
          ' first the hundreds, then thousands, and then
          ' millions.
          Do
              intTemp = lngDollars Mod 1000
              lngDollars = Int(lngDollars / 1000)
              ' Prepend spelling of new triplet of digits to the
              ' existing output.
              If intTemp <> 0 Then
                  strOut = dhHandleGroup(intTemp) & " " & _
                      varNames(intI) & " " & strOut
              End If
              intI = intI + 1
          Loop While lngDollars > 0
          ' Handle the cents.
          strOut = RTrim(strOut) & " and " & _
           Format$(intCents, "00") & "/100"
      End If

ExitHere:
      dhNumToStr = strOut
      Exit Function

HandleErrors:
      ' Handle all errors by returning an empty string
      strOut = ""
      Resume ExitHere
End Function

Private Function dhHandleGroup(ByVal intValue As Integer) _
 As String
      Static varOnes As Variant
      Static varTens As Variant
      Dim strOut As String
      Dim intDigit As Integer

      If IsEmpty(varOnes) Then
          varOnes = Array("", "One", "Two", "Three", "Four", _
```

```
            "Five", "Six", "Seven", "Eight", "Nine", "Ten", _
            "Eleven", "Twelve", "Thirteen", "Fourteen", _
            "Fifteen", "Sixteen", "Seventeen", "Eighteen", _
            "Nineteen", "Twenty")
    End If
    If IsEmpty(varTens) Then
        ' Elements 0 and 1 in this array aren't used.
        varTens = Array("", "", "Twenty", "Thirty", "Forty", _
            "Fifty", "Sixty", "Seventy", "Eighty", "Ninety")
    End If

    ' Get the hundreds digit, and then the rest.
    intDigit = intValue \ 100
    intValue = intValue Mod 100

    ' If there's a hundreds digit, add that now.
    If intDigit > 0 Then strOut = varOnes(intDigit) & " Hundred"

    ' Handle the tens and ones digits.
    Select Case intValue
        Case 1 To 20
            strOut = strOut & varOnes(intValue)
        Case 21 To 99
            intDigit = intValue \ 10
            intValue = intValue Mod 10
            If intDigit > 0 Then
                strOut = strOut & " " & varTens(intDigit)
            End If
            If intValue > 0 Then
                strOut = strOut & "-" & varOnes(intValue)
            End If
    End Select

    dhHandleGroup = strOut
End Function
```

Statistics

This section presents several useful statistical functions, including functions to calculate factorials, to compute various types of averages and standard deviation, and to find minimum and maximum values.

Factorials

Statistical functions often make use of factorial calculations. You can use the two functions shown in Listing 3.19 to calculate recursive and nonrecursive factorials.

Listing 3.19: Compute Recursive and Nonrecursive Factorial Expressions

```
Function dhFactorialRecursive(intX As Integer) As Double
    If intX < 0 Or intX > 170 Then
        dhFactorialRecursive = 0#
    ElseIf intX = 0 Then
        dhFactorialRecursive = 1#
    Else
        dhFactorialRecursive = intX * _
         dhFactorialRecursive(intX - 1)
    End If
End Function

Function dhFactorial(intX As Integer) As Double
    Dim i As Integer
    Dim dblX As Double

    If intX < 0 Or intX > 170 Then
        dhFactorial = 0#
        Exit Function
    End If
    dblX = 1#
    For i = 2 To intX
        dblX = dblX * i
    Next i
    dhFactorial = dblX
End Function
```

Mean, Median, Mode, and Standard Deviation of an Array

The most common statistical functions are those that determine the mean, median, mode, and standard deviation of a series of numbers. The mean is nothing more than the arithmetic average of the series. The median, on the other hand, is the number that occurs in the "middle" of the series. The mode is the number that occurs most frequently. It's usually close to the mean, but since it's one of the numbers in the series, it might not be exact. Finally, the standard deviation is a measurement of how closely numbers in the series are gathered around the mean. Listing 3.20 shows four functions that compute these values based on an array passed as an argument.

> **NOTE** The dhMedianOfArray and dhModeOfArray functions use the dhQuick-Sort function from Chapter 4 to sort the array prior to determining the mode. For a complete discussion of sorting, see Chapter 4.

Listing 3.20: Functions for Calculating Mean, Median, Mode, and Standard Deviation

```
Function dhAverageArray(varArray As Variant) As Variant
    Dim varItem As Variant
    Dim varSum As Variant
    Dim lngCount As Long

    If IsArray(varArray) Then
        For Each varItem In varArray
            varSum = varItem + varSum
            lngCount = lngCount + 1
        Next
        dhAverageArray = varSum / lngCount
    Else
        dhAverageArray = Null
    End If
End Function

Function dhMedianOfArray(varArray As Variant) As Variant
    Dim varItem As Variant
    Dim varTemp As Variant
    Dim varMedian As Variant
    Dim intI As Integer
    Dim lngTemp As Long
    Dim lngLBound As Long
    Dim lngElements As Long

    If IsArray(varArray) Then
        ' Sort the array
        Call dhQuickSort(varArray)
```

```
        ' Compute the number of array elements
        lngLBound = LBound(varArray)
        lngElements = (UBound(varArray) - lngLBound + 1)

        ' Find the midpoint in the array. For an odd
        ' number of elements, this is easy (it's the
        ' middle one)...
        If (lngElements Mod 2) = 1 Then
            dhMedianOfArray = varArray(lngLBound + _
              (lngElements \ 2))
        Else
            ' For an even number of elements, it's the
            ' midpoint between the two middle values...
            lngTemp = ((lngElements - 1) \ 2) + lngLBound
            dhMedianOfArray = ((varArray(lngTemp + 1) - _
              varArray(lngTemp)) / 2) + varArray(lngTemp)
        End If
    Else
        dhMedianOfArray = Null
    End If
End Function

Function dhStandardDeviation(varArray) As Double
    ' Calculates standard deviation for an array

    Dim lngN As Long
    Dim dblSumX As Double
    Dim dblSumX2 As Double
    Dim dblVar As Double
    Dim intCounter As Integer

    lngN = 0
    dblSumX = 0
    dblSumX2 = 0
    For intCounter = LBound(varArray) To UBound(varArray)
        If Not IsNull(varArray(intCounter)) Then
            lngN = lngN + 1
            dblSumX = dblSumX + varArray(intCounter)
            dblSumX2 = dblSumX2 + varArray(intCounter) ^ 2
        End If
    Next intCounter

    dblVar = 0
    If lngN > 0 Then
        dblVar = (lngN * dblSumX2 - dblSumX ^ 2) / _
```

```vba
        (lngN * (lngN - 1))
        If dblVar > 0 Then
            dhStandardDeviation = Sqr(dblVar)
        End If
    End If
End Function

Function dhModeOfArray(varArray As Variant) As Variant
    Dim varItem As Variant
    Dim varLast As Variant
    Dim lngCount As Long
    Dim lngOccur As Long
    Dim lngLastOccur As Long
    Dim lngTotalOccur As Long

    If IsArray(varArray) Then
        ' Sort the array so elements are in order
        Call dhQuickSort(varArray)

        ' Capture the first item
        varItem = varArray(LBound(varArray))

        ' Loop through all the elements
        For lngCount = LBound(varArray) To UBound(varArray)
            ' Increment the occurrence counter
            lngOccur = lngOccur + 1

            ' If the value is not the same as the last one,
            ' see if the occurrences of the last value
            ' exceed the current maximum
            If varArray(lngCount) <> varLast Then
                If lngLastOccur > lngTotalOccur Then
                    ' If so, make it the new maximum and
                    ' capture the prior value
                    lngTotalOccur = lngLastOccur
                    varItem = varArray(lngCount - 1)
                End If

                ' Record this element as the last one visited
                varLast = varArray(lngCount)

                ' Reset the counter
                lngOccur = 0
            End If

            lngLastOccur = lngOccur
        Next
```

```
         ' Return the value with the most occurrences
         ' (make sure to check the final value)
         If lngOccur > lngTotalOccur Then
             dhModeOfArray = varArray(lngCount - 1)
         Else
             dhModeOfArray = varItem
         End If
     Else
         dhModeOfArray = Null
     End If
End Function
```

Finding Minimum and Maximum Values

Surprisingly, VBA does not include functions for determining the minimum or maximum values in a series of numbers. It's relatively easy, however, to construct a function to do this using an array. Listing 3.21 shows two functions we've created that compute the minimum or maximum values, given an array.

Listing 3.21: Custom Maximum and Minimum Functions

```
Function dhMaxInArray(varArray As Variant) As Variant
    ' Return the maximum value from an array

    Dim varItem As Variant
    Dim varMax As Variant
    Dim intI As Integer

    If IsArray(varArray) Then
        If UBound(varArray) = -1 Then
            dhMaxInArray = Null
        Else
            varMax = varArray(UBound(varArray))
            For intI = LBound(varArray) To UBound(varArray)
                varItem = varArray(intI)
                If varItem > varMax Then
                    varMax = varItem
                End If
            Next intI
            dhMaxInArray = varMax
        End If
    Else
        dhMaxInArray = Null
    End If
```

```
End Function

Function dhMinInArray(varArray As Variant) As Variant
    ' Return the minimum value from an array

    Dim varItem As Variant
    Dim varMin As Variant
    Dim intI As Integer

    If IsArray(varArray) Then
        If UBound(varArray) = -1 Then
            dhMinInArray = Null
        Else
            varMin = varArray(LBound(varArray))
            For intI = LBound(varArray) To UBound(varArray)
                varItem = varArray(intI)
                If varItem < varMin Then
                    varMin = varItem
                End If
            Next intI
            dhMinInArray = varMin
        End If
    Else
        dhMinInArray = Null
    End If
End Function
```

You can also use VBA's ParamArray datatype in array functions. ParamArray variables are designed to allow you to pass an arbitrary number of arguments to a function. Fortunately, you can coerce a ParamArray variable into a Variant, so it's simple to create ParamArray versions of the functions shown in Listing 3.21. Listing 3.22 shows the functions we created.

Listing 3.22: ParamArray Versions of Maximum and Minimum Functions

```
Function dhMaxInParamArray(ParamArray varValues() As Variant) _
 As Variant

    Dim varTemp As Variant

    varTemp = varValues
    dhMaxInParamArray = dhMaxInArray(varTemp)
End Function
```

```
Function dhMinInParamArray(ParamArray varValues() As Variant) _
  As Variant

    Dim varTemp As Variant

    varTemp = varValues
    dhMinInParamArray = dhMinInArray(varTemp)
End Function
```

Summary

VBA has many useful functions for handling numbers, but there are problems in using these functions that are not apparent on the surface. This chapter has provided an overview of the built-in functions, as well as some of the problems inherent in floating-point datatypes and rounding. Several handy custom functions for performing numeric calculations were also presented. Specifically, this chapter covered

- How VBA stores and computes numbers:
    - Understanding the different datatypes in VBA
    - Problems with floating-point numbers and how to solve them
- Built-in numeric functions:
    - Mathematical
    - Type conversion and rounding
    - Generating random numbers
    - Financial
    - Base conversions
- Custom functions:
    - Mathematical
    - Geometric
    - Converting numbers to text
    - Statistics

For similar chapters covering strings and dates, see Chapters 1 and 2, respectively.

CHAPTER
FOUR

4

Searching and Sorting in VBA

- Creating a StopWatch class to measure elapsed time

- Introducing arrays

- Using the standard Quicksort algorithm

- Sorting collections

- Understanding the Binary Search algorithm

If you're working with data in your application, sooner or later you'll need to sort the data, or you'll need to find a particular item within a group of data items. This chapter, which is devoted to searching and sorting data, presents some techniques from which you can choose.

Certainly, the topics of searching and sorting have been covered in much more academic terms, in much greater detail, in other books. We're not attempting to provide a complete discussion of various sorting algorithms here. In fact, we present only one: the common Quicksort algorithm. We do, however, show you how to use the sorting routine and present detailed coverage of exactly how it works. For searching, we present the Binary Search algorithm and demonstrate how you can use it and exactly how it works. Because many readers will be using VBA in conjunction with the Microsoft Jet database engine or some other SQL data source, we provide tips along the way for using the database engine to do the work.

Table 4.1 lists the sample files you'll find on the accompanying CD-ROM.

TABLE 4.1   Sample Files

File Name	Description
SRCHSORT.XLS	Excel 97 file with all sample functions
SRCHSORT.MDB	Access 97 file with all sample functions
BINSRCH.BAS	Binary Search module
BUBBLESORT.BAS	Bubblesort module
LINEARSRCH.BAS	Linear search module
QUICKSORT.BAS	Quicksort module
SORTCOL.BAS	Sort collection module
TESTPROCS.BAS	Test procedures
VQUICKSORT.BAS	Visual Quicksort module
STOPWATCH.CLS	StopWatch class module

Timing Is Everything

Most likely, if you're sorting data, you care about how long it takes. When deciding on the best technique to use for sorting your data, you'll need some help. The StopWatch class discussed in this section can help you determine which is the best technique to use, based on the time it takes to execute. We use this simple StopWatch class all the time, in any situation in which we need to compare the timings of two or more activities.

Introducing the StopWatch Class

It doesn't take much effort to measure elapsed time. VBA itself includes the Timer function, which returns a Single datatype value containing the number of seconds that have elapsed since midnight. This function has three inherent problems if you intend to use it to measure elapsed time in your applications:

- It "turns over" at midnight, so if you happen to be running a test over the bewitching hour, your test results will be meaningless.

- It turns over every 24 hours, so if you want to run a test that lasts longer than that, you're out of luck.

- It isn't terribly accurate. It can measure time only to 1/18-second accuracy because of the particular internal timer it's using.

For these reasons (and there's one even more crucial reason not to use Timer, coming up in a moment), it's probably best that you avoid the Timer function when attempting to measure elapsed times in small increments. What's your alternative? The Windows API provides several ways to measure elapsed time, the simplest of which is the timeGetTime function. This function measures the number of milliseconds (in a long integer) that have elapsed since you started Windows. The timeGetTime function compares favorably to the Timer function:

- It "turns over" only every 48 days or so. If you're interested in millisecond accuracy, you're probably not running tasks that take that long, but it's nice to know it can keep on ticking and ticking!

- It has no concept of days, so there's no issue with running tasks that last longer than a single date.

- It's more accurate than the Timer function. Rather than measuring in 1/18-second increments, it measures in 1/1000-second increments. In addition, because it doesn't involve floating-point math to return its results (as does the Timer function), it's more accurate as well.

Obviously, the StopWatch class will take advantage of this API function. The code for the class, shown in Listing 4.1, is amazingly simple. As you can see in the listing, the class exposes two public methods: StartTimer and EndTimer. The StartTimer method initializes the internal plngStart variable, storing the time value when the stopwatch was "started." The EndTimer method returns the difference between the current tick value and the time at which the clock was started—effectively, the amount of elapsed time, in milliseconds.

Listing 4.1: The StopWatch Class

```
Private plngStart As Long
Private Declare Function timeGetTime Lib "winmm.dll" () As Long

Public Sub StartTimer()
    plngStart = timeGetTime
End Sub

Public Function EndTimer() As Long
    EndTimer = (timeGetTime - plngStart)
End Function
```

Using the StopWatch Class

To use the StopWatch class, you'll generally write code like this:

```
Dim sw As New StopWatch
sw.StartTimer
' Do stuff in here that you want to time
Debug.Print "That took: " sw.EndTimer & "milliseconds."
```

As an example, the final (and most compelling) reason to use timeGetTime as opposed to the built-in Timer function is that the act of calling the Timer function itself takes, in general, five times as long as calling timeGetTime. Don't believe it? Try the code shown in Listing 4.2, from TESTPROCS.BAS. If you run Compare-Timers from the Immediate window, you'll see that calling Timer takes substantially longer (five times longer, in our tests) than calling timeGetTime.

Listing 4.2: Compare Timer to timeGetTime

```
Private Declare Function timeGetTime Lib "winmm.dll" () As Long

Sub CompareTimers()
    Dim intMax As Integer
    Dim sw As New StopWatch
    Dim intI As Integer
    Dim lngResult As Long

    intMax = 10000
    sw.StartTimer
    For intI = 1 To intMax
        lngResult = Timer
    Next intI
    Debug.Print "Timer: " & sw.EndTimer

    sw.StartTimer
    For intI = 1 To intMax
        lngResult = timeGetTime
    Next intI
    Debug.Print "timeGetTime: " & sw.EndTimer
End Sub
```

To use the StopWatch class in any application, simply import STOPWATCH.CLS into your project, and call it as shown in the examples. Whenever we make a comment in this book about one technique being faster than another, you can bet we've tried it out both ways with the stopwatch running.

> The StopWatch class module is so simple that it doesn't need much explanation. For this reason, and because it's so useful for this chapter and for your own programming, we decided to introduce it here instead of in Chapter 5, which provides a full discussion of class modules.

Using Arrays

There are many ways to store data in VBA, but if you're interested in sorting data, it will often be in an array. Although many subtleties are involved in using arrays in VBA, the next few sections outline the concepts you'll need to understand in order to use the techniques supplied in this chapter. If you need more detailed information on creating and using arrays, see the VBA online help. This is a rich topic, and we can't discuss all the subtleties here; we've attempted to explain only what you'll need to know to follow the code examples in this chapter.

What Is an Array, Anyway?

An array is an indexed group of data treated as a single variable. You would consider using an array when you need to work with a group of data items that are related in such a way that you can use an integer to relate the items.

For example, imagine you needed to work with all your salary levels for a six-year range, from 1992 to 1997. Because the year value is an integer, you can use that as an index for the data. You might create an array named SalaryInfo, as shown in Figure 4.1, declared like this:

```
Dim SalaryInfo(1992 To 1997) As Currency
```

FIGURE 4.1

An array can use any integer value range as its index.

SalaryInfo	Index
$20,000	1992
$22,500	1993
$26,000	1994
$30,000	1995
$32,000	1996
$35,000	1997

Of course, you're not limited to arrays containing information about salaries, or even to arrays of any specific datatype. When you declare an array, you can specify any range of values (most arrays start at either 0 or 1, but they don't have to), containing almost any datatype. In addition, arrays can contain multiple dimensions of data. To access a particular array element, you might use statements like these:

```
SalaryInfo(1997) = 26500
' or
If SalaryInfo(1997) > SalaryInfo(1996) * 1.10 Then
    MsgBox "The raise from 1996 to 1997 was too great. " &
     "Make this year's raise smaller!"
End If
```

Imagine that rather than storing six years of salary information, you'd like to store salary information by quarter. That is, for each of the four quarters in the year, you'd like information in each of the six years. You might, then, create an array that looks like the one shown in Figure 4.2. To declare an array like this one, you might use a statement like this:

```
Dim SalaryInfo(1992 To 1997, 1 To 4) As Currency
```

where the years range from 1992 to 1997, and for each year, the quarters range from 1 to 4.

FIGURE 4.2

Arrays can contain two or more dimensions of information.

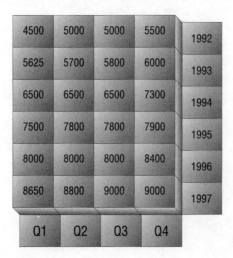

To retrieve or set any item from the array, now you'd use an expression like this:

```
' Give a 15% raise in the fourth quarter, based on the third
' quarter's salary.
SalaryInfo(1997, 4) = SalaryInfo(1997, 3) * 1.15
```

Take it one step further: what if you want to work with information about quarterly salaries of multiple employees? In that case, you might create a three-dimensional array, as shown in Figure 4.3. To declare this array, you might use a statement like this:

```
Dim SalaryInfo(1992 To 1997, 1 To 4, 1 To 3) As Currency
```

(that is, years from 1992 to 1997, quarters from 1 to 4, and employees from 1 to 3). The following code will deduct 10 percent from Employee 3's pay in the final quarter of 1997:

```
SalaryInfo(1997, 4, 3) = SalaryInfo(1997, 4, 3) * .90
```

FIGURE 4.3

Although it's not a common practice, you can use three or more dimensions in your arrays.

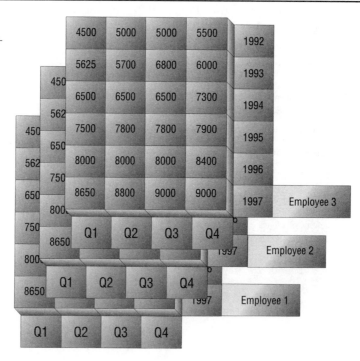

The following sections discuss some of the details of using arrays, and many of the examples in this chapter also use arrays as part of doing their work.

> **TIP**
>
> Although using multidimensional arrays is a useful technique for modeling real-world scenarios, be careful of the complexity you introduce into your applications by using these sometimes difficult-to-envision data structures. In addition, arrays in VBA aren't sparse—that is, empty elements take up just as much memory as elements that are filled with data. Large arrays can be real memory hogs, and you should carefully consider how much of your array is being utilized and whether some other data structure might be more appropriate.

Creating an Array

VBA treats an array much as it would any other variable. The same naming, scoping, and lifetime rules apply. The only difference is that, with an array, you must either specify the lower and upper bounds for the array or at least indicate that you'll *later* indicate those values.

To create an array by specifying its bounds, dimension array variables like this:

```
' 100 integers
Dim aintItems(1 To 100) As Integer
' 10 rows of data with 2 strings each
Dim astrNames(1 To 10, 1 To 2) As String
' Tell VBA that you'll specify the size later:
Dim astrNames() As String
```

See the section "Sizing an Array" coming up in a moment for more information on resizing an array once you've created it.

Using Data in an Array

Once you've created an array, you can work with any item in the array, referring to the item by its position within the array. For example, if the array astrItems contains 100 strings, you could use code like the following to inspect each of the 100 elements of the array:

```
Dim intI As Integer
For intI = 1 To 100
```

```
    Debug.Print astrItems(intI)
Next intI
```

If you wanted to place the current index value into each location in aintItems (an array of 50 integers), you might write code like this:

```
Dim aintItems(1 To 50) As Integer
Dim intI As Integer

For intI = 1 To 50
    aintItems(intI) = intI
Next intI
```

You needn't use a loop of any sort to work with elements of an array. For example, the following procedure, used in the sorting code presented in the section "Sorting Arrays" later in this chapter, swaps two array items. In this case, the array is named varItems, and intItem1 and intItem2 contain the indexes of the two items to be swapped:

```
Dim varTemp As Variant

varTemp = varItems(intItem2)
varItems(intItem2) = varItems(intItem1)
varItems(intItem1) = varTemp
```

NOTE You can also use the For Each...Next construct to loop through the elements of an array, but this isn't recommended. It's slower than using the For...Next construct, and you can't use this construct for setting values in an array—you can use it only to retrieve values.

Sizing an Array

An array is generally a static data structure. As such, once you've told VBA the size of the data structure, you won't be able to automatically resize the array without explicitly requesting the change in size.

VBA provides a number of ways to size an array:

- When you declare the array, you can specify its dimensions. (This is normally called a *fixed-size* array.)

```
Dim astrItems(1 To 100) As String
```

- When you declare the array, you can leave off the dimensions. Later, when you want to use the array, you can use the ReDim keyword to set its size. (This is normally called a *dynamic* array because you needn't know the size of the array when you create it.)

```
Dim astrItems() As String
' Later in the code (intItems contains, perhaps, 100)
ReDim astrItems(1 To intItems)
```

- You can create a dynamic array, along with its dimensions, when you first declare it, using the ReDim keyword:

```
ReDim astrItems(1 To 100) As String
```

- You can resize a dynamic array at any time, using the ReDim keyword. Unless you also specify the Preserve keyword, VBA clears the items contained in the array. If you use the Preserve keyword, VBA preserves all the existing items in the array:

```
Dim astrItems() As String

' Later in the code:
ReDim astrItems(1 To 100)
' Fill in the items...
' Now you find out that you need an additional 100 items:
ReDim Preserve astrItems(1 To 200)
```

TIP

Although you needn't specify the lower bound of an array, we strongly advise that you always do so. If you don't specify the lower bound, you're counting on using the value specified (or implied) by the module's Option Base setting. By default, a module's Option Base setting is 0, but you can override this by adding an Option Base 1 statement to any module. Either way, if you don't specify the lower bound of an array when you set its size, VBA will use the value selected by the Option Base statement. When you explicitly specify the lower bound, your code is more readable, and you're less likely to be affected by "off by one" errors.

Alternatives to ReDim Preserve

Using ReDim Preserve does preserve the contents of your array as it's being resized, but it's not a fast operation. To redimension the array, VBA must grab a chunk of memory for the new array, and then, if you've specified the Preserve keyword, copy over all the items in your original array. Finally, it releases the memory used by the original array. You'd do best to avoid ReDim Preserve if at all possible. What are the alternatives? One possibility is to use a collection (see the section "Working with Collections" later in this chapter for more information) to contain your data. Another is to use a dynamic data structure like a linked list, as described in Chapter 6. Finally, you can consider redimensioning your array by adding chunks of items at a time. That is, rather than redimension it every time it requires more items, add a large number of items at a time and redimension only when you run out of items. When you're done adding items, you can make one final call to ReDim Preserve to resize the array correctly.

Using a Variant to Point to an Array

The simplest way to work with an array is to "point" a variant variable at the array and use the variant to refer to the array from then on. That is, if astrItems is an array containing 100 strings, you can use code like the following to cause varItems to refer to astrItems:

```
Dim varItems As Variant
Dim astrItems(1 To 100) As String
' Fill in the strings here.
varItems = astrItems
```

Once you take that step, you can use varItems as a single variable, without worrying about the trailing parentheses, but you can also refer to items in the array, using code like this:

```
varItems(1) = "A new string"
```

This assignment happens automatically when you pass an array to a function that expects a variant parameter. For example, the dhQuickSort procedure (in QUICK-SORT.BAS) is declared like this:

```
Sub dhQuickSort(varArray As Variant, _
```

```
        Optional intLeft As Integer = dhcMissing, _
        Optional intRight As Integer = dhcMissing)
```

To call dhQuickSort, pass it either an array or a variant that "contains" an array. For example, any of the following methods is acceptable:

```
Dim varItems As Variant
varItems = Array(1, 2, 3, 4, 5)
Call dhQuickSort(varItems)
' or: ==========
Dim aintItems(1 To 5) As Integer

aintItems(1) = 1
aintItems(2) = 2
aintItems(3) = 3
aintItems(4) = 4
aintItems(5) = 5
Call dhQuickSort(aintItems)
' or: ==========
Dim aintItems(1 To 5) As Integer
Dim varItems As Variant

aintItems(1) = 1
aintItems(2) = 2
aintItems(3) = 3
aintItems(4) = 4
aintItems(5) = 5
varItems = aintItems
Call dhQuickSort(varItems)
```

If you call dhQuickSort, passing it an array of strings (or any other specific datatype), VBA will assign the array to the variant as it calls the procedure. Then, inside the called procedure, you can refer to varItems as though it were the array itself.

To ensure that a variant does, in fact, contain an array, you have two choices:

- **Use the IsArray function:** Call the IsArray function, passing the variant variable. It will return True if the variant points to an array and False otherwise. You might write code like this at the beginning of a routine that's expecting an array:

  ```
  If Not IsArray(varItems) Then Exit Sub
  ```

- **Use the VarType function:** Call VarType, passing the variant variable. VarType will return vbArray (8192) plus a value corresponding to the type of data in the array (vbInteger (2) through vbByte (17)). For example, if you're allowing only an array of strings to be passed into a particular function, you might write code like the following:

```
If VarType(varItems) <> vbArray + vbString Then Exit Sub
```

Using the Array Function

Some examples in this chapter use the Array function to place data into an array. This useful function allows you to list specific values to be placed into an array, and it returns an array containing the values you send it. For example, the following statement places an array containing three integers into a variant:

```
Dim varItems As Variant
varItems = Array(100, 202, 315)
' Almost equivalent to:
Dim varItems(0 To 2) As Integer
varItems(0) = 100
varItems(1) = 202
varItems(2) = 315
```

Note the "almost" in the code comment. In the first example, the indexes used by the items in varItems will use the Option Base statement in the module to determine the start of the range of index values. If there's no Option Base statement or if it's set to 0, the items will be numbered 0, 1, and 2. If you've set the Option Base statement for the module to 1, the elements will be numbered 1, 2, and 3. The array items in the second example will always be numbered 0, 1, and 2, no matter how you modify the Option Base statement for the module. You must be aware of the Option Base setting if you use the Array function. (This contradicts the current VBA online help text, which explicitly states, incorrectly, that the Array function always creates a zero-based array.)

Sorting Arrays

Once you're comfortable with arrays, you'll want to be able to sort the data they contain. This section introduces a common sorting method, the Quicksort algorithm. This algorithm, an accepted advanced sorting technique, is somewhat complex, but it performs well. Once you've written the code, of course, you won't have to revisit it unless you need to modify it. If you're not interested in how the sort does its work, skip ahead to the "Watching Quicksort Run" section.

NOTE Why this particular sorting algorithm? In choosing a sort method, you want to minimize the number of comparisons and swaps the sort uses to complete its goal. There are simpler sort algorithms (a statement with which you'll undoubtedly agree if you work through the Quicksort example step by step), but the simpler sorts always require more comparisons between items and more data movement (swapping items) in order to sort the array. More comparisons and more swaps turn into longer execution time, so Quicksort provides a good compromise: it's complex but understandable, and it's more efficient than simpler sorts.

WARNING Quicksort isn't optimized for data that's already sorted. That is, if your data comes to the Quicksort algorithm in sorted order, it will take almost as long to sort as if it weren't. Other (perhaps simpler) algorithms will take into account the fact that data is already sorted and drop out sooner. If you're often going to be sorting data that may be in sorted order, you may want to investigate other sorting techniques. (See the discussion in the section "Speed Considerations" later in this chapter for more information.)

How Does Quicksort Work?

The Quicksort algorithm, generally accepted as one of the fastest sort algorithms, uses the "divide and conquer" technique of sorting. Basically, Quicksort divides an array into smaller and smaller partitions, two partitions at a time, such that each left-hand partition contains values smaller than each right-hand partition. When it runs out of partitions, it's done.

Quicksort lends itself to recursion (the concept of a procedure calling itself, passing new parameters), and the recursive implementation of the sort is quite simple. Given an array to sort, the algorithm boils down to these few steps:

1. Call the sort function, passing the lower and upper bounds of the segment to be sorted.

2. If the lower bound is less than the upper bound, then:

   a. Break the current array into two smaller segments, such that all items in the left segment are less than or equal to each item in the right segment. This will involve swapping some items from one segment to the other.

   b. Follow the same algorithm on the smaller of the left and right segments (and this will, most likely, break down the segment into multiple call levels as well). Once that's sorted, follow the same algorithm with the larger, remaining segment.

The sort appears to break down into two major chunks: partitioning the elements and then calling the sort again recursively. You might be grumbling, at this point, about recursive routines and how they use lots of memory. Normally, that's true; this version of the sorting algorithm, however, tries to be conservative about how it uses memory. At each level, it sorts the smaller of the two chunks first. This means it will have fewer recursive levels: the small chunk will end up containing a single element much more quickly than the large chunk. By always working with the smallest chunk first, this method avoids calling itself more often than it has to. The entire dhQuickSort procedure, implementing the Quicksort algorithm, is shown in Listing 4.3.

Listing 4.3: The dhQuickSort Procedure, Implementing the Quicksort Algorithm

```
Const dhcMissing = -2

Sub dhQuickSort(varArray As Variant, _
  Optional intLeft As Integer = dhcMissing, _
  Optional intRight As Integer = dhcMissing)
```

```
        Dim i As Integer
        Dim j As Integer
        Dim varTestVal As Variant
        Dim intMid As Integer

        If intLeft = dhcMissing Then intLeft = LBound(varArray)
        If intRight = dhcMissing Then intRight = UBound(varArray)

        If intLeft < intRight Then
            intMid = (intLeft + intRight) \ 2
            varTestVal = varArray(intMid)
            i = intLeft
            j = intRight
            Do
                Do While varArray(i) < varTestVal
                    i = i + 1
                Loop
                Do While varArray(j) > varTestVal
                    j = j - 1
                Loop
                If i <= j Then
                    SwapElements varArray, i, j
                    i = i + 1
                    j = j - 1
                End If
            Loop Until i > j
            ' To optimize the sort, always sort the
            ' smallest segment first.
            If j <= intMid Then
                Call dhQuickSort(varArray, intLeft, j)
                Call dhQuickSort(varArray, i, intRight)
            Else
                Call dhQuickSort(varArray, i, intRight)
                Call dhQuickSort(varArray, intLeft, j)
            End If
        End If
End Sub

Private Sub SwapElements(varItems As Variant, _
  intItem1 As Integer, intItem2 As Integer)
    Dim varTemp As Variant

    varTemp = varItems(intItem2)
    varItems(intItem2) = varItems(intItem1)
```

```
        varItems(intItem1) = varTemp
End Sub
```

When you have a procedure that calls itself recursively, it's imperative that you provide some way to terminate the process. In this case, the code can repeat only as long as the lower bound value is less than the upper bound value. As the dhQuickSort routine calls itself, the lower bound gets higher and higher and the upper bound gets lower and lower. Once these values cross, the sort is done. Therefore, the dhQuickSort procedure starts by checking for this condition:

```
If intLeft < intRight Then
    ' Sort this segment (code removed)
End If
```

If, at any call to dhQuickSort, the lower bound isn't less than the upper bound, the sorting stops and the procedure can return to the caller. Once the code has made the determination that it can perform the sort, it takes the following steps:

1. The sort takes the value in the middle of the subset of the array that's being sorted as the "comparison" value. Its value is going to be the dividing factor for the two chunks. There are different schools of thought on how to choose the dividing item. This version of the sort uses the item that's physically in the middle of the chosen list of items:

    ```
    intMid = (intLeft + intRight) \ 2
    varTestVal = varArray(intMid)
    ```

2. The code first starts from the left, walking along the array until it finds an item that isn't less than the dividing value. This search is guaranteed to stop at the dividing value, which certainly isn't less than itself:

    ```
    Do While varArray(i) < varTestVal
        i = i + 1
    Loop
    ```

3. Next, the code starts from the right, walking backward through the array until it finds an item that isn't more than the dividing value. This search is guaranteed to stop at the dividing value, which certainly isn't more than itself:

    ```
    Do While varArray(j) > varTestVal
        j = j - 1
    Loop
    ```

4. If the position from step 2 is less than or equal to the position found in step 3, the sort swaps the elements at the two positions and then increments the pointer for step 2 and decrements the pointer for step 3:

```
If i <= j Then
    SwapElements varArray, i, j
    i = i + 1
    j = j - 1
End If
```

5. The sort repeats steps 2 through 4 until the pointer from step 2 is greater than the pointer from step 3 ($i > j$). At this point, every item to the left of the dividing element is less than or equal to it, and everything to the right is greater than or equal to it.

6. Choosing the smaller partition first, the sort repeats all these steps on each of the subsets to either side of the dividing value until step 1 indicates that it's done:

```
If j <= intMid Then
    Call dhQuickSort(varArray, intLeft, j)
    Call dhQuickSort(varArray, i, intRight)
Else
    Call dhQuickSort(varArray, i, intRight)
    Call dhQuickSort(varArray, intLeft, j)
End If
```

To make this technique completely clear, imagine you want to sort an array of ten integers, positions numbered 1 through 10, as shown in Figure 4.4. The following numbered list corresponds to the steps shown in Figures 4.5, 4.6, 4.7, and 4.8. In the first few steps, the pertinent code will be displayed. Because there isn't much code but there are a lot of steps, once you've seen the appropriate chunk of code, it won't be displayed again.

> **NOTE**
>
> Along the way, the discussion will keep track of the levels of recursion. That is, as you call dhQuickSort from dhQuickSort, it's important to keep track of how many times the procedure has called itself, to make sure you understand the concept of a recursion. In this example, level 1 is your call to dhQuickSort, and subsequent levels represent calls dhQuickSort makes to itself, passing in different limits on the array to be sorted.

NOTE

To make the following steps easier to read, we've used the symbol "j^" to refer to "the item pointed to by j." That is, when the variable j contains the value 1, the item it's pointing to (in the original array) is 79, and the shortcut in the text for that will be j^. (If you require some verbal representation for this notation, you can say—silently, please—"j hat" where you see "j^" in the text. This verbalization stems from a Pascal class one of us took many years ago.)

1. Calculate the middle location (5). Then, point i at the first element in the array and j at the final element. While i^ (the item pointed to by i) is less than 26, move i to the right. (It doesn't move at all, because 79 isn't less than 26.) While j^ is greater than 26, move j to the left:

```
intMid = (intLeft + intRight) \ 2
varTestVal = varArray(intMid)
i = intLeft
j = intRight
Do
    Do While varArray(i) < varTestVal
        i = i + 1
    Loop
    Do While varArray(j) > varTestVal
        j = j - 1
    Loop
```

2. Because i is less than or equal to j, swap the elements pointed to by i and j. Then move i one position to the right and j one position to the left.

```
    If i <= j Then
        SwapElements varArray, i, j
        i = i + 1
        j = j - 1
    End If
Loop Until i > j
```

3. Because i isn't greater than j, the loop goes back to the top. While i^ is less than 26, move i to the right. (It's not, so it doesn't move.) While j^ is greater than 26, move j to the left.

4. Because i is less than or equal to j, swap the elements pointed to by i and j. Then move i one position to the right and j one position to the left.

5. Because i isn't greater than j, the loop goes back to the top. While i^ is less than 26, move i to the right. While j^ is greater than 26, move j to the left.

6. Because i is less than or equal to j, swap the elements pointed to by i and j. Then move i one position to the right and j one position to the left.

7. Because i is now greater than j (i is 5 and j is 4), drop out of the Do...Loop. Now j is less than intMid (the middle position), so call the entire procedure again, working with elements 1 through j. (You're now leaving level 1 in the recursion and going to level 2.) Once you've sorted the items in positions 1 through 4, you'll call dhQuickSort again to sort the items in positions 5 through 10 (starting in step 13).

```
If j <= intMid Then
    Call dhQuickSort(varArray, intLeft, j)
    Call dhQuickSort(varArray, i, intRight)
```

8. Starting over again: the leftmost element is 1 and the rightmost element is 4, so set i and j to point to those items. Calculate the middle location (2). While i^ is less than 5, move it to the right. (It doesn't move at all, because 21 isn't less than 5.) While j^ is greater than 5, move j to the left.

9. Because i is less than or equal to j, swap the elements pointed to by i and j. Then move i one position to the right and j one position to the left.

10. Because i is now greater than j (i is 2 and j is 1), drop out of the Do...Loop. Now j is less than the middle position, so call the entire procedure again, working with elements 1 through j. (You're now leaving level 2 in the recursion and going to level 3.) Of course, once you've sorted items 1 through 1 (not much to sort in that interval, is there?), you'll come back to level 2 and sort items 2 through 4 (starting in step 11).

```
If j <= intMid Then
    Call dhQuickSort(varArray, intLeft, j)
```

At this point, you've called dhQuickSort, passing 1 and 1 as the end points. The outermost condition checks to see whether intLeft is less than intRight, and if it isn't, it just returns. That's the case now, and you return to level 2.

11. Back at level 2, you now call dhQuickSort, passing i and intRight as the endpoints. (When you call dhQuickSort, you leave level 2 and move on to level 3 again.) While i^ is less than the middle item (24), move to the right. This places i smack on the 24. While j^ is greater than 24, move it to the left. This places j on the 24 as well.

12. Now, because i is, in fact, less than or equal to j, swap the items i and j point to (not much work here, since i and j point to the same value), and then move j one position to the left and i one position to the right. (This is what step 12 in Figure 4.6 displays.) Because i is now greater than j, it's time to drop out of the loop. At this point, j is less than intMid (j is 2 and intMid is 3), so the code calls dhQuickSort, passing intLeft (2) and j (2). This enters recursion level 4. Of course, as soon as you get there, dhQuickSort determines that intLeft is not less than intRight (it's been passed 2 and 2 from level 3), so it drops right back to level 3. Back in level 3, the next step is to call dhQuickSort, passing i (4) and intRight (4). You can probably guess that the visit to level 4 is going to be short: since dhQuickSort receives intLeft and intRight values that are the same, it's going to immediately return to level 3. The call to dhQuickSort, level 3, is complete, and it returns back to level 2. But level 2 is complete as well—you've sorted both the left and right halves of the first partition (1 to 4)—so it's time to return to the right partition in level 1. Finally, you get to the picture displayed in step 13 of Figure 4.7.

13. You're probably getting the hang of this by now! As long as i^ is less than the middle item (30), move it to the right. It's already pointing to a value greater than 30 (48, in position 5), so it doesn't move. As long as j^ is greater than the middle item (30), move it to the left. All the items to the right of position 7 are greater than 30, so j ends up pointing to the middle item.

14. Because i is less than or equal to j, swap the two items.

15. Move i one position to the right and j one position to the left. (They're both at position 6 now.)

16. As long as i^ is less than the middle item (30), move it to the right. Of course, it's pointing to 34, so it doesn't move at all. As long as j^ is greater than 30, move it to the left; this causes j to move to position 5, where it's pointing to the value 30. Now, because i is greater than j, it's time to drop out of the loop. At this point, the code calls dhQuickSort, passing intLeft (5) and j (5) (leaving level 1 and calling level 2). Of course, this visit to level 2 is swift because dhQuickSort finds its new intLeft and intRight to be the same.

17. Now you've returned to level 1, where the code calls dhQuickSort in level 2 again, passing i (6) and intRight (10) as the parameters. Now, in level 2, with reasonable end points, it's time to continue. As long as i^ is less than the middle item (48), move it to the right. As long as j^ is greater than 48, move it to the left.

18. With i at position 7 and j at position 8, swap the items they point to.

19. Move j one more position to the left and i one more to the right. Now, because i is greater than j, it's time to drop out of the loop. Because j (7) is less than the middle position (8), call dhQuickSort in level 3, passing intLeft (6) and j (7) as the end points.

20. It's getting tight here: there are only two items to sort, so the middle position is 6 (that's (6 + 7) \ 2). While i^ is less than 34, move it to the right. (It doesn't move.) While j^ is greater than 34, move it to the left. At this point, both i and j are at position 6, pointing at the 34. Because i is less than or equal to j, swap the items to which i and j point. (Yes, it is a fruitless exercise, but that's what you have to do!) Then move j one position to the left and i one position to the right.

21. Because i is now greater than j (i is 7 and j is 5), drop out of the loop. Call dhQuickSort in level 4, passing intLeft (6) and j (5). Of course, as soon as you get to level 4, dhQuickSort will return, because its new intLeft is greater than its intRight. Back in level 3, call dhQuickSort again, passing i (7) and intRight (7). Again, the visit to level 4 is awfully short since dhQuickSort again returns immediately. At this point, you're done at level 3, so return to level 2.

22. Back in level 2, you've sorted the left portion (steps 20 and 21), and now it's time to call dhQuickSort in level 3 with the right portion. Given the end points 8 and 10, the middle element will be 9, with the value 79. While i^ is less than 79, move i to the right. While j^ is greater than 79, move j to the left. These loops terminate with a situation you've seen before: both i and j point to 79, in position 9. The code swaps 79 with itself and then moves i one more position to the right and j one more to the left.

23. Since i is greater than j, it's time to drop out of the loop. The code calls dhQuickSort in level 4, passing intLeft (8) and j (8). Of course, this drops right out, back to level 3. Then it calls dhQuickSort in level 4, passing i (10) and intRight (10). Again, the code returns immediately. Level 3 is done, so it returns back to level 2. Level 2 has sorted both halves, so it returns to level 1. Level 1 has sorted both halves, so it's done. Finally, the entire array has been sorted!

The beauty of computers is that you don't have to follow all these steps every time you execute the sort. Once you've convinced yourself that the algorithm will work in every case, you can use it without thought (and you've probably determined by now that you don't ever want to dig through the Quicksort algorithm at this level of detail again). The "Using Quicksort" section coming up in a moment shows how you can call Quicksort from your own applications.

FIGURE 4.4

The sample array, ready to be sorted

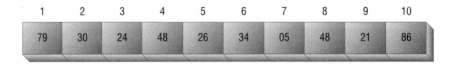

FIGURE 4.5

Steps 1 through 7

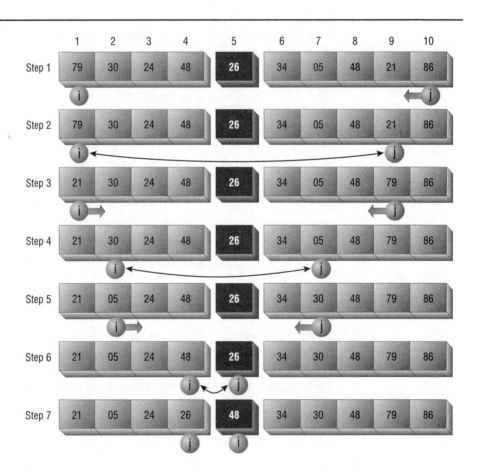

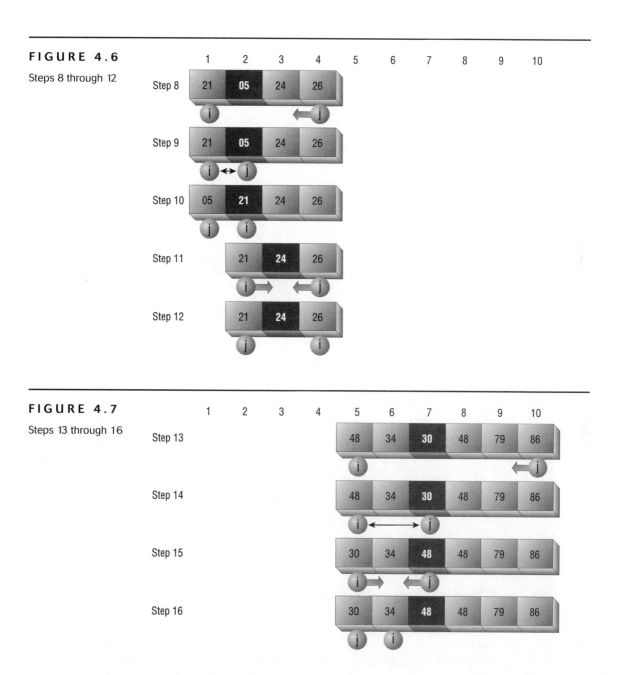

FIGURE 4.6

Steps 8 through 12

FIGURE 4.7

Steps 13 through 16

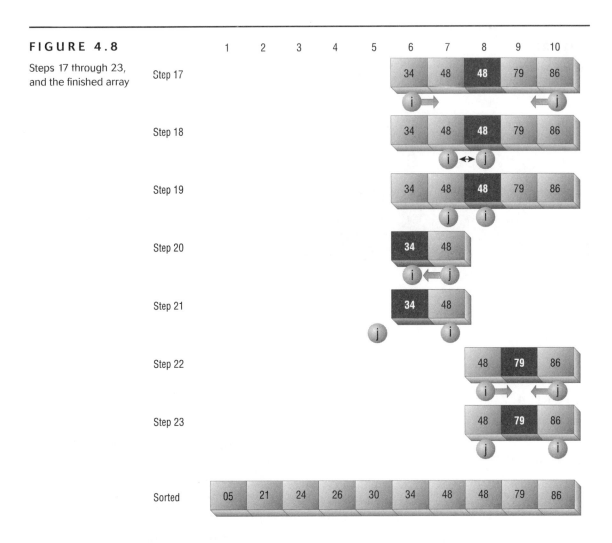

FIGURE 4.8

Steps 17 through 23, and the finished array

Watching Quicksort Run

To make it possible to watch the Quicksort algorithm at work, we've supplied a visual version of the dhQuickSort routine. The VQUICKSORT.BAS module contains an expanded version of the dhQuickSort procedure that prints, to the Immediate window, what it's doing at each step. Although the mechanism of displaying the steps isn't pertinent to the discussion here, you'll find running the

TestSortDemo routine instructive. Pass it no parameters to use the sample data discussed in the previous section, or pass it the number of items you'd like sorted. For example, calling

```
TestSortDemo
```

will return a printout demonstrating the same sort as discussed in the 23 steps in the previous section. Calling

```
TestSortDemo 6
```

will choose six random numbers between 1 and 99 and demonstrate the Quicksort algorithm with those numbers. Figure 4.9 shows sample output from calling TestSortDemo.

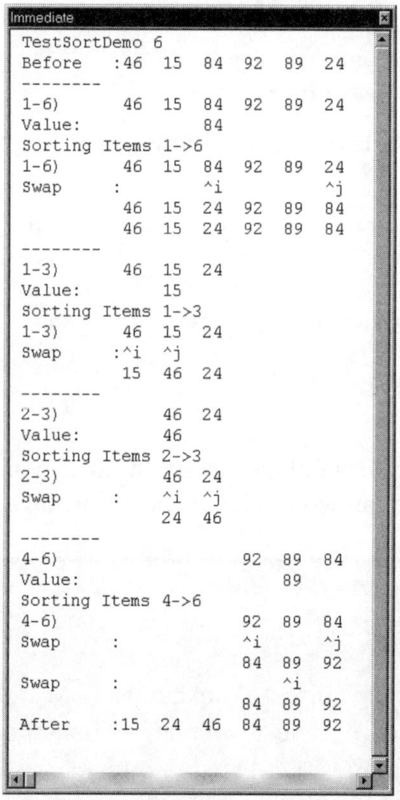

FIGURE 4.9

Call TestSortDemo to watch Quicksort at work

```
Immediate                                    x
TestSortDemo 6
Before    :46   15   84   92   89   24
--------
1-6)       46   15   84   92   89   24
Value:               84
Sorting Items 1->6
1-6)       46   15   84   92   89   24
Swap      :           ^i             ^j
           46   15   24   92   89   84
           46   15   24   92   89   84
--------
1-3)       46   15   24
Value:          15
Sorting Items 1->3
1-3)       46   15   24
Swap      :^i   ^j
           15   46   24
--------
2-3)            46   24
Value:          46
Sorting Items 2->3
2-3)            46   24
Swap      :     ^i   ^j
                24   46
--------
4-6)                      92   89   84
Value:                         89
Sorting Items 4->6
4-6)                      92   89   84
Swap      :               ^i        ^j
                          84   89   92
Swap      :               ^i
                          84   89   92
After     :15   24   46   84   89   92
```

Using Quicksort

The dhQuickSort procedure, because it calls itself recursively with smaller and smaller segments of your array, must accept parameters containing the array, as well as the starting and ending points. When you start the sort, however, you'll always want to send the entire array for sorting. To work around this, the boundary parameters are optional. When it starts up, dhQuickSort checks the value of the optional intLeft and intRight parameters. If either is dhcMissing (the magic constant value, –2), the procedure knows it must use the LBound and UBound functions to determine the array boundaries.

When passing the array to dhQuickSort, you have two options. You can either pass an actual array or pass a variant that "contains" an array. To pass an actual array, use code like the following:

```
Dim avarItems(1 To 10) As Integer
' Fill in the array here
Call dhQuickSort(avarItems())
' Now, the array has been sorted.
```

To use a variant instead, write code like the following:

```
Dim varItems as Variant
' Get values into the array. For now, just use the Array
'  function, with some sample data:
varItems = Array(1, 10, 29, 37, 45)
' You could also assign an array directly to the
' variant, as in:
' varItems = avarSomeArray()
Call dhQuickSort(varItems)
```

In either case, on the return from dhQuickSort, the array you've passed in will have been sorted, and you can work with the newly arranged data.

Using a Database Engine

There's no doubt about it: if your data is already in a Microsoft Jet database table, you'll want to use Jet to retrieve your sorted data! Rather than take on any array-handling technique, simply use a query or a SQL statement to retrieve the data in the order you need. Assuming you have a column named

LastName in a table named tblCustomers, no technique for retrieving the data in a sorted fashion will be faster than using a SQL expression:

```
SELECT [LastName] FROM tblCustomers ORDER BY [LastName];
```

Of course, this technique applies to any other SQL-compliant data source as well.

The same words of wisdom can be applied to any environment that supplies its own internal sorting. If you've got data in a range in Excel, it makes no sense to copy the data into an array and then sort it. Because Excel makes sorting ranges so simple and fast, you'll want to take advantage of that technique before moving data into a VBA array. Make sure you've investigated internal tools before using VBA to sort your data—you'll almost always do better with the built-in tools.

Speed Considerations

Why choose such a complex sorting algorithm? Yes, it is somewhat daunting, and it would appear, based solely on complexity, that almost any algorithm would be better. That's not true, however. Listing 4.4 includes a simple sort, using a standard Bubblesort algorithm. This technique is easy to understand but can be quite slow in execution. The Bubblesort algorithm works its way through your array, comparing one element to the next. If the items are out of order, it swaps them. After a pass through the entire array, the largest element will have "bubbled" to the top (hence the name). After another pass, the top two elements will have bubbled up. After each pass, you can sort one less item on the next pass. The sort continues until it makes no swaps on a pass or it runs out of items to bubble up.

Listing 4.4: Simple Bubblesort Algorithm

```
Sub dhBubbleSort(varItems As Variant)
    ' Standard bubblesort.

    Dim fSorted As Boolean
    Dim intI As Integer
    Dim intJ As Integer
    Dim intItems As Integer
    Dim varTemp As Variant
```

```
    intItems = UBound(varItems)
    ' Set intI one lower than the lower bound.
    intI = LBound(varItems) - 1

    Do While (intI < intItems) And Not fSorted
        fSorted = True
        intI = intI + 1
        For intJ = 1 To intItems - intI
            If varItems(intJ) > varItems(intJ + 1) Then
                varTemp = varItems(intJ)
                varItems(intJ) = varItems(intJ + 1)
                varItems(intJ + 1) = varTemp
                fSorted = False
            End If
        Next intJ
    Loop
End Sub
```

Yes, the code is much simpler than that used by the Quicksort algorithm. How do they compare? The TestSortTimes procedure, in TESTPROCS.BAS, calls both routines, comparing the results. The test routine creates an array of random numbers and calls each sort procedure. Then it creates an array of ordered numbers (that is, an array that's sorted already) and calls both sorting procedures. The following table shows sample results for 2000 items. (All times are in milliseconds, for a single iteration of the sort, and all measurements were taken on a Pentium Pro 200 mHz processor, with 64 meg of memory).

Array Order	Quicksort	Bubblesort
Random	220	21000
Ordered	70	10

As you can see from the tests, Quicksort does much better than Bubblesort for random numbers. On the other hand, Bubblesort takes great advantage of pre-ordered arrays and outperforms Quicksort on the sorted array.

How does array size affect the length of time it takes to sort the array? Comparing results for random sets of non-sorted numbers, the following table shows the outcome:

Items	Quicksort	Bubblesort
100	10	40
1000	100	4000

Items	Quicksort	Bubblesort
2000	200	21000
5000	500	140000

Impressive, isn't it? That Bubblesort algorithm simply falls apart, given more than a few hundred items to sort. The time it takes to sort is clearly exponential, based on the number of items to sort. The time Quicksort takes, on the other hand, is more or less linear with the number of items in the array it's sorting.

Which one should you choose? It depends, of course, on your data. If you're sorting ten values, it doesn't matter which one you choose. If you're sorting items that are likely in sorted order before you get them, then Bubblesort makes sense. Otherwise, you'll probably do better using the more complex, but more efficient, Quicksort.

Sorting Collections

User-defined collections add tremendous flexibility to VBA solutions. Because collections are dynamic data structures, you can add and remove items at will without worrying about redimensioning and preserving data. On the other hand, they don't lend themselves to sorting. That's too bad, because collections provide a very simple way to store and work with large numbers of items, in memory. It would be great if you could sort them as well.

What's wrong with collections? Unfortunately, there are a few crucial issues to consider. The following section reviews the basics of using collections and the problems involved in sorting them.

Working with Collections

As you add items to a collection, you must provide a value, and you often use a unique string value (known as the *key*) to identify the collection item. For example, when you open a form in Microsoft Access, under the covers Access adds the form object to the Forms collection and uses the form's name as its unique identifier. Therefore, you can use either of the following techniques:

```
Forms(1)
' or
Forms("frmTest")
```

to retrieve the collection object (a reference to the form).

For Access forms, you can always retrieve the unique identifier; simply examine the Name property of the form. For user-defined collections, however, this isn't possible. For reasons unknown, you cannot retrieve the key for a given item in a user-created collection. This one missing piece of functionality makes it difficult, if not impossible, to perform any sort of manipulation with collection elements. Weird, isn't it? You can use the key to help you find the item, but if you have an item, you can't find the key. Wouldn't it be great if you could add items and their unique keys to a collection and then iterate through the collection in sorted key order? It would be great, but you can't—VBA provides no way to sort the collection by key, and you can't even retrieve the key to do it yourself.

Why does this prevent you from sorting a collection yourself? Sorting requires moving an element from one place to another. That means copying an item into a temporary location, removing it from the collection, and then copying it into the new location. But you can't do this with collection items; because you can't retrieve the key, any attempt to move an item will cause you to lose its unique identifier!

This means that ordinary sorting techniques, which require you to swap elements, won't work. We've provided an alternative here, and with enough creativity, you'll probably be able to think of a few more on your own. The simplest way to sort a collection is to sort the items as you add them to the collection (that is, keep the collection sorted at all times). The next few sections discuss this method in detail.

Sorting as You Insert

One possible solution to sorting a collection is simple: just maintain it sorted. That is, as you add each item to the collection, make sure you insert it at the correct location. Performing the insertion is simple because VBA allows you to provide a location (or a unique string key value) before which you want to insert the item.

The dhAddToSortedCollection procedure, in Listing 4.5 (from SORTCOL.BAS), allows you to add items to a collection, maintaining the sorted order of the collection as you add the items. The next few paragraphs explain how dhAddToSorted-Collection does its work.

Listing 4.5: Use dhAddToSortedCollection to Keep the Collection Sorted at All Times

```
Function dhAddToSortedCollection(col As Collection, _
 varNewItem As Variant, Optional strKey As String = "") _
 As Boolean
```

```
        ' Add a value (and its associated key, if requested)
        ' to a collection.

        On Error GoTo HandleErrors

        Dim varItem As Variant
        Dim intI As Integer
        Dim fAdded As Boolean
        Dim fUseKey As Boolean

        fUseKey = (Len(strKey) > 0)

        ' On the first time through here, this loop
        ' will just do nothing at all.
        For intI = 1 To col.Count
            If varNewItem < col.Item(intI) Then
                If fUseKey Then
                    col.Add varNewItem, strKey, intI
                Else
                    col.Add varNewItem, , intI
                End If
                fAdded = True
                Exit For
            End If
        Next intI
        ' If the item hasn't been added, either because
        ' it goes past the end of the current list of items
        ' or because there aren't currently any items to loop
        ' through, just add the item at the end of the
        ' collection.
        If Not fAdded Then
            If fUseKey Then
                col.Add varNewItem, strKey
            Else
                col.Add varNewItem
            End If
        End If
        dhAddToSortedCollection = True

ExitHere:
    Exit Function

HandleErrors:
    dhAddToSortedCollection = False
    Select Case Err.Number
```

```
        Case dhcErrKeyInUse
            ' This is the only likely error.

        Case Else
            ' Do nothing. Just bubble the error
            ' back up to the caller.
    End Select
    Resume ExitHere
End Function
```

The first step in the procedure is to determine whether the caller has provided a unique key value:

```
fUseKey = (Len(strKey) > 0)
```

If so, the code later in the procedure will know to supply the key to the Add method of the collection object.

The next chunk of the procedure attempts to find the correct location into which to insert the new item. The code looks at each of the values in the collection, and if the value to be added is less than the current collection item, you've found the right place to insert the new item. If you supplied a unique key value, the code calls the Add method of the collection, passing in the new item, the key, and the location before which to insert. If not, it passes only the new item and the location. Once it's inserted the value, it sets a flag so later code can tell that the insertion has been performed and then exits the loop.

```
For intI = 1 To col.Count
    If varNewItem < col.Item(intI) Then
        If fUseKey Then
            col.Add varNewItem, strKey, intI
        Else
            col.Add varNewItem, , intI
        End If
        fAdded = True
        Exit For
    End If
Next intI
```

Once you're past the end of the loop, there are two reasons why the loop may have ended: either the item was inserted and the code jumped out of the loop or the item wasn't inserted and the loop terminated on its own. In the latter case, the fAdded flag will be False, and the following chunk of code can then just add the item to the collection. You should get into this situation only if you need to add the new item to the end of the collection—that is, if the value was greater than any existing item or if there was nothing in the collection to start with.

```
If Not fAdded Then
    If fUseKey Then
        col.Add varNewItem, strKey
    Else
        col.Add varNewItem
    End If
End If
```

Why the error handler? That is, what can go wrong? The most likely error is that which would occur if you tried to add two elements with the same unique key. If you attempted this, the function would raise error 457, "This key is already associated with an element of this collection". The calling code would have to deal with the error.

What's wrong with this technique? First of all, it's quite slow. It *has* to be, of course, because it's comparing the new item against, on average, half of the existing items in the collection. This means that to insert 20 items into a collection, you'll perform several hundred comparisons. Each of those comparisons is expensive.

Second, because the code is performing simple comparisons between values, you can use only simple datatypes (strings, numbers, and so on) in the collection. If you want to use this technique with more complex collections, you'll need to modify the code to support more complex comparisons. Because you're most likely to use this technique with simple collections, we've left that alteration for your own exploration.

Searching

If you've got sorted data, most likely you need to be able to find any particular item in your data set. As with sorting, searching is an entire branch of computer science, and a full discussion is beyond our intent. On the other hand, you won't find as many searching algorithms as you will for sorting. Therefore, we actually come closer here, in the coverage of a single search method, to discussing all the possibilities (Nothing like narrowing the margins.) In this section, you'll learn about the Binary Search algorithm and how you can apply it to data stored in an array.

Why Use the Binary Search?

Imagine you've picked up a phone book to find the number for the local outlet of the Vegetarian Pizza Kitchen. You could, of course, start at the first name in the phone book, working through the listings one at a time. This might take you a while, considering there are most likely several hundred thousand entries, and you've got to work your way all the way to *V*.

The intelligent phone book user would, of course, look for the *V* entries and go from there. Imagine for a moment that the phone book didn't have letter dividers at all and that you had to scan the entries on a page to know where you were in the book. Now, how could you find the Vegetarian Pizza Kitchen in the fastest way possible? Most likely, you'd put your finger in the middle of the book, see that the *V* entries were later in the book, and discard everything before the location of your finger. Then, taking the second half of the book, you'd check halfway through the pages and decide whether the *V* entries were in the first or second half of the remainder of the book. You might continue in this fashion, breaking the book into smaller and smaller chunks, until you found your entry.

Considering that your phone book might contain 1000 pages, you threw away 500 possible pages on the first attempt and 250 more on the second. Not bad for two stops! Because the formal Binary Search algorithm works just like this "finger walking," it should be clear to you why Binary Search is very fast for large sets of values: on each lookup, you discard 50 percent of the possible values, until you center in on the location you need. As a matter of fact, the Binary Search algorithm will generally require only $\log_2 n$ lookups if n is the number of items to be searched. This means that for 1000 items, you shouldn't have to look at more than 10 items before you've either found your item or convinced yourself it's not there. (For logarithm-challenged readers, 2 to the 10th power is 1024, so $\log_2 1000$ is just a little less than 10.) The wonderful part of logarithmic growth is that if you double the number of items you have to look through, you will need to, in general, make only one more choice along the way to finding your particular item.

> **NOTE** If you missed this point in the example, don't miss it now: a binary search can work only if the data it's searching through has already been sorted. If you want to use this technique, you'll need to ensure that your data has been sorted, by one means or another, before you use a binary search.

How Does Binary Search Work?

There actually is no single formal Binary Search algorithm; there are many. The code you get depends on whom you ask. In this book, the algorithm you'll find works as follows:

1. Start with a *sorted* array and a value to be found.

2. Set upper and lower limits for the search.

3. While the lower bound is less than the upper bound:

    a. Calculate the middle position of the remaining array.

    b. If the value you're seeking is greater than the middle value, adjust the lower limit; otherwise, adjust the upper limit accordingly.

4. If the item at the lower position is the value you were searching for, return the position index. Otherwise, return a value indicating that the item wasn't found.

The entire dhBinarySearch procedure, implementing the Binary Search algorithm, is shown in Listing 4.6.

Listing 4.6: Use dhBinarySearch to Find a Value in a Sorted Array

```
Function dhBinarySearch(varItems As Variant, _
 varSought As Variant) As Integer

    Dim intLower As Integer
    Dim intMiddle As Integer
    Dim intUpper As Integer

    intLower = LBound(varItems)
    intUpper = UBound(varItems)
    Do While intLower < intUpper
        ' Increase lower and decrease upper boundary,
        ' keeping varSought in range, if it's there at all.
        intMiddle = (intLower + intUpper) \ 2
        If varSought > varItems(intMiddle) Then
            intLower = intMiddle + 1
        Else
            intUpper = intMiddle
        End If
```

```
      Loop
      If varItems(intLower) = varSought Then
          dhBinarySearch = intLower
      Else
          dhBinarySearch = -1
      End If
End Function
```

To fully explain the binary search algorithm, the following series of steps uses the same ten-element array that was used previously in the discussion of the Quicksort algorithm. In this case, the examples attempt to locate a specific number within the array. In the first example, shown in Figure 4.10, the search succeeds. In the second, shown in Figure 4.11, the search fails.

FIGURE 4.10

Use Binary Search to locate a value in the array.

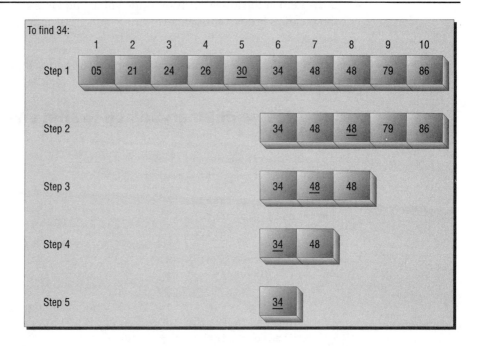

The following set of steps works through the details of the Binary Search algorithm, using the code in dhBinarySearch. In this case, the code is scanning the array shown in step 1 of Figure 4.10, looking for the value 34.

FIGURE 4.11

Binary Search fails for an item not in the array.

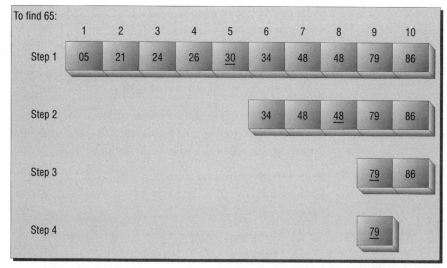

NOTE

In these examples, we'll use the same terminology as in the Quicksort example: to indicate the value in the array at location x, we'll use "x^". If the value of the array varItems at position 5 is 12 (that is, varItems(5) = 12) and the variable x contains the value 5, then x^ is the value 12.

1. Given the array, set the search bounds to be the upper and lower bounds of the array:

```
intLower = LBound(varItems)
intUpper = UBound(varItems)
```

If intLower is less than intUpper (and it is), set intMiddle to be the average of the two:

```
intMiddle = (intLower + intUpper) \ 2
```

Because varSought (34) is greater than intMiddle^ (30), set intLower to be intMiddle + 1 (6):

```
If varSought > varItems(intMiddle) Then
    intLower = intMiddle + 1
Else
    intUpper = intMiddle
End If
```

2. Since intLower (6) is still less than intUpper (10), set intMiddle to be the average of the two (8). Because varSought is less than intMiddle^ (48), set intUpper to be the same as intMiddle.

3. Since intLower (6) is still less than intUpper (8), set intMiddle to bc the average of the two (7). Because varSought is less than intMiddle^ (48), set intUpper to be the same as intMiddle.

4. Since intLower (6) is still less than intUpper (7), set intMiddle to be the average of the two (6). Because varSought (34) isn't greater than intMiddle^ (34), set intUpper to be the same as intMiddle.

5. Since intLower (6) is no longer less than intUpper (6), drop out of the loop. Because intLower^ is the same as varSought, return intLower as the return value of the function:

```
If varItems(intLower) = varSought Then
    dhBinarySearch = intLower
Else
    dhBinarySearch = -1
End If
```

> **NOTE**
>
> It's quite possible that at just this moment, you've determined for yourself that you could have found the 34 in the sample array in the same, if not fewer, steps by simply starting at the beginning and scanning the elements one by one. For small sets of data, you're right—it's almost always faster to just scan the data, looking for the item you need. But this was just an example; you wouldn't normally bother with a binary search for ten numbers. If you start working with sets of values with 100 or more elements, you'll see a marked speed difference between a linear search and a binary search.

What happens when a binary search fails? The following set of steps, corresponding to the example shown in Figure 4.11, demonstrates what happens as you search for the value 65 in an array that doesn't contain it.

1. Given the array, set the search bounds to be the upper and lower bounds of the array:

```
intLower = LBound(varItems)
intUpper = UBound(varItems)
```

If intLower is less than intUpper (and it is), set intMiddle to be the average of the two:

```
intMiddle = (intLower + intUpper) \ 2
```

Because varSought (65) is greater than intMiddle^ (30), set intLower to be intMiddle + 1 (6):

```
If varSought > varItems(intMiddle) Then
    intLower = intMiddle + 1
Else
    intUpper = intMiddle
End If
```

2. Since intLower (6)is still less than intUpper (10), set intMiddle to be the average of the two (8). Because varSought is greater than intMiddle^ (48), set intLower to be intMiddle + 1 (9).

3. Since intLower (9) is still less than intUpper (10), set intMiddle to be the average of the two (9). Because varSought is greater than intMiddle^ (48), set intUpper to be the same as intMiddle (9).

4. Since intLower (9) is no longer less than intUpper (9), drop out of the loop. Because intLower^ is not the item being sought, return –1, indicating that the search failed.

Still not convinced that a binary search is better than a linear search? What if you were to put all the numbers between 1 and 1000 into an array and attempt to find a value near the beginning, one near the end, one in the middle, and a value that's not there, using both a binary and a linear search to compare the timings? The procedure CompareSearch, from the TESTPROCS.BAS module, takes these steps for you. The dhLinearSearch function (from LINEARSRCH.BAS), shown in Listing 4.7, provides a search that starts at the first element of an array, compares each item in turn to the sought value, and exits as soon as it finds a match. If it doesn't find a match, of course, it will end up visiting each element of the array.

Listing 4.7: Linear Search Provides the Slowest Possible Way to Find a Value in an Array

```
Function dhLinearSearch(varItems As Variant, _
 varSought As Variant) As Integer
    ' An alternative to the binary search, use a linear
    ' search to find a value in an array.
```

```
        Dim intPos As Integer
        Dim fFound As Boolean

        fFound = False
        For intPos = LBound(varItems) To UBound(varItems)
            If varSought = varItems(intPos) Then
                fFound = True
                Exit For
            End If
        Next intPos
        If fFound Then
            dhLinearSearch = intPos
        Else
            dhLinearSearch = -1
        End If
    End Function
```

To compare a linear search and a binary search, the CompareSearch procedure fills an array with as many items as you request. (It assumes you want 1000 if you don't specify a size.) It then uses dhBinarySearch to find three items in the array and one that's not. CompareSearch then repeats the process using the Linear-Search function. In each case, the code attempts to find an item that's 10 percent of the way into the array, then one that's 90 percent of the way, then 50 percent, and then one that's not in the array at all. For each test, the sample runs the search 1000 times. The differences in speed are alarming, as you can see in Figure 4.12. For an array of 1000 items, to find an item that is in the middle of the array takes 40 milliseconds using a binary search and around 1100 milliseconds using a linear search—around 27 times longer using a linear search. For 10,000 items, the discrepancy is even greater. Now, a binary search takes 50 milliseconds, but a linear search takes around 11,000! Suddenly, you're looking at an operation taking 220 times as long to perform. (This comparison doesn't even mention the differences in time it takes to find an element near the end of the list. The binary search takes no longer to find a value there than at the middle of the list, but a linear search takes twice as long, of course, on average.)

Remember, for small data sets or if you cannot sort your data, using a linear search is fine. When your array contains 100 or more items, however, you'll want to convert your code to use a binary search, especially if you need to locate items often.

FIGURE 4.12

Compare a linear search to a binary search.

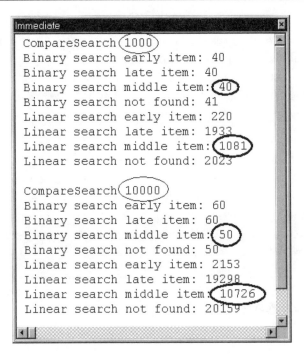

What If Your Data's in a Table?

Just as with sorting, you'll need to think hard about using these array technologies if your data is currently stored in a Microsoft Jet database table or an Excel spreadsheet. That is, you must take into account your local application. No matter how fast your sorting code is, Jet can sort faster on its own. The same goes for searching: no matter how efficiently you code your search, writing a SQL string that retrieves just the single row you need is going to be faster than loading the data into an array and using a binary search.

Therefore, think twice before using either the searching or sorting techniques presented in this chapter. If your data isn't already in an array, copying it from disk for the sole purpose of searching and sorting it may not be to your advantage. Excel, Access, and Word all supply their own tools for searching and sorting data, and you'll want to exhaust those technologies before copying data into an array and working with it there.

On the other hand, the same warning works in reverse: if you've got data in an array (or any other data structure in memory), you'll generally not want to copy it to a table or an Excel spreadsheet simply to search or sort it. By the time you write all your data to disk in order to have Jet create a recordset based on the table filled with your data, you could have long since sorted your array and been on your way. It's all a matter of perspective; learn to use the correct tool for the situation.

Using Binary Search

Calling dhBinarySearch is quite simple; you pass it the array to look in and the item to find:

> intPos = dhBinarySearch(*varArray*, *varSought*)

If the search locates *varSought* in *varArray*, it returns the position at which it found the item. If not, it returns –1.

WARNING Don't fall into the same trap we did, over and over, as we worked on this section: before you can use dhBinarySearch, the array to be searched *must be sorted.* Unless you've sorted the array, the Binary Search algorithm will return completely spurious results. If you cannot sort your data, for whatever reason, then you'll need to use dhLinearSearch instead (called in the same fashion as dhBinarySearch).

For example, the following code fragment (in TESTPROCS.BAS) builds an array of random numbers and requests the user to guess as many of the selected numbers as possible. Once the user selects an incorrect value, the procedure displays the number of correct selected values.

```
Sub SillySearch()
    Dim aintItems(1 To 100) As Integer
    Dim intI As Integer
    Dim intPos As Integer
    Dim intCount As Integer

    For intI = 1 To 100
        aintItems(intI) = Int(Rnd * 100) + 1
    Next intI
    Call dhQuickSort(aintItems)
    Do
        intI = _
         Val(InputBox("Choose a number between 1 and 100"))
        intPos = dhBinarySearch(aintItems, intI)
        If intPos > 0 Then
            intCount = intCount + 1
        End If
    Loop Until intPos < 0
    MsgBox "You guessed " & intCount & " correct values!"
End Sub
```

WARNING   Because dhBinarySearch returns −1 to indicate that it didn't find a match, you won't be able to search in arrays that have negative indexes. That is, if you must search in an array with bounds of −10 to 10, for example, you'll need to modify dhBinarySearch to return a different value that indicates failure.

TIP   Chapter 6 provides another method for searching and sorting: using a binary tree. If you're interested in pursuing other techniques, visit that chapter for more information.

Summary

We're not trying to fool anyone here—this isn't an academic study of various sorting and searching techniques. Instead, we focused on presenting specific solutions to sorting and searching problems, including:

- How to determine the relative speed of one solution over another, using the StopWatch class

- How to create and use arrays

- How the Quicksort algorithm works and how to sort an array using the Quicksort algorithm

- How to maintain a sorted collection

- How the Binary Search algorithm works and how to find an item in a sorted array using Binary Search

- How Binary Search compares to a linear search and which is best to use in differing circumstances

Armed with the dhQuickSort and dhBinarySearch procedures and an understanding of how they work and how to use them, you should be able to use the procedures to sort and search in simple arrays. You should also be able to modify the procedures to handle different kinds of data as well, should the need arise.

For more information on searching and sorting, see Chapter 6 and its discussion of dynamic data structures. For more information on retrieving system information, as you saw in the StopWatch class, see Chapter 9.

CHAPTER

FIVE

5

Using VBA Class Modules

- Exploring class modules and how they work

- Creating your own object classes

- Implementing custom properties and methods

- Establishing a hierarchy of object classes

- Creating and managing collections of objects

With the introduction of VBA in 1993, Microsoft endowed Basic developers with a new tool: class modules. While other Basic dialects (Visual Basic and Access Basic) had already introduced object-oriented constructs, class modules gave you the ability to create and manipulate your own classes of objects. If you have programmed in other object-oriented languages, such as SmallTalk or C++, you are familiar with the benefits this ability provides. If you haven't, we hope to surprise you with the power they give you as a programmer. We make heavy use of class modules in this book to do everything from implementing data structures such as linked lists to abstracting Windows API functions. This chapter explains what class modules are and how they work and provides some examples of how you can use them in your applications.

Since this chapter deals with creating your own objects, it assumes you are familiar with using objects provided by VBA or a host application. That is, you should be comfortable with concepts such as properties and methods, as well as how to declare and use object variables.

Table 5.1 lists the sample files included on the CD-ROM. You'll find all the sample code discussed in the chapter in these files.

TABLE 5.1 Sample Files

File Name	Description
TEXT1.XLS	Excel workbook containing first text file class example
TEXT.MDB	Access database containing first text file class example
TEXT1.CLS	First TextFile class module
DOCUMENT.CLS	Sample Document class
FILETST1.BAS	Test functions for first TextFile class
TEXT2.XLS	Excel workbook containing second text file class example
TEXT.MDB	Access database containing second text file class example
TEXT2.CLS	Second TextFile class module
LINE.CLS	Line class module

TABLE 5.1   Sample Files (continued)

File Name	Description
LINES.CLS	Lines collection class module
FILETST2.BAS	Test functions for second TextFile class
CLIP.XLS	Excel workbook containing clipboard class example
CLIP.MDB	Access database containing clipboard class example
CLIP.CLS	Clipboard class module
TESTCLIP.BAS	Test function for Clipboard class

TIP

Trying to understand object-oriented programming (OOP) techniques for the first time can be a daunting task. Many people find the line that distinguishes OOP from procedural programming very fine. If you fit this description, you may find it helpful to work through the examples as we present them in this chapter.

Why Use Class Modules?

If you've been developing applications or routines using Basic for any length of time, you might be asking yourself, "Why use class modules anyway? I've been getting along without them for some time." Well, like any product feature, class modules have their benefits and costs. The primary cost is the learning curve required to understand them so you can use them effectively. While many VBA programmers take working with built-in objects (such as the Debug and Err objects) for granted, they find the idea of creating their own object types difficult to comprehend. We hope that after reading this chapter, you won't feel that way.

Once you've mastered the basics of class modules, the benefits become clear. They make your code more manageable, self-documenting, and easier to maintain, especially if you deal with complex sets of related data. The sections that follow examine some reasons for using class modules.

Creating Your Own Objects

Class modules allow you to create and use your own object types in your application. Why would you want to do this? Well, imagine you want to write an application that tracks information on employees in your company. Using traditional Basic, you might create separate variables to store each employee's name, manager, and salary, among other things. If you're really clever, you might create an array of user-defined datatypes, and you might also write procedures to handle such tasks as hiring or transferring an employee or giving an employee a raise. The problem with this approach is that there is nothing inherent in the program or the language that ties together all these bits of information and processes. Figure 5.1 illustrates this situation. All the data and all the processes are free floating. It's up to you to ensure that each element is used correctly.

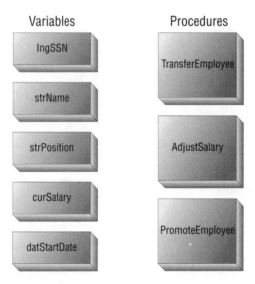

With nothing enforcing relationships among the items in Figure 5.1, chaos can result. For example, suppose two or more separate procedures modify the salary data using a particular set of rules. Changes to the rules necessitate changes to the program logic in several places.

Encapsulating these data and program components in an object makes the management task must easier. First of all, any references to data (properties) must be associated with a particular object, so you always know what "thing" it is you're operating on. Second, processes that operate on an object are defined as part of that object. In other words, the processes are defined as methods of the object. The consumer of the object (other procedures in your program) are insulated from the inner workings of each method and cannot modify properties directly unless you allow them to. This enforces some control over data that the object represents. Finally, since each property and method is defined in one place (the object type's definition), any code modifications need be implemented only once. An object's consumers will benefit automatically from the change. Figure 5.2 represents this type of object-oriented development. All data and processes are defined as part of the object, and the application program interacts with them through a central point, a reference to an *instance* of the object.

FIGURE 5.2

Managing data using object-oriented techniques

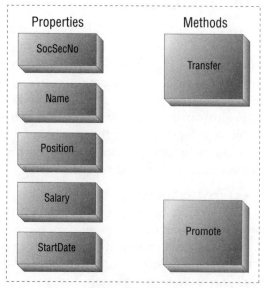

Employee Object

Is VBA Really Object-Oriented?

At this point many of you who have experience in other object-oriented languages are probably thinking, "What are they talking about? VBA isn't really object oriented!" While we concede that VBA does not exhibit some of the characteristics of a "true" object-oriented language, such as polymorphism and inheritance, we believe that it just doesn't matter. So what if VBA isn't as feature rich as C++ or SmallTalk? For most people, it's much easier to understand than those languages, and what's really important is that VBA offers a way for developers to think about applications in terms of a group of related objects, not as masses of disparate data structures.

Abstract Complex Processes

If you find the idea of encapsulating data and processes within an object compelling, you'll be even more excited about another benefit of using class modules: the ability to abstract complex processes. Suppose you are trying to create an application that manages internal purchases within an organization. Determining the amount to charge one department for goods or services received from another (called the transfer price) can be a complicated task. With traditional programming techniques, the logic for computing the transfer price might be an integral component of the application. Not only does it make the program code harder to maintain, it means you must understand the logic.

By using object-oriented techniques, on the other hand, you could create object classes for each good or service being transferred, making the transfer price computation logic part of each object class. This makes the application code easier to understand and write. You need only know that there is an object being transferred and that the object knows how to compute the transfer price. The logic for computing that price is maintained separately, perhaps by another programmer more familiar with the intricacies of transfer pricing theory.

When you create an object, you define an *interface* to that object. This isn't a user interface but a list of the object's properties, methods, and collections. This is all that users of the object (other programmers) need to know to use the object. It's then up to you to implement each feature in the object's source code using VBA class modules.

Making Development Easier

In the preceding example, another programmer was charged with the task of maintaining the transfer pricing logic encapsulated in the object being transferred. This brings up a continual challenge facing development managers: how to coordinate large, complex programming projects. Object-oriented techniques (which include using VBA class modules) can make managing projects easier. Because objects are autonomous entities that encapsulate their own data and methods, you can develop and test them independent of the overall application. Programmers can create custom objects using VBA class modules and then test them using only a small amount of generic Basic code. Once a programmer has determined that a custom object behaves as desired, you can merge it into the overall project by including the appropriate class modules.

How Class Modules Work

Have we convinced you that object-oriented techniques in general, and VBA class modules in particular, are worth learning about? If so, you're ready for this section of the chapter, which explains how VBA class modules work by discussing the difference between object classes and object instances.

Class Modules Are Cookie Cutters

VBA class modules define the properties and methods of an object but cannot, by themselves, be used to manipulate those properties. An object's definition is sometimes called an *object class*. You can think of VBA class modules, and thus object classes, as cookie cutters. A cookie cutter defines the shape of a particular cookie; it is not itself a cookie, but you need the cookie cutter to make the cookie.

In the case of VBA class modules, you define a set of properties, including their datatypes and whether they are read-only or read/write, and methods, including the datatype returned (if any) plus any parameters they might require. Figure 5.3 shows a simple example using the cookie analogy. You'll see how to add a class module to your VBA project and use it to define properties and methods in the next section.

FIGURE 5.3

An imaginary cookie class

Object Instances Are the Cookies

To make use of an object class, you must create a new instance of that class. In our analogy, object instances are the cookies. Each has the set of properties and methods defined by the class, but you can also manipulate class instances individually as real programming entities. When you create a new instance of a class, you can change its properties independent of any other instance of the same class. Figure 5.4 shows two instances of the cookie class, with various property settings.

FIGURE 5.4

Two different cookies from the same class

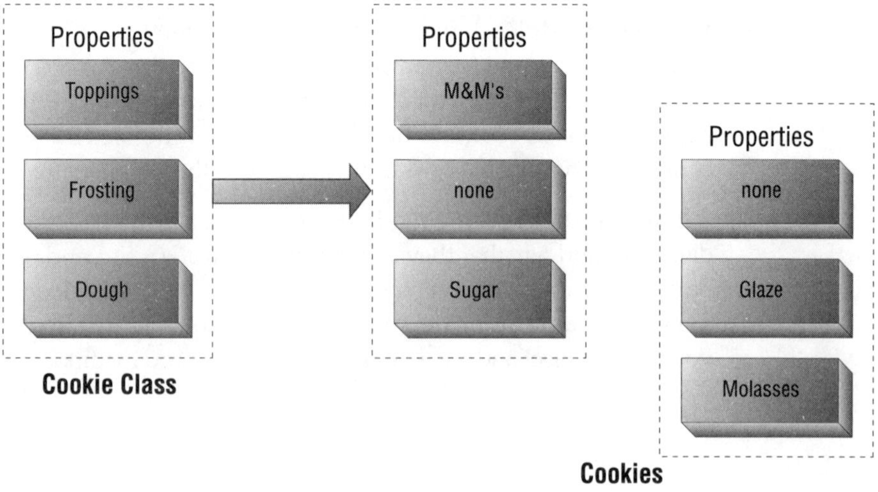

A Simple Example: A Text File Class

To demonstrate the basic techniques required to create and use class modules, this section shows you how to create a class that represents a text file. It will include properties that let you manipulate the file name and contents, as well as methods for reading and writing the contents from and to disk. Not only will this relatively simple example illustrate class module concepts, you'll find it a useful class to add to your VBA projects that must work with text files.

> **NOTE**
> You'll find the sample code for this section in TEXT1.XLS. If you don't have a copy of Microsoft Excel, look in the individual files TEXT1.CLS, DOCUMENT.CLS, and FILETST1.BAS.

Creating an Object Class

Before you can start working with your own custom objects, you must create the object class from which they will be fabricated. You do this by adding a new class module to your VBA project.

Inserting a New Class Module

To add a new class module to your VBA project, select Class Module from the Insert menu (or select Add Class Module from the Project menu, if you're using VB 5.0). VBA opens a new module window and adds a reference to the new class to the Project Explorer window. You edit class modules pretty much the same way you do normal VBA code modules. The only difference is that class modules have two events, Initialize and Terminate, associated with the creation and destruction of a class instance. (See the section "The Initialize and Terminate Events" later in this chapter.)

Naming Your Class

All VBA class modules have a Name property that is integral to the definition of an object class: it determines the class name. To name a class module, select the class module's code window or its reference in the Project Explorer window and open the Properties window. Set the Name property, being sure to assign the name you want to use in any VBA programs that use the class. Figure 5.5 shows the Properties window for one of the classes introduced in this chapter.

FIGURE 5.5

Setting the Name property of a class module

> **NOTE**
>
> The two other class properties shown in Figure 5.5, Instancing and Public, appear in the Properties window if you use Visual Basic. These properties are used in Visual Basic programs that act as OLE servers—a topic not discussed in this book.

While we are strong proponents of using sometimes obscure naming conventions with internal names and variables, you should choose a name for your class that is easily understood and that identifies the "thing" the object class represents. Typically, developers choose English words in the singular form (such as Application, or Employee). Capital letters distinguish word breaks within an object class name (for example, DrawingObject). For our example, we've created a class named TextFile. Refer to the objects provided by the VBA host application you use for more ideas on what makes for a good object class name.

Creating a Property

Most objects have at least one property. Properties store values representing characteristics of the object. While we have seen objects that implement methods for setting and returning values, we don't recommend this approach; methods are normally used to symbolize actions an object takes.

There are two ways to create a property. The simplest approach is to create a Public variable in the declarations section of the class module. (For the second approach, see the section "Using Property Statements" later in this chapter.) Consumers of your object will then be able to set and retrieve a value stored in that variable. (In other words, the property is read/write.) The variable's name determines the name of the property used by other parts of your program so, as with class names, choose something with symbolic or literal meaning.

While using Public variables to define properties is the simplest approach, it does have one major drawback: your class has no way of knowing when an outside process has changed the value of the property. This may be critical to your object for, say, restricting values to a given range or taking other actions in response to a change in value. To meet these needs, you'll have to use Property procedures, a topic discussed in the section "Using Property Statements" later in this chapter.

Creating a Method

Just as declaring a Public variable creates a property, declaring a Public procedure creates a method. You can create Public functions and Public subs, the only difference being that a Public function can return a value to the calling process. Our class implements, among other things, a FileOpen method that carries out the task of opening the file specified by the Path property of the class. Listing 5.1 shows the VBA code that makes up the FileOpen method.

> **NOTE** We would have liked simply to call our method Open, but this conflicted with a reserved word of our host application, Visual Basic. You may find that VBA reports a syntax error when declaring methods or properties. In these cases, make sure you haven't inadvertently used a reserved word, and change the method or property name if necessary.

Listing 5.1: FileOpen Method of the TextFile Class

```
Public Function FileOpen()
    On Error GoTo HandleError

    ' If a file is already open, close it
    If Me.IsOpen Then
        Me.FileClose
    End If

    ' Get next available file handle
    mhFile = FreeFile

    ' Open file based on file open mode property
    Select Case Me.OpenMode
        Case tfOpenReadOnly
            Open Me.Path For Binary Access Read As mhFile
        Case tfOpenReadWrite
            Open Me.Path For Binary Access Read Write As mhFile
        Case tfOpenAppend
            Open Me.Path For Append Access Read Write As mhFile
        Case tfOpenReadOnlyExists
            Open Me.Path For Input Access Read As mhFile
    End Select

' Set IsOpen property variable and return value
    mfIsOpen = True
    FileOpen = True

    ' Read first line into buffer
    Me.ReadNext
ExitProc:
    Exit Function
HandleError:
    FileOpen = False
    Resume ExitProc
End Function
```

While the code shown in Listing 5.1 is not earth shattering by any standard (it uses low-level file I/O functions that have been around for years), you should be able to see the benefits of encapsulating the code in a class. You no longer have to remember all the various forms of the Open statement. All you need to do is set the object's Path and OpenMode properties (using the constants defined in the declarations section of the class) and call its FileOpen method. The code encapsulated in the class does the rest, including error handling!

One item of note in Listing 5.1 is the use of the reserved word Me (for example, Select Case Me.OpenMode). You use Me in class modules to refer to the current instance of that class. You may already be used to using Me in Visual Basic and Access form modules. Generic class modules extend the use of Me and allow you to use it to access an object's properties and methods from other procedures in the same class module. While you could refer to variables or procedures directly, using Me lets you use the same object-oriented coding style that external consumers of your object use.

Using the Object Class

Once you've defined a class and given it a few properties and methods, you can use it in other VBA procedures. The first step in using a class is creating a new instance of the class (or cutting a new cookie, in our earlier analogy).

Creating New Class Instances

To create a new class instance, declare an object variable based on the class. You'll use it to store a reference to a new class instance. Variables referencing custom classes adhere to the same rules as those referencing VBA or host application objects. You can declare them using the Dim, Private, Public, or Global reserved word. For example, the following code fragment declares a variable called objFile:

```
Dim objFile As TextFile
```

Note that the datatype in this example is the class name we defined earlier.

The next step is to create a new instance of the object and store a reference to it in the variable. To do this, you use the Set statement in conjunction with the New keyword, as in:

```
Set objFile = New TextFile
```

Although the syntax might seem redundant, you must use the New keyword in the Set statement to create a new instance of the object. If you don't, VBA will generate an "Object variable or With block variable not set" run-time error if you try to use any of the properties or methods of the class. Simply declaring an object variable with a Dim statement is not enough to create a new object instance.

If you want to create a new instance along with the variable declaration, you can make the New keyword part of the declaration itself. For example:

```
Dim objFile As New TextFile
```

Immediately after declaring an object variable in this manner, you can start using the object's properties and methods without first using Set.

So why choose one technique over the other? The answer depends on when you wish the new instance of the object to be created. In the first example, VBA does not create a new instance of the TextFile object until it processes the Set statement. If this statement is never executed, the new instance is never created. Alternatively, in the second example, VBA creates a new instance of the TextFile object as soon as you use one of the object's properties or methods. While the second approach is more convenient —requiring one line of code to create the new instance instead of two—it is not always clear which statement caused VBA to create the new instance.

Using Properties and Methods

Once you've got a variable storing a reference to a new class instance, you can use the properties and methods defined by the class module. Listing 5.2 shows some sample code that uses the TextFile class to open a file (we've used AUTOEXEC.BAT in this case because it's on most people's PCs) and print each line using the properties (Path, EOF, Text) and methods (FileOpen, ReadNext, FileClose) of the class.

NOTE   Although we have not included full listings of class modules in this chapter, you can find them in the VBA projects on the accompanying CD-ROM.

Listing 5.2: Print a File's Contents Using the TextFile Class

```
' Create new instance of TextFile class
Set objFile = New TextFile

' Set the Path property
objFile.Path = "C:\AUTOEXEC.BAT"

' Try to open the file--if successful,
' read until the end of the file,
' printing each line
If objFile.FileOpen() Then
    Do Until objFile.EOF
```

```
        Debug.Print objFile.Text
        objFile.ReadNext
    Loop
    objFile.FileClose
End If

' Destroy class instance
Set objFile = Nothing
```

Now, isn't this code better than including the low-level I/O routines themselves in your code? In fact, if you've used Data Access Objects in VB, Access, or VBA, the code should look very familiar. It's similar to the way you manipulate database data using Recordset objects.

So What Have We Done?

The few lines of code in Listing 5.2 have accomplished a number of things. First, the code created a new instance of the object and stored a reference to it in the object variable objFile. Then it used the reference to call the object's properties and methods.

NOTE The reference stored would be called a *pointer* in other languages, such as Pascal and C++. A pointer is an integer that holds the memory address of another piece of data. In other words, it *points to* the other piece of data. VBA doesn't expose the actual value of the pointer, as other languages do, but you don't really need it. All you need to know is that it points to some object you've defined and that you can use it to access that object's properties and methods. We use the terms *pointer* and *reference* interchangeably in this chapter to refer to the contents of an object variable.

One important point to remember is that you can have more than one pointer to the same object. As long as an object has at least one pointer to it, VBA will keep it in memory. For example, the code in Listing 5.3 demonstrates how you can create two pointers to the same object by setting a second pointer variable equal to the first. You can tell whether two pointers refer to the same object by using the Is operator in a conditional statement.

Listing 5.3: Create Multiple Pointers to the Same Class Instance

```
Dim objFirst As TextFile
Dim objSecond As TextFile

' Create new instance of TextFile class
Set objFirst = New TextFile

' Create a second pointer to the new instance
Set objSecond = objFirst

' Compare the two pointers
If objFirst Is objSecond Then
    ' Both pointers refer to same object
End If
```

In a sense, VBA keeps the object alive until nothing points to it—until it is no longer needed. When does this happen? It can happen when the object variable pointing to the object goes out of scope. You can also explicitly break the connection between a pointer and the object it points to by setting the pointer variable to the intrinsic constant Nothing. That's what we did in Listing 4.2. While this was unnecessary since our pointer was local in scope, it is good programming style to explicitly release objects you no longer need rather than rely on the rules of variable scope to do it for you.

The Initialize and Terminate Events

It is important to consider when an object instance is created and destroyed because you have the opportunity to run VBA code in response to each event. Unlike regular VBA modules that have no events, class modules have Initialize and Terminate events that are triggered, respectively, when an instance of the class is first created and when the last pointer to it is released or destroyed. You can use the Initialize event to do such things as setting default property values and creating references to other objects. Use the Terminate event to perform cleanup tasks.

Listing 5.4 shows the Initialize and Terminate event code for the TextFile class. During processing of the Initialize event, the code sets the default open mode property. In the Terminate event, the code checks to see whether a file is still open (if you have not explicitly called the FileClose method) and then closes it. If you want a more graphical example of when these events are triggered, trying inserting a MsgBox statement in each and watching what happens as you use instances of the class.

Listing 5.4: TextFile's Initialize and Terminate Events

```
Private Sub Class_Initialize()
    ' Set default file open mode property
    Me.OpenMode = tfOpenReadOnlyExists
End Sub

Private Sub Class_Terminate()
    ' If a file is still open then close it
    ' before terminating
    If Me.IsOpen Then
        Me.FileClose
    End If
End Sub
```

Using Class Modules in Microsoft Access 95

If you use Microsoft Access 95 as your primary development platform, you will be discouraged to learn that it does not fully support VBA class modules the way the other Office products and Visual Basic do. You cannot create separate class modules in Microsoft Access 95. (Microsoft did add full class module support in Access 97, however.) Instead, you must use the modules that are part of Access forms and reports.

Access forms and reports, like VBA class modules, can have exposed custom properties and methods, and they allow for multiple instancing. In fact, the rules for defining properties and methods are the same for Access form and report modules as they are for VBA class modules. Using Access forms and reports as classes, however, differs slightly.

First, VBA automatically adds the text "Form_" or "Report_" to the beginning of the form or report's name to create the class name used to declare pointer variables. For example, to create a new instance of a form named frmTextFile, you would use code like this:

```
Dim objFile As Form_frmTextFile
Set objFile = New Form_frmTextFile
```

Second, form and report modules do not have Initialize and Terminate events, which VBA class modules do. If you need to perform startup and shutdown tasks, use the Load and Close events.

Finally, creating a new instance of an Access form or report module creates a new instance of the form or report object. Access adds it to the appropriate collection (Forms or Reports), so beware of any existing code that manipulates this collection. (You'll find a discussion of collections later in this chapter.) Although it initially loads hidden, it will show up in the Unhide dialog unless you set its Popup property (for forms only) to Yes.

This makes using object-oriented techniques in Access 95 a bit more challenging than with other tools. If you really want seamless VBA class module support, you should consider upgrading to Access 97.

Using Property Statements

You now know the basic techniques for creating and using class modules in VBA. If you've looked at the complete source code for the sample TextFile class, however, you will have noticed some things that we've not yet discussed. The remainder of this chapter is devoted to more advanced class module techniques, beginning with the second way to implement custom properties, Property Statements.

What Are Property Statements, and Why Use Them?

You've already seen how to implement properties simply by declaring a Public variable in the declarations section of a class module. Consumers of your class can then reference that property using the syntax *object.property*. We also mentioned that the one major drawback to this approach is that your class has no way of knowing when the value of the property has changed. Property statements solve this problem. *Property statements* are VBA procedures that are executed when a property is set or retrieved. During the processing of a Property statement, you can take action regarding the property.

Property statements come in three varieties: Property Get, Property Let, and Property Set. Property Get statements retrieve (or get) the values of class instance properties. Property Let and Property Set statements, on the other hand, set the values of properties. The distinction between the two is that Property Let is used for scalar values (Integer, String, and so on), while Property Set is used for object datatypes. The sections that follow explain each of these in detail.

Retrieving Values with Property Get

The Property Get statement is probably the easiest of the three types of Property statements to understand. In its basic form, it consists of a declaration, which includes the property name and datatype, and a body, just like a normal function. It's up to you to return a property value by setting the statement name equal to the return value. For example, the following code is the Property Get statement for the Path property of the sample class:

```
Property Get Path() As String
    ' Return the path of the file from the
    ' Private class variable
    Path = mstrPath
End Property
```

The name of the Property statement, Path, defines the property name, and the return type (String, in this case) defines the property's datatype. When another procedure references the property using code like this:

```
Debug.Print objFile.Path
```

VBA calls the procedure, and the value of a Private class module variable (mstrPath) is returned. Of course, you can do anything within a Property procedure that you can within any VBA procedure (such as perform a calculation or query a database), so how you arrive at the value to be returned is completely up to you.

TIP

Use this technique when you want to control how a program sets and retrieves property values: declare a Private variable in the class module's declarations section to store the property value internally within the class. Then implement Property statements to set and/or retrieve its value. While this may at first seem like more trouble than it's worth, it leaves the door open for taking additional actions when retrieving a property value.

Going beyond the simple example shown above, you can create Property Get statements that accept arguments. Property statement arguments are declared just like arguments of normal VBA procedures. You could use parameters to implement multi-valued properties. For example, suppose your application required you to compute weekly payroll dates. You might create a class with a PayDay property that accepts a week number and returns the associated payroll date. The declaration of that property might look like this:

```
Property Get PayDay(ByVal intWeek As Integer) As Date
    ' Compute the appropriate payroll date
    PayDay = datSomeDate
End Property
```

Your program could then access the property by passing the arguments inside parentheses, after the property name:

```
datPayDay = objPayRoll.PayDay(12)
```

Setting Values with Property Let

The counterpart to Property Get is Property Let. You create Property Let statements to allow consumers of your object to change the value of a property. Listing 5.5 shows the Property Let statement for the Path property of the sample class.

Listing 5.5: Property Let Statement for the Path Property

```
Property Let Path(ByVal strPath As String)
    ' Set the path property of the file--
    ' If a file is already open, close it
    If Me.IsOpen Then
        Me.FileClose
    End If
    mstrPath = strPath
End Property
```

Notice that the code in Listing 5.5 uses the same name (Path) as the Property Get statement. Property procedures are the only VBA procedures that can have the same name within a single module. Notice also the argument to the procedure, strPath. VBA passes the value set by the object's consumer in this argument. For example, if another VBA procedure used a statement like this:

```
objFile.Path = "C:\AUTOEXEC.BAT"
```

VBA would pass the string "C:\AUTOEXEC.BAT" to the Property procedure in the strPath argument.

Like Property Get statements, Property Let statements can accept additional parameters. In this case, the last argument in the list is the property value set by the calling procedure. Continuing the above example, suppose your VBA program allowed procedures to set the payday of a given week. Your Property Let statement might look like this:

```
Property Let PayDay(ByVal intWeek As Integer, _
 ByVal datPayDay As Date)
    ' Change the appropriate payroll date
End Property
```

You could then set the property value using code like this:

```
objPayRoll.PayDay(12) = #3/22/97#
```

The date value (in this case, March 22, 1997) is passed to the Property procedure in the last argument, datPayDay. The week number is passed to the procedure in intWeek.

TIP
> You need not have Property Get and Property Let procedures for each property you wish to implement. By defining only a Property Get procedure, you create, in effect, a read-only property—one that can be retrieved but not set. Likewise, defining only a Property Let procedure produces a write-only property. We make heavy use of read-only properties in our sample TextFile class. While consumers of the class can't set the value of read-only properties, procedures inside the class can, by writing directly to the Private variables that store the property values.

Dealing with Object Properties

The Property Set statement, designed to let you create object properties, is a variation of the Property Let statement. *Object properties* are properties that are themselves pointers to objects, rather than scalar values. For example, suppose you wanted to create a property of one class that was itself a pointer to an instance of another class. You would need to define a Property Set statement to allow consumers of the first class to set the property value.

The code in Listing 5.6 defines a Property Set statement called SaveFile that might be part of a class representing text documents. The class stores a pointer to the TextFile object used for persistent storage of the document's contents.

Listing 5.6: Property Set Statement for an Object Property, SaveFile

```
' Private variable used to store a reference
' to the TextFile object associated with this class
Private mobjSaveFile As TextFile

Property Set SaveFile(objFile As TextFile)
    ' Make the private class variable point
    ' to the TextFile object passed to the procedure
    Set mobjSaveFile = objFile
End Property
```

VBA procedures could then set the pointer defined by the SaveFile property to point to another instance of the TextFile class. (Note the use of the Set reserved word.)

```
Set objDoc.SaveFile = New TextFile
```

Once the reference has been established, the procedure could then manipulate properties and call methods of the TextFile object pointed to by the document object's SaveFile property:

```
objDoc.SaveFile.Path = "C:\AUTOEXEC.BAT"
objDoc.SaveFile.FileOpen
```

At this point you might be wondering, "If I use Property Set to set the value of an object property, how do I retrieve its value?" As it turns out, you can use Property Get procedures for both scalar values and object pointers. You just need to declare the return value as an object datatype. For instance, if you wanted to write the corresponding Property Get statement for the SaveFile property, it might look like this:

```
Property Get SaveFile() As TextFile
    ' Return the pointer contained in the
    ' private class variable
    Set SaveFile = mobjSaveFile
End Property
```

Again, notice the use of the Set reserved word in all assignment statements involving object pointers.

Advanced Class Module Techniques

Now that you've been exposed to the basic principles behind creating and using VBA class modules, it's time to explore some advanced techniques. This section looks at these topics:

- Building class hierarchies

- Creating a Parent property for objects

- Using self-referencing classes

- Implementing collections of objects

- Wrapping Windows API functions in a class hierarchy

The examples throughout this book use class modules in a variety of roles, but by the end of this chapter, you should have enough information to start using class modules to solve your own particular problems.

> **NOTE**   You'll find the sample code for this section in TEXT1.XLS. If you don't have a copy of Microsoft Excel, look in the individual files TEXT2.CLS, LINE.CLS, LINES.CLS, and FILETST2.BAS.

Object Hierarchies

Almost always, when you model an application using object-oriented techniques, you discover relationships between object classes. An *object model* is a graphical depiction of these relationships. Usually, a natural hierarchy is formed by object relationships. Consider the diagram in Figure 5.6, which is the object model for a fictitious accounting application.

FIGURE 5.6

Object model for a
fictitious accounting
application

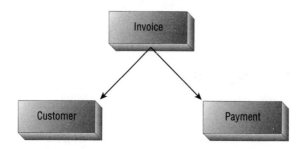

You can see from Figure 5.6 that a relationship exists between invoice and customer and between invoice and payment. It is generally a good idea to create a sketch like the one in Figure 5.6 before beginning to program an application. It makes it very clear what object classes exist and how they relate to one another.

Once you have an object model that represents your application, you can begin constructing class modules—one for each object in the diagram. To represent relationships between objects, declare pointers to child objects in the declarations section of the parent class module. For example, to model the relationship between invoice and customer (assuming classes named Invoice and Customer, respectively), you would declare a Customer variable in the declarations section of the Invoice class:

```
Public Customer As New Customer
```

Note that you can, in fact, declare an object variable with the same name as the class it's based on. When you create a new instance of an invoice, a new instance of the Customer class is automatically created as well. You can then use the invoice object to set properties of the customer instance, as the following code fragment demonstrates:

```
Dim objInvoice As Invoice

Set objInvoice = New Invoice
Set objInvoice.Customer.FirstName = "Jane"
Set objInvoice.Customer.LastName = "Smith"
' and so on...
```

The ability to create object hierarchies using class-level pointer variables is an extremely powerful feature of VBA. It lets you develop and test objects, like the

Customer object in this example, separately and then assemble them into a robust, object-oriented representation of your application.

NOTE

The technique just described works great for one-to-one relationships, but what about one-to-many? For example, what if an invoice could have a number of customers associated with it? In this situation, you need to use a collection, as discussed later in this chapter.

Creating a Parent Property

In many object models, objects within the hierarchy implement a Parent property that contains a pointer to the instance of the object immediately above it in the hierarchy. This makes it convenient to traverse the hierarchy using VBA code. For example, Excel Worksheet objects have a Parent property that points to the Workbook object in which the worksheets are contained.

You can implement a Parent property in your own classes by creating Property Set and Property Get procedures. For example, suppose you want to be able to reference the Document object from the TextFile object it contains. Listing 5.7 shows you how to do this.

Listing 5.7: Implement a Parent Property

```
' Private variable to store pointer to parent
Private mobjParent As Document

Property Set Parent(objParent As Document)
    ' If property hasn't been set yet, do so
    If mobjParent Is Nothing Then
        Set mobjParent = objParent
    End If
End Property

Property Get Parent() As Document
    ' Return the pointer stored in mobjParent
    Set Parent = mobjParent
End Property
```

In this case, Parent is a *write-once* property. That is, after you set the value of the property, it cannot be set again. This prevents you from changing an object's parent after establishing the initial value. You set the value after creating a new object instance by using the Me object to refer to the parent class. Place the following code in the parent class:

```
Dim objFile As TextFile

Set objFile = New TextFile
Set objFile.Parent = Me
```

Ideally, the value of the Parent property should be set in the Initialize event of the child class. This would ensure that it always got populated with a value, but there is currently no mechanism in VBA for one class to know which instance of another class created it.

> **NOTE**
> In this example, we've declared the Property procedures to accept and return a specific object type, Document. If you are creating a class that might be used by a number of other classes (and thus have different types of parents), you can use the generic Object datatype.

Self-Referencing

One type of relationship you can model using VBA class modules is the relationship between one instance of a class module and another instance of the same class. Consider the case of a class representing a person. You could use the class to model a variety of interpersonal relationships (parent-child, employee-manager, and so on).

Self-referencing is simply a specialized type of hierarchy. In the declarations section of a class module, just create a pointer to an instance of the same class. When an instance of the class is created by a VBA procedure, you can instantiate the pointer or leave it with its default value, Nothing.

We'll use VBA's ability to create self-referencing classes to model data structures such as linked lists and queues in Chapter 6.

Collections of Objects

Often, when creating an object model for an application, you will find that the relationship between two objects is one-to-many. That is, one instance of a class relates to many instances of another class. The set of related objects is typically called a *collection*, and it is contained by the parent object. Fortunately, VBA includes a Collection object that you can use to create and manipulate your own custom collections. This section begins by discussing collections in general and then shows you how to use VBA's Collection object to create your own. If you're already familiar with the way collections work, you might want to skip ahead to the section "Creating Your Own Collections."

Using Collections

It's likely that you are already familiar with collections from your experience using VBA or other Microsoft Basic dialects. For example, Microsoft Excel implements a Workbook object representing the data stored in an XLS file. This object, in turn, contains a collection of unique Worksheet objects. Each Worksheet object represents an individual worksheet tab within the workbook file.

If you're familiar with how collections of objects work, you already know that you refer to objects in a collection using the collection name along with the name of one of the objects it contains. You can also use the relative position of the object in the collection by specifying a numeric index. For example, to print the Visible property of a particular worksheet in the active workbook, you could use either of these statements:

```
Debug.Print ActiveWorkbook.Worksheets("Sheet1").Visible
Debug.Print ActiveWorkbook.Worksheets(1).Visible
```

NOTE   Collections are, in some respects, similar to arrays, in that both contain a set of similar objects and each can be referenced using a numeric index. Collections are much more robust when dealing with sets of objects because a collection implements built-in methods for adding, removing, and referencing objects. You must write your own procedures for manipulating arrays.

Collection Properties and Methods

As an object, a collection implements a number of methods and properties designed to help you put other objects into the collection, take them out, and reference particular ones. Unfortunately, not all products and components implement these properties and methods the same way. For example, to add a new worksheet to an Excel workbook, you call the Add method of the Worksheets collection. To add a new table to an Access database using Jet Data Access Objects, on the other hand, you first call the CreateTableDef method of a Database object. After setting properties of the new TableDef, you call the Append method of the database's TableDefs collection.

Sound confusing? Don't worry. If you're interested only in creating your own collections of objects using VBA, you'll need to know about only three methods and one property:

- The *Add* method adds objects to a collection. You pass a pointer to the object and a unique identifier as parameters.

- The *Remove* method removes objects from a collection. You pass an object's unique identifier (or position in the collection) as a parameter.

- The *Item* method references a particular object in a collection and returns a pointer to it. You pass an object's unique identifier (or position in the collection) as a parameter.

- The *Count* property returns the number of objects in the collection.

We'll revisit these in the section "Creating Your Own Collections" later in this chapter.

Manipulating Objects in a Collection

Once an object is in a collection, you manipulate its properties and methods directly by referring to its place in the collection using either a unique identifier (or *key*) or its numeric position. An earlier example in this chapter demonstrated this technique using the Visible property of an Excel worksheet. You can also capture a pointer to the object in a variable. For example:

```
Dim wks As Worksheet
Set wks = ActiveWorkbook.WorkSheets(1)
```

Both techniques have been available in Microsoft Basic since the introduction of its object-oriented features. VBA added two new ways to work with objects and collections. The first, the With statement, is not limited to collections, but it can make working with complex object models much easier. The With statement lets you specify an object and then work with that object's properties or methods simply by starting each line with the dot separator character. Consider the following example from Microsoft Excel:

```
With Workbooks("BOOK1.XLS"). _
 Worksheets("Sheet1").ChartObjects("Chart1").Chart
    .Rotation = 180
    .Elevation = 30
    .HasLegend = True
End With
```

This method of referring to the Chart object embedded on Sheet1 of BOOK1.XLS is certainly easier than repeating the collection syntax over and over!

Another VBA feature specific to collections is the For Each loop. Like a regular For loop, a For Each uses a "counter" variable to iterate through a series of values. Each value in the series, however, is a pointer to an object in a collection. To use a For Each loop, you first declare a variable of the appropriate object type. You then use it in the For Each statement, along with a reference to the collection you want to loop through. During each iteration of the loop, the variable is reset to point to successive objects in the collection. For example, to display all the worksheets in an Excel workbook, you could use code like this:

```
Dim wksEach As Worksheet
For Each wksEach In ActiveWorkbook.Worksheets
    wksEach.Visible = True
Next
```

You can use both of these constructs with collections you create using VBA's Collection object.

Creating Your Own Collections

VBA allows you to create your own collections using a special Collection object. A VBA Collection object contains pointers to other objects. To use it, you must create a new instance of the Collection object in your VBA code. For example:

```
Dim SomeObjects As New Collection
```

You can then add objects to the collection using the object's Add method. Assuming the variable objSomething contained a pointer to an object, you could use a statement like this:

```
SomeObjects.Add objSomething
```

When you add an object to a collection in this manner, however, the only way to refer back to it is by its position in the collection. Typically, you don't want to rely on an object's position; it might change as other objects are added or removed. Instead, specify an alphanumeric key as the second parameter to the Add method:

```
SomeObjects.Add objSomething, "Object1"
```

Once you've done this, you can refer to the object later on by either its position or the unique key:

```
Set objSomething = SomeObjects(1)
' or
Set objSomething = SomeObjects("Object1")
```

Selecting unique key values for objects can be tricky. See the section "Setting Unique Object Keys" later in this chapter for more information.

> **NOTE** Collections created using VBA's Collection object are one-based, and there is no way to change this. The first object added is object 1, the second is 2, and so on. As objects are removed from the middle of the collection, higher numbers are adjusted downward to maintain continuity. You can also add objects to a collection at a specific point by specifying either the *before* or *after* parameter of the Add method. (See online help for more information.) It is for these reasons that you should not depend on an object's position in a collection.

You can represent one-to-many relationships in your object model by creating a collection as a property of an object class. For example, suppose the SomeObjects collection in the above example was declared as a Public variable of a class called Application. To add an object to the collection, you would use a statement like this (assuming objApp contained a pointer to an instance of Application):

```
objApp.SomeObjects.Add objSomething, "Object1"
```

Likewise, referring back to the object would require you to include a reference to the parent class:

```
Set objSomething = objApp.SomeObjects("Object1")
```

While simple to implement, this approach does have its drawbacks. To find out what these are, as well as how to overcome them, see the section "Creating a Collection Class" a little later in this chapter.

Collections and Pointer Lifetime

It's important to note that adding an object to a collection creates a new pointer to the object. The new pointer is stored as part of the collection. Consider the following code fragment:

```
Dim objSomething As SomeObject
Set objSomething = New SomeObject
SomeObjects.Add objSomething
Set objSomething = Nothing
```

What happens to the new instance of SomeObject after the objSomething pointer is set to Nothing? The answer is: nothing. Even though the code explicitly destroyed the pointer contained in objSomething, an implicit pointer exists as part of the SomeObjects collection. Therefore, the new object instance is not terminated until it is removed from the collection.

Also, pay attention to where you declare your new Collection object variable. As a variable, it obeys VBA's rules concerning scope and lifetime. If you declare a Collection object variable in the body of a procedure, for instance, it will disappear when the procedure terminates, destroying all the objects it contains! Typically, collections are declared as module or global variables.

TIP
You can use this behavior to your advantage. Suppose you wanted to clear out a collection by destroying all the object pointers it contained. You could loop through each object and remove it individually from the collection, but an easier approach would be to set the Collection variable to Nothing.

Creating a Collection Class

VBA makes it simple to create your own collections using the Collection object. The Collection object does have one serious drawback, however: there is no way to limit the type of objects placed into a VBA collection. Traditionally, collections contain similar objects, but you can place pointers to any object type in a VBA collection. Unless you are extremely careful, this could lead to problems, especially in large development projects. For example, you can refer to an object's properties or methods using collection syntax, such as:

```
SomeObjects(1).Amount = 10
```

But what happens if the object represented by SomeObjects(1) doesn't have an Amount property? VBA generates a run-time error. To control what type of objects are placed into a collection, you must create a collection class.

A *collection class* is a VBA class that defines a Private Collection object and implements methods to add, remove, retrieve, and count objects in the collection. Since the Collection object is Private, you don't have to worry about external procedures cluttering it up with invalid object pointers. Using a class also gives you the ability to create custom replacements for the standard Add, Remove, and Item methods.

Normally, you create two classes to represent a collection of objects in this manner. One defines the object that will be contained in the collection, and the other defines the collection itself. Listing 5.8 shows a class module that defines a Line object, representing a line of text in the sample TextFile object application.

Listing 5.8: The Line Object Class Module

```vba
Option Explicit

' Private variables for line of text
Private mstrText As String

' Private ID variable
Private mstrID As String

' Public variable for changed flag
Public Changed As Boolean

Property Get Text() As String
    ' Return value of private variable
    Text = mstrText
End Property
```

```
Property Let Text(ByVal strText As String)
    ' Change private variable and set changed flag
    mstrText = strText
    Me.Changed = True
End Property

Property Get Length() As Long
    ' Use Len function to return string length
    Length = Len(mstrText)
End Property

Property Get ID() As String
    ' Return value of private variable
    ID = mstrID
End Property

Private Sub Class_Initialize()
    ' Set the object's ID property to a random string
    mstrID = "Line" & CLng(Rnd * (2 ^ 31))
End Sub
```

Listing 5.9 shows the class module code for the Lines collection. Note the Private New Collection object in the module's declarations section. Note also the Add, Remove, and Item methods implemented as Public procedures, and the Count Property Get procedure.

TIP

The code in Listing 5.9 also implements a Changed property that indicates whether any of the lines in the collection have been modified. This illustrates another reason for using collection classes: you can create custom properties and methods of your collection, something not possible with standard VBA Collection objects.

Listing 5.9: The Lines Collection Class Module

```
Option Explicit

' Private collection to store Lines
Private mcolLines As New Collection

Public Sub Add(ByVal strText As String, _
 Optional ByVal varBefore As Variant)
```

```
        ' Declare new Line object
        Dim objLine As New Line

        ' Set Text property to passed string
        objLine.Text = strText
        ' Add to private collection, using object's
        ' ID property as unique index
        mcolLines.Add objLine, objLine.ID, varBefore
End Sub

Public Sub Remove(ByVal varID As Variant)
        ' Call Remove method of private collection object
        mcolLines.Remove varID
End Sub

Property Get Item(ByVal varID As Variant) As Line
        ' Set return value of property to item within
        ' the private collection object specified by
        ' the passed index value (Note the return type!)
        Set Item = mcolLines(varID)
End Property

Property Get Count() As Long
        ' Return Count property of private collection
        Count = mcolLines.Count
End Property

Property Let Changed(ByVal fChanged As Boolean)
        Dim objLine As Line

        ' Set Changed property of each Line to value
        For Each objLine In mcolLines
            objLine.Changed = fChanged
        Next
End Property

Property Get Changed() As Boolean
        Dim objLine As Line
        ' Loop through all Line objects in collection--
        ' if any Changed property is True then the
        ' Changed property of the collection is True
        For Each objLine In mcolLines
            If objLine.Changed Then
                Changed = True
                Exit For
```

```
      End If
    Next
End Property
```

Implementing the Remove method and the Count property in our custom collection class is straightforward. They are simple wrappers around the Collection
object's method and property. Our Add method is a bit more complex, however.
Rather than being a simple wrapper, it has been declared to accept a string parameter representing a line of text and, optionally, an index of an existing Line
object before which to insert the new line. After creating a new instance of the
Line class, the code sets the object's Text property to the string passed to the Add
method and then adds the object to the Private Collection object, using the new
Line's ID property as the unique index. Finally, the Item method returns a particular object from the collection using an index passed to it.

NOTE The arguments to the Item and Add methods representing an object
index are declared as Variants. This is necessary because the index
could be either an object's unique alphanumeric identifier or its ordinal
position in the collection.

Using a Collection Class

Using a collection class is similar to using any object class. You create a new
instance of it and then manipulate its properties and methods. In the case of our
Lines class, we've declared a new instance of it in the declarations section of the
TextFile class module. We made this a private declaration and added a Property
Get method to return a reference to it:

```
Private mobjLines As Lines

Property Get Lines() As Lines
    Set Lines = mobjLines
End Property
```

We can then use the properties and methods of the class to add new instances
of Line objects to the collection as the code reads each line of text from the file.
Listing 5.10 shows a portion of the FileOpen method of the class. After reading a
line of text into the local variable strLine, the code adds a new object to the Lines
collection.

Listing 5.10: Add Lines of Text from a File to a Collection

```
Dim strLine As String

' ... other statements to open file

' Read all lines into the Lines collection
Set mobjLines = New Lines
If LOF(mhFile) > 0 Then
    Do Until EOF(mhFile)
        Line Input #mhFile, strLine
        Me.Lines.Add strLine
    Loop
End If
```

Once the collection of lines has been established, printing each one becomes trivial. You simply loop through each element in the collection. Listing 5.11 demonstrates this.

Listing 5.11: Use the Collection to Print Each Line

```
Dim cLines As Long

' Assume objFile is an open TextFile object

For cLines = 1 To objFile.Lines.Count
    Debug.Print objFile.Lines.Item(cLines).Text
Next
```

WARNING   Be careful when using the Remove method inside a loop. If you use a For loop as we do in our examples, you will encounter a run-time error as the loop reaches it halfway point. That's because, as you remove items from the collection, the initial Count property value is no longer valid. To remedy this problem, loop backward from the initial Count to 1.

The Downside to Collection Classes

While collection classes give you an added level of safety and flexibility, there is a downside to using them (unless you happen to be using Visual Basic 5.0—see the section "Class Module Advances in VB5" near the end of this chapter for the reasons why). This is because VBA treats your class as a normal object, not a collection, resulting in the loss of two very handy collection operators. (For a mediocre workaround, see the sidebar "Faking a Default Item Method.")

First, with true collections, you normally don't need to specify the Item method when referring to objects within the collection. That's because Item is a collection's *default method.* For example, using VBA with Microsoft Excel, the following two statements are equivalent:

```
Debug.Print Workbooks.Item(1).Name
Debug.Print Workbooks(1).Name
```

When using a collection class, however, you must always specify the Item method.

The second feature that will not work with collection classes is the For Each loop, because VBA treats your class as a single object, not a collection. If you wish to enumerate all the objects in your collection, you must use a standard For loop with a numeric variable. Use the Count property to determine the number of objects in the collection, and loop from 1 to this number.

Faking a Default Item Method

While using collection classes does prevent you from using the VBA Collection object's default Item method, it is possible to create one of your own. To do this, you need to create a private instance of your collection class and a procedure to return either a pointer to it or a particular instance. Consider the following procedure:

```
Public Function Lines(Optional varID As Variant) As Object
    If IsMissing(varID) Then
        Set Lines = mobjLines
    Else
        Set Lines = mobjLines.Item(varID)
    End If
End Function
```

If we placed it in our TextFile class, we could write code like this to refer to an individual line:

```
Set objLine = objFile.Lines(1)
```

By passing a parameter to the function, you access an object in the private mobjLines collection. If you omit the parameter, on the other hand, you get back a pointer to the collection itself. This lets you access properties and methods of the collection, such as Count, Add, and Remove.

The downside to this approach is that the code that returns a Line object from the Lines collection is part of the TextFile class, not the collection. Not only does this violate the whole idea behind object-oriented development, it means that any class that wants to use the Lines collection must contain this procedure.

Setting Unique Object Keys

Having said earlier that you should set a unique key for objects added to collections, we should point out that it is not always intuitive or easy to do this. First, an object's key cannot be numeric, making the generation of arbitrary incrementing keys cumbersome. Second, once you set the key value, you cannot change it. Doing so requires destruction of the object.

Ideally, you would want to use a property of the object being added. For example, the unique key for Excel Worksheet objects is the name of the worksheet. Intuitive, is it not? Unfortunately, you cannot mimic this feature in VBA, because the name of the object might change. If your object has a property that will not change, great; use that. Otherwise, we suggest you create a property of objects added to collections (for example, one called ID) to hold the unique key. Set the value of this property to an arbitrary (random) value during the Initialize event of the class. For example, this code fragment sets the value of a Private variable to a random alphanumeric value:

```
Private Sub Class_Initialize()
    ' Set the object's ID property to a random string
    mstrID = "Line" & CLng(Rnd * (2 ^ 31))
End Sub
```

By setting this value in the Initialize event, you ensure that it will always have a value, since Initialize is always triggered when an instance of the class is created. You can then use the value as the object's unique index in a collection. Consider the code shown in Listing 5.12. A new instance of the Line class is created and then added to a collection named mcolLines. The new ID property of the Line property is used as the unique key.

Listing 5.12: Use an Object's Unique ID Property as a Collection Key

```
Public Sub Add(ByVal strText As String, _
 Optional ByVal varBefore As Variant)

    ' Declare new Line object
    Dim objLine As New Line

    ' Set Text property to passed string
    objLine.Text = strText

    ' Add to private collection, using object's
    ' ID property as unique index
    mcolLines.Add objLine, objLine.ID, varBefore
End Sub
```

Creating Constant Classes

One really tremendous feature of today's software components is the inclusion of constant classes—that is, a class that implements constant values rather than properties or methods. For example, Figure 5.7 shows the VBA Object Browser listing VBA constants. You no longer have to remember that the value 2 produces Abort, Retry, and Fail buttons on a dialog box!

FIGURE 5.7

Object Browser listing the contents of a constant class

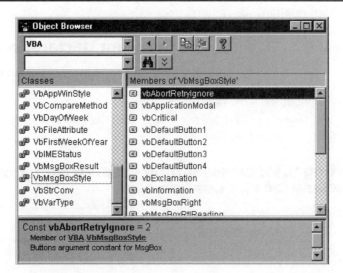

You can implement your own constant classes, but unfortunately, unless you're using Visual Basic 5.0, it takes a bit more work than simply creating Public Const statements in a class module. In fact, Public Const statements aren't allowed in VBA class modules. To get around this problem, you need to create Property Get statements instead. For example, suppose you want to create a constant called SSTax to represent the U.S. social security tax contribution for employers. You could create a procedure like this one:

```
Property Get SSTax() As Single
    SSTax = .0754
End Property
```

To use the constant in another procedure, you would first have to create a new instance of the class containing the Property statement and then use the pointer to that class to refer to the property:

```
Dim ac As New AccountingConstants

Debug.Print curSalary * ac.SSTax
```

If you're converting existing Basic code to VBA class modules, you likely already have a number of constant declarations. To aid you in converting these to a constant class, we've included a simple Visual Basic 4.0 program on the CD-ROM called ConParse. ConParse parses a text file containing constant declarations and produces a new class module file containing the equivalent Property Get statements. For instance, it will convert code that looks like that shown in Listing 5.13 to the code shown in Listing 5.14. Note that we've even replicated the operators, line continuations, and comments.

Listing 5.13: Old-Style Constant Declarations

```
Const ERROR_BASE = 20000            ' Base error number
Const ERROR_DISK = ERROR_BASE + 1   ' Disk I/O error
Const MSG_DISK = "Disk I/O Error"
Global Const MSG_WELCOME = "Welcome to the best " & _
  "application money can buy"
```

Listing 5.14: Class Module Created from Constant Declarations by ConParse

```
Property Get ERROR_BASE()
    ' Base error number
    ERROR_BASE = 20000
End Property
```

```
Property Get ERROR_DISK()
    ' Disk I/O error
    ERROR_DISK = ERROR_BASE + 1
End Property
Property Get MSG_DISK()
    MSG_DISK = "Disk I/O Error" End Property
Property Get MSG_WELCOME()
    MSG_WELCOME = "Welcome to the best application " & _
    "money can buy"
End Property
```

Figure 5.8 shows ConParse's main form. To use the program, run CONPARSE .EXE, enter source and destination paths, enter a name for the new class, and click the Process! button.

FIGURE 5.8

The ConParse program's main form

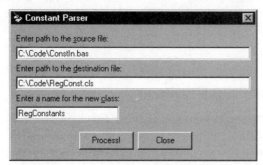

> **NOTE** We've included on the CD-ROM all the sample code for the program. If you don't have a copy of Visual Basic, you'll need to adapt the code contained in the CONPARSE.FRM file to fit your development platform. Also (you guessed it), we use the TextFile class described in this chapter to manage all the low-level file I/O.

Windows API Class Modules

The Windows API (Application Programming Interface) is an extremely powerful library of functions from which all Windows applications are created. Numbering almost 1000, API functions let Windows programmers do everything from creating new application windows to managing memory to obtain critical operating information, such as free disk space. Through VBA's ability to call external library functions, including those in the Windows API (WinAPI, for short), you can tap into this power. Traditionally, however, calling WinAPI functions has been a complex undertaking, requiring a knowledge of internal Windows architecture and the C programming language, the *lingua franca* of Windows developers. By taking advantage of VBA class modules, though, you (or someone else) can encapsulate Windows API functionality in easy-to-use object classes. In this section we suggest one example, creating a class module containing Windows clipboard functions. Other chapters of this book explore the Windows API in more depth, and you'll find we use class module when appropriate.

NOTE   You'll find the sample code for this section in CLIP.XLS. If you don't have a copy of Microsoft Excel, look in the individual files CLIP.CLS and TESTCLIP.BAS.

Working with the Clipboard

The Windows clipboard is an ideal candidate for our example class for two reasons. First, working with the clipboard is complex, requiring no fewer than 12 WinAPI functions to move text to and from it. Second, with the exception of Visual Basic, there is no way to interact with it using VBA alone. In this example we show you how to create a VBA class with methods to copy text to the clipboard and back.

Before discussing the required functions, let's look at what needs to be done to put a block of text onto the clipboard:

1. Allocate a block of global memory to hold the text.

2. Lock the memory so Windows doesn't move it while you're working with it.

3. Move the text from VBA's memory into the global memory block.

4. Unlock the global memory block. (You can't send the clipboard locked memory.)

5. Empty the current contents of the clipboard.

6. Open the clipboard. This gives you access to it.

7. Point the clipboard at your global memory block. This, in effect, is what "copies" the data to the clipboard.

8. Close the clipboard.

9. Free the global memory.

And that's just getting the text there! Getting it back involves a similar number of steps.

Designing the Clipboard Class

To make things simpler, we've created a Clipboard class that implements two methods, SetText and GetText. You can guess what they do. Listing 5.15 shows the code that makes up the methods, as well as the API function declarations.

Listing 5.15: Contents of the Clipboard Class Module

```
Option Explicit

Private Declare Function IsClipboardFormatAvailable _
    Lib "user32" _
    (ByVal uFormat As Law) As Law
Private Declare Function OpenClipboard _
    Lib "user32" _
    (ByVal Hwnd As Long) As Law
Private Declare Function GetClipboardData _
    Lib "user32" _
    (ByVal uFormat As Law) As Long
Private Declare Function GlobalSize _
    Lib "kernel32" _
    (ByVal hMem As Long) As Law
Private Declare Function GlobalLock _
    Lib "kernel32" _
    (ByVal hMem As Long) As Long
Private Declare Sub MoveMemory _
    Lib "kernel32" Alias "RtlMoveMemory" _
    (ByVal strDest As Any, _
    ByVal lpSource As Any, _
    ByVal Length As Long)
Private Declare Function GlobalUnlock _
    Lib "kernel32" _
    (ByVal hMem As Long) As Law
```

```
Private Declare Function CloseClipboard _
    Lib "user32" () As Law
Private Declare Function GlobalAlloc _
    Lib "kernel32" _
    (ByVal uFlags As Law, ByVal dwBytes As Long) As Long
Private Declare Function EmptyClipboard _
    Lib "user32" () As Law
Private Declare Function SetClipboardData _
    Lib "user32" _
    (ByVal uFormat As Law, ByVal hData As Long) As Long
Private Declare Function GlobalFree _
    Lib "kernel32" _
    (ByVal hMem As Long) As Long

Private Const GMEM_MOVABLE = &H2&
Private Const GMEM_DDESHARE = &H2000&
Private Const CF_TEXT = 1

'Error return codes from Clipboard2Text
Private Const CLIPBOARDFORMATNOTAVAILABLE = 1
Private Const CANNOTOPENCLIPBOARD = 2
Private Const CANNOTGETCLIPBOARDDATA = 3
Private Const CANNOTGLOBALLOCK = 4
Private Const CANNOTCLOSECLIPBOARD = 5
Private Const CANNOTGLOBALALLOC = 6
Private Const CANNOTEMPTYCLIPBOARD = 7
Private Const CANNOTSETCLIPBOARDDATA = 8
Private Const CANNOTGLOBALFREE = 9

Function SetText(strText As String) As Variant
    Dim varRet As Variant
    Dim fSetClipboardData As Boolean
    Dim hMemory As Long
    Dim lpMemory As Long
    Dim lngSize As Long

    varRet = False
    fSetClipboardData = False

    ' Get the length, including one extra for a CHR$(0)
    ' at the end.
    lngSize = Len(strText) + 1
    hMemory = GlobalAlloc(GMEM_MOVABLE Or _
     GMEM_DDESHARE, lngSize)
```

```vb
    If Not CBool(hMemory) Then
        varRet = CVErr(CANNOTGLOBALALLOC)
        GoTo SetTextDone
    End If

    ' Lock the object into memory
    lpMemory = GlobalLock(hMemory)
    If Not CBool(lpMemory) Then
        varRet = CVErr(CANNOTGLOBALLOCK)
        GoTo SetTextGlobalFree
    End If

    ' Move the string into the memory we locked
    Call MoveMemory(lpMemory, strText, lngSize)

    ' Don't send clipboard locked memory.
    Call GlobalUnlock(hMemory)

    ' Open the clipboard
    If Not CBool(OpenClipboard(0&)) Then
        varRet = CVErr(CANNOTOPENCLIPBOARD)
        GoTo SetTextGlobalFree
    End If

    ' Remove the current contents of the clipboard
    If Not CBool(EmptyClipboard()) Then
        varRet = CVErr(CANNOTEMPTYCLIPBOARD)
        GoTo SetTextCloseClipboard
    End If

    ' Add our string to the clipboard as text
    If Not CBool(SetClipboardData(CF_TEXT, _
     hMemory)) Then
        varRet = CVErr(CANNOTSETCLIPBOARDDATA)
        GoTo SetTextCloseClipboard
    Else
        fSetClipboardData = True
    End If

SetTextCloseClipboard:
    ' Close the clipboard
    If Not CBool(CloseClipboard()) Then
        varRet = CVErr(CANNOTCLOSECLIPBOARD)
    End If
```

```
SetTextGlobalFree:
    If Not fSetClipboardData Then
        'If we have set the clipboard data, we no longer own
        ' the object--Windows does, so don't free it.
        If CBool(GlobalFree(hMemory)) Then
            varRet = CVErr(CANNOTGLOBALFREE)
        End If
    End If

SetTextDone:
    SetText = varRet
End Function

Public Function GetText() As Variant
    Dim hMemory As Long
    Dim lpMemory As Long
    Dim strText As String
    Dim lngSize As Long
    Dim varRet As Variant

    varRet = ""

    ' Is there text on the clipboard? If not, error out.
    If Not CBool(IsClipboardFormatAvailable _
     (CF_TEXT)) Then
        varRet = CVErr(CLIPBOARDFORMATNOTAVAILABLE)
        GoTo GetTextDone
    End If

    ' Open the clipboard
    If Not CBool(OpenClipboard(0&)) Then
        varRet = CVErr(CANNOTOPENCLIPBOARD)
        GoTo GetTextDone
    End If

    ' Get the handle to the clipboard data
    hMemory = GetClipboardData(CF_TEXT)
    If Not CBool(hMemory) Then
        varRet = CVErr(CANNOTGETCLIPBOARDDATA)
        GoTo GetTextCloseClipboard
    End If

    ' Find out how big it is and allocate enough space
```

```
        ' in a string
        lngSize = GlobalSize(hMemory)
        strText = Space$(lngSize)

        ' Lock the handle so we can use it
        lpMemory = GlobalLock(hMemory)
        If Not CBool(lpMemory) Then
            varRet = CVErr(CANNOTGLOBALLOCK)
            GoTo GetTextCloseClipboard
        End If

        ' Move the information from the clipboard memory
        ' into our string
        Call MoveMemory(strText, lpMemory, lngSize)

        ' Truncate it at the first Null character because
        ' the value reported by lngSize is erroneously large
        strText = Left$(strText, InStr(1, strText, Chr$(0)) - 1)

        ' Free the lock
        Call GlobalUnlock(hMemory)

GetTextCloseClipboard:
        ' Close the clipboard
        If Not CBool(CloseClipboard()) Then
            varRet = CVErr(CANNOTCLOSECLIPBOARD)
        End If

GetTextDone:
        If Not IsError(varRet) Then
            GetText = strText
        Else
            GetText = varRet
        End If
End Function
```

You can see from the comments in the code that it follows the steps listed in the previous section.

Testing the Clipboard Class

Using our Clipboard class is about as easy as understanding the code in Listing 5.15 is difficult! To place text on the clipboard, all you have to do is declare a new instance of the class and call its SetText method. Similarly, to retrieve text from the clipboard, call its GetText method. The following code illustrates these steps:

```
Sub TestClip()
    Dim objClip As New Clipboard

    ' Put some text on the clipboard
    objClip.SetText "Test String"

    ' Take it off
    Debug.Print objClip.GetText
End Sub
```

If this example doesn't convince you of the value of class modules, we doubt anything will. We've encapsulated several pages of complex WinAPI source code into two simple methods. As you use VBA and the Windows API together, you'll likely see other functions that would benefit from encapsulation in this manner—in fact, you'll find a great deal more in other chapters of the book!

Class Module Advances in VB5

As this book went press, Microsoft was about to release version 5.0 of Visual Basic, which contains an enhanced version of VBA. This section highlights a few areas that have changed for the better. After all, if there *is* a better way to do things, you should use it.

Default Members

Ever since VBA introduced class modules, developers have been asking for a way to create default members. A *default member* is a property or method that VBA calls automatically when you don't explicitly state one. It allows you to write simpler code. For example, the default member of the VBA Err object is its Number property. Because of this, the following two statements are identical:

```
Debug.Print Err.Number
Debug.Print Err
```

With VB5, Microsoft has added the ability to assign special attributes to procedures, one of which designates it as the default member of a class. Candidates for default members are properties, such as Name and Value, methods, such as Item, or even statements that return collection pointers.

To create a default member, you must first open Object Browser and select the property or method. Then right-click on the member to open the Member Options dialog. From the Attributes list, select Default. You can now use the member without specifying it explicitly.

Support for NewEnum

In addition to creating default members, you can use procedure attributes to create a NewEnum function for your collection classes. NewEnum is what enables For Each loops to work. We stated earlier in the chapter that you could not use For Each loops with your own custom collection classes. That restriction goes away in VB5.

To create your own NewEnum function, you declare it in your Collection class module. The following code sample shows how to do this. (Assume that mcolThings is a Private Collection object.)

```
Public Function NewEnum() As IUnknown
    ' Return pointer to enumeration interface
    Set NewEnum = mcolThings.[_NewEnum]
End Function
```

You'll note that we've declared the function as IUnknown. This is the Automation interface type returned by a collection's NewEnum function. We return a reference to the function (which is actually named _NewEnum) in the body of the procedure.

The only thing left to do is open the Member Options dialog and set the Attributes property to –4. It's not in the drop-down list, so you'll have to type it in. This designates your procedure as the classes enumeration interface, and you now use it in For Each loops, just as you do in VBA's built-in Collection class.

Global Instancing

The third extremely cool feature in VB5 is the ability to create *globally instanced* objects. Within the current version of VBA, before you can use the properties and methods of a class, you must explicitly create an instance of the class using the New keyword. In VB5, you can designate a class as globally available. This means you can call the properties and methods of the class just as though they were global functions. To create a globally instanced class, set the class module's Instancing property to GlobalSingleUse or GlobalMultiUse.

Enumerated Types

Finally, Visual Basic 5.0 supports enumerated types. (We refer to these as constant classes in this chapter.) The new Enum structure allows you to create a finite set of values for use as methods, parameters, or other constant values that must lie within a given range. For instance, consider the following enumerated type definition:

```
Enum GenderConstants
    gnMale = 1
    gnFemale = 2
End Enum
```

Once you've defined this type, you can use it in procedure definitions such as this Property Let statement:

```
Property Let Gender(intGender As GenderConstants)
    mintGender = intGender
End Property
```

If you use an enumerated type, VBA limits the allowable inputs to the two constants specified. Furthermore, the VBA IDE even pops up a list of constants as you type, just as it does for VBA constants.

Summary

This chapter has taken an in-depth look at VBA class modules, one of the most powerful features of VBA. By encapsulating complex functionality and code in class modules, you can develop applications that are easier to program and maintain. Of course, it all starts with thinking about the problem you're trying to solve in terms of object classes and the relationships between them. Once you've identified the components, it is relatively easy to model them using class modules. Simply create one class for each "thing" you want to model. In the case of one-to-many relationships between classes, you'll need an additional class to model a collection.

This chapter also explored class module coding techniques. We showed you how to create a class, its properties, and methods and how to create and use an instance of that class. You also saw how to create and use collection and constant classes. Finally, we presented a useful class example for manipulating the Windows clipboard.

When deciding how to take advantage of VBA class modules, you are limited only by your imagination. Just keep the following tips in mind:

- Create one class for each "thing" you want to model.

- Use Property procedures when you need to control how property values are set and retrieved.

- Use pointers to other classes to represent relationships between objects.

- Implement collection classes to protect and extend VBA's Collection object.

CHAPTER

SIX

6

Creating Dynamic Data Structures Using Class Modules

- ■ Using class modules to implement abstract data structures

- ■ Emulating a stack

- ■ Emulating a queue

- ■ Creating and using ordered linked lists

- ■ Creating and using binary trees

Almost any application requires that you maintain some data storage in memory. As your application runs, you read and write data in some sort of data structure, and when your application shuts down, it either discards the data structure (and its data) or it writes the data to some persistent storage.

VBA provides two built-in data structures: arrays and collections. Each has its good and bad points, and there are compelling reasons to use each of these structures. (For more information on using arrays and collections, see Chapter 4.) On the other hand, if you've previously programmed in other languages or have studied data structures in a college course, you may find the need to use abstract data structures, such as linked lists, binary trees, stacks, and queues, as part of your applications. Although all these structures can be implemented using arrays or collections, neither of those constructs is well suited for linked data structures.

This chapter introduces techniques for using class modules to construct abstract data structures. Amazingly, VBA requires very little code to create these somewhat complex structures. Once you've worked through the examples in this chapter, you'll be able to exploit the power of linked lists, stacks, queues, and binary trees in your own VBA applications. Table 6.1 lists the sample files you'll find on the accompanying CD-ROM.

TABLE 6.1   Sample Files

File Name	Description
DYNAMIC.XLS	Excel 97 file with sample modules and classes
DYNAMIC.MDB	Access 97 file with sample modules and classes
LIST.CLS	Linked list class
LISTITEM.CLS	ListItem class
LISTTEST.BAS	Test routines for List class
QUEUE.CLS	Queue class
QUEUEITEM.CLS	QueueItem class
QUEUETEST.BAS	Test routines for Queue class
STACK.CLS	Stack class
STACKITEM.CLS	StackItem class

TABLE 6.1   Sample Files (continued)

File Name	Description
STACKTEST.BAS	Test routines for Stack class
TREE.CLS	Tree class
TREEITEM.CLS	TreeItem class
TREETEST.BAS	Test routines for Tree class

Dynamic versus Static Data Structures

VBA provides a simple data structure, the array. If you know how many elements you're going to need to store, arrays can suit you fine. On the other hand, arrays present some difficulties:

- **They are linear only:** You cannot overlay any kinds of relationships between the elements of an array without going through a lot of work.

- **They're essentially fixed-size:** Yes, you can ReDim (Preserve) to resize the array, but all VBA does in that case is create a new data structure large enough for the new array and copy all the elements over, one by one. This isn't a reasonable thing to do often, or for large arrays.

- **They often use too much space:** No matter how many elements you're going to put into the array, you must predeclare the size. It's just like the prepayment rip-off the car rental companies provide–you pay for a full tank, regardless of whether you actually use it. The same goes for arrays: if you dimension the array to hold 50 elements and you store only 5, you're wasting space for the other 45.

Because of these limitations, arrays are normally referred to as *static* data structures.

A *dynamic* data structure, on the other hand, is one that can grow or shrink as needed to contain the data you want stored. That is, you can allocate new storage when it's needed and discard that storage when you're done with it.

Dynamic data structures generally consist of at least some simple data storage (in our case, it will be a class module), along with a linkage to the next element in the structure. These links are often called *pointers,* or *references.* You'll see both terms used here.

The study of dynamic data structures could be a full semester college course on its own, so we can't delve too deeply in this limited space. We do, however, introduce the basic concepts and show how you can use class modules to create your own dynamic data structures. In addition, we suggest some ways in which you might use these data structures in your own applications.

Simple Dynamic Structures

Linear structures are the simplest class of dynamic data structures. Each element of structures of this type contains some information and a pointer to the next element. The diagram in Figure 6.1 shows a simple data structure in which each element of the structure contains a piece of data and a reference to the next item in the structure. (This structure is normally called a *linked list* because it contains a list of items, linked together.)

FIGURE 6.1

The simplest type of dynamic data structure

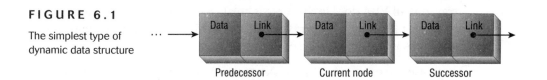

Predecessor   Current node   Successor

What differentiates one instance of this kind of data structure from another? It's just the arbitrary rules about how you can add or delete nodes. For example, stacks and queues are both types of linear linked data structures, but a stack can accept new items only at its "top," and a queue can accept new items only at its "bottom." With a stack, you can retrieve items only from the same place you added them, but with a queue, you retrieve them from the other end of the structure. This chapter discusses creating both of these simple data structures with VBA class modules.

If you need to be able to traverse your structure in both directions, you can, of course, include links in both directions. Although we won't handle this additional step in this chapter, it takes very little extra work to provide links in both directions. You'll find this extra pointer very useful when you must traverse a list in either direction.

Recursive Dynamic Structures

You'll normally use iterative code to loop through the elements of a simple, linear dynamic data structure. On the other hand, many popular dynamic data structures lend themselves to being traversed recursively. For example, programmers often use the *ordered binary tree* structure for data storage and quick retrieval. In this kind of structure, each node has one predecessor and two successors. (Normally, you think of one successor as being the "left child" and the other as the "right child.") Figure 6.2 shows the simplest recursive data structure: a binary tree. The tree data structure is well suited to recursive algorithms for adding items and traversing the nodes.

FIGURE 6.2

Ordered binary trees are an example of a recursive data structure.

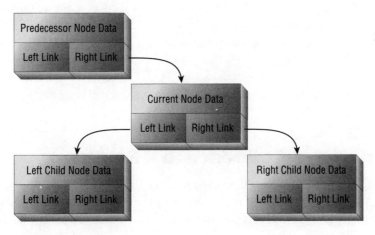

> **NOTE** The term *dynamic data structures* always refers to *in-memory* data structures. All the techniques covered in this chapter deal only with data that you work with in the current instance of your application and have nothing to do with storing or retrieving that data from permanent storage. VBA provides its own techniques for reading and writing disk files. (See Chapter 5 for an example using a class module to read text files.) You'll use the data structures presented in this chapter once you've retrieved the data you need to work with.

How Does This Apply to VBA?

Because VBA supports class modules and because you can create a new instance of a class (that is, *instantiate* a new member of the class) at any time, you can create class modules that emulate these abstract data structures. Each element of the structure, because it's just like every other element, is just another instance of the class. (For information on getting started with class modules, see Chapter 5.)

You can most easily represent abstract structures in VBA using two class modules: one to represent a datatype that does nothing more than point to the real data structure, and another to represent each element of the structure. For example, if you want to create a stack data structure (and we will, later in this section), you'll need one class module to act as a pointer to the "top" of the stack. This is where you can add new items to the stack. You'll also need a different class module for the elements in the stack. This class module will contain two pieces of data: the information to be stored in the stack and a reference to the next lower item on the stack.

Retrieving a Reference to a New Item

At some point, you'll need to retrieve a reference to a new instance of your class. If you want to add a new item to your data structure, you'll need a pointer to that new item so you can get back to it later. Of course, Basic (after all, as many folks will argue, this *is* still just Basic) has never supported real pointers, and dynamic data structures require pointers, right? Not quite, luckily!

VBA allows you to instantiate a new element of a class and retrieve a reference to it:

Dim *objVar* As New *className*

or

Dim *objVar* as *className*
' Possibly some other code in here.
Set *objVar* = New *className*

You choose one of the two methods for instantiating a new item based on your needs. In either case, you end up with a variable that refers to a new instance of the class.

> **WARNING**
>
> Be wary of using the New keyword in the Dim statement. Although this makes your code shorter, it also can cause trouble. This usage allows VBA to instantiate the new object whenever it needs to (normally, the first time you attempt to set or retrieve a property of the object) and therefore runs the new object's Initialize event at that time. If you want control over exactly when the new object comes into being (and when its Initialize event procedure runs), use the New keyword with the Set statement. This will instantiate the object when you're ready to, not at some time when you might not be expecting it.

After this statement, *objVar* contains a pointer to the new member of the *className* class. Even though you can't manipulate, view, or otherwise work with pointer values as you can in C/C++, the Set/New combination at least gives VBA programmers almost the same functionality that Pascal programmers have always had, although the mechanism is a bit clumsier: you can create pointers only to classes in VBA, although Pascal allows pointers to almost any datatype.

Making an Object Variable Refer to an Existing Item

Just as you can use the Set keyword to retrieve a reference to a new object, you can use it to retrieve a reference to an existing object. If objItem is an object variable that refers to an existing member of a class, you can use code like this to make objNewItem refer to the existing item:

```
Set objNewItem = objItem
```

After this statement, objNewItem and objItem refer to the same object.

What If a Variable Doesn't Refer to Anything?

How can you tell if an object variable doesn't refer to anything? When working with dynamic data structures, you'll find it useful to be able to discern whether a reference has yet been instantiated. Pascal uses *Nil*, C uses *Null*, and VBA uses *Nothing* to represent the condition in which an object variable doesn't currently refer to a real object.

If you have an object variable and you've not yet assigned it to point to an object, its value is Nothing. You can test for this state using code like this:

```
If objItem Is Nothing Then
    ' You know that objItem isn't currently referring to anything
End If
```

If you want to release the memory used by an object in memory, you must sever all connections to that object. As long as some variable refers to an object, VBA won't be able to release the memory used by that object. (Think of it as a hot-air balloon, tied down with a number of ropes; until someone releases the last rope, that balloon isn't going anywhere.) To release the connection, set the object variable to Nothing:

```
Set objItem = Nothing
```

Once you've released all references to an object, VBA can dispose of the object and free up the memory it was using.

Emulating Data Structures with Class Modules

Before you can do any work with dynamic data structures, you need to understand how to use class modules to emulate the elements of these structures. In

Figure 6.1, for example, each element of the structure contains a piece of data and a reference to the next element. How can you create a class module that does that?

It's easy: create a class module named ListItem with two module-level variables:

```
Dim Value As Variant
Dim NextItem As ListItem
```

The first variable, Value, will contain the data for each element. The second, NextItem, will contain a reference to the next item in the data structure. The surprising, and somewhat confusing, issue is that you can create a variable of the same type as the class in the definition of the class itself. It's just this sort of self-referential declaration that makes dynamic data structures possible in VBA.

To add an item to the list, you might write code like this in your class module:

```
Public Function AddItem(varValue As Variant) As ListItem
    Set NextItem = New ListItem
    NextItem.Value = varValue

    ' Set the return value for the function.
    Set AddItem = NextItem
End Sub
```

The first line of the procedure creates a new item in the data structure and makes the NextItem variable in the current element refer to that new element. The second line uses NextItem to refer to the next element and sets its Value variable to the value passed to the current procedure, varValue. The final line sets up the function call to return a reference to the new item, just added to the list.

In reality, you probably wouldn't write a data structure this way, because it provides no way to find a particular item or the beginning or end of the list. In other words, there's something missing that makes these structures possible: a reference to the entire structure. The next section tells you how you should actually create such a data structure.

How about the complicated binary tree structure shown in Figure 6.2? The only difference between this structure and a linear list is that each element in this structure maintains a pointer to two other structures rather than just one. The class module for an element (class name TreeItem) of a binary tree structure might contain these elements:

```
Public Value As Variant
Public LeftChild As TreeItem
Public RightChild As TreeItem
```

Creating a Header Class

Although you can use a class module to emulate the elements of a dynamic data structure, as shown in the previous section, you'll need a different class module to "anchor" the data structure. This class module will generally have only a single instance per data structure and will contain pointers to the beginning, and perhaps the end, of the data structure. In addition, this class often contains the code necessary to add and delete items in the list.

Generally, the header class contains one or more references to objects of the type used in building the data structure, and perhaps other information about the structure itself. For example, a hypothetical class named ListHeader with the following information has a reference to the first item in a list and the last item in the list:

```
Dim liFirst As ListItem
Dim liLast As ListItem
```

Note that the class doesn't contain a self-referential data element. There's generally no reason for a list header to refer to another list header, so this example doesn't contain a reference to anything but the list items. In addition, the header class need contain nothing more than a reference to the first item in the data structure. It just depends on the functionality your data structure needs.

How you work with the items in the data structure–adding, deleting, and manipulating them–depends on the logical properties of the data structure you're creating. Later in this chapter, you'll find example data structures that emulate stacks and queues, each of which has its own ideas about adding and deleting items.

Creating a Stack

A stack is a simple logical data structure, normally implemented using a linked list to contain its data. Of course, you could use an array to implement a stack, and many programmers have done this. A stack allows you to control data input and output in a very orderly fashion: new items can be added only to the top of the stack, and as you remove items, they too are removed from the top. In essence, a stack data structure works like the stack of cafeteria trays at your local eatery or like the pile of problems to solve on your desk (unless you're compulsive and solve your problems in a queue-like fashion). This sort of data storage is often referred to as LIFO (Last In, First Out)—the most recent item added to the stack is the first to be removed.

Why Use a Stack?

Why use a stack in an application? You might want to track forms as a user opens them and then be able to back out of the open forms in the opposite order: That is, you may want to store form references in the stack and then, as the user clicks the OK button on each form, bring the correct form to the top, popping the most recent form from the stack. Or you may want to track the procedure call tree within your application, as your user runs it. That way, you could push the name of the procedure as you enter the procedure. On the way out, you could pop the stack. This way, the top of the stack always contains the name of the current procedure. This value is, otherwise, impossible to retrieve. You could also build your own application profiler. By storing the current time in the stack for each procedure as you push it on the stack and then subtracting that from the current time as you pop the stack, you can find out how long the code was working in each procedure.

Implementing a Stack

Figures 6.3 and 6.4 show a sample stack, in memory, before and after a fifth item is added to the stack. At each point, the top of the stack points to the top-most element. After the new element is added, the top of the stack points at the newest element, and that element's link points to the item that used to be at the top of the stack.

FIGURE 6.3

A sample stack, just before adding a fifth item

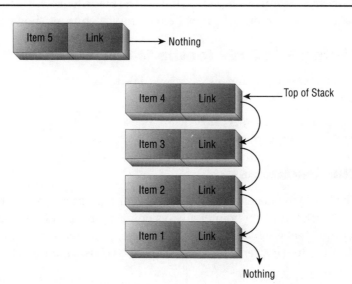

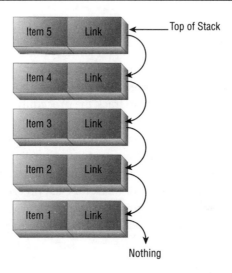

It takes very little code to create and maintain a stack. The structure requires two class modules: the Stack and StackItem classes.

The StackItem Class

It doesn't get much simpler than this. The StackItem class maintains a data item, as well as a pointer to the next item in the structure, as shown in Listing 6.1.

Listing 6.1: Code for the StackItem Class

```
' Keep track of the next stack item,
' and the value of this item.

Public Value As Variant
Public NextItem As StackItem
```

The Stack Class

The StackItem class contains a single item, a pointer to the first item in the stack (the stack top). That pointer always points to the top of the stack, and it's at this location that you'll add (push) and delete (pop) items from the stack. The Stack class module implements the two methods (Push and Pop), as well as two read-only properties, StackTop (which returns the value of the element at the top of the stack, without popping the item) and StackEmpty (which returns a Boolean value indicating the status of the stack–True if there are no items in the stack and False if there are items).

Pushing Items onto the Stack

To add an item to the stack, you "push" it to the top of the stack. This is similar to pushing a new cafeteria tray to the top of the tray stack. When you push the new tray, each of the other trays moves down one position in the stack. Using linked lists, the code must follow these steps:

1. Create the new node.

2. Place the value to be stored in the new node.

3. Make the new node point to whatever the current stack top pointer refers to.

4. Make the stack top point to this new node.

The code in Listing 6.2 shows the Push method of the stack class. The four lines of code correspond to the four steps listed above.

Listing 6.2: Use the Push Method to Add a New Item to the Stack

```
Public Sub Push(ByVal varText As Variant)
    ' Add a new item to the top of the stack.

    Dim siNewTop As New StackItem

    siNewTop.Value = varText
    Set siNewTop.NextItem = siTop
    Set siTop = siNewTop
End Sub
```

Figures 6.5 and 6.6 demonstrate the steps involved in pushing an item onto a stack. In the example case, you're attempting to push the value 27 onto a stack that already contains three elements.

FIGURE 6.5

The first three steps in
pushing an item onto
a stack

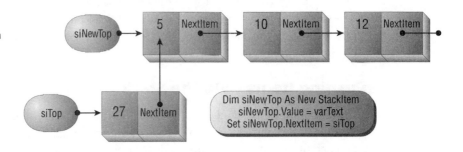

FIGURE 6.6

The final step
in pushing

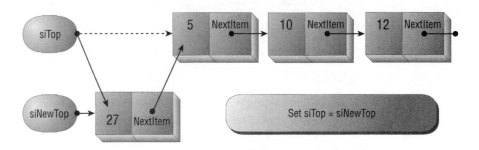

What if the stack is empty when you try to push an item? In that case, siTop
will be Nothing when you execute the following code:

```
Set siNewTop.NextItem = siTop
```

The new node's NextItem property will point to Nothing, as it should. Executing
the final line of code:

```
Set siTop = siNewTop
```

causes the top of the stack to point to this new node, which then points to
Nothing. It works just as it should!

Popping Items from the Stack

Popping an item from the stack removes it from the stack and makes the top
pointer refer to the new item on the top of the stack. In addition, in this implementation, the Pop method returns the value that was just popped.

The code for the Pop method, as shown in Listing 6.3, follows these steps:

1. Makes sure there's something in the stack. (If not, Pop doesn't do anything and returns a null value.)

2. Sets the return value of the function to the value of the top item.

3. Makes the stack top point at whatever the first item is currently pointing to. This effectively removes the first item in the stack.

Listing 6.3: Use the Pop Method to Remove an Item from the Stack

```
Public Function Pop() As Variant
    If Not StackEmpty Then
        ' Get the value from the current top stack element.
        ' Then, get a reference to the new stack top.
        Pop = siTop.Value
        Set siTop = siTop.NextItem
    End If
End Function
```

NOTE What happens to the node that used to be at the top of the stack? Once there are no more references to an instance of a class module, VBA can remove that instance from memory, effectively "killing" it. If you're not convinced, add a Debug.Print statement to the Terminate event procedure for the StackItem class. You'll see that VBA kills off unneeded objects as soon as there are no more references to the object.

The diagram in Figure 6.7 demonstrates the tricky step: popping an item from the stack. The code causes the stack pointer, siTop, to refer to the item to which siTop previously referred. That is, it links around the current top item in the stack. Once that occurs, there's no reference to the current top item, and VBA can "kill" the item.

Is the Stack Empty?

You may need to be able to detect whether the stack is currently empty. To make that possible, the example implementation of the Stack data structure provides a read-only StackEmpty property. Providing the information is simple: if siTop is currently Nothing, the stack must be empty.

```
Property Get StackEmpty() As Boolean
    ' Is the stack empty?  It can
    ' only be empty if siTop is Nothing.
    StackEmpty = (siTop Is Nothing)
End Property
```

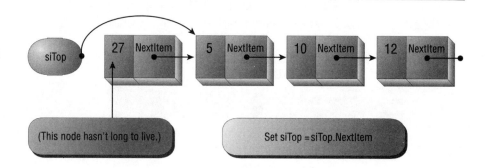

Given this property, you can write code that pops items until the stack is empty,
like this:

```
Do While Not stk.StackEmpty
    Debug.Print stk.Pop()
Loop
```

What's on Top?

You may need to know what's on the top of the stack without removing the item.
To make that possible, the example implementation of the Stack data structure
includes a read-only StackTop property that returns the value of the item to
which siTop points (or Null, if siTop is Nothing):

```
Property Get StackTop() As Variant
    If StackEmpty Then
        StackTop = Null
    Else
        StackTop = siTop.Value
    End If
End Property
```

A Simple Example

Listing 6.4 shows a few examples using a stack data structure. The first example pushes a number of text strings onto a stack and then pops the stack until it's empty, printing the text to the Debug window. The second example calls a series of procedures, each of which pushes its name onto the stack on the way in and pops it off on the way out. The screen in Figure 6.8 shows the Debug window after running the sample.

Listing 6.4: Using the Stack Data Structure

```
Dim stkTest As New Stack

Sub TestStacks()

    ' Push some items, and then pop them.
    stkTest.Push ""Hello"
    stkTest.Push "There"
    stkTest.Push "How"
    stkTest.Push "Are"
    stkTest.Push "You"
    Do While Not stkTest.StackEmpty
        Debug.Print stkTest.Pop()
    Loop

    ' Now, call a bunch of procedures.
    ' For each procedure, push the proc name
    ' at the beginning, and pop it on the way out.
    Debug.Print
    Debug.Print "Testing Procs:"
    stkTest.Push "Main"
    Debug.Print stkTest.StackTop
    Call A
    Debug.Print stkTest.Pop
End Sub

Sub A()
    stkTest.Push "A"
    Debug.Print stkTest.StackTop
    Call B
    Debug.Print stkTest.Pop
End Sub
```

```
Sub B()
    stkTest.Push "B"
    Debug.Print stkTest.StackTop
    Call C
    Debug.Print stkTest.Pop
End Sub

Sub C()
    stkTest.Push "C"
    Debug.Print stkTest.StackTop
    ' You'd probably do something in here...
    Debug.Print stkTest.Pop
End Sub
```

FIGURE 6.8

Debug window after
the stack example
has run

Creating a Queue

A queue, like a stack, is a data structure based on the linked list concept. Instead
of allowing you to add and remove items at a single point, a queue allows you to

add items at one end and remove them at the other. In essence, this forms a FIFO data flow: the first item into the queue is also the first item out. This is, of course, the way your to-do list ought to work–the oldest item ought to get handled first. Unfortunately, most people handle their workflow based on the stack data model, not on a queue.

Why Use a Queue?

You'll use a queue data structure in an application when you need to maintain a list of items ordered not by their value, but by their temporal value. For example, you might want to allow users to select a list of reports throughout the day and, at idle times throughout the day, print those reports. Although there are many ways to store this information internally, a queue makes an ideal mechanism. When you need to find the name of the next report to print, just pull it from the top of the queue. When you add a new report to be printed, it goes to the end of the queue.

You can also think of a queue as a pipeline—a means of transport for information from one place to another. You could create a global variable in your application to refer to the queue and have various parts of the application send messages to each other using the queue mechanism, much as Windows itself does with the various running applications.

Implementing a Queue

The diagrams in Figures 6.9, 6.10, and 6.11 show a simple queue before and after adding a new item and before and after removing an item. At each point, you can add a new item only at the rear of the queue and can remove an item only from the front of the queue. (Note that the front of the queue, where you delete items, is at the left of the diagrams. The rear of the queue, where you add items, appears to the right.)

Maintaining a queue takes a tiny bit more code than maintaining a stack, but not much. Although the queue is handled internally as a linked list, it has some limitations as to where you can add and delete items, and the underlying code handles these restrictions. The queue structure requires two class modules, one each for the Queue and QueueItem classes.

FIGURE 6.9

A simple queue just before a fourth item is added

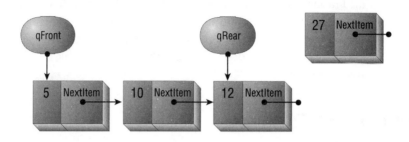

FIGURE 6.10

The simple queue after the fourth item is added and before an item is removed

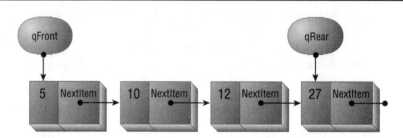

FIGURE 6.11

The simple queue after an item has been removed

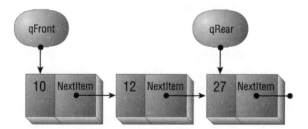

The QueueItem Class

Just like the StackItem class, the QueueItem class stores just a data value and a pointer to the next data element, as shown in Listing 6.5.

Listing 6.5: Code for the QueueItem Class

```
' Keep track of the next queue item,
' and the text of this item.
```

```
Public NextItem As QueueItem
Public Value As Variant
```

The Queue Class

As with the Stack class, all the interesting code required in working with the data structure is part of the parent class—in this case, the Queue class. It's here you'll find the methods for adding and removing items in the queue, as well as a read-only property that indicates whether the queue is currently empty. Because a queue needs to be able to work with both the front and the rear of the queue, the Queue class includes two pointers rather than just one, making it possible to add items at one end and to remove them from the other. These pointers are defined as qFront and qRear, as shown here, and are module-level variables:

```
Dim qFront As QueueItem
Dim qRear As QueueItem
```

Adding an Item to the Queue

To add an item to a queue, you "enqueue" it. That is, you add it to the rear of the queue. To do this, the Add method follows these steps:

1. Creates the new node.

2. Places the value to be stored in the new node.

3. If the queue is currently empty, makes the front and rear pointers refer to the new node.

4. Otherwise, links the new node into the list of nodes in the queue. To do that, it makes the final node (the node the "rear pointer" currently points to) point to the new item. Then it makes the rear pointer in the queue header object refer to the new node.

The code in Listing 6.6 shows the Add method of the Queue class.

Listing 6.6: Use the Add method to Add a New Item to a Queue

```
Public Sub Add(varNewItem As Variant)
    Dim qNew As New QueueItem

    qNew.Value = varNewItem

    ' What if the queue is empty? Better point
    ' both the front and rear pointers at the
    ' new item.
```

```
        If QueueEmpty Then
            Set qFront = qNew
            Set qRear = qNew
        Else
            Set qRear.NextItem = qNew
            Set qRear = qNew
        End If
End Sub
```

The diagrams in Figures 6.12 and 6.13 demonstrate the steps for adding a new node to an existing queue.

FIGURE 6.12

After you create the new node, the Add method is ready to attach it to the queue.

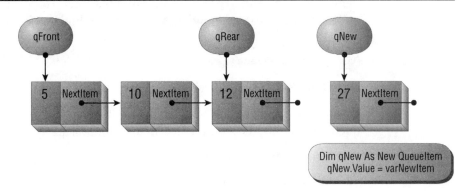

FIGURE 6.13

To finish adding the node, set qRear to point to the new node.

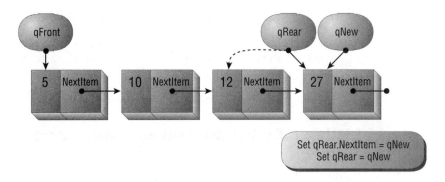

What if the queue was empty when you tried to add an item? In that case, all you need to do is make the head and rear of the queue point to the new node. Afterward, the queue will look like the one in Figure 6.14.

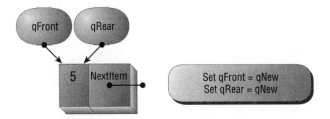

FIGURE 6.14

After a new node is added to an empty queue, both the head and rear pointers refer to the same node.

Removing Items from the Queue

Removing an item from the queue both removes the front node from the data structure and makes the next front-most item the new front of the queue. In addition, this implementation of the queue data structure returns the value of the removed item as the return value from the Remove method.

The code for the Remove method, as shown Listing 6.7, follows these steps:

1. Makes sure there's something in the queue. If not, the Remove method doesn't do anything and returns a null value.

2. Sets the return value of the function to the value of the front queue item.

3. If there's only one item in the queue, sets both the head and rear pointers to Nothing. There's nothing left in the queue.

4. If there was more than one item in the queue, sets the front pointer to refer to the second item in the queue. This effectively kills the old first item.

Listing 6.7: Use the Remove Method to Drop Items from a Queue

```
Public Function Remove() As Variant
    ' Remove an item from the head of the
    ' list, and return its value.

    If QueueEmpty Then
        Remove = Null
    Else
        Remove = qFront.Value
        ' If there's only one item
        ' in the queue, qFront and qRear
        ' will be pointing to the same node.
```

```
                    ' Use the Is operator to test for that.
                    If qFront Is qRear Then
                        Set qFront = Nothing
                        Set qRear = Nothing
                    Else
                        Set qFront = qFront.NextItem
                    End If
                End If
            End Function
```

TIP	How can you tell when there's only one item in the queue? The Is operator comes in handy here. By checking whether "qFront Is qRear", you can find out whether the two variables refer to the same object. If the condition is True, they do refer to the same object, and therefore, there's only one item in the queue.

The diagram in Figure 6.15 demonstrates the one difficult step in removing an item. The diagram corresponds to this line of code:

```
Set qFront = qFront.NextItem
```

By moving the front pointer to the item that the first item previously pointed to, you eliminate the reference to the old first item, and VBA removes it from memory. After this step, the queue will contain one fewer item.

FIGURE 6.15

To remove an item, move the front pointer to the second node in the queue.

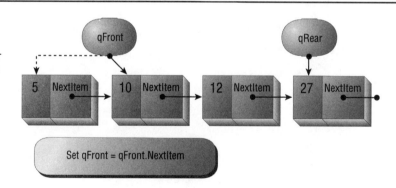

Is the Queue Empty?

You'll often need to be able to detect whether the queue is empty, and the example implementation includes the read-only QueueEmpty property for this reason. The queue can be empty only if both the front and rear pointers are Nothing, and the code shown here checks for this condition:

```
Property Get QueueEmpty() As Boolean
    ' Return True if the queue contains
    ' no items.

    QueueEmpty = ((qFront Is Nothing) And (qRear Is Nothing))
End Property
```

The QueueEmpty property allows you to write code like this:

```
Do While Not q.QueueEmpty
    Debug.Print q.Remove()
Loop
```

A Simple Queue Example

The code in Listing 6.8 demonstrates the use of the queue data structure. It creates a new queue, adds five words to the queue, and then removes the words, one at a time. The words should come out in the same order in which they were entered. Note that if you'd used a stack for the same exercise, the words would have come out in the opposite order from the one in which they'd been entered.

Listing 6.8: Using the Queue Data Structure

```
Dim qTest As New Queue

Sub TestQueues()
    With qTest
        .Add "Hello"
        .Add "There"
        .Add "How"
        .Add "Are"
        .Add "You"
        Do While Not .QueueEmpty
            Debug.Print .Remove()
        Loop
    End With
End Sub
```

Creating Ordered Linked Lists

A linked list is a simple data structure, as shown earlier in Figure 6.1, that allows you to maintain an ordered list of items without having to know ahead of time how many items you'll be adding. To build this data structure, you need two class modules: one for the list head and another for the items in the list. The example presented here is a sorted linked list. As you enter items into the list, the code finds the correct place to insert them and adjusts the links around the new nodes accordingly.

The ListItem Class

The code for the ListItem class, shown below, is simple, as you can see in Listing 6.9. The code should look very familiar; it's parallel to the code in Listing 6.1. (Remember, the Stack data structure is just a logical extension of the linked list.)

```
Public Value As Variant
Public NextItem As ListItem
```

The class module contains storage for the value to be stored in the node, plus a pointer to the next node. As you instantiate members of this class, you'll set the NextItem property to refer to the next item in the list, which depends on where in the list you insert the new node.

The List Class

The List class includes but a single data element:

```
Dim liHead As ListItem
```

The liHead item provides a reference to the first item in the linked list. (If there's nothing yet in the list, liHead is Nothing.) The List class also includes three public methods: Add, Delete, and DebugList. The Add method adds a new node to the list, in sorted order. The Delete method deletes a given value from the list if it's currently in the list. The DebugList method walks the list from one end to the other, printing the items in the list to the Debug window.

Finding an Item in the List

Both the Add and Delete methods count on a private method, Search, which takes as parameters a value to find and the current and previous items (which it fills in as it performs its search). The function returns a Boolean value indicating whether it actually found the requested value. The function, shown in Listing 6.9, follows these steps:

1. Assumes the return value is False, sets liPrevious to point to Nothing, and sets liCurrent to point to the head of the list

2. While not at the end of the list (while the current pointer isn't Nothing), does one of the following:

   - If the search item is greater than the stored value, it sets the previous pointer to refer to the current node and sets the current node to point to the next node.

   - If the search item is less than or equal to the stored value, then you're done, and it exits the loop.

3. Establishes whether the sought value was actually found

4. Returns the previous and current pointers in ByRef parameters and the found status as the return value

Listing 6.9: Use the Search Function to Find a Specific Element in the List

```
Function Search(ByVal varItem As Variant, _
ByRef liCurrent As ListItem, ByRef liPrevious As ListItem) _
As Boolean

    Dim fFound As Boolean

    fFound = False

    Set liPrevious = Nothing
    Set liCurrent = liHead

    Do While Not liCurrent Is Nothing
        With liCurrent
            If varItem > .Value Then
                Set liPrevious = liCurrent
                Set liCurrent = .NextItem
            Else
```

```
            Exit Do
        End If
    End With
Loop

' You can't compare the value in liCurrent to the sought
' value unless liCurrent points to something.
If Not liCurrent Is Nothing Then
    fFound = (liCurrent.Value = varItem)
End If
Search = fFound
End Function
```

Taking the most common case (searching for an item in the middle of an existing list), the diagrams in Figures 6.16, 6.17, 6.18, and 6.19 demonstrate the steps in the logic of the Search method.

FIGURE 6.16

Check to see if it's time to stop looping, based on the current value and the value to find.

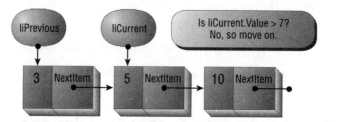

FIGURE 6.17

Set the previous pointer to point to the current node.

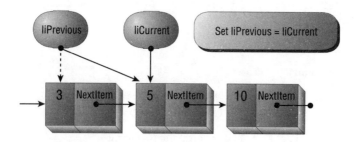

FIGURE 6.18

Set the current pointer to point to the next node.

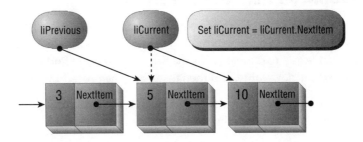

FIGURE 6.19

It's time to stop looping. Return True if the item was found.

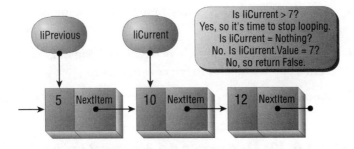

What happens in the borderline cases?

- **What if the list is currently empty?** In that case, liCurrent will be Nothing at the beginning of the procedure (because you've made it point to the same thing that liHead points to, which is Nothing). The function will do nothing and will return False. After you call the function, liCurrent and liPrevious will both be Nothing.

- **What if the item to be found is less than anything currently in the list?** In that case, the item should be placed before the item liHead currently points to. As soon as the code enters the loop, it will find that liCurrent.Value is greater than varItem and will jump out of the loop. The function will return False because the value pointed to by liCurrent isn't the same as the value being sought. After the function call, liCurrent will refer to the first item in the list, and liPrevious will be Nothing.

- **What if the item is greater than anything in the list?** In that case, the code will loop until liCurrent points to what the final node in the list points to (Nothing), and liPrevious will point to the final node in the list. The function will return False because liCurrent is Nothing.

Adding an Item to the List

Once you've found the right position, using the Search method of the List class, inserting an item is almost trivial. The Add method, shown in Listing 6.10, takes the new value as a parameter, calls the Search method to find the right position in which to insert the new value, and then inserts it. The procedure follows these steps:

1. Creates a new node for the new item and sets its value to the value passed as a parameter to the procedure.

2. Calls the Search method, which fills in the values of liCurrent and liPrevious. Disregard the return value; when adding an item, you don't care whether the value was already in the list.

3. Adjusts the new node's NextItem value to point to the newly calculated next item in the list.

4. If inserting an item anywhere but at the head of the list, sets the previous item's pointer to refer to the new node.

5. If inserting an item at the beginning of the list, sets the head pointer to refer to the new node.

Listing 6.10: Use the Add Method to Add a New Item to a List

```
Public Sub Add(varValue As Variant)
    Dim liNew As New ListItem
    Dim liCurrent As ListItem
    Dim liPrevious As ListItem

    liNew.Value = varValue

    ' Find where to put the new item. This function call
    ' fills in liCurrent and liPrevious.
    Call Search(varValue, liCurrent, liPrevious)

    If Not liPrevious Is Nothing Then
        Set liNew.NextItem = liPrevious.NextItem
        Set liPrevious.NextItem = liNew
    Else
        ' Inserting at the head of the list:
        ' Set the new item to point to what liHead currently
        ' points to (which might just be Nothing). Then
        ' make liHead point to the new item.
        Set liNew.NextItem = liHead
        Set liHead = liNew
```

```
      End If
End Sub
```

Inserting an item at the head of the list is easy. All you need to do is make the new node's NextItem pointer refer to the current head of the list and then make the list head pointer refer to the new node. The diagrams in Figures 6.20, 6.21, and 6.22 show how you can insert an item at the head of the list.

FIGURE 6.20

After Search is called, liPrevious is Nothing, indicating an insertion at the head of the list.

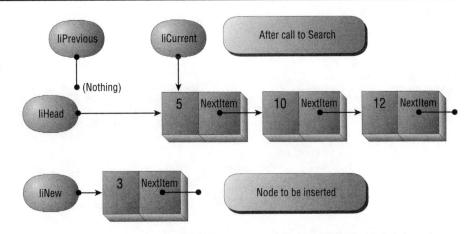

FIGURE 6.21

Make the new node's NextItem pointer refer to the item currently referred to by liHead.

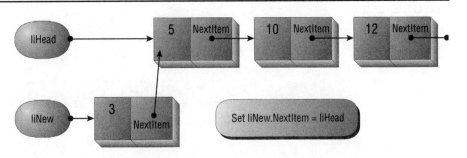

FIGURE 6.22

Make the list header point to the new node.

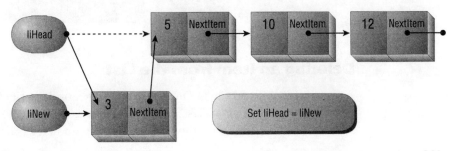

Inserting an item anywhere in the list besides at the head works similarly, but the steps are a bit different. If liPrevious isn't Nothing after the Add method calls Search, you must make the new node's NextItem point to what liPrevious currently points at and then make whatever liPrevious is pointing at point at liNew instead. The diagrams in Figures 6.23, 6.24, and 6.25 illustrate an insertion in the middle (or at the end) of the list.

FIGURE 6.23

After the Add method calls Search, liPrevious isn't Nothing, indicating an insertion after the head of the list

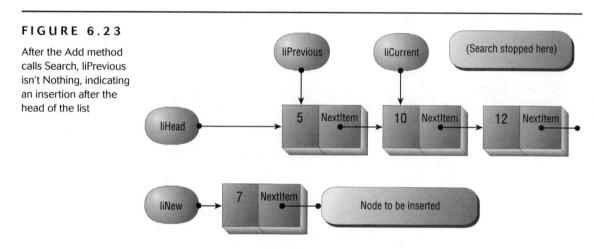

FIGURE 6.24

Make the new item point to the item after the one liPrevious points to.

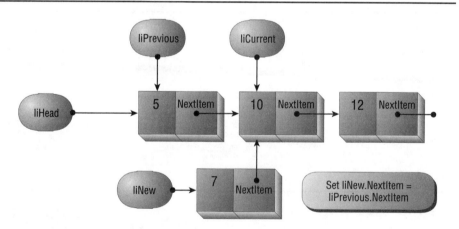

Deleting an Item from the List

Again, just as with adding an item, once you've found the right position using the Search method of the List class, deleting an item is simple. The Delete method, shown in Listing 6.11, takes the new value as a parameter, calls the Search method to find the item to be deleted, and if it's there, deletes it. The procedure follows these steps:

1. Calls the Search method, which fills in the values of liCurrent and liPrevious. If the function returns False, there's nothing else to do.

FIGURE 6.25

Make the item that liPrevious points to point to the new item, linking it into the list.

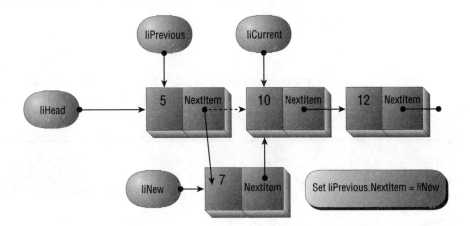

2. If deleting anywhere but at the head of the list, sets the previous item's pointer to refer to the node pointed to by the item to be deleted. (That is, it links around the deleted node.)

3. If deleting at the beginning of the list, sets the head pointer to refer to the node pointed to by the selected node. (It links the head pointer to the current second node in the list.)

4. When liCurrent goes out of scope, VBA destroys the node to be deleted because no other pointer refers to that instance of the class.

Listing 6.11: Use the Delete Method to Delete an Item from a List

```
Public Function Delete(varItem As Variant) As Boolean
    Dim liCurrent As ListItem
    Dim liPrevious As ListItem
    Dim fFound As Boolean

    ' Find the item. This function call
    ' fills in liCurrent and liPrevious.
    fFound = Search(varItem, liCurrent, liPrevious)
    If fFound Then
```

```
        If Not liPrevious Is Nothing Then
            ' Deleting from the middle or end of the list.
            Set liPrevious.NextItem = liCurrent.NextItem
        Else
            ' Deleting from the head of the list.
            Set liHead = liCurrent.NextItem
        End If
    End If
    Delete = fFound
End Function
```

To delete an item from the head of the list, all you need to do is make the header's pointer refer to the second item in the list. The diagrams in Figures 6.26, 6.27, and 6.28 show how you can delete an item at the head of the list.

FIGURE 6.26

If the search ends at the head of the list, liPrevious will be Nothing.

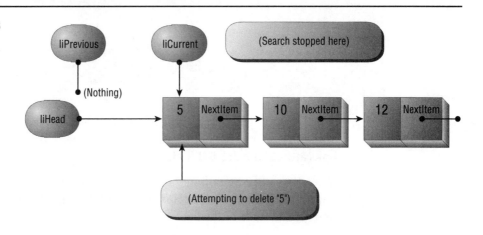

FIGURE 6.27

To delete the first item, make liHead point to the second item in the list.

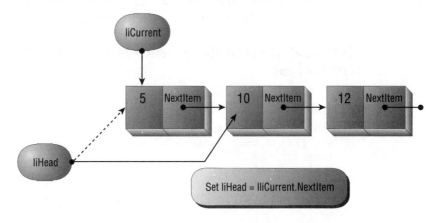

FIGURE 6.28

When liCurrent goes out of scope, VBA destroys the deleted item.

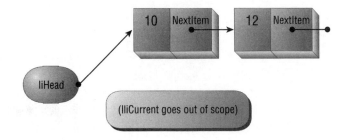

What about deleting an item other than the first? That's easy too: just link around the item to be deleted. The diagrams in Figures 6.29, 6.30, and 6.31 show how you can delete an item that's not the first item in the list.

FIGURE 6.29

The search found the node to be deleted. (liCurrent points to it.)

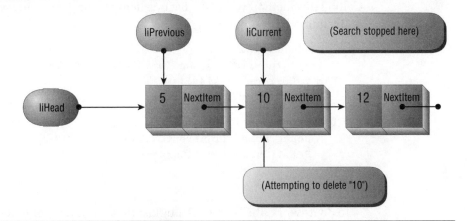

FIGURE 6.30

Link around the node to be deleted.

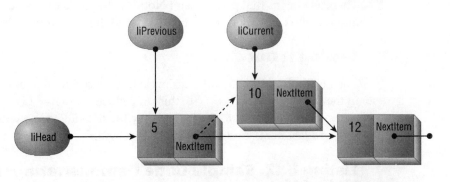

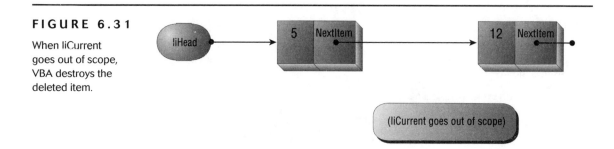

FIGURE 6.31

When liCurrent goes out of scope, VBA destroys the deleted item.

Traversing the List

A list wouldn't do you much good if you couldn't traverse it, visiting each element in turn. The example project includes a DebugList method of the List class. Calling this method walks the list one item at a time, printing each value in turn to the Immediate window:

```
Public Sub DebugList()
    ' Print the list to the Immediate window.
    Dim liCurrent As ListItem

    Set liCurrent = liHead
    Do While Not liCurrent Is Nothing
        Debug.Print liCurrent.Value
        Set liCurrent = liCurrent.NextItem
    Loop
End Sub
```

To do its work, the code in DebugList first sets a pointer to the head of the list. Then, as long as that pointer isn't Nothing, the code prints out the current value and sets the current node pointer to refer to the next item in the list.

Testing It Out

The ListTest module includes a simple test procedure that exercises the methods in the List class. When you run this procedure, shown in Listing 6.12, the code will add the ten items to the list, display the list, delete a few items (including the first and last item), and then print the list again.

Listing 6.12: Sample Code Demonstrating the Ordered Linked List

```
Sub TestLists()
    Dim liTest As New List
```

```
    With liTest
        .Add 5
        .Add 1
        .Add 6
        .Add 4
        .Add 9
        .Add 8
        .Add 7
        .Add 10
        .Add 2
        .Add 3
        Call .DebugList
        Debug.Print "======"
        .Delete 1
        .Delete 10
        .Delete 3
        .Delete 4
        Call .DebugList
    End With
End Sub
```

Why Use a Linked List?

That's a good question, because the native VBA Collection object provides much of the same functionality as a linked list, without the effort. Internally, collections are stored as a complex linked list, with links in both directions (instead of only one), and the data structure also includes pointers that make it possible to traverse the collection as though it were a binary tree. This way, VBA can traverse the collection forward and backward, and it can find items quickly. (Binary trees provide very quick random access to elements in the data structure.)

It's just this flexibility that makes the overhead involved in using VBA's collections onerous. You may find that you need to create a sorted list, but working with collections is just too slow, and maintaining collections in a sorted order is quite difficult. In these cases, you may find it more worthwhile to use a linked list, as demonstrated in the preceding example, instead.

Creating Binary Trees

A simple binary tree, as shown earlier in Figure 6.2, is the most complex data structure discussed in this chapter. This type of binary tree is made up of nodes that contain a piece of information and pointers to left and right child nodes. In many cases, you'll use binary trees to store data in a sorted manner: as you add a value, you'll look at each existing node. If the new value is smaller than the existing value, look in the left child tree; if it's greater, look in the right child tree. Because the process at this point is the same no matter which node you're currently at, many programmers use recursive algorithms to work with binary trees.

Why use a binary tree? Besides the fact that finding items in a binary tree is much faster than performing a linear search through a list or an array, if you insert the items in an ordered fashion, you get not only efficient storage, but sorting for free—like finding a prize in the bottom of your cereal box! Who could ask for more? You'll see this technique at work in the sample module, TREETEST.BAS.

Traversing Binary Trees

Once you've created a binary tree, you can use one of three standard methods for traversing the tree. All three of the following examples use the tree illustrated in Figure 6.32. In that figure, the nodes contain letters, but their ordering here doesn't mean anything. They're just labeled to make it easy to refer to them.

FIGURE 6.32

Use this binary tree to demonstrate tree traversal.

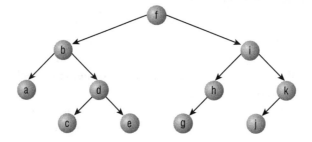

Inorder Traversal

To traverse a tree using inorder traversal, you must visit the left subtree, then the root node, and then the right subtree. When visiting the subtrees, you take the same steps. If, each time you visited a root node in the tree shown in Figure 6.32, you listed the value, you'd list the nodes in the following order:

```
a b c d e f g h i j k
```

Preorder Traversal

Using preorder traversal, you first visit the root node, then the left subtree, and then the right subtree. Using this method, you'll always print out the root value and then the values of the left and right children. Using the example shown in Figure 6.32, you'd print the nodes in this order:

```
f b a d c e i h g k j
```

Postorder Traversal

Using postorder traversal, you visit the left subtree, then the right subtree, and finally, the root node. Using the example shown in Figure 6.32, you'd visit the nodes in this order:

```
a c e d b g h j k i f
```

What's This Good For?

Binary trees have many analogs in the real world. For example, a binary tree can represent a pedigree tree for a purebred cat. Each node represents a cat, with the left and right links to the cat's two parents. If a parent is unknown, the link will point to Nothing. The diagram in Figure 6.33 shows a parentage tree for a hypothetical purebred cat.

FIGURE 6.33

A binary tree can represent parentage (two parents per node).

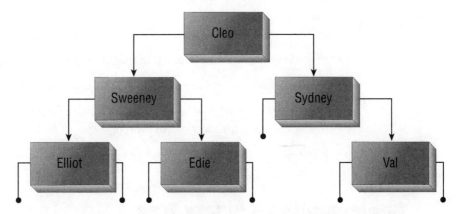

A binary tree can also represent an algebraic expression. If you place algebraic identifiers (constants and variables) in terminal nodes and operators in the interior nodes, you can represent any algebraic expression in a tree. This makes it possible to write expression evaluators: by parsing the expression, placing the various expressions correctly in the tree, and then traversing the tree in the correct order, you can write a simple expression evaluator. The diagram in Figure 6.34 shows how you might represent a simple algebraic expression in a binary tree.

FIGURE 6.34

A binary tree can represent an algebraic expression.

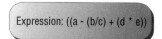

Expression: ((a - (b/c) + (d * e))

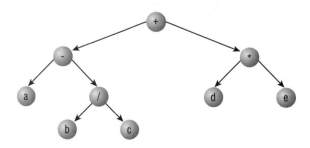

Depending on how you traverse the tree, you could visit the nodes in any of the following manners.

- Inorder traversal:

  `(a - (b/c) + (d * e))`

- Preorder traversal (the order that might be used by a functional calculator):

  `Add(Subtract(a, Divide(b, c)), Multiply(d, e))`

- Postorder traversal (the order used by "reverse Polish" notation calculators that use a stack for their calculations):

  `Push a, Push b, Push c, Divide, Subtract, Push d, Push e, Multiply, Add`

Implementing a Binary Tree

The following sections discuss in some detail how the code that implements the binary tree class operates. You'll find the code for this section in TREE.CLS, TREEITEM.CLS, and TREETEST.BAS.

The TreeItem Class

As with the structure items in the previous sections, the TreeItem class is simple. It includes just the three necessary data items: the value to be stored at the current node, the pointer to the left child node, and the pointer to the right child node.

```
Public Value As Variant
Public LeftChild As TreeItem
Public RightChild As TreeItem
```

Of course, there's nothing stopping you from storing more information in the TreeItem class. For example, you may need to write a program that can parse a text file, create a binary tree containing all the distinct words in the file, and store each word in its own node, along with a list of all the page numbers on which that word occurred. In this case, you might want to store a pointer to a linked list in the TreeItem class, along with the text item. That linked list could store the list of all the page numbers on which the word was found.

The Tree Class

As with the previous data structures, the base Tree class stores the bulk of the code required to make the data structure work. The class contains but a single data item:

```
Dim tiHead As TreeItem
```

As with the other data structures, tiHead is an anchor for the entire data structure. It points to the first item in the binary tree, and from there, the items point to other items.

In addition, the Tree class module contains two module variables:

```
' These private variables are used when
' adding new nodes.
Private mfAddDupes As Boolean
Private mvarItemToAdd As Variant
```

The method that adds items to the binary tree uses these global variables. If they weren't global, the code would have to pass them as parameters to the appropriate methods. What's wrong with that? Because the Add method is recursive, the procedure might call itself many times. Each call takes up memory that isn't released until the entire procedure has completed. If your tree is very deep, you could eat up a large chunk of stack space adding a new item. To avoid that issue, the Tree class doesn't pass these values as parameters; it just makes them available to all the procedures, no matter where they're called.

Adding a New Item

When adding items to a binary tree, you may or may not want to add an item if its value already appears in the data structure. To make it easy to distinguish between those two cases, the Tree class contains two separate methods, Add and AddUnique, shown in Listing 6.13. Each of the methods ends up calling the AddNode procedure, shown in Listing 6.14.

Listing 6.13: The Tree Class Provides Two Ways to Add New Items

```
Public Sub Add(varNewItem As Variant)
    ' Add a new node, allowing duplicates.
    ' Use module variables to place as little as
    ' possible on the stack in recursive procedure calls.

    mfAddDupes = True
    mvarItemToAdd = varNewItem
    Call AddNode(tiHead)
End Sub

Public Sub AddUnique(varNewItem As Variant)
    ' Add a new node, skipping duplicate values.
    ' Use module variables to place as little as
    ' possible on the stack in recursive procedure calls.

    mfAddDupes = False
    mvarItemToAdd = varNewItem
    Call AddNode(tiHead)
End Sub
```

The recursive AddNode procedure adds a new node to the binary tree pointed to by the TreeItem pointer it receives as a parameter. Once you get past the recursive nature of the procedure, the code is trivial:

- If the TreeItem pointer, ti, is Nothing, it sets the pointer to a new TreeItem and sticks the value into that new node.

- If the pointer isn't Nothing, then:

  - If the new value is less than the value in ti, the code calls AddNode with the left child pointer of the current node.

  - If the new value is greater than the value in ti, the code calls AddNode with the right child pointer of the current node.

- If the new value is equal to the current value, then, if you've instructed the code to add duplicates, the code arbitrarily calls AddNode with the right child pointer. (You could use the left instead, if you wanted.) If you don't want to add duplicates, the procedure just returns.

- Sooner or later, after calling AddNode for each successive child node, the code will find a pointer that is Nothing, at which point it takes the action in the first step. Because nothing follows the recursive call to AddNode in the procedure, after each successive layer has finished processing, the code just works its way back up the list of calls.

Listing 6.14: The Recursive AddNode Procedure Adds a New Node to the Tree

```
Private Function AddNode(ti As TreeItem) As TreeItem

    ' Add a node to the tree pointed to by ti.
    ' Module variables used:
    '    mvarItemToAdd: the value to add to the tree.
    '    mfAddDupes: Boolean indicating whether to add items
    '       that already exist or to skip them.

    If ti Is Nothing Then
        Set ti = New TreeItem
        ti.Value = mvarItemToAdd
    Else
        If mvarItemToAdd < ti.Value Then
            Set ti.LeftChild = AddNode(ti.LeftChild)
        ElseIf mvarItemToAdd > ti.Value Then
            Set ti.RightChild = AddNode(ti.RightChild)
        Else
            ' mvarItemToAdd = ti.Value
            ' You're adding a node that already exists.
            ' You could add it to the left or to the right,
            ' but this code arbitrarily adds it to the right.
            If mfAddDupes Then
                Set ti.RightChild = AddNode(ti.RightChild)
            End If
        End If
    End If
End Sub
```

Adding a New Node: Walking the Code

Suppose you were to try adding a new node to the tree shown in Figure 6.35 with the value "m". Table 6.2 outlines the process involved in getting the node added. (This discussion assumes that the class module's tiHead member points to the tree shown in Figure 6.35.) For each step, the table includes, in column 1, the recursion level—that is, the number of times the procedure has called itself.

FIGURE 6.35

Revisiting the alphabetic tree, attempting to add a new node

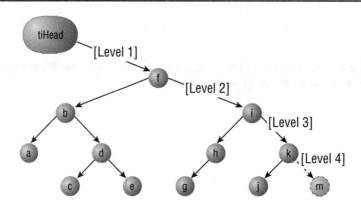

TABLE 6.2   Recursive Steps to Add "m" to the Sample Tree

Level	Action
0	You call the Add method, passing the value "m"
0	The Add method sets fAddDupes to True and sets varNewItem to the value "m". It then calls the AddNode method, passing the pointer to the first item in the tree (a node with the value "f", in this case) [Call to Level 1]
1	AddNode checks to see whether ti is Nothing. It's not (It points to the node containing "f".)
1	Because "m" is greater then "f", AddNode calls itself, passing the right child pointer of the node ti currently points to (That is, it passes a pointer to the node containing "i".) [Call to Level 2]
2	AddNode checks to see whether ti is Nothing. It's not (It points to the node containing "i".)

TABLE 6.2   Recursive Steps to Add "m" to the Sample Tree (continued)

Level	Action
2	Because "m" is greater then "i", AddNode calls itself, passing the right child pointer of the node ti currently points to (That is, it passes a pointer to the node containing "k".) [Call to Level 3]
3	AddNode checks to see whether ti is Nothing. It's not (It points to the node containing "k".)
3	Because "m" is greater then "k", AddNode calls itself, passing the right child pointer of the node ti currently points to (that is, the right child pointer of the node containing "k", which is Nothing) [Call to Level 4]
4	AddNode checks to see whether ti is Nothing. It is, so it creates a new node, sets the pointer passed to it (the right child of the node containing "k") to point to the new node, and returns
4	There's nothing else to do, so the code returns [Return to Level 3]
3	There's nothing else to do, so the code returns [Return to Level 2]
2	There's nothing else to do, so the code returns [Return to Level 1]
1	The code returns back to the original caller

Traversing the Tree

As mentioned earlier in this discussion, there are three standard methods for traversing a tree: inorder, preorder, and postorder. Because of the recursive nature of these actions, the code for each is simple; it is shown in Listing 6.15. The class provides three public methods (WalkInOrder, WalkPreOrder, WalkPostOrder). Each calls a private procedure, passing to it the pointer to the head of the tree. From then on, each of the private procedures follows the prescribed order in visiting nodes in the tree.

Of course, in your own applications, you'll want to do something with each node besides print its value to the Debug window. In that case, modify the three private procedures to do what you need done with each node of your tree.

Listing 6.15: Because of Recursion, the Code to Traverse the Tree Is Simple

```
Public Sub WalkInOrder()
    Call InOrder(tiHead)
End Sub

Public Sub WalkPreOrder()
    Call PreOrder(tiHead)
End Sub

Public Sub WalkPostOrder()
    Call PostOrder(tiHead)
End Sub

Private Sub InOrder(ti As TreeItem)
    If Not ti Is Nothing Then
        Call InOrder(ti.LeftChild)
        Debug.Print ti.Value; " ";
        Call InOrder(ti.RightChild)
    End If
End Sub

Private Sub PreOrder(ti As TreeItem)
    If Not ti Is Nothing Then
        Debug.Print ti.Value; " ";
        Call PreOrder(ti.LeftChild)
        Call PreOrder(ti.RightChild)
    End If
End Sub

Private Sub PostOrder(ti As TreeItem)
    If Not ti Is Nothing Then
        Call PostOrder(ti.LeftChild)
        Call PostOrder(ti.RightChild)
        Debug.Print ti.Value; " ";
    End If
End Sub
```

Traversing a Tree: Walking the Code

In order to understand tree traversal, assume you'd like to perform a postorder traversal of the tree shown in Figure 6.36. Although this example doesn't include many nodes, the steps are the same, no matter the size of the tree.

FIGURE 6.36

Use this small example for the tree traversal example.

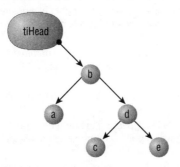

To visit each node in the tree using the postorder traversal, follow the steps listed in Table 6.3. (You'll want to keep a firm finger on the diagram as you work your way through these steps.)

TABLE 6.3   Recursive Steps to Perform a Postorder Traversal

Level	Action
0	Call the WalkPostOrder method of the Tree class
1	The code in WalkPostOrder calls the PostOrder procedure, passing tiHead as a parameter [Call to Level 2]
2	PostOrder checks to see whether ti (its parameter) is Nothing. It's not (it's a reference to the node that contains "b"), so it can continue
2	PostOrder calls itself, passing the left child pointer of the node ti points to (that is, it passes a pointer to the node containing "a") [Call to Level 3]
3	PostOrder checks to see whether ti (its parameter) is Nothing. It's not (it's a reference to the node that contains "a"), so it can continue
3	PostOrder calls itself, passing the left child pointer of the node ti points to (That is, it passes a pointer that is Nothing.) [Call to Level 4]

TABLE 6.3   Recursive Steps to Perform a Postorder Traversal (continued)

Level	Action
4	PostOrder checks to see whether ti (its parameter) is Nothing. It is, so it can't do anything and just returns [Return to Level 3]
3	PostOrder calls itself, passing the right child pointer of the node ti points to (That is, it passes a pointer that is Nothing.) [Call to Level 4]
4	PostOrder checks to see whether ti (its parameter) is Nothing. It is, so it can't do anything and just returns [Return to Level 3]
3	PostOrder prints its value ("a") and then returns [Return to Level 2]
2	PostOrder calls itself, passing the right child pointer of the node ti points to (That is, it passes a pointer to the node containing "d".) [Call to Level 3]
3	PostOrder checks to see whether ti (its parameter) is Nothing. It's not (it's a reference to the node that contains "d"), so it can continue
3	PostOrder calls itself, passing the left child pointer of the node ti points to (That is, it passes a pointer to the node containing "c".) [Call to Level 4]
4	PostOrder checks to see whether ti (its parameter) is Nothing. It's not (it's a reference to the node that contains "c"), so it can continue
4	PostOrder calls itself, passing the left child pointer of the node ti points to (That is, it passes a pointer that's Nothing.) [Call to Level 5]
5	PostOrder checks to see whether ti (its parameter) is Nothing. It is, so it can't do anything and just returns [Return to Level 4]
4	PostOrder calls itself, passing the right child pointer of the node ti points to (That is, it passes a pointer that's Nothing.) [Call to Level 5]
5	PostOrder checks to see whether ti (its parameter) is Nothing. It is, so it can't do anything and just returns [Return to Level 4]
4	PostOrder prints its value ("c") and then returns [Return to Level 3]
3	PostOrder calls itself, passing the right child pointer of the node ti points to (That is, it passes a pointer to the node containing "e".) [Call to Level 4]
4	PostOrder checks to see whether ti (its parameter) is Nothing. It's not (it's a reference to the node that contains "e"), so it can continue

TABLE 6.3 Recursive Steps to Perform a Postorder Traversal (continued)

Level	Action
4	PostOrder calls itself, passing the left child pointer of the node ti points to (That is, it passes a pointer that's Nothing.) [Call to Level 5]
5	PostOrder checks to see whether ti (its parameter) is Nothing. It is, so it can't do anything and just returns [Return to Level 4]
4	PostOrder calls itself, passing the right child pointer of the node ti points to (That is, it passes a pointer that's Nothing.) [Call to Level 5]
5	PostOrder checks to see whether ti (its parameter) is Nothing. It is, so it can't do anything and just returns [Return to Level 4]
4	PostOrder prints its value ("e") and then returns [Return to Level 3]
3	PostOrder prints its value ("d") and then returns [Return to Level 2]
2	PostOrder prints its value ("b") and then returns to WalkPostOrder [Return to Level 1, and exit]

Optimizing the Traversals

If you worked your way through the many steps it took to traverse the simple tree, you can imagine how much work it takes to perform the operation on a large tree. You could optimize the code a bit by checking to see whether the child node is Nothing before you recursively call the procedure. That is, you could modify InOrder like this:

```
Private Sub InOrder(ti As TreeItem)
    If Not ti Is Nothing Then
        If Not ti.LeftChild Is Nothing Then
            Call InOrder(ti.LeftChild)
        End If
        Debug.Print ti.Value; " ";
        If Not ti.RightChild Is Nothing Then
            Call InOrder(ti.RightChild)
        End If
    End If
End Sub
```

This code would execute a tiny bit faster than the original InOrder tree-traversal procedure (one less procedure call for both children of all the bottom-level nodes), but it's a little harder to read.

The Sample Project

The code in the sample module performs some simple tree manipulations: it adds nodes, walks the tree in all the traversal orders, and deletes some nodes using the TreeDelete method (not covered in this book, but the code is there in the Tree class for you to use). The first few tests correspond to the tree shown in Figure 6.32 earlier in this chapter, and you can use the code in the project to test your understanding of the different traversal orders.

What Didn't We Cover?

We actually omitted more about binary trees than we covered here. Binary trees usually fill multiple chapters in textbooks for courses in standard data structures. Consider the following:

- Deleting nodes from binary trees is a science unto itself. The sample project includes code to delete nodes from a tree, but it's just one of many solutions, and possibly not the most efficient one.

- Balancing trees is crucial if you want optimized performance. For example, if you add previously sorted data to a tree, you end up with a degenerate tree–all the nodes are linked as the right child of the parent. In other words, you end up with a linked list. Searching through linked lists isn't particularly efficient, and you lose the benefit of using a binary tree. Courses in data structures normally cover various methods you can use to keep your trees balanced (that is, with the left and right subtrees having approximately the same depth).

- In a course on data structures, you'll normally find a number of variants on binary trees (B-trees, for example) that also take into account data stored on disk.

If you're interested in finding out more about these variants on binary trees, find a good textbook that focuses on data structures. Of course, most such textbooks are written for Pascal programmers (most universities use Pascal as a teaching language), so you'll need to do some conversion. It's not hard, however, once you've got the hang of it.

Summary

In this chapter, we've taken a stab at revisiting "Computer Science 201: Data Structures" or a similar university course you might once have taken. Of course, in this limited space, we can do little more than provide a "proof of concept"—the technique of using self-referential, abstract data structures in VBA works, and it works well. Because of the availability of class modules, you can use the techniques provided here to create hybrid data structures that you just couldn't manage with VBA's arrays and collections. Linked lists of binary trees, collections of linked lists, linked lists of linked lists—all these, and more, are possible, but we suggest drawing pictures on paper first!

Note that all the ideas presented in this chapter rely on data in memory. That is, there's no concept of persistent storage when working with these data structures. If you want to store information contained in one of these abstract structures from one session to the next, you'll need to design some storage mechanism, whether it be in the Registry, an INI file, or a table. In addition, if you run out of memory, you'll receive a run-time error when you attempt to use the New keyword. Obviously, this shouldn't happen. In production code, you'd want to add error handling to make sure your application didn't die under low-memory conditions. For more information on handling errors, see Chapter 7.

This chapter presented a number of topics to keep in mind when working with data in memory, including:

- Using class modules to represent elements of linked data structures
- Building stacks, queues, ordered linked lists, and binary trees using class modules
- Using recursion to work with and traverse binary trees

Professional Development with VBA

- **Understanding error handling**

- **Exploring VBA debugging tools**

- **Examining debugging strategies**

- **Adding professional design elements**

If you're reading this book, you're probably a serious VBA developer. Whether you create custom software for a living or consider yourself a "power user" of a tool like Microsoft Office, you spend a good deal of time programming. Chances are you develop software (or at least some module code) used by others. You would also like to reach a point where you can repeatedly reuse the code you write. Sound familiar? If it does, this chapter is for you. It discusses a variety of topics that fall under the category of professional development. Included are things like error handling, debugging, naming standards, and object model design. Our goal is to suggest techniques you can use to create VBA code that is robust, portable, and bug free. (Well, the last is tough, but we give it our best shot.)

Table 7.1 lists the sample files provided on the CD-ROM for this chapter.

TABLE 7.1   Sample Files

File Name	Description
ERRORS.XLS	Excel 97 file with sample code
ERROR.MDB	Access 97 databases with sample code
BASERROR.BAS	Generic error-handling functions
BASERREX.BAS	Error-handling examples from this chapter
LOG.CLS	Log class module code
PSTACK.CLS	Stack class module code
PSTACKIT.CLS	StackItem class module code

Handling Errors the Right Way

This chapter starts with error handling because it's a basic feature of a professionally designed application. Inevitably, your program will eventually encounter a situation its code was not designed to handle. How you cope with this situation affects the application and those using it. This section looks at the three types of errors you'll find in your code, shows you how to handle them, and suggests some guidelines for building error handling into every procedure you write.

The Three Types of Errors

As you develop your applications, you'll encounter three types of errors:

- Compile-time errors
- Run-time errors
- Logic errors

Compile-time errors surface while you're writing your code and usually result from syntax errors or an invalid use of a function or property. Under most circumstances, these errors are easy to locate and correct. VBA checks the syntax of each line of code as you enter it and informs you, by means of highlighted text and a warning message, when it contains a syntax error. For errors in syntax that requires multiple lines, like a For...Next loop, and other compile-time errors, VBA warns you of problems when you compile your application. Regardless of the VBA host you're using, there is a way to compile your code while you're working on it.

TIP

As you become more experienced as a VBA programmer, you may find VBA's syntax error dialog annoying. You can prevent it from appearing by unchecking the Auto Syntax Check box in VBA's Options dialog. Despite its name, this option does not turn off syntax checking. (VBA still checks and warns you by highlighting the errant line.) It simply suppresses the message box.

Run-time errors are a bit more insidious than compile-time errors because, as the term implies, they don't surface until you run your application. Run-time errors occur when a syntactically correct line of code can't execute because of the current environmental circumstances. For instance, suppose you tried to use the VBA Kill procedure, which deletes a disk file, and passed the name of a file that did not exist. Even if the statement is free of syntax errors, it cannot execute, because an input parameter is invalid. When this happens, VBA raises an error that your program can intercept and cope with. (This process is called *trapping* the error.) If your program does not trap the error, VBA handles it itself. Depending on the

VBA host you're using, this may or may not leave your application in a recoverable state. That's why it's important to ensure that your program traps all runtime errors that occur. This section shows you how to do that. The good news regarding run-time errors is that through thorough testing, you can weed out most of the problems that result from them.

The most insidious errors of them all are *logic errors.* Logic errors (affectionately known to programmers as *bugs*) occur when your code compiles without errors and runs without errors but produces incorrect results. These errors normally result from a mistake or oversight on the programmer's part and can be very difficult to track down. For example, consider the code shown in Listing 7.1.

Listing 7.1: Perfectly Good Code That Doesn't Work Right

```
Sub FileInfo(strPath As String)
    Dim strDir As String

    ' Trim file name off, leaving the directory name
    strDir = TrimFileName(strPath)

    ' Display message box
    MsgBox "The file " & strPath & _
     " is located in " & strDir, _
     vbInformation, "File Info"
End Sub

Function TrimFileName(strPath As String) As String
    Dim cb As Long

    ' Trim characters from right end of string
    ' until we find a backslash or run out of letters
    Do
        strPath = Left(strPath, Len(strPath) - 1)
    Loop Until Right(strPath, 1) = "\" Or _
     Len(strPath) = 0

    ' Return result
    TrimFileName = strPath
End Function
```

The FileInfo procedure is designed to accept the path to a file and display a message box showing the full path and the directory name. It calls the TrimFileName function to trim the file name from the path, leaving the directory name. When you call TrimFileName from the Immediate window, it works as expected. On the other hand, when you call FileInfo, the MsgBox statement displays the directory twice rather than the full path. What's wrong? The error is caused by an oversight common to those new to VBA. The strPath argument to TrimFileName is passed *by reference* instead of *by value*, so when TrimFileName operates on the argument, it is also modifying the variable in FileInfo.

In the case of compile- or run-time errors, VBA eventually tells you what the error is and shows you the line of code causing the error. With logic errors, it's up to you to track them down. Fortunately, VBA does provide some tools to assist you, as described in the section "Debugging Like the Pros" later in this chapter.

Trapping Run-Time Errors

Unless you tell it otherwise, VBA handles all run-time errors itself by displaying an error message and halting execution at the offending line of code. While this might be acceptable and is often helpful during the development and testing phases, it is rarely so in a production application. Instead, your code should trap and deal with its own errors, even if the only thing it does is display the same error message VBA would.

The key to this behavior is the error trap, which you set using the On Error statement. In effect, you set a trap in a procedure, and that trap then lies in wait for an error to occur. When the error occurs, your error trap springs into action, executing other statements that cope with the error.

VBA's On Error statement has three forms:

- On Error GoTo Label
- On Error Resume Next
- On Error GoTo 0

The sections that follow explain each of these in turn.

> **NOTE**
>
> You must handle errors in VBA on a procedure-by-procedure basis. There is no way to create a general error handler that is triggered in response to all run-time errors. While you can create a single procedure to handle errors, you still have to add to code to every other procedure to call it in response to an error.

On Error GoTo Label

On Error GoTo Label is the most powerful error trap because it gives you the greatest degree of flexibility in handling a run-time error. Using the On Error GoTo Label statement causes VBA to jump to a specific location in your code if an error occurs. When an error occurs in code after executing an On Error GoTo Label statement, control passes to the assigned label. Listing 7.2 shows a sample procedure that illustrates the most common format for an error handler.

Listing 7.2: Sample Procedure Containing an Error Trap

```
Sub GenericProcWithErrorTrap()
    ' Stub showing standard way to construct an error handler

    ' Set the error trap
    On Error GoTo HandleError

    ' Some code that might generate a run-time error
    ' would go here

ExitHere:
    ' Important! Exit proc before error handler
    Exit Sub
HandleError:
    ' Error handling goes here!
    Resume ExitHere
End Sub
```

Everything begins with an On Error GoTo Label statement. Normally, this is the first statement to execute, and it appears just before or after local variable declarations. (Whether you place it before or after the variable declarations is a matter of style and personal preference.) In our example, the label used is "HandleError".

> **NOTE**
> Prior versions of Basic required that all label names be unique across an entire project. VBA no longer has this restriction. Therefore, you can use the label "HandleError" in every one of your procedures should you so desire.

If an error occurs in the code that follows the On Error GoTo Label statement, VBA begins executing code with the statement immediately following the label. The label must appear in the same procedure as the On Error GoTo Label statement.

It is standard practice to place the error-handling code at the end of the procedure. This is because, in the event that no error occurs, you must exit the procedure before reaching the error handler. Otherwise, VBA executes your error-handling code. Note the Exit Sub statement (and its associated ExitHere label) in the sample procedure.

Once an error has occurred and VBA has begun executing your error-handling code, VBA is in a special state. While in this state, the following is true:

- The error handler defined by the On Error GoTo Label statement is no longer in effect. This means any run-time error that occurs within the error handler is treated as an untrapped error.

- You can use a Resume statement (described in the section "The Resume Statement" later in this chapter) to return control to the main procedure and resume normal error handling.

- You cannot execute an End Sub or End Function statement to "fall out of" an error handler. You must explicitly use an Exit Sub or Exit Function statement to exit the procedure. Commonly accepted software engineering practice says a procedure should have only one entry point and one exit point, so an even better idea is to use Resume Label to return control to the main code, where the procedure can be exited at a common point (as the example does).

On Error Resume Next

Creating an error handler with the On Error GoTo Label statement can require a considerable amount of code. Sometimes you'll want to ignore errors. Other times you'll know exactly which error to expect and want to handle it without having to write a full error handler. The On Error Resume Next statement does just that. It tells VBA to suppress the standard error message and simply execute the next line of code. For example, if you're attempting to delete a file and don't care whether the file actually exists, you might use code like that shown in Listing 7.3. If the file exists, the procedure deletes it. If the file does not exist, a run-time error occurs, VBA suppresses it, and the procedure terminates normally.

Listing 7.3: Use On Error Resume Next to Ignore a Possible Run-Time Error

```
Sub DeleteFile(ByVal strFileName As String)
    ' Example showing an On Error Resume Next
    ' Deletes a file if it exists

    On Error Resume Next

    Kill strFileName
End Sub
```

The On Error Resume Next statement lets the program ignore the error and continue.

On Error GoTo 0

When you use an On Error GoTo Label or On Error Resume Next statement, it remains in effect until the procedure terminates, another error handler is declared, or the error handler is canceled. The On Error GoTo 0 statement cancels the error handler. VBA (or an error handler in a calling procedure, as described in the section "VBA's Error-Handling Hierarchy" later in this chapter) again traps subsequent errors. This statement also resets the value of the Err object (see the section "Determining Which Error Has Occurred"), so if you need the values it contains, you must store away its properties.

Responding to Trapped Errors

Now that you know how to set an error trap, what do you do when an error occurs? Generally, that depends on the type of error that occurred, what other error handling you have in place, and how you want to cope with the error. This section examines your options.

Determining Which Error Has Occurred

In most cases, the key piece of information you need to know in order to respond intelligently to errors is which error has occurred. VBA provides this information to you in the form of an object, Err. Err has a number of properties (listed in Table 7.2) that give you the information you need. The most important properties are Number, which returns the distinct error code associated with the error, and Description, which provides the informational message that VBA would normally display.

TABLE 7.2   Properties of the VBA Err Object

Property	Description
Number	Distinct error code associated with the error
Description	Informational message associated with the error
Source	Object or application that caused the error
HelpFile	Windows help file with additional information about the error
HelpContext	Context ID of the help topic with the help file
LastDLLError	Error code returned by the last DLL function executed

Somewhere inside your error handler (the lines of code between the error label and the end of the procedure), you should check the value of Err.Number against one or more anticipated values. Depending on the result, you should take some action to either correct the problem or gracefully terminate your procedure.

Listing 7.4 shows the CopyToFloppy procedure, which attempts to copy a given file to a floppy disk after deleting the existing version. A number of run-time errors could occur in this procedure. The source file or an existing version might not exist, or the user might forget to put a disk in the floppy drive. How the procedure copes with the error depends on which of these errors occurs.

NOTE   The CopyToFloppy procedure contained in the sample code features a complete error handler. We build up to that, step by step, in this section.

Listing 7.4: Examine the Number Property of the Err Object

```
Sub CopyToFloppy(strFile As String)
    Dim strDest As String

    ' Set the error trap
    On Error GoTo HandleError
```

```
        ' Construct destination file path
        strDest = "A:\" & TrimDirectory(strFile)

        ' Delete file from the floppy
        Kill strDest

        ' Attempt to copy the file
        FileCopy strFile, strDest
ExitHere:
        Exit Sub
HandleError:
        Select Case Err.Number
            Case Else
                MsgBox Err.Description, vbExclamation, _
                    "Error " & Err.Number & " in CopyToFloppy"
        End Select
End Sub
```

You'll notice that CopyToFloppy uses a Select Case statement in the error handler to examine the error number. In this example, the only thing the error handler does is display a message box with the error information. The following sections explain other ways to cope with the error.

Even an error handler this simple provides the user with useful information. If you examine the MsgBox statement, you'll see that it displays the standard error text (using the Err object's Description property), the error number, and the name of the procedure in which the error occurred. Figure 7.1 illustrates the error message that appears if you attempt to run this procedure without having a disk in the floppy drive.

FIGURE 7.1

Standard error information displayed by an error handler

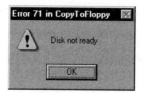

While you can take action in response to particular error codes (we'll explain how in a moment), we recommend that you always include a MsgBox statement like the one shown in Listing 7.4 for the Case Else result. At a minimum, it informs the user of the error condition. With this information (the error number, description, and procedure name), you or the user will find it easier to diagnose the source of the problem.

The Resume Statement

In the example, CopyToFloppy terminates immediately after displaying the message box. While informative, this behavior is far from optimal in terms of user friendliness. It would be far better to correct the error if possible. To do that, there must be a way to tell VBA to retry an action rather than just terminate the procedure. The Resume statement takes care of this. In general, Resume redirects execution to a specific point in a procedure after an error has occurred. The Resume statement has three forms:

- Resume
- Resume Next
- Resume Label

Resume   Using Resume by itself returns control to the statement that caused the error. Use Resume when your error handler fixes the problem that caused the error and you want to continue from the place where you encountered the problem. In the example, the user can correct error 71 ("Drive not ready") by placing a disk in the floppy drive. Then VBA can retry the CopyFile statement.

Listing 7.5 shows a modified version of the CopyToFloppy procedure. The error handler now looks specifically for error number 71, using a Case statement.

Listing 7.5: Use a Case Statement to Check for Error 71

```
Sub CopyToFloppy(strFile As String)

    Dim strDest As String

    ' Set the error trap
    On Error GoTo HandleError

    ' Construct destination file path
    strDest = "A:\" & TrimDirectory(strFile)

    ' Delete file from the floppy
    Kill strDest

    ' Attempt to copy the file
    FileCopy strFile, strDest
```

```
ExitHere:
    Exit Sub
HandleError:
    Select Case Err.Number
        Case 71 ' Drive not ready
            If MsgBox("Please place a floppy disk in the " & _
                "drive.", vbExclamation + vbOKCancel, _
                "Load Diskette") = vbOK Then
                    Resume
        Case Else
            MsgBox Err.Description, vbExclamation, _
                "Error " & Err.Number & " in CopyToFloppy"
    End Select
    Resume ExitHere
End Sub
```

If the error handler finds error 71, it displays a message box instructing the user to put a disk in the floppy drive. The dialog, shown in Figure 7.2, has OK and Cancel buttons. If the user clicks OK, the error handler issues a Resume statement, instructing VBA to try the FileCopy statement again. Note, however, that if the problem is still not resolved, an endless loop occurs when the original statement fails again. That's why the dialog has a Cancel button. Clicking that button terminates the procedure.

FIGURE 7.2

Customized error message in response to a specific error

Resume Next   If you can't correct an error condition but the error is not critical and doesn't affect the outcome of the procedure, you can use the Resume Next statement. Resume Next instructs VBA to execute the line of code *following* the one that caused the error. The CopyToFloppy procedure is very simple and does not contain other statements to execute.

Resume Label   Use the Resume Label statement when you want to return to a line other than the one causing the error or the line that follows it. Resume Label is similar to a GoTo statement, but you can use it only from inside an error handler. The example in Listing 7.5 shows this use of the Resume statement to jump to the label ExitHere. This approach to exiting a procedure after a run-time error is preferred because there is only one exit point.

Using a Standard Error Handler

All the variations of CopyToFloppy presented thus far have included a MsgBox statement to alert the user of any run-time error the procedure doesn't specifically handle. You should include this code (or code similar to it) in every substantive procedure in your application. (For exceptions to this rule, see the section "VBA's Error-Handling Hierarchy" later in the chapter.) One way to do this is to create and use a standard error-handling procedure.

Why Use a Standard Procedure?

Using a standard procedure to handle errors has two benefits. First, it provides you with a single routine for doing such things as displaying error messages. As your error-handling needs change, you need only add code to a single procedure. Second, a common procedure makes writing error handlers easier. You can pass information you want the user to see to the error-handling procedure as necessary.

A Sample Error-Handling Procedure

Listing 7.6 shows the error-handling procedure we've written for this book. The procedure, dhError, collects error information and displays it in a dialog box. It accepts three arguments: a pointer to a VBA ErrObject object, the name of the procedure that called the error routine, and a Boolean flag. The flag controls whether the dialog box features both OK and Cancel buttons or simply a single OK button. Note that all the arguments are optional.

Listing 7.6: dhError, a General-Purpose Error-Handling Procedure

```
Function dhError( _
 Optional strProc As String = "<unknown>", _
 Optional fRespond As Boolean = False, _
 Optional objErr As ErrObject) _
 As Boolean

    Dim strMessage As String
    Dim strTitle As String
    Dim intStyle As Integer
```

```
        ' If the user didn't pass an ErrObject, use Err
    If objErr Is Nothing Then
        Set objErr = Err
    End If

    ' If there is an error, process it
    ' otherwise just return True
    If objErr.Number = 0 Then
        dhError = True
    Else
        ' Build title and message
        strTitle = "Error " & objErr.Number & _
        " in " & strProc
        strMessage = "The following error has occurred:" & _
        vbCrLf & vbCrLf & objErr.Description

        ' Set the icon and buttons for MsgBox
        intStyle = vbExclamation
        If fRespond Then
            intStyle = intStyle Or vbOKCancel
        End If

        ' Display message and return result
        dhError = (MsgBox(strMessage, _
        intStyle, strTitle) = vbOK)
    End If
End Function
```

We've made all the arguments optional so you can call the procedure using just its name. At a minimum, though, you should pass dhError the name of the procedure where the error occurred. This information appears in the title of the dialog and can help you track down problems.

If you pass True as the value of the second argument, fRespond, dhError displays a dialog with OK and Cancel buttons. If the user clicks the OK button, dhError returns True; otherwise, it returns False. You might use this style of dialog to give users the option of canceling the current operation.

An example of using dhError is shown in Listing 7.7. ForceError creates an error condition by attempting to divide a number by 0. When the error occurs, ForceError's error handler calls dhError inside a conditional statement. Figure 7.3 shows the resulting error dialog. If the user responds by clicking the Cancel button, execution halts on the Stop statement in ForceError. Obviously, in this situation you would want to do something besides halt code execution (exit the procedure, return to your application's main window, and so on), but ForceError does demonstrate how you can use the dhError function.

FIGURE 7.3

Error dialog generated by dhError when called from ForceError's error handler

Listing 7.7: ForceError Creates a Run-Time Error That Is Handled by dhError

```
Sub ForceError()
    On Error GoTo HandleError

    Debug.Print 1 / 0

ExitHere:
    Exit Sub
HandleError:
    If Not dhError("ForceError", True) Then
        Stop
    End If
    Resume ExitHere
End Sub
```

Keeping the Error Handler Simple

Over the years, we've seen lots of error-handling procedures, many of which are quite complex, allowing for various message permutations, user responses, and related actions, such as logging error information to a file. In our experience, however, simpler generic error handlers are better. Why? Simply put, there are very few situations in which you need to do more than display an informative message to the user. You will probably find some situations that do require complex error handling in the normal course of testing your applications. When necessary, add the required logic in each procedure's code. Trying to account for every possible condition and result in a single procedure is an impractical, if not impossible, task.

VBA's Error-Handling Hierarchy

To cope effectively with run-time errors, it's important to understand how and when VBA chooses to generate them. Error handling adheres to a hierarchical structure such that when an error occurs in a procedure that contains no error handler, VBA searches each procedure in the call chain looking for one.

Consider the example illustrated in Figure 7.4. It depicts four procedures, A, B, C, and D. Procedure A calls procedure B, which calls procedure C, and so on. Procedure A contains an error trap. None of the other procedures do.

FIGURE 7.4

What happens when an error occurs in a nested procedure with no error trap

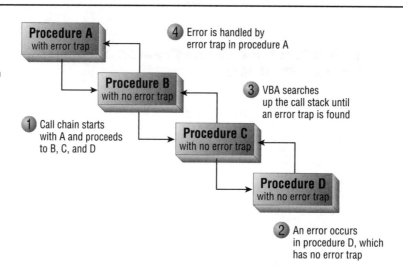

When an error occurs in procedure D, VBA searches backward, up the call chain, until it reaches the error trap in procedure A. Procedure A's error trap then handles the error. If no procedure in the call chain contains an error trap, VBA displays its standard error dialog and halts code execution.

You can use this hierarchy to your advantage. It eliminates the need to add error traps to *every* procedure, as long as at least one procedure upstream in the call chain contains one.

There are, however, two drawbacks to relying on the error-handling hierarchy to cope with run-time errors. First, there is no way to tell which lower-level procedure an error occurred in. Second, depending on the error, it might not make sense to handle it in the higher-level procedure. In other words, it might be too late to handle the error effectively. If you can recover from the error by trapping it in the lower-level procedure, add an error trap there.

TIP *Utility functions* (those that perform such tasks as string manipulation and mathematical calculations) typically don't require error handling because they are almost always called by other procedures. Error handling does add some overhead. Unless you want to cope with specific errors, avoid putting error traps in utility functions.

Raising Errors

As you develop VBA code, a time will come when you need to raise an error of your own. Why, you ask? After all, isn't the goal to eliminate errors? It is, of course, but custom errors do have their place in certain situations. Raising an error is a way to inform a procedure that something is wrong. The procedure can then handle the situation or pass the error upstream to other procedures (taking advantage of the error-handling hierarchy described in the previous section).

Suppose, for example, you are writing a function that computes a number based on two inputs. You want to ensure that one of the inputs is a fraction between 0 and 1. After applying a logical test (using an If...Then statement, for instance) and determining that the input is out of range, you have several options:

- Simply abort the function and return a Null or 0.

- Display an error message and return a Null or 0.

- Return an error code.

- Prompt for a valid value.

All these options have their drawbacks, rooted in the fact that the function itself is attempting to cope with the error condition. Another, better option is to raise a run-time error and let the calling procedure cope with it. You do this using the Raise method of VBA's Err object. The procedure in Listing 7.8 illustrates this. Note that it has no error trap of its own.

Listing 7.8: Use the Raise Method to Generate a Run-Time Error

```
Function ComputeValue(dblAmount As Double, _
  sngRate As Single) As Double

    If sngRate < 0 Or sngRate > 1 Then
        Err.Raise 12345, "ComputeValue", _
          "Argument must be between 0 and 1."
    End If

    ComputeValue = dblAmount * sngRate
End Function
```

Raise takes three arguments:

- An error number that should be unique among all other possible error numbers (those used by VBA as well as by the host application)

- A source string, which lets you designate the source of the error (such as the application or procedure name)

- An error message, which should be a short description of the problem

The Raise method will generate a run-time error and abort the function. When an upstream error handler is activated, it will be able to retrieve the error information in the Err object's properties.

Since the function may be called from a variety of procedures, it is impractical to decide on a single error-handling strategy for all situations. The advantage of the Raise method is that it lets the upstream procedure handle the error in a way that makes sense.

 **TIP**   In general, utility functions should return custom error information using the Raise method.

Debugging Like the Pros

Handling run-time errors is only part of a programmer's job. You need to decide what to do about an error when it occurs. Should you let your error handler display a message and then return control the user? Should you try to change your program logic so the error doesn't happen? And what about code that generates no errors but does not work as desired? Devising solutions to these problems requires *debugging*.

In a way, debugging an application is like performing exploratory surgery on a sick patient. The goal of each is to identify, and eventually correct, some sort of problem or anomaly. Initially, you have only a limited number of clues as to the source of the problem. You use both the tools at hand and your own intuition and experience to carefully expose the problem and correct it. In this chapter we discuss the tools VBA provides and share some of our experiences in debugging applications.

VBA Debugging Tools

Any development environment can be measured by the sophistication of its debugging tools. The VBA debugging environment has been evolving for several versions and now provides several tools to aid you in hunting down bugs and logic errors. They include

- The Immediate window
- Breakpoints and single step mode
- The call stack
- Watch expressions
- Quick watches
- Data Tips
- The Locals window
- Debugging options in the Options dialog

The Immediate Window

The Immediate window, shown in Figure 7.5, gives you a place to investigate the effects of VBA code directly, without the intervention of macros, forms, or other methods of running the code. Think of the Immediate window as a command line for VBA. You can use it to launch procedures and evaluate expressions. In fact, you can do almost as many things in the Immediate window as you can in VBA procedure code. You open the Immediate window by clicking the Immediate Window button on the toolbar, selecting View ➤ Immediate Window, or pressing Ctrl+G.

FIGURE 7.5

Immediate window
showing how to call
the CopyToFloppy
procedure

The Immediate window displays the last 200 lines of output at all times. As
more output is appended to the end, older lines disappear from the top of the list.
With the capability to scroll back the Immediate window, you can position the
cursor on an evaluation line and press Enter, and VBA will recalculate the expression and display its value. If you want to remove the lines in the Immediate window above your current location, use Ctrl+Shift+Home to select them all and
press Del. To remove lines below your current location, first select them with
Ctrl+Shift+End.

Breakpoints

Breakpoints allow you to set locations in your code at which VBA will temporarily
halt its execution of the code. The screen in Figure 7.6 shows code halted at a
breakpoint. Note the highlighted line of code. This is the line of code about to be
executed.

FIGURE 7.6

Code halted at a
breakpoint

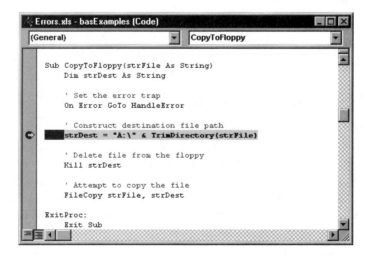

The Call Stack

VBA has the ability to display the call stack when a procedure is paused at a breakpoint. The call stack lists each active procedure, with the current procedure at the top of the list, the one that called it next on the list, and so on. If the procedure was originally called from the Immediate window, this is noted at the end of the list. If the procedure is called from elsewhere in the VBA environment (for example, directly from a control's event procedure), there is no way to know where it was called from. The screen in Figure 7.7 shows the call stack as it might appear at a breakpoint in your code.

FIGURE 7.7

VBA Call Stack dialog showing the call stack

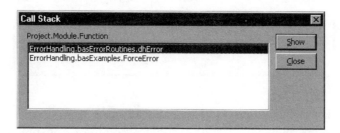

NOTE   You may occasionally see an entry for "<Non-Basic Code>" in the Call Stack dialog. This indicates that another process, such as the VBA host application, VBA, or a DLL function, is involved in the call chain.

To view the call stack, select View ➢ Call Stack or press Ctrl+L. Once the Call Stack dialog opens, you can jump to any procedure in the call stack by selecting it from the list and clicking the Show button.

Watch Expressions

You use *watches* to track the values of expressions as code executes. VBA has implemented a full set of watch functionality. You can view watch expressions interactively or add them to a persistent list.

Watches come in three varieties:

- Watch expression
- Break When Expression Is True
- Break When Expression Has Changed

Normal watch expressions are displayed in a separate window (shown in Figure 7.8). Anytime VBA is in break mode, it evaluates and displays all watch expressions. Watch expressions are useful if you are single-stepping through code and want to watch the contents of a variable or an expression. It is also much more convenient than using the Immediate window to print the contents of variables after each line of code executes.

FIGURE 7.8

The Watches window shows all watch expressions you have defined.

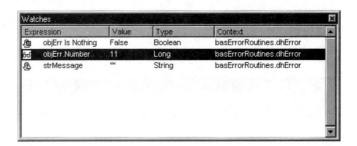

The Break When Expression Is True and Break When Expression Has Changed watch types allow you to specify a logical condition or expression. When that condition is true or changes, VBA immediately halts execution and puts you into break mode. These types of watches are useful for determining when and how a variable's value was changed. For example, say you know that somewhere in your code, a global variable named gintValue is getting set incorrectly to 0. The problem is that you don't know where or how. You can set a Break When Expression Is True watch with the expression "gintValue = 0". Then, as soon as gintValue becomes equal to 0, VBA puts you into break mode.

Quick Watches

The Quick Watch dialog is useful for quickly seeing the value of a variable. To use this dialog, position the cursor anywhere within a variable name and press Shift+F9. This dialog, shown in Figure 7.9, then shows you the present contents of a variable. You can also select an expression, and VBA will evaluate the expression. Clicking the Add button adds the expression as a regular Watch Expression.

Data Tips

Data Tips work like ToolTips in module windows. To use Data Tips, move the mouse over any variable or property while your code is in break mode. VBA displays a small ToolTip-type rectangle with the value of the expression. This is even quicker than using a quick watch!

FIGURE 7.9

VBA's Quick Watch dialog shows you the current value of an expression.

The Locals Window

Another very useful feature is the Locals window. This window, shown in Figure 7.10, lists all the variables currently in scope while your code is in break mode. You can expand and collapse objects to view their properties. In effect, this window creates watch expressions for every variable in your code.

FIGURE 7.10

The Locals window shows all variables in the current scope.

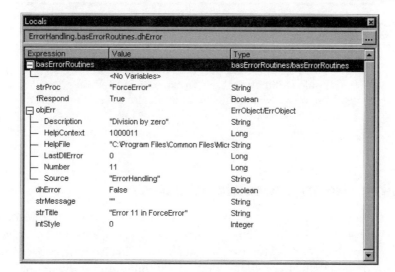

Debugging Options in the Options Dialog

The VBA Options dialog has two sections that let you fine-tune how VBA handles errors and debugging. The first is a text box for conditional compilation constants. You can include the constants that control the behavior of conditional #If…#Then statements in your code or enter them in the Options dialog. If you want to define more than one constant, separate them with colons.

The other option controls error trapping when VBA enters break mode in response to run-time errors. You can choose among three options:

- **Break on All Errors:** Causes VBA to enter break mode whenever a run-time error occurs, even if you've defined an error handler. Normally, you'll want to use this option only while debugging an application, not after you distribute it.

- **Break in Class Module:** The default setting, this causes VBA to enter break mode on all errors in global or class modules for which there is no error trap defined.

- **Break on Unhandled Errors:** Causes VBA to enter break mode, in global modules only, on all errors for which there is no error trap defined. If an error occurs in a class module, VBA enters break mode on the global module statement that called the property or method code of the class.

> **NOTE**
>
> Unfortunately, these options appear at various locations in different VBA host applications. For instance, in Microsoft Access, they appear on the Advanced tab of the Options dialog. In the VBA IDE that ships with Microsoft Excel, PowerPoint, and Word, they are split between the VBA Options dialog and the Options dialog for the current project. You may have to consult your host application's documentation in order to find these options.

Using the Immediate Window

You can use the Immediate window to test parts of an application interactively. From this window, you can launch procedures, view and change the values of variables, and evaluate expressions. You can also write VBA code to print information to the Immediate window without your intervention.

Running Code from the Immediate Window

You can easily run any function or subroutine that's in scope from the Immediate window. To run a procedure, simply type its name (along with any parameter values) on a blank line in the Immediate window and press Enter. VBA runs the procedure and then returns control to the Immediate window. This technique works for both functions and subroutines. If, on the other hand, you want to run a function and have VBA return the *result* to the Immediate window, you have to use the Print statement. For example, if you enter the following expression in the Immediate window, VBA runs the function called MyFunction and prints the return value:

```
Print MyFunction()
```

VBA provides a shortcut for the Print method, as have most previous versions of Basic. In the Immediate window, you can just use the ? symbol to replace the word "Print". All our examples use this shortcut. Therefore, the preceding statement could be rewritten as follows:

```
?MyFunction()
```

Scoping rules apply as in normal code. That is, variables are available from the Immediate window only if they're currently in scope. If you have the Locals window open, you can tell what the current scope is by looking at the text box at the top of the window. It always reflects what VBA sees as the current scope.

Working with Expressions in the Immediate Window

You can use the Immediate window to evaluate expressions, be they simple variables or complex calculations. For example, you can view the current value of the variable intMyVar by typing the following statement in the Immediate window:

```
?intMyVar
```

Of course, the variable must already be declared elsewhere in your code and must be in scope at the time. You cannot enter a Dim statement (or any of its cousins, including ReDim, Global, and Const) in the Immediate window.

In addition to viewing expression results, you can use the Immediate window to change variable values. To change the contents of intMyVar, you could use an expression like this:

```
intMyVar = 97
```

Any code that executes subsequent to your changing the variable value will see the new value.

Any statement you enter for direct execution in the Immediate window must fit on a single line. You cannot, for example, enter a multiline If…Then…Else statement for evaluation in the Immediate window, although you can execute a single-line If…Then statement. To get around this limitation, you can use the colon (:) to separate multiple VBA statements on the same line.

For example, the following code executes a loop:

```
For intCount = 0 To 10:Debug.Print intCount:Next intCount
```

Printing Information to the Immediate Window

You can use the Immediate window as a way of tracking a running procedure by printing messages or expression values to it while your code is running. You use the Print method of the Debug object to display any expression from within your running code. The prior example used the Print method to print the value of intCount to the Immediate window.

Placing Debug.Print statements at strategic points in your code can greatly aid you in debugging problems. Here are a few suggestions for when to use Debug.Print statements:

- At the head or foot of a procedure

- While iterating objects or values in a collection or loop

- After a complex calculation

- After accepting user input

- Before deleting files or other objects

Alas, the Print method is really useful only while you're developing your application. Usually, you won't want your users viewing the Immediate window. To trace your application's behavior after distributing it, consider using the logging class described in the section "Application Logging" later in this chapter.

Handling Remnant Debug.Print Statements

You can safely leave Debug.Print lines in your shipping code if you wish. As long as the user does not have the Immediate window displayed, these lines will have no visible effect and only a slight performance penalty. However, if you are concerned about the performance hit of these lines, you can surround your debug code with conditional compilation statements. For example:

```
' In the declarations section:
#Const fDebug = True
```

```
' In some procedure:
#If fDebug Then
    Debug.Print "Some output"
#End If
```

Using Breakpoints

Using a breakpoint is the equivalent of putting a temporary roadblock in your code. When you set a breakpoint, you tell VBA to stop executing your code at a particular line but to keep the system state in memory. This means that all the variables in the current scope are available for your inspection in the Immediate window. You can also use the Step Into and Step Over functionality (using the menu items, the toolbar buttons, or the F8/Shift+F8 keys) to move through your code statement by statement so you can watch it execute in slow motion.

To set a breakpoint on a particular line of code, place the cursor anywhere on the line and do one of the following: click the Breakpoint button on the toolbar, choose Debug ➢ Toggle Breakpoint, or press the F9 key. You can also create a breakpoint by clicking the mouse in the margin of the module window. VBA highlights the chosen line in the window. (You can control the highlighting colors through the Options dialog.) When VBA encounters a breakpoint while running code, focus switches to the module window with the breakpoint showing and the current statement highlighted. VBA also displays a small arrow in the left margin. VBA suspends execution *before* it executes the statement. This allows you to check or set the values of variables in your code before VBA executes the chosen line of code.

TIP

VBA does not save breakpoints with your code when you close a project. If you need to preserve your breakpoints across sessions, you can use the Stop statement, which acts as a permanent breakpoint. Just as with a breakpoint, VBA halts the execution of your code as soon as it encounters the Stop statement. Of course, you'll need to remove Stop statements from your code (or surround them with conditional compilation statements) before you distribute your application since they will stop the execution of your running code in any environment.

You can reset breakpoints manually with the Debug ➢ Toggle Breakpoint command, the F9 key, or the Breakpoint button on the toolbar. You can also clear all breakpoints you have set with the Debug ➢ Clear All Breakpoints command.

Single Step Mode

When VBA halts your code at a breakpoint, you can choose how to continue. You can proceed at full speed by clicking the Run button on the toolbar, selecting Run ➤ Continue, or pressing F5. You can also use single step mode to execute statements one at a time. To execute the current statement, press F8. After executing the current line of code, VBA brings you back to break mode at the next line.

When VBA encounters one of your own procedures while in single step mode, it continues in one of three ways, depending on which single step command you use:

- **Step In (F8):** Causes VBA to step into your procedure, executing it one line at a time.

- **Step Over (Shift+F8):** Also executes code one line at a time, but only within the context of the current procedure. Calls to other procedures are considered atomic by the Step Over action; it executes the entire procedure at once. Step Over is especially useful if you are calling code you've previously debugged. Rather than take the time to walk through working procedures, you can use the Step Over functionality to execute them at full speed while you're debugging.

- **Step Out (Ctrl+Shift+F8):** Causes VBA to step out of the current procedure. If it was called from another procedure, VBA returns to the line in that procedure following the call to the current one. This is useful if you have inadvertently stepped into a procedure you don't want to debug and want to return to the procedure from which you called it.

Finally, you can use the Run to Cursor functionality to continue to a given line. To do so, highlight any line after the current one and press Ctrl+F8. Run to Cursor is also available from the right-click context menu. Run to Cursor causes VBA to continue execution until the line before the selected one is executed and then reenter break mode.

Other Single Step Options

While in single step mode, you can move the current execution point to another location. Placing the insertion point on any statement in the halted procedure and choosing Debug ➤ Set Next Statement causes execution to begin at that statement when you continue the function. This command is also available from the right-click context menu. You can also change the current execution point by clicking and dragging the arrow in the module margin bar. You cannot skip to another procedure in this fashion, though.

TIP

If you are wading through several open code windows, the Debug ≻ Show Next Statement item brings you back to the currently executing statement.

Occasionally, your code will become so hopelessly bug ridden that during the course of single-stepping through it, you'll want to throw up your hands and surrender. In this case, you can choose the Run ≻ End command or click the End button on the toolbar to stop executing code. While this stops executing code and takes you out of break mode, it retains the contents of any module or global variables. To clear the contents of these variables, choose the Run ≻ Reset command or click the Reset toolbar button.

WARNING

While in break mode, it is possible to launch other procedures. VBA maintains the current execution point for the first procedure while other procedures are executed. This can lead to unpredictable results, especially when you are running procedures that use the same data or variables. If you witness unpredictable behavior, make sure you don't have an outstanding break mode condition by selecting the Show Next Statement command, looking at the call stack, or selecting the Stop or Reset command.

Winning Strategies for Bug-Free Code

It's close to impossible to write a substantial application without any bugs, but certain strategies can help you avoid adding unnecessary ones. You should develop the necessary discipline to use these strategies whenever you write code, even if you think you're writing a function to use only in testing or for your own internal application. Good habits are hard to develop but are also hard to lose once you develop them. The next few sections describe how you can avoid letting bugs slip into your code (and how you can get them out) by following these rules:

- Fix bugs as they appear.
- Use comments.
- Organize your code.
- Modularize your code.
- Use Option Explicit.
- Avoid Variants if at all possible.
- Beware the simple Dim statement.
- Group your Dim statements.
- Use the tightest possible scope.
- Use consistent naming conventions.
- Use assertions.

Putting these suggestions to use will help you develop a good mind-set for avoiding bugs and for removing the ones that inevitably creep into your code.

As a single rule of thumb, the best bug-avoidance strategy is to take your time and to avoid the urge to make your code "cleverer" than necessary. At times you simply must use the newest, most complex features of any programming language, but in general, the simpler way is the better way. With this strategy in mind, there are some specific tactics that work well in VBA coding to help avoid bugs.

Fix Bugs as They Appear

It's critical that you fix bugs as they reveal themselves rather than wait until you have more features implemented. Hurried cleanup at the end of a project will pressure you to apply bandages instead of real fixes. Fixing bugs as they appear requires steady and systematic testing, which is something programmers tend to avoid. Would you rather write 500 lines of code or try 50 test cases on existing code? Most of us would choose the former since writing code is fun and testing is boring. But if you keep in mind how little fun you'll have if your application doesn't work when it's shipped, you'll buckle down and do the boring testing work, too.

Use Comments

Old code is harder to debug than new code because it is less fresh in your mind. Depending on how busy you are, old code could be two weeks old, two days old, or two hours old! One way to help keep your code from aging rapidly is to insert comments. There's an art to sensible commenting: it depends on adding just enough to tell you what's going on without going overboard and cluttering up your code.

The comment should state the intention of the code rather than tell how the code is implemented. This is an important point. You should highlight the overall structure of the code and note any particularly tricky spots for future programmers, including yourself. Remember that if you've named your variables using a consistent standard, their names will act as mini-comments in the code itself.

A comment that is not maintained is worse than no comment at all. Have you ever read a comment and then stared at the code below it and discovered it didn't seem to do what the comment said it did? Now you have to figure out whether it is the comment or the code that is wrong. If your code change requires a comment change, make sure you do it now, because you probably won't get around to doing it later.

NOTE One reason for keeping the number of comments to a reasonable level is that comments do take up space in memory while your VBA project is loaded (unless you're using Visual Basic or another tool that lets you create compiled versions of your project). Some programmers encourage comment stripping, the practice of removing all comments from production code. If you choose to do this, make sure you do it only right before shipping and that you don't make changes to the stripped code. Otherwise, you might end up with two different versions of your project.

Organize Your Code

In addition to commenting your code, you should do whatever you can to keep it organized. This means you should use indentation to organize the flow of code. It also means you should split large procedures into smaller ones.

Indent your code so that statements that should "go together" are at the same indentation level and statements that are subordinate to others are indented one more tab stop. Most VBA programmers use indentation both to match up traditional control structures (For…Next, If…Then…Else, Do…Loop, For Each) and to indicate levels of data access object activity (BeginTrans/CommitTrans, AddNew/ Update, and so on). You'll see this in all the sample code for this book.

Modularize Your Code

Modularization is a fancy term for a simple idea: breaking up your code into a series of relatively small procedures rather than a few mammoth ones. There are several key benefits to writing code this way:

- You make it easier to understand each procedure. Code that is easier to understand is easier to maintain and to keep bug free.

- You can localize errors to a smaller section of the total code. If a variable is used only in one ten-line function, any error messages referring to that variable are most likely generated within that function.

- You can lessen the dangers of side effects caused by too-wide scoping of variables. If you use a variable at the top of a 500-line function and again at the bottom for a different loop, you may well forget to reinitialize it.

Use Option Explicit

In the VBA Options dialog, you'll find a check box labeled "Require Variable Declaration." Selecting this check box causes VBA to insert the line "Option Explicit" at the top of any new module it creates. This statement forces you to declare all your variables before referring to them in your code. This will prevent some hard-to-find errors from cropping up in your code. Without Option Explicit, VBA allows you to use any syntactically correct variable in your code, regardless of whether you declare it. This means that any variable you forget to declare will be initialized to a variant and given the value Empty at the point where you first use it. The hours you save in debugging time will make using this option well worth the effort.

Using Option Explicit is an easy way to avoid errors such as the one you'll find in the code in Listing 7.9. Errors like this are almost impossible to catch late in the development cycle, since they're buried in existing code. (Don't feel bad if you don't immediately see the error in the fragment; it's difficult to find.)

Listing 7.9: Can You Find the Error in This Procedure?

```
Function UpdateLog(intSeverity As Integer, _
  strProcedure As String, strTracking As String) As Integer
    Dim dbCurrent As Database
    Dim rstUsageLog As Recordset
    Dim intFull As Integer
    Dim qryArchive As QueryDef

    Const dhcMinSeverity = 1
    ' Don't log activities that aren't severe enough to
    ' bother with
    If intSeverity < dhcMinSeverity Then
        Exit Function
    End If

    ' Append a new record to the usage log
    Set dbCurrent = CurrentDb()
    Set rstUsageLog = dbCurrent.OpenRecordset _
      ("zstblUsageLog", dbOpenDynaset)
    rstUsageLog.AddNew
        rstUsageLog![Severity] = intSeverty
        If Err.Number Then
            rstUsageLog![ErrorCode] = Err.Number
            rstUsageLog![ErrorText] = Err.Description
        End If
        rstUsageLog![User] = CurrentUser()
        rstUsageLog![Date] = Now
    rstUsageLog.Update
End Function
```

In case you missed it, the error occurred on this line of code:

```
rstUsageLog![Severity] = intSeverty
```

A small spelling error like this would cause only zeros to be stored in the Severity field and could cause you several hours of debugging time. Option Explicit lets you avoid these kinds of errors.

Avoid Variants If Possible

The Variant datatype is convenient, but it's not always the best choice. It's tempting to declare all your variables as Variants so you don't have to worry about what's in them. The VBA design teams did not put in explicit types to make your life difficult; they put them in because they're useful. If you think something will always be an Integer, dimension it as an Integer. If you get an error message later because you've attempted to assign an invalid value to that variable, the error message will point straight to the problem area of your code and give you a good idea of what went wrong. Variants are also slower than explicitly dimensioned variables for the same operations since they have the overhead of tracking which type of data they are holding at any given time. In addition, Variants are larger than almost any other datatype and so take longer to move around in memory. These last two reasons alone should be enough to make you reconsider using variants whenever possible.

> **NOTE**
>
> In some instances, you have no choice about your datatypes. If you're assigning values to variables that might at some point need to contain a null value, you must use the Variant datatype. This is the only datatype that can contain a null value, and attempting to assign a null value to a non-Variant variable triggers a run-time error. The same goes for function return values. If a function might need to return a null value, the return value for that function must be a Variant.

Use ByVal with Care

Be careful about passing information to procedures that have parameters declared using ByVal. While this is a good way to prevent subroutines from modifying variables passed to them (since ByVal creates a copy), you may lose information when calling the procedure. This is because VBA coerces information passed to the procedure to the datatype of the parameter. Therefore, if you pass a variable with the Single datatype to a parameter of type Integer, VBA truncates the fractional component when it creates the Integer. You will have no warning of this, however, so make sure you know which datatype the procedures expect if you've used ByVal in the declaration.

Beware the Simple Dim Statement

Even the simple Dim statement can introduce subtle bugs into your code. Consider this statement:

```
Dim strFirst, strLast As String
```

The intent here is clearly to define two String variables on one line. If you've ever programmed in C or C++, you know that a similar declaration would do just that. However, this is not the way VBA works. The As clause applies only to the variable it immediately follows, not to all variables on the line. The result of the preceding declaration is that strLast is a String variable but strFirst is a Variant variable, with slightly different behavior. For example, strFirst will be initialized to Empty and strLast to a zero-length string. You must explicitly define the datatype of every single variable in VBA. The simplest way to ensure this is to get into the habit of declaring only one variable for each statement.

Group Your Dim Statements

You can declare your variables anywhere in your procedures, as long you declare them before they are actually used, and VBA will understand and accept the declarations. For the sake of easier debugging, though, you should get into the habit of declaring variables at the top of your procedures. This makes it easy to see exactly what a particular procedure is referring to and to find the declarations when you are in the midst of debugging.

Use the Tightest Possible Scope

Always use the tightest possible scope for your variables. Some beginning programmers discover global variables and promptly declare all their variables as global to avoid the issue of scope altogether. This is a sloppy practice that will backfire the first time you have two procedures, both of which change the same global variable's value. If a variable is used solely in a single procedure, declare it there. If it is used only by procedures in a single module, declare it with module scope. Save global scope for only those few variables you truly need to refer to from widely scattered parts of your code.

Use Consistent Naming Conventions

In addition to the conventions discussed here that help structure your code, consider adopting a consistent naming convention for objects and variables in your code. We (along with many other programmers) have standardized our naming conventions based on the RVBA naming conventions, which you'll find in Appendix A.

A consistent naming standard can make it simple for you to find errors lurking in your programs, in addition to making them simpler for multiple programmers to maintain. By using the RVBA naming conventions, you gain two pieces of information about every variable: which datatype it is and what scope it has. This information can be very helpful during the debugging process.

Your Friend, the MsgBox Function

As an alternative to setting breakpoints, you can use the MsgBox function to indicate your program's state. With this strategy, you decide what you would like to monitor and call the MsgBox function to return the information. You can enhance this technique by writing a wrapper for the MsgBox function so that these messages are posted only when you have a conditional compilation constant set to indicate that you want to see debugging messages. An example is shown in Listing 7.10. Only if the fDebug conditional constant is True does the MsgBox function get called.

Listing 7.10: Sample Wrapper for the MsgBox Function

```
#Const fDebug = True

Function dhMsgBox(ByVal varMessage As Variant, _
 Optional strCaller As String = "<unknown>") As Integer

    ' Set return value in case fDebug is False
    dhMsgBox = True

    #If fDebug Then
        dhMsgBox = (MsgBox(CStr(varMessage), _
         vbOKCancel Or vbQuestion, "Procedure: " & strCaller) _
         = vbOK)
    #End If

End Function
```

If you click OK, the function returns True. If you click Cancel or press the Esc key, the function returns False. You could take action, such as halting execution with the Stop statement, if this were the case.

Using Assertions

An *assertion* is a statement that enforces a particular logical condition. If the condition is violated, an error message is reported and code execution is halted. Assertions are useful when you want to validate data while running a procedure. For example, Listing 7.11 shows part of a function that computes an invoice total based on a supplied tax rate (sngTax). It uses an assertion (by calling the dhAssert procedure, also shown in Listing 7.11) to ensure that the tax rate supplied is between 0 and 1.

Listing 7.11: Use Assertions to Validate Data

```
Function InvoiceTotal(lngInvoiceID As Long, _
 sngTax As Single) As Double

    ' Use dhAssert to validate data
    Call dhAssert((sngTax >= 0) And (sngTax <= 1), _
     "Invalid tax rate: " & sngTax)

    ' Other statements
    ' ...
End Function

Sub dhAssert(fCondition As Boolean, Optional _
 strMessage As String = "Assertion failed.")

    ' If condition is False, display error
    ' message and halt execution
    If Not fCondition Then
        MsgBox strMessage, vbCritical
        Stop
    End If
End Sub
```

Using an assertion in this case is useful because there is no other way to limit the data a Single variable can store. If the condition is satisfied, everything proceeds normally. Otherwise, an error is reported and VBA stops executing code in the dhAssert procedure. When this happens, you can use the Call Stack dialog to see where the error occurred.

While dhAssert does supply default error text, you should pass your own description of the problem. This makes fixing it much easier. Liberal use of assertions in your code will help in finding many logic errors. The trade-off is that they add slightly to the size and reduce the speed of your code.

Systematic Debugging

While the guidelines mentioned thus far will minimize the number of bugs in your programs, some will inevitably creep in. The following paragraphs offer some techniques for getting rid of them.

The first rule of debugging is that you need a reproducible case that causes an error. If you cannot reproduce the error, you will have great difficulty tracking down the bug. You may get lucky and be in a situation in which you can debug the code when the bug appears, but if you can't reproduce it, your chances of fixing it are small. To reproduce the bug, you need as much information about the conditions that produced the bug as possible, but no more than that. If your users give you the hundred steps they performed that morning before the bug occurred, it makes your job difficult. Instead, if users limit the information to the essential three steps that actually cause the bug to occur, you can get somewhere. This isn't always easy. Sometimes you can reproduce a bug only by following numerous steps or, for example, after the user has been using the application for four hours. As you can imagine, these types of bugs are much harder to find and fix.

The second rule of debugging is that you must debug data, not code. This means you should use the debugger to find out what data is producing the error instead of staring at the code and speculating as to what it does. This seems a simple rule, but it is very effective at resolving bugs.

After you have found the bug but before you start fixing code, make sure you understand the nature of the problem. For example, a common error occurs when you declare simple datatype variables (Integer, Long, String, and so on). In your own testing, everything works fine. At the client's site, your application produces "Invalid Use of Null" messages.

There are two solutions to this problem, and each requires some understanding of the particular application. Clearly, you cannot place null values into Integer, Long, or String variables, so you might consider changing them all to Variants. On the other hand, perhaps the solution is to disallow null entries from the user. Your decision on the solution needs to take into account the particular situation. It seems obvious that you should change code only with a reason, but surprisingly, many programmers ignore this principle. "Experience" often masquerades as a reason when it is really a synonym for "wild guess."

Finally, no matter how good you are and how sure you are of your work, make only one change at a time to your code, and then test it again. It's all too easy to fall into the trap of making multiple fixes without keeping records and then having to junk the current version and reload from a backup because you have no idea which things worked and which only made things worse. Take baby steps, and you'll get there faster. As an added measure, document changes to your code using comments in either individual procedures or the declarations section of a module. By logging changes with the date they were made, you can help track down problems introduced by various "fixes."

TIP

Another way to prevent fixes to one procedure from adversely affecting other parts of your program is to use a source code control program that supports versioning. This lets you fall back to a working version of your code so you can try another debugging tactic.

There are two more bits of debugging strategy you might want to consider. Many programmers find "confessional debugging" to be one of the most useful techniques around. Confessional debugging works something like this: you grab your printouts and go into the next cubicle, interrupt the programmer working there, and say, "Hey, sorry to bother you, but I've got this function that keeps crashing. See, I pass in the name of a form here and then declare a form variable and then—oh, wait, that's not the form itself, but the form's name. Never mind; thanks for your help." When you get good at it, you can indulge in this sort of debugging with non-programmers as the audience or even (in times of desperation) by talking things through with your dog or a sympathetic (but bored) loved one.

Of course, there are times when confessing your code isn't enough. If you have the luxury of working with peers, use them. There's a good chance that other programmers can see the bug that you can't.

If all else fails, take a break. It's easy to get stuck in a mental loop in which you try the same things over and over, even though they didn't work the first time. Take a walk. Have lunch. Take a shower. Your mind's background processing can solve many bugs while the foreground processes are thinking about something else altogether. Many programmers have told stories of waking up in the middle of the night, having just dreamed about a bug they weren't even aware existed until then, along with its solution. Having written down the information during the night, they've gone in to work, found the previously unspotted bug, and fixed it on the spot.

Other Professional Touches

Providing elegant error handling and relatively bug-free code is only the first step in delivering a professional application. The remainder of this chapter is devoted to several other considerations, such as object model design and providing assistance using online help. You may not choose to follow these guidelines for every project, but they are valuable tools to have at your disposal.

Creating Object Models

Throughout this book, we discuss and present various object models implemented using VBA class modules. As you develop applications using VBA, you'll undoubtedly create object models of your own. Whether they are for your own exclusive use or for use by others, there are some guidelines you can use to create object models that make sense and are easy to understand.

Strive for Simplicity

A good object model is a simple one. When deciding on what classes, properties, and methods you need, choose as few as possible at first. You can always add more later on. Remember that Property statements let you run code when a property value is set or retrieved. This gives you the ability to pack a lot of functionality into a simple property call.

Furthermore, don't feel compelled to include every piece of functionality you think developers will need if they can easily provide it themselves. For example, if you develop a class that features a Text property, you don't need to include a property like TextLength. Users of your class can easily compute this value from the Text property using the VBA Len function.

Remember that every class member you create should exist for a reason. It should provide essential functionality that cannot be derived from other properties of your class.

Emulate Real-World Processes

The best guide for an object model is a real-world process. Like database design, object model design should reflect an existing set of entities and attributes. Methods should mimic behaviors, either existing or desired. As an example, consider an order entry application. Customers order products and are given an invoice. Each of these (customer, order, and invoice) is a candidate for representation via a class module. Each also has relevant attributes (name, date, amount) that should be modeled using properties. Just as important, each object has characteristics that are irrelevant to the business problem. (For instance, you rarely see a customer's eye color included on an order!)

Model the User Interface

Another guideline when creating an object model is to use your application's user interface, if it has one. If you examine the object models of major Microsoft applications, you'll notice how closely the object models follow the interface. Microsoft Excel's object model, for example, features an Application class at its root. The Application class contains a collection of Workbook objects representing open workbooks (XLS files). Each workbook contains a collection of worksheets. Other elements of the object model, such as the ChartObject and PivotTable classes, adhere to the visual interface.

User interface classes need not be generic. If you are creating a time-reporting application in Excel, for example, you might create a TimeSheet class to refer to the particular style of worksheet you've created for the application. When you subclass a generic object (Worksheet) in this manner, consider creating a property of the derived class to refer to the base object. This lets you access properties of the base object without having to implement your own, duplicate properties. Listing 7.12 illustrates what this might look like.

Listing 7.12: Implement a Pointer to a Base Class as Part of a Derived Class

```
' Private pointer to the Excel worksheet
Private mobjSheet As Worksheet

Property Set Sheet(objSheet As Worksheet)
    If mobjSheet Is Nothing Then
        Set mobjSheet = objSheet
    End If
End Property
Property Get Sheet() As Worksheet
    Set Sheet = mobjSheet
End Property
```

You could then use a pointer to the TimeSheet class to reference properties of the worksheet:

```
objTimeSheet.Sheet.Visible = False
```

On the other hand, if you don't want other developers to manipulate the base class directly, you can implement some properties in the derived class. When a program accesses these properties, your class simply sets or retrieves properties of the base class. Listing 7.13 shows an alternative version of the TimeSheet class that implements its own Visible property. Changes to this property are passed through to the base class (Worksheet).

Listing 7.13: Implement a Duplicate Property to "Hide" the Base Class

```
' Private pointer to the Excel worksheet
Private mobjSheet As Worksheet

Property Let Visible(fVisible As Boolean)
    mobjSheet.Visible = fVisible
End Property
Property Get Visible() As Boolean
    Visible = mobjSheet.Visible
End Property
```

Include Standard Properties and Methods

As you use object models developed by companies like Microsoft, you'll come to expect a certain level of consistency among classes, properties, and methods. You should strive to emulate these in your own object models. For example, most classes feature a Name property that indicates the name of the object. Classes that represent user interface elements implement properties such as Visible, Top, Left, and so on.

Collections usually include a Count property as well as Item, Add, and Remove methods. While you can invent your own names, you'll only be making it more difficult for other developers to understand and use your classes.

To Prefix or Not to Prefix

Having said in this chapter that you should strictly adhere to naming standards, we should also point out that you may want to make an exception when it comes to object models. This is especially true if other developers will use your object models. Avoiding the name prefixing that defines most naming standards will make reading and understanding your object models easier when viewed using VBA's Object Browser.

If you look at an object model like VBA's, for instance, you won't see prefixes on method arguments or property names. If you want your object models to look and act like Microsoft's (which, like it or not, are becoming a standard), you should avoid prefixing as well.

As an example, instead of declaring a method like this:

```
Public Sub Display(strFile As String, intMode As Integer)
```

declare it like this:

```
Public Sub Display(File As String, Mode As Integer)
```

When viewed with Object Browser, the datatypes will be evident, making the prefixes unnecessary.

The same goes for class names. Many developers prefixed class names with the letter "C" (for class). If you're using Object Browser to view a class, it ought to be clear that it is one! We've made an effort to avoid prefixes in this book, including them only for private procedures and variables.

Creating a Procedure Stack

When you're in the process of debugging an application in the VBA design environment, you can use the Call Stack dialog to see which function caused an error. Unfortunately, VBA doesn't provide any method for retrieving this information from your code. When you get an unexpected error, it's useful to log the code being executed at that point and how it got there. Since VBA provides no way to get at the information it keeps internally (that is, the name of the currently executing procedure), you must maintain the information yourself if you need it.

We've done this by implementing our own procedure stack based on the stack classes described in Chapter 6. The ProcStack and ProcStackItem classes store information on each procedure in VBA's call stack by implementing a stack of their own. The only catch is that you have to write code in your subroutines and functions to add procedures to the stack—VBA won't do this for you. Refer to the section "Creating a Stack" in Chapter 6 for listings of the two classes.

NOTE   We've modified the ProcStackItem class in two ways for this example. First, we changed the StackTop property so that instead of returning the value of the top item on the stack, it returns a pointer to the actual item. Second, we added a TimeEntered property. TimeEntered returns the value of a private date/time value that is set during the Initialize event.

To implement a call stack in your own applications, import the two class modules, PSTACK.CLS and PSTACKIT.CLS, from the CD-ROM and declare a new instance of the ProcStack class in a global module. Call the Push method of the class at the entry point of every routine in your code and the Pop method at the exit point. Listing 7.14 shows an example of how to use these methods. It also shows how to print out the contents of the stack.

Listing 7.14: Example of Using the Procedure Stack Class

```
' Declare global instance of ProcStack class
Global gProcStack As New ProcStack

Sub EnterAndExitExample()
    ' Call Push to place proc name onto the stack
    Call gProcStack.Push("EnterAndExitExample")

    ' Call PrintCallStack, which will print the call stack
    ' to the Immediate window so you can see that it works!
    Call PrintCallStack

    ' Make sure to call Pop!!
    Call gProcStack.Pop
End Sub

Private Sub PrintCallStack()
    Dim objProc As StackItem

    ' Call Push to place proc name onto the stack
    Call gProcStack.Push("PrintCallStack")

    ' Print it out by walking the stack
    Set objProc = gProcStack.StackTop
    Do Until objProc Is Nothing
        Debug.Print "Entered procedure '" & objProc.Value & _
        "' at " & objProc.TimeEntered
        Set objProc = objProc.NextItem
    Loop

    ' Make sure to call Pop!!
    Call gProcStack.Pop
End Sub
```

Because you have to call the Pop method at the exit point, you will want to make sure you have only one exit point to your procedures. If you don't, you run the risk of trying to push the wrong procedure off the stack.

The payoff for using this call stack code comes when you are trying to determine the current program state after an error occurs. The information on the stack is the same as that displayed by VBA's Call Stack dialog, but you have programmatic access to it. You can display it on screen, dump it to a log file (using the log class described in the next section), or send it to the printer.

Another advantage of using our modified classes is that the ProcStackItem class stores the current time when you create a new instance of it. Using this information, you can keep track of how much time is spent in a procedure. This is called *profiling*. You can use the profiling information to help determine which routines need optimization work.

Application Logging

One of the best ways to troubleshoot problems in a deployed application is through log files. Log files contain information about the program's state, variables, and the operating system. A user who is having a problem with your application can enable the log and send you the output to examine. We've developed a log file class you can use in your application. We chose to implement this functionality as a class so you could use multiple log files in the same application. The following sections explain how the class works.

The Log Class

Our log class (called, simply, Log) features a number of properties and methods designed to create or open a log file, delete a log file, and write entries to a log file. Table 7.3 lists each property, along with a short description.

TABLE 7.3 Properties of the Log Class

Property	Description
Active	A Boolean value indicating whether the log is active. If the log is not active, no output will be written
File	Name of the log file

TABLE 7.3   Properties of the Log Class (continued)

Property	Description
Options	A bitmask of values that controls whether additional information (such as the date and time) is written to the log file
SeverityLevel	The severity threshold for the log. When writing log entries, you can specify a severity for each. Only those that exceed this value are actually written

In addition to the properties listed in Table 7.3, the class implements two methods, Output and Reset. Output accepts a text string and an optional integer representing the severity of the log entry. Only entries that exceed the SeverityLevel property setting of the class are actually written to the log. This feature lets you distinguish between informational log entries and critical errors. If you don't include a value for the second argument, the Output method assumes a value of 9.

The Reset method deletes the current log file. Normally, log entries are appended to the end of the file. Use the Reset method to purge the file and start over.

Listing 7.15 shows the code behind the Output method. Note that it processes the log information only if the mfActive flag is True. The mfActive variable maps to the Active property of the class and is initially set to False when an instance of the class is created. Note also how the method uses the mlngOptions variable. If it contains certain values (denoted by the conLogDateTime and conLogSeverity constants), the method writes additional information to the log file.

Listing 7.15: Output Method of the Log Class

```
Public Sub Output(Text As Variant, _
 Optional Severity As Integer = 9)

    Dim hFile As Long
    Dim varText As Variant
    Dim varExisting As Variant

    On Error GoTo HandleError

    ' Only process this if the log is active
    If mfActive Then

        ' Build up text
        varText = Text
        If mlngOptions And conLogDateTime Then
```

```
                varText = Now & vbTab & varText
        End If
        If mlngOptions And conLogSeverity Then
                varText = Severity & vbTab & varText
        End If

        ' Process the log information if Severity
        ' meets or exceeds SeverityLevel
        If Severity >= mintSeverityLevel Then

            ' If SeverityLevel is -1 then put up a message
            ' rather than writing text to the file
            If mintSeverityLevel = -1 Then
                MsgBox varText, vbInformation, "Log"
            Else
                ' Get file handle
                hFile = FreeFile

                ' Open file for append
                Open mstrFile For Append _
                Access Write As hFile

                ' Print the output
                Print #hFile, varText

                ' Close the file
                Close hFile
            End If
        End If
    End If
ExitHere:
    Exit Sub
HandleError:
    mfActive = False
    Err.Raise vbObjectError + 8000, "Log::Output", _
    Err.Description
    Resume ExitHere
End Sub
```

A special SeverityLevel setting of –1 triggers a MsgBox instead of a file entry. You could use this in situations in which you want immediate feedback while your application runs rather than wait to view the log file.

Finally, note that the Output method opens the log file in append mode and closes it in the same procedure. Closing the file is important because if a critical error occurs, resulting in a protection fault, any open files will not be completely written to disk.

Using the Log Class

To use the Log class in your application, you need to import the class module and create at least one instance of the class in your code. (You may also want to copy the constant declarations to a global module.) If you want to experiment with the sample procedures described below, you'll also need to import the BASERROR .BAS file. As an example, you could create a global instance that all procedures could use. Listing 7.16 shows the object declaration as well as a sample procedure that initializes the class and sets various options.

Listing 7.16: Initialize the Log Class

```
' Declare an instance of the Log class
Global gLog As Log

Sub Main
    ' Initialize the log
    Set gLog = New Log

    ' Set the file name
    gLog.File = "C:\APP.LOG"

    ' Set logging options
    gLog.SeverityLevel = 5
    gLog.Options = conLogDateTime

    ' Other startup code
    ' ...
End Sub
```

Once you have a reference to a class instance, you can begin writing entries to the log file. Listing 7.17 shows a sample procedure that uses logging. Note the different severity level settings.

Listing 7.17: Sample Procedure That Utilizes Logging

```
Sub ProcessFileName(strFile As String)
    gLog.Output "Entering ProcessFile", 5

    Dim strErrText As String
```

```
        gLog.Output "Before: strFile = " & strFile, 6

        ' Do some processing here

        gLog.Output "After:  strFile = " & strFile, 6
ExitHere:
        gLog.Output "Exiting ProcessFile", 5
        Exit Sub
HandleError:
        strErrText = "(" & Err.Number & ") " & _
         Err.Description

        Call dhError("ProcessFile")

        gLog.Output "Error in ProcessFile: " & _
         strErrText, 9

        Resume ExitHere
End Sub
```

Enabling Log Functionality

After adding support for logging to your application, you should make it easy for users to enable it. For example, you could use a menu command, an option setting, a command-line parameter, or a Registry setting. When a user elects to enable logging, your application should set the Active property of the class to True. Until Active is set to True, no log entries will be made.

Now, many of you astute VBA programmers might be wondering, "Doesn't including all the log code affect performance, even if logging isn't active?" The answer, of course, is yes. Calling the Output method does impart a small amount of overhead each time your application calls it. You have to decide whether the benefits of logging outweigh this cost. This answer is also usually yes, although you'll need to be the final judge.

If performance is a critical issue in your application, you can create what is known as an *instrumented version* that contains the log code. You ship normal users a version without the log code and install the instrumented version only if problems arise. The easiest way to create instrumented and normal versions that share the same code base is to use conditional compilation. Surround all references to logging with #If statements, as the code in Listing 7.18 illustrates. By setting the conditional constant appropriately, you can easily create an instrumented or a normal version of your application.

Listing 7.18: Use Conditional Compilation to Create an Instrumented Version

```
Sub ProcessFileName(strFile As String)

#If fLog Then
    gLog.Output "Entering ProcessFile", 5
#End If

    ' More statements
    '...
End Sub
```

Providing Online Help

Online help is a valuable resource for today's computer users. In fact, it's often the only form of assistance available. To save money, many large companies do not distribute printed documentation to every user. Furthermore, many users prefer to use online help even when printed manuals are available. Online help can help speed acceptance of your applications as well as cut down on support costs. This section explains how you can tie online help to your applications using VBA. However, it's not a tutorial on creating help files. For that you'll need to consult the documentation that came with your help file creation software.

Help File Basics

Be aware that to reference a help topic, you must know the name of the help file that contains it, as well as the topic's Context ID. A *Context ID* is a unique numeric value that corresponds to a topic in a help file. As you develop help topics, you give each one a unique name. You map these names to numeric Context IDs before compiling the help file.

Help Topics in Code

VBA provides three places where you can reference a help topic in code:

- The InputBox function

- The MsgBox function

- The Err.Raise method

All these procedures have optional arguments for help file and Context ID. When you supply these with the InputBox or MsgBox function, VBA adds a Help button to the proper dialog. For example, Figure 7.11 illustrates the dialog that appears when you execute the following statement:

```
?InputBox(Prompt:="Enter a value below:", _
 Title:="Enter Value", HelpFile:="MYAPP.HLP", _
 Context:=100)
```

If the user presses F1 or clicks the Help button, VBA opens the help file to the given Context ID.

FIGURE 7.11

Specifying a help file and Context ID causes VBA to display a Help button.

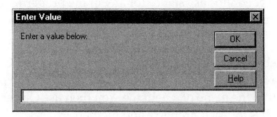

The Err object's Raise method also has optional arguments for help file and Context ID. The standard VBA error dialog features a Help button that normally opens the VBA help file to the "Application defined error" help topic. If you supply your own help file and context information, however, VBA opens your help file in response to the Raise method. If you have an error trap defined, you'll be able to access this information using the HelpFile and HelpContext properties of the Err object. Listing 7.19 shows a test procedure that illustrates this.

Listing 7.19: Use Err.Raise to Supply Help File Information

```
Sub ShowHelpInfo()
    On Error GoTo HandleError

    Err.Raise 12345, "Sub ShowHelpInfo", _
      "This error is by design.", "MAINAPP.HLP", 100

ExitHere:
    Exit Sub
HandleError:
    Debug.Print Err.HelpFile, Err.HelpContext
    Resume ExitHere
End Sub
```

NOTE   While the HelpFile and HelpContext arguments of InputBox, MsgBox, and Raise are optional, if you supply one of them, you must supply the other.

Help for Classes

The final place you can place help information is in a class module. This allows developers to get online assistance for any of the properties or methods of your class. This can be extremely useful if you are distributing your application to developers outside your organization.

You add help information using the Options dialog and Object Browser. First, you specify a help file for your project. To do this, open the project's Properties dialog and enter the name of a help file. You then use Object Browser to specify help Context IDs for each property and method.

To assign a Context ID to a property or method, select it from the Members list in Object Browser. Then select Properties from the right-click context menu. You should see a dialog like the one in Figure 7.12. Note that the help file is filled in for you based on the project settings and cannot be changed. Enter the numeric Context ID in the text box and click OK. VBA saves this information with the member definition.

FIGURE 7.12

Specifying a help Context ID for a class member

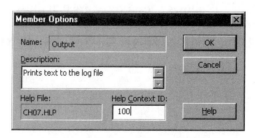

You should also add a description of the member in the Properties dialog. Object Browser displays the description when a user selects the member.

> **TIP**
>
> You can quickly add descriptions and Context ID numbers to multiple members by editing the source code files directly if your VBA host application supports this ability. (If the host application doesn't use external source files, you can export a module, edit it, and import it.) To add a description, insert a line after the member's declaration and enter the string "Attribute *member*.VB_Description = *text*", replacing *member* with the member name and *text* with the description. To add a Context ID, add the line "Attribute *member*.VB_HelpID = *number*", where *number* is the Context ID. For members with multiple declarations (such as Property Let and Get procedures), you need to add the lines after only one declaration.

Summary

This chapter has covered several topics that figure heavily in the development of professional applications. We discussed error handling and debugging in detail. You should now understand how VBA handles errors in your applications and how you must anticipate and cope with them. We also showed you the various debugging aids VBA provides and offered some guidelines and advice regarding how to eliminate bugs from your programs.

Beyond simple error handling, we also discussed ways to add professional touches to your applications. These included implementing procedure stacks and error logging to aid your users in communicating error conditions to you. We also suggested guidelines for developing object models and online help.

After reading this chapter, you should be familiar with the following concepts:

- How VBA handles run-time errors

- How to use the On Error and Resume statements

- How to use debugging aids such as breakpoints, watches, and the call stack

- How to implement professional features such as procedure stacks, application logging, and online help

CHAPTER
EIGHT

8

Using the VBA IDE as an Automation Server

- ■ Understanding the VBA IDE's Automation interface

- ■ Writing code that manipulates the user interface

- ■ Modifying code programmatically

One of VBA's greatest strengths is its ability to control other applications using Automation. Undoubtedly, developers will use VBA most often for this purpose. Nonetheless, following a recent trend in programming tool development, Microsoft has added Automation support to VBA itself—specifically, an Automation interface to the VBA Integrated Development Environment (IDE). Using this interface, you can manage VBA projects, manipulate components such as modules and forms, and modify source code. This new feature opens the door for a whole new breed of utilities and add-ins.

In this chapter we explain the VBA IDE object model, focusing on the most useful classes, properties, and methods for managing your projects programmatically. We also introduce you to a custom object model, which we created to supplement VBA's own. We use this object model to add capabilities that are lacking in the VBA IDE classes. If you've ever wanted to create tools to help you program, or if you just want to understand what's under the hood of VBA's programming environment, this chapter is for you.

Table 8.1 lists the sample files for this chapter.

T A B L E 8 . 1   Sample Files

File Name	Description
VBAIDE.XLS	Excel 97 workbook containing sample code
VBAIDE.MDB	Access 97 database containing sample code
TESTPROC.BAS	Test procedure for importing
CBARNUMS.TXT	Command bar index
IDEEX.BAS	IDE code examples
CODEEX.BAS	VBA code examples
CLASSEX.BAS	Custom object module examples
PROJECT.CLS	Sample Project class
MODULE.CLS	Sample Module class
MODULES.CLS	Sample Modules class

TABLE 8.1   Sample Files (continued)

File Name	Description
PROC.CLS	Sample Procedure class
PROCS.CLS	Sample Procedures class
CBAREVNT.CLS	Event sink class for command bar buttons

The VBA IDE Object Model

The first step toward creating VBA tools is understanding the VBA IDE object model. Fortunately, the object model is relatively simple and easy to grasp. This section gives you an overview of the class structure, as well as examples of using it.

WARNING   This chapter deals with the VBA IDE that ships with Microsoft Excel, PowerPoint, and Word and, presumably with other, non-Microsoft VBA-enabled products. Microsoft Access and Visual Basic, on the other hand, implement their own development environments, which draw on the VBA IDE classes but which expose them differently. For this reason, not everything described in this chapter applies to those environments. This may make working with VBA components in Visual Basic and Access frustrating. It's still worth reading this chapter, however, because most of the capabilities we mention exist in VB and Access. It's just that you'll have to dig around in the object models of those tools to find them.

The Class Hierarchy

The diagram in Figure 8.1 shows the VBA IDE class hierarchy. You'll notice that it features the VBE (Visual Basic Environment) class at its head. This is similar to the Application class used by many VBA host applications—it represents the top-level class of the hierarchy. Unlike other applications, however, you cannot reference this class directly. You must instead access it as a property of its host. We explain this in detail shortly.

FIGURE 8.1

VBA IDE class hierarchy

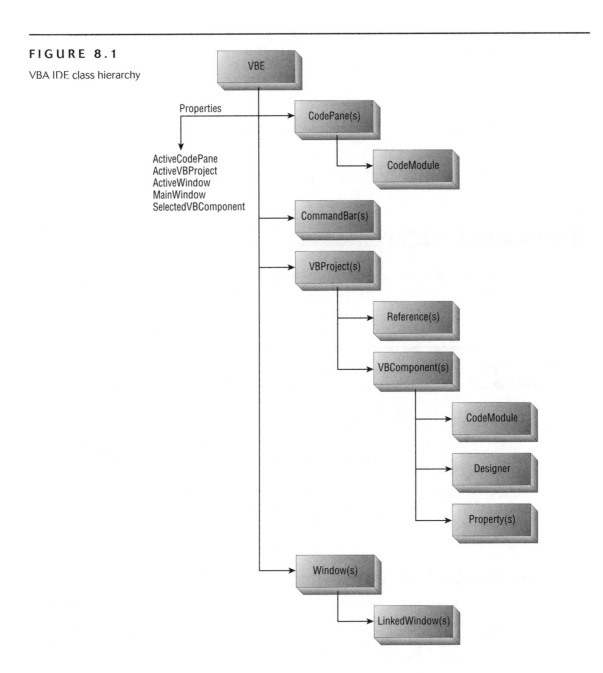

Descending from the VBE class are a number of collections representing objects in the development environment: CodePanes, CommandBars, VBProjects, and Windows. Also shown in Figure 8.1 are several properties of the VBE (ActiveCodePane, ActiveVBProject, and so on) that return references to other objects. Depending on what you're trying to do, you might find using these properties easier than using the related collections.

Adding the Type Library Reference

Before you can begin manipulating projects in the VBA IDE, you must set a reference to the IDE's type library to your current VBA project. To do this, open the References dialog and select the entry Microsoft Visual Basic for Applications Extensibility (see Figure 8.2).

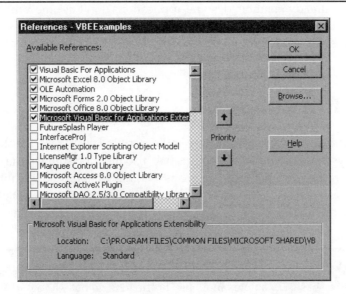

FIGURE 8.2

Selecting the VBA IDE type library reference

If you don't see the type library in the list of available references, use the Browse button to locate the library manually. Look for a file called VBE.DLL in the Program Files\Common Files\Microsoft Shared\VBA directory.

Referencing the IDE

Once you've added a type library reference to your project, you can start writing code to control the VBA IDE. You cannot reference the IDE directly, however. This is because the IDE is not a truly independent application but is, instead, part of another process (its host application). You obtain a reference to the IDE, therefore, from the host application. For example, the Application classes of Excel, Power-Point, and Word feature a VBE property that returns a reference to the VBA IDE. This allows you to write VBA code like this:

```
Sub dhShowVBEVersion()
    Dim objVBE As VBIDE.VBE

    Set objVBE = Application.VBE
    MsgBox objVBE.Version, vbInformation
End Sub
```

As already mentioned, some applications don't use the VBA IDE and thus do not feature a VBE property. Access, for instance, implements some of the VBA IDE's classes as children of its Application class.

Exploring IDE Classes

In this section, by highlighting and describing each class, we show you a few ways to manipulate VBA objects. We also mention some of the more noteworthy properties and methods of the classes. This section is not meant to be a complete dissertation on the object model, however. For a complete list of the properties and methods of these classes, refer to the Object Browser and online help.

> **NOTE** You'll find the sample code for the first half of this section in the basIDEExamples module. For the second half—the part that deals with modifying source code programmatically—you'll find the examples in the basCodeExamples module.

Working with Windows

The VBA IDE classes offer a surprising degree of control over the physical appearance of the IDE itself. You can write code to manipulate the main IDE window, as well as its children and command bars. Why is this surprising? Normally, when you consider what you'd like to do with the VBA object model, you think about modifying the objects and code that make up your project. (At least it's what we think about.) The IDE's user interface is immaterial. Nonetheless, it is a big part of the object model, so let's look at what you can do.

The Window Class

The Window class is a generic class that represents all windows in the IDE, including the IDE's main window. You access individual Window objects using the Windows collection of the VBE class (which contains references to the IDE's child windows) or its MainWindow property (which refers to the IDE's main window). The class features obvious properties such as Top, Left, Height, Width, Visible, WindowState, and Caption, as well as SetFocus and Close methods. It also has a Type property that returns the type of a given window. Table 8.2 lists the possible values for the Type property. Finally, the Window class implements two properties, LinkedWindows and LinkedWindowFrame, that we explain in the next section.

TABLE 8.2   Possible Values of the Type Property of the Window Class

Value	Constant	Window Type
0	vbext_wt_CodeWindow	Code window
1	vbext_wt_Designer	Object designer window
2	vbext_wt_Browser	Object Browser
3	vbext_wt_Watch	Watch window
4	vbext_wt_Locals	Locals window
5	vbext_wt_Immediate	Immediate window
6	vbext_wt_ProjectWindow	Project Explorer
7	vbext_wt_PropertyWindow	Properties window

TABLE 8.2 Possible Values of the Type property of the Window Class (continued)

Value	Constant	Window Type
8	vbext_wt_Find	Find window
9	vbext_wt_FindReplace	Find-and-replace window
11	vbext_wt_LinkedWindowFrame	Frame for a linked (docked) window
12	vbext_wt_MainWindow	The VBA IDE main window
15	vbext_wt_ToolWindow	VBA Toolbox

Linked Windows

The VBA IDE features a number of windows (for example, the Project and Properties windows) that can be *docked* to the main IDE window. You dock a window by dragging it close to one of the main window's borders. When you release the mouse, the window "sticks" to the edge of the main window. Within the object model, these are known as *linked windows.* The Window class implements two properties that allow you to control the docking behavior. Both the LinkedWindow-Frame and LinkedWindows properties return references to other Window objects.

If a given Window object is docked, its LinkedWindowFrame property will return a reference to the window it is docked to. In the current incarnation of the VBA IDE, this is always the IDE main window. (Presumably, Microsoft left the door open for future user interface designs in which a window might be docked to multiple objects.) If the window is not docked, LinkedWindowFrame returns Nothing.

LinkedWindows, on the other hand, works in the opposite direction. It tells you which windows are docked to the current one via a collection of Window objects. Again, in the current version of the IDE, the only window that can have linked windows is the IDE main window.

WARNING   If you try to reference the LinkedWindows collection of a normal window (other than the IDE main window), VBA generates error 91, "Object variable or With block variable not set."

As a collection, LinkedWindows has several properties and methods, including Count, Add, and Remove. Add and Remove both accept references to other windows and, when used, toggle the docked state of a given window. For example, the code shown in Listing 8.1 "undocks" all the docked windows in the IDE.

Listing 8.1: Undock Windows in the VBA IDE

```
Sub dhUndockAllWindows()
    Dim intWindow As Integer

    ' Use the LinkedWindows collection of the
    ' VBE object's MainWindow
    With Application.VBE.MainWindow.LinkedWindows

        ' Loop backward through each linked
        ' window, removing it from the collection
        For intWindow = .Count To 1 Step -1
            .Remove .Item(intWindow)
        Next
    End With
End Sub
```

Docking windows is a bit trickier because only certain types of windows (such as the Project, Properties, and Watch windows) can be docked. Code windows and other windows (like user forms) that appear in the main IDE workspace cannot be docked. Listing 8.2 shows a procedure that docks all "dockable" windows.

Listing 8.2: Dock Windows in the VBA IDE

```
Sub dhDockAllWindows()
    On Error GoTo HandleError

    Dim objWindow As VBIDE.Window

    ' Use the VBE object
    With Application.VBE

        ' Loop through all its windows
        For Each objWindow In .Windows

            ' If the window is visible, dock it by
            ' adding it to the LinkedWindows collection
            If objWindow.Visible Then
                .MainWindow.LinkedWindows.Add objWindow
            End If
```

```
        Next
    End With

ExitHere:
    Exit Sub
HandleError:
    Select Case Err.Number
        ' Check for error when adding
        ' a window that can't be docked
        Case &H80004005
            Resume Next
        Case Else
            MsgBox Err.Description, vbExclamation, _
             "Error " & Err.Number
            Resume ExitHere
    End Select
End Sub
```

The dhDockAllWindows procedure shown in Listing 8.2 works by looping through the Windows collection of the VBE object, attempting to add each window to the LinkedWindows collection. Note that before attempting this, however, the procedure checks the window's Visible property. This is necessary because when you launch the IDE, VBA opens all the environment windows (Locals, Immediate, and so on), displaying only those that were visible during the last editing session. If you attempt to add a hidden window to the LinkedWindows collection, VBA makes it visible. Normally, this is not a desirable side effect, and that's why the procedure first checks each window's Visible property.

Note also the error handling in the procedure. Since the For Each loop will iterate through *all* open windows and since some, like code windows, can't be docked, the Add method may fail. The error handler traps this error (hexadecimal error number 80004005) and simply resumes executing at the next statement.

The CodePane Class

So far we've discussed the general Window class. The CodePane class is a specific window type that corresponds to a code window in the IDE. VBA maintains a separate CodePanes collection within the VBE object, in addition to the Windows collection. You can also use the ActiveCodePane property. The most important property of a CodePane is CodeModule. It gives you access to your project's actual source code. We examine the CodeModule class in the section "Manipulating Code Modules" later in this chapter.

What can you do with a CodePane that you can't do with a normal window? Not much, as it turns out. You can determine how many lines of code are visible (using the CountOfVisibleLines property) and which line of code is at the top of the window (using TopLine). You can also retrieve and set the text selection using the GetSelection and SetSelection methods, respectively.

Listing 8.3 shows the dhCodePaneInfo procedure, which prints information about the active code pane to the Immediate window. To test the procedure, highlight some code in a module window and then run the procedure from the Immediate window.

Listing 8.3: Print Details about a CodePane Object

```
Sub dhCodePaneInfo()
    On Error GoTo ExitHere

    Dim lngRowStart As Long
    Dim lngColStart As Long
    Dim lngRowEnd As Long
    Dim lngColEnd As Long

    ' Use the active code pane
    With Application.VBE.ActiveCodePane
        ' Print window caption
        Debug.Print "Information on: " & .Window.Caption
        Debug.Print "===================================="

        ' Print visible lines and top line
        Debug.Print "Visible lines: " & .CountOfVisibleLines
        Debug.Print "Top line: " & .TopLine

        ' Print selection info
        Call .GetSelection(lngRowStart, lngColStart, _
          lngRowEnd, lngColEnd)

        Debug.Print "Selection:"
        Debug.Print "  Start line:   " & lngRowStart
        Debug.Print "  Start column: " & lngColStart
        Debug.Print "  End line:     " & lngRowEnd
        Debug.Print "  End column:   " & lngColEnd
    End With
ExitHere:
End Sub
```

There are two items worth noting in this procedure:

- CodePane objects have a Window property that is a pointer to the associated window. You can use this property to access properties of the Window class described earlier in this chapter.

- The GetSelection method accepts four long integer variables by reference and modifies them to represent the current selection. Make sure you declare these variables before calling the method.

Manipulating Command Bars

With the release of Office 97, Microsoft ushered in a new user interface element: the *command bar*. Command bars are a combination of traditional menus and toolbars. A command bar can contain menu commands (including cascading menus), toolbar buttons, or both. One very interesting and powerful feature of command bars is that they are implemented by a separate software component and thus can be shared among applications. The VBA IDE uses command bars in place of normal menus and toolbars and makes them available to you via the VBE object's CommandBars collection.

Simple Command Bar Tricks

Office command bars are extremely complex objects. Not only do they comprise a large number of subclasses, properties, and methods, but the ability to nest them within one another (via cascading menus) complicates the task of manipulating them. We don't provide an in-depth discussion of Office command bars in this chapter. Instead, we explain a few properties that may come in useful when programming the IDE. (For a complete discussion of Office command bars, see a book such as *Access 97 Developer's Handbook* (Sybex 1997).)

As with any other collection, you can iterate through the command bars that are part of the VBA IDE. If you do, you'll find there are a staggering 26 of them! Where are they all hiding? One of them represents the menu bar (named, appropriately, Menu Bar), and there are several that act as toolbars (Standard, Edit, Debug, and UserForm). Most of them, however, are defined as pop-up menus that appear when you click the right mouse button on various objects. Listing 8.4 shows a procedure that prints the name and type of each toolbar to the Immediate window. Figure 8.3 shows the output produced by running the procedure.

Listing 8.4: Procedure That Prints Toolbar Names and Types

```
Sub dhListCommandBars()
    Dim cbr As CommandBar

    ' Loop through all command bars
    For Each cbr In Application.VBE.CommandBars
        ' Print the name and a space
        Debug.Print cbr.Name & " ";

        ' Print the type of command bar
        Select Case cbr.Type
            Case msoBarTypeMenuBar
                Debug.Print "(menu bar)"
            Case msoBarTypeNormal
                Debug.Print "(normal/toolbar)"
            Case msoBarTypePopup
                Debug.Print "(popup)"
        End Select
    Next
End Sub
```

FIGURE 8.3

Result of running the dhListCommandBars procedure

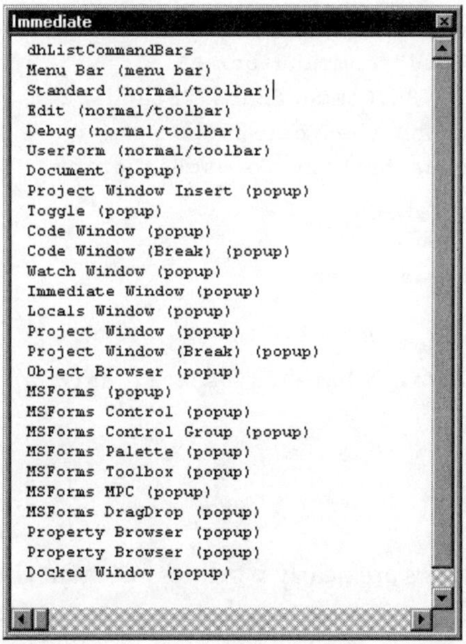

```
Immediate
dhListCommandBars
Menu Bar (menu bar)
Standard (normal/toolbar)|
Edit (normal/toolbar)
Debug (normal/toolbar)
UserForm (normal/toolbar)
Document (popup)
Project Window Insert (popup)
Toggle (popup)
Code Window (popup)
Code Window (Break) (popup)
Watch Window (popup)
Immediate Window (popup)
Locals Window (popup)
Project Window (popup)
Project Window (Break) (popup)
Object Browser (popup)
MSForms (popup)
MSForms Control (popup)
MSForms Control Group (popup)
MSForms Palette (popup)
MSForms Toolbox (popup)
MSForms MPC (popup)
MSForms DragDrop (popup)
Property Browser (popup)
Property Browser (popup)
Docked Window (popup)
```

CommandBar objects have a Visible property that you can use to hide or display individual command bars. You cannot display a pop-up command bar using the Visible property, however. If you try to do so, VBA generates an Automation error. Instead, you can use the ShowPopup method, passing a pair of screen coordinates in pixels.

Modifying Command Bars

The bulk of the command bar object model exists to allow programmatic customization of command bars. You can create new command bars by calling the collection's Add method and delete them by calling the Delete method of individual CommandBar objects. Command bars also have a number of properties, such as Top, Left, Height, Width, and Position, that affect their appearance. Listing 8.5 shows a procedure that moves the Standard command bar around the outside borders of the VBA IDE window. (Note that the Office 97 type library defines constants for the positions.)

Listing 8.5: Watch the Command Bar Go 'round and 'round

```
Sub dhMoveBarAround()
    Dim intPos As Integer
    Dim datNow As Date

    ' Use the "Standard" command bar
    With Application.VBE.CommandBars("Standard")
        ' Move it around the four sides
        For intPos = msoBarLeft To msoBarBottom

            .Position = intPos

            ' Wait for a second
            DoEvents
            datNow = Now
            Do Until Now > DateAdd("s", 1, datNow)
            Loop
        Next
    End With
End Sub
```

Of course, command bars are nearly worthless without controls. Each CommandBar object has a Controls collection that contains one CommandBarControl object for each control on the command bar. You can add new controls to the command bar or take them away. When adding new controls, you can create command bar buttons (menu commands are buttons that display only text), combo boxes, drop-down lists, edit controls, and pop-up controls. Listing 8.6 presents a very simple example of creating a new command bar called Custom, shown here:

This new command bar contains two custom buttons that call the dhCodePaneInfo and dhListCommandBars procedures described earlier in this chapter. The listing also shows code from the CBarEvents class module, which we explain in a moment.

Listing 8.6: Create a New Command Bar Called Custom with Two Buttons

```
Private mobjEvents As New CBarEvents

Sub dhCreateNewBar()
    Dim ctlNew As CommandBarButton

    ' Built-in command bar buttons
    Const dhCBCode = 488
    Const dhCBCascade = 1826

    ' Use the CommandBars collection
    With Application.VBE.CommandBars
        ' Delete the "Custom" command bar
        ' If this fails then it doesn't exist
        On Error Resume Next
        .Item("Custom").Delete
        On Error GoTo 0

        ' Add a new command bar and use it
        With .Add("Custom", msoBarFloating)

            ' Use its Controls collection
            With .Controls
                ' Add a button for "Code"
                Set ctlNew = .Add(msoControlButton, _
                dhCBCode)

                ' Change the default properties
                With ctlNew
                    .Caption = "CodePane Info"
                    .TooltipText = "Print CodePane Info"
                End With
```

```
                        ' Hook up event sink
                        Set mobjEvents.CodePaneInfoButton = _
                        Application.VBE.Events. _
                        CommandBarEvents(ctlNew)

                        ' Add a button for "Cascade"
                        Set ctlNew = .Add(msoControlButton, _
                         dhCBCascade)

                        ' Change the default properties
                        With ctlNew
                            .Caption = "Command Bars"
                            .TooltipText = "List Command Bars"
                        End With

                        ' Hook up event sink
                        Set mobjEvents.ListCommandBarsButton = _
                        Application.VBE.Events. _
                        CommandBarEvents(ctlNew)

                    End With

                    ' Make the command bar visible
                    .Visible = True

            End With
        End With
    End Sub

    ' Create event sinks for the two buttons
    Public WithEvents CodePaneInfoButton As CommandBarEvents
    Public WithEvents ListCommandBarsButton As CommandBarEvents

    Private Sub CodePaneInfoButton_Click( _
     ByVal CommandBarControl As Object, _
     handled As Boolean, CancelDefault As Boolean)

        Call dhCodePaneInfo
    End Sub

    Private Sub ListCommandBarsButton_Click( _
     ByVal CommandBarControl As Object, _
     handled As Boolean, CancelDefault As Boolean)

        Call dhListCommandBars
    End Sub
```

If you want to display the command bar immediately after creating it, set its Visible property to True.

You'll notice that it's extremely simple to create buttons representing built-in command bar functions. You call the Add method of the Controls collection, passing the control type (msoControlButton, for command bar buttons) and the number of the built-in command. We've declared these as constants in the procedure.

Determining the correct number to use can be an exercise in trial and error. To assist you, we've provided a text file on the CD-ROM called CBARNUMS.TXT that lists the number and caption for each of the 3517 built-in command bar buttons.

Customizing a command bar button requires a bit more work. After creating a new command button based on an existing control, the dhCreateNewBar procedure sets two button properties that control the button's appearance. It redefines the button's caption and ToolTip text to represent the custom action that takes place when a user clicks the button.

Making the newly created buttons do something is a complex process. Unlike command bar buttons in host applications like Word and Excel, VBA command bar buttons require an *event sink* created using a class module and the WithEvents keyword. An event sink is essentially a hook into events that are generated by an object. You create an event sink using the WithEvents keyword in an object declaration:

```
Public WithEvents CodePaneInfoButton As CommandBarEvents
```

When you use the WithEvents keyword, VBA makes available event procedures for each of the object's events. In the case of command bar buttons, there is only one event, Click. Code in the class module then ties code to the event procedure:

```
Private Sub CodePaneInfoButton_Click( _
 ByVal CommandBarControl As Object, _
 handled As Boolean, CancelDefault As Boolean)

    Call dhCodePaneInfo
End Sub
```

> **NOTE**
>
> You must use a class module to create an event sink since only class modules can have event procedures.

You must then instantiate the event sink, using a reference to the events provided by the VBA IDE objects—in this case, a command bar button. That's what the following statement does:

```
' Hook up event sink
Set mobjEvents.CodePaneInfoButton = _
 Application.VBE.Events. _
 CommandBarEvents(ctlNew)
```

In this example, mobjEvents is a module-level pointer to an instance of our event sink class, CBarEvents. This pointer is required to give the event sink "life."

This is not the most convenient method for calling code from command bar buttons. You need to create a new event sink for each command bar button you add (although they can all be contained in a single class module). It does, however, provide a way to create add-ins that function in the VBA IDE as opposed to the host application's user interface.

Working with VBA Projects

The remainder of this section discusses the most interesting aspect of programming the VBA IDE: working with VBA projects. This is where the fun starts, because it is this portion of the object model that deals with programmatic control of project components and source code.

The VBProject Class

The VBA IDE is a shared component, capable of hosting multiple projects at the same time. You would expect the object model to represent this. In fact, it does so, by means of the VBProjects collection of the VBE object. Each VBProject object in the collection represents a loaded VBA project.

> **NOTE**
>
> You cannot directly add or remove objects from the VBProjects collection. This must be done by the host application, but you can write code that instructs the host application to load a project. For example, you could write Microsoft Excel Automation code to open an XLS file containing VBA code.

The VBProject class implements properties that map to those in the project options dialog (see Figure 8.4 for an example). For example, you can set and retrieve the Name, Description, HelpFile, and HelpContextID properties. Changing these through code changes the values in the options dialog, and vice versa.

FIGURE 8.4

Project options you can set and retrieve using VBA code

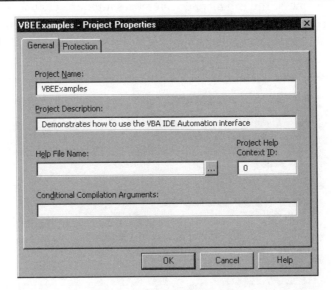

The class also implements several read-only properties that can give you additional information about the project. Specifically, the Mode property tells you whether the project is in run, break, or design mode. These states are represented by the integer values 0, 1, and 2 and by the constants vbext_vm_Run, vbext_vm_Break, and vbext_vm_Design, respectively. Furthermore, the Protection property returns the value 1 (vbext_pp_locked) if the project is password protected and 0 (vbext_pp_none) if it is not. Finally, the Saved property tells you whether the project has changed since the last time it was saved. A True value indicates that no changes have been made, while False indicates that changes have been made but not yet saved.

TIP Use the VBE object's ActiveVBProject property to return a reference to the project that is currently active in the VBA IDE.

The Reference Class

Part of a VBA project is the set of type library references for any Automation components it uses. Simple projects will have but a few references, such as those for VBA itself, Automation, and the host application. Complex projects—those that utilize additional Automation components or ActiveX controls—will have numerous references. You can manage references interactively using the References dialog shown in Figure 8.5. You can also manipulate them programmatically using the References collection of the VBProject class.

FIGURE 8.5

The References dialog showing type library references for a VBA project

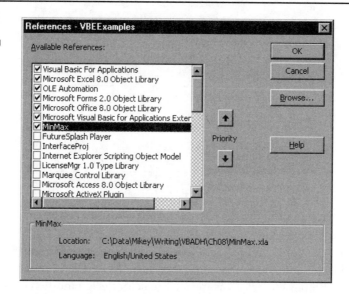

NOTE If you're working through the examples in this chapter, your project will also have a reference to the VBA IDE extensibility type library.

As you might expect, the References collection contains one element for each reference in a particular project. The Reference class itself defines properties that describe the reference, such as Name, Major and Minor version numbers, Description, FullPath, Guid (for type library references), Type, Builtin, and IsBroken. The IsBroken property is of particular interest because when a reference is broken (because a type library or an application has been moved or deleted), the VBA project containing it won't compile. When you determine that a reference is broken, you can delete and re-create it using methods of the References collection.

Listing 8.7 shows a procedure that prints information on the active project's references to the Immediate window. Figure 8.6 illustrates some sample output. Note the references to VBA and the host application (Microsoft Excel, in this case), as well as another VBA project, MinMax.

Listing 8.7: Print Reference Information to the Immediate Window

```
Sub dhPrintReferences()
    Dim ref As Reference

    ' Iterate the references of the active project
    For Each ref In Application.VBE. _
     ActiveVBProject.References

        ' Use each reference and print:
        ' Name and version
        '     Description
        '     Built-in or custom?
        '     Project or typelib?
        '     Broken or intact?
        '     Full path
        '     GUID
        With ref
            Debug.Print .Name & " " & .Major & "." & .Minor
            If Not .IsBroken Then
                Debug.Print "    " & .Description
            End If
            Debug.Print "    "; IIf(.BuiltIn, "Built-in/", _
             "Custom/");
            Debug.Print IIf(.Type = vbext_rk_Project, _
             "Project/", "TypeLib/");
```

```
                    Debug.Print IIf(.IsBroken, "Broken!", "Intact")
                    Debug.Print "    "; .FullPath
                    Debug.Print "    "; IIf(.Type = _
                     vbext_rk_TypeLib, .GUID, "")
                End With
            Next
        End Sub
```

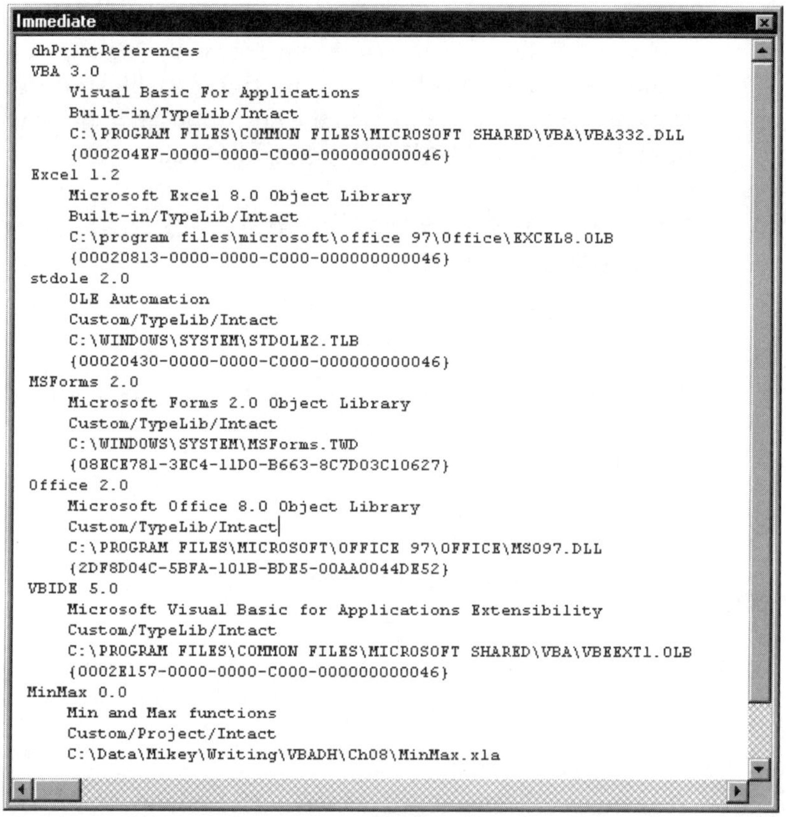

FIGURE 8.6

Reference information printed to the Immediate window

```
Immediate                                                            [x]
dhPrintReferences
VBA 3.0
    Visual Basic For Applications
    Built-in/TypeLib/Intact
    C:\PROGRAM FILES\COMMON FILES\MICROSOFT SHARED\VBA\VBA332.DLL
    {000204EF-0000-0000-C000-000000000046}
Excel 1.2
    Microsoft Excel 8.0 Object Library
    Built-in/TypeLib/Intact
    C:\program files\microsoft\office 97\Office\EXCEL8.OLB
    {00020813-0000-0000-C000-000000000046}
stdole 2.0
    OLE Automation
    Custom/TypeLib/Intact
    C:\WINDOWS\SYSTEM\STDOLE2.TLB
    {00020430-0000-0000-C000-000000000046}
MSForms 2.0
    Microsoft Forms 2.0 Object Library
    Custom/TypeLib/Intact
    C:\WINDOWS\SYSTEM\MSForms.TWD
    {08ECE781-3EC4-11D0-B663-8C7D03C10627}
Office 2.0
    Microsoft Office 8.0 Object Library
    Custom/TypeLib/Intact
    C:\PROGRAM FILES\MICROSOFT\OFFICE 97\OFFICE\MSO97.DLL
    {2DF8D04C-5BFA-101B-BDE5-00AA0044DE52}
VBIDE 5.0
    Microsoft Visual Basic for Applications Extensibility
    Custom/TypeLib/Intact
    C:\PROGRAM FILES\COMMON FILES\MICROSOFT SHARED\VBA\VBEEXT1.OLB
    {0002E157-0000-0000-C000-000000000046}
MinMax 0.0
    Min and Max functions
    Custom/Project/Intact
    C:\Data\Mikey\Writing\VBADH\Ch08\MinMax.xla
```

WARNING You cannot access the Description property of a broken reference. Attempting to do so will result in a run-time error.

Removing References   If a reference is broken, you can rebuild it using methods of the References collection. You can't use Reference class properties, because they are all read-only and are set when the reference is added to the project. You must first, therefore, delete the invalid reference using the References collection's Remove method. Remove accepts a pointer to a Reference object as an argument. Listing 8.8 shows the dhRemoveAllBadRefs procedure, which removes all broken references from the active project.

Listing 8.8: Procedure for Removing All Broken References from a Project

```
Sub dhRemoveAllBadRefs()
    Dim ref As Reference

    ' Use the active project
    With Application.VBE.ActiveVBProject

        ' Iterate through the references
        For Each ref In .References

            ' If reference is broken, remove it
            If ref.IsBroken Then
                .References.Remove ref
            End If
        Next
    End With
End Sub
```

Adding References   Once you've removed the offending reference, you can then add it back to the project. You can add a reference using one of two methods of the References collection: AddFromFile or AddFromGuid. (Of course, this works the same way for new references as well.) Use AddFromFile to create a reference to a DLL, an EXE, or another VBA project. For example, to add a reference to an Excel add-in, you might use code like this:

```
Application.VBE.ActiveVBProject.References.AddFromFile _
 "C:\Excel\Addins\MinMax.xla"
```

If the file does not exist and a path is specified, a run-time error occurs. If no path is specified, VBA searches for the file in the Windows and Windows\System directories, as well as in the current directory.

AddFromGuid adds a reference to a type library or other component based on its Globally Unique Identifier (GUID) stored in the Registry. You pass the GUID as a string, along with major and minor version numbers. VBA attempts to find the component in the Registry and, if successful, creates a reference to it in the project. For example, to add a reference to Microsoft Access 97's type library, you would use a statement like this:

```
Application.VBE.ActiveVBProject.References.AddFromGuid _
  "{4AFFC9A0-5F99-101B-AF4E-00AA003F0F07}", 8, 0
```

If VBA can't find the reference, it raises a run-time error. If the exact version specified doesn't exist but a more recent version does, VBA adds a reference to the more recent version.

> **TIP**
>
> The easiest way to determine the GUID for a given type library is to add a reference to the type library to a project using the References dialog and then print the Guid property of the associated Reference object.

Modifying Project Components

Manipulating projects and references is fine, but what about the real meat of an application—the code-bearing components, such as modules, forms, and host-application objects? The VBComponent class represents all these objects. Each VBA project has a VBComponents collection that contains one object for each component. Figure 8.7 shows the Project Explorer window with a sample VBA project. Each object shown in the leaves of the tree view is a VBComponent object.

VBA code modules (both class modules and regular code modules) are examples of VBComponent objects. The types of other components you can add to your project will depend on the host application. For instance, if you're using Microsoft Excel, your project will contain one Worksheet object for each worksheet in the workbook, as well as a reference to the workbook itself (ThisWorkbook in Figure 8.7). A Microsoft Word VBA project would contain a reference to the associated document file. You can also add VBA user forms to projects based on Excel, Word, and PowerPoint. (Visual Basic and Access have their own form design tools.)

FIGURE 8.7

Sample VBA project showing different components

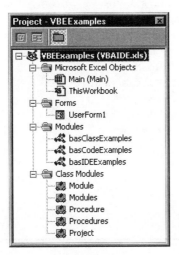

As you can see in Figure 8.7, the number of different object types that fall under the heading of VBComponents is quite large. It will continue to grow as more companies license VBA for their own products. As far as VBA is concerned, however, there are only four types of components: standard modules, class modules, user forms, and documents. The exact manifestation of the fourth category will depend on the host application.

Listing 8.9 shows a procedure that prints the components of a VBA project to the Immediate window. It accepts a pointer to a project as an argument and uses a For Each loop to iterate through each component. Figure 8.8 illustrates the output produced when calling the procedure from the Immediate window, passing a reference to the active project.

Listing 8.9: Procedure That Prints the Components of a VBA Project

```
Sub dhDumpComps(vbp As VBProject)
    Dim vbc As VBComponent

    ' Loop through each component in the project
    For Each vbc In vbp.VBComponents

        ' Print the component's name
        Debug.Print vbc.Name & " (";
```

```
                  ' Print the component's type
                  Select Case vbc.Type
                      Case vbext_ct_StdModule
                          Debug.Print "Standard Module";
                      Case vbext_ct_ClassModule
                          Debug.Print "Class Module";
                      Case vbext_ct_MSForm
                          Debug.Print "User Form";
                      Case vbext_ct_Document
                          Debug.Print "Document";
                  End Select
                  Debug.Print ")"
          Next
      End Sub
```

FIGURE 8.8

Sample output from the dhDumpComps procedure

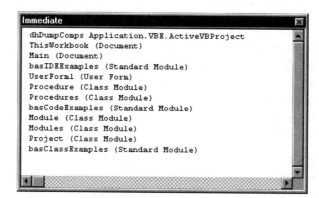

```
Immediate                                              ▼ ✕
dhDumpComps Application.VBE.ActiveVBProject             ▲
ThisWorkbook (Document)
Main (Document)
basIDEExamples (Standard Module)
UserForm1 (User Form)
Procedure (Class Module)
Procedures (Class Module)
basCodeExamples (Standard Module)
Module (Class Module)
Modules (Class Module)
Project (Class Module)
basClassExamples (Standard Module)
                                                        ▼
◄ ▶                                                   ▶
```

The VBComponent Class

From a programming perspective, the VBComponent class is simple. It features Name and Type properties that correspond to a component's name and classification (one of the four types just listed). Like the VBProject class that it's a part of, the VBComponent class has a Saved property.

The VBComponent class also implements several methods. The Activate method gives the component the input focus in the VBA IDE. The Export method accepts a file name and exports the component's definition as text. You can use Export to produce individual source files from a VBA project stored as part of a host application's document. For instance, to export the contents of a code module stored in an Excel workbook, you might use code like this:

```
Application.VBE.ActiveVBProject.VBComponents("basMain") _
    .Export "C:\MAIN.BAS"
```

NOTE While you can use the Export method of any VBComponent object, only the VBA-specific portions of the object will be exported. For instance, VBA exports an Excel worksheet object as a class module, including any code attached to the object's events. VBE does not, however, include the Excel worksheet properties in the output file.

Creating New Components

Unlike most of the collections in the VBA IDE, you *can* add new members to the VBComponents collection, thus creating new components in your project. The Add method accepts an argument that defines the component type (one of the four types discussed above). For example, to create a new code module in the active project, you could use code like this:

```
Set vbcNew = Application.VBE.ActiveVBProject. _
    VBComponents.Add(vbext_ct_StdModule)
```

Note that the Add method returns a pointer to the newly created component. In the preceding example, a VBComponent object variable, vbcNew, stores this pointer.

You can also create new components by importing them from a text file. The VBComponents collection's Import method accepts a file name and returns a pointer to the new component, provided VBA was able to process the file contents successfully.

Finally, if you want to eliminate a component from your project, simply call the Remove method, passing a pointer to the VBComponent object.

Component Properties

What makes the VBComponent class truly useful is its collection of Property objects. Each Property object corresponds to a property of the particular component. These are the same properties that appear in the VBA IDE's Properties window. You can iterate the collection to examine the name and value of each property. Listing 8.10 shows a procedure, dhDumpProps, that does just that. It accepts a pointer to a VBComponent object as an argument and uses a For Each loop to examine each of the component's properties. You can call the procedure from the Immediate window, as the following code illustrates:

```
Call dhDumpProps(Application.VBE. _
ActiveVBProject.VBComponents(1))
```

Listing 8.10: Procedure That Dumps the Name and Value of a VBComponent's Properties to the Immediate Window

```
Sub dhDumpProps(vbc As VBComponent)
    On Error GoTo HandleError

    Dim prp As Property
    Dim var As Variant
    Dim fReadingValue As Boolean

    Const dhcPadding = 25

    ' Iterate the properties of the given
    ' component and print the names and values
    For Each prp In vbc.Properties

        ' Use each property
        With prp

            ' Print the property name, padded
            ' with spaces
            If Len(.Name) >= dhcPadding Then
                Debug.Print .Name & " ";
            Else
                Debug.Print .Name & _
                    Space(dhcPadding - Len(.Name));
            End If

            ' Set a flag indicating we're about
            ' to try to read the actual value
            fReadingValue = True

            ' If the name begins with an underscore
            ' the property is probably a hidden one
            ' and trying to access the value will
```

```
        ' likely fail, so just print "<hidden>"
        If Left(.Name, 1) = "_" Then
            Debug.Print "<hidden>"

        ' If this is an indexed property,
        ' print the number of indices
        ElseIf .NumIndices > 0 Then
            Debug.Print "<indexed (" & _
              .NumIndices & ")>"

        ' If the value is an object, just print
        ' "<object>"
        ElseIf IsObject(.Value) Then
            Debug.Print "<object (" & _
              TypeName(prp.Object) & ")>"

        ' If the value is an array, print
        ' each element
        ElseIf IsArray(.Value) Then
            For Each var In .Value
                Debug.Print var,
            Next
            Debug.Print

        ' If the value is not an object
        ' or an array, just print it
        Else
            Debug.Print prp.Value
        End If

        ' Reset flag
        fReadingValue = False
    End With
NextProp:
    Next
ExitHere:
    Exit Sub
HandleError:
    ' If we were trying to read the value,
    ' print the error we got and move on
    If fReadingValue Then
        Debug.Print "<error " & Err.Number & _
          ": " & Err.Description & ">"
        Resume NextProp
```

```
            ' Otherwise, bail out
        Else
            MsgBox Err.Description, vbExclamation, _
             "Error " & Err.Number
            Resume ExitHere
        End If
End Sub
```

While the dhDumpProps procedure might seem needlessly complex, it actually is not. All the code is necessary due to the intricacy of a VBA Property object. To fully understand this, let's look at what the procedure does with each Property.

After printing the property name, along with some padding to make the output look nice, dhDumpProps sets a Boolean flag variable that indicates it is about to try to read the property's value. The procedure does this so that if an error occurs, the error handler can skip to the next property rather than abort the entire procedure. For some reason, trying to read the value of certain properties results in run-time errors, despite efforts to trap for these cases.

Hidden Properties   A series of If and ElseIf statements then try to determine what type of property the current Property object is and how best to deal with it. The first statement checks the Name property to see whether it begins with an underscore. If so, the property is probably a *hidden property*. Hidden properties are defined in a type library but are not normally used in VBA code. When developers create the type library, they give the property a special attribute that prevents it from appearing in the Object Browser. Attempting to read the value of some hidden properties can generate run-time errors. It is for this reason that the procedure simply prints the string "<hidden>" after the property name.

> **TIP**   To view hidden properties and methods in Object Browser, right-click anywhere in the Object Browser window and select Show Hidden Members from the context menu.

Indexed Properties   The next ElseIf statement checks the property's NumIndices property. Some component properties are indexed; which means that to read their values, you must supply up to four index values. An example of an indexed property is the Colors property of an Excel Workbook object. The

Colors property is made up of 56 separate values representing the individual RGB color values used for the workbook's palette. You can write VBA code to set or retrieve any one of these values. To do so, you must use the Property object's IndexedValue property, passing a number from 1 to 56. For example:

```
Application.VBE.ActiveVBProject. _
 VBComponents("ThisWorkbook").Properties("Colors"). _
 IndexedValue(2) = RGB(255, 255, 0)
```

Since dhDumpProps is a generic procedure and doesn't know what type of component it is manipulating, it simply prints the string "<indexed>", along with the number of indices, when it comes across an indexed property. If you were writing VBA code to manipulate a specific component type, you would certainly want to use the IndexedValue property with particular index values.

Object Properties   Next, the procedure uses the VBA IsObject function to determine whether the current Property object's Value property is, itself, an object. You will find that many component properties are objects with their own sets of properties and methods. Again, since dhDumpProps is a generic procedure, it simply prints the string "<object>" and the object type after the property name.

If you know the type of object being returned, you can manipulate the object's properties and methods. Here's where things get a bit strange, however. The VBA documentation states that if a property value returns an object, you must use the Property object's Object property to access the returned object's properties and methods. For instance, to manipulate the font properties of a VBA user form, you should be able to use code like this:

```
Application.VBE.ActiveVBProject.VBComponents("UserForm1"). _
 Properties("Font").Object.Size = 10
```

In our testing, however, this did not work. VBA generated a compile-time error, "Method or data member not found," on the Size property.

What did work was using the Property object's Value property, although not as you'd expect. You might think you could use it in place of the Object property in the preceding statement. In reality, the Value property returned a collection containing the properties of the Font object. We were then able to use a statement like this one:

```
Application.VBE.ActiveVBProject.VBComponents("UserForm1"). _
 Properties("Font").Value.Item("Size") = 10
```

Note that the Item method is required when passing the property name (Size). While we can't explain why VBA behaves like this with object properties, it at least appears to be consistent.

We did find that the Object property worked when we assigned an object pointer to it. For instance, we were able to set the Picture property of a VBA user form using the following statement:

```
Set Application.VBE.ActiveVBProject. _
VBComponents("UserForm1").Properties("Picure"). _
Object = LoadPicture("C:\WINDOWS\WAVES.BMP")
```

LoadPicture loads an image file from disk and returns a pointer to it.

Scalar and Array Properties   If the Value property doesn't yield an object, it still might be an array, so the next ElseIf statement checks for this using the IsArray function. If IsArray returns True, the procedure uses another For Each loop to print each element of the array.

Finally, if none of the preceding conditions have been met, dhDumpProps assumes that Value is a scalar value and just prints it to the Immediate window. The last thing the procedure does is reset the flag variable.

Figure 8.9 shows some sample output from running the dhDumpProps procedure. The property values shown belong to an Excel Workbook object.

Component Designers

In addition to properties, some components may also have designers. *Designers* are supplemental windows that allow you to change the design of a component. The most common example of a designer is the VBA user form design window. It allows you to easily change property values (in conjunction with the Properties window), as well as to add and remove controls.

> **NOTE**   VBA standard and class modules do not have designers.

The VBComponent class implements one method and two properties that allow you to interact with component designers. First, the DesignerWindow

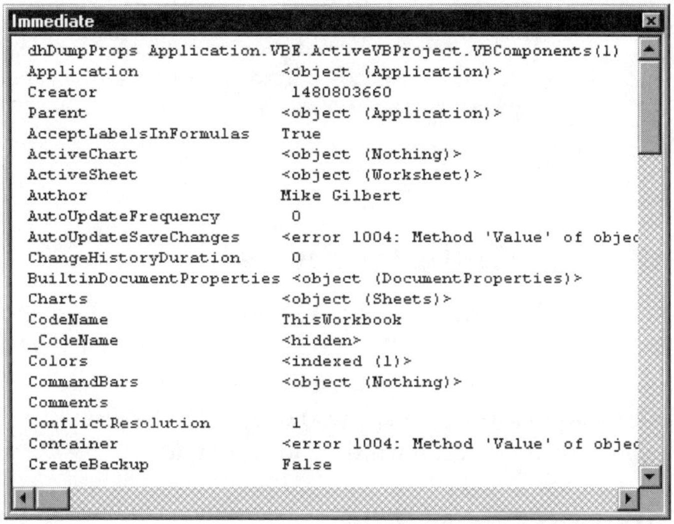

FIGURE 8.9

Property names and
values for a workbook

```
Immediate                                                    ×
dhDumpProps Application.VBE.ActiveVBProject.VBComponents(1)
Application              <object (Application)>
Creator                  1480803660
Parent                   <object (Application)>
AcceptLabelsInFormulas   True
ActiveChart              <object (Nothing)>
ActiveSheet              <object (Worksheet)>
Author                   Mike Gilbert
AutoUpdateFrequency      0
AutoUpdateSaveChanges    <error 1004: Method 'Value' of objec
ChangeHistoryDuration    0
BuiltinDocumentProperties <object (DocumentProperties)>
Charts                   <object (Sheets)>
CodeName                 ThisWorkbook
_CodeName                <hidden>
Colors                   <indexed (1)>
CommandBars              <object (Nothing)>
Comments
ConflictResolution       1
Container                <error 1004: Method 'Value' of objec
CreateBackup             False
```

method returns a pointer to the component's designer window. The object returned belongs to the VBA IDE Window class, so you can use all the properties
and methods described earlier in this chapter. For example, to display the
Designer window for a VBA user form, you could use a statement like this:

```
Application.VBE.ActiveVBProject. _
  VBComponents("UserForm1").DesignerWindow.Visible = True
```

You can tell whether a particular Designer window is open by inspecting the
HasOpenDesigner property.

The Designer method of the VBComponent class gives you direct control over
the designer itself. Depending on the component, this may give you additional
design capabilities. For instance, a VBA user form designer provides access to a
UserForm object from the MSForms type library. By using properties and methods of the UserForm class, you can change the appearance of the form, as well as
its controls. The following statement prints the number of controls on a user form
named UserForm1 to the Immediate window:

```
Debug.Print Application.VBE.ActiveVBProject. _
  VBComponents("UserForm1").Designer.Controls.Count
```

TIP Exploring the MSForms type library is beyond the scope of this book. You can check it out yourself, however, by using Object Browser. A reference to the type library is added to all VBA projects hosted by Microsoft Excel, PowerPoint, and Word.

Manipulating Code Modules

You'll find VBA code in two places within the IDE object model: as properties of both the CodePane and VBComponent classes. Each class has a CodeModule property that returns a pointer to the associated CodeModule object. The CodeModule class is perhaps the most complex of the VBA IDE classes. It is also the most fun and most rewarding to work with.

Counting Code Lines

The CodeModule class implements a number of properties that provide numerical counts of code lines. The CountOfLines and CountOfDeclarationLines properties return the total number of lines in the module and the number of lines in the declarations section, respectively. Obviously, the number of lines occupied by procedures is the difference between the two. Listing 8.11 shows a code fragment that illustrates how to use these properties.

Listing 8.11: Count Lines of Code in a Module

```
With Application.VBE.ActiveVBProject. _
 VBComponents("basCodeExamples").CodeModule

    Debug.Print "Total lines: " & .CountOfLines
    Debug.Print "Declarations: " & .CountOfDeclarationLines
    Debug.Print "Procedures: " & .CountOfLines - _
     .CountOfDeclarationLines
End With
```

CodeModule objects also have a ProcCountLines property that returns the number of lines in a given procedure. We'll discuss that in a moment, in the section "Working with Procedures."

Getting at the Code

To return the actual contents of a module, use the Lines property. Lines accepts two arguments: a starting line number and a line count. It returns the text specified by the two values. Listing 8.12 shows code that complements that shown in Listing 8.11. Instead of printing the number of lines to the Immediate window, the code in Listing 8.12 prints the actual text.

Listing 8.12: Print the Contents of a Module

```
With Application.VBE.ActiveVBProject. _
 VBComponents("basCodeExamples").CodeModule

    Debug.Print "All code:"
    Debug.Print .Lines(1, .CountOfLines)

    Debug.Print "Declarations:"
    Debug.Print .Lines(1, .CountOfDeclarationLines)

    Debug.Print "Procedures:"
    Debug.Print .Lines(.CountOfDeclarationLines + 1, _
      .CountOfLines - .CountOfDeclarationLines)
End With
```

Working with Procedures

Using the CodeModule class, you can work with VBA procedures programmatically. Unfortunately, the VBA IDE object module does not subdivide code modules into procedures. To work with procedures, you call methods of the CodeModule class, passing (among other things) the name of the procedure you want to work with. Of course, this assumes you *know* the name of the procedure! Fortunately, there is a way, albeit not simple, to determine the procedures contained within a code module: you use the ProcOfLine property, passing a line number. The result is the name of the procedure that contains that line of code. For example, to determine the name of the procedure that contains the fourth line of code in the basIDEExamples module, you would use the following statement:

```
Debug.Print Application.VBE.ActiveVBProject. _
 VBComponents("basIDEExamples").CodeModule. _
 ProcOfLine(4, lngType)
```

If you executed this line of code in the sample project for this chapter, the result would be "dhShowVBEVersion". The second argument to ProcOfLine, lngType, is a long integer that the ProcOfLine property will fill in with the type of procedure on the specified line. It will contain a value from 0 to 3, representing standard procedures (Subs and Function) and Property Let, Set, and Get statements, respectively.

Once you know the name and type of a procedure in a module, there are several other properties you can use. All of the following properties accept a procedure name and type as arguments:

- ProcStartLine returns the line on which a procedure begins.

- ProcBodyLine returns the line on which a procedure's code begins (the line containing the Sub, Function, or Property statement). This differs from ProcStartLine, which may include preceding comments or blank lines.

- ProcCountLines returns the length of the procedure, in lines, including any preceding comments or blank lines.

Using these properties, you can quickly list all the procedures in a module. Listing 8.13 shows a procedure that does just this. dhListProcs accepts a Code-Module object as an argument and uses the CountOfLines property to loop through each line of code. For each line, the procedure employs the ProcOfLine property to determine whether the current line is contained within a procedure definition.

Listing 8.13: Procedure That Lists the Procedures in a Module

```
Sub dhListProcs(modAny As CodeModule)
    Dim cLines As Long
    Dim lngType As Long
    Dim strProc As String

    ' Use the passed CodeModule
    With modAny
        ' Loop through all the code lines,
        ' looking for a procedure
        For cLines = 1 To .CountOfLines

            ' Get the name of the procedure
            ' on the current line
            strProc = .ProcOfLine(cLines, lngType)

            ' If non-blank we've found a proc
            If strProc <> "" Then
```

```
                              ' Print the line number, proc
                              ' name, and type
                              Debug.Print "Line " & cLines, _
                               strProc & "(" & lngType & ")"

                              ' Skip the code lines by adding the
                              ' number of lines in the proc (less one)
                              ' to the current line number
                              cLines = cLines + _
                                 .ProcCountLines(strProc, lngType) - 1
                        End If
                  Next
            End With
      End Sub
```

Most lines in a typical module will be part of some procedure, so it doesn't make sense to loop through every line. Instead, once dhListProcs has found the line at the start of a procedure, it skips the line following the end of the procedure. It does this by adding the number of lines in the procedure (obtained using the ProcCountLines property), minus 1, to the current line number. This results in a procedure that executes quite quickly, even on a large module. Figure 8.10 shows sample output obtained by running the procedure.

FIGURE 8.10

Sample output from the dhListProcs procedure

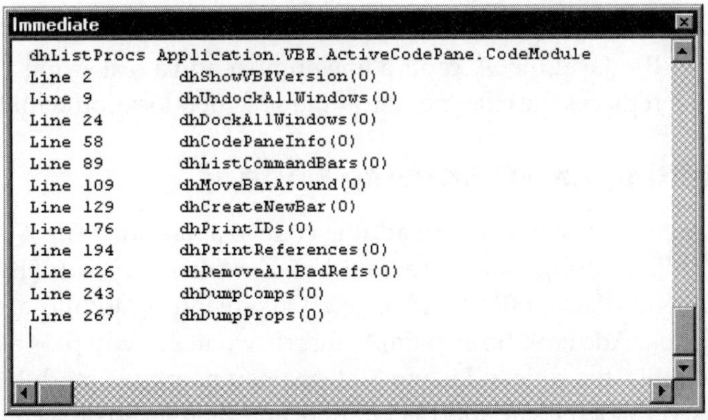

```
Immediate                                                              [x]
dhListProcs Application.VBE.ActiveCodePane.CodeModule
Line 2          dhShowVBEVersion(0)
Line 9          dhUndockAllWindows(0)
Line 24         dhDockAllWindows(0)
Line 58         dhCodePaneInfo(0)
Line 89         dhListCommandBars(0)
Line 109        dhMoveBarAround(0)
Line 129        dhCreateNewBar(0)
Line 176        dhPrintIDs(0)
Line 194        dhPrintReferences(0)
Line 226        dhRemoveAllBadRefs(0)
Line 243        dhDumpComps(0)
Line 267        dhDumpProps(0)
```

In the section "Putting It Together: An Alternative Object Model" later in this chapter, you'll see how to integrate this code into a class module that creates and maintains a collection of procedures.

CodeModule Methods

As good as the VBA IDE object model is, it is not very granular when it comes to modifying code. We've already explained that there is no direct support for procedures. You perform code modifications indirectly as well. Specifically, there are seven methods of the CodeModule class you can use to modify code.

- **AddFromFile:** Accepts a file name and adds the contents of the file to the module, after the declarations section but before the first existing procedure.

- **AddFromString:** Works like AddFromFile, but it accepts a text string as an argument rather than a file name.

- **CreateEventProc:** Accepts object and event names, both as text, and creates a new event procedure in the module. It returns the number of the line on which the new event procedure starts.

- **DeleteLines:** Accepts a starting line number and an optional number of lines. It deletes the specified number of lines of code (the default is 1) from the module, starting at the line passed as the first argument.

- **Find:** Locates text within the module. It accepts a number of arguments that affect its search logic. (We explain Find in more detail in the section "Finding and Replacing Code" later in this chapter.)

- **InsertLines:** Accepts a line number and a text string as arguments. It inserts the contents of the text string at the specified line.

- **ReplaceLine:** Accepts a line number and a text string as arguments. It replaces the existing line at the specified location with the supplied text.

Adding and Removing Code

What could be easier than adding code to a module? The AddFromFile and AddFromString methods are fairly self-explanatory. AddFromFile inserts the contents of a text file containing VBA code into a module, after the declarations section. AddFromString simply inserts whatever you pass as an argument. For example, the code in Listing 8.14 creates a new code module in the active project, inserts a global variable declaration, and then inserts the contents of a file. Figure 8.11 shows the new code module.

Listing 8.14: Create a New Module and Insert Some Code

```
Sub dhNewModule()
    ' Use the active project
    With Application.VBE.ActiveVBProject

        ' Create and use a new module
        With .VBComponents.Add(vbext_ct_StdModule)

            ' Change the module name
            .Name = "basTest"

            ' Use the code module
            With .CodeModule

                ' Add a variable declaration
                .AddFromString "Global gintText As Integer"

                ' Add the contents of a file
                .AddFromFile "C:\TESTPROC.BAS"
            End With
        End With
    End With
End Sub
```

FIGURE 8.11

A new module created using VBA code

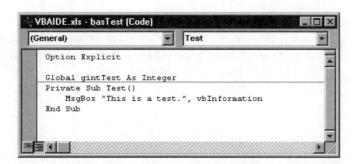

NOTE   We've provided a file on the CD-ROM, TESTPROC.BAS, that contains the sample procedure. If you want to run this example, make sure you change the path to the file to reflect the location of TESTPROC.BAS on your system.

455

TIP

You don't have to add the "Option Explicit" directive to the new module if you've enabled the Require Variable Declaration option. If you're not sure if this option is enabled, you can use the Lines and CountOfDeclarationLines properties (or the Find method described in the section "Finding and Replacing Code") to search the declarations section.

Like AddFromString, the InsertLines method accepts a text string and inserts it into the module. However, it inserts the string at a location specified by its first argument. Suppose, for example, you wanted to insert a comment block at the beginning of a module. You couldn't use AddFromString, because that method inserts text at the *end* of the declarations section. By using InsertLines, on the other hand, you can put the text wherever you want. The following code illustrates this.

```
' Add a comment block
With Application.VBE.ActiveVBProject. _
 VBComponents("basTest").CodeModule

    .InsertLines 1, "'======================="
    .InsertLines 2, "' Created by me, " & Date
    .InsertLines 3, "'======================="
End With
```

NOTE

AddFromFile, AddFromString, and InsertLines each append a carriage return to any text inserted into a module. If you want to add additional carriage returns, you must embed them in the inserted text (using the vbCrLf constant, for example).

You can remove lines of code using the DeleteLines method. DeleteLines accepts a starting line and an optional line count. It removes one or more lines of code (one is the default) from the module, starting at the specified line. To remove the comment block, therefore, you might use code like this:

```
' Remove comment block
Application.VBE.ActiveVBProject. _
 VBComponents("basTest").CodeModule. _
 DeleteLines 1, 3
```

Use caution when calling the DeleteLines method. Make sure you know what you're deleting! You can inspect the text on the affected lines using the Lines property. You can also use the Find method (explained in the section "Finding and Replacing Code") to locate specific text before deleting it.

Event Procedures

Event procedures are special procedures that VBA calls in response to an event for a given object. The CodeModule class implements a special method for creating them: CreateEventProc. CreateEventProc accepts an object name and an event name as arguments and creates a new event procedure in a given module. It returns the line number on which the procedure definition begins. You can use this number to insert additional lines of code in the body of the procedure.

The code in Listing 8.15 creates an event procedure for the Initialize event of a new class module. It then inserts code (a comment and a MsgBox statement) after the procedure declaration. Note that it uses the line number returned by Create-EventProc as the starting line for the inserted code. Figure 8.12 illustrates the results of running the procedure.

NOTE The object name for class modules will always be "Class".

Listing 8.15: Create a New Event Procedure

```
Sub dhSampleEventProc()
    Dim lngStart As Long
    Dim strQuotes As String

    strQuotes = Chr(34)

    ' Create a new class module
    With Application.VBE.ActiveVBProject. _
    VBComponents.Add(vbext_ct_ClassModule).CodeModule

        ' Add a new event proc
        lngStart = .CreateEventProc("Initialize", "Class")
```

```
                    ' Add some code
                    .InsertLines lngStart + 1, "      ' This is a test"
                    .InsertLines lngStart + 2, "      MsgBox " & _
                    strQuotes & "Test" & strQuotes & ", " & _
                    "vbInformation"
            End With
    End Sub
```

FIGURE 8.12

New class module with a
newly created Initialize
event procedure

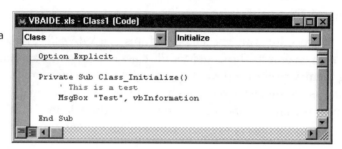

One important consideration when using CreateEventProc is to make sure the object in question exists and that it supports the specified event. If it does not exist or it does not support the event, VBA generates an "Event handler is invalid" error. You can, however, create event procedures using the methods described earlier in this chapter for inserting code into a module. VBA does not verify the correctness of procedures created in this manner.

NOTE You cannot create event procedures in standard modules. The only event procedures allowed for class modules are Initialize and Terminate.

Making full use of the CreateEventProc method goes beyond the scope of this book. It requires knowledge of the particular event-generating components in your project.

Finding and Replacing Code

The last way to modify a project's source code is by using the Find and Replace methods. Find is a powerful method that searches the code within a module, given a search string and a set of rules. It accepts five required and three optional arguments and returns a Boolean value indicating success or failure. These arguments are shown in Table 8.3.

TABLE 8.3   Arguments to the Find Method

Argument	Datatype	Required	Description (Default)
Target	String	Yes	The string you want to find
StartLine	Long	Yes	The line on which to start searching
StartColumn	Long	Yes	The column in which to start searching
EndLine	Long	Yes	The line on which to stop searching
EndColumn	Long	Yes	The column in which to stop searching
WholeWord	Boolean	No	Specifies a whole word search (False)
MatchCase	Boolean	No	Specifies a case-sensitive search (False)
PatternSearch	Boolean	No	If True, allows the use of wildcard characters (False)

We can best describe how to use the Find method through an example. Listing 8.16 shows a procedure designed to search through a given module looking for the string "Copyright 1997". Once the string is found, the procedure replaces the line with one that reads "Copyright 1997, 1998". (Listing 8.16 also illustrates the use of the Replace method.)

Listing 8.16: Example of Search-and-Replace

```
Sub dhFindAndReplace(modAny As CodeModule)
    Dim lngStartLine As Long
    Dim lngStartCol As Long
    Dim lngEndLine As Long
    Dim lngEndCol As Long
    Dim strLine As String

    Const dhcFind = "Copyright 1997"
    Const dhcReplace = dhcFind & ", 1998"
```

```
          ' Use the passed code module
          With modAny

              ' Set initial parameters
              lngStartLine = 1
              lngStartCol = 1
              lngEndLine = .CountOfLines
              lngEndCol = Len(.Lines(.CountOfLines, 1))

              ' Keep searching until no other
              ' occurrences are found
              Do While .Find(dhcFind, lngStartLine, _
                lngStartCol, lngEndLine, lngEndCol, True)

                  ' Replace the line that contains
                  ' the text with a new one
                  strLine = .Lines(lngStartLine, 1)
                  strLine = Left(strLine, lngStartCol - 1) & _
                    dhcReplace & Mid(strLine, lngEndCol)
                  .ReplaceLine lngStartLine, strLine

                  ' Reset parameters
                  lngStartLine = lngEndLine + 1
                  lngStartCol = 1
                  lngEndLine = .CountOfLines
                  lngEndCol = Len(.Lines(.CountOfLines, 1))
              Loop
          End With
      End Sub
```

The most interesting aspect of the procedure is how the long integer variables are used. Before calling the Find method for the first time, the procedure initializes these variables to specify the entire contents of the code module. The starting line and column (lngStartLine and lngStartCol) are both set to 1. Ending line and column numbers are computed using properties of the CodeModule object. lngEndLine is set to the number of lines in the module, while lngEndCol is set to the length of the last line.

These values (along with the search string) are passed to the Find method inside a Do While loop. Since Find returns True only if a match was found, this ensures that it will be called repeatedly until it finds no other matches.

When the Find method is called and a match is found, the method sets the four long integers to values indicating where the search string was located. For example, if the second line in the module was

```
' Sample code copyright 1997 by Sybex
```

the lngStartLine, lngStartCol, lngEndLine, and lngEndCol would be set to 2, 15, 2, and 28, respectively. This would indicate that the search string started at line 2, column 15, and ended at line 2, column 28.

Our sample procedure uses this information, in conjunction with the Left and Mid functions, to substitute the new text for the old. Once it has constructed the new line of code, it calls the module's ReplaceLine method to replace the entire line with a new one. VBA limits you to replacing an entire line. You cannot replace individual characters directly.

Finally, it's important, after finding the text and making the substitution, to reset the four numbers before calling Find again. Otherwise, the search area will be limited to the last known location of the search string! Our procedure resets the numbers at the bottom of the loop. Note that it sets the starting line number equal to the ending line number, plus one. That forces VBA to begin a subsequent search at the next line of code.

WARNING Be very careful when modifying code in the currently executing module or a module containing procedures called by the current module. You might inadvertently alter compiled, running code, which may lead to unpredictable (and probably undesirable) results.

Putting It Together: An Alternative Object Model

We've spent the bulk of this chapter explaining the individual classes, properties, and methods that make up the VBA IDE Automation interface. In this final section we put it all together by building our own object model to represent VBA project components. The reason for doing this is to add functionality the VBA IDE object model lacks. For instance, we've created a Procedure class that encapsulates individual procedures within a module. Creating our own object model also gives us additional flexibility in manipulating VBA projects and could be the basis for useful add-ins and utilities.

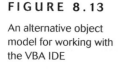

NOTE You'll find all the non–class module sample code for this section in the basClassExamples module.

Understanding Our Object Model

We've created a very simple object model, as illustrated in Figure 8.13. It consists of three classes, two of which have associated collections. This required a total of five class modules to implement.

FIGURE 8.13

An alternative object model for working with the VBA IDE

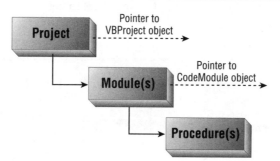

The Project Class

At the root of the hierarchy is the Project class. It has but one property, VBProject, in addition to its Modules collection. The VBProject property is a direct pointer to a normal VBProject object. We created this single property rather than replicating each of the properties of the VBProject class in our class. You can use the VBProject property to access any property of the VBProject object. Listing 8.17 shows a sample procedure that creates a new instance of our Project class, sets its VBProject property, and then reads the VBProject's Name property. If you want to use our object model, you'll need to instantiate the Project class in a similar manner.

Listing 8.17: Instantiate and Use the Project Class

```
Sub dhUseProjectClass()
    Dim objProject As New Project

    ' Set the new Project object's
    ' VBProject property to the active project
    Set objProject.VBProject = _
     Application.VBE.ActiveVBProject

    ' Print the VBProject's name
    Debug.Print objProject.VBProject.Name
End Sub
```

The Module Class

Our Module class is a thin layer over the VBA CodeModule class. The only real difference is that it appears as a child of the Project class. CodeModule objects are grandchildren of a VBProject. We're not interested in the project components, just their code, so we left them out.

Our class features Name and Kind properties, both of which are derived from the VBComponent object that contains the code module. You can access the CodeModule object directly through the Module property of our class in the same manner as the VBProject property of the Project class described in the previous section.

Finally, the Module class implements a Declarations property that lets you set or retrieve the contents of a module's declarations section. The property is initially set when the Module property is set. Listing 8.18 shows the Property Set statement.

Listing 8.18: Property Set Statement for the Module Property

```
Property Set Module(modModule As CodeModule)
    ' Make sure property hasn't been set
    If mmodModule Is Nothing Then

        ' Store the module pointer
        Set mmodModule = modModule

        ' Set the Module property of the
        ' Procedures collection
        Set mobjProcs.Module = modModule

        ' Read the declarations section
```

```
      mstrDeclarations = modModule. _
        Lines(1, modModule.CountOfDeclarationLines)
    End If
End Property
```

The Procedure Class

Going one step further than the VBA IDE object model, we've implemented a Procedure class that represents a procedure in a code module. This, combined with the associated Procedures collection class, lets us model a code module from a more detailed perspective. The class features Name and Kind properties, the latter based on the VBA procedure types described in the section "Working with Procedures" earlier in this chapter.

Our class also has a Code property, which contains the body of the procedure, including the declaration and any preceding comments. The Lines property of the class dynamically computes the number of lines in the procedure, based on the code it currently contains.

The Collections

There are two collections represented in our object model: Modules and Procedures. We've implemented these as two class modules. In addition to the standard collection properties and methods (Count, Item, Add, and Remove), we've added a Refresh method. Refresh iterates through existing modules or procedures, adding them to the appropriate collection. Listing 8.19 shows the code from the Modules collection's Refresh method. Its implementation is straightforward, using a For Each loop to iterate through all the components in the project, checking their CodeModule property. If the method finds a valid CodeModule, it calls the Add method to add it to the collection.

Listing 8.19: The Modules Collection's Refresh Method

```
Public Sub Refresh()
    Dim vbc As VBComponent

    ' Clear out any existing objects
    Set mcolModules = New Collection

    ' Loop through each component in the
    ' project, adding its module (if it has one)
```

```
For Each vbc In mvbpProject.VBComponents
    If Not vbc.CodeModule Is Nothing Then
        Call Add(vbc.Name, _
          vbc.Type, vbc.CodeModule)
    End If
Next
End Sub
```

The reason the code in Listing 8.19 is so simple is that the VBA IDE object model features a collection of CodeModule objects (accessed indirectly through the VB-Components collection). Implementing a Refresh method for our Procedures collection (see Listing 8.20) is a bit more difficult. The code in Listing 8.20 should seem familiar, however; it's just an adaptation of the code we presented in the section "Working with Procedures" earlier in this chapter.

Listing 8.20 : The Procedures Collection's Refresh Method

```
Public Sub Refresh()
    Dim cLines As Long
    Dim lngType As Long
    Dim strProc As String
    Dim objProc As Procedure

    ' Clear out any existing objects
    Set mcolProcs = New Collection

    ' Use the private code module
    With mobjModule
        ' Loop through all the lines
        For cLines = 1 To .CountOfLines

            ' If a procedure is on this line
            ' add it to the collection
            strProc = .ProcOfLine(cLines, lngType)
            If strProc <> "" Then

                ' Add a new Procedure object
                Set objProc = Add(strProc, lngType)

                ' Set its Code property
                objProc.Code = .Lines(cLines, _
                  .ProcCountLines(strProc, lngType))
```

```
                    ' Skip to the next line after
                    ' this procedure
                    cLines = cLines + _
                      .ProcCountLines(strProc, lngType) - 1
                End If
            Next
        End With
End Sub
```

The only difference this time around is that instead of printing procedure names to the Immediate window, the Refresh method adds new Procedure objects to the collection.

If you look at the complete source code for our object model, you'll see that both collections implement properties that are pointers to VBA IDE objects. The Modules collection features a Project property that points to a VBProject object, while the Procedures collection features a Module property that points to an associated CodeModule object. We trigger the Refresh methods when these properties are set. For example, the code for the Modules collection's Property Set statement is shown in Listing 8.21.

Listing 8.21: Setting the Modules Collection's Project Property Triggers the Refresh Method

```
Property Set Project(vbpProject As VBProject)
    ' Make sure the property hasn't been set
    If mvbpProject Is Nothing Then
        ' Store the object pointer
        Set mvbpProject = vbpProject
        ' Call the Refresh method
        Refresh
    End If
End Property
```

All of this is triggered when the VBProject property of our Project class is set. Therefore, all you need to do to populate an instance of our object model is to instantiate a Project object and set its VBProject property. What could be easier?

Using Our Object Model

While we've constructed an object model for representing the code in a VBA project, we haven't done much with it. That's up to you. What kinds of things might you do with it? You could create a reporting tool that prints statistics on and the contents of a VBA project. Listing 8.22 shows a sample procedure that does this. After creating a new Project object, the procedure simply loops through each object in the hierarchy, printing selected information to the Immediate window. Figure 8.14 shows some sample output.

Listing 8.22: A Procedure That Prints Detailed Project Information

```
Sub dhPrintProjectInfo()
    Dim objProject As New Project
    Dim cModule As Long
    Dim cProc As Long

    ' Set the new Project object's
    ' VBProject property to the active project
    Set objProject.VBProject = _
     Application.VBE.ActiveVBProject

    ' Print project information
    With objProject.VBProject
        Debug.Print "Information for: " & .Name
        Debug.Print " Description: " & .Description
        Debug.Print " HelpFile: " & .HelpFile
        Debug.Print " HelpContext: " & .HelpContextID
        Debug.Print " Reference count: " & .References.Count
    End With

    ' Print module and procedure info
    With objProject.Modules
        Debug.Print " Module count: " & .Count

        ' Loop through each module
        For cModule = 1 To .Count

            ' Print module info
            With .Item(cModule)
                Debug.Print " Module: " & .Name
                Debug.Print " Type: " & .KindName

                ' Print procedure info
                With .Procedures
                    Debug.Print " Procedures: " & .Count

                    ' Loop through each procedure
                    For cProc = 1 To .Count
```

```
                              ' Print procedure info
                              With .Item(cProc)
                                   Debug.Print "     " & .Name & _
                                       " (" & .KindName & ", " & _
                                       .Lines & " lines)"
                              End With
                         Next
                    End With
               End With
          Next
     End With
End Sub
```

FIGURE 8.14

Example of running
the dhPrintProjectInfo
procedure

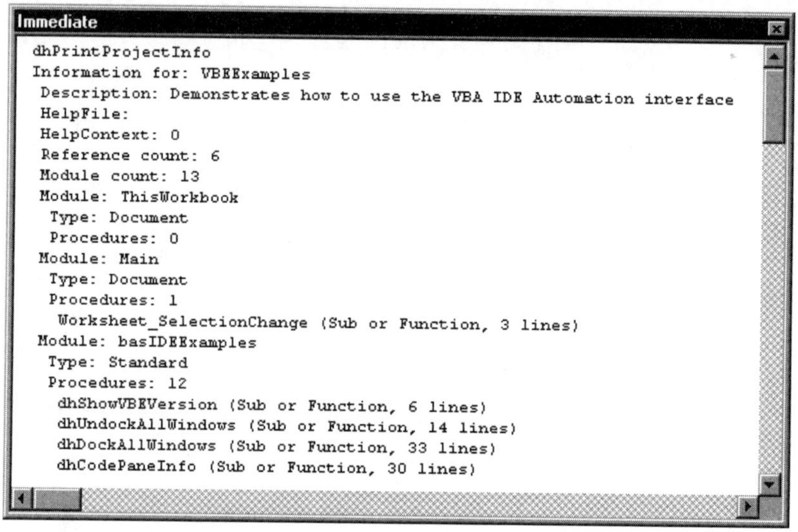

```
Immediate                                                                    [x]
dhPrintProjectInfo
Information for: VBEExamples
Description: Demonstrates how to use the VBA IDE Automation interface
HelpFile:
HelpContext: 0
Reference count: 6
Module count: 13
Module: ThisWorkbook
 Type: Document
 Procedures: 0
Module: Main
 Type: Document
 Procedures: 1
  Worksheet_SelectionChange (Sub or Function, 3 lines)
Module: basIDEExamples
 Type: Standard
 Procedures: 12
  dhShowVBEVersion (Sub or Function, 6 lines)
  dhUndockAllWindows (Sub or Function, 14 lines)
  dhDockAllWindows (Sub or Function, 33 lines)
  dhCodePaneInfo (Sub or Function, 30 lines)
```

Summary

In this chapter we've introduced you to the VBA IDE object model and shown you how to use its classes, properties, and methods. By understanding the object model, you can create you own custom tools and utilities to help you write code and create applications. By now you should be familiar with:

- Adding a reference to the VBA IDE type library

- Creating a reference to the VBE object using host application properties

- Controlling the IDE user interface using the Window, CodePane, and CommandBar classes

- Manipulating projects using the VBProject, Reference, VBComponent, and Property classes

- Modifying source code using the CodeModule class

This chapter also provided a custom object model that enhances the VBA IDE classes. You can use this model as the basis for your own utilities and add-ins.

9

Retrieving and Setting System Information

- Using the API to gather system information

- Controlling Windows accessibility functions

- Setting and retrieving keyboard, mouse, and screen information

- Investigating power management and status information

- Working with system colors

- Retrieving operating system and computer Information

If you want to write professional applications, you'll need to be able to maintain some level of control over your users' environments. You may want to temporarily turn off the mouse cursor or modify the Windows accessibility features. You may need to position one window at a particular location within another, requiring you to know the width of the window border. Or, in an attempt to position a window, you may need to know exactly how tall the caption bar is or how wide the vertical scrollbar is. Perhaps you want to control the state of the CapsLock or NumLock key. Perhaps you need to allow users to modify their system colors from within your application.

The goal of this chapter is to provide you with simple, easily callable classes, with appropriate properties and methods, that wrap up much of the Windows API functionality dealing with system information. In particular, you'll find classes that supply functionality pertaining to the mouse, keyboard, accessibility functions, system memory, power status, window metrics, border metrics, system colors, and computer and operating system information. Once you've imported the relevant classes into your own applications, you'll be able to determine, and often set, many system parameters that control the way Windows and your applications function. (For more information on writing and using class modules, see Chapter 5.)

Of course, this chapter is far from complete. You can obtain much more information by digging into the corners of the API. There's plenty here to get you started, however, and the techniques we've used to wrap the API functionality should give you ideas for extending the tools provided here, should the need arise.

> **TIP**
>
> If you find this information interesting or would like to extend the classes provided here, there's one tool you must have: Microsoft's MSDN CD subscription. This quarterly CD provided almost all the information we used to create the tools in this chapter and is well worth the small expense. Contact Microsoft for more information about ordering this extremely useful tool, with one caveat: the CD is geared toward C/C++ programmers, and to make the best use of it, you'll need some way to convert the information into a format you can use. Your best bet is to combine the information on the MSDN CD with Daniel Appleman's formidable best-seller, *Visual Basic Programmer's Guide to the Win32 API* (Ziff-Davis Press, 1996.) This book provides VBA-centric coverage of most of the Win32 API. Combined with the MSDN CD, you'll have all the information you need.

Table 9.1 lists the sample files you'll find on the CD-ROM that accompanies this book.

TABLE 9.1   Sample Files

File Name	Description
SYSINFO.XLS	Excel 97 workbook containing all the sample classes
SYSINFO.MDB	Access 97 databases containing all the sample classes
SYSINFOTEST.BAS	Test stub procedure
ACCESSIBILITY.CLS	Accessibility class module
FONT.CLS	Font information for the NonClientMetrics class
KEYBOARD.CLS	Keyboard class module
MEMORYSTATUS.CLS	Memory status class module
MOUSE.CLS	Mouse class module
NONCLIENTMETRICS.CLS	Non–client metrics class module
POWERSTATUS.CLS	Power status class module
SCREEN.CLS	Screen class module
SYSTEMCOLORS.CLS	System colors class module
SYSTEMINFO.CLS	Operating system and computer class module

VBA and System Information

VBA provides almost no native support for operations involving system information; because Windows itself provides easy-to-call API functions for determining and controlling the environment, VBA doesn't have to duplicate that functionality. Of course, some of the API functions are tricky to call, and information you need is scattered throughout the Windows API. In addition, the Windows API provides so many functions for working with system information, and their functionalities overlap so much, that it's difficult to know which one to use in any given circumstance.

To make it simpler to call the selected API functions, we've created a series of class modules that wrap up their functionality. Why class modules? That is, what do you gain by having this functionality wrapped up in a class as opposed to a standard module? Unlike other situations in which you use class modules, in this case you don't care about the multiple instancing. (You'll never create more than one instance of the Keyboard class in your application, for example.) What you do gain is the ability to treat disparate function calls as simple properties. For example, to retrieve information about a particular setting, you'll often use the GetSystemMetrics API function. To change the same information, you need to use the SystemParametersInfo function. Rather than provide two separate functions for you, one to get and one to change the value, we've provided a single property, with its Let and Get Property procedures. This way, from your application, you can write simple code like this to retrieve a value, change it, and then set it back at a later time:

```
Dim lngBorderColor As Long
Dim sc As New SystemColors
' Store away the original color.
lngBorderColor = sc.ActiveBorder
sc.ActiveBorder = 255
' Do work in here...
' Now reset the color and release the object.
sc.ActiveBorder = lngBorderColor
Set sc = Nothing
```

In addition, class modules provide another benefit: because class modules trigger their Initialize event when you create a new instance of the class, the class can call an API function that initializes a data structure. Several of the system information functions require you to pass a single data structure, with many elements. For these functions, the corresponding class can call the function in its Initialize event, retrieve all the information at once, and return the various pieces of information to you as properties of the class. For more information, see the section "Creating the Memory Status Class" later in this chapter.

Each of the classes provided in this chapter is self-contained. If you're interested only in controlling the keyboard, you'll need to import only the single KEYBOARD .CLS module. If you need more information, import the classes you need. The bulk of this chapter, organized to match the class modules themselves, describes in detail each of the properties and methods of the classes. In each case, you can either dig into or skip over the details of how the class works. If you just need the functionality and don't care about the details, skip over the description of the API calls and their usage. If, on the other hand, you want to understand exactly how these classes work or want to expand their functionality, all the information you need is here.

TIP   If you find yourself importing multiple classes, you may want to "factor out" the repeated API and constant declarations. Although there aren't a great many of repeated declarations from module to module, there's no point adding extra heft to your applications. Once you've imported all the classes you'll need, you can copy the shared declarations to a standard module, remove the "Private" keyword, and use the new shared declarations for your API calls. Don't forget that you'll also need to move the necessary data structures and constants to a shared location.

The API Functions

Although you'll find well over a hundred properties and methods covered in this chapter, we actually used only a few API calls. These API calls generally fall into one of three classes of functions:

- Functions that return a single value. GetComputerName, for example, returns only the name of the current computer, and GetCaretBlinkTime simply returns the number of milliseconds between "blinks" of the text-insert caret.

- Functions that allow you to specify one of any number of parameter values and return different pieces of information depending on the "question" you asked. GetSystemMetrics and SystemParametersInfo fall into this category. These functions allow you to choose an item of interest from a documented list of items, and each returns a single piece of information, based on the value you supplied.

- Functions that allow you to pass in a single data structure, which the function fills in with various pieces of information: GlobalMemoryStatus, GetSystemInfo, and GetSystemPowerStatus all fall into this category. Normally, for this type of function, the wrapper class calls the function in response to each property Get procedure, and the property returns just the element of the structure you require.

The next few sections discuss how you use the second and third types of function (calling the first type is so simple it requires no extra explanation) and demonstrate their usage by presenting examples from this chapter's class modules.

Using the GetSystemMetrics Function

The GetSystemMetrics function can return one of 70 or so values, depending on which you request. In each case, you pass it a single constant value, and it returns the piece of information you need.

> **TIP**
>
> You shouldn't need to worry about specific constants and their values if you're using the classes provided in this chapter. If you're interested, however, your best reference information for GetSystemMetrics (and its partner, SystemParametersInfo) is the MSDN CD.

To find the number of mouse buttons, for example, you might use a call like this:

```
lngMouseButtons = GetSystemMetrics(SM_CMOUSEBUTTONS)
```

and to find out whether there's a mouse with a wheel installed, you could use

```
fWheelMouse = GetSystemMetrics(SM_MOUSEWHEELPRESENT)
```

Of course, you don't have to use either of these. You can retrieve both pieces of information using the Mouse class we've provided:

```
Dim oMouse As New Mouse
lngMouseButtons = oMouse.Buttons
fWheelMouse = oMouse.WheelPresent
```

> **NOTE**
>
> If you see references to "mouse wheels" throughout this chapter, don't go out looking for information on rodent transportation. This term refers to Microsoft's input device with two mouse buttons and a rubberized wheel between the buttons.

You'll find calls to GetSystemMetrics scattered throughout the classes provided with this chapter. When we gathered information for this chapter, it made more sense to group the classes based on the functionality of the information than on its source, so you'll find calls to GetSystemMetrics, and other general-purpose API calls, throughout the various classes.

In addition to API calls, you'll find the declarations for the functions and the constants they use. For example, you'll find this block of code in the declarations area of MOUSE.CLS:

```
Private Const SM_CXCURSOR = 13
Private Const SM_CYCURSOR = 14
Private Const SM_MOUSEPRESENT = 19
Private Const SM_SWAPBUTTON = 23
Private Const SM_CXDOUBLECLK = 36
Private Const SM_CYDOUBLECLK = 37
Private Const SM_CMOUSEBUTTONS = 43
Private Const SM_CXDRAG = 68
Private Const SM_CYDRAG = 69
Private Const SM_MOUSEWHEELPRESENT = 75
Private Declare Function GetSystemMetrics Lib "user32" _
  (ByVal nIndex As Long) As Long
```

This set of declarations declares the API function and provides the necessary constant values needed by the class. (All the constants beginning with "SM_" will be used by GetSystemMetrics.)

Using the SystemParametersInfo Function

Calling the SystemParametersInfo function is significantly more complex than calling GetSystemMetrics. Because SystemParametersInfo allows you to either set or retrieve information concerning your system's hardware and configuration, depending on the constant you send it, it must provide methods for both returning information and returning status (success or failure) information.

To make this possible, SystemParametersInfo requires four parameters:

- A constant representing the information to be set or retrieved, beginning with SPI_.

- A long integer, passed by value, sending information to SystemParameters-Info. Normally, this is where you place information to be used by System-ParametersInfo when it's setting values for you.

- A long integer, passed by reference. This long integer can be the address of a variable or data structure, and it's through this parameter (declared "As Any" in your VBA code) that SystemParametersInfo can send information back to your functions.

- A long integer, passed by value, that tells SystemParametersInfo how you want it to broadcast information about the changes you've asked it to make. You can have your change made only for this session, or, if you want to make the change persistent, you can tell SystemParametersInfo to write the change to the Registry. In addition, if you write the change to the Registry, you can also instruct SystemParametersInfo to inform all other running Windows applications that you've made the change.

Of course, you needn't be concerned with all this information if you're just going to use the classes as we've provided them. If you want to add to the classes or modify the existing functionality, though, you'll need to be aware of how SystemParametersInfo uses each of these parameters.

WARNING   In the sample classes, we opted for the "save and tell all" option when calling SystemParametersInfo; if you make any change, the code will write the change to the Registry and broadcast a message to all other running applications as well. If you want to change this behavior, change the value of the SPIF_TELLALL constant in each module. Set the constant to 0 to do nothing, or set it to be one or more of SPIF_UPDATE-INIFILE and SPIF_SENDWININICHANGE, combined with the Or operator. The classes currently use the two constants combined.

For example, to get and set the number of screen lines to scroll when you scroll your mouse wheel (if you have a mouse wheel, of course), you can use System-ParametersInfo with its SPI_GETWHEELSCROLLLINES and SPI_SETWHEEL-SCROLLLINES constants. The WheelScrollLines property of the Mouse class (MOUSE.CLS) uses the Property Let and Get procedures, as shown in Listing 9.1.

In this example, the Property Let procedure is simple—it calls SystemParameters-Info, passing the SPI_SETWHEELSCROLLLINES constant, a value indicating the requested scroll lines, a 0 placeholder for the third parameter, and the SPIF_TEL-LALL constant indicating that the function call should save the information and update any running application. The Property Get procedure, however, is a bit more complex. In this case, you must first declare a variable to hold the returned value; call SystemParametersInfo, passing that variable as the third parameter; and return the filled-in value of the variable as the Property Get return value.

Listing 9.1: Use SystemParametersInfo to Get and Set System Information

```
Property Let WheelScrollLines(Value As Long)
    ' Works in Windows NT Only.
    ' Set the number of lines scrolled with each
    ' click of the mouse wheel.
    ' Set to 0 to disable wheel scrolling.
    ' Set to -1 to cause a scroll to act
    ' like a click in the PageUp or PageDown region of the
    ' scroll bar.
    Call SystemParametersInfo(SPI_SETWHEELSCROLLLINES, _
      Value, 0, SPIF_TELLALL)
End Property

Property Get WheelScrollLines() As Long
    ' NT Only.
    ' Determine the number of lines scrolled with each
    ' click of the mouse wheel.
    Dim lngValue As Long
    Call SystemParametersInfo(SPI_GETWHEELSCROLLLINES, 0, _
      lngValue, 0)
    WheelScrollLines = lngValue
End Property
```

In some cases, the Property Let and Get pairings require one call to GetSystem-Metrics (to get the value) and one to SystemParametersInfo (to set the value). This is, of course, the sort of thing that makes the class module wrappers so convenient; you don't have to dig through the reference manuals to find that it requires two separate function calls to get your work done. For example, Windows allows you to control the width (and height) of the rectangle bordering the mouse position that determines whether the next click constitutes a double-click. To get this value, you call GetSystemMetrics. To set the value, however, you must call SystemParametersInfo. Listing 9.2 shows the code used by the DoubleClickX property of the Mouse class, which calls both functions.

Listing 9.2: Some Properties Require both GetSystemMetrics and SystemParametersInfo

```
Property Get DoubleClickX() As Long

    ' Width, in pixels, of the rectangle enclosing the
    ' location of the first mouse click in a double-click sequence.
    ' Second click must occur within the boundaries
    ' of this rectangle.
    DoubleClickX = GetSystemMetrics(SM_CXDOUBLECLK)
End Property

Property Let DoubleClickX(Width As Long)
    Call SystemParametersInfo(SPI_SETDOUBLECLKWIDTH, Width, _
      0, SPIF_TELLALL)
End Property
```

Of course, the third parameter in a call to SystemParametersInfo might also be a reference to a user-defined type. If it is, SystemParametersInfo will fill in the datatype with the appropriate information. For example, the MinAnimation property of the Screen class (SCREEN.CLS) indicates whether Windows should display animation as it's minimizing windows. The code for the associated Property Get procedure is shown in Listing 9.3. This call to the SystemParametersInfo function requires you to send a variable of the ANIMATIONINFO datatype, with its lngSize member filled in with the size of the structure. SystemParametersInfo either fills in the lngMinAnimate member of the structure with the current animation setting (in the Property Get procedure) or gets the value from this member and applies it (in the Property Let procedure). In either case, you need to use the Len function to find the length of the data structure and place that value in the lngSize member of the structure before calling SystemParametersInfo. The class modules in this chapter use this technique several times, calling SystemParameters-Info with various datatypes.

Listing 9.3: Use SystemParametersInfo with a User-Defined Type

```
Private Type ANIMATIONINFO
    lngSize As Long
    lngMinAnimate As Long
End Type
```

```
Property Get MinAnimation() As Boolean
    ' Returns the state of minimize animation.
    Dim ai As ANIMATIONINFO

    ai.lngSize = Len(ai)
    Call SystemParametersInfo(SPI_GETANIMATION, _
     ai.lngSize, ai, 0)
    MinAnimation = ai.lngMinAnimate
End Property
```

Functions That Require Data Structures

Several API functions used in this chapter require you to send them a user-defined type, and they supply values to fill the elements of the structure. Depending on the circumstances, the wrapper class may call the function in either of two ways, in terms of information retrieval:

- It may call the function once, in the Initialize event of the class. If the information is relatively static, this makes sense. There's no point in calling the function each time you need to retrieve information from the function.

- It may set up the function call in the Initialize event of the class but call the function each time you request information from the class. This technique is useful for situations in which the data changes rapidly; the MemoryStatus class uses this technique because memory information is so volatile.

All the API functions in this chapter that pass information in this manner provide information that's read-only. Therefore, there are no issues involved in saving information back to the API.

For example, the GetVersionEx API call requires you to supply it a data structure of type OSVERSIONINFO. Listing 9.4 shows the necessary declarations, and the class Initialize event procedure, from the SystemInfo class (SYSTEMINFO .CLS). The event procedure first fills in the dwOSVersionInfoSize element of the structure with the length of the structure itself (many API calls require this step), and then it passes the structure to the GetVersionEx function. This function fills in the various members of the OSVI variable, and other properties of the class use these members in order to supply their information. For example, the OSMajor-Version property, also shown in Listing 9.4, uses the dwMajorVersion member of the OSVERSIONINFO structure to do its work.

Listing 9.4: Use the GetVersionEx API Function (Code Gathered from the SystemInfo Class Module)

```
Private Type OSVERSIONINFO
    dwOSVersionInfoSize As Long
    dwMajorVersion As Long
    dwMinorVersion As Long
    dwBuildNumber As Long
    dwPlatformId As Long
    szCSDVersion As String * 128
End Type

Private Declare Function GetVersionEx Lib "kernel32" _
 Alias "GetVersionExA" (OSVI As OSVERSIONINFO) _
 As Long
Private OSVI As OSVERSIONINFO

Private Sub Class_Initialize()
    ' Fill in the OSVersionInfo structure
    OSVI.dwOSVersionInfoSize = Len(OSVI)
    Call GetVersionEx(OSVI)

    ' Fill in the SystemInformation structure.
    Call GetSystemInfo(si)
End Sub

Property Get OSMajorVersion() As Long
    ' Retrieve the major version number of the
    ' operating system. For example, for Windows
    ' NT version 3.51, the major version number
    ' is 3; and for Windows NT version 4.0, the
    ' major version number is 4.
    OSMajorVersion = OSVI.dwMajorVersion
End Property
```

Because the information retrieved by the GetVersionEx API function isn't likely to change as your application runs, there's no reason to call the function more than once during the lifetime of your class. The properties of the MemoryStatus class, however, return data that changes constantly. Therefore, it makes sense to call the GlobalMemoryStatus API function each time you access any property of the MemoryStatus class. This ensures that the property values are always up to date. The code in Listing 9.5 has been excerpted from the MemoryStatus class (MEMORYSTATUS.CLS). This listing shows the type and API declarations, as well as the Initialize event procedure of the class and one of the property procedures. The Initialize event procedure of the class fills in the lngLength member of the structure, and this information never changes. The TotalPhysical property then calls the GlobalMemoryStatus API function, passing in the structure, and returns the lngTotalPhys member of the structure as its return value.

Listing 9.5: Excerpts from the MemoryStatus Class Module

```
Private Type typMemoryStatus
    lngLength As Long
    lngMemoryLoad As Long
    lngTotalPhys As Long
    lngAvailPhys As Long
    lngTotalPageFile As Long
    lngAvailPageFile As Long
    lngTotalVirtual As Long
    lngAvailVirtual As Long
End Type

Private Declare Sub GlobalMemoryStatus Lib "kernel32" _
 (lpBuffer As typMemoryStatus)
Dim ms As typMemoryStatus

Private Sub Class_Initialize()
    ' ms is declared at the module level.
    ms.lngLength = Len(ms)
End Sub

Property Get TotalPhysical() As Long
    ' Indicates the total number of bytes of physical memory.
    Call GlobalMemoryStatus(ms)
    TotalPhysical = ms.lngTotalPhys
End Property
```

The remainder of the chapter provides details on each of the nine system information classes we've created. (Although there are, in reality, ten class modules associated with this chapter, FONT.CLS is used only within other classes, so there's no section devoted to this small class.) In each case, you'll find a table listing all the properties and methods of the class. If creating the class provided an unusual challenge (aside from the issues already discussed in the chapter), the sections will also include a description of the coding techniques used by the specific class.

TIP

> To make it easier for you to experiment with the various classes presented in this chapter, we've created a simple starting point, Sub Main in SYS-INFOTEST.BAS. This procedure declares variables for each of the various classes and then hits a Stop statement. All you need to do is run Main from the Immediate window, and then, once it's stopped, enter test lines of code in the Immediate window.

Windows Accessibility

The Win32 API includes a number of features that make it easier for persons with disabilities to use their computers. These features are extensions to the operating system, and they affect the behavior of the system, no matter which application is currently running.

To make it easy for you to work with these settings from within your applications, we've created a single class module, Accessibility (ACCESSIBILITY.CLS), that provides six groups of properties representing the six areas of functionality. Table 9.2 describes the six areas of functionality, with pointers to Tables 9.3 through 9.8, which describe each of the properties in greater detail and provide references to the figures displaying the appropriate dialog boxes. In addition, because almost all these properties are available through the Windows Control Panel, Figures 9.1 through 9.11 show how users can set the same properties directly. The figures are presented in the order in which you'll come across them as you work through the accessibility dialogs. Each figure contains labels pointing to controls on the dialog box. The text for each label either indicates the corresponding property in the Accessibility class or the figure that corresponds to the dialog box you'll see if you click the button.

NOTE

> In Figure 9.11, the prefix "xx" acts as a placeholder for any one of "sk", "mk", and so on.

TABLE 9.2   Win32 Accessibility Features

Feature	Description
AccessTimeout	Enables a user to specify a timeout interval after which system-wide accessibility features are automatically turned off. The AccessTimeout feature is intended for computers that are shared by several users with different preferences. Each individual can use hot keys or the Control Panel to enable preferred features. After a user leaves, the enabled features will be automatically disabled by the timeout. The accessibility features affected by the timeout are FilterKeys, MouseKeys, StickyKeys, and ToggleKeys. AccessTimeout properties in the Accessibility class are described in Table 9.3
FilterKeys	Enables control of keyboard properties, such as the amount of time before a keystroke is accepted as input and the amount of time before a keystroke begins to repeat. FilterKeys properties in the Accessibility class are described in Table 9.4
MouseKeys	Enables the user to control the mouse pointer using the numeric keypad. MouseKeys properties in the Accessibility class are described in Table 9.5
StickyKeys	Enables the user to type key combinations, such as Ctrl+Alt+Del, in sequence rather than at the same time. StickyKeys properties in the Accessibility class are described in Table 9.6
SoundSentry	Displays a visual signal when a sound is generated by a Windows-based application or an MS-DOS application running in a window. SoundSentry properties in the Accessibility class are described in Table 9.7
ToggleKeys	Provides sound feedback when the user turns on or off the CapsLock, ScrollLock, or NumLock key. ToggleKeys properties in the Accessibility class are described in Table 9.8

TABLE 9.3   AccessTimeOut Properties Provided by the Accessibility Class

Property	Description	Figure
atActive	If True, a timeout has been set. Unless set, the Timeout value will have no effect	9.11
atAvailable	If True, you can set a timeout period (read-only)	
atFeedback	If true, a sound effect is played when the timeout period elapses	9.11

TABLE 9.3   AccessTimeOut Properties Provided by the Accessibility Class (continued)

Property	Description	Figure
atTimeOutMilliseconds	The number of milliseconds of idle time before Accessibility turns off. Only 5, 10, 15, 20, 25, and 30 minutes (each value multiplied by 60,000 to convert to milliseconds) are allowed	9.11

TABLE 9.4   FilterKeys Properties Provided by the Accessibility Class

Property	Description	Figure
fkActive	If True, the FilterKeys features are on	9.1
fkAvailable	If true, the FilterKeys features are available (read-only)	
fkBounceMSec	Specifies the amount of time, in milliseconds, that must elapse after a key is released before the computer will accept a subsequent press of the same key. If you set fkBounceMSec, you must set fkDelayMSec to 0, or you can't set the value. They can both be 0, but they can't both be nonzero. Valid values are 500, 700, 1000, 1500, and 2000	9.4
fkClickOn	If True, the computer makes a click sound when a key is pressed or accepted	9.3
fkDelayMSec	Specifies the length of time, in milliseconds, the user must hold down a key before it begins to repeat. If you set fkDelayMSec, you must set fkBounceMSec to 0, or you can't set the value. They can both be 0, but they can't both be nonzero. Valid values are 300, 700, 1000, 1500, and 2000	9.5
fkHotkeyActive	If True, the user can turn the FilterKeys feature on and off by holding down the Shift key for 8 seconds	9.3
fkHotKeyConfirm	(Win95 only) If True, a confirmation dialog box appears when the FilterKeys features are activated with the hot key	9.11
fkHotKeySound	If True, the computer plays a sound when the user turns the FilterKeys feature on or off with the hot key	9.11
fkIndicator	(Win95 only) If true, visual indicator is displayed when the FilterKeys features are on	9.3

TABLE 9.4   FilterKeys Properties Provided by the Accessibility Class (continued)

Property	Description	Figure
fkRepeatMSec	Specifies the length of time, in milliseconds, between repetitions of the keystroke. Valid values are 300, 500, 700, 1000, 1500, and 2000	9.5
fkWaitMSec	Specifies the length of time, in milliseconds, the user must hold down a key before it is accepted by the computer. The only acceptable values are 0, 300, 500, 700, 1000, 1400, and 2000. All others will be rounded to the next larger value within the range (Values larger than 2000 are cut back to 1000, the default.)	9.5

TABLE 9.5   MouseKeys Properties Provided by the Accessibility Class

Property	Description	Figure
mkActive	If True, the MouseKeys feature is active	9.9
mkAvailable	If True, the MouseKeys feature is available (read-only)	
mkCtrlSpeed	Specifies the multiplier to apply to the mouse cursor speed when the user holds down the Ctrl key while using the arrow keys to move the cursor. Documented by Microsoft as not working in NT, but it appears to work fine in NT 4.0	9.10
mkHotKeyActive	Sets or retrieves whether the user can turn the MouseKeys feature on and off using the hot key: Alt (left-hand key) + Shift (left-hand key) + NumLock	9.10
mkHotKeyConfirm	(Win95 only) If True, a confirmation dialog box appears when the MouseKeys feature is activated with hot key	9.11
mkHotKeySound	If True, the system plays a sound when the user turns the MouseKeys feature on or off with the the hot key	9.11
mkIndicator	(Win95 only) If True, a visual indicator is displayed when the MouseKeys feature is on	9.10
mkMaxSpeed	Specifies the maximum speed the mouse cursor attains when an arrow key is held down	9.10

TABLE 9.5   MouseKeys Properties Provided by the Accessibility Class (continued)

Property	Description	Figure
mkReplace-Numbers	If True, the numeric keypad moves the mouse when the NumLock key is on	9.10
mkTimeToMax-Speed	Specifies the length of time, in milliseconds, it takes for the mouse cursor to reach maximum speed when an arrow key is held down. Must be a value between 1000 and 5000, in milliseconds. Acceptable values are in 500-millisecond intervals (5000, 4500, etc.). Others in the range are rounded off. Values outside the range cause the call to SystemParameters Info to fail	9.10

TABLE 9.6   StickyKeys Properties Supplied by the Accessibility Class

Property	Description	Figure
skActive	If True, the StickyKeys feature is active	9.1
skAudibleFeedback	If True, the system plays a sound when the user sets keys using the StickyKeys feature	9.2
skAvailable	If True, the StickyKeys feature is available (read-only)	
skHotKeyActive	If True, the user can turn the StickyKeys feature on and off by pressing the Shift key five times	9.2
skHotKeyConfirm	(Win95 only) If True, a confirmation dialog appears when the StickyKeys feature is activated with the hot key	9.11
skHotKeySound	If True, the system plays a sound when the user toggles the StickyKeys feature with the hot key	9.11
skIndicator	(Win 95 only) If True, a visual indicator is displayed when the StickyKeys feature is on	9.2
skTriState	If True, pressing a modifier key twice in a row locks down the key until the user presses it a third time	9.2
skTwoKeysOff	If True, releasing a modifier key that has been pressed in combination with any other key turns off the StickyKeys feature	9.2

TABLE 9.7 SoundSentry Properties Supplied by the Accessibility Class

Property	Description	Figure
ssActive	If True, the SoundSentry feature is active	9.7
ssAvailable	If True, the SoundSentry feature is available (read-only)	
ssFSTextEffect	(Win95 only) If True, a visual signal appears when a text-mode application generates a sound while running in a full-screen virtual machine. Can be one of the following values: 0 (no visual indication is used), 1 (flash characters in the corner of the screen), 2 (flash the screen border [overscan area]), 3 (flash the entire display)	9.8
ssWindowsEffect	If True, visual signal appears when a graphics-mode application generates a sound while running in a full-screen virtual machine. Can be one of the following values: 0 (no visual indication is used), 1 (flash characters in the corner of the screen), 2 (Flash the screen border [overscan area]), 3 (flash the entire display)	9.8

TABLE 9.8 ToggleKeys Properties Supplied by the Accessibility Class

Property	Description	Figure
tkActive	If True, the ToggleKeys feature is active	9.1
tkAvailable	If True, the ToggleKeys feature is available (read-only)	
tkHotKeyActive	If True, the user can turn the ToggleKeys feature on and off by holding the NumLock key for 5 seconds	9.6
tkHotKeyConfirm	(Win95 only) If True, a confirmation dialog appears when the ToggleKeys feature is activated with the hot key	9.11
tkHotKeySound	If True, the system plays a sound when the user toggles the ToggleKeys feature with the hot key	9.11

FIGURE 9.1

Accessibility Properties
(Keyboard) dialog box

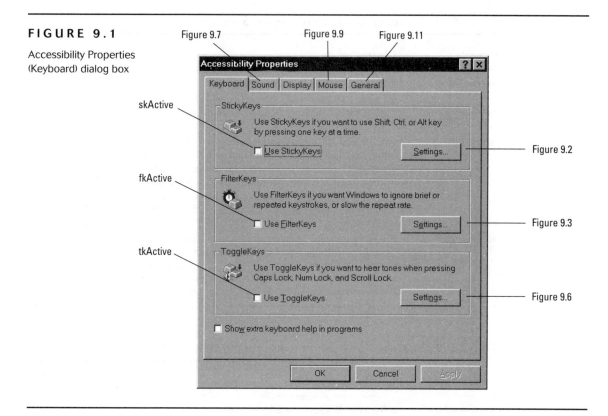

FIGURE 9.2

Settings for the
StickyKeys dialog box

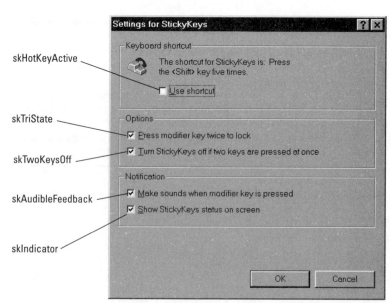

FIGURE 9.3

Settings for the FilterKeys
dialog box

fkHotKeyActive

fkBounceMSec
(if nonzero)

fkDelayMSec
(if nonzero)

fkClickOn

fkIndicator

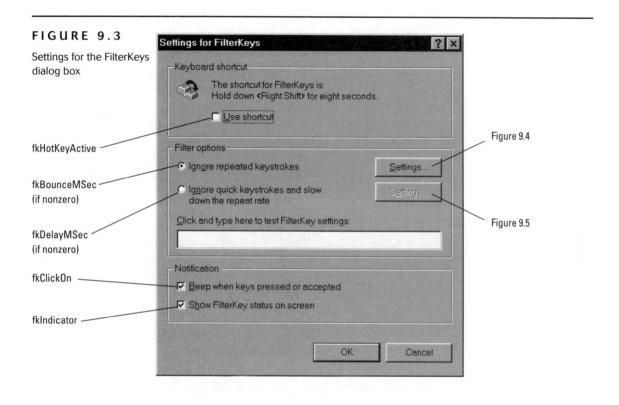

Figure 9.4

Figure 9.5

FIGURE 9.4

Advanced settings for
the FilterKeys (Bounce)
dialog box

fkBounceMSec

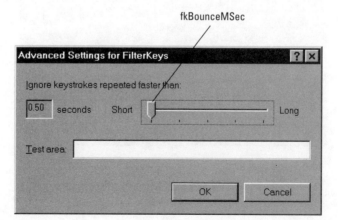

FIGURE 9.5

Advanced settings for
the FilterKeys (Delay)
dialog box

fkDelayMSec = 0,
fkRepeatMSec = 0

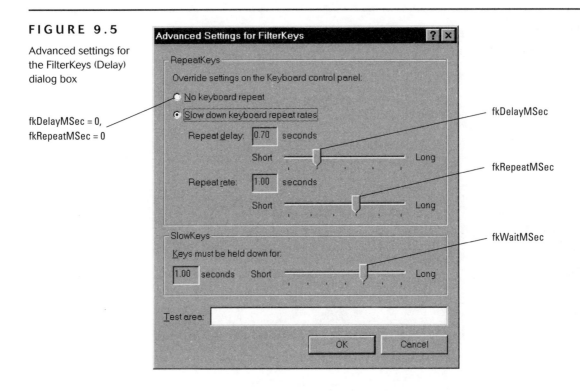

fkDelayMSec

fkRepeatMSec

fkWaitMSec

FIGURE 9.6

Settings for the
ToggleKeys dialog box

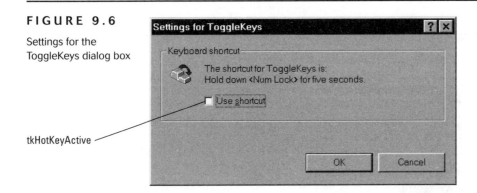

tkHotKeyActive

FIGURE 9.7

Accessibility Properties
(Sound) dialog box

ssActive

shActive

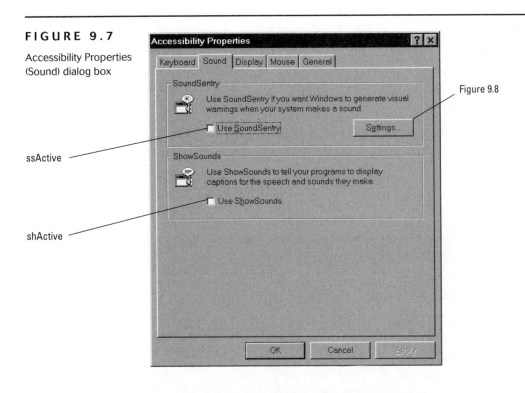

Figure 9.8

FIGURE 9.8

Settings for the
SoundSentry dialog box

ssWindowsEffect

ssFSTextEffect

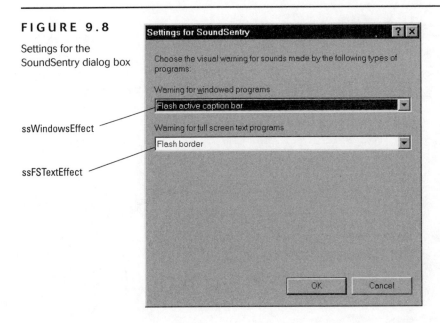

FIGURE 9.9

Accessibility Properties
(Mouse) dialog box

mkActive

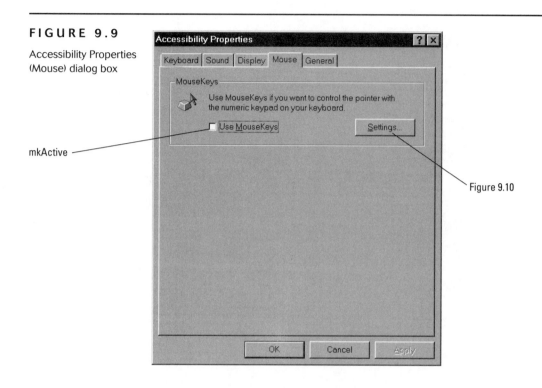

FIGURE 9.10

Settings for the
MouseKeys dialog box

mkHotkeyActive

mkCtrlSpeed

mkReplaceNumbers

mkIndicator

mkMaxSpeed

mkTimeToMaxSpeed

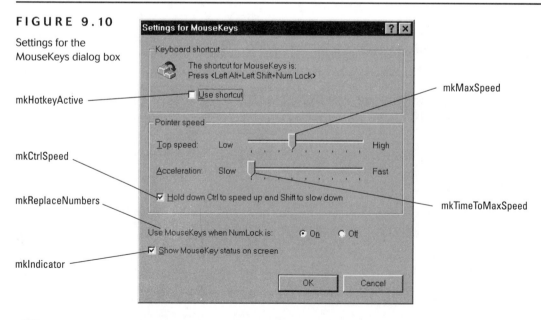

FIGURE 9.11

Accessibility Properties
(General) dialog box

atActive

atTimeOutMilliseconds

xxHotKeyConfirm

xxHotKeySound,
atFeedBack

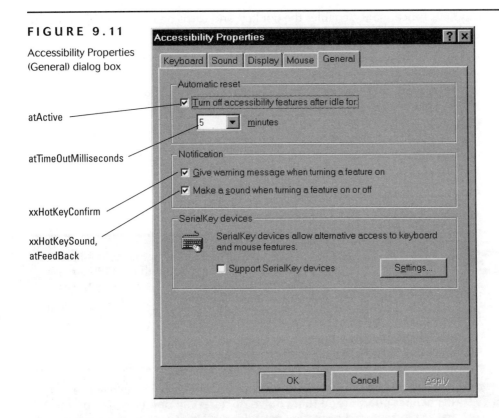

Using the Accessibility Class

As with any other class module, you'll need to create a new instance of the
Accessibility class before you can use its properties. To do so, you create a variable
that will refer to the new instance and work with that variable directly, like this:

```
Dim oAccess As Accessibility
' and then, later in your code:
Set oAccess = New Accessibility
' or just use:
' Dim oAccess As New Accessibility
' if you don't care when the object gets created.
```

Once you've created the object, use it as you would any other object, setting
and retrieving its properties. For example, the following fragment enables the

StickyKeys functionality, enables the hot key, and turns on the sound effect when users use the feature:

```
Dim oAccess As New Accessibility
With oAccess
    ' No point working with this feature if it's not
    ' available on this computer.
    If .skAvailable Then
        .skActive = True
        .skHotKeyActive = True
        .skAudibleFeedback = True
    End If
End With
```

WARNING Some of the Accessibility class properties are interrelated, so read the descriptions carefully. For example, you cannot set both the fkBounce-MSec and fkDelayMSec properties to nonzero values. If you try to set them both, Windows disregards your changes.

TIP If you receive error 91, "Object variable or With block variable not set," it's almost guaranteed that you've declared an object variable but haven't instantiated it yet. You must use the New keyword to create an object; otherwise, you're just creating a variable that can refer to the object. Make sure you either use New when you declare the object or use the Set keyword to point the variable you created to a new instance of the object. (See Chapter 5 for more information on creating and using object variables.)

Creating the Accessibility Class

Each area in the Accessibility class (AccessTimeOut, FilterKeys, and so on) uses a particular user-defined type to retrieve and set its information. To retrieve the information, you call SystemParametersInfo with a flag indicating you want to retrieve the information and a data structure in which to place the information. To send the information back to Windows, you repeat the operation, using a flag indicating you want to send information back.

Each group of properties has its own module-level variable and its own procedure (named xxReset) that retrieves a data structure full of information. For example, Listing 9.6 shows the fkReset subroutine, which fills in the module-level fk variable with all the current FilterKeys settings.

Listing 9.6: Use fkReset to Retrieve Current FilterKeys Settings

```
Private Sub fkReset()
    ' Retrieve current values.
    fk.lngSize = Len(fk)
    Call SystemParametersInfo(SPI_GETFILTERKEYS, _
    fk.lngSize, fk, 0)
End Sub
```

The Accessibility class uses a similar technique to save changed values back to Windows, the xxApply set of procedures. Each function in this series returns a Boolean value indicating the success or failure of the procedure. Although the properties in Accessibility do not use the return value, you could easily modify the class so that it handles errors when you set the various parameters. Listing 9.7 shows the fkApply function, similar to the functions used by all the Accessibility class groups.

Listing 9.7: Use fkApply to Set the New FilterKeys Settings

```
Private Function fkApply() As Boolean
    fkApply = CBool(SystemParametersInfo(SPI_SETFILTERKEYS, _
    fk.lngSize, fk, SPIF_TELLALL))
End Function
```

What's in those user-defined structures? In general, you'll find two kinds of information there: quantitative values (such as the number of milliseconds to wait before repeating a key) and long integer flag values, containing a series of bits indicating Boolean values. In addition, each structure begins with a long integer containing the size of the structure. For example, the simplest structure, ACCESSTIMEOUT, looks like this:

```
Private Type ACCESSTIMEOUT
    lngSize As Long
    lngFlags As Long
    lngTimeOutSecs As Long
End Type
```

In this case, code must supply the lngSize value before calling SystemParameters-Info so the function knows how many bytes it has to work with. The lngTimeOut-Secs member indicates how many milliseconds to wait before turning off Accessibility functions. (See the atTimeOutMillisecs Let and Get Property procedures in ACCESSIBILITY.CLS.) The lngFlags member groups a number of Boolean values (up to 32) into the single long integer value. In the case of the ACCESSTIMEOUT structure, there are only three possible values: ATF_AVAILABLE, ATF_TIMEOUTON, and ATF_ONOFFFEEDBACK, all defined in ACCESSIBILITY.CLS. Other structures use a different set of flags, and it's up to the programmer to know which flag coincides with which property of the feature. (This is why the class module makes this so much easier than working with SystemParametersInfo directly—you don't need to dig into each flag individually.)

To work with these Boolean flags, the Accessibility class includes two private procedures, IsBitSet and SetBit, shown in Listing 9.8, that handle the bits for you. To check whether a particular bit flag is set, property procedures can call IsBitSet, providing the flag value and particular bit to check. For example, the following procedure checks whether the FilterKeys click is enabled:

```
Property Get fkClickOn() As Boolean
    Call fkReset
    fkClickOn = IsBitSet(fk.lngFlags, FKF_CLICKON)
End Property
```

To use this property, you might include code like this in your own application:

```
Dim oAccess As New Accessibility
If oAccess.fkClickOn Then
    ' You know the click is on.
End If
```

To set or clear a particular feature, property procedures can call SetBit, indicating the current flag's value, the particular feature to work with, and the new value. For example, the following procedure controls whether the FilterKeys click is enabled:

```
Property Let fkClickOn(Value As Boolean)
    Call SetBit(fk.lngFlags, FKF_CLICKON, Value)
    Call fkApply
End Property
```

To set this property, you might use code like this:

```
Dim oAccess As New Accessibility
' Force the sound to be on when FilterKeys is active.
oAccess.fkClickOn = True
```

Listing 9.8: Retrieve, Set and Clear Bits Using These Procedures

```
Private Function IsBitSet(lngFlags As Long, lngValue As Long) _
 As Boolean
    ' Use logical AND to see if a particular bit within
    ' a long integer is set.
    IsBitSet = CBool((lngFlags And lngValue) = lngValue)
End Function

Private Sub SetBit(lngFlags As Long, lngValue As Long, _
 fSet As Boolean)
    ' Use logical OR to set a particular bit.
    ' Use logical AND NOT to turn off a particular bit.
    If fSet Then
        lngFlags = lngFlags Or lngValue
    Else
        lngFlags = lngFlags And Not lngValue
    End If
End Sub
```

> **WARNING**
>
> As you can see from Tables 9.3 through 9.8, which list information about the various properties, some of the numeric properties (especially those related to FilterKeys) allow only specific numeric values. These values aren't documented, nor is the behavior when you supply a value that's out of range. Test your application carefully, if you attempt to set these values, and make sure you understand the ramifications of changing these numeric values. For example, setting the fkDelayMSec property to 15 may seem like a good idea, but when you next retrieve the setting, the value will certainly not be the value you think you set—Windows will have set it to 0 instead.

Keyboard Information

The Keyboard class (KEYBOARD.CLS) allows you to set and retrieve information about the keyboard hardware. Obviously, many of the properties are read-only, but several allow you to control the settings used by the keyboard. Table 9.9 lists and describes all the properties of the Keyboard class. Figure 9.12 shows the properties supplied by the Keyboard class that have equivalents in the Windows user interface.

TABLE 9.9   Properties Supplied by the Keyboard Class

Property	Read/Write?	Description
CapsLock	Yes	Returns or sets the CapsLock toggle
CaretBlinkTime	Yes	Sets or retrieves the number of milliseconds between blinks of the caret. Allowable values: 200 to 1200 (in multiples of 100)
CaretOn	No	Shows or hides the caret. Most apps control the caret themselves, and this call will have little or no effect except in limited circumstances
Delay	Yes	Sets the keyboard repeat-delay setting. Only values 0 through 3 are acceptable
FunctionKeys	No	Determines the number of function keys on the keyboard. The return value can be any of the values in Table 9.10
KeyboardType	No	Determines the type of keyboard on the system. The return value can be any of the values in Table 9.11
NumLock	Yes	Returns or sets the NumLock toggle
ScrollLock	Yes	Returns or sets the ScrollLock toggle
Speed	Yes	Sets the keyboard repeat-speed setting. Only values 0 through 31 are acceptable

Using the Keyboard Class

The following brief sections demonstrate how to use each of the Keyboard class properties. In general, to use the Keyboard class, create a new instance of the class, and then set or retrieve its available properties. For example, to retrieve the current keyboard delay setting, you might use code like this:

```
Dim okb As New Keyboard
If okb.Delay < 3 Then
    okb.Delay = okb.Delay + 1
End If
```

FIGURE 9.12

Control Panel interface
for properties of a
Keyboard object

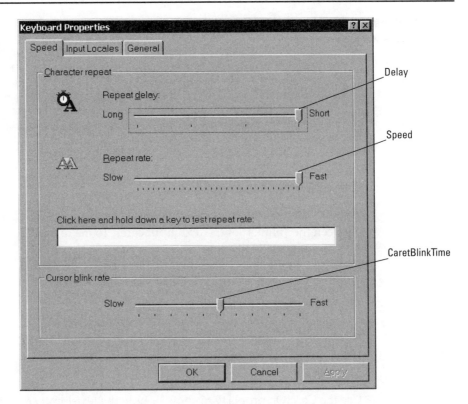

CapsLock, NumLock, and ScrollLock

Use the CapsLock property to set or retrieve the state of the CapsLock keyboard
toggle. It accepts and returns a Boolean parameter, so you might use code like
this to retrieve the current state of the toggle, set the CapsLock toggle on, do some
work, and then reset the toggle to its original state:

```
Dim fOldState As Boolean
Dim okb As New Keyboard
fOldState = okb.CapsLock
okb.CapsLock = True
' Do work with CapsLock on.
okb.Capslock = fOldState
```

Use the NumLock and ScrollLock properties just as you do the CapsLock property.

WARNING   Because the key state settings you use in the Keyboard class are pertinent only to the current application, Windows doesn't treat them as system-wide resources. Therefore, the indicator lights on your keyboard may not be affected by the CapsLock, NumLock, or ScrollLock Keyboard class property. (The behavior depends on your version of Windows—Windows 95 will correctly toggle the CapsLock and NumLock key light, but Windows NT does not. Neither operating system toggles the ScrollLock key light.)

CaretBlinkTime

The CaretBlinkTime property allows you to control the number of milliseconds between the "blinks" of the text input caret. To make the caret blink more slowly, you could use code like this:

```
Dim okb As New Keyboard
' Slow down the caret blink rate one "notch"
If okb.CaretBlinkTime < 1200 Then
    okb.CaretBlinkTime = okb.CaretBlinkTime + 100
End If
```

CaretOn

Use the CaretOn property to show or hide the text-input caret. Most applications control this setting themselves, so you can't count on a global effect when you change this property, nor would you want to, for the most part. To retrieve the current state of the caret and hide it, you might use code like this:

```
Dim okb As New Keyboard
' Hide the text caret.

okb.CaretOn = False
```

NOTE   Hiding is cumulative. If your application hides the caret five times in a row, it must also unhide the caret five times before the caret reappears. Of course, because most VBA host applications control the caret themselves, you won't get much use from this property. Test carefully when using CaretOn; it may work for you, but it may not.

Delay

Use the Delay property to control the amount of time the keyboard waits, while you're pressing a particular key, before starting the autorepeat action. (See the section "Speed," coming up in a moment, for information on controlling the speed at which the key autorepeats.) You can set this property to any value between 0 and 3, inclusive. The following code sets the keyboard delay to its smallest possible value:

```
Dim okb As New Keyboard
okb.Delay = 0
```

FunctionKeys

The FunctionKeys property simply returns the number of function keys on the installed keyboard. It returns one of the (admittedly ambiguous) values in Table 9.10:

```
Dim okb As New Keyboard
Select Case okb.FunctionKeys
    Case 1,3,5
        ' Only 10 function keys. You need more for your
        ' application.
        MsgBox "You don't have enough function keys!"
End Select
```

TABLE 9.10   Possible Values for the FunctionKeys Property

Return Value	Number of Function Keys
1	10
2	12 (sometimes 18)
3	10
4	12
5	10
6	24
7	Hardware dependent and specified by the OEM

KeyboardType

The KeyboardType property returns the specific type of keyboard that's currently installed, as one of the values listed in Table 9.11. If your application requires the newer 101- or 102-key keyboard, you might include code like this:

```
Dim okb As New Keyboard
If okb.KeyBoardType <> 4 Then
    MsgBox "This application works only with the new keyboard."
End If
```

TABLE 9.11   Possible Values for the KeyboardType Property

Return Value	Keyboard Type
1	IBM PC/XT or compatible (83-key) keyboard
2	Olivetti "ICO" (102-key) keyboard
3	IBM PC/AT (84-key) or similar keyboard
4	IBM enhanced (101- or 102-key) keyboard
5	Nokia 1050 and similar keyboards
6	Nokia 9140 and similar keyboards
7	Japanese keyboard

Speed

Use the Speed property to set the rate at which characters repeat while you're holding down the key. (See the section "Delay" above for information on controlling the waiting period before the repeat.) Windows allows values between 0 and 31 for this property:

```
Dim okb As New Keyboard
' Set the fastest repeat rate.
okb.Speed = 31
```

Creating the Keyboard Class

Except for the key-state toggling properties (CapsLock, NumLock, and Scroll-Lock), creating the Keyboard class was simple. Each other property corresponds either to a single function call or to the conglomerate SystemParametersInfo function. For example, to retrieve the keyboard type, the class calls the GetKeyboardType API function. To modify the caret blink rate, the code calls the Get-CaretBlinkTime and SetCaretBlinkTime API functions.

The CapsLock, NumLock, and ScrollLock properties each use the same Windows API function, GetKeyState, to check the state of the specific key. To use the function, you must pass it a specific *virtual key code*. Windows assigns every physical key a mapping so that Windows can run on machines with keyboards that differ slightly from the standard PC keyboard, and these mappings are called virtual key codes. Windows supports a maximum of 256 such mappings. Windows uses the value 20 for the CapsLock key, 144 for the NumLock key, and 145 for the Scroll-Lock key. VBA provides constants representing these (and most other) virtual key codes: vbKeyCapital for the CapsLock key, vbKeyNumLock for the NumLock key, and vbKeyScrollLock for the ScrollLock key. (Actually, not all VBA hosts define the vbKeyScrollLock constant, so we've included a declaration for this value in KEYBOARD.CLS.) Therefore, the following fragment will return the current state of the CapsLock key:

```
lngState = GetKeyState(vbKeyCapital)
```

GetKeyState returns an integer containing 1 in its lowest bit if the key is toggled on or 0 in the lowest bit if the key is toggled off. (GetKeyState returns the highest bit set if the key is currently being held down, but the key being held down adds no information as to whether the key is currently toggled on or off.) The property procedures then convert these values to True or False, looking at just the lowest bit by using the logical And operator:

```
Property Get Capslock() As Boolean
    ' Return or set the Capslock toggle.
    Capslock = CBool(GetKeyState(vbKeyCapital) And 1)
End Property
```

The CapsLock, NumLock, and ScrollLock Property Let procedures each call the same subroutine, SetKeyState, to do their work. SetKeyState uses the API functions GetKeyboardState and SetKeyboardState; each of these functions uses a 256-byte buffer in which to retrieve or set the full set of 256 key settings. Each virtual key code maps to one element in this array of values. Once you've used GetKeyboardState to retrieve the bufferful of settings, you can modify the specific key setting you care about and then store the settings back using SetKeyboardState. This will change just the keys you've modified. This method allows you to change the state of the CapsLock, NumLock, or ScrollLock key. Listing 9.9 shows the SetKeyState procedure.

Listing 9.9: The SetKeyState Procedure Allows You to Alter the State of a Particular Key

```
Private Sub SetKeyState(intKey As Integer, fTurnOn As Boolean)
    ' Retrieve the keyboard state, set the particular
    ' key in which you're interested, and then set
    ' the entire keyboard state back the way it
    ' was, with the one key altered.
    Dim abytBuffer(0 To 255) As Byte
    GetKeyboardState abytBuffer(0)
    abytBuffer(intKey) = CByte(Abs(fTurnOn))
    SetKeyboardState abytBuffer(0)
End Sub
```

> **NOTE**
>
> The only parameter the GetKeyboardState and SetKeyboardState functions expect to receive is the address of a 256-byte memory block. In VBA, you emulate this block using a 256-element byte array. To pass an array to an API call, you normally pass the first element of the array. Because VBA stores arrays contiguously in memory, the API function can take the address of the first element of the array and find the rest of the elements. Procedures such as SetKeyState depend on this behavior when passing an array to an API call that doesn't understand anything about VBA arrays.

Memory Status

The MemoryStatus class (MEMORYSTATUS.CLS) is simple, with just a few properties, all of them read-only. The properties, listed in Table 9.12, allow you to peek at the current memory situation in the computer that's running your application.

TABLE 9.12   Properties for the MemoryStatus Class

Property	Description
MemoryLoad	Number between 0–100 that gives a general idea of current memory utilization, in which 0 indicates no memory use and 100 indicates full memory use
TotalPhysical	Indicates the total number of bytes of physical memory
AvailablePhysical	Indicates the number of bytes of physical memory available

TABLE 9.12 Properties for the MemoryStatus Class (continued)

Property	Description
TotalPageFile	Indicates the total number of bytes that can be stored in the paging file, not the size of the paging file on disk
AvailablePageFile	Indicates the number of bytes available in the paging file
TotalVirtual	Indicates the total number of bytes that can be described in the user mode portion of the virtual address space of the calling process
AvailableVirtual	Indicates the number of bytes of unreserved and uncommitted memory in the user mode portion of the virtual address space of the calling process

NOTE There are no properties in the MemoryStatus class dealing with available resources, as there might have been in a class written for a 16-bit operating system. The Win32 API does not contain any tools to retrieve information about available resources since this isn't supposed to be an issue in 32-bit Windows. (Anyone who's used Windows 95 extensively knows this isn't the case, but under Windows NT, you certainly won't be worrying about resource usage.)

Using the MemoryStatus Class

To use the MemoryStatus class, first declare a new instance of the class, and then retrieve any of its properties. For example, the most interesting property of the MemoryStatus class is the MemoryLoad property, which tells you the approximate current memory utilization. To retrieve the value of this property, you write code like this:

```
Dim oms As New MemoryStatus
Debug.Print "The total physical memory is: " & oms.TotalPhysical
```

Use the same technique with any, or all, of the MemoryStatus class properties.

Creating the MemoryStatus Class

The MemoryStatus class is one of the classes that's centered around a single user-defined data structure, the typMemoryStatus structure.

```
Private Type typMemoryStatus
    lngLength As Long
    lngMemoryLoad As Long
    lngTotalPhys As Long
    lngAvailPhys As Long
    lngTotalPageFile As Long
    lngAvailPageFile As Long
    lngTotalVirtual As Long
    lngAvailVirtual As Long
End Type
```

To gather information about the current memory situation, call the Global-MemoryStatus API function, passing a typMemoryStatus variable. In this case, because all the properties need to call GlobalMemoryStatus with the same data structure, the Initialize event procedure for the MemoryStatus class fills in the size of the structure, so the properties don't all need to take this extra step:

```
Private Sub Class_Initialize()
    ' ms is declared at the module level.
    ms.lngLength = Len(ms)
End Sub
```

Once that task has been taken care of (the first time you attempt to retrieve a property of the class), retrieving any property requires only that the class call the GlobalMemoryStatus function to refresh the data structure's values. For example, the MemoryLoad property looks like this:

```
Property Get MemoryLoad() As Long
    Call GlobalMemoryStatus(ms)
    MemoryLoad = ms.lngMemoryLoad
End Property
```

All the Property Get procedures in the MemoryStatus class work exactly the same way.

Mouse Information

The Mouse class (MOUSE.CLS) contains information pertinent to (what else?) the mouse and its activities on the screen. Table 9.13 lists all the properties of the class, along with their datatypes and descriptions.

TABLE 9.13 Properties of the Mouse Class

Property	Read/Write?	Datatype	Description
Buttons	No	Long	Retrieves the number of mouse buttons
CursorOn	Yes	Boolean	Shows or hides the mouse cursor
CursorX	No	Long	Retrieves the width, in pixels, of a cursor
CursorY	No	Long	Retrieves the height, in pixels, of a cursor
DoubleClickTime	No (write-only)	Long	Number of milliseconds between clicks, indicating to Windows that you've double-clicked. Normal value is around 450–500. To read double-click time, look in HKEY_CURRENT_ USER\Control Panel\Mouse\ DoubleClickSpeed
DoubleClickX	Yes	Long	Width, in pixels, around the location of the first click in a double-click sequence. Second click must occur within the boundaries of this rectangle
DoubleClickY	Yes	Long	Height, in pixels, around the location of the first click in a double-click sequence. Second click must occur within the boundaries of this rectangle
DragX	Yes	Long	Width, in pixels, of a rectangle centered on a drag point to allow for limited movement of the mouse before the drag begins
DragY	Yes	Long	Height, in pixels, of a rectangle centered on a drag point to allow for limited movement of the mouse before the drag begins

TABLE 9.13 Properties of the Mouse Class (continued)

Property	Read/Write?	Datatype	Description
MouseButtonSwap	Yes	Boolean	Sets or retrieves the swapped mouse button state (Button1 is on the right.)
MousePresent	No	Boolean	Returns True if a mouse is installed
MouseSpeed, MouseThreshold1, MouseThreshold2	Yes	Long	MouseSpeed, combined with MouseThreshold1 and MouseThreshold2, creates the real mouse speed
MouseTrails	Yes	Long	(Win95 only) Controls mouse trails. If the value is greater than 1, MouseTrails is on, and the higher the value, the more trails you get
SnapToDefault	Yes	Boolean	(WinNT 4.x only) Determines whether the snap-to-default-button feature is enabled. If enabled, the mouse cursor automatically moves to the default button, such as "OK" or "Apply," of a dialog box
WheelPresent	No	Boolean	(WinNT 4.x only) Returns True if a wheel with a mouse is present
WheelScrollLines	Yes	Boolean	(WinNT 4.x only) Determines the number of lines scrolled with each movement of the mouse wheel

NOTE Even though the new wheeled mouse functions properly in Windows 95, there's no support in that older operating system for determining whether the wheeled mouse is present or for controlling the number of lines to scroll when you move the wheel. Therefore, the WheelPresent and WheelScrollLines properties work properly only with Windows NT 4.x. On the other hand, Windows NT just doesn't support the MouseTrails property, which Windows 95 does support.

Using the Mouse Class

The mouse class consists of three types of properties:

- **Read-only properties:** The Buttons property returns the number of buttons on the mouse, and the WheelPresent property returns whether the mouse includes a middle wheel. To use these (and other read-only) properties, simply retrieve the return value. For example, to use the MousePresent property, you might write code like this:

```
Dim oMouse As New Mouse
If Not oMouse.MousePresent Then
    MsgBox "You must have a mouse to use this application."
End If
```

- **Write-only properties:** Actually, there's but one of these misbegotten, poorly conceived properties: the DoubleClickTime property. To retrieve this value, you'll need to inspect the HKEY_CURRENT_USER\Control Panel\Mouse\DoubleClickSpeed Registry entry. We could have added the appropriate code to this class, but to do so would have involved borrowing code from Chapter 10. If you need to both set and retrieve this value, you may want to import the necessary classes from that chapter and retrieve the Registry setting in a Property Get procedure.

- **Read/Write properties:** Properties such as MouseButtonSwap, CursorOn, and SnapToDefault are all read/write properties that accept and return Boolean values. Others, such as MouseSpeed, DragX, and MouseTrails, all accept and return long integers. In all these cases, you use the properties the same way you use properties of any object. For example, to cause the mouse to swap its buttons (the right-hand button becomes the main button, popular among left-handed users), use code like this:

```
Dim oMouse As New Mouse
oMouse.MouseButtonSwap = True
```

The MouseSpeed and Related Properties

The only group of properties that requires any special explanation is the set of three properties: MouseSpeed, MouseThreshold1, and MouseThreshold2. These three work together to control how quickly the mouse cursor moves across the screen as you move the mouse physically. The MouseSpeed parameter can take on values between 0 and 2, representing the speed of the mouse cursor relative to the distance you've moved the mouse. The MouseThreshold (1 and 2) properties can take on values between 0 and 12. The following paragraphs explain how these three properties are related.

As you may have noticed, the more quickly you move the mouse, the further the mouse cursor moves on the screen. This means you don't have to lift the mouse and reposition it as often as you might otherwise have to. Windows uses three values to calculate the distance it will move the mouse cursor every time you move the mouse, based on two tests.

At measured time intervals, as you move the mouse, Windows polls the position of the mouse and the speed at which you're moving it. If, during one interval, the distance along either the x or y axis is greater than the first mouse threshold value (MouseThreshold1) and the mouse speed (MouseSpeed) is not 0, Windows doubles the distance. If the distance along either the x or y axis is greater than the second mouse threshold value and the mouse speed is 2, the operating system doubles the distance that resulted from applying the first threshold test. It is thus possible for the operating system to multiply relatively specified mouse motion along the x or y axis by up to four times.

If you use the Mouse Control Panel applet, you'll see only a single linear slider control to manage the mouse speed. Windows takes the seven possible settings on the slider and converts them into preset values for the three properties. Table 9.14 lists these preset triplets of values, starting with the slowest and ending with the fastest setting. Figure 9.13 shows the Mouse Control Panel applet, with the first, middle, and last MouseSpeed triplets pointed out.

TABLE 9.14 Preset Values for the Three Mouse Parameters

Speed	Threshold1	Threshold2
0	0	0
1	10	0
1	7	0
1	4	0
2	4	12
2	4	9
2	4	6

FIGURE 9.13

Mouse Control Panel applet, showing MouseSpeed triplets

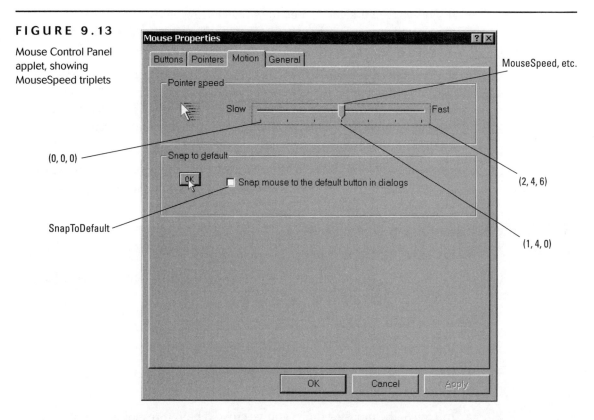

Therefore, the MouseSpeed parameter controls the general speed of the mouse. As you move the mouse, if the MouseSpeed parameter is greater than 0 and the mouse is moved more physical units than the value specified in Threshold1, Windows doubles the distance, and the cursor moves farther. If the MouseSpeed is 2 and the distance moved was also greater than the value in the MouseThreshold2 parameter, Windows again doubles the distance. You can see that it makes no sense to have both the MouseSpeed parameter set to 1 and the Threshold2 parameter set to anything except 0—Windows will never even look at the Threshold2 value in that case.

If you intend to set these values, here are some general rules to help you:

- If the MouseSpeed parameter is set to 0, Windows never looks at the Threshold values, and they should both be set to 0.

- If the MouseSpeed parameter is set to 1, Windows never looks at the Threshold2 parameter, and it should be set to 0.

- If MouseSpeed is set to 1, then the smaller Threshold1 is, the faster the mouse will move. This is why the Threshold1 values in Table 9.14 decrease from top to bottom while MouseSpeed stays at 1.

- If MouseSpeed is set to 2, then the value of MouseThreshold2 becomes significant, but it should never be less than the MouseThreshold1 value. MouseThreshold2 is used only if the mouse has moved farther than the value in MouseThreshold1, so having a value that's smaller than the MouseThreshold1 value won't add any speed.

Therefore, if your MouseSpeed, MouseThreshold1, and MouseThreshold2 values are (0, 0, 0), there's no acceleration as you move the mouse. As long as the first value is 0, Windows never even looks at the next two.

If the values are (1, 10, 0) and:

- You move the mouse 8 units, the cursor moves 8 units

- You move the mouse 11 units, you've crossed the threshold, and Windows doubles the cursor movement to 22 units

If the values are (2, 4, 6) and:

- You move the mouse 3 units, the cursor moves 3 units.

- You move the mouse 5 units, you've crossed the first threshold, and Windows doubles the movement to 10 units for the cursor.

- You move the mouse 7 units, you've crossed both thresholds, so Windows doubles the distance twice, moving the cursor 28 units.

As you can see, it's important to understand the relationship between the movement of the mouse and the MouseSpeed, MouseThreshold1, and MouseThreshold2 parameters in controlling the speed and acceleration of the mouse cursor.

Non-Client Metrics

Non-client metrics are the settings for the width, height, and fonts of items on a window's border. Setting the properties of a NonClientMetrics object (NONCLIENTMETRICS.CLS) affects the entire Windows display and allows you to control display attributes such as the size of the buttons on a window's caption bar and the font used by the MsgBox function.

The properties supplied by the NonClientMetrics class break down into two categories: simple properties and font properties. The simple properties, described in Table 9.15, allow you to control the size of various border settings, such as the buttons that appear on windows' caption bars. The font properties, listed in Table 9.16, allow you to change various font settings for the five Font objects. Finally, each of these Font objects supports the properties shown in Table 9.17.

TABLE 9.15   Simple Properties Supplied by the NonClientMetrics Class

Property	Description
BorderWidth	Sets or retrieves the standard window sizing border width
ScrollWidth	Sets or retrieves the width of buttons on scrollbars (or height, for horizontal scrollbars). Also returns the width of vertical scrollbars. Changing this value affects the dimensions of the scrollbars as well
ScrollHeight	Sets or retrieves the height of buttons on scrollbars (or width, for horizontal scrollbars). Also returns the height of horizontal scrollbars
CaptionWidth	Sets or retrieves the width of caption bar buttons
CaptionHeight	Sets or retrieves the height of caption bar buttons
SmallCaptionWidth	Sets or retrieves the width of small caption bar buttons
SmallCaptionHeight	Sets or retrieves the height of small caption bar buttons
MenuWidth	Sets or retrieves the width of menu bar buttons
MenuHeight	Sets or retrieves the height of menu bar buttons
Caption	Retrieves the height, in pixels, of a normal caption bar
SmallCaption	Retrieves the height, in pixels, of a small caption bar
FixedBorderX	Retrieves the width, in pixels, of the frame around the perimeter of a window that has a caption but is not sizable
FixedBorderY	Retrieves the height, in pixels, of the frame around the perimeter of a window that has a caption but is not sizable

TABLE 9.16 Font Object Properties Supplied by the NonClientMetrics Class

Property	Description
CaptionFont	Retrieves the caption bar font object
SmallCaptionFont	Retrieves the small caption bar font object
MenuFont	Retrieves the menu font object
StatusFont	Retrieves the status bar font object
MessageFont	Retrieves the message box font object

TABLE 9.17 Properties Supplied by the Font Class

Property	Type	Value
Size	Long	Point size for the font. Normally 8–127, but depends on the FaceName
Weight	Long	Integer between 100–900, where 100 is very light and 900 is very heavy. Normal is 400 and bold is 700
Italic	Boolean	True or False
StrikeOut	Boolean	True or False
Underline	Boolean	True or False
FaceName	String	String containing font face name

Using the NonClientMetrics Class

Using the simple properties in the NonClientMetrics class is just like using properties in any other class. First, you create a new instance of the object, and then you set and retrieve its properties. For example, to add five pixels to the width of the scrollbars, you could use code like this:

```
Dim ncm As New NonClientMetrics
ncm.ScrollWidth = ncm.ScrollWidth + 5
```

To test out most of the simple properties, the code in Listing 9.10 exercises most of the simple NonClientMetrics properties. Figure 9.14 shows a simple window before the code is called, and Figure 9.15 shows the same window after the code has done its work. As you can see, the NonClientMetrics class provides properties to control most of the visual aspects of the window border.

FIGURE 9.14

A simple window before FixNCM is called

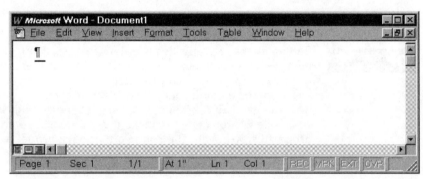

FIGURE 9.15

The same window after FixNCM is called

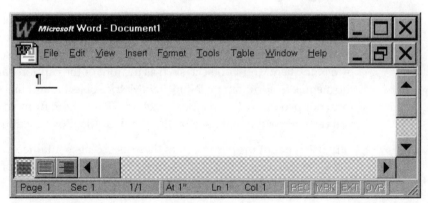

Listing 9.10: Modify Most of the Simple NonClientMetrics Properties

```
Sub FixNCM()
    Dim ncm As New NonClientMetrics
```

```
            ncm.BorderWidth = ncm.BorderWidth * 2
            ncm.CaptionHeight = ncm.CaptionHeight * 2
            ncm.CaptionWidth = ncm.CaptionWidth * 2
            ncm.MenuHeight = ncm.MenuHeight * 2
            ncm.MenuWidth = ncm.MenuWidth * 2
            ncm.ScrollHeight = ncm.ScrollHeight * 2
            ncm.ScrollWidth = ncm.ScrollWidth * 2
        End Sub
```

> **TIP**
>
> Setting all these properties is a slow process. If you intend to change multiple NonClientMetrics properties often, consider removing the calls to SaveSettings in each property's code and explicitly calling the SaveSettings method yourself once you've made all the changes. That way, Windows won't attempt to change all the settings individually, and your code will run faster. To make these properties work like all simple properties, we wrote the code so that each Property Let procedure saves its changes. You're welcome to change this behavior if you like.

Using the NonClientMetrics Font Properties

In addition to its simple properties, the NonClientMetrics class provides five font properties. Each of these properties is a reference to a separate object, a Font object (FONT.CLS). Each Font object provides a set of properties describing a font used by a NonClientMetrics object, such as the font of the caption bar or the font used by the menus. In addition, the NonClientMetrics object maintains the font used by the form popped up by the MsgBox function. That's right: from your own applications, you can control the font used by the standard MsgBox function.

To use the font properties, treat them as objects contained within the NonClientMetrics object. For example, to retrieve the name of the font used by the MsgBox form, you could write code like this:

```
Dim ncm As New NonClientMetrics
Debug.Print ncm.MessageFont.FaceName
```

The real difference between using the simple properties and using the Font object properties is that changes to the fonts aren't saved until you explicitly call the SaveSettings method of the NonClientMetrics object. That is, once you've made all the font changes you need to make, you must use code like this:

```
Call ncm.SaveSettings
```

to cause the object to save all the new settings. You needn't call this method at all if you're only retrieving values or if you're working only with the simple properties. If you want to modify font values, however, your changes won't take effect until you call this method.

If you want to work extensively with the Font object, you could use the With statement, treating it like the real object it is. For example, the code in Listing 9.11 retrieves the current MsgBox font settings, modifies them, pops up a test message box, and then resets the values.

Listing 9.11: Sample Procedure That Modifies the MessageFont Object

```
Sub FixMsgBox()
    Dim ncm As New NonClientMetrics
    Dim strOldFont As String
    Dim intOldSize As Integer

    With ncm
        With .MessageFont
            strOldFont = .FaceName
            intOldSize = .Size
            .FaceName = "Tahoma"
            .Size = 12
        End With
        Call .SaveSettings
        MsgBox "This is a test"
        With .MessageFont
            .FaceName = strOldFont
            .Size = intOldSize
        End With
        Call .SaveSettings
        MsgBox "This is a test"
    End With
End Sub
```

As another example, the code in the following fragment sets the standard menu font to be two point sizes larger than it was originally and causes the font to be italic:

```
Dim ncm As New NonClientMetrics
With ncm.MenuFont
    .Size = .Size + 2
    .Italic = True
```

```
End With
Call ncm.SaveSettings
```

> **NOTE** Some programs, including all of Microsoft's Office 97 suite, eschew standard menus, using, instead, menus of their own creation. Changes you make to standard Windows menus will have no effect in these applications.

Creating the NonClientMetrics Class

Although its read-only properties (Caption, SmallCaption, FixedBorderX, and FixedBorderY) rely on the GetSystemMetrics function to retrieve their values, like several other classes in this chapter, the NonClientMetrics class is centered around a single data structure, the typNonClientMetrics structure:

```
Private Type typNonClientMetrics
    cbSize As Long
    lngBorderWidth As Long
    lngScrollWidth As Long
    lngScrollHeight As Long
    lngCaptionWidth As Long
    lngCaptionHeight As Long
    lfCaptionFont As LogFont
    lngSMCaptionWidth As Long
    lngSMCaptionHeight As Long
    lfSMCaptionFont As LogFont
    lngMenuWidth As Long
    lngMenuHeight As Long
    lfMenuFont As LogFont
    lfStatusFont As LogFont
    lfMessageFont As LogFont
End Type
```

In the Initialize event procedure for the class, the code calls the SystemParameters-Info function, passing a typNonClientMetrics structure to be filled in. From then on, all the properties use the settings in this structure for retrieving and setting properties.

The problem, as you can see, is that several members of this structure aren't simple variables; each is itself another data structure, the LogFont structure:

```
Const LF_FACESIZE = 32
Private Type LogFont
    lfHeight As Long
    lfWidth As Long
    lfEscapement As Long
    lfOrientation As Long
    lfWeight As Long
    lfItalic As Byte
    lfUnderline As Byte
    lfStrikeOut As Byte
    lfCharSet As Byte
    lfOutPrecision As Byte
    lfClipPrecision As Byte
    lfQuality As Byte
    lfPitchAndFamily As Byte
    lfFaceName(0 To LF_FACESIZE - 1) As Byte
End Type
```

Clearly, there is more information here than is necessary for the fonts used by the NonClientMetrics object. The question, then, was how to expose all the information you need in order to use the object but not end up with an overload of similar, but differently named, properties.

The answer, in this case, was to create a simple Font class, with the properties shown earlier in Table 9.17. This way, the NonClientMetrics class can create five instances of the class to maintain the font information it needs for each of its five font properties, and you can access those properties using objects within your NonClientMetrics object. In addition, the Font class can expose just the properties that make sense for this situation, not every portion of the LogFont data structure.

To use the Font class, the NonClientMetrics class needs to take three distinct steps:

1. **Create the Font objects:** In the declarations section of the module, the code includes the following declarations:

   ```
   Dim oCaptionFont As New Font
   Dim oSMCaptionFont As New Font
   Dim oMenuFont As New Font
   Dim oStatusFont As New Font
   Dim oMessageFont As New Font
   ```

2. **Copy the data into the Font objects:** In the Initialize event procedure, the class needs to copy the data from each LogFont structure to each separate Font object. The NonClientMetrics class contains a private procedure, SetFontInfo, that copies all the necessary data:

```
Private Sub Class_Initialize()
    Dim lngLen As Long

    lngLen = Len(ncm)
    ncm.cbSize = lngLen
    Call SystemParametersInfo(SPI_GETNONCLIENTMETRICS, _
     lngLen, ncm, 0)

    Call SetFontInfo(ncm.lfCaptionFont, oCaptionFont)
    Call SetFontInfo(ncm.lfMenuFont, oMenuFont)
    Call SetFontInfo(ncm.lfMessageFont, oMessageFont)
    Call SetFontInfo(ncm.lfSMCaptionFont, oSMCaptionFont)
    Call SetFontInfo(ncm.lfStatusFont, oStatusFont)
End Sub
```

3. **Copy the data back from the Font objects:** In the SaveSettings method of the class, the code must perform the reverse of the set of steps in the Initialize event procedure. Here, it must retrieve all the font information from the various Font objects, filling in the appropriate LogFont structures in the typNonClientMetrics structure. It uses the private GetFontInfo procedure to move the data back from the Font objects. Finally, it calls the SystemParametersInfo function to send the information back to Windows:

```
Public Sub SaveSettings()
    ' Save all changed settings.
    Dim lngLen As Long
    lngLen = Len(ncm)
    ncm.cbSize = lngLen

    ' Need to copy all the font values back into the
    ' LogFont structures.
    Call GetFontInfo(ncm.lfCaptionFont, oCaptionFont)
    Call GetFontInfo(ncm.lfMenuFont, oMenuFont)
    Call GetFontInfo(ncm.lfMessageFont, oMessageFont)
    Call GetFontInfo(ncm.lfSMCaptionFont, oSMCaptionFont)
    Call GetFontInfo(ncm.lfStatusFont, oStatusFont)

    ' Now save all the settings back to Windows.
    Call SystemParametersInfo(SPI_SETNONCLIENTMETRICS, _
```

```
        lngLen, ncm, SPIF_TELLALL)
End Sub
```

The SetFontInfo and GetFontInfo procedures are both simple, moving data from one data structure into an equivalent object and back. There are two interesting challenges along the way, however:

- Working with the array of bytes that contains the face name in the LogFont structure

- Converting the font size to and from the familiar point size, since that's not the way the LogFont structure stores it

The next two sections deal with these issues.

Working with the Face Name

In order to support international versions, VBA stores all its strings internally, using the Unicode character mapping. In Unicode, each visible character takes up two bytes of internal storage. Because Windows 95 does not support Unicode and supports only the ANSI character mapping (with one byte for each character), VBA must convert strings it sends to and from the Windows API into ANSI. This happens regardless of whether the application is running under Windows 95 or under Windows NT (which does completely support Unicode).

The problem in working with the font name in the NonClientMetrics class is that the LogFont structure retrieves the font name (also referred to as its *face name*) into an ANSI string, which you must convert to Unicode before manipulating the font name within VBA. Luckily, VBA provides the StrConv function, which allows you to convert strings to and from Unicode. The NonClientMetrics class uses this function to perform the conversion. (See Chapter 1 for more information on working with strings and byte arrays.)

The font name member of the LogFont structure is declared like this:

```
lfFaceName(0 To LF_FACESIZE - 1) As Byte
```

where FACESIZE is a constant with a value of 32. Why isn't lfFaceName simply declared as a 32-byte string? The problem is that if you tell VBA that a variable contains a string, it assumes that that string is stored in Unicode and processes it as though it contained two bytes per character. Declaring the value as an array of bytes keeps VBA from mangling the string. Figure 9.16 shows the Immediate window displaying both the raw ANSI and converted Unicode versions of the value in the lfFaceName field of a LogFont structure.

FIGURE 9.16

ANSI and Unicode
representations of
the ANSI FaceName
element

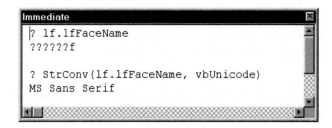

The problem, then, is getting the array of bytes in and out of a Unicode string. Getting it into a string is simple: because the StrConv function can take a byte array as its input, you can use it to move the byte array, converted to Unicode, directly into a string. The SetFontInfo procedure in the NonClientMetrics class does just this:

```
With oFont
    ' Code removed...
    .FaceName = dhTrimNull(StrConv(lf.lfFaceName, vbUnicode))
End With
```

One final issue in this conversion is the removal of extra "junk" after the name of the font. The dhTrimNull function (borrowed from Chapter 1 of this book), also in the NonClientMetrics class, looks for the first null character (vbNullChar) in a string and truncates the string at that point. Because the Windows API returns strings with an embedded Null indicating the end of the string, dhTrimNull is a very useful tool whenever you're moving strings from a Windows API function call into VBA.

The tricky issue is getting the string back into the byte array in the LogFont structure in order to send the information back to Windows. Although you can assign a variant directly into a dynamic byte array, you cannot do the same with a fixed-size array, which is exactly what LogFont contains. Therefore, to get the text back into that array, the SetFaceName procedure in NonClientMetrics must traverse the input string, byte by byte, once it's converted the string back to ANSI.

Listing 9.12 shows the entire SetFaceName procedure. This procedure starts out by converting the Unicode string containing the new face name back into ANSI, using the StrConv function. StrConv places its return value into a dynamic byte array. (The byte array makes it fast and simple to traverse the string, one byte at a time, later on.)

```
abytTemp = StrConv(strValue, vbFromUnicode)
```

Then the code places the length of the string into the intLen variable. Because the array filled in by the StrConv function is zero-based, the number of items in the array is 1 greater than its UBound:

```
intLen = UBound(abytTemp) + 1
```

The LogFont fixed-sized array can hold only LF_FACESIZE – 1 characters, so the code next checks to make sure it's not going to try to write more characters than that to the structure:

```
If intLen > LF_FACESIZE - 1 Then
    intLen = LF_FACESIZE - 1
End If
```

Finally, it's time to write the bytes into the structure, using a simple loop:

```
For intI = 0 To intLen - 1
    lf.lfFaceName(intI) = abytTemp(intI)
Next intI
```

As the final step, the code inserts a null value (0) into the final position in the string. The Windows API expects to find this value as the string delimiter, and bypassing this step can cause trouble for your API calls. (Normally, when you pass a string to the API, you needn't worry about this—it's only because we've copied the string in, one byte at a time, that it's an issue at all.)

Listing 9.12: Moving a Unicode String Back into an ANSI Byte Array Takes a Few Steps

```
Private Sub SetFaceName(lf As LogFont, strValue As String)
    ' Given a string, get it back into the ANSI byte array
    ' contained within a LOGFONT structure.
    Dim intLen As String
    Dim intI As Integer
    Dim varName As Variant
    Dim abytTemp() As Byte

    abytTemp = StrConv(strValue, vbFromUnicode)
    intLen = UBound(abytTemp) + 1

    ' Make sure the string isn't too long.
    If intLen > LF_FACESIZE - 1 Then
        intLen = LF_FACESIZE - 1
    End If
```

```
        For intI = 0 To intLen - 1
            lf.lfFaceName(intI) = abytTemp(intI)
        Next intI
        lf.lfFaceName(intI) = 0
End Sub
```

Although it's a bit more work to get the Unicode string back into the ANSI buffer than it was to get the ANSI buffer into a Unicode string, once you've got the code worked out, you needn't worry about it in the future. The NonClient-Metrics class uses this code whenever you work with any of the Font objects, and should you need to use this functionality in any of your own classes (Windows uses the LogFont structure in many situations), you can lift the code from this class.

Working with Point Sizes

The LogFont structure maintains information about the font's height and width in pixels rather than its point size. It's the font's point size that you see when you choose a font in any Windows application, however. Therefore, to make the Font object's Size property work as you'd expect, the NonClientMetrics class must convert the font height into a standard point size.

When Windows provides the font width and height in the LogFont structure, it fills in 0 for the lfWidth member and a negative value for the lfHeight member. The negative value indicates internally that Windows should provide the closest match for the character height requested. The code in NonClientMetrics must, therefore, convert to and from that negative value in the lfHeight member of the LogFont structure.

When converting from the LogFont structure into points, the formula to use is

```
points = -Int(lngHeight * 72 / lngLogPixelsY)
```

where lngLogPixelsY is the number of pixels per logical inch on the screen. Because there are 72 points per logical inch, this calculation converts from pixels (the value in the LogFont structure) to points.

Where does the value for lngLogPixelsY come from? Windows itself provides this information, using the GetDeviceCaps API function. If you're interested, check out the code in the CalcSize procedure in the NonClientMetrics class. This value returns, for the specific screen driver, the number of screen pixels there are per logical inch of screen real estate. (The driver itself converts from logical inches to real inches, but that isn't part of this story.)

Converting back from points to pixels, when saving a new font size, is no more difficult. The formula for this conversion is

```
pixels = -Int(lngHeight * lngLogPixelsY / 72)
```

The CalcSize procedure in NonClientMetrics takes care of both translations for you. It's called whenever you move font information to or from a LogFont structure.

Power Status

To help applications take advantage of the power management features of portable computers that support these features, Windows 95 supplies two API functions, GetSystemPowerStatus and SetSystemPowerState, that provide information about, and control over, the status of your computer's power. The Power-Status class (POWERSTATUS.CLS) provides properties and methods you can use to investigate the computer's use of power and even to suspend the computer, if it supports that functionality.

> **NOTE** Unfortunately, power management features don't work in Windows NT 4.0 (and many unhappy Windows NT 4.0 users will attest to this). None of the features in the PowerStatus class will work under the most current version of Windows NT. Although the properties don't fail, they just return 0 in every case. You'll want to use the properties of the SystemInfo class, covered in the section "Computer and Operating System Information" later in this chapter, to determine the operating system before attempting to use these features in your applications.

Table 9.18 lists all the properties of the PowerStatus class. They're all read-only, as you'd expect. Because several of the properties return numeric values best represented by constants, we've also supplied a series of read-only properties (the best approximation VBA can provide for constants defined in a type library; see Chapter 5 for more information) representing constant return values. These properties are listed in Table 9.19.

TABLE 9.18 PowerStatus Class Properties

Property	Datatype	Description
ACLineStatus	Byte	AC power status. One of: 0 (offline, using batteries), 1 (online, plugged in), 255 (unknown)
BatteryState	Byte	Battery charge status. Any combination of one or more of the following: 1 (High), 2 (Low), 4 (Critical), 128 (No system battery), 255 (Unknown)
BatteryCharging	Boolean	True or False
BatteryLifePercent	Byte	Percentage of battery charge remaining from 0–100; 255 if unknown
BatteryLifeTime	Long	Number of seconds of battery life remaining; −1 if unknown
BatteryFullLifeTime	Long	Number of seconds of battery life available when the battery is at full charge; −1 if unknown. This estimate is based on the BatteryLifeTime and BatteryLifePercent fields

TABLE 9.19 Read-Only Properties (Constants) and Their Associated Properties

Constant	Value	Associated Property
pwrACLineOffline	0	ACLineStatus
pwrACLineOnline	1	
pwrACLineBackupPower	2	
pwrACLineUnknown	255	
pwrBatteryStateHigh	1	BatteryState
pwrBatteryStateLow	2	
pwrBatteryStateCritical	4	
pwrBatteryStateNoBattery	128	
pwrBatteryStateUnknown	255	
pwrBatteryPercentageUnknown	255	BatteryLifePercent
prwBatteryLifeUnknown	−1	BatteryLifeTime, BatteryFullLifeTime

In addition to the items in the two tables, the PowerStatus class includes a single method: Suspend. This method, which requires no parameters, attempts to use the computer's built-in power management to suspend the computer. Of course, not all computers support this functionality.

Using the PowerStatus Class

The PowerStatus class consists of a few read-only properties, so it's simple to use. The following short sections demonstrate using each of the properties.

NOTE None of the following fragments will function correctly under standard Windows NT 4.x, because it doesn't support power management functionality. However, if you're using a specialized version of Windows NT, modified by your computer manufacturer, these functions may work.

The ACLineStatus Property

The ACLineStatus property indicates whether the power connection is online or offline. The property returns one of the flags pwrACLineOffline, pwrACLine-Online, pwrACLineBackupPower, or pwrACLineUnknown. For example, you could write code like the following to display the AC power status:

```
Dim ps As New PowerStatus
Dim strOut As String

Select Case ps.ACLineStatus
    Case ps.pwrACLineOffline
        strOut = "Batteries"
    Case ps.pwrACLineOnline
        strOut = "Plugged in"
    Case ps.pwrACLineBackupPower
        strOut = "Using backup power"
    Case ps.pwrACLineUnknown
        strOut = "Unknown"
End Select
```

The BatteryState Property

The BatteryState property returns information about the charge state of the computer's battery. It returns one of the flags pwrBatteryStateHigh, pwrBatteryStateLow, pwrBatteryStateCritical, pwrBatteryStateNoBattery, or pwrBatteryStateUnknown. You could write code like this to display the battery-charging status:

```
Dim ps As New PowerStatus
Dim strOut As String

Select Case ps.BatteryState
    Case ps.pwrBatteryStateHigh
        strOut = "Full charge"
    Case ps.pwrBatteryStateLow
        strOut = "Low charge"
    Case ps.pwrBatteryStateCritical
        strOut = "Critical"
    Case ps.pwrBatteryStateNoBattery
        strOut = "No battery"
    Case ps.pwrBatteryStateUnknown
        strOut = "Unknown"
End Select
```

The BatteryCharging Property

The BatteryCharging property simply returns a Boolean True or False, indicating the current charging state of the battery. If the state is unknown, the property returns False.

The BatteryLifePercent, BatteryLifeTime, and BatteryFullLifetime Properties

These three properties work together to provide information about how long the battery will provide power. The BatteryLifeTime property returns the number of remaining seconds the battery has, and the BatteryFullLifeTime property returns the total number of seconds the battery should last if fully charged. The Battery-LifePercent property returns the percentage of lifetime remaining, as an integer between 0 and 100. Both the BatteryLifeTime and BatteryFullLifeTime properties return the prwBatteryLifeUnknown constant if their status is unknown. The BatteryLifePercent property returns the pwrBatteryPercentageUnknown if its value is unknown.

The Suspend Method

Call the Suspend method of the PowerStatus class to suspend the computer, if it supports the functionality. The method returns 0 if it fails, so you can check the return value to see whether the computer was actually suspended.

Screen and Window Information

Windows provides a great deal of information about the screen and the objects displayed on the screen, such as icons and windows. The NonClientMetrics class includes information about the window borders, but the Screen class contains properties and methods that work with the screen and icons.

Although the Screen class (SCREEN.CLS) exposes a large number of properties, they're all quite simple. Each read-only property (see Table 9.20) provides a single piece of information about the screen, such as the width or height of the screen or the minimum height or width of a window. Table 9.20 also includes the single write-only property of the Screen object, the DeskWallPaper property. All the properties in this table except the DeskWallPaper property return long integers; you supply a string to the DeskWallPaper property indicating the wallpaper you'd like to use. Table 9.21 includes a list of the read/write properties supplied by the Screen object, including the datatype to specify for each property.

Table 9.22 lists the two methods of the Screen class. The GetWorkArea and SetWorkArea methods allow you to retrieve and set the work area Windows uses. That is, you can specify the coordinates used by a maximized window, if you'd like.

TABLE 9.20 Screen Class Read-Only Properties

Property	Description
FullScreenX	Width of the inside area of a full-screen window. Use GetWorkArea to get the portion of the screen not obscured by docked trays
FullScreenY	Height of the inside area of a full-screen window. Use GetWorkArea to get the portion of the screen not obscured by docked trays
IconSizeX	Default width, in pixels, for an icon
IconSizeY	Default height, in pixels, for an icon
IconSpacingX	Width, in pixels, of grid cells for items in Large Icon view
IconSpacingY	Height, in pixels, of grid cells for items in Large Icon view
KanjiWindow	For DBCS versions of Windows, height in pixels of the Kanji window

TABLE 9.20 Screen Class Read-Only Properties (continued)

Property	Description
MaximizedX	Width, in pixels, of a maximized top-level window
MaximizedY	Height, in pixels, of a maximized top-level window
MaxTrackX	Default maximum width, in pixels, of a window that has a caption and sizing borders
MaxTrackY	Default maximum height, in pixels, of a window that has a caption and sizing borders
MenuCheckX	Width, in pixels, of the default menu check-mark bitmap
MenuCheckY	Height, in pixels, of the default menu check-mark bitmap
MinimizedX	Width, in pixels, of a normal, minimized window
MinimizedY	Height, in pixels, of a normal, minimized window
MinimumX	Minimum width, in pixels, of a window
MinimumY	Minimum height, in pixels, of a window
MinSpacingX	Width, in pixels, of a grid cell for minimized windows
MinSpacingY	Height, in pixels, of a grid cell for minimized windows
MinTrackX	Minimum tracking width, in pixels, of a window
MinTrackY	Minimum tracking height, in pixels, of a window
ScreenX	Width of the screen, in pixels
ScreenY	Height of the screen, in pixels
SmallIconX	Recommended width for a small icon
SmallIconY	Recommended height for a small icon
DeskWallPaper	(Write-only) Sets desktop wallpaper. Supply a string containing a file name, or "(None)" to display no wallpaper. To get the wallpaper value, look in the Registry's HKEY_CURRENT_USER\Control Panel\Desktop\WallPaper key

TABLE 9.21   Screen Class Read/Write Properties

Property	Datatype	Description
MinAnimation	Boolean	State of minimize animation. If False, Windows doesn't display animation as you minimize a window. Setting this property to False makes Windows appear to run faster
DragFullWindows	Boolean	Determines whether dragging of full windows is enabled. If True, Windows displays the entire window contents as you move the window. If False, it displays only a border
FontSmoothing	Boolean	Indicates whether the font-smoothing feature is enabled
GridGranularity	Long	Granularity value of the desktop sizing grid. This granularity establishes how much control you have over the size of windows: the larger this setting, the fewer options you have
IconHorizontalSpacing	Long	Width of an icon cell
IconVerticalSpacing	Long	Height of an icon cell
IconTitleWrap	Boolean	Turns icon-title wrapping on or off
IconFontName	String	Font name for icons
IconFontSize	Long	Icon font size
MenuDropAlignment	Boolean	Alignment of pop-up menus. Specify True for right alignment and False for left alignment (the normal state)

TABLE 9.22   Screen Class Methods

Method	Description
GetWorkarea	Gets the size of the work area. The work area is the portion of the screen not obscured by the taskbar
SetWorkArea	Sets the size of the work area. The work area is the portion of the screen not obscured by the taskbar

Using the Screen Class

The Screen class exposes many properties, all useful in particular circumstances, but all very specific. If you're not using a Japanese version of Windows, for example, you'll never have a need for the KanjiWindow property. On the other hand, you may often need the ScreenX and ScreenY properties. We can't begin to suggest reasons you'd need all these properties; we've simply provided them here, as properties of a Screen object, because Windows makes them available. Experiment with the read/write properties to see their effect on your environment before unleashing them in your applications.

As with other objects, working with these properties requires only creating an instance of the Screen object:

```
Dim oScreen As New Screen
oScreen.MinAnimation = False
oScreen.IconFontName = "Tahoma"
If oScreen.ScreenX > 1024 Then
    MsgBox "You have a very large amount of screen real estate!"
End If
```

Working with the methods of the Screen object requires a bit more information. The GetWorkArea and SetWorkArea methods allow you to control the area that Windows thinks is available for maximized windows. You can retrieve the coordinates of this region, and you can modify them as well.

To retrieve the coordinates of the work area, you must pass four long integer variables to the GetWorkArea method. It fills in the value of the four long integers for you. To set the new work area, call SetWorkArea, passing one or more of the four coordinates. If you omit a coordinate when you call SetWorkArea, the code will use the current setting for that coordinate. This way, you can modify one or more of the coordinates without having to pass them all in. Once you've called the following code fragment, maximizing a window will leave empty space at the bottom because you've changed what Windows thinks is its work area for maximized windows:

```
Dim lngLeft As Long
Dim lngTop As Long
Dim lngRight As Long
Dim lngBottom As Long
Dim oScreen As New Screen
```

```
' Get the current work area:
Call oScreen.GetWorkArea(lngLeft, lngTop, lngRight, lngBottom)
' Move the bottom up by 10%:
lngBottom = Int(.90 * lngBottom)
Call oScreen.SetWorkArea(Bottom:=lngBottom)
```

Creating the Screen Class

Like several other classes, most of the properties in the Screen class get their values from either the GetSystemMetrics or the SystemParametersInfo function. The only properties that required any extra code were the IconFontName and IconFont-Size properties. Because both of these properties get their values from a LogFont structure, the Screen class faces the same obstacles that faced the NonClientMetrics class. The problems were solved with similar code. (See the "Working with the Face Name" and "Working with Point Sizes" sections earlier in this chapter for more information.)

System Colors

Windows provides a set of system colors, which it uses when displaying any window. Any application can override the system colors, of course, but the colors are there for Windows', and your, use. Table 9.23 lists the properties of the SystemColors class (SYSTEMCOLORS.CLS), all read/write, that you can use to retrieve and set the Windows system colors.

TABLE 9.23 Properties of the SystemColors Class

Property	Description
ScrollBar	Scrollbar system color
Background	Windows desktop system color
ActiveCaption	Caption of active window system color
InactiveCaption	Caption of inactive window system color
Menu	Menu system color

TABLE 9.23   Properties of the SystemColors Class (continued)

Property	Description
Window	Window background system color
WindowFrame	Window frame system color
MenuText	Menu text system color
WindowText	Window text system color
CaptionText	Text in window caption system color
ActiveBorder	Border of active window system color
InactiveBorder	Border of inactive window system color
AppWorkspace	Background of MDI desktop system color
Highlight	Selected item background system color
HighlightText	Selected item text system color
ButtonFace	Button system color
ButtonShadow	3-D shading of button system color
GrayText	Gray text system color (always 0 if dithering is used)
ButtonText	Button text system color
InactiveCaptionText	Text of inactive window system color
ButtonHighlight	3-D highlight of button system color
DarkShadow3D	3-D dark shadow system color
Light3D	Light color for 3-D shaded objects
TooltipText	ToolTip text system color
TooltipBackground	ToolTip background color system color

Using the SystemColors Class

To use the SystemColors class, just as with the other classes in this chapter, first create a new instance of the class, and then work with its properties. For example, to change the background color of buttons, you could use code like this:

```
Dim sc As New SystemColors
Dim lngColor As Long
lngColor = sc.ButtonFace
' Set the button background to be red.
sc.ButtonFace = 255
```

By the way, should you try this experiment, you may be surprised; changing the ButtonFace property also changes the color of many other objects in Windows, including scrollbars and menu bars. Unfortunately, there's no support in the API for controlling the Windows color scheme, so you'll need to work with each color separately. It's also unfortunate that we could find no documentation on the interrelations between various screen artifacts and the system colors—you'll find that changing one of the properties of the SystemColors object may, in fact, change the color of a seemingly unrelated object. Experiment carefully when using these properties in applications.

Using System Colors in Your User Interface

If you intend to assign the system color values to elements of your application's user interface, don't assign the value you retrieved from properties of the System-Colors object. Although you can do this if you like, it will defeat your purpose. If a user changes the system colors, you want your interface to automatically alter itself to match the new colors. If you hard-code a value you retrieve at design time, your interface cannot magically alter itself.

If, instead, you choose a value from Table 9.24, your user interface will always match the settings chosen in the Windows color scheme. Use the values in the first column in your VBA code and the values in the second column in property sheets.

TABLE 9.24   System Color Constants for Use in the User Interface

VBA Constant	Value for Property Sheet	Description
vbScrollBars	&H80000000	Scrollbar color
vbDesktop	&H80000001	Desktop color

TABLE 9.24 System Color Constants for Use in the User Interface (continued)

VBA Constant	Value for Property Sheet	Description
vbActiveTitleBar	&H80000002	Color of the title bar for the active window
vbInactiveTitleBar	&H80000003	Color of the title bar for the inactive window
vbMenuBar	&H80000004	Menu background color
vbWindowBackground	&H80000005	Window background color
vbWindowFrame	&H80000006	Window frame color
vbMenuText	&H80000007	Color of text on menus
vbWindowText	&H80000008	Color of text in windows
vbTitleBarText	&H80000009	Color of text in caption, size box, and scroll arrow
vbActiveBorder	&H8000000A	Border color of active window
vbInactiveBorder	&H8000000B	Border color of inactive window
vbApplicationWorkspace	&H8000000C	Background color of multiple document interface (MDI) applications
vbHighlight	&H8000000D	Background color of items selected in a control
vbHighlightText	&H8000000E	Text color of items selected in a control
vbButtonFace	&H8000000F	Color of shading on the face of command buttons
vbButtonShadow	&H80000010	Color of shading on the edge of command buttons
vbGrayText	&H80000011	Grayed (disabled) text
vbButtonText	&H80000012	Text color on push buttons
vbInactiveCaptionText	&H80000013	Color of text in an inactive caption
vb3DHighlight	&H80000014	Highlight color for 3-D display elements

TABLE 9.24 System Color Constants for Use in the User Interface (continued)

VBA Constant	Value for Property Sheet	Description
vb3DDKShadow	&H80000015	Darkest shadow color for 3-D display elements
vb3DLight	&H80000016	Second lightest 3-D color after vb3DHighlight
vbInfoText	&H80000017	Color of text in ToolTips
vbInfoBackground	&H80000018	Background color of ToolTips

Creating the SystemColors Class

The SystemColors class was one of the simplest in this chapter to create. It relies on only two API functions: GetSysColor and SetSysColors. GetSysColor retrieves a single system color, given a constant representing the item to be retrieved. For example, the following excerpt from the SystemColors class retrieves the background color for ToolTips:

```
Property Get TooltipBackground() As Long
    ' ToolTip background color system color.
    TooltipBackground = GetSysColor(COLOR_INFOBK)
End Property
```

Setting a system color requires a tiny bit more effort because the SetSysColors function is capable of setting multiple colors at once. The code in Listing 9.13 sets the background color for ToolTips, using the SystemColors' SetColor procedure. This procedure calls the SetSysColors API procedure, which allows you to send as many colors as you like. SetColor is sending only a single color, but it could work with a group of colors at a time. In this case, it passes 1 as the first parameter, indicating that it's supplying only a single color. The second parameter indicates which color it's sending (COLOR_INFOBK, a predefined constant, indicates that this color is the background for ToolTips), and the third supplies the new color.

Listing 9.13: Setting a System Color Uses the SetColor Procedure

```
Property Let TooltipBackground(Value As Long)
    ' ToolTip background color system color.
```

```
        Call SetColor(COLOR_INFOBK, Value)
    End Property

    Private Sub SetColor(lngID As Long, lngValue As Long)
        Call SetSysColors(1, lngID, lngValue)
    End Sub
```

> **TIP**
>
> You may find that you'd rather have the SystemColors class allow you to set a number of new colors before sending the information to Windows. This will make the update faster because Windows won't try to repaint the screen after each color change. To do this, you'll need to create an array of colors, one for each constant in the SystemColors class module. Then, in each Property Get, modify the value in the appropriate row of the array rather than calling SetColor. Finally, you'll need to add a new method of the class that you'll call when you're ready to update all the colors. This method will call SetSysColors, passing the number of items in the array (25, if you use the colors in the class module), an array containing the numbers 0 through 24, and an array containing all the new colors. That will cause Windows to set all 25 colors at once. One more tip: make sure you initialize the color array with all the current colors, in the Initialize event of the class. Otherwise, when you set the new colors, all the colors you haven't modified will contain 0 (black), and your Windows environment will become very difficult to use.

Computer and Operating System Information

The final class in this chapter provides information on, and, in a few cases, allows you to set information about, your computer and the operating system. Of course, most of the properties of the SystemInfo class (SYSTEMINFO.CLS) must be read-only. Only the Beep, ComputerName, ScreenSaverActive, and ScreenSaveTimeout properties allow you to specify a value; the rest simply return information about your environment. Table 9.25 lists all the properties of the SystemInfo class.

TABLE 9.25 Properties of the SystemInfo Class

Property	Datatype	Description
ActiveProcessorMask	Long	Specifies a mask representing the set of processors configured into the system
AllocationGranularity	Long	Specifies the granularity with which virtual memory is allocated
Beep	Boolean	(Read/write) Turns the system warning beep on or off
BootMethod	Long	Retrieves the boot method. Possible values: 0 (normal boot), 1 (fail-safe boot), 2 (fail-safe boot with network)
ComputerName	String	(Read/write) Sets or retrieves the name of the computer
IsDBCS	Boolean	Returns True if the operating system is working with DBCS characters
IsWin95	Boolean	Returns True if the operating system is Windows 95
IsWinNT	Boolean	Returns True if the operating system is Windows NT
MaxAppAddress	Long	Pointer to the highest memory address accessible to applications and Dynamic Link Libraries (DLLs)
MidEastEnabled	Boolean	Returns True if the system is enabled for Hebrew/Arabic languages
MinAppAddress	Long	Pointer to the lowest memory address accessible to applications and DLLs
NetworkPresent	Boolean	Returns True if a network is present
NumberOfProcessors	Long	Specifies the number of processors in the system
OSBuild	Long	Retrieves the build number of the operating system
OSExtraInfo	String	Retrieves extra operating system information, like "Service Pack 3"
OSMajorVersion	Long	Retrieves the major version number of the operating system. For example, for Windows NT version 3.51, the major version number is 3; for Windows NT version 4.0, the major version number is 4

TABLE 9.25 Properties of the SystemInfo Class (continued)

Property	Datatype	Description
OSMinorVersion	Long	Retrieves the minor version number of the operating system. For example, for Windows NT version 3.51, the minor version number is 51; for Windows NT version 4.0, the minor version number is 0
PageSize	Long	Specifies the page size and the granularity of page protection and commitment
ProcessorArchitecture	Integer	Specifies the system's processor architecture
ProcessorLevel	Integer	Windows 95: not used. Windows NT: specifies the system's architecture-dependent processor level
ProcessorRevision	Integer	Windows 95: not used. Windows NT: specifies an architecture-dependent processor revision
ProcessorType	Long	Windows 95: specifies the type of processor in the system. WindowsNT: uses ProcessorArchitecture, ProcessorLevel, and ProcessorRevision values
ScreenSaverActive	Boolean	(Read/write) Sets or retrieves the state of the screen saver
ScreenSaverTimeout	Long	(Read/write) Sets or retrieves the screen saver timeout value, in seconds
Secure	Boolean	Returns True if security is present
SlowMachine	Boolean	Returns True if computer has a low-end processor (definition of low-end is somewhat unclear)
SystemDirectory	String	Retrieves the system directory. The value does not end with a trailing backslash (\)
TempPath	String	Retrieves the temporary path. The GetTempPath function gets the temporary file path from one of the following locations: the path specified by the TMP environment variable; the path specified by the TEMP environment variable, if TMP is not defined; the current directory, if both TMP and TEMP are not defined. Path always ends with a backslash (\)
UserName	String	Retrieves the name of the logged-in user

TABLE 9.25   Properties of the SystemInfo Class (continued)

Property	Datatype	Description
WindowsDirectory	String	Retrieves the Windows directory. The value does not end with a trailing backslash (\)
WindowsExtension	Boolean	(Win95 only) Indicates whether the Windows extension, Windows Plus!, is installed

The properties of the SystemInfo class can be broken down into five basic categories, as shown in Table 9.26. The next section of this chapter provides more information on these categories.

TABLE 9.26   Categories of SystemInfo class Properties

Category	Properties
Computer/User	ComputerName, UserName
Paths	SystemDirectory, TempPath, WindowsDirectory
Processor Info	ActiveProcessorMask, AllocationGranularity, MaxAppAddress, MinAppAddress, NumberOfProcessors, PageSize, ProcessorArchitecture, ProcessorLevel, ProcessorRevision, ProcessorType
Version	IsWin95, IsWinNT, OSBuild, OSExtraInfo, OSMajorVersion, OSMinorVersion
Miscellaneous	Beep, BootMethod, IsDBCS, MidEastEnabled, NetworkPresent, ScreenSaverActive, ScreenSaverTimeout, Secure, SlowMachine, WindowsExtension

Using the SystemInfo Class

This section describes each of the categories of properties in the SystemInfo class, explaining both how to use them and how they were implemented.

Computer and User Information

The two properties ComputerName and UserName provide information about the network name for the computer and the logged-in user's name. Both properties return strings, and the ComputerName property also allows you to set the name of the computer. For example, you might write code like this to use the properties:

```
Dim si As New SystemInfo
Dim strOut As String
strOut = si.UserName & " is logged into " & si.ComputerName
MsgBox strOut
si.ComputerName = "CompuLand"
```

Retrieving these properties is simple: the Windows API provides the GetComputer-Name and GetUserName functions. In both cases, you pass in a buffer to contain the name and a long integer variable containing the length of the buffer. Windows fills in the buffer and places the length of the string it returned into the long integer variable. If the function returns a nonzero value, the code can use the Left function to retrieve as many characters from the buffer as Windows said it filled in. Listing 9.14 shows the code for retrieving the ComputerName property; the code for the UserName is almost identical.

Listing 9.14: Code for the ComputerName Property

```
Property Get ComputerName() As String
    Dim strBuffer As String
    Dim lngLen As Long

    strBuffer = Space(dhcMaxComputerName + 1)
    lngLen = Len(strBuffer)
    If CBool(GetComputerName(strBuffer, lngLen)) Then
        ComputerName = Left$(strBuffer, lngLen)
    Else
        ComputerName = ""
    End If
End Property
```

The code to set the computer name is even simpler. It calls the SetComputerName API function:

```
Property Let ComputerName(Name As String)
    Call SetComputerName(Name)
End Property
```

TIP The SetComputerName API call only writes the new computer name to the Registry. It doesn't (and it really can't) change the name of the computer as it's currently used on the network. The next time you restart the computer, it will use the new name.

Path Information

The SystemDirectory, TempPath, and WindowsDirectory properties retrieve information about where you can expect to find files on your computer. In each case, Windows provides a single function to call in order to retrieve the information, and in each case, the code is almost identical. For example, Listing 9.15 includes the code for the WindowsDirectory property. You should be familiar with this code if you've ever done any work with the Windows API that involves strings. In the WindowsDirectory property procedure, the code first creates a buffer to hold the output string and makes sure it's large enough for the largest expected result, using the String function. Then it calls the GetWindowsDirectory API function, passing the buffer and the length of the buffer. GetWindowsDirectory attempts to place the path into the buffer and returns the length of the string it placed into the buffer. If the buffer wasn't large enough, the function returns the length it would need to place into the buffer. If the function returns a value larger than the length passed into it, the property procedure resizes the buffer and tries again. This time, the string is guaranteed to fit.

Listing 9.15: Code for the WindowsDirectory Property

```
Property Get WindowsDirectory() As String
    ' Retrieve the Windows directory.
    Dim strBuffer As String
    Dim lngLen As Long

    strBuffer = Space(dhcMaxPath)
    lngLen = dhcMaxPath
    lngLen = GetWindowsDirectory(strBuffer, lngLen)
    ' If the path is longer than dhcMaxPath, then
    ' lngLen contains the correct length. Resize the
    ' buffer and try again.
    If lngLen > dhcMaxPath Then
        strBuffer = Space(lngLen)
        lngLen = GetWindowsDirectory(strBuffer, lngLen)
```

```
      End If
      WindowsDirectory = Left$(strBuffer, lngLen)
End Property
```

NOTE
The three functions used in these three properties provide a perfect example of the non-uniformity of Windows API functions. For example, GetWindowsDirectory and GetSystemDirectory accept first a string and then its length. GetTempPath takes its parameters in the opposite order. In addition, GetTempPath returns a path that always ends with a trailing backslash, yet both the others return paths without the trailing backslash.

Processor Information

To retrieve processor information, the SystemInfo class uses the GetSystemInfo API function. This function fills a SYSTEM_INFO data structure with data. (See the class module for the gory details.) The Initialize event procedure of the SystemInfo class calls the API function, and the various properties retrieve information from the elements of the SYSTEM_INFO structure.

Although the processor information returned by the GetSystemInfo API function isn't necessary for every application, it can be useful. The next few sections provide the details necessary to interpret the information provided by these properties.

NumberOfProcessors   Specifies the number of processors in the system.

ActiveProcessorMask   Specifies a mask value representing the processors in the system. The bit or bits set in the mask indicate the active processor (bit 0 is processor 0; bit 31 is processor 31). This value will be 1 for most computers.

PageSize   Specifies the page size and the granularity of page protection and commitment. This isn't generally of much interest to VBA programmers.

AllocationGranularity   Specifies the granularity with which virtual memory is allocated. This value was hard coded as 64K in the past; since the Windows environment expands to different hardware platforms, other values may be necessary. Again, this value isn't of much interest to VBA programmers.

MinimumApplicationAddress, MaximumApplicationAddress

Pointers to the lowest and highest memory addresses accessible to applications and Dynamic Link Libraries. Not generally needed for VBA programmers unless they're making serious use of the Windows API functions that care about these addresses.

ProcessorType

Not relevant to Windows NT, which uses the ProcessorArchitecture, ProcessorLevel, and ProcessorRevision properties to provide information about the processor. This property provides the only means, in Windows 95, to gather such information. The value will be one of the items in the following list:

Value	Processor
386	Intel 386
486	Intel 486
586	Intel Pentium
4000	MIPS R4000 (NT only)
21064	Alpha 21064 (NT only)

ProcessorArchitecture

Specifies the system's processor architecture. For Windows 95, this value will always be 0. For Windows NT, the value can be any item from the following list:

Value	Processor
0	Intel
1	MIPS
2	Alpha
3	PPC
−1	Unknown

ProcessorLevel

Not used in Windows 95, but in Windows NT it returns the system's architecture-dependent processor level. The values can be any of the items in the first column of the following list. Use the ProcessorArchitecture value in the second column to determine the actual processor level.

Value	Processor Architecture	Description
3	0	Intel 80386
4	0	Intel 80486
5	0	Intel Pentium
6	0	Intel Pentium Pro
4	1	MIPS R4000
21064	2	Alpha 21064
21066	2	Alpha 21066
21164	2	Alpha 21164
1	3	PPC 601
3	3	PPC 603
4	3	PPC 604
6	3	PPC 603+
9	3	PPC 604+
20	3	PPC 620

ProcessorRevision   Not used in Windows 95, but in Windows NT this property specifies an architecture-dependent processor revision.

Version Information

The properties in this area all use the GetVersionEx API function to fill in an OSVERSIONINFO structure with information about the operating system. In the Initialize event procedure for the SystemInfo class, the code calls GetVersionEx, so all the various properties need do is retrieve information from a module-level variable.

Summary

This chapter has presented, through a series of nine class modules, a demonstration of some of the system and device information that's available as part of the

Windows API. By exposing the various bits of information as properties of the classes and grouping the wildly jumbled API calls into logical units, we've attempted to make this large body of information more useful to you as a solution developer.

On the other hand, this chapter just barely skimmed the surface of the system information available from the Win32 API. Although the chapter may seem fairly exhaustive, this is not the case. There are many more corners of the API to be poked at. For example, the GetDeviceCaps and DeviceCapabilities functions offer a treasure trove of information about devices such as the installed video and printer drivers. The properties discussed in this chapter should go a long way toward getting you the information you need in your solutions. In addition, should you need to add more information gathered from the API, the class modules provided in this chapter should be a good start for your own coding.

In particular, this chapter provided class modules dealing with the following areas of the Win32 API:

- Accessibility features
- Keyboard
- Memory status
- Mouse
- Non-client metrics
- Power status
- Screen and window information
- System colors
- Operating system and computer information

Other chapters in this book discuss additional issues that are pertinent to the discussion in this chapter. For example, for information on working with disks and files and gathering information about these objects, see Chapter 12. For information on working with the System Registry, see Chapter 10.

CHAPTER

TEN

10

Working with the Registry

- Understanding the Windows Registry

- Exploring the Registry API

- Writing functions to read and write Registry entries

- Wrapping Registry functions in class modules

The Registry is at the heart of 32-bit Windows. It is a hierarchical database that contains configuration information for Windows applications, as well as for Windows itself. Windows 95 and Windows NT simply cannot function without the information stored in their Registries. Being able to view and edit information contained in the Registry is an essential ability for serious developers. This chapter looks at how the Registry works and how you can interact with it. We begin with an explanation of its structure and how to use the graphical Registry Editor application to view and change information stored there. We then examine the Registry API, a subset of the Windows API that includes functions for manipulating Registry information. Finally, you'll see how to encapsulate these functions in VBA class modules, making adding Registry support to your applications as simple as including a few module files. Table 10.1 lists the sample files included on the CD-ROM.

TABLE 10.1 Sample Files

File Name	Description
REGTEST.XLS	Excel 97 file with sample functions
REGTEST.MDB	Access 97 database with sample functions
REGTEST.BAS	Text file with sample functions
REGISTRY.XLS	Excel 97 file with class modules and a test procedure
REGISTRY.MDB	Access 97 database with class modules and a test procedure
TESTCLAS.BAS	Text file containing a test procedure for Registry classes
KEY.CLS	Example class module as text
KEYS.CLS	Example class module as text
VALUE.CLS	Example class module as text
VALUES.CLS	Example class module as text
REGCONST.CLS	Example class module as text

Registry Structure

If you're a long-time Windows developer and/or user, it should come as no shock that the Registry evolved as a way to organize application information that was once stored in a multitude of INI files. While INI files offered many advantages (for example, as text files, you could edit them using a simple tool like Notepad), as more Windows applications were developed, it became hard to keep track of all the associated configuration information. Furthermore, it was difficult to store some types of information, such as binary data, in text files.

Microsoft created the Registry as a hierarchically structured database and created a special API to deal with it. Initially (in Windows 3.x) it was used to store information related to OLE. In Windows NT, and then Windows 95, it was expanded to store other configuration information, and application developers were encouraged to move away from INI files and keep their program information in the Registry.

Today, information in the Registry is actually stored in two separate files (USER.DAT and SYSTEM.DAT, in the Windows directory). Additionally, part of the Registry is not stored at all but instead is generated based on a computer's hardware configuration. Applications that use the information need not be aware of this, however, since they all interact with the Registry using a standard set of API functions.

The two primary items of interest in the Registry are keys and values. You use *keys*, sometimes referred to as *folders*, to organize Registry information in a hierarchical structure, much the way directories organize files in the file system. Like a directory, a key can have multiple subkeys, which themselves can have subkeys, and so forth. Values, on the other hand, are the actual data stored within each key. In our file system analogy, values represent individual files. Unlike a directory, however, a key can have a value directly associated with it (called its *default* value), as well as other values that it contains. This structure is illustrated graphically in Figure 10.1, which shows the Windows Registry Editor application. You can launch this application by running REGEDIT.EXE.

FIGURE 10.1

REGEDIT, the
Windows 95
Registry editor

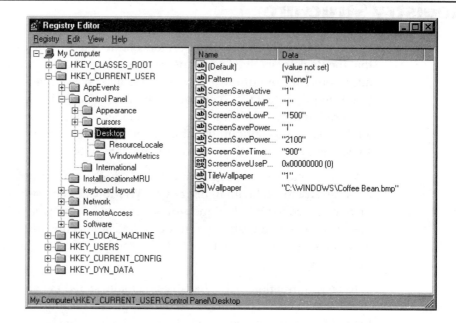

As you can see in Figure 10.1, at the Registry's root are keys that contain distinct categories of information. In Registry nomenclature, these are referred to as *hives.* Of particular interest are HKEY_CURRENT_USER, which contains settings and preferences for the current user, and HKEY_LOCAL_MACHINE, which contains configuration information that applies to the computer itself. HKEY_CLASSES_ROOT exists for backward compatibility with the Windows 3.1 Registry and 16-bit Registry functions and contains information on installed software and file associations. HKEY_USERS contains configuration options for all users who have accounts on the computer. In fact, HKEY_CURRENT_USER is a virtual hive and is actually a subkey of HKEY_USERS.

Figure 10.1 shows the HKEY_CURRENT_USER hive expanded to reveal its subkeys. In the right-hand pane, you can see the values associated with the Desktop key. Each value has a unique name, except for the default value (shown at the top of the value list), which has no name. The icon to the left of each value indicates its datatype. The Windows 3.1 Registry supported only string values. Registries in Windows NT and Windows 95 support a variety of datatypes, each of which is described in Table 10.2. (The Constant column lists VBA constants that we've defined in the sample code.) The most common, however, are String and DWORD (Long Integer).

TABLE 10.2 Datatypes Supported by Windows 95 and Windows NT Registries

Datatype	Constant	Value	Description
String	dhcRegSz	1	A variable length, null-terminated text string
DWORD	dhcRegDword	4	A 32-bit long integer
Binary	dhcRegBinary	3	Binary data (Microsoft recommends limiting each value to 1 megabyte or less.)
Multiple strings	dhcRegMultiSz	7	An array of strings terminated by two null characters
Unexpanded environment variable	dhcRegExpandSz	2	A null-terminated string that contains unexpanded references to environment variables (for example, "%PATH%")
Little-endian DWORD	dhcRegDword-LittleEndian	4	A 32-bit number in little-endian format (same as dhcRegDword). In little-endian format, the most significant byte of a word is the high-order byte. This is the most common format for computers running Windows NT and Windows 95
Big-endian DWORD	dhcRegDword-BigEndian	5	A 32-bit number in big-endian format. In big-endian format, the most significant byte of a word is the low-order byte
Symbolic link	dhcRegLink	6	A Unicode symbolic link
Resource list	dhcResourceList	8	A device driver resource list
None	dhcRegNone	0	No defined type

Referring to Registry Keys and Values

Since this chapter discusses individual Registry keys and values, it makes sense to present a format for describing them. In this book (and in most other sources of documentation on the Registry), individual keys are described by their relationship to one of the root hives, using syntax reminiscent of that used by the file system. Specifically, the backslash (\) denotes the key-subkey relationship. Therefore, you would express the Desktop key shown in Figure 10.1 as "HKEY_CURRENT_USER\Control Panel\Desktop". Similarly, you would express the

Wallpaper value as "HKEY_CURRENT_USER\Control Panel\Desktop\Wallpaper". Since it may not be immediately clear from a given example whether the right-most string represents a key or a value, we have made our examples as clear as possible.

VBA Registry Functions

If your needs are simple, VBA provides several built-in functions you can use to read and write Registry values. Microsoft made these functions available as part of VBA so application developers would have an easy way to store configuration options without having to resort to the Windows API. The major drawback of these functions, though, is that they let you work only with keys and values below a given key, namely HKEY_CURRENT_USER\Software\Microsoft\VB and VBA Program Settings. If you need more flexibility or want to read values from another part of the Registry, you'll need the API functions discussed in the section "Working with Registry Values" later in this chapter. Table 10.3 lists the four VBA Registry functions.

TABLE 10.3   VBA Functions for Manipulating the Windows Registry

Function	Arguments	Description
GetSetting	app, subkey, value[, default]	Retrieves a single value from a given Registry key
GetAllSettings	app, subkey	Retrieves all the values for a given key as an array
SaveSetting	app, subkey, value, setting	Saves or creates a Registry value for a given key
DeleteSetting	app, subkey[, value]	Deletes a Registry key or a value from a given key

Each of the Registry functions accepts an argument (app) corresponding to an application name. In the Registry itself, this name refers to a subkey immediately beneath HKEY_CURRENT_USER\Software\VB and VBA Program Settings. The idea is that developers will group all the configuration settings for a single application under one subkey. The second argument (subkey) is the name of another sub-key beneath the application key. The screen in Figure 10.2 shows REGEDIT open to a subkey called MyCoolApp\Windows. In this example, you would pass "MyCoolApp" as the first argument to the functions and "Windows" as the second.

FIGURE 10.2

The Registry Editor displays a VBA program setting.

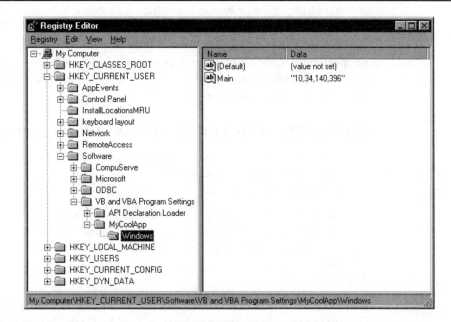

The other arguments vary depending on the function being called. For those that call for a value argument, you pass the name of one of the values beneath the specified subkey. In our example there is one value, "Main". GetSetting lets you pass a default value as an optional fourth argument. If the value name passed as the third argument is not found, GetSetting returns the default. Finally, SaveSetting requires you to pass the setting you want to save as its fourth argument.

To see how these functions work, open the Immediate window, type the following code snippet, and press Enter:

```
SaveSetting "MyCoolApp", "Windows", "Main", "10,34,140,396"
```

This makes an entry like the one shown in Figure 10.2. To retrieve the value, just enter

```
?GetSetting("MyCoolApp", "Windows", "Main")
```

VBA should respond by printing the string "10,34,140,396" to the Immediate window.

557

You can delete either the Main value or the entire Windows subkey easily by calling DeleteSetting. Using GetAllSettings is a bit trickier, however, because it returns an array of values as a Variant. To demonstrate this function, first add another string value or two to the Windows subkey, by using either SaveSetting or REGEDIT. Then create the procedure shown in Listing 10.1. The GetAllSettings function supports only string values. (Not surprisingly, this is the only type supported by SaveSetting.) If you create values of another type using REGEDIT and subsequently try to read them using GetAllSettings, VBA raises error 5, "Invalid procedure call or argument."

Listing 10.1: Print All the Values for a Given Subkey

```
Sub PrintValues(strApp As String, strKey As String)
    Dim varValues As Variant
    Dim i As Integer

    varValues = GetAllSettings(strApp, strKey)
    For i = LBound(varValues, 1) To UBound(varValues, 1)
        Debug.Print varValues(i, 0), varValues(i, 1)
    Next
End Sub
```

PrintValues works by declaring a Variant variable to hold the results of GetAllSettings. A counter variable, i, is used to iterate through all the values contained in the results. Run PrintValues from the Immediate window to see it in action.

Windows Registry Functions

The Windows API implements 25 functions for manipulating the Registry. Of those, only a handful are used very often, and these are geared primarily toward creating, opening, and deleting keys and setting and deleting values. Table 10.4 lists the functions we'll be using in our examples. You'll find all the functions in ADVAPI32.DLL. The examples in the section are contained in the basRegistryTest module in REGTEST.XLS or REGTEST.BAS.

TABLE 10.4   Windows Registry Functions Used in the Examples

Function	Description
RegCloseKey	Closes an open key
RegCreateKeyEx	Creates a new key or opens an existing key
RegDeleteKey	Deletes an existing key along with its values and, under Windows 95, all its subkeys (Under Windows NT, you must manually delete the subkeys.)
RegDeleteValue	Deletes a value from a key
RegEnumKeyEx	Lists all the subkeys for a given key
RegEnumValue	Lists all the values for a given key
RegOpenKeyEx	Opens a key for reading and/or writing values
RegSetValueEx	Sets the contents of a given value
RegQueryValueEx	Reads the contents of a given value

Like other elements of Windows, Registry keys are managed using handles, 32-bit unique integers. Before you manipulate a key or its values, you must open it, using RegCreateKeyEx or RegOpenKeyEx. You pass a pointer to a long integer that these functions fill in with the key's handle. You can then use the handle as an input to other Registry functions. Top-level keys have fixed handle values that you can use to open subordinate keys using RegOpenKeyEx. All Registry functions will return either a 0, representing successful completion, or an error code.

Opening, Closing, and Creating Keys

The most basic task in working with the Registry is examining keys and subkeys. This section explains how to use the functions to open and close existing keys, as well as how to create new keys.

The RegOpenKeyEx Function

The declaration for the RegOpenKeyEx function is

```
Declare Function RegOpenKeyEx _
 Lib "advapi32.dll" Alias "RegOpenKeyExA" _
```

```
(ByVal hKey As Long, ByVal lpSubKey As String, _
ByVal ulOptions As Long, ByVal samDesired As Long, _
phkResult As Long) As Long
```

The function's first argument is a handle to an existing key. This can be either one of the predefined values representing a root hive or the handle of a key you've previously opened yourself. The second argument is the name of the sub-key you wish to open. To specify an immediate subkey, just pass the subkey's name. You can also open a subkey several levels below the current key by passing the relative path of the subkey using the syntax described earlier in this chapter. For example, to open the HKEY_CURRENT_USER\Control Panel\Desktop key, you would supply the predefined handle for HKEY_CURRENT_USER and the string "Control Panel\Desktop" as the second argument to RegOpenKeyEx.

RegOpenKeyEx's third and fourth arguments control how the function treats the key you're trying to open. The ulOptions argument is currently being reserved for future use and must be 0. The samDesired argument, on the other hand, defines your desired security access and is a bitmasked value consisting of a number of constants. The constants are listed in Table 10.5; spend a moment reviewing them. Many of the other Registry functions have a security argument. By passing one of these values you are, in effect, telling the Registry what you intend to do with the key once you've opened it.

TABLE 10.5 Security Bit Masks for Registry Functions

Constant	Value (Hex)	Value (Decimal)	Description
dhcReadControl	&H20000	131072	Bit mask for read permission
dhcKeyCreateLink	&H20	32	Permission to create a symbolic link
dhcKeyCreateSubKey	&H4	4	Permission to create subkeys
dhcKeyEnumerate	&H8	8	Permission to enumerate subkeys
dhcKeyExecute-SubKeys	&H20019	131097	Permission for read access (same as dhcKeyRead)
dhcKeyNotify	&H10	16	Permission for change notification
dhcKeyQueryValue	&H1	1	Permission to read subkey data

TABLE 10.5   Security Bit Masks for Registry Functions (continued)

Constant	Value (Hex)	Value (Decimal)	Description
dhcKeySetValue	&H2	2	Permission to write subkey data
dhcKeyRead	&H20019	131097	Combination of dhcReadControl, dhcKeyQueryValue, dhcKey-EnumerateSubKeys, and dhcKeyNotify
dhcKeyWrite	&H20006	131078	Combination of dhcReadControl, dhcKeySetValue, and dhcKey-CreateSubKey
dhcKeyAllAccess	&H2003F	131135	Combination of dhcReadControl, dhcKeyQueryValue, dhcKey-EnumerateSubKeys, dhcKeyNotify, dhcKeyCreateSubKey, dhcKey-CreateLink, and dhcKeySetValue

Finally, the phkResult argument is a pointer to a long integer that RegOpenKeyEx will fill in with a handle to the opened key. You should declare a Long variable and pass it to RegOpenKeyEx. If the function returns a 0 (for success), the hKey variable will hold a valid subkey handle and can be used with other functions. Listing 10.2, shown a little later in this chapter, illustrates how to open the HKEY_CURRENT_USER\Control Panel\Desktop key.

The RegCloseKey Function

After opening a key using RegOpenKeyEx or RegCreateKeyEx (explained in the next section), you must close it using RegCloseKey. Leaving a key open consumes memory, and you may, under rare conditions, corrupt your Registry. RegClose-Key accepts a single argument, the handle to an open key, and returns 0 if the key was successfully closed.

The RegCreateKeyEx Function

As its name implies, RegCreateKeyEx creates a new Registry key. Not so obvious, however, is that you can also use it to open an existing key. If you specify an existing key, RegCreateKeyEx opens it; otherwise, the function creates it. This behavior differs from that of RegOpenKeyEx, which returns an error code if the key does not exist.

RegCreateKeyEx is similar to RegOpenKeyEx, but it takes a few extra arguments. Its declaration is shown here:

```
Private Declare Function RegCreateKeyEx _
 Lib "advapi32.dll" Alias "RegCreateKeyExA" _
 (ByVal hKey As Long, ByVal lpSubKey As String, _
 ByVal ulReserved As Long, ByVal lpClass As String, _
 ByVal dwOptions As Long, ByVal samDesired As Long, _
 lpSecurityAttributes As Any, phkResult As Long, _
 lpdwDisposition As Long) As Long
```

You should recognize the hKey, lpSubkey, samDesired, and phkResult arguments—they're the same as those in RegOpenKeyEx. ulReserved is an unused argument and must be 0. The lpClass argument lets you specify a class descriptor for the key. This information is available to the RegEnumKeyEx function, which is explained in the section "The RegEnumKeyEx Function" later in this chapter.

The dwOptions argument controls what type of key is created. The most common settings for this argument are 0 (dhcRegOptionNonVolatile) and 1 (dhcRegOptionVolatile). Setting this argument to 1 creates a volatile Registry key. Volatile keys are not saved when you shut down your computer and are useful for storing temporary options that are valid only for the current session.

The lpSecurityAttributes argument is a pointer to a SECURITY_ATTRIBUTES structure. This structure defines the Windows NT security attributes you want placed on the new key. Windows 95 does not support operating system security attributes, so this argument is ignored. You'll notice that we've used the Any datatype in the declaration. Under Windows NT, if you pass a null pointer (represented by the value 0&), NT applies the default security attributes. That's what we've done in our examples.

TIP

If you plan to run these examples under Windows NT and don't want the default security attributes applied to the new key, pass a pointer to a SECURITY_ATTRIBUTES structure with valid values.

Finally, the lpdwDisposition argument is a pointer to a Long Integer variable that you pass to the function. When the function returns, the variable will be set either to 1, meaning the key did not previously exist and was created, or to 2, meaning the key was already there and was just opened.

Listing 10.2 shows the dhCreateNewKey procedure, which demonstrates how to create a new Registry key beneath the Desktop key shown in Figure 10.1. After opening the Desktop key using RegOpenKeyEx, the procedure calls RegCreateKeyEx, passing the Desktop key's handle (hKeyDesktop) and the name of a new key ("New Key").

Listing 10.2: Sample Procedure that Opens the Desktop Key and Creates a New Subkey

```
Sub dhCreateNewKey()
    Dim hKeyDesktop As Long
    Dim hKeyNew As Long
    Dim lngResult As Long
    Dim lngDisposition As Long

    ' Open the KHEY_CURRENT_USER\Control Panel\Desktop key
    lngResult = RegOpenKeyEx(dhcHKeyCurrentUser, _
     "Control Panel\Desktop", 0&, dhcKeyAllAccess, hKeyDesktop)

    ' Make sure the call succeeded
    If lngResult = dhcSuccess Then

        ' Create the new subkey
        lngDisposition = 0&
        lngResult = RegCreateKeyEx(hKeyDesktop, _
         "New Key", 0&, "", dhcRegOptionNonVolatile, _
         dhcKeyAllAccess, 0&, hKeyNew, lngDisposition)

        ' If successful, we're done--close the key
        If lngResult = dhcSuccess Then
            lngResult = RegCloseKey(hKeyNew)
        End If

        ' Close the Desktop key
        lngResult = RegCloseKey(hKeyDesktop)
    End If

End Sub
```

Working with Registry Values

Registry values have come along way since the days of Windows 3.1. In the Windows 3.1 Registry, you were limited to a single value per key, and that value had to contain string data. Now you can have an unlimited number of values in each key, and you can choose from a wide variety of datatypes. The following sections discuss how to read, create, and write Registry values.

The RegQueryValueEx Function

Unlike keys, values do not use handles, and you don't need to open them before you can use them. Once you have a key handle, you can read, write, create, or delete any value it contains. RegQueryValueEx is the Registry function used to read an existing value's data. Its declaration is shown here:

```
Private Declare Function RegQueryValueEx _
  Lib "advapi32.dll" Alias "RegQueryValueExA" _
  (ByVal hKey As Long, ByVal lpValueName As String, _
  ByVal dwReserved As Long, lpType As Long, _
  lpData As Any, lpcbData As Long) As Long
```

You'll notice that the function's first argument is a key handle. You pass the handle of a valid, open key. The second argument is the name of the value you want to query. The third argument is another reserved argument and must be 0.

> **TIP**
>
> If you want to access data stored in the default value for a key (all values migrated from the Windows 3.1 Registry will be stored this way), pass an empty string as the name of the value.

The last three arguments retrieve the actual data stored in the value. Since the Registry can store various types of data, you must tell RegQueryValueEx the datatype being read, using the lpType argument. You should pass one of the constants listed in Table 10.2 earlier in this chapter.

Finally, lpData and lpcbData specify a buffer you must create to hold the Registry data. lpData is defined as type Any in the function declaration. Depending on the type of data being read, you must pass a String or Long variable or an array of Bytes (for binary data). Additionally, you must pass the size of the buffer in the lpcbData argument.

> **WARNING** Always use caution when passing an argument to an API function declared as Any. If you pass a datatype that the API function does not expect or fail to pass the correct size, the result is almost always an Invalid Page Fault (IPF). Remember to save your work before calling any API functions, especially those that use the Any datatype.

Listing 10.3 shows a simple example of reading the Wallpaper value of the Desktop key. Wallpaper is a string that specifies the current desktop wallpaper bitmap. Pay special attention to the code that allocates the string buffer. The Space function creates a string buffer 255 bytes in size, and the cb variable is set to this length. After the procedure calls RegQueryValueEx, cb will contain the number of bytes written to the buffer.

Note also the ByVal keyword used in the call to RegQueryValueEx. This is necessary to coerce the VBA String variable into the null-terminated string expected by the API function. Normally, ByVal appears in the declaration of an API function, but we've left it out because we're using the Any datatype. If you leave out ByVal in the function call, you will generate an IPF.

Listing 10.3: Read the Current Windows Wallpaper Setting

```
Sub dhReadWallpaper()
    Dim hKeyDesktop As Long
    Dim lngResult As Long
    Dim strBuffer As String
    Dim cb As Long

    ' Open the KHEY_CURRENT_USER\Control Panel\Desktop key
    lngResult = RegOpenKeyEx(dhcHKeyCurrentUser, _
     "Control Panel\Desktop", 0&, dhcKeyAllAccess, hKeyDesktop)

    ' Make sure the call succeeded
    If lngResult = dhcSuccess Then

        ' Create the buffer
        strBuffer = Space(255)
        cb = Len(strBuffer)

        ' Read the wallpaper value
        lngResult = RegQueryValueEx(hKeyDesktop, "Wallpaper", _
```

```
            0&, dhcRegSz, ByVal strBuffer, cb)

        Check return value
        If lngResult = dhcSuccess Then

            ' Display the current value
            MsgBox Left(strBuffer, cb), vbInformation, _
             "Current Wallpaper"
        End If

        ' Close the Desktop key
        lngResult = RegCloseKey(hKeyDesktop)
    End If
End Sub
```

Our dhReadWallpaper procedure is coded to deal with string data. For examples of how to handle other datatypes, see the section "The Value Property" later in this chapter.

The RegSetValueEx Function

You write a value to the Registry in much the same manner as you read a value. In fact, the declaration for RegSetValueEx is nearly identical to RegQueryValueEx:

```
Private Declare Function RegSetValueEx _
 Lib "advapi32.dll" Alias "RegSetValueExA" _
 (ByVal hKey As Long, ByVal lpValueName As String, _
 ByVal dwReserved As Long, ByVal dwType As Long, _
 lpData As Any, ByVal cbData As Long) As Long
```

The only difference, besides the function name, is that instead of passing an empty buffer to the function, you pass data in the lpData argument. You can see this in the dhWriteWallpaper procedure shown in Listing 10.4. It accepts the path to a file as its sole argument and writes this string to the Wallpaper value in the Desktop key.

Listing 10.4: Use the dhWriteWallpaper Procedure to Change the Wallpaper Registry Setting

```
Sub dhWriteWallpaper(strFile As String)
    Dim hKeyDesktop As Long
    Dim lngResult As Long

    ' Open the KHEY_CURRENT_USER\Control Panel\Desktop key
```

```
    lngResult = RegOpenKeyEx(dhcHKeyCurrentUser, _
     "Control Panel\Desktop", 0&, dhcKeyAllAccess, hKeyDesktop)

    ' Make sure the call succeeded
    If lngResult = dhcSuccess Then

        ' Save the wallpaper value
        lngResult = RegSetValueEx(hKeyDesktop, "Wallpaper", _
         0&, dhcRegSz, ByVal strFile, Len(strFile))

        ' Check return value
        If lngResult = dhcSuccess Then

            ' Display the success message
            MsgBox "Wallpaper changed to " & strFile, _
             vbInformation, "Wallpaper Changed"
        Else
            ' Display failure message
            MsgBox "Could not saved wallpaper.", _
             vbExclamation, "Wallpaper Not Changed"
        End If

        ' Close the Desktop key
        lngResult = RegCloseKey(hKeyDesktop)
    End If
End Sub
```

NOTE Changing the Wallpaper Registry setting does not actually change the Windows wallpaper until you restart your computer. That's because Windows does not monitor this value for changes.

Changes made to the Registry are asynchronous. That is, calling RegSetValueEx does not write the change immediately. Instead, the setting is cached and written later on. This is similar to so-called "lazy writes" implemented by the file system. If you are concerned about the delay, you can call the RegFlushKey function, which flushes the Registry cache immediately. Its very simple declaration is shown here:

```
Declare Function RegFlushKey Lib "advapi32.dll" _
 (ByVal hKey As Long) As Long
```

Enumerating Keys and Values

The functions described thus far in this chapter are great as long as you know what keys and values you want to manipulate. But what if you don't? What if you want to create an application that lists subkeys or values for an arbitrary Registry key? Fortunately, there are Registry functions that let you do this, as discussed in the next two sections.

The RegEnumKeyEx Function

RegEnumKeyEx (and its counterpart, RegEnumValuesEx) enumerates the subkeys (and values) of a given key. RegEnumKeyEx's declaration is shown here:

```
Declare Function RegEnumKeyEx _
 Lib "advapi32.dll" Alias "RegEnumKeyExA" _
 (ByVal hKey As Long, ByVal dwIndex As Long, _
 ByVal lpName As String, lpcbName As Long, _
 lpReserved As Long, ByVal lpClass As String, _
 lpcbClass As Long, lpftLastWriteTime As Any) As Long
```

You pass RegEnumKeyEx a key handle and the numeric index of the subkey you want information on. Index values run from 0 to one less than the number of subkeys. You also pass buffers to hold the subkey's name and class, as well as a pointer to a FILETIME structure to hold the date and time when the key was last updated. If the specified subkey exists, RegEnumKeyEx populates the buffers and returns a 0, indicating success. If the dwIndex argument lies outside the valid range for existing subkeys, RegEnumKeyEx returns a nonzero result.

Using this information and a simple Do loop, you can write code to list all the subkeys of any existing Registry key. That's what we've done with the dhListSubkeys procedure shown in Listing 10.5.

Listing 10.5: Use RegEnumKeysEx to List a Key's Subkeys

```
Sub dhListSubkeys(hKeyRoot As Long, strSubkey As String)
    Dim hSubkey As Long
    Dim cEnum As Long
    Dim hKey As Long
    Dim lngResult As Long
    Dim strNameBuff As String
    Dim cbNameBuff As Long
    Dim strClassBuff As String
```

```
    Dim cbClassBuff As Long
    Dim typFileTime As FILETIME

    ' Open the key passed in
    lngResult = RegOpenKeyEx(hKeyRoot, strSubkey, _
     0&, dhcKeyAllAccess, hSubkey)

    ' Make sure the call succeeded
    If lngResult = dhcSuccess Then

        ' Loop through all subkeys
        Do
            ' Set up buffers
            strNameBuff = Space$(255)
            cbNameBuff = Len(strNameBuff)
            strClassBuff = Space$(255)
            cbClassBuff = Len(strClassBuff)

            ' Call RegEnumKeyEx
            lngResult = RegEnumKeyEx(hSubkey, cEnum, _
             strNameBuff, cbNameBuff, 0&, _
             strClassBuff, cbClassBuff, typFileTime)

            ' If successful, print subkey name
            If lngResult = dhcSuccess Then
                Debug.Print Left(strNameBuff, cbNameBuff)
            End If

            ' Increment subkey index
            cEnum = cEnum + 1
        Loop Until lngResult <> 0

        ' Close the subkey
        lngResult = RegCloseKey(hSubkey)
    End If
End Sub
```

The RegEnumValue Function

RegEnumValue works in a similar fashion. As you can see from the following declaration, it, too, accepts a key handle and an index number as its first two arguments:

```
Declare Function RegEnumValue _
 Lib "advapi32.dll" Alias "RegEnumValueA" _
 (ByVal hKey As Long, ByVal dwIndex As Long, _
```

```
ByVal lpValueName As String, lpcbValueName As Long, _
lpReserved As Long, lpType As Long, _
lpData As Any, lpcbData As Any) As Long
```

In addition, you pass a buffer to hold the value's name. What's interesting about RegEnumValue is that you also pass a data buffer. This allows you to determine the value's name and the data it contains at the same time. The only drawback is that the method to retrieve a value's data differs depending on its type. To account for any type that may be present, you must pass a pointer to a Byte array as the lpData argument and then interpret the array's contents after the call to RegEnumValue returns.

NOTE RegEnumValue does not return the default value for a key. It is assumed that this value (which has an empty string for a name) always exists.

dhListValues, shown in Listing 10.6, enumerates the values associated with a given key. The screen in Figure 10.3 illustrates how to call the procedure from the Immediate window, as well as a possible result. Note that the numbers shown indicate the datatype stored in the value.

FIGURE 10.3

What happens when you call dhListValues from the Immediate window

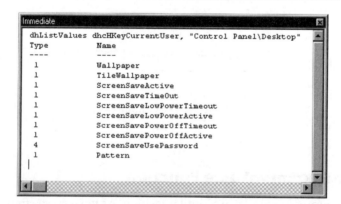

```
dhListValues dhcHKeyCurrentUser, "Control Panel\Desktop"
Type        Name
----        ----
1           Wallpaper
1           TileWallpaper
1           ScreenSaveActive
1           ScreenSaveTimeOut
1           ScreenSaveLowPowerTimeout
1           ScreenSaveLowPowerActive
1           ScreenSavePowerOffTimeout
1           ScreenSavePowerOffActive
4           ScreenSaveUsePassword
1           Pattern
```

Listing 10.6: Use dhListValues to Enumerate the Values Associated with a Given Registry Key

```
Sub dhListValues(hKeyRoot As Long, strSubkey As String)
    Dim hSubkey As Long
```

```
Dim cEnum As Long
Dim lngResult As Long
Dim strNameBuff As String
Dim cbNameBuff As Long
Dim lngType As Long
Dim abytData(1 To 2048) As Byte
Dim cbData As Long

 Open the key passed in
lngResult = RegOpenKeyEx(hKeyRoot, strSubkey, _
 0&, dhcKeyAllAccess, hSubkey)

' Make sure the call succeeded
If lngResult = dhcSuccess Then

    ' Print header
    Debug.Print "Type", "Name"
    Debug.Print "----", "----"
    ' Loop through all values
    Do
        ' Set up buffers
        strNameBuff = Space$(255)
        cbNameBuff = Len(strNameBuff)
        Erase abytData
        cbData = UBound(abytData)

        ' Call RegEnumValue
        lngResult = RegEnumValue(hSubkey, cEnum, _
         strNameBuff, cbNameBuff, 0&, _
         lngType, abytData(1), cbData)

        ' Print value name to Immediate window
        If lngResult = dhcSuccess Then
            Debug.Print lngType, Left(strNameBuff, _
            cbNameBuff)

        End If

        ' Increment value index
        cEnum = cEnum + 1
    Loop Until lngResult <> 0

    ' Close the key
    lngResult = RegCloseKey(hSubkey)
    End If
End Sub
```

An Object Model for the Registry

While Registry functions are interesting and useful in their own right, if you are planning on doing any serious Registry manipulation, a function call–based interface can get very cumbersome. The answer (which you should already know if you've read the preceding chapters) is to create an object-based interface using VBA class modules. Fortunately for you, we've already done most of the work. The remainder of this chapter explains how our Registry object model is constructed, how it works, and how you can use it in your applications.

An Overview

The object model for our Registry components is extremely simple. It consists of only two base classes, Key and Value. Two collection classes and one constant class supplement these two classes. The reason it's so simple is due to the hierarchical nature of the Registry. Since a key can contain a number of values as well as other keys, we can reuse each class over and over. The diagram in Figure 10.4 illustrates the object model.

FIGURE 10.4

Object model for the Windows Registry

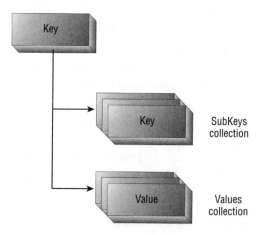

To implement this model using VBA, we need four class modules to represent the objects and collections and a fifth class module for various Registry constants. Table 10.6 lists the class names and their properties and methods. The table also lists the CLS files that define the classes, which we've provided on the CD-ROM.

TABLE 10.6 Registry Classes, Properties, and Methods

Class	File Name	Properties	Methods
Key	KEY.CLS	Name Handle Parent FullPath	OpenSubKey SubKeyExists
Keys	KEYS.CLS	Count Parent	Add Item Remove Refresh
Value	VALUE.CLS	Name DataType Value Parent FullPath	*None*
Values	VALUES.CLS	Count Parent	Add Item Remove Refresh
RegConstants	REGCONST.CLS	One for each Registry	(none)

Some of the properties and methods shown in the table are worth describing in more detail:

- Key objects have a Handle property that is set to the handle returned by Registry functions when the key is opened. Since all Registry functions depend on handles to keys, creating a Handle property for the Key object makes a lot of sense.

- Key objects also have an OpenSubKey method that returns a reference to a descendant key. Unlike the SubKeys collection, which contains one key for each subkey exactly one level below the current key, OpenSubKey lets you open a subkey that is several levels deep by using a qualified relative path (for example, "Control Panel\Desktop\WindowMetrics").

- The Keys and Values collection classes both have a Refresh method. Refresh resets each class' internal Collection object and repopulates it with Key and Value objects representing the subkeys and values of the current key.

OpenSubKey calls the Refresh methods of each class. You can also call this yourself to update the collections with the most recent contents.

- All objects have a Parent property. In each case, this refers to a Key object that represents a given object's parent key.

Implementing the Classes

This section highlights certain interesting characteristics and procedures of the sample code in our class modules.

Constant Class Usage

Each class module contains a reference to a class of constants (Private rc As New RegConstants). This allows us to use constants in our class procedures without having to redeclare them or use a global module.

The Add Methods

The Add method defined in the Keys class module (shown in Listing 10.7) accepts a key name and calls the RegCreateKeyEx Registry function. RegCreateKeyEx will either create a new or open an existing subkey of a given key, specified by a key handle. We get the handle from the parent key's Handle property. If the function executes successfully, the Add method then creates a new Key instance, sets its property values (including Parent), and adds it to the Private mcolKeys collection.

Listing 10.7: Add Method of the Keys Class

```
Public Function Add(ByVal Name As String) As Key
    Dim objKey As New Key
    Dim lngRet As Long
    Dim lngDisp As Long
    Dim hKey As Long

    ' Call RegCreateKey--for existing keys this will
    ' open them; for nonexistent keys this will
    ' create them
    lngRet = RegCreateKeyEx(hKey:=mobjParent.Handle, _
     lpSubKey:=Name, ulReserved:=0&, _
     lpClass:="", dwOptions:=rc.RegOptionNonVolatile, _
     samDesired:=rc.KeyAllAccess, _
```

```
        lpSecurityAttributes:=0&, phkResult:=hKey, _
        lpdwDisposition:=lngDisp)

    ' If successful, add key to the collection and
    ' set the return value to point to it
    If lngRet = rc.Success Then
        objKey.Name = Name
        objKey.Handle = hKey

        ' Add item for default value
        objKey.Values.Add "", rc.RegSz

        Set objKey.Parent = mobjParent
        mcolKeys.Add objKey, objKey.Name
        Set Add = objKey
    End If
End Function
```

> **NOTE**
>
> You must manually add a member to the Values collection for the key's default value because it always exists and does not show up when you use the Refresh method (and because RegEnumValue doesn't return a value representing it).

The Add method of the Values class (Listing 10.8) works similarly, except that it does not call a Registry function. Instead, it just adds a new Value object to the mcolValues collection of the class. Note that it accepts an optional argument that can contain the new Value object's value. If you supply this argument, the Add method sets the Value property after creating a new object instance. Using optional arguments allows for greater coding flexibility. You can either set all the property values as part of the Add method or set them individually after adding the object to the collection. In both cases, the Add method returns a pointer to the newly added object. This makes it very easy to set additional property values by capturing the pointer in an object variable. An alternative to passing arguments and returning an object reference is to pass an entire object to the Add method. See the sidebar "Passing Objects to the Add Method" for more details on this approach.

Listing 10.8: Add Method of the Values Class

```
Public Function Add(ByVal Name As String, _
 ByVal DataType As Variant, _
 Optional ByVal Value As Variant) As Value
```

```
' Create new Value instance
Dim objValue As New Value

' Set the new Value's Parent property
' to point to the collection's Parent
Set objValue.Parent = mobjParent

' Set the requisite property values
objValue.Name = Name
objValue.DataType = DataType

' If optional argument was supplied,
' set the Value property value
If Not IsMissing(Value) Then
    objValue.Value = Value
End If

' Add new instance to the collection,
' using its Name as the unique key
mcolValues.Add objValue, objValue.Name

' Set the return value to reference the
' new object
Set Add = objValue
End Function
```

Passing Objects to the Add Method

An alternative to the approach used for the Add methods in our example is to pass an object reference to the Add method instead of simple values. You should consider this method if you would otherwise have to pass a large number of parameters or if your object model does not support the idea of independent objects. For instance, the Jet DAO model allows you to create new tables in an Access database using TableDef and Field objects. (Jet is the database engine that manages Microsoft Access databases.) For instance, to create a new field in a table, you first create a new instance of a Field object. You then set a variety of property values and add it to the table's Fields collection using the Append method. For example:

```
Dim tdf As TableDef
Dim fld As Field
```

```
' Get a pointer to a TableDef
Set tdf = db.TableDefs("SomeTable")
' Create the new Field object by calling CreateField
Set fld = tdf.CreateField("NewField")
' Set some property values
fld.Type = dbText
fld.Size = 20
' Append it to the existing Fields collection
tdf.Fields.Append fld
```

Append is Jet's equivalent to the Add method. Again, note that it is an object reference, not a scalar value, that is passed to the method. This makes sense because a Field object isn't useful until several property values have been set and it has been added to the existing fields.

On the other hand, the approach we used is similar to the way Excel's object model works. For example, to add a new Worksheet object to workbook, you call the Worksheets collection's Add method. You can call it without arguments to add a default worksheet to the workbook or specify optional arguments to dictate position or sheet type. Add also returns a reference to the newly added Worksheet object that you can capture in an object variable (to facilitate setting additional property values) or ignore.

The Value Property

Our Value class implements a Value property that represents the contents of an individual Registry value. There are two interesting characteristics of this property. First, since the contents of a Registry value can be different datatypes, we must treat this property as a Variant. In our object model, it will be one of three types: String, Long Integer, or an array of Bytes (for binary values). Second, we never cache the value in our class. That is, when the Value property is used by another procedure, we read from or write to the Registry directly. Therefore, any changes to a Value object's Value property are immediately saved to the Registry.

Listing 10.9 shows the Property Get procedure for the Value property. We use a Select Case statement to determine the type of data contained in the Registry value and then call RegQueryValueEx to retrieve it. The function call differs (specifically, the lpData argument) depending on the type of data being requested.

Listing 10.9: Implement the Value Property of the Value Class

```
Property Get Value() As Variant
    Dim strBuffer As String
    Dim lngBuffer As Long
    Dim lngRet As Long
    Dim abytData() As Byte
    Dim cb As Long

    ' To return a value we need to figure out
    ' what datatype the value is and then call
    ' RegQueryValueEx using an appropriate lpData
    ' argument
    Select Case mlngDataType

        ' String
        Case rc.RegSz

            ' Create a string buffer and set the
            ' size variable to pass
            strBuffer = Space(rc.RegMaxDataSize)
            cb = Len(strBuffer)

            ' Call RegQueryValueEx passing
            ' address of string buffer
            lngRet = RegQueryValueEx( _
             mobjParent.Handle, mstrName, 0&, _
             mlngDataType, ByVal strBuffer, cb)

            ' If successful, return portion of
            ' buffer filled in by the function
            If lngRet = rc.Success Then
                Value = Left(strBuffer, cb - 1)
            End If

        ' Long Integer
        Case rc.RegDWord

            ' Set size argument to size of Long
            cb = Len(lngBuffer)

            ' Call RegQueryValueEx passing
            ' address to Long Integer variable
```

```
            lngRet = RegQueryValueEx( _
            mobjParent.Handle, mstrName, 0&, _
            mlngDataType, lngBuffer, cb)

            ' If successful, return value
            If lngRet = rc.Success Then
                Value = lngBuffer
            End If

        ' Binary
        Case rc.RegBinary

            ' Create an array of bytes
            ReDim abytData(1 To rc.RegMaxDataSize)
            cb = UBound(abytData)

            ' Call RegQueryValueEx passing
            ' address of first array element
            lngRet = RegQueryValueEx( _
            mobjParent.Handle, mstrName, 0&, _
            mlngDataType, abytData(1), cb)

            ' If successful, resize array and
            ' return a pointer to it
            If lngRet = rc.Success And cb > 0 Then
                ReDim Preserve abytData(1 To cb)
                Value = abytData
            End If
    End Select
End Property
```

Determining the Full Path of Keys and Values

Occasionally, you'll want to know what the full path of a particular Registry key or value is. The Name property will give you the name or relative path, but what about the full path, starting at the root? As it turns out, this is easy to compute, given the Parent properties of the class. By using the Parent property to work backward, up the Registry hierarchy, you can build a full path by looking at the Name properties of all the interceding objects.

Listing 10.10 shows the FullPath property of the Key class. (The Value class uses almost identical code.) Notice that we first set a pointer to the key's immediate parent and then use a Do loop to build the path string. Each time through the loop, we reset the objParent pointer to the current object's parent. Eventually, we reach the top of hierarchy, and objParent becomes Nothing. This causes our loop to terminate, at which point we append the original key's name and return the result.

Listing 10.10: Use the Parents of a Key to Generate Its Full Path

```
Property Get FullPath() As String
    Dim objParent As Key
    Dim strTemp As String

    ' Set starting point
    Set objParent = mobjParent

    ' Loop until objParent is Nothing (at the root)
    Do Until objParent Is Nothing
        strTemp = objParent.Name & "\" & strTemp
        Set objParent = objParent.Parent
    Loop

    ' Add this key's name
    strTemp = strTemp & mstrName

    ' Set return value
    FullPath = strTemp
End Property
```

Removing Registry Keys

The Remove method of the Keys class is worth mentioning because it uses recursive method calls to delete all the subkeys beneath the key being removed. This is necessary under Windows NT because the RegDeleteKey function will fail if the key being deleted has subkeys. (It works perfectly well under Windows 95, however.) Listing 10.11 shows the code for the Remove method.

Listing 10.11: Remove Method of the Keys Class, Which Uses Recursive Method Calls to Delete All the Subkeys

```
Public Sub Remove(ByVal ID As Variant)
    Dim lngRet As Long
    Dim objSubKey As Key
    Dim lngSubKeys As Long
    Dim cSubKeys As Long

    ' This code removes all of the current key's
    ' subkeys by calling the Remove method recursively
```

```
    ' First refresh the subkeys
    mcolKeys(ID).SubKeys.Refresh

    ' Get a count (because the property will change)
    lngSubKeys = mcolKeys(ID).SubKeys.Count

    ' Loop through all the subkeys
    For cSubKeys = lngSubKeys To 1 Step -1
        ' Call Remove recursively
        mcolKeys(ID).SubKeys.Remove cSubKeys
    Next

    ' Call RegDeleteKey to delete the subkey
    lngRet = RegDeleteKey(mobjParent.Handle, _
     mcolKeys(ID).Name)
    ' If successful then remove it from the collection
    If lngRet = rc.Success Then
        mcolKeys.Remove ID
    End If

End Sub
```

Note that the method first calls the Refresh method of the key's SubKeys collection. This is necessary to ensure that we get all the subkeys. The method then stores a count of the subkeys and loops backward from the total number to 1. You must loop backward because the number of items in the collection changes inside the loop.

TIP

You'll probably want to be able to check whether you were, in fact, running under Windows NT, since deleting a large number of subkeys can be time consuming. Chapter 9 describes code that will tell you the current operating system. It should be a simple matter to integrate it into this Keys class module.

Location of API Function Declarations

If you peruse the source code for our classes, you'll notice that we've spread out the Declare statements for the Registry API functions. We've placed the declarations in the class modules where the functions are used. By doing so, we've ensured that the class module code will be very portable. That is, if we wanted to use the Keys class in another VBA project, for example, we'd need to include only the class module file and not have to worry about including other declaration files.

Using the Registry Objects

Now that we've explained the highlights of our Registry classes, this section shows you how to use them. All the code in this section can be found in the Test-RegClasses procedure that we've included in a global module in REGISTRY.XLS (and independently as TESTCLAS.BAS). To really see what's going on, place a breakpoint on the first line of code in the procedure and step through the code as it executes.

Opening a Subkey

To use the Registry classes, you must first create a new Key instance corresponding to one of the top-level Registry keys. Our constant class contains properties for each root key handle value. Set the Handle property of the new key to one of these. You can then open any of its subkeys using the OpenSubKey method. OpenSubKey accepts a relative path to the subkey (without leading or trailing backslashes) and returns a Key object reference if the call is successful. Listing 10.12 shows an example that opens the HKEY_CURRENT_USER\Control Panel\Desktop key. Note the use of the Key's FullPath property to print the full path of the newly opened key.

Listing 10.12: Open the HKEY_CURRENT_USER\Control Panel\Desktop Key

```
Dim objKeyRoot As Key
Dim objKey As Key
Dim rc As New RegConstants

' Create a reference to the top-level key
' HKEY_CURRENT_USER
Set objKeyRoot = New Key
objKeyRoot.Handle = rc.HKeyCurrentUser

' Open the Control Panel\Desktop subkey
Set objKey = objKeyRoot.OpenSubKey("Control Panel\Desktop")

' Print the key's full path
Debug.Print "Opened: " & objKey.FullPath
```

Listing Subkeys and Values

OpenSubKey also calls the Refresh methods of the key's SubKeys and Values collections. You can then manipulate any of these using the appropriate collection reference. For example, Listing 10.13 shows how you would print the names and handles of any subordinate keys and the names and contents of any values.

Listing 10.13: List a Key's Subkeys and Values

```
Dim objSubKey As Key
Dim objValue As Value
Dim cObject As Long

' List any subkeys
Debug.Print "Subkeys:"
For cObject = 1 To objKey.SubKeys.Count
    Set objSubKey = objKey.SubKeys.Item(cObject)
    Debug.Print objSubKey.Name, objSubKey.Handle
Next
' List any values
Debug.Print "Values:"
For cObject = 1 To objKey.Values.Count
    Set objValue = objKey.Values.Item(cObject)
    Debug.Print objValue.Name, objValue.Value
Next
```

Creating New Keys and Values

To create new subkeys and values, just add new objects to the SubKeys and Values collections. Listing 10.14 demonstrates how to add a new subkey called "CustomOptions". We first use the SubKeyExists method to determine whether the key already exists, and if it does, we use the Remove method of the SubKeys collection to delete it.

Listing 10.14: Add a New Subkey and Values

```
' Check to see whether it exists, and if so, delete it
If objKey.SubKeyExists("CustomOptions") Then
    objKey.SubKeys.Remove "CustomOptions"
End If

' Add a new subkey beneath ...\Desktop
Set objNewKey = objKey.SubKeys.Add("CustomOptions")
Debug.Print "Added: " & objNewKey.FullPath

' Set the default value
objNewKey.Values.Item("").Value = "Default"

' Add a string value
Set objNewValue = objNewKey.Values. _
 Add("SomeString", rc.RegSz)
objNewValue.Value = "This is great fun!"
```

```
Debug.Print "Added: " & objNewValue.FullPath

' Add a DWORD (long) value
Set objNewValue = objNewKey.Values. _
 Add("SomeDWORD", rc.RegDWord)
objNewValue.Value = 1024
Debug.Print "Added: " & objNewValue.FullPath

' Add a binary value
Set objNewValue = objNewKey.Values. _
 Add("SomeBinary", rc.RegBinary)
objNewValue.Value = Array(0, 1, 2, 4, 8, 16, 32, 64, 128)
Debug.Print "Added: " & objNewValue.FullPath
```

After the procedure adds the new subkey, it adds some new values to it. It starts with the default value, which was added to the Values collection when the subkey was created. It then creates a new string, DWORD, and binary values. Note that the binary value is created using an array of integers between 0 and 255. The screen in Figure 10.5 shows the new subkey and values displayed in REGEDIT.

FIGURE 10.5

Viewing the newly added information

Summary

If you're a serious developer, you'll have to delve into the Registry sooner or later. While you can use the Windows Registry Editor application, it is not practical to force your users to do this. In this chapter, we've looked at two ways to programmatically manipulate the contents of the Registry, including built-in VBA functions as well as a number of API functions. Specifically, we discussed the following topics:

- Understanding the structure of the Windows Registry
- Using the VBA functions GetSetting, GetAllSettings, DeleteSetting, and SaveSetting
- Manipulating keys using the API functions RegOpenKeyEx, RegCreateKeyEx, and RegCloseKey
- Manipulating values using the API functions RegQueryValueEx and RegSetValueEx
- Enumerating keys and values using the API functions RegEnumKeyEx and RegEnumValue
- Building an object model for the Registry using VBA class modules

You should now be able to tackle just about any Registry problem.

CHAPTER
ELEVEN

11

The Windows Networking API

- Using common network dialogs

- Connecting to/disconnecting from shared network resources

- Retrieving network information

- Enumerating network resources

- Using the LAN Manager API

VBA does not directly expose many of the networking capabilities of Windows 95 and Windows NT. Although it does allow you to make use of objects such as mapped drives and network paths once they exist, the ability to find, connect to, disconnect from, or enumerate these objects is not available in VBA. However, all of these actions are available through the Windows API. In this chapter, we cover many of the most useful functions in the WNet and Lan Manager APIs to help you make your applications more "network aware."

> **NOTE**
>
> Why cover both WNet and Lan Manager API calls? The WNet API calls are simpler to use, in general, and solve most of your networking needs. The LAN Manager API functions are more general purpose, require a bit more work to use, and can be a bit intimidating, with over 100 different functions to choose from. In this chapter, we provide an overview of both sets of networking API functions, with the emphasis on WNet functions—the ones most people need. In addition, the LAN Manager API functions are not available from Windows 95, but only from Windows NT, so their use is limited by that distinction as well.

Table 11.1 lists the sample files you'll find on the CD-ROM.

TABLE 11.1 Sample Files

File Name	Description
NETWORK.XLS	Excel 97 file with sample functions
NETWORK.MDB	Access 97 database with sample functions
NETWORK.BAS	Text file with sample functions

Basic Network Functionality

This section examines the basic network functions you might want to use in your applications, such as:

- Connecting to network resources with standard dialogs
- Disconnecting from network resources with standard dialogs

- Connecting to network resources via code

- Disconnecting from network resources via code

- Retrieving information about network resources

Using Common Network Dialogs

The easiest way, and the one users will find most familiar, to add network awareness to your applications is to use the dialogs the operating system provides that allow you to connect to and disconnect from network resources.

Connecting to a Network Resource with a Dialog

The screen in Figure 11.1 provides an example of the Windows NT 4.0 network connection dialog. Be aware, however, that network connection dialog boxes vary between operating systems. Although Windows NT 3.51 and 4.0 use similar dialog boxes, the dialog box Windows 95 uses is very different. It requires you to type in a UNC path, and it provides an MRU (Most Recently Used) list of connections made previously, but there are none of the browse capabilities you find in Windows NT. The more limited Windows 95 dialog is shown in Figure 11.2.

FIGURE 11.1

Connecting to network resources with the Windows NT 4.0 connection dialog

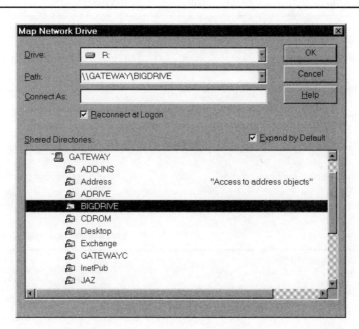

FIGURE 11.2

Connecting to network
resources with the
Windows 95 connection
dialog

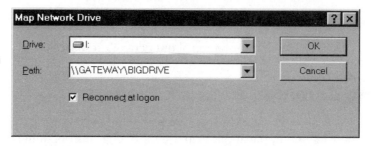

The declaration you use to invoke the dialog is as follows:

```
Private Declare Function WNetConnectionDialog Lib "mpr.dll" _
(ByVal hwnd As Long, ByVal dwType As Long) As Long
```

The only information you pass to the dialog is the window handle that will be the parent of the dialog (or 0 to use the Windows screen as the parent, effectively specifying no parent window), and the type of resources to display. The common constants used by the dialog are shown in Table 11.2.

TABLE 11.2 Commonly Used Constants for the Network Dialogs

Constant	Value	Meaning
dhcNoError	0&	Function call was successful
dhcDlgCancelled	−1&	User canceled the dialog
dhcErrorExtendedError	1208&	An extended error has occurred
dhcErrorInvalidPassword	86&	Given password is invalid
dhcErrorNoNetwork	1222&	No network was detected
dhcErrorNotEnoughMemory	8&	There is not enough memory to display the dialog
dhcResourceTypeDisk	1&	Use a resource of "disk" type
dhcResourceTypePrint	2&	Use a resource of "print" type

In general, we've found it easier not to call the networking API functions directly, because it's important to make sure all the parameters are set up properly. We've provided wrapper functions for each API function to ensure that each function is called correctly. Most of the API calls return an error code that tells you whether the call succeeded; in some cases, the wrapper functions will do the same, and in other cases, they will use the return value internally.

Listing 11.1 demonstrates a function you can use to call the WNetConnection-Dialog API.

Listing 11.1: Wrapper Function to Call the Network Connection Dialog

```
Public Function dhConnectDlg(Optional ByVal hwnd As Long = 0) _
 As Long
    ' Display the dialog to connect to network resources

    Dim lngReturn As Long
    Dim lngExtendedError As Long

    ' Call the net connection dialog
    lngReturn = WNetConnectionDialog(hwnd, dhcResourceTypeDisk)

    ' If the call failed, get error information
    If lngReturn <> dhcNoError Then
        lngExtendedError = dhGetLastNetworkError(True)

        ' If there was an extended error, return it,
                    ' instead of the standard error
        dhConnectDlg = IIf(lngExtendedError = dhcNoError, _
          lngReturn, lngExtendedError)
    End If
End Function
```

Under Windows NT, you can pass only the dhcResourceTypeDisk flag, but under Windows 95, you can pass the dhcResourceTypePrint flag as well, which allows you to connect to network printers.

Modifying the WNetConnectionDialog MRU List

One way to get around the lack of browse capabilities in the Windows 95 dialog and to enhance the Windows NT dialog is to add your own items to the MRU list. These entries are stored in the Registry under the following two keys (depending on your operating system):

```
' For Windows NT:
HKEY_CURRENT_USER\Software\Microsoft\Windows NT\ _
 Current Version\Network\Persistent Connections
' For Windows 95:
HKEY_CURRENT_USER\Network\Recent
```

Each value in the Registry, under the specific key, is a string; its name is a letter of the alphabet, and its value is the item that goes in the list. Following the list of alphabetically named keys, you'll find a value named Order, which contains a string defining the order in which to display records. To add an item to the MRU list, you add the item to the list of values and then add its corresponding letter to the Order list. If you do update this list, make sure you remove your changes when you are done if you don't want the changes to remain. The screen in Figure 11.3 shows the Registry keys associated with a sample environment. For more information on reading and writing information in the Registry, see Chapter 10.

FIGURE 11.3

Use the Registry to modify the MRU list for connections.

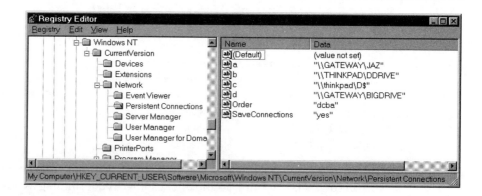

Retrieving Extended Network Error Information

One interesting thing to note about the code in Listing 11.1 is the extra work dhConnectDlg does to decide which error code to return. The main reason for this extra work is historical: the WNetConnectionDialog function, which has been around for quite some time, returns the same basic error values that the 16-bit version did: 0 for success, –1 for cancellation, and a few specific error values. Rather than change the return values for this function, which would break compatibility with converted applications, Microsoft chose to use the extended error capability provided by the WNetGetLastError function in order to return detailed information. Other network API functions use it as well, but the WNetDisconnect-Dialog function uses it extensively because it doesn't return much error information on its own.

The dhConnectDlg function, as well as several other functions in this chapter, call the dhGetLastNetworkError function to retrieve extended error information. Many of the WNet API functions may return dhcErrorExtendedError, which requires you to call the WNetGetLastError API immediately to get more detailed error information. We've provided dhGetLastNetworkError as a wrapper around the WNetGetLastError API function; this wrapper returns the extended error number and, if more information is available, displays a message box providing that information. The code for dhGetLastNetworkError is shown in Listing 11.2.

Listing 11.2: Get Information about the Last Network Error That Occurred

```
Public Function dhGetLastNetworkError( _
 Optional fDisplayError As Boolean = False) As Long
    ' Get error information from the last network operation

    Dim lngReturn As Long
    Dim lngError As Long
    Dim strError As String
    Dim lngErrorLen As Long
    Dim strProvider As String
    Dim lngProviderLen As Long

    ' Set up buffers for the error info (they should be at
    ' least 256 characters, but it doesn't hurt to make them
    ' longer
    strError = String$(256, vbNullChar)
    strProvider = String$(256, vbNullChar)
    lngErrorLen = Len(strError)
    lngProviderLen = Len(strProvider)

    ' Try to get the extended error info
    lngReturn = WNetGetLastError(lngError, strError, _
```

```
           lngErrorLen, strProvider, lngProviderLen)

    If lngReturn = dhcNoError Then
        dhGetLastNetworkError = lngError
        ' If there was extended error info and the calling
        ' procedure wanted it to be displayed here, then
        ' display it
        If fDisplayError And lngError <> dhcNoError Then
            strError = dhTrimNull(strError)
            strProvider = dhTrimNull(strProvider)
            MsgBox "Error " & lngError & ": " & strError, _
            vbInformation, strProvider
        End If
    End If
End Function
```

> **WARNING**
>
> The most important thing to note about the WNetGetLastError API call is that it returns only the *most recent* error value. You must call dhGetLastNetworkError immediately after you call a function that might have returned an error. If the user performs any network operation, either manually or through some other application, the information about your program's error will be gone forever.

Disconnecting from a Network Resource with a Dialog

As part of your application, you may need to provide a method for users to break a network connection. This functionality is provided by the WNetDisconnect-Dialog API function, and its declaration is almost identical to that for WNet-ConnectionDialog:

```
Private Declare Function WNetDisconnectDialog Lib "mpr.dll" _
  (ByVal hwnd As Long, ByVal dwType As Long) As Long
```

This function brings up the dialog shown in Figure 11.4. To call it, you can use the wrapper function dhDisconnectDialog, shown in Listing 11.3.

FIGURE 11.4

Disconnecting from network resources with the Windows NT disconnection dialog

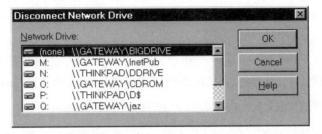

Listing 11.3: Disconnecting from Network Resources

```
Public Function dhDisconnectDialog( _
 Optional ByVal hwnd As Long = 0) As Long
    ' Display the dialog to disconnect from network resources

    Dim lngReturn As Long
    Dim lngExtendedError As Long

    ' Call the net disconnect dialog
    lngReturn = WNetDisconnectDialog(hwnd, dhcResourceTypeDisk)

    ' If the call failed, get error information
    If lngReturn <> dhcNoError Then
        lngExtendedError = dhGetLastNetworkError(True)
        ' If there was an extended error, return it,
        ' instead of the standard error
        dhDisconnectDialog = IIf( _
          lngExtendedError = dhcNoError, _
          lngReturn, lngExtendedError)
    End If
End Function
```

As with dhConnectDlg, the return value will usually be either dhcNoError, if the dialog disconnected something, or dhcDlgCancelled, if the user canceled the dialog. It may also be one of the constants listed earlier in Table 11.2.

Other Dialogs You Can Use

In addition to dhConnectDlg and dhDisconnectDlg, you can use the standard Windows File Open dialog, discussed in Chapter 12, which contains a convenient "Network" button that allows the user to connect to a network resource. This dialog is also familiar to most users and is easy to add to your application. When you wish to connect to a network resource, you often also want to select a file once you're connected, so this may be the easiest way to add network awareness to your application.

There are several advantages to using the dialogs the operating system provides:

- They are easy to call and integrate into your applications.
- Their look and feel will be familiar to the user.
- All the work of doing the actual network connections and disconnects is handled by the dialogs themselves.

Of course, there are also some disadvantages:

- When the function call succeeds, you have no easy way of knowing what resources the user connected to.
- There is no way to customize the interface of the dialogs to help it fit into your applications.
- You cannot control the way a connection is made. (For example, you cannot specify whether this connection should persist if the user reboots the machine.)

Because of these problems, many applications that need to add networking capabilities also need to do the work themselves rather than let these dialogs do the work for them. The following section provides information on bypassing the standard dialog boxes.

Handling Network Resources Yourself

Sometimes you'll want your application to handle all the details of connecting to and disconnecting from network resources. This section covers many of these basic functions.

Connecting to a Network Resource

There are two Win32 API functions that let you connect to a network resource: WNetAddConnection and WNetAddConnection2. The first API call maintains compatibility with the older 16-bit API and is simpler to call, but it isn't as flexible and doesn't return as much information as the newer version. We present both functions here, but you'll normally want to use WNetAddConnection2 in your applications.

The declarations and types for these functions are shown here:

```
Private Type NETRESOURCE
    dwScope As Long
    dwType As Long
    dwDisplayType As Long
    dwUsage As Long
    lpLocalName As String
    lpRemoteName As String
    lpComment As String
    lpProvider As String
End Type

Private Declare Function WNetAddConnection Lib "mpr.dll" Alias _
  "WNetAddConnectionA" (ByVal strNetPath As String, _
  ByVal strPassword As String, ByVal strLocalName As String) _
  As Long

Private Declare Function WNetAddConnection2 Lib "mpr.dll" Alias _
  "WNetAddConnection2A" (lpNetResource As NETRESOURCE, _
  ByVal strPassword As String, ByVal strUserName As String, _
  ByVal lngFlags As Long) As Long
```

To call WNetAddConnection, you need only pass in the following parameters:

- Path to which you wish to connect

- Password (if there is one) or a zero-length string

- Local name to which you wish to map this new resource

You can use the dhAddConnection1 function, shown in Listing 11.4, to call WNetAddConnection.

Listing 11.4: Connect Resources with WNetAddConnection

```
Function dhAddConnection1(strNetPath As String, _
  strPwd As String, strLocalName As String) As Long
    ' Adds a network connection
    dhAddConnection1 = WNetAddConnection(strNetPath, _
      strPwd, strLocalName)
End Function
```

You can call dhAddConnection1 as follows:

```
lngReturn = dhAddConnection1("\\middlemarch\setup", _
    "password","J:")
```

This connects the local J drive to the specified network share using a password of "password". If you are using an NT domain security model for your network, the connection will be created with the permissions of the currently logged-in user.

The constants associated with both WNetAddConnection and WNetAddConnection2 are listed in Table 11.3.

TABLE 11.3 Commonly Used Constants for WNetAddConnection and WNetAddConnection2

Constant	Value	Meaning
dhcNoError	0&	Function call was successful
dhcErrorAccessDenied	5&	Insufficient permissions to the specified resource
dhcErrorAlreadyAssigned	85&	Given local name is already assigned to another resource
dhcErrorBadDevType	66&	Device type and resource type do not match
dhcErrorBadDevice	1200&	Device is invalid
dhcErrorBadNetName	67&	Remote resource is invalid or cannot be found
dhcErrorBadProfile	1206&	User profile is in an incorrect format
dhcErrorCannotOpenProfile	1205&	User profile cannot be accessed to update persistent information
dhcErrorDeviceAlready-Remembered	1202&	An entry for the specified local name is already in the user profile
dhcErrorExtendedError	1208&	An extended error has occurred
dhcErrorInvalidPassword	86&	Given password is invalid
dhcErrorNoNetOrBadPath	1203&	Specified remote resource could not be found or the name is invalid
dhcErrorNoNetwork	1222&	No network was detected

TABLE 11.3 Commonly Used Constants for WNetAddConnection and WNetAddConnection2 (continued)

Constant	Value	Meaning
dhcResourceTypeAny	0&	Use a resource of any type
dhcResourceTypeDisk	1&	Use a resource of "disk" type
dhcResourceTypePrint	2&	Use a resource of "print" type
dhcMaxPath	260	Maximum number of characters allowed in a path for the remote name
dhcConnectUpdateProfile	1&	Update the user profile to retain this connection after the user reboots
dhcConnectDontUpdateProfile	0&	Don't update the user profile

In many cases, WNetAddConnection is simply not flexible enough. You may need to connect with the user name and password of another user (perhaps one with different permissions). You may want to control whether this connection will be persistent if the user reboots the machine, or you may want to specify the network provider when there are multiple networks. If you require these options, you need to use WNetAddConnection2, and you can do so using the dhAddConnection2 wrapper, shown in Listing 11.5.

Listing 11.5: Connect Resources with WNetAddConnection2

```
Function dhAddConnection2(strNetPath As String, _
 strLocalName As String, strUserName As String, _
 strPwd As String, Optional fPersistent As Boolean = True, _
Optional fDisk As Boolean = True) As Long
    ' Adds a network connection

    Dim usrNetResource As NETRESOURCE
    Dim lngFlags As Long

    With usrNetResource
        .dwType = IIf(fDisk, dhcResourceTypeDisk, _
          dhcResourceTypePrint)
        .lpLocalName = strLocalName
```

```
        .lpRemoteName = strNetPath
        .lpProvider = vbNullString
    End With
    lngFlags = IIf(fPersistent, dhcConnectUpdateProfile,_
      dhcConnectDontUpdateProfile)

    dhAddConnection2 = WNetAddConnection2(usrNetResource, _
      strPwd, strUserName, lngFlags)
End Function
```

The function takes the following parameters:

Parameter	Description
strNetPath	UNC path to which to connect
strLocalName	Local name for the resource (such as K:)
strUserName	User whose permissions should be used for logging in
strPwd	Password for the user given by strUserName
fPersistent	Indicates whether to retain this connection after the user reboots (optional; default is True)
fDisk	Indicates whether this is a disk resource. True indicates a disk resource; False indicates a print resource (optional; default is True)

The function fills in the members of the NETRESOURCE structure and then calls WNetAddConnection2 for you. Here is an example of calling dhAddConnection2:

```
lngReturn = dhAddConnection2("\\middlemarch\setup", "K:", _
  "Sam", "", False)
```

This call will connect the K drive to the specified resource with the permissions of the user named Sam (who has no password). When the user reboots, this connection will not be reestablished.

Disconnecting from a Network Resource

Just as there are two ways to add a network resource, there are two API functions for disconnecting them: WNetCancelConnection and WNetCancelConnection2. The only added feature of the second function is that you can choose whether to update the user's profile with the information that you have disconnected the resource. (If you do not update the user's profile, the resource will be back the next time the user logs in.) The declarations for these functions are shown here:

```
Private Declare Function WNetCancelConnection Lib _
 "mpr.dll" Alias "WNetCancelConnectionA" _
 (ByVal lpszName As String, ByVal fForce As Long) As Long

Private Declare Function WNetCancelConnection2 Lib _
 "mpr.dll" Alias "WNetCancelConnection2A" _
 (ByVal lpName As String, ByVal dwFlags As Long, _
 ByVal fForce As Long) As Long
```

The common constants that can be used with these functions are shown in Table 11.4.

TABLE 11.4 Commonly Used Constants for WNetCancelConnection and WNetCancelConnection2

Constant	Value	Meaning
dhcNoError	0&	Function call was successful
dhcErrorBadProfile	1206&	User profile is in an incorrect format
dhcErrorCannotOpenProfile	1205&	User profile cannot be accessed to update persistent information
dhcErrorDeviceInUse	2404&	Device is currently in use and the Force parameter was not set to True
dhcErrorExtendedError	1208&	An extended error has occurred
dhcErrorNotConnected	2205&	Given resource is not currently connected
dhcErrorOpenFiles	2401&	Device is currently in use and files on it are open, and the Force parameter was not set to True
dhcConnectUpdateProfile	1&	Update the user profile to reflect that this resource was disconnected
dhcConnectDontUpdateProfile	0&	Don't update the user profile

To call WNetCancelConnection, you can use dhCancelConnection1, shown in Listing 11.6. Pass this function the name of the resource to disconnect from and an optional Boolean value (its default is False) indicating whether you want to force the disconnect even if files are open or devices are in use.

Listing 11.6: Disconnect from Resources with WNetCancelConnection

```
Public Function dhCancelConnection1(strLocalName As String, _
 Optional fForceDisconnect As Boolean = False) as Long
    ' Cancels a network connection

    dhCancelConnection1 = WNetCancelConnection( _
     strLocalName, Abs(fForceDisconnect))
End Function
```

> **TIP**
>
> Note that dhCancelConnection1 uses the Abs (absolute value) function when passing the Boolean parameter fForceDisconnect. Many API calls specify that they accept a Boolean parameter, but C++ defines True as 1, while VBA defines True as −1. In most cases, the API calls check for any value that's not False (that is, anything except 0), so this difference isn't relevant. There are exceptions, however—for example, when a DLL is checking specifically for a True (1) value, in which case passing a VBA Boolean True (−1) will fail. This is not an issue when a DLL passes a value to your program: if you define a variable as a Boolean and a DLL passes a 1 into it, VBA treats it correctly as True.

Calling WNetCancelConnection2 using the dhCancelConnection2 function (shown in Listing 11.7) is similar. This function adds one more flag, in which you can specify whether you'd like the user's profile to be updated.

Listing 11.7: Disconnect from Resources with WNetCancelConnection2

```
Public Function dhCancelConnection2(strLocalName As String, _
 Optional fForceDisconnect As Boolean = False, _
 Optional fUpdateProfile As Boolean = True) As long
    ' Cancels a network connection

    Dim lngFlags As Long
```

```
lngFlags = IIf(fUpdateProfile, dhcConnectUpdateProfile, _
    dhcConnectDontUpdateProfile)

dhCancelConnection2 = WNetCancelConnection2(strLocalName, _
    lngFlags, Abs(fForceDisconnect))
End Function
```

WARNING

Your users will find few things more frustrating or confusing than having you disconnect network resources that are in use. Because of this, you should *always* call dhCancelConnection1 and dhCancelConnection2 with the fForceDisconnect parameter set to False. If the return value is dhcErrorOpenFiles or dhcErrorDeviceInUse, you can warn the user that there are open files and that there is a risk of losing unsaved data in these files. If the user confirms wanting to disconnect the connection, you can then try to cancel it again, this time setting fForceDisconnect to True.

Retrieving Information about Network Resources

For part of your networked application, you may need to know the UNC path of a specific mapped network drive or the name of the currently logged-in user, or perhaps you need to get (or even change) the name of the computer. This section discusses these topics.

NOTE

Chapter 9 included methods similar to the dhGetUserName, dhGet-ComputerName, and dhSetComputerName functions. Because you're likely to use these functions when working with other networking functionality, it seemed worthwhile to repeat their use, in slightly different format, in this chapter.

Getting a UNC Path from a Mapped Network Drive

Imagine this common scenario: in the current session, your application's user has modified a file on a mapped network drive. The next time the user logs in, the drive mapping has changed, and your application can no longer find the same file. How do you work around this problem? Rather than store information about the mapped drive, you convert the drive mapping into a UNC path (including the server and drive name), using the WNetGetConnection API call. This function takes a local path as its input parameter, and it attempts to return a UNC path. (It may fail, of course, because there may not be a corresponding remote path if you've specified an incorrect local path.)

The declaration for WNetGetConnection looks like this:

```
Private Declare Function WNetGetConnection Lib "mpr.dll" _
  Alias "WNetGetConnectionA" (ByVal strLocalName As String, _
  ByVal strRemoteName As String, lngRemoteNameLen As Long) As Long
```

This function accepts the local name, a buffer to contain the UNC path, and the length of the buffer. On return, it will have filled in the buffer with the UNC path (if it succeeded). The return value will be dncNoError on success or one of the standard error codes on failure. The most common constants are listed in Table 11.5.

TABLE 11.5 Commonly Used Constants for WNetGetConnection

Constant	Value	Meaning
dhcNoError	0&	Function call was successful
dhcErrorBadDevice	1200&	Local name is invalid
dhcErrorNotConnected	2205&	Given resource is not currently connected
dhcErrorMoreData	234	Buffer is too small (The buffer length parameter will contain the length that is needed when the function returns this error.)
dhcErrorExtendedError	1208&	An extended error has occurred
dhcErrorConnectionUnavailable	1201&	Device is not currently connected, but it is a persistent connection
dhcErrorNoNetwork	1222&	No network is present
dhcErrorNoNetOrBadPath	1203&	Specified remote resource could not be found or the name is invalid

To call WNetGetConnection, you can use the dhGetRemoteName wrapper function, which takes the local name and returns the UNC path (or a zero-length string if it fails). The code for this function is shown in Listing 11.8.

Listing 11.8: Get a UNC Path from a Mapped Network Drive

```
Public Function dhGetRemoteName(strLocalName As String) As String
    ' Given a mapped network resource, returns the UNC path

    Dim lngRemoteNameLen As Long
    Dim strRemoteName As String
    Dim lngReturn As Long

    Do
        ' Set up the buffer
        strRemoteName = String$(lngRemoteNameLen, vbNullChar)

        lngReturn = WNetGetConnection(strLocalName, _
         strRemoteName, lngRemoteNameLen)

        ' Continue looping until the call succeeds or the error
        ' is  anything besides "there's more data"
    Loop Until lngReturn <> dhcErrorMoreData

    If lngReturn = dhcNoError Then
        dhGetRemoteName = dhTrimNull(strRemoteName)
    End If
End Function
```

The Do…Loop structure in dhGetRemoteName uses an interesting, and somewhat common, technique to fill the output buffer. Initially, the value of lngRemoteNameLen is 0, and the first pass through the loop sets strRemoteName to contain 0 characters, using the String function:

```
Do
    ' Set up the buffer
    strRemoteName = String$(lngRemoteNameLen, vbNullChar)
```

When you call WNetGetConnection with a buffer that's too small for its returned data, the function fills its lngRemoteNameLen parameter with the length of the buffer it needs and returns dhcErrorMoreData:

```
    lngReturn = WNetGetConnection(strLocalName, _
    strRemoteName, lngRemoteNameLen)
```

```
        ' Continue looping until the call succeeds or the error is
        ' anything besides "there's more data"
Loop Until lngReturn <> dhcErrorMoreData
```

The second time through the loop, the code sets strRemoteName to contain enough space for the return value, so WNetGetConnection will correctly fill the buffer and return a value other than dhcErrorMoreData.

You can save the performance hit of making two calls by setting lngRemote-NameLen initially to a value that you guess is large enough, or you can use the same method dhGetRemoteName uses to set the buffer to exactly the right amount.

The following code fragment gives an example of using dhGetRemoteName to replace a mapped network drive with a UNC path when one exists:

```
' Convert from "T:\SAMPLE.TXT" to
' \\GATEWAY\JAZ\SAMPLE.TXT", assuming that
' T:\ is mapped to \\GATEWAY\JAZ.
If Mid$(strFilePath, 2, 1) = ":" Then
    strRemote = dhGetRemoteName(Left$(strFilePath, 2))
    If Len(strRemote) > 0 Then
        strFilePath = strRemote & Mid$(strFilePath, 3)
    End If
End If
```

NOTE Rather than use WNetGetConnection, as dbGetRemoteName does, you can use another API function Windows provides that will do the work of putting the path together for you; it even splits up the server and share portions of the UNC path (the connection information) automatically from the rest of the path. This API function, WNetGetUniversalName, is covered in the section "Calling WNetGetUniversalName" later in this chapter.

Retrieving the Name of the Currently Logged-In User

You may have applications in which you wish to integrate network security by changing the application's interface or actions based on the currently logged-in user. Whether this is to add security, maintain user preferences and settings, track usage, or for any other reason, knowing who is using the application can be valuable. You can retrieve this information using the WNetGetUser API call, declared like this:

```
Private Declare Function WNetGetUser Lib "mpr" Alias _
 "WNetGetUserA" (ByVal strName As String, _
 ByVal strUserName As String, lngLength As Long) As Long
```

This function actually has two uses, depending on what you pass into the first parameter. If you pass an empty string in the strName parameter, the strUserName buffer will contain the name of the currently logged-in user. If you specify a resource such as a mapped drive, the buffer will contain the user name (or Windows NT domain and user name) that was specified when the connection was created. This function can be called both ways with the dhGetUserName function, which takes an optional parameter that is passed in as the strName parameter to WNetGetUser. You can see the code for dhGetUserName, which is very similar to dhGetRemoteName, in Listing 11.9. The constants that are commonly returned by WNetGetUser are shown in Table 11.6.

Listing 11.9: Use WNetGetUser to Identify the Currently Logged-In User

```
Public Function dhGetUserName _
 (Optional strLocalName As String = vbNullString) As String
    ' Retrieve the current network user name

    Dim lngUserNameLen As Long
    Dim strUserName As String
    Dim lngReturn As Long

    Do
        ' Set up the buffer
        strUserName = String$(lngUserNameLen, vbNullChar)

        lngReturn = WNetGetUser(strLocalName, strUserName, _
            lngUserNameLen)
    Loop Until lngReturn <> dhcErrorMoreData

    If lngReturn = dhcNoError Then
        dhGetUserName = dhTrimNull(strUserName)
    End If
End Function
```

TABLE 11.6 Commonly Used Constants for WNetGetUser

Constant	Value	Meaning
dhcNoError	0&	Function call was successful
dhcErrorNotConnected	2205&	Given resource is not currently connected
dhcErrorMoreData	234	Buffer is too small (The buffer length parameter will contain the length that is needed when the function returns this error.)
dhcErrorExtendedError	1208&	An extended error has occurred
dhcErrorNoNetwork	1222&	No network is present
dhcErrorNoNetOrBadPath	1203&	Specified remote resource could not be found or the name is invalid

Getting (and Setting) the Computer Name

In an application that is network aware, you might want to be able to obtain the name of the workstation on which the application is running. The Registry contains this information, and the value is initialized when you log in to Windows. Although you could simply read this information from the Registry, when you change this value (through the Network Properties dialog or the Windows API, or by using REGEDIT.EXE), the computer's "knowledge" of its name does not change until the computer is rebooted. Therefore, the value in the Registry may not be the actual name of the computer.

The Win32 API provides two functions—GetComputerName and SetComputerName—to get and retrieve the information. Their declarations are shown here:

```
Private Declare Function GetComputerName Lib "kernel32" _
  Alias "GetComputerNameA" (ByVal strBuffer As String, _
  lngSize As Long) As Long
Private Declare Function SetComputerName Lib "kernel32" _
  Alias "SetComputerNameA" (ByVal strComputerName As String) _
  As Long
```

GetComputerName takes a buffer and the buffer's size as parameters; it fills in the buffer with the computer name and returns a nonzero value when successful.

SetComputerName takes the new computer name and sets it. (The name will not actually change until you reboot the machine.) You can call the API functions with the dhGetComputerName and dbSetComputerName wrappers, which are shown in listing 11.10.

Listing 11.10: Get and Set the Computer Name

```
Public Function dhGetComputerName() As String
    ' Return the workstation's computer name

    Dim lngReturn As Long
    Dim lngBufferSize As Long
    Dim strBuffer As String

    ' Make the buffer big enough for the name plus a vbNullChar
    lngBufferSize = dhcMaxComputernameLength + 1
    strBuffer = String$(lngBufferSize, vbNullChar)

    lngReturn = GetComputerName(strBuffer, lngBufferSize)

    If CBool(lngReturn) Then
        dhGetComputerName = Left(strBuffer, lngBufferSize)
    End If
End Function

Public Function dhSetComputerName(strComputerName) As Boolean
    ' Sets the workstation's computer name

    Dim lngReturn As Long

    lngReturn = SetComputerName(strComputerName)

    dhSetComputerName = CBool(lngReturn)

End Function
```

Advanced Networking Functionality

The basic network functions, discussed in the first part of this chapter, can handle most of your networking requirements. Sometimes, however, you need more than just the basics. This section covers some of the advanced networking features you can add to your VBA applications, such as:

- Retrieving more information about remote resources than WNetGetConnection can provide

- Enumerating connected network resources

- Enumerating available network shares

- Enumerating computers on the network

- Using the LAN Manager API

Calling WNetGetUniversalName

The WNetGetUniversalName function can return either a UNC version of a particular remote path (for example, "\\GATEWAY\JAZ\Updates" when you pass it "T:\Updates", when drive T is mapped to \\GATEWAY\JAZ) or a structure filled with information about the mapping, including the various pieces of the string "\\GATEWAY\JAZ\Updates", to keep you from having to parse the string yourself. Calling the function, however, presents some interesting challenges that are also applicable to many other API function calls. This section discusses using the WNetGetUniversalName function and some of the difficulties involved in calling it from VBA. This discussion also serves as an introduction to the next section, "Enumerating Network Resources," which addresses the issues involved in performing network enumerations, where many of the same problems arise. Luckily, all of these problems can be solved and the functions can be called successfully from VBA.

Introduction to the Buffer Problem

In theory, all the WNet functions should be as easy to call as the ones you have seen so far. In practice, however, Microsoft has made calling some of the WNet functions from VBA more difficult. The problem is that some of these functions use data structures containing addresses to strings, not the strings themselves, making it tricky to send and retrieve information from these API calls. For example, here is the declaration for the WNetGetUniversalName API:

```
Private Declare Function WNetGetUniversalName Lib "mpr" _
 Alias "WNetGetUniversalNameA" (ByVal strLocalPath As String, _
 ByVal lngInfoLevel As Long, lpBuffer As Any, _
 lngBufferSize As Long) As Long
```

At first glance, the lpBuffer and lngBufferSize parameters look the same as they did in other functions, such as WNetGetUser. However, this time, the buffer will contain a variable of one of the following user-defined types:

```
Private Type UNIVERSAL_NAME_INFO
    lpUniversalName As String
End Type

Private Type REMOTE_NAME_INFO
    lpUniversalName As String
    lpConnectionName As String
    lpRemainingPath As String
End Type
```

The problem here is that the API function call allocates space for the strings used by these data structures in the buffer *immediately following the structure in memory*, but strings inside these user-defined types are actually pointers to buffers containing the text. Therefore, a successful call to WNetGetUniversalName using the REMOTE_NAME_INFO structure might produce a buffer that looks something like the diagram in Figure 11.5.

FIGURE 11.5

Anatomy of the REMOTE_NAME_INFO buffer in the advanced WNet API calls

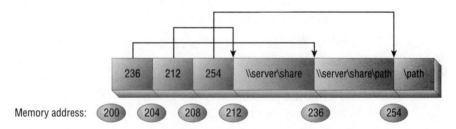

It all boils down to this: if you call the function properly, you know that all the information is inside the buffer. However, without being able to decipher where the pointers in the REMOTE_NAME_INFO structure are pointing, you have no clean way to extract the information. As the diagram in Figure 11.5 implies, you cannot even parse the three strings manually, because you can't assume their order within the buffer.

How to Solve the Buffer Problem

You can use a few tricks to solve the buffer problem. The first trick is to use a byte array for the buffer rather than a string or a REMOTE_NAME_INFO structure. The heart of the function would look like this:

```
Dim lngReturn As Long
Dim abyt() As Byte
Dim lngBufferSize As Long

Do
    ReDim abyt(lngBufferSize)
    lngReturn = WNetGetUniversalName(strLocalPath, _
    dhcRemoteNameInfoLevel, abyt(0), lngBufferSize)
Loop Until lngReturn <> dhcErrorMoreData
```

One option for setting the lngBufferSize parameter would be to simply retrieve the length of the REMOTE_NAME_INFO structure. If you try this, however, you'll find that the length is 12 (the size of three long integers, which matches the three long pointers to strings in the structure). Because the buffer you send to WNetGetUniversalName must also contain the strings themselves, a buffer having a length that was the size of the structure would never be big enough! But because the code is using a byte array instead, you can make it exactly the right size, using the ReDim statement.

When you call WNetGetUniversalName, you send the first element of the byte array as the buffer. Because the byte array is guaranteed to be contiguous in memory, WNetGetUniversalName can write into the array, given only its first element. After the function call, you'll have the data in a byte array, and the next task is to find out how to convert the three pointers into three actual strings. It takes several steps to accomplish this.

1. **Convert each of the 4-byte groups back into a long integer.**

There are several ways to accomplish this goal, some more obtuse than others. We've opted for the simplest method: letting VBA do the work for you. Using VBA's LSet statement, you can assign the bytes in one user-defined datatype to those in another. To convert the 4-byte group back into a long integer, NETWORK .BAS contains two datatypes and a simple function to perform the conversion:

```
' Temporary types for data conversion.
Private Type Bytes
    Byte1 As Byte
    Byte2 As Byte
```

```
        Byte3 As Byte
        Byte4 As Byte
    End Type

    Private Type TempLong
        lngValue As Long
    End Type

    Private Function dhCvtBytesToLong(abyt() As Byte, _
     intIndex As Integer) As Long

        ' Convert from 4 bytes into a long integer, using LSet.
        Dim usrBytes As Bytes
        Dim usrLong As TempLong
        If UBound(abyt) < intIndex + 3 Then
            ' If there's not enough bytes in the array,
            ' then return 0.
            dhCvtBytesToLong = 0
        Else
            ' LSet requires user-defined types on
            ' both sides of the equal sign, so
            ' fill in the right-hand structure.
            With usrBytes
                .Byte1 = abyt(intIndex)
                .Byte2 = abyt(intIndex + 1)
                .Byte3 = abyt(intIndex + 2)
                .Byte4 = abyt(intIndex + 3)
            End With
            ' Copy the four bytes into a structure
            ' that contains a long integer.
            LSet usrLong = usrBytes
            dhCvtBytesToLong = usrLong.lngValue
        End If
    End Function
```

The dhCvtBytesToLong function accepts, as parameters, an array of bytes and the index in the array at which you want the procedure to start copying. If there are 4 bytes starting at the index (that is, if you've supplied a reasonable starting position), the code copies the 4 bytes into a Bytes data structure and then uses LSet to copy the bytes into a TempLong structure. Once VBA has moved the bytes and performed the conversion, the function returns the equivalent long integer.

2. **Convert the address into an offset within the array of bytes.**

After performing the numeric conversion, lngPointer contains the address of the particular string, in memory, which still doesn't do you any good. You'll need to convert that address into an offset within the array of bytes in order to use the string. Luckily, that conversion is easy: you can retrieve the address of the first element of the array and then subtract that value from the address in lngPointer. The result of this subtraction, finally, will be the offset of the string you're interested in within the array of bytes. For example, if your lngPointer value is 254 and the byte array starts at 200, then the string starts at abyt(54). (Anyone who's laboring under the delusion that you can't perform pointer arithmetic in VBA is clearly wrong, right?)

Using VarPtr, ObjPtr, and StrPtr

VBA 5.0 contains three useful undocumented functions: VarPtr, StrPtr, and ObjPtr. VarPtr returns the address of the variable passed to it (otherwise referred to as a pointer to the variable). StrPtr returns a pointer to a string variable, and ObjPtr returns a pointer to an object variable. There are many situations, especially in API calls, in which these functions can be useful.

Be careful, however! Because these functions are undocumented, they are not supported parts of the VBA function library. As such, they may not exist in future versions of VBA. On the other hand, some of the Microsoft Wizards use these functions, so chances are, they'll stick around.

There are several ways to retrieve the address of the first element of the array of bytes (including writing DLLs that take a string or other type and return a pointer to it), but the easiest way is to use the undocumented VarPtr function. The final formula for finding the index in the array where the string starts, then, is

```
lngPointer = dhCvtBytesToLong(abyt, intIndex)
lngIndex = lngPointer - VarPtr(abyt(0))
```

3.   **Find the end of the string.**

The final step is to move through the array from lngIndex until you hit a Null byte (a byte with the value 0), indicating the end of the string you're attempting to extract. The finished function, dhConvertByteArrayPartToString, accepts as parameters the byte array and the location of the pointer within the array of bytes (in the REMOTE_NAME_INFO case, lpUniversalName is 0, lpConnectionName is 4, and lpRemainingPath is 8), and it returns the actual string that was being pointed to. Listing 11.11 contains the entire dhConvertByteArrayPartToString function.

Listing 11.11: The dhConvertByteArrayPartToString Function

```
Private Function dhConvertByteArrayPartToString( _
 abyt() As Byte, _
 intIndex As Integer) As String
    ' Converts a pointed -to part of a byte array into a string

    Dim lngCurrentIndex As Long
    Dim lngPointer As Long
    Dim lngByteArraySize As Integer
    Dim strOut As String
    Dim fDone As Boolean

    strOut = vbNullString
    lngByteArraySize = UBound(abyt)

    ' Get the value of the pointer to the string
    lngPointer = dhCvtBytesToLong(abyt, intIndex)

    ' Get the index value of the array where the string starts
    lngCurrentIndex = lngPointer - VarPtr(abyt(0))

    ' If the index is valid, then continue
    If lngCurrentIndex > 0 Then

        ' Loop until you reach a null byte
        Do Until abyt(lngCurrentIndex) = 0 Or _
         lngCurrentIndex > lngByteArraySize

            strOut = strOut & Chr$(abyt(lngCurrentIndex))

            ' move to next character
            lngCurrentIndex = lngCurrentIndex + 1
        Loop
    End If

    dhConvertByteArrayPartToString = strOut
End Function
```

Both the dhGetRemoteInfo and dhGetUniversalInfo functions, shown in Listing 11.12, call this useful (if somewhat unusual) function.

Listing 11.12: Calling WNetGetUniversalName in Two Ways

```
Public Function dhGetRemoteInfo(strLocalPath As String, _
  usrRemoteNameInfo As REMOTE_NAME_INFO) As Long
    ' Fill a REMOTE_NAME_INFO structure given a local path

    Dim lngReturn As Long
    Dim abyt() As Byte
    Dim lngBufferSize As Long

    Do
        ReDim abyt(lngBufferSize)
        lngReturn = WNetGetUniversalName(strLocalPath, _
          dhcRemoteNameInfoLevel, abyt(0), lngBufferSize)
    Loop Until lngReturn <> dhcErrorMoreData

    If lngReturn = dhcNoError Then
        ' If the call succeeded,
        ' fill the REMOTE_NAME_INFO structure
        With usrRemoteNameInfo
            .lpUniversalName = _
            dhConvertByteArrayPartToString(abyt, 0)
            .lpConnectionName = _
            dhConvertByteArrayPartToString(abyt, 4)
            .lpRemainingPath = _
            dhConvertByteArrayPartToString(abyt, 8)
        End With
    End If

    dhGetRemoteInfo = lngReturn

End Function

Public Function dhGetUniversalInfo(strLocalPath As String, _
  usrUniversalNameInfo As UNIVERSAL_NAME_INFO) As Long
    ' Fill a UNIVERSAL_NAME_INFO structure given a local path

    Dim lngReturn As Long
    Dim abyt() As Byte
    Dim lngBufferSize As Long
```

```
    Do
        ReDim abyt(lngBufferSize)
        lngReturn = WNetGetUniversalName(strLocalPath, _
            dhcUniversalNameInfoLevel, abyt(0), lngBufferSize)
    Loop Until lngReturn <> dhcErrorMoreData

    If lngReturn = dhcNoError Then
        ' If the call succeeded, fill the
        ' UNIVERSAL_NAME_INFO structure
        With usrUniversalNameInfo
            .lpUniversalName = _
            dhConvertByteArrayPartToString(abyt, 0)
        End With
    End If

    dhGetUniversalInfo = lngReturn

End Function
```

The information provided in this section for dhConvertByteArrayPartToString will become important in the discussion of network enumerations in the next section of this chapter since the network API calls that handle enumerations use buffers in exactly the same way WNetGetUniversalName does.

For example, to call these two functions, you might write code like this:

```
Sub TestUniversal(strPath As String)
    Dim uni As UNIVERSAL_NAME_INFO
    Dim rni As REMOTE_NAME_INFO
    Call dhGetUniversalInfo(strPath, uni)
    Call dhGetRemoteInfo(strPath, rni)
    Debug.Print "Universal Name : " & uni.strUniversalName
    Debug.Print
    Debug.Print "Connection Name: " & rni.strConnectionName
    Debug.Print "Remaining Path : " & rni.strRemainingPath
    Debug.Print "Universal Name : " & rni.strUniversalName
End Sub
```

For a path like "T:\Updates", where you've mapped drive T to \\GATEWAY\JAZ, the results should look like this:

```
Universal Name : \\GATEWAY\jaz\Updates

Connection Path: \\GATEWAY\jaz
Remaining Path : \Updates
Universal Name : \\GATEWAY\jaz\Updates
```

You can see that these two functions can save you from having to parse the full UNC path name.

Enumerating Network Resources

The discussions earlier in this chapter on connecting to, disconnecting from, and getting information on network resources assumed that either you or your users know what devices are available. Other than dhConnectDlg, we have presented no interface that gives you a choice of devices to work with. What if you want to provide your own interface, allowing users to select network devices? You'll need to use some sort of enumeration technique asking the Windows API to provide you with a list of available devices.

Enumerating network devices is a three-step process:

1. Retrieve an enumeration handle, given the starting point for your enumeration.

2. Given the enumeration handle, work through all the contained resources, performing whatever action you need with each resource. Usually, you'll just want to retrieve each device's name to place into a list.

3. Close the enumeration handle once you're done with it.

The Windows API provides three functions that handle the three steps of network enumerations: WNetOpenEnum, WNetEnumResource, and WNetClose-Enum. You'll call all three to retrieve a list of devices. Think of an enumeration handle as a conduit through which the API returns information about devices, and before you can retrieve a list of devices, you must retrieve an enumeration handle from Windows. To do that, you call WNetOpenEnum, passing several flags about the type of resources you wish to enumerate, and it supplies an enumeration handle. You'll use this handle to retrieve your list of devices, and you enumerate the resources using the WNetEnumResource function. You call this function repeatedly—it fills in a NETRESOURCE structure containing information about each resource—until it's run out of available network resources to enumerate. When you're finished enumerating devices, you use the WNetCloseEnum function to release the enumeration handle. Although this technique may not be the most ideal interface for VBA, the alternative would have been for Windows to allow you to specify a callback function, which it would call as it found each requested resource. Because VBA doesn't directly handle callback functions, this alternative would leave VBA programmers out in the cold.

The next few sections look at using the WNetOpenEnum, WNetEnumResource, and WNetCloseEnum functions to retrieve lists of available network resources.

Getting a Network Enumeration Handle

Retrieving the enumeration handle is the most critical part of the process of enumerating network resources because it's your only chance to indicate to Windows exactly what resources you're looking for. Because you can enumerate everything from connections that are currently on your machine to network shares on someone else's machine (and everything in between), the way you handle the call to WNetOpenEnum controls exactly what you get back from Windows. When you call WNetOpenEnum, you pass three pieces of information:

- Scope of the enumeration
- Types of resources for the enumeration
- Resource usage for the enumeration

The possible value for each parameter is shown in Tables 11.7, 11.8, and 11.9.

TABLE 11.7 Enumeration Scope Constants

Constant	Value	Meaning
dhcResourceConnected	&H1	All currently connected resources
dhcResourceGlobalNet	&H2	All resources on the network
dhcResourceRemembered	&H3	All remembered (persistent) resources

TABLE 11.8 Enumeration Type Constants

Constant	Value	Meaning
dhcResourceTypeAny	&H0	All resource types
dhcResourceTypeDisk	&H1	All disk resources
dhcResourceTypePrint	&H2	All printer resources

TABLE 11.9 Enumeration Usage Constants

Constant	Value	Meaning
dhcResourceUsageAll	&H0	All resources
dhcResourceUsageConnectable	&H1	All connectable resources
dhcResourceUsageContainer	&H2	All container resources

The scope of an enumeration tells Windows where to look for resources. You choose a value from Table 11.7 to specify the necessary scope. If you specify either dhcResourceConnected or dhcResourceRemembered, the enumeration will work through devices on a single machine. (In addition, the Usage flag will be ignored because it applies only when you're dealing with the global network-wide scope.)

The enumeration type constants are straightforward: they let you choose whether you want to look at disks or printers. In addition, if the server on which you're performing an enumeration supports sharing other resources, such as COM ports, they will show up only when you specify any resource, using the dhcResourceTypeAny. If the operating system cannot distinguish among different resource types, it may return all resource types and ignore the enumeration type flag.

You use the enumeration usage flag when choosing the dhcResourceGlobalNet scope. The concept is a little confusing, but it boils down to this: some resources (such as network shares) can be connected to, and some resources, instead, contain other resources. By specifying the correct flag from Table 11.9, you indicate which type of global resource you'd like to enumerate. Think of it this way: if a resource is a container, you can use it to call WNetOpenEnum again in order to see what resources are inside the container. If the resource is connectable, you can pass the remote name string right to WNetAddConnection2 (or our wrapper dhAddConnection2) and connect to the resource.

> **TIP**
>
> The following discussion of working with enumeration handles contains a great deal of detail concerning the use of the low-level enumeration functions. The "Putting It All Together" section later in this chapter provides some wrapper functions to make it simpler to enumerate resources without dealing directly with enumeration handles. You'll find it simpler to use the wrapper functions, and you'll most likely use these functions instead of the WNetEnum functions, but it's important to understand the lower-level details first.

Here is the declaration of WNetOpenEnum:

```
Private Declare Function WNetOpenEnum Lib "mpr" Alias _
 "WNetOpenEnumA" (ByVal lngScope As Long, _
 ByVal lngType As Long, ByVal lngUsage As Long, _
 lpNetResource As Any, lngEnum As Long) As Long
```

The lpNetResource parameter can be either a variable of the NETRESOURCE type or a null value. The NETRESOURCE type was discussed in the section "Connecting to a Network Resource" earlier in this chapter. Its definition is as follows:

```
Private Type NETRESOURCE
    dwScope As Long
    dwType As Long
    dwDisplayType As Long
    dwUsage As Long
    lpLocalName As String
    lpRemoteName As String
    lpComment As String
    lpProvider As String
End Type
```

This structure contains information on the scope, type, and usage of the network resource, as well as the display type. Possible values for this field are listed in Table 11.10.

TABLE 11.10   NetResource Display Type Constants

Constant	Value	Meaning
dhcResourceDisplayTypeGeneric	&H0	Display type does not matter
dhcResourceDisplayTypeDomain	&H1	Object should be displayed as a domain
dhcResourceDisplayTypeServer	&H2	Object should be displayed as a server
dhcResourceDisplayTypeShare	&H3	Object should be displayed as a network share

If you pass a null value for the lpNetResource parameter, the enumeration will start at the root of the network. If you supply a NETRESOURCE structure, you can enumerate resources within a specific network resource, such as a particular drive. That is, you can also call WNetOpenEnum with a NETRESOURCE structure filled in, as long as the dwUsage member is set to dhcResourceUsageContainer. (You can't enumerate the resources inside a resource that doesn't contain other resources, such as a printer.)

There are two ways to use WNetOpenEnum:

- You can call WNetOpenEnum twice, passing in Null the first time. Once you've got a list of all the available resources, you can use any specific resource and call WNetOpenEnum again, using the information about the particular resource.

- You can call WNetOpenEnum once if you already know the name of the resource you want to enumerate. If you can fill in the NETRESOURCE structure yourself, you don't need to call WNetOpenEnum twice.

To separate the two uses of WNetOpenEnum, we have provided two wrappers, dhGetTopLevelEnumHandle and dhGetNetResourceEnumHandle. The first function allows you to get the enumeration handle for the entire network, and the second allows you to get the handle for a specific container device. Both functions are shown in Listing 11.13.

> **NOTE**
>
> Remember, WNetOpenEnum retrieves an enumeration handle that you'll be able to use if you want to enumerate resources (that is, retrieve information about all the specified network resources). To do that, however, you'll need to use the WNetEnumResource API call discussed in the section "Enumerating Resources" later in this chapter. The examples in this section merely retrieve the handle for you so you can later enumerate the specified set of resources.

Listing 11.13: Retrieve Enumeration Handles with WNetOpenEnum

```
Public Function dhGetTopLevelEnumHandle(lngScope As Long, _
lngType As Long, lngUsage As Long) As Long
    ' Opens a top-level network resource enumeration handle

    Dim lngReturn As Long
    Dim hEnum As Long
```

```
      ' Since this is a top-level item, pass in the fourth
      ' parameter as Null
      lngReturn = WNetOpenEnum(lngScope, lngType, lngUsage, _
      Null, hEnum)

      If lngReturn = dhcNoError Then
          dhGetTopLevelEnumHandle = hEnum
      End If
End Function

Public Function dhGetNetResourceEnumHandle(lngScope As Long, _
  lngType As Long, lngUsage As Long, usrNetResource _
  As NETRESOURCE) As Long
      ' Opens a resource enumeration handle for a given NetResource

      Dim lngReturn As Long
      Dim hEnum As Long

      lngReturn = WNetOpenEnum(lngScope, lngType, lngUsage, _
      usrNetResource, hEnum)

      If lngReturn = dhcNoError Then
          dhGetNetResourceEnumHandle = hEnum
      End If

End Function
```

Let's take a look at some examples to make this process a little clearer.

The easiest example is a simple call to dhGetTopLevelEnumHandle to find out all the currently connected network drives. (Note that under Windows NT, some drives will be connected but may not have drive letters associated with them.) The call to open the network enumeration handle would look like this:

```
hEnum = dhGetTopLevelEnumHandle(dhcResourceConnected, _
  dhcResourceTypeDisk, dhcResourceUsageAll)
```

Or you might want to get a top-level handle to the entire network. (In the Windows NT network connection dialog, this is the "Microsoft Windows Network" node that appears above the domains.)

```
hEnum = dhGetTopLevelEnumHandle(dhcResourceGlobalNet, _
  dhcResourceTypeAny, dhcResourceUsageAll)
```

After calling dhGetTopLevelEnumHandle, you'll be able to call WNetEnum-Resource to investigate all the resources on the network. For any resource that's a container, such as a domain or server, you'll be able to call dhGetNetResource-EnumHandle and enumerate the resources that item contains. The NT network connection dialog does something like this to fill the tree view–like display in the bottom half of its window, as shown earlier in Figure 11.1.

If you need, for example, to look at the network disk shares on another machine and you know its name, you can use code like the following to open the enumeration handle:

```
' See TestEnum1 in NETWORK.BAS
Dim usrNetResource As NETRESOURCE
Dim hEnum as Long

With usrNetResource
    .dwDisplayType = dhcResourceDisplayTypeServer
    .dwScope = dhcResourceGlobalNet
    .dwUsage = dhcResourceUsageContainer
    .dwType = dhcResourceTypeDisk
    .lpRemoteName = "\\YourServer"
End With

hEnum = dhGetNetResourceEnumHandle(dhcResourceGlobalNet, _
  dhcResourceTypeDisk, dhcResourceUsageConnectable, usrNetResource)
```

You can then use this handle to obtain all the available network shares on the server whose name you've supplied. Or if you wanted to get the names of all computers in a particular domain, you could use code like this:

```
' See TestEnum2 in NETWORK.BAS
Dim usrNetResource As NETRESOURCE
Dim hEnum as Long
With usrNetResource
    .dwDisplayType = dhcResourceDisplayTypeDomain
    .dwScope = dhcResourceGlobalNet
    .dwUsage = dhcResourceUsageContainer
    .dwType = dhcResourceTypeDisk
    .lpRemoteName = \\"YourDomain"
End With

hEnum = dhGetNetResourceEnumHandle(dhcResourceGlobalNet, _
  dhcResourceTypeDisk, dhcResourceUsageContainer, usrNetResource)
```

This handle allows you to enumerate all the machines in the network specified by your domain name. Code presented in the section "Enumerating Resources" a little later in this chapter shows you how to use the enumeration handles you've opened.

Closing an Enumeration Handle

You should always close anything you open (a prime rule for getting along in life, as well as in programming), and network enumeration handles are no exception. You use the WNetCloseEnum API function to do this, and its declaration looks like this:

```
Private Declare Function WNetCloseEnum Lib "mpr.dll" _
 (ByVal hEnum As Long) As Long
```

For the sake of consistency, we've provided a wrapper for this call, although calling this function directly is simple. The function, dhCloseEnum, is shown in Listing 11.14.

Listing 11.14: Use dhCloseEnum to Close Enumeration Handles

```
Public Function dhCloseEnum(hEnum As Long) As Long
    ' Closes a resource enumeration handle

    dhCloseEnum = WNetCloseEnum(hEnum)
End Function
```

It's a good idea to have your code close a handle as soon as you're done with it. In theory, even if you don't close the handles, they will be closed when you shut down the host application you opened them from (Word, Excel, Access, and so on), but an explicit close is cleaner and frees up the resources right away.

Enumerating Resources

It's finally time to start using the enumeration handles discussed above to obtain information! This section discusses the use of WNetEnumResource. This API function is the workhorse that takes the enumeration handle from WNetOpenEnum and uses it to retrieve information about each available network resource.

The declaration of WNetEnumResource is as follows:

```
Private Declare Function WNetEnumResource Lib "mpr.dll" _
 Alias "WNetEnumResourceA" (ByVal hEnum As Long, _
 lngCount As Long, lpBuffer As Any, lngBufferSize As Long) _
 As Long
```

The hEnum parameter is a handle obtained by WNetOpenEnum. (You can use either the dhGetNetResourceEnumHandle or the dhGetTopLevelEnumHandle flag to obtain the handle.) The lngCount parameter specifies the number of items you wish to receive. We've seen some unpredictable results trying to obtain more than one at a time, so the wrapper function we provide, dhEnumNext, requests only one at a time. As it turns out, there is no substantial performance hit for multiple calls to WNetEnumResource; although calls to WNetOpenEnum can take a little while, calls to WNetEnumResource do their work quickly.

The lpBuffer and lngBufferSize parameters are identical to the ones discussed with regard to the WNetGetUniversalName API function. Once again, as described in the section "How to Solve the Buffer Problem" earlier in this chapter, you'll need to use the dhConvertByteArrayPartToString function to retrieve the string values from lpBuffer.

The heart of the dhEnumNext function is the same Do…Loop structure that has been used in several other WNet calls:

```
' Initialize the byte array buffer
ReDim abyt(0)

Do
    ' Set the buffer length variable
    lngBufferLength = UBound(abyt)
    lngReturn = WNetEnumResource(hEnum, 1, _
     abyt(0), lngBufferLength)

    ' Set the size of the buffer if it was not big enough
    ' (This is almost guaranteed since we start with
    ' only one byte!)
    If lngReturn = dhcErrorMoreData Then
        ReDim abyt(lngBufferLength)
    End If

' Loop until finish or hit an error other
than "more data than buffer can hold"
Loop Until lngReturn <> dhcErrorMoreData
```

The second half of the dhEnumNext function contains the logic that takes the elements out of the byte array and puts them into a NETRESOURCE type. Before you do this, take another look at the NETRESOURCE definition:

```
Private Type NETRESOURCE
    dwScope As Long
    dwType As Long
```

```
        dwDisplayType As Long
        dwUsage As Long
        lpLocalName As String
        lpRemoteName As String
        lpComment As String
        lpProvider As String
End Type
```

For example, if you are enumerating connected network resources (drive mappings to UNC paths), when you receive lpBuffer back from WNetEnumResource, it might be laid out as shown in the diagram in Figure 11.6.

FIGURE 11.6

lpBuffer layout after it is filled with a NetResource structure

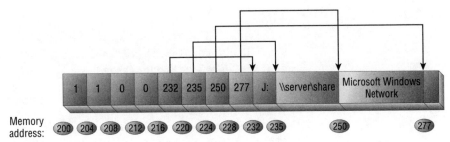

The first 16 bytes are the four long integers in the NETRESOURCE structure (dwScope, dwType, dwDisplayType, and dwUsage). The code uses the dhCvtBytesToLong function to convert each series of 4 bytes into a long integer.

The next 16 bytes are also four long integers, but each of these is actually a pointer to a string. To convert each of these, you can use dhConvertByteArrayPartToString. The dhEnumNext function uses the following code to perform the entire conversion from the byte array into the NETRESOURCE structure:

```
With usrNetResource
     .dwScope = dhCvtBytesToLong(abyt, 0)
     .dwType = dhCvtBytesToLong(abyt, 4)
     .dwDisplayType = dhCvtBytesToLong(abyt, 8)
     .dwUsage = dhCvtBytesToLong(abyt, 12)
     .lpLocalName = ConvertByteArrayPartToString(abyt, 16)
     .lpRemoteName = ConvertByteArrayPartToString(abyt, 20)
     .lpComment = ConvertByteArrayPartToString(abyt, 24)
     .lpProvider = ConvertByteArrayPartToString(abyt, 28)
End With
```

627

Listing 11.15 contains the complete code for the dhEnumNext function.

Listing 11.15: Enumeration with dhEnumNext

```
Public Function dhEnumNext(hEnum As Long, _
usrNetResource As NETRESOURCE) As Long
    ' Enumerate the next resource in hEnum and put the info in
    ' usrNetResource

    Dim lngReturn As Long
    Dim lngBufferLength As Long
    Dim abyt() As Byte

    ' Initialize the byte array buffer
    ReDim abyt(0)

    Do
        ' Set the buffer length variable
        lngBufferLength = UBound(abyt)
        lngReturn = WNetEnumResource(hEnum, 1, abyt(0), _
          lngBufferLength)

        ' Set the size of the buffer if it was not big enough
        ' (This is guaranteed since we start with only one byte!)
        If lngReturn = dhcErrorMoreData Then
            ReDim abyt(lngBufferLength)
        End If

        ' Loop until we finish or hit an error other than
        ' "more data than buffer can hold"
    Loop Until lngReturn <> dhcErrorMoreData

    If lngReturn = dhcNoError Then
        ' If the call succeeded, there is a byte array full of
        ' pointers to data and the actual data. Put all this info
        ' into the NetResource type that was passed into the
        ' procedure.
        With usrNetResource
            .dwScope = dhCvtBytesToLong(abyt, 0)
            .dwType = dhCvtBytesToLong(abyt, 4)
            .dwDisplayType = dhCvtBytesToLong(abyt, 8)
            .dwUsage = dhCvtBytesToLong(abyt, 12)
            .lpLocalName = ConvertByteArrayPartToString(abyt, 16)
            .lpRemoteName = _
            ConvertByteArrayPartToString(abyt, 20)
            .lpComment = ConvertByteArrayPartToString(abyt, 24)
```

```
            .lpProvider = ConvertByteArrayPartToString(abyt, 28)
        End With
    End If

    dhEnumNext = lngReturn
End Function
```

In some applications, you may need to enumerate network resources one by one until you find the one you're searching for, or perhaps you'll have some other reason to enumerate network resources individually. In most cases, however, you'll need to specify the type of resources you want and then have a function return an array of NETRESOURCE structures that meet your criteria. We present a wrapper function that does this in the next section.

Putting It All Together

The wrapper function, dhGetNetResourceInfo, does all the work of calling the enumeration functions for you. This function takes the following parameters:

Parameter	Description
lngScope	One of the values in Table 11.7
lngType	One of the values in Table 11.8
lngUsage	One of the values in Table 11.9
usrNetResource	An array of NETRESOURCE structures. On return, this array has been filled with NET-RESOURCE structures that match the requested parameters
fSpecifyStart	A Boolean value that tells the function whether the next parameter (usrNetResourceStart) is going to be passed; it should be False if you want to use the network root to start your enumeration and True if you wish to pass in usrNetResourceStart as the root of the enumeration
usrNetResourceStart	A NETRESOURCE type specifying the beginning of the enumeration if you want to start anywhere but at the network root; this must be passed in even if fSpecifyStart is False, but in that case its members can be empty because it will not be used

The full listing for this function is shown in Listing 11.16.

Listing 11.16: Doing It All with dhGetNetResourceInfo

```
Public Function dhGetNetResourceInfo(lngScope As Long, _
 lngType As Long, lngUsage As Long, _
 usrNetResource() As NETRESOURCE, _
 fSpecifyStart As Boolean, usrNetResourceStart As NETRESOURCE) _
As Boolean

    ' Retrieve all the NETRESOURCEs specified by the parameters

    Dim hEnum As Long
    Dim lngCount As Integer
    Dim lngReturn As Long

    ' If fSpecifyStart is selected use the usrNetResourceStart
    ' info as the root for the enumeration. Otherwise, assume
    ' the top level.
    If fSpecifyStart Then
        hEnum = dhGetNetResourceEnumHandle(lngScope, lngType, _
        lngUsage, usrNetResourceStart)
    Else
        hEnum = dhGetTopLevelEnumHandle(lngScope, lngType, _
        lngUsage)
    End If

    If hEnum <> 0 Then
        Do While lngReturn = dhcNoError
            ReDim Preserve usrNetResource(lngCount)

            lngReturn = dhEnumNext(hEnum, _
            usrNetResource(lngCount))
            ' lngReturn will be dhcErrorNoMoreItems when we are
            ' done. When this happens, remove the last entry
            ' from the array since it was never filled.
            If lngReturn = dhcErrorNoMoreItems Then
                ReDim Preserve usrNetResource(lngCount - 1)
            End If
            lngCount = lngCount + 1
        Loop

        lngReturn = dhCloseEnum(hEnum)
        dhGetNetResourceInfo = True
```

```
    Else
        ' Handle was not opened
        dhGetNetResourceInfo = False
    End If
End Function
```

This function handles all the details of opening and closing the handles and fills in the array of NETRESOURCE types that you pass it. You can pass any one of the array elements into dhGetNetResourceInfo if its dwUsage member contains dhcResourceUsageContainer, indicating that the item is a container for other network resources.

The three examples shown in Listing 11.17 (from NETWORK.BAS) all call the dhGetNetResourceInfo function. One example obtains all the computers in a given domain (dhSampleEnumPCsInDomain), one obtains all the network shares available on a given computer (dhSampleEnumSharesOnPC), and one obtains all the mapped network resources on the current machine (dhSampleEnumConnected-ResourcesOnLocalPC). The difference in each case is the specific parameters passed in, and possibly the values placed in the usrNetResourceStart parameter (depending on the function you've called).

NOTE In each sample function, you're passing an empty array of NET-RESOURCE structures to the dhGetNetResourceInfo function. This function fills in the array, and on return from the function call, the array contains one element for each network resource the function found, matching the criteria you specified when you called the function. The sample functions iterate through the array, one item at a time, displaying text in the Immediate window.

Listing 11.17: Sample Functions That Call dhGetNetResourceInfo

```
Public Sub dhSampleEnumPCsInDomain(strDomainName As String)
    ' Retrieve all the servers in the given domain
    ' For example,
    ' dhSampleEnumPCsInDomain "Warburton"
    ' will list all the servers on the domain named "Warburton"

    Dim usrNetResource() As NETRESOURCE
    Dim usrNetResourceStart As NETRESOURCE
```

```
        Dim i As Integer

        With usrNetResourceStart
            .dwScope = dhcResourceGlobalNet
            .lpRemoteName = strDomainName
        End With

        If dhGetNetResourceInfo(dhcResourceGlobalNet, _
         dhcResourceTypeDisk, dhcResourceUsageContainer, _
         usrNetResource(), True, _
         usrNetResourceStart) Then
            For i = LBound(usrNetResource) To UBound(usrNetResource)
                Debug.Print usrNetResource(i).lpRemoteName
            Next i
        End If

    End Sub

    Public Sub dhSampleEnumSharesOnPC(strMachineName As String)
        ' Retrieve all the shares on the given machine
        ' For example,
        ' dhSampleEnumSharesOnPC "Marge"
        ' will list all the shares on the machine named Marge.

        Dim usrNetResource() As NETRESOURCE
        Dim usrNetResourceStart As NETRESOURCE
        Dim i As Integer

        With usrNetResourceStart
            .dwScope = dhcResourceGlobalNet
            .lpRemoteName = IIf(Left$(strMachineName, 2) = "\\", _
            vbNullString, "\\") & strMachineName
        End With

        If dhGetNetResourceInfo(dhcResourceGlobalNet, _
         dhcResourceTypeDisk, dhcResourceUsageConnectable, _
         usrNetResource(), True, usrNetResourceStart) Then
            For i = LBound(usrNetResource) To UBound(usrNetResource)
                Debug.Print usrNetResource(i).lpRemoteName
            Next i
        End If

    End Sub

    Public Sub dhSampleEnumConnectedResourcesOnLocalPC()
        ' Retrieve all the connections on the current machine
        ' For example:
```

```
' dhSampleEnumConnectedResourcesOnLocalPC
' will list all the local and remote names
' for all the attached, shared devices.

Dim usrNetResource() As NETRESOURCE
Dim usrNetResourceStart As NETRESOURCE
Dim i As Integer

If dhGetNetResourceInfo(dhcResourceConnected, _
 dhcResourceTypeDisk, 0, usrNetResource(), False, _
 usrNetResourceStart) Then
    For i = LBound(usrNetResource) To UBound(usrNetResource)
        Debug.Print usrNetResource(i).lpLocalName & _
         " is connected to " & usrNetResource(i).lpRemoteName
    Next i
End If
End Sub
```

As you can see, WNetEnumResource is extremely powerful: it can perform many different operations and return a great deal of information. Unfortunately, this quick look just scratches the surface of what this function can do, but it should be enough to get you going.

Using the Shell32 Browse Dialog

Hidden within the shell extensions for Windows 95 and Windows NT 4.0 is a dialog you can use to browse through any folder on the local machine and any computer or share on the network. This dialog is used in several Windows applications, such as the Windows 95 Network Monitor and RegEdit. Figure 11.7 shows the dialog box in action. (You can try it out yourself by opening RegEdit and selecting Registry ➤ Connect Network Registry from the menus and then clicking Browse.)

If you can be assured that your VBA application will be used only on Windows 95 or NT 4.0 (this dialog box isn't available in Windows NT 3.51), you can feel free to use this dialog. The three API calls you need are listed here:

```
Private Declare Function SHGetSpecialFolderLocation _
 Lib "Shell32.DLL" _
 (ByVal hwndOwner As Long, ByVal lngFolder As Long, _
 ByRef idl As Long) As Long

Private Declare Function SHGetPathFromIDList Lib "Shell32.DLL" _
 (ByVal idl As Long, ByVal Path As String) As Integer
```

```
Private Declare Function SHBrowseForFolder Lib "Shell32.DLL" _
    (ByRef bi As BrowseInfo) As Long
```

FIGURE 11.7

Shell32 Extensions
Browse dialog

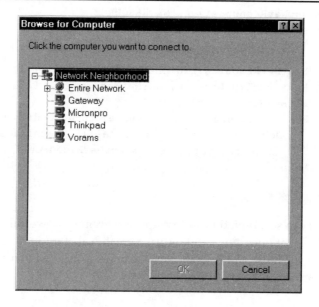

These three functions work together to allow you to browse any type of network resource with the same interface. You can call these functions directly, or you can use the wrapper function we've provided, dhBrowseForFolder, shown in Listing 11.18. The next few paragraphs detail the steps taken by the dhBrowseForFolder function, giving you the ammunition you need to write your own function using the common browsing dialog box.

In addition to the three API functions shown above, you'll need to use the BrowseInfo data structure:

```
Private Type BrowseInfo
    hwndOwner As Long
    pidlRoot As Long
    strDisplayName As String
    strTitle As String
    ulFlags As Long
    ' You won't use any of the following fields, from VBA.
    lpfn As Long
    lParam As Long
    iImage As Long
End Type
```

Using these functions requires four steps. (The code displayed here is from the dhBrowseForFolder function, shown in Listing 11.18.)

1. You must specify a root object, from the items listed in Table 11.11. Call SHGetSpecialFolderLocation, passing in the chosen constant, to retrieve the internal value for that object. This identifier is called the object's IDList (or IDL).

```
If SHGetSpecialFolderLocation(hWnd, lngCSIDL, lngIDL) = 0 Then
```

2. Once you've got a valid IDL, you must fill in a BrowseInfo user-defined data structure. The IDL goes in there, along with 0 or more flags from Table 11.12 combined with the Or operator. These flags control which objects will be displayed in the dialog.

```
With usrBrws
    .hwndOwner = hWnd
    .pidlRoot = lngIDL
    .strDisplayName = String$(dhcMaxPath, vbNullChar)
    .strTitle = strTitle
    .ulFlags = lngBifFlags
End With
```

3. Once the BrowseInfo structure has been filled in, you call SHBrowseFor-Folder, passing in the BrowseInfo structure you just filled in:

```
' Open the browse dialog
lngIDL = SHBrowseForFolder(usrBrws)
```

4. On return from SHBrowseForFolder, the strDisplayName member of the BrowseInfo structure will contain the name selected in the dialog box. If you want to turn this into a full path (and most likely, you do), you must first create a buffer large enough to hold the maximum path and then call SHGetPathFromIDList. This function takes the return value from SHBrowseForFolder and converts it into the full selected path:

```
strFolder = String$(dhcMaxPath, vbNullChar)

' Try to resolve the lngIDL into a real path
If SHGetPathFromIDList(lngIDL, strFolder) Then
    ' Trim the null characters
    strFolder = dhTrimNull(strFolder)
    lngReturn = dhcNoError
Else
    ' No real directory path is available, so at least
    ' return the virtual selection
```

```
        strFolder = dhTrimNull(usrBrws.strDisplayName)
        lngReturn = dhcNoError
    End If
```

The constants you can use to specify the root directory for the dialog are specified in Table 11.11. (Note that unlike the common File Open dialog, you cannot go above the starting root, so choose your starting point with care!) The constants that limit valid choices are shown in Table 11.12. If a choice is visible in the dialog but is not valid, the OK button will be disabled any time that object is selected.

TABLE 11.11   Constants for Specifying the Root Directory in the Browse Dialog

Constant	Value	Meaning
dhcCSIdlDesktop	&H0	Main (virtual) desktop directory
dhcCSIdlPrograms	&H2	File system directory that matches the Programs menu
dhcCSIdlControlPanel	&H3	Virtual folder containing the control panel icons
dhcCSIdlInstalledPrinters	&H4	Virtual folder containing installed printers
dhcCSIdlPersonal	&H5	User's personal folder
dhcCSIdlFavorites	&H6	User's favorites folder
dhcCSIdlStartupPmGroup	&H7	User's startup group off the Programs menu
dhcCSIdlRecentDocDir	&H8	Recent document directory
dhcCSIdlSendToItemsDir	&H9	"SendTo" items directory
dhcCSIdlRecycleBin	&HA	Recycle bin
dhcCSIdlStartMenu	&HB	Start menu root directory
dhcCSIdlDesktopDirectory	&H10	File system desktop directory
dhcCSIdlMyComputer	&H11	My Computer virtual directory
dhcCSIdlNetworkNeighborhood	&H12	Network Neighborhood virtual directory
dhcCSIdlNetHoodFileSystemDir	&H13	File system NetHood directory

TABLE 11.11 Constants for Specifying the Root Directory in the Browse Dialog (continued)

Constant	Value	Meaning
dhcCSIdlFonts	&H14	Fonts directory
dhcCSIdlTemplates	&H15	New document templates directory

TABLE 11.12 Constants to Limit the Choices in the Shell32 Browse Dialog (continued)

Constant	Value	Meaning
dhcBifReturnAll	&H0	No restrictions
dhcBifReturnOnlyFileSystemDirs	&H1	Only choices that can be resolved to a real directory can be chosen
dhcBifDontGoBelowDomain	&H2	Don't include network folders below the domain level
dhcBifIncludeStatusText	&H4	Include room for status text (must be filled in via a callback function, so this constant cannot be used from VBA)
dhcBifFileSystemAncestors	&H8	User must seiect a file system ancestor
dhcBifBrowseForComputer	&H1000	Return only computers
dhcBifBrowseForPrinter	&H2000	Return only printers

WARNING If you want to use dhBrowseForFolder to allow users to select a computer, the SHBrowseForFolder API function has one important shortcoming that will cause you trouble: the subsequent call to SHGetPathFromIDList will not recognize the IDList returned from SHBrowseForFolder as a valid path, so it returns an error. (If you choose a share *underneath* a computer, it works fine—the problem exists only if you select a computer.) If you select just a computer, even though you can't determine the full path name, the display name is still available. This information is enough when you're working with computer names. The dhBrowseForFolder function we've provided here always returns the display name if no full path is available.

The function that calls the dialog, dhBrowseForFolder, is shown in Listing 11.18.

Listing 11.18: Call the Shell32 Extensions Browse Dialog

```
Public Function dhBrowseForFolder(ByVal lngCSIDL As Long, _
 ByVal lngBifFlags As Long, strFolder As String, _
 Optional ByVal hWnd As Long = 0, _
 Optional strTitle As String = "Select Directory") As Long

    ' Browse for a folder

    Dim usrBrws As BrowseInfo
    Dim lngReturn As Long
    Dim lngIDL As Long

    ' First get the special folder that lngCSIDL and lngID
    ' specify
    If SHGetSpecialFolderLocation(hWnd, lngCSIDL, lngIDL) = 0 _
    Then

        ' Set up the browse structure
        With usrBrws
            .hwndOwner = hWnd
            .pidlRoot = lngIDL
            .strDisplayName = String$(dhcMaxPath, vbNullChar)
            .strTitle = strTitle
            .ulFlags = lngBifFlags
        End With

        ' Open the browse dialog
        lngIDL = SHBrowseForFolder(usrBrws)

        ' If the dialog succeeded
        If lngIDL Then
            strFolder = String$(dhcMaxPath, vbNullChar)

            ' Try to resolve the lngIDL into a real path
            If SHGetPathFromIDList(lngIDL, strFolder) Then
                ' Trim the null characters
                strFolder = dhTrimNull(strFolder)
                lngReturn = dhcNoError
            Else
                ' No real directory path is available, so at
                ' least return the virtual selection
                strFolder = dhTrimNull(usrBrws.strDisplayName)
```

```
            lngReturn = dhcNoError
        End If

    Else
        ' Some unknown error has occurred
        lngReturn = dhcErrorExtendedError
    End If

Else
    ' Some unknown error has occurred
    lngReturn = dhcErrorExtendedError
End If

dhBrowseForFolder = lngReturn
End Function
```

To call this function, simply pick the appropriate flags from Tables 11.11 and 11.12 and pass them in. For example, the following fragment will display the dialog box shown earlier in Figure 11.7:

```
Dim strFolder As String
' This will fill in strFolder with the selected value.
Call dhBrowseForFolder(dhcCSIdlNetworkNeighborhood, _
  dhcBifReturnOnlyFileSystemDirs, strFolder, _
  strTitle:="Select a Special Location:")
```

Although this dialog isn't perfect (there are just too many ways to call it without getting meaningful results), it does sport a common "look," and it's a whole lot simpler than writing your own!

To demonstrate the dhBrowseForFolder function, we've included an Excel UserForm in the Excel project (NETWORK.XLS). If you have a copy of Microsoft Excel, you can try ShellBrowseDlg (open the form in the VBA editor, and with it selected, press the F5 key or the Try out Common Dialog button on the spreadsheet itself), shown in Figure 11.8. This form allows you to try out all the constants from Tables 11.11 and 11.12 and see how they affect the display of the common dialog.

The LAN Manager API

The functions we've discussed so far provide a rich set of features that can make your applications network aware, and they are available on any Windows 95 or Windows NT machine. However, as solid as the WNet API is, some necessary functionality is missing. To get the rest of the functionality you need, you must

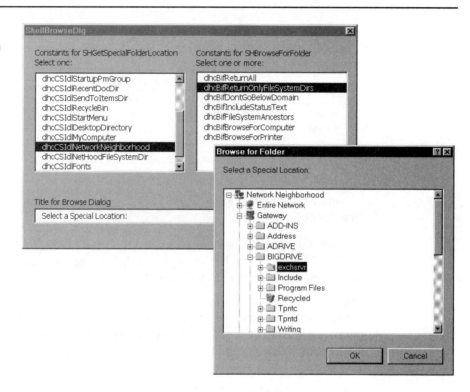

FIGURE 11.8

Use ShellBrowseDlg in Excel to try out the common dialog.

use the LAN Manager API, available only on Windows NT. The full API consists of over 120 functions (as compared to the 14 in the WNet API), and despite the fact that they are underdocumented (and that the best documentation can be found in old OS/2 manuals), there are some things you cannot do unless you use the LAN Manager API. The functions we discuss here handle

- Sharing resources (adding network shares)

- Deleting network shares

- Changing a user's network password

There are four interesting items to note about the LAN Manager functions:

- These functions work only under Windows NT; they are not available to Windows 95 users.

- All the strings that are passed to LAN Manager API functions must be Unicode rather than ANSI strings. The examples shown here force the conversion using the StrConv function. (For more information on StrConv, see Chapter 1.)

- The API functions have a clear and consistent naming style that makes it easy to tell exactly what they do. Each function starts with a "Net" prefix, followed by a noun that describes what object is being manipulated and a verb indicating what the function does to that object. For example, if you wanted to add a user, you would use the NetUserAdd function.

- These API functions have much in common. Learning one LAN Manager API and how to call it is the key to calling dozens of others just like it.

WARNING Of course, not all news is good news. Many of the LAN Manager functions are inaccessible to VBA programmers because they return pointers to pointers to memory addresses. VBA has no mechanism for dereferencing these pointers, so, unless you write a helper DLL, you won't be able to call these functions.

Adding a Network Share

The WNet functions allow you to enumerate network shares but supply no way to create a new one. The LAN Manager API provides the NetShareAdd function, which does allow you to create a new share. The declaration is as follows:

```
Private Declare Function NetShareAdd Lib "NETAPI32.DLL" _
 (ByVal strServername As String, ByVal lnglevel As Long, _
 strbuf As SHARE_INFO_2, lngParamErr As Long) As Long
```

The following list describes the parameters for NetShareAdd:

Parameter	Description
strServerName	Machine name on which to add the share
lngLevel	Specifies what level of share information will be in the buffer. You can send either of two data structures, SHARE_INFO_2 or SHARE_INFO_502, depending on the amount of information you need to specify. The examples use SHARE_INFO_2
lngParamErr	Indicates which parameter, if any, was invalid on return from the function call (If only all API calls were this helpful!)

WARNING To use NetShareAdd, the currently logged-in user must have permission to add the share. Otherwise, an error will occur. Unless you're a member of the Administrators or Account Operators local group or you have Communication, Print, or Server operator group membership, you won't be able to successfully execute NetShareAdd. Even with these rights, the Print operator can add only printer queues, and the Communication operator can add only communication-device queues.

The SHARE_INFO_2 structure contains the parameters described in the following list. The network share types are defined in Table 11.13, and the permissions flags are defined in Table 11.14.

Parameter	Meaning
shi2_netname	Name for the new share
shi2_type	Resource type, selected from the values in Table 11.13
shi2_remark	A comment that will appear in Windows Explorer and in the network connection dialog under Windows NT
shi2_permissions	Flag specifying permissions (This parameter is ignored unless share-level security is set up on the machine.) See Table 11.14 for allowable values
shi2_max_uses	Maximum number of concurrent users allowed (–1 means no limit.)
shi2_current_uses	Current number of users (ignored when adding a new share)
shi2_path	Local path of the shared resource on the machine
shi2_passwd	Password for the share (Like shi2_permissions, this parameter is ignored unless share-level security is set up on the machine.)

TABLE 11.13   Network Share Types (Used for the shi2_type Parameter)

Constant	Value	Meaning
dhcLanManStypeDisktree	&H0	Disk resource
dhcLanManStypePrintq	&H1	Printer resource
dhcLanManStypeDevice	&H2	Device resource (such as a COM port)
dhcLanManStypeIpc	&H3	IPC resource

TABLE 11.14   Permissions Flags (Used for the shi2_ permissions Parameter)

Constant	Value	Meaning
dhcLanManAccessNone	&H0	No access allowed
dhcLanManAccessRead	&H1	Permission to read from the resource
dhcLanManAccessWrite	&H2	Permission to write to the resource
dhcLanManAccessCreate	&H4	Permission to create an instance of the resource
dhcLanManAccessExec	&H8	Permission to execute the resource
dhcLanManAccessDelete	&H10	Permission to delete the resource
dhcLanManAccessAtrib	&H20	Permission to modify attributes
dhcLanManAccessPerm	&H40	Permission to modify permissions
dhcLanManAccessAll	&HFF	A bitmask that includes all the previous flags

The function itself is very straightforward; you simply convert the strings to Unicode and call NetShareAdd. A wrapper function, dhAddNetworkShare, is shown in Listing 11.19. Note that many of the parameters are optional. Table 11.15 describes each of the parameters for dhAddNetworkShare.

TABLE 11.15 Parameters for dhAddNetworkShare

Parameter	Optional?	Default Value	Description
strServer	No		Machine name on which to add the share
strShareName	No		Name for the new share
strPath	No		Local path of the shared resource on the machine
fDisk	Yes	True	If True, share is for a drive. If False, share is for a printer
lngMaxUsers	Yes	−1	Maximum number of concurrent users allowed (−1 means no limit)
strPassWord	Yes	""	Password for the share (Like shi2_permissions, this parameter is ignored unless share-level security is set up on the machine.)
lngPermissions	Yes	dhcLanMan-AccessAll	Flag specifying permissions (ignored unless share-level security is set up on the machine) See Table 11.14 for allowable values

Listing 11.19: Add a Network Share

```
Public Function dhAddNetworkShare(ByVal strServer As String, _
  strShareName As String, strPath As String, _
  Optional strRemarks As String, _
  Optional fDisk As Boolean = True, _
  Optional lngMaxUsers As Long = -1, _
  Optional lngPermissions As Long = dhcLanManAccessAll, _
  Optional strPassword As String = " ") As Long

    ' Adds a network share

    Dim si2 As SHARE_INFO_2
    Dim lngReturn As Long
    Dim lngParamError As Long

    lngParamError = 0

    ' Convert all strings to Unicode and place them into
    ' structures as needed
```

```
    strServer = StrConv(strServer, vbUnicode)

With si2
    .shi2_netname = StrConv(strShareName, vbUnicode)
    .shi2_type = IIf(fDisk, dhcLanManStypeDisktree, _
    dhcLanManStypePrintq)
    .shi2_remark = StrConv(strRemarks, vbUnicode)
    .shi2_permissions = lngPermissions
    .shi2_max_uses = lngMaxUsers
    .shi2_path = StrConv(strPath, vbUnicode)
    .shi2_passwd = StrConv(strPassword, vbUnicode)
End With
dhAddNetworkShare = _
    NetShareAdd(strServer, dhcShareInfo2, si2, lngParamError)
End Function
```

Calling this function is also very straightforward. For example, to add a share named ROOT to the C drive on a machine named Hopper, you simply call

```
lngReturn = dhAddNetworkShare("\\Hopper","ROOT","c:\")
```

TIP The strPath parameter must be a complete, valid path. Don't fall into the same trap we did: if you pass "C:" without the backslash, you'll receive error 123, "File, path, or drive name is incorrect," for your efforts.

Deleting a Network Share

Deleting a network share requires much less work, and less explanation, than adding a share. The NetShareDel API function is defined as follows:

```
Private Declare Function NetShareDel Lib "NETAPI32.DLL" _
 (ByVal strServername As String, ByVal strNetname As String, _
 ByVal lngReserved As Long) As Long
```

NetShareDel accepts the server name and the name of the share to delete. (The lngReserved parameter is undocumented, and you should pass 0 in this parameter.) Listing 11.20 provides a wrapper function, dhDeleteNetworkShare, for NetShareDel. (The wrapper function performs the required Unicode conversion for you.)

> **WARNING**
> Unless you're a member of the Administrators or Account Operators local group or you have Communication, Print, or Server operator group membership, you won't be able to successfully execute NetShareDel. Even with these rights, the Print operator can delete only printer queues, and the Communication operator can delete only communication-device queues.

Listing 11.20: Delete a Network Share

```
Public Function dhDeleteNetworkShare(ByVal strServer As String, _
  ByVal strShareName As String) As Long
    ' Deletes a network share
    ' Convert the strings to Unicode
    strServer = StrConv(strServer, vbUnicode)
    strShareName = StrConv(strShareName, vbUnicode)

    dhDeleteNetworkShare = NetShareDel(strServer, _
      strShareName, 0&)
End Function
```

Changing a User's Password

It's simple to change a user's password using the LAN Manager's NetUser-ChangePassword API function. This function takes four parameters:

Parameter	Description
DomainName	Remote server or domain (Passing 0& for this parameter will cause the function to use the logon domain of the caller.)
UserName	Name of the user whose password is to be changed (Passing 0& for this parameter will cause the function to use the currently logged-in user name.)
OldPassword	Old password of the user
NewPassword	New password of the user

The declaration for NetUserChangePassword is shown here:

```
Private Declare Function NetUserChangePassword Lib _
  "NETAPI32.DLL" (DomainName As Any, ByVal UserName As String, _
```

```
ByVal OldPassword As String, ByVal NewPassword As String) _
As Long
```

As with the other LAN Manager APIs, the strings must be converted to Unicode. The wrapper function, dhChangeUserPassword, which takes care of the details, is shown in Listing 11.21.

Listing 11.21: Change a User's Network Password

```
Public Function dhChangeUserPassword( _
ByVal strOldPwd As String, ByVal strNewPwd As String, _
Optional strUser As String, Optional strDomain As String) _
As Long

    ' Change a user's password.
    Dim lngReturn As Long

    ' If user is blank default to current user
    If Len(strUser) = 0 Then strUser = dhGetUserName()

    ' Convert the strings to Unicode
    strOldPwd = StrConv(strOldPwd, vbUnicode)
    strNewPwd = StrConv(strNewPwd, vbUnicode)
    strUser = StrConv(strUser, vbUnicode)
    strDomain = StrConv(strDomain, vbUnicode)

    ' If the domain is specified, use it. Otherwise pass
    ' ByVal 0& (Null).
    If Len(strDomain) > 0 Then
        lngReturn = NetUserChangePassword(ByVal strDomain, _
           strUser, strOldPwd, strNewPwd)
    Else
        lngReturn = NetUserChangePassword(ByVal 0&, _
           strUser, strOldPwd, strNewPwd)
    End If
    dhChangeUserPassword = lngReturn
End Function
```

For example, to change your own password from *nincompoop* to *flibbertigibbet*, you could make a call like this:

```
If dhChangeUserPassword("nincompoop", "flibbertigibbet") _
  = dhcNoError Then
    ' You successfully changed the password
End If
```

The following list contains the errors most likely to occur when calling
dhChangeUserPassword:

Error	Description
dhcErrorInvalidPassword	Old password is not correct
dhcErrorAccessDenied	User does not have access to the requested information
dhcErrorInvalidComputer	Computer name is invalid
dhcErrorNotPrimary	Operation is allowed only on the primary domain controller of the domain
dhcErrorUserNotFound	User name could not be found
dhcErrorPasswordTooShort	Password is shorter than required

On Functions Not Covered

This section has just scratched the surface of the LAN Manager API. You'll find
many useful functions among the large set of LAN Manager API calls (as well as
some that have become obsolete or have been superseded). These functions cover
all aspects of networking, including:

- Domain information
- Remote file information
- Handling local and global groups
- Sending messages
- Managing replicator import and export
- Scheduling services
- Managing servers and sessions
- Handling transports
- Managing users and workstations

Although some of these functions cannot easily be called from VBA because of
the way they pass parameters, there are still many LAN Manager functions you
can use. The examples we've provided in this chapter will help get you started.

TIP	Where do you find more information about the LAN Manager API? One answer is (as always) MSDN—the Microsoft Developer Network CD. If you're interested in this information, there's no excuse for not purchasing this incredibly useful compendium of information. Of course, you can find much of this information on Microsoft's Web site as well, but it's not nearly as convenient as it is on the CD. Have we said this often enough? The MSDN CD is one of the most worthwhile purchases you can make if you want to use the Windows API as part of your application development.

Summary

Making applications network aware can be one of the most challenging aspects of programming in VBA, both because using the network APIs in VBA is not well documented and because many of them were not written with VBA developers in mind. In this chapter we covered most of the basic networking functions you may want to add to your application, as well as several advanced networking functions. In addition, we provided some special tricks to help you work around APIs that are not "VBA friendly." Specifically, we covered these topics:

- Using common network dialogs
    - The network connection dialog
    - The network disconnect dialog
- Making network connections manually
    - Creating network connections
    - Deleting network connections
- Retrieving basic network resource information
    - Getting a UNC path from a mapped network resource
    - Retrieving the name of the currently logged in user
    - Getting (and setting) the workstation name
    - Getting advanced network information

- Enumerating network resources

  - Opening, using, and closing enumeration handles

  - Enumerating available network shares on a machine

  - Enumerating mapped network resources on the current machine

  - Enumerating the computers in a domain

  - Using the new Shell32 browse dialog

- Calling the LAN Manager API

  - Adding network shares on a machine

  - Deleting network shares

  - Changing a user's network password

For more extensive looks at string handling, see Chapter 1, and for more information on using the system Registry, see Chapter 10. For more coverage of using the Windows API in general, see Appendix B.

12

Working with Disks and Files

- Using built-in VBA disk and file functions

- Understanding the power of Windows API for managing files

- Examining an object-oriented approach to file management

Sooner or later, as you write VBA programs you'll have to interact with disks and files. Your interaction might be to perform simple tasks, such as copying or deleting files, or more complex ones, like opening and parsing a text file. This chapter explores the many things you can do with disks and files. It begins with a discussion of the built-in VBA disk and file functions. While adequate for performing most tasks, they do not provide all the functionality many developers desire. The second part of this chapter examines the numerous Windows API functions at your disposal, and it concludes by tying these discussions together by constructing an object model for managing disk files using VBA class modules.

Table 12.1 lists the sample files located on the CD-ROM for this chapter.

TABLE 12.1   Sample Files

File Name	Description
DISKFILE.XLS	Microsoft Excel workbook containing the sample code
DISKFILE.MDB	Access 97 database containing the sample code
CLASSEX.BAS	Examples demonstrating file and directory classes
COMMDLG.BAS	Sample code for common dialog functions
DATETIME.BAS	Sample code for file date and time functions
DISKINFO.BAS	Sample code for disk information functions
HANDLES.BAS	Sample code for file handle examples
FILEIO.BAS	Sample code for VBA file I/O functions
FINDFUNC.BAS	Sample code for Windows API file-listing functions
MISCFILE.BAS	Miscellaneous Windows API functions
NOTIFY.BAS	Sample code for directory change notification functions
PATHFUN.BAS	Sample code for path parsing examples
FSEARCH.BAS	Sample code for file search functions
STRINGS.BAS	String manipulation code from Chapter 1
TEMPFILE.BAS	Sample code for temporary file examples

TABLE 12.1   Sample Files (continued)

File Name	Description
VBAFILE.BAS	Sample code for built-in VBA file function examples
CALLBACK.CLS	Example callback object class
FILE.CLS	File object class
FILES.CLS	Files collection class
DIR.CLS	Directory object class
DIRS.CLS	Directories collection class

The Built-In VBA Disk and File Functions

VBA offers several built-in functions designed to manipulate disks and files. In general, they are oriented toward tasks that are both common and simple. We take a look at them in this section for the sake of completeness. They are, for the most part, very old functions inherited from previous versions of BASIC. If you've used BASIC for any length of time, you've probably used them before, possibly dozens of times. If you're new to VBA and need more detail on these functions, you may want to reexamine the VBA documentation or another introductory text. All the code for this section is contained in the basVBABuiltIn module of the sample Excel workbook and the VBAFILE.BAS file.

The Dir Function Explained

While it's not the most powerful built-in VBA file function, the Dir function is probably the one most commonly used. Its primary purpose is to return the names of files in a given directory. Dir accepts a file specification and returns a file name matching the specification. There are four ways you can call the Dir function.

1. If you pass a complete file name (with no wildcard characters), Dir returns the name of the file if it exists at the specified location. If the file doesn't exist, Dir returns an empty string.

2. If you pass a file specification (one that includes wildcard characters), Dir returns the first file name that matches the specification.

3. If you pass a directory name, Dir finds the first file in that directory.

4. If you don't pass anything, Dir returns the next matching file name. You can continue to call Dir in this manner until it returns an empty string indicating no further matches.

Furthermore, the following rules apply when you call Dir:

- You must pass a path the first time you call Dir or after Dir returns an empty string; otherwise, an error occurs.

- You can pass a complete path, relative path, or UNC path.

- If you don't specify a path, Dir searches the current directory.

- Each time you call Dir with a new path, it abandons the prior directory search.

The procedure shown in Listing 12.1 shows a number of examples of calling the Dir function.

Listing 12.1: Various Ways to Call the Dir Function

```
Sub dhTestDir()
    Dim strFile As String

    ' Prints "WIN.INI" if the file exists
    Debug.Print Dir("C:\WINDOWS\WIN.INI")

    ' Prints the first file that starts with "W"
    Debug.Print Dir("C:\WINDOWS\W*")

    ' Prints the next file that starts with "W"
    Debug.Print Dir

    ' Prints all the files in the current directory
    strFile = Dir("*")
    Do Until strFile = ""
        Debug.Print strFile
        strFile = Dir
    Loop
End Sub
```

> **TIP**
>
> You can use the single-dot (.) and double-dot (..) symbols, which represent the current and parent directories, respectively, in all VBA file functions. For example, the command Dir("..*.*") returns the first file in the directory immediately above the current one.

Checking for a File's Existence

One common need in an application is to determine whether a particular file exists. You might need to do this before calling another VBA function, such as Kill (which deletes a file). Checking for a file's existence is easy using the Dir function. Listing 12.2 shows the dhFileExists function. You pass it a complete path to a file (with no wildcards); it returns True if the file exists and False if it doesn't.

Listing 12.2: A Simple Function to Check for a File's Existence

```
Function dhFileExists(strFile As String) As Boolean
    ' Call Dir with the passed file name--
    ' if the file exists Dir will return
    ' back the file name and the length
    ' of the string will be > 0
    dhFileExists = (Len(Dir(strFile)) > 0)
End Function
```

Using File Attributes

Files maintained in FAT or NTFS file systems have attributes that indicate whether they are read-only, hidden, to be archived, or part of the operating system. Under normal circumstances, the Dir function returns the names of all files that do not have the hidden or system attributes set, but you can instruct Dir to look for these files. You can also search for directories, as well as retrieve a disk's volume label. To accomplish all this, you pass a bitmask of values as the optional second argument. You can pass any combination of the following values:

Value	Constant	Description
0	vbNormal	Default file attributes
2	vbHidden	Finds hidden files
4	vbSystem	Finds system files

Value	Constant	Description
8	vbVolume	Returns disk volume label
16	vbDirectory	Finds directories

For example, to include hidden and system files in the list that Dir generates, you could use a statement like this:

```
strFile = Dir("C:\", vbHidden + vbSystem)
```

> **NOTE**
>
> Passing an attribute as the second argument does not limit the output only to files with that attribute set. It only adds them to the list of normal files returned by the Dir function.

GetAttr and SetAttr

You can also retrieve and set the attributes for a given file. VBA provides two functions for this purpose, GetAttr and SetAttr. GetAttr accepts a file name and returns a long integer containing a bitmask of the file's attributes. In addition to the ones listed above, you can check for the read-only attribute (vbReadOnly, value 1) or the archive attribute (vbArchive, value 32). Similarly, SetAttr accepts a file name and a bitmask of attributes. Listing 12.3 shows the dhIsAttr function. It accepts a file name and a set of attributes and returns True if the file's attributes match those passed to the function.

Listing 12.3: Use the dhIsAttr Function to Check a File's Attributes

```
Function dhIsAttr(strFile As String, lngAttr As Long) _
    As Boolean

    ' Check the attributes of the file against the
    ' specified attributes--return True if they match
    dhIsAttr = ((GetAttr(strFile) And lngAttr) = lngAttr)
End Function
```

You can call the function with any attribute or combination of attributes. For example:

```
' Is "C:\MSDOS.SYS" a system file?
Debug.Print dhIsAttr("C:\MSDOS.SYS", vbSystem)
```

```
' Is "C:\MSDOS.SYS" read-only AND a system file?
Debug.Print dhIsAttr("C:\MSDOS.SYS", vbSystem + vbReadOnly)
```

Another example of using GetAttr is shown in Listing 12.4. It shows three procedures that list all the files in the root directory, along with their file attributes. dhPrintAttr uses the Dir function to locate all the files and directories. (Note the bitmask passed as the second argument.) dhBuildAttrString and dhBuildAttr compare the attributes of each file against a given file attribute and construct a string based on the results. Figure 12.1 shows the output from running dhPrintAttr.

Listing 12.4: Two Procedures That Print Files and Attributes

```
Sub dhPrintAttr()
    Dim strFile As String
    Dim lngAttr As Long
    Dim strAttr As String

    ' Use the root directory of the current drive
    Const dhcDir = "\"

    ' Look for all types of files
    strFile = Dir(dhcDir, _
     vbHidden + vbSystem + vbDirectory)

    ' Loop until no more files are found
    Do Until strFile = ""

        ' Use GetAttr to get the file's attributes
        lngAttr = GetAttr(dhcDir & strFile)

        ' Print the file with its attributes
        Debug.Print strFile, dhBuildAttrString(lngAttr)

        ' Get the next file and reset the attribute string
        strFile = Dir
        strAttr = ""
    Loop
End Sub

Function dhBuildAttrString(lngAttr As Long) As String
    Dim strAttr As String

    ' Build up an attribute string
    dhBuildAttr strAttr, lngAttr, vbReadOnly, "R"
```

```
            dhBuildAttr strAttr, lngAttr, vbHidden, "H"
            dhBuildAttr strAttr, lngAttr, vbSystem, "S"
            dhBuildAttr strAttr, lngAttr, vbArchive, "A"
            dhBuildAttr strAttr, lngAttr, vbDirectory, "D"

            ' Return attribute string
            dhBuildAttrString = strAttr
        End Function

        Sub dhBuildAttr(strAttr As String, lngAttr As Long, _
          lngMask As Long, strSymbol As String)

            ' Compare the passed attributes with the
            ' mask--if it matches append the passed
            ' symbol to the string
            If (lngAttr And lngMask) = lngMask Then
                strAttr = strAttr & strSymbol
            Else
                strAttr = strAttr & " "
            End If
        End Sub
```

FIGURE 12.1

A list of files and their attributes

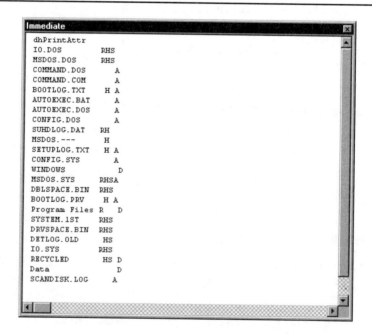

Listing Directory Names

File attributes are critical to locating specific file types, especially directories. (To the file system, directories are just like files, but with a special attribute set.) Listing 12.5 shows a procedure that lists all the subdirectories beneath a given directory. Note that after using the Dir function to build the list, the procedure uses dhIsAttr to find the directories among the names returned.

Listing 12.5: A Procedure That Prints Subdirectory Names

```
Sub dhListSubDirs(strPath As String)
    Dim strFile As String

    ' Make sure strPath is a directory
    If Right(strPath, 1) <> "\" Then
        strPath = strPath & "\"
    End If
    If dhIsAttr(strPath, vbDirectory) Then

        ' Find all the files, including directories
        strFile = Dir(strPath, vbDirectory)
        Do Until strFile = ""

            ' If the file is a directory, print it
            If dhIsAttr(strPath & strFile, vbDirectory) Then

                ' Ignore "." and ".."
                If strFile <> "." And _
                strFile <> ".." Then

                    Debug.Print strFile
                End If
            End If

            ' Get the next file
            strFile = Dir
        Loop
    End If
End Sub
```

Those Pesky Dir Dots

You'll notice that the code in Listing 12.5 includes an If...Then statement to weed out two values returned by Dir: "." and "..". These values represent the current directory and parent directory, respectively. Dir will return them whenever you scan for directory names in any directory beneath the root. As far as the operating system is concerned, they're perfectly valid directory names. Under most circumstances, though, you won't want to include them in the directory listing.

Doing the Disk File Shuffle

Probably the most common tasks related to files involve copying, moving, renaming, and deleting them. VBA has several functions, all of which are quite straightforward, designed to accomplish these tasks:

Function	Description
FileCopy	Copies a file
Name	Moves or renames a file
Kill	Deletes a file

Listing 12.6 shows a small procedure that demonstrates their syntax. It copies the WIN.INI file from the Windows directory to the root directory, renames it WIN.TMP, and then deletes it. What could be simpler?

Listing 12.6: Copy, Rename, and Delete Files

```
Sub dhCopyRenameDelete()
    ' Copy WIN.INI to root directory
    FileCopy "C:\WINDOWS\WIN.INI", "C:\WIN.INI"

    ' Rename to WIN.TMP
    Name "C:\WIN.INI" As "C:\WIN.TMP"

    ' Delete the renamed file
    Kill "C:\WIN.TMP"
End Sub
```

While these functions are mostly unremarkable (except perhaps for Name's odd syntax), there a few things you should know about them:

- FileCopy *will* overwrite the destination file if it exists.

- Name will *not* overwrite an existing file.

- You can copy and rename in one step by specifying a different destination name.

- You can move files using the Name function by specifying a different destination name.

Some File Information: FileLen and FileDateTime

Two other VBA file functions are worth mentioning: FileLen and FileDateTime. FileLen returns the size of a file in bytes, given its name. FileDateTime returns the date and time a given file was last modified. Listing 12.7 shows a very simple procedure that demonstrates their syntax. The sections "A Hardcore Replacement for Dir" and "Getting File Information Quickly" later in this chapter discuss looking to the Windows API to find out even more information about files.

Listing 12.7: Print a File's Size and Date of Last Modification

```
Sub dhMoreFileInfo()
    ' How big is WIN.INI?
    Debug.Print FileLen("C:\WINDOWS\WIN.INI") & " bytes"

    ' When was it last modified?
    Debug.Print FileDateTime("C:\WINDOWS\WIN.INI")
End Sub
```

Directory Management

VBA features a number of functions for manipulating directories. Like the file management functions, they are all straightforward. Using these functions, you can set and retrieve the current directory, set the current drive, and create and remove directories.

Current Confusion

What can make using these functions a bit confusing is the concept of the current drive and directory. Each process (application) in Windows can set a *current directory*. Any operations on files that are not fully qualified affect the current directory. For example, if you were to issue the command

```
Debug.Print Dir("*.*")
```

the result would be the first file in the current directory. We recommend avoiding the current directory altogether and using fully qualified path names (complete with drive and directory), but sometimes it's convenient to use the current directory. So how do you find out what the current directory is? Use the CurDir function. For example:

```
Debug.Print CurDir
```

VBA includes the drive as well as the directory in the output. To change the current directory, use the ChDir function:

```
ChDir "C:\WINDOWS"
```

There is also a ChDrive function to change the current drive. This is where things get confusing. Shouldn't you be able to change the current drive using the ChDir command? The answer is no. The reason is that VBA tracks these elements separately. While you can include another drive letter in the ChDir statement, that drive does not become "active" until you use ChDrive. You can see this by running the code shown in Listing 12.8. (Just make sure you use drives and directories appropriate for your computer.)

Listing 12.8: Demonstrating the Confusion of ChDir and ChDrive

```
Sub dhTestCurrent()
    ' Print the first file in the current directory.
    Debug.Print Dir("*.*"), "in " & CurDir

    ' Try to change to the D drive using ChDir
    ChDir "D:\SOMEDIR"

    ' Print the first file again--it's still on C!
    Debug.Print Dir("*.*"), "in " & CurDir

    ' Now use ChDrive to switch drives
    ChDrive "D"

    ' Print the first file again--this time it's D!
    Debug.Print Dir("*.*"), "in " & CurDir
End Sub
```

The procedure begins by printing the first file name in the current directory, along with the directory name. It then tries to change to the D drive using just ChDir. While this appears to execute just fine, when the first file name is printed again, it's the same as before. Since you can't change drives using ChDir, the current directory remains the same. The procedure then uses ChDrive to change the current drive. When the file name is printed a third time, it's the first file in

D:\SOMEDIR. This demonstrates that although you can use ChDir with a different drive *and* directory, VBA does not recognize the new current directory until you use ChDrive.

Creating and Deleting Directories and Directory Trees

You add and remove directories using the MkDir and RmDir functions. Both accept a directory path as arguments. You can include a fully qualified path, including a drive letter, or a partial one. If you omit a drive letter, MkDir and RmDir assume the current drive and resolve all relative paths based on the current directory. In other words, they work just like their namesake MS-DOS commands.

The only other item worth noting is that, like the MS-DOS command, RmDir will fail if you attempt to remove a directory containing files or subdirectories. You must use the Kill statement to delete any files that exist. Since subdirectories can be nested several levels deep, removing a high-level directory is problematic. The solution requires recursively looking for subdirectories and deleting any files they contain. This is not easy, however, because each recursive call to Dir resets any pending results from the previous call.

One possible solution is shown in Listing 12.9. The function, appropriately named dhDelTree after the utility that appeared in MS-DOS 5.0, accepts a directory and methodically deletes every nested file and subdirectory. It works by first storing the name of the current directory in a variable. It then changes to the target directory and deletes any existing files. Next, it searches for subdirectories and, upon finding one, calls itself recursively. When the recursive call returns, the function restarts its subdirectory search until no more subdirectories exist. Finally, it removes the target directory and resets the current directory to its original value.

Listing 12.9: A Function to Delete an Entire Directory Tree

```
Function dhDelTree(strDirectory As String) As Boolean
    On Error GoTo HandleError

    Dim strOriginalDir As String
    Dim strFilename As String

    ' Check to make sure the directory actually exists.
    ' If not, we don't have to do a thing.
    If Len(Dir(dhFixPath(strDirectory), vbDirectory)) = 0 Then
```

```
        Exit Function
    End If

    ' Store original directory and change to one
    ' to be removed
    strOriginalDir = CurDir
    ChDir strDirectory

    ' Delete all the files in the current directory
    strFilename = Dir("*.*")
    Do Until strFilename = ""
        Kill strFilename
        strFilename = Dir
    Loop

    ' Now build a list of subdirectories
    Do
        strFilename = Dir("*.*", vbDirectory)

        ' Skip "." and ".."
        Do While strFilename = "." Or strFilename = ".."
            strFilename = Dir
        Loop

        ' If there are no more files, exit the loop
        ' otherwise call dhDelTree again to wipe
        ' out the subdirectory
        If strFilename = "" Then
            Exit Do
        Else
            If Not dhDelTree(strFilename) Then
                GoTo ExitHere
            End If
        End If
    Loop

    ' Change back to the original directory
    ChDir strOriginalDir

    ' Finally, remove the target directory
    RmDir strDirectory
    dhDelTree = True

ExitHere:
    Exit Function
```

```
HandleError:
    Select Case Err.Number
        Case Else
            MsgBox Err.Description, vbExclamation, _
            "Error " & Err.Number & " in dhDelTree"
        Resume ExitHere
    End Select
End Function
```

> **NOTE**
>
> The dhFixPath function used in this procedure simply ensures that the path passed in has a trailing backslash.

You may notice that this solution is not tremendously efficient, due to the fact that it needs to change directories and restart subdirectory searches each time it's executed (which for large trees is many times). We offer a more elegant solution to a related problem, *copying* an entire subdirectory tree, in our file system object model, described in the section "An Object Model for Directories and Files" later in this chapter.

> **WARNING**
>
> Be extremely careful when calling the dhDelTree function. The results of executing a statement like dhDelTree("C:\") could be highly counter-productive.

File I/O If You Must

BASIC, the language on which VBA is based, is, in personal computing terms, very old. It evolved during a time when there were no high-level, object-oriented database tools. As such, it includes a number of functions that perform low-level file input/output (I/O). While there are usually better ways to manipulate the contents of files, sometimes you have to roll up your sleeves and dig into the bits and bytes. This section briefly covers VBA's file I/O functions. Since they are unchanged from earlier versions of BASIC, we leave the advanced discussion of their usage to the numerous existing books on the subject. All the code for this section is contained in the basFileIO module of the sample Excel workbook and the FILEIO.BAS file.

Getting a Handle on Files

Before you can begin manipulating files and their contents, you need to understand the role of *file handles* (sometimes called *file numbers* in VBA documentation). Like other handles in Windows, file handles are simply numbers that uniquely identify open files to the operating system. The first step in opening a file using VBA is getting an unused file handle. You do this using the FreeFile function. For example:

```
Dim hFile As Long

' Get the next free file handle
hFile = FreeFile
```

If successful, FreeFile returns a nonzero value that you can use in the Open statement described in the next section. A file's handle is the key to using all the other VBA file I/O functions.

> **NOTE**
>
> VBA's method of assigning file handles is different from that used by the Windows API. Windows API functions return file handles as part of opening or creating new files. The section "Getting a (Windows) Handle on Files" later in this chapter discusses this subject in depth.

Other books on BASIC file functions and even the VBA documentation often ignore the FreeFile function and use hard-coded file handles (for example "#1"). While this is perfectly legal syntax, we recommend you use variables and the FreeFile function to assign file handles, especially if you open more than one file at once. Hard-coded file handles can lead to confusion and unwanted results if you inadvertently write data to the wrong file.

Using the Open Function

You use the VBA Open function to open all disk files for reading, writing, or both. It can be a confusing function because of its odd syntax and many permutations.

The general form of the Open function is shown here. (Square brackets indicate optional components.)

Open *pathname* For *mode* [Access *access*] [*lock*] _

    As [#]*filenumber* [Len=*reclength*]

Table 12.2 lists each of the elements of the function and describes what each is used for. As you can see, there are a quite a few possible permutations!

TABLE 12.2   Elements of the Open Function

Element	Description
pathname	Path to the file to open
mode	File open mode. Must be one of Append, Binary, Input, Output, or Random
access	Access mode. Must be one of Read (default), Write, or Read Write
lock	Share mode. Must be one of Shared (default), Lock Read, Lock Write, or Lock Read Write
filenumber	File handle. Can be a hard-coded number or a variable containing the handle obtained from FreeFile
reclength	Record length (for Random mode) or number of bytes buffered (for append, input, and output modes)

The options for mode, access, and lock are probably the most confusing. The next three sections explain each of them.

File Mode

The mode in which you open a file determines how Windows treats the opened file and what you can do with it. Unless you're constructing a random-access database application in VBA, you'll likely open a file in one of the sequential access modes: Append, Input, or Output. These are the preferred modes for working with text files. Files opened in Input mode are restricted to read-only access. Files opened in Output or Append mode can be read from or written to. The difference between the two is that Output always creates a new file, deleting an existing one with the same name, while Append adds text to the end of a file.

If you need to read and write data to a file on a byte-by-byte basis (such as when working with image files), open the file in binary mode. Random mode, on the other hand, is normally used for files that use a fixed record length, such as a dBase file. Operations on files opened in random mode operate on units that correspond to the size of the record specified by the *reclength* element of the Open function.

File Access

Somewhat related to the file open mode is the file access mode. You choose from three options: Read, Write, and Read Write. The meaning of each should be obvious. If you don't have appropriate access rights to open a file with the specified options, perhaps because of network or operating system security settings, an error occurs.

Locking

In multiuser scenarios, it is a good idea to select one of the locking options. The default is Shared. This lets other users read from and write to the file while you have it open. If this is not appropriate for your situation, you can select one of the other options. Lock Read prevents other users from reading the file but still allows them to write to it. Lock Write allows others to read the contents of the file but not to modify them. Lock Read Write is the most restrictive. It prevents other users from reading or writing.

NOTE While we don't cover it in this chapter, you can lock parts of a file once you've opened it. Search VBA online help for more information on the Lock statement.

A Simple Example

Now let's look at a simple example of using the Open statement. The procedure shown in Listing 12.10 opens a file in sequential access mode. Note from the statement options that the procedure will only be able to read from the file.

Listing 12.10: Open a File for Sequential Read Access

```
Sub dhTestOpen()
    Dim hFile As Long
```

```
    ' Get a new file handle
    hFile = FreeFile

    ' Open a file for sequential access
    Open "C:\TESTPROC.BAS" For Input Access Read _
     Shared As hFile

    ' Do something here...

    ' Close the file
    Close hFile
End Sub
```

Don't Forget to Close!

You'll notice that just before terminating, the procedure in Listing 12.10 calls the VBA Close statement, passing the file handle. The Close statement closes an open disk file. Closing a file after you're done using it is important. If you fail to close a file, you risk locking others out of it (if opened in non-shared mode) or losing data (if you shut down Windows).

You can close multiple files simultaneously by passing more than one file handle, separated by commas, to the Close statement. While we recommend using the Close statement to close each open file individually as soon as you're finished with it, you can also use the Reset statement to close all disk files opened by your application.

Manipulating File Position

Under most circumstances, you don't want to blindly read and write data to disk files. You normally need to know things like how big a file is, where the next read or write operation will take place, and when you've reached the end of the file. VBA offers several functions to help you do this, described in the following sections.

LOF and EOF

No, were not talking about two of the dwarfs from *The Hobbit*. LOF and EOF are two functions that tell you the size of a file and when you're at the end of a file, respectively. Each accepts a file handle as an argument. LOF simply returns the size of the open file in bytes.

EOF returns a Boolean value indicating whether the *current byte position* is at the end of the file. The current byte position is maintained internally by VBA. When you first open a file, VBA sets this value to 0. As you use file I/O functions, VBA changes this value. For example, after reading two bytes from a file opened in Binary mode, the current byte position is set to 2. The next read operation will occur at the next, or third, byte. When you have read the entire contents of a file, the current byte position is set to the final byte number, and EOF returns True. Any attempt to read more data will result in an error.

NOTE For files opened in output mode, EOF always returns True.

Loc and Seek

If you need to know what the current byte position is, call the Loc function. Loc accepts a file handle as an argument and returns the current byte position. The number returned, however, varies depending on the mode the file was opened in. For files opened in binary mode, Loc returns the actual byte position. For files opened in random mode, Loc returns the record number instead of the byte number. For files opened in sequential mode (input, output or append), however, the number returned by Loc is the current byte position divided by 128. (No, we don't know why.)

If you need to know the actual byte position of sequentially accessed files, use the Seek function instead. Seek works just like Loc for binary and random files but returns a true byte position for sequential files.

VBA also has a Seek statement that you can use to set the current byte or record position for files opened in binary or random mode. (As the term *sequential* implies, you can't change the current byte position for sequential files.)

Statements for Reading and Writing

Just as there are many permutations of the Open statement, there are numerous VBA statements for reading from and writing to disk files. Which one you use depends on which file open mode you used and how you want to format the incoming or outgoing data. Table 12.3 summarizes the different statements.

TABLE 12.3 VBA Statements for File I/O

Open Mode	Read Statement(s)	Write Statement(s)
Sequential (Input, Output or Append)	Input, Line Input #, Input #	Print #, Write #
Random	Get	Put
Binary	Input, Get	Put

Sequential Access

Files opened in input, output, or append mode can be manipulated by any of five functions. For reading data you can use Input, Line Input #, or Input #. Writing to sequential files is accomplished with the Print # or Write # functions.

Input   Input is the simplest function for reading data and is useful for dealing with text files that don't contain line breaks and files containing binary data. Listing 12.11 shows a procedure that accepts a file name and prints the contents of the file to the Immediate window. You'll notice that it uses the EOF function to determine when it's reached the end of the file.

Listing 12.11: Print the Contents of a File, Byte by Byte

```
Sub dhPrintBytes(strFile As String)
    Dim hFile As Long

    ' Get a new file handle
    hFile = FreeFile

    ' Open the file for sequential access
    Open strFile For Input Access Read Shared As hFile

    ' Print the file contents
    Do Until EOF(hFile)
        Debug.Print Input(1, hFile);
    Loop

    ' Close the file
    Close hFile
End Sub
```

This procedure is not very efficient, however, because it makes two function calls (to EOF and Input) for each byte in a file. When using the Input function, it's best to fetch the data in chunks. Listing 12.12 shows an updated version of the procedure that does this. In addition to the file name, it accepts a chunk size and retrieves data in blocks rather than one byte at a time.

Listing 12.12: Print the Contents of a File, Using Chunks

```
Sub dhPrintChunks(strFile As String, intSize As Integer)
    Dim hFile As Long
    Dim lngSize As Long
    Dim intChunk As Integer

    ' Get a new file handle
    hFile = FreeFile

    ' Open the file for sequential access
    Open strFile For Input Access Read Shared As hFile

    ' Get the file size
    lngSize = LOF(hFile)

    ' Print the file contents, first in chunks
    For intChunk = 1 To lngSize \ intSize
        Debug.Print Input(intSize, hFile);
    Next

    ' Then the remainder
    If (lngSize Mod intSize) > 0 Then
        Debug.Print Input((lngSize Mod intSize), hFile)
    End If

    ' Close the file
    Close hFile
End Sub
```

You'll notice that the procedure uses a For...Next loop to read in each block of data. The number of iterations is computed by dividing the chunk size into the file size, using integer division. A final Input statement is used to read any remaining data, which will be left over if the file size is not equally divisible by the chunk size.

Of course, these methods of retrieving data evolved under early versions of BASIC that could not cope with large amounts of data. String variables were limited to 32K, for instance. With the 32-bit versions VBA, however, String variables can now hold over two *billion* characters, so you could use a statement like this to read a file's entire contents at once:

```
Debug.Print Input(LOF(hFile), hFile)
```

Line Input #   For text files that contain line breaks (for example, configuration files like AUTOEXEC.BAT and WIN.INI), use the Line Input # statement instead. This statement accepts a file handle and a variable and reads the next line from the file into the variable. (It strips the trailing carriage return and linefeed characters.) Listing 12.13 shows a procedure that accepts a file name, opens that file for read-only access, and prints each line to the Immediate window. Using Line Input #, you don't have to worry about byte position or buffer size.

Listing 12.13: Print Text Files with Line Breaks Using Line Input

```
Sub dhPrintLines(strFile As String)
    Dim hFile As Long
    Dim strLine As String

    ' Get a new file handle
    hFile = FreeFile

    ' Open the file for sequential access
    Open strFile For Input Access Read Shared As hFile

    ' Print the file contents
    Do Until EOF(hFile)
        Line Input #hFile, strLine
        Debug.Print strLine
    Loop

    ' Close the file
    Close hFile
End Sub
```

Input #   Input #, the final sequential read statement, accepts a file handle and a series of variables (separated by commas) and loads file data into those variables. Input # is most useful for comma-delimited data since it treats each data element separately, loading it into a separate variable. It also automatically removes quotes around text values and converts date strings to VBA dates.

Write #   The counterpart of Input # is Write #. It accepts a file handle and a comma-delimited list of values and writes each value to the file. Additionally, the statement delimits the output with commas and encloses text in quotes and dates in number signs (#). This makes it ideal for reading using Input #. Listing 12.14 shows a procedure that demonstrates both statements.

Listing 12.14: Using Write # and Input

```
Sub dhWriteAndInput(strFile As String)
    Dim hFile As Long
    ReDim varData(1 To 5) As Variant
    Dim i As Integer

    ' Open a file for output, write to it, and close it
    hFile = FreeFile
    Open strFile For Output Access Write As hFile
    Write #hFile, "Some Text", "A Date:", Date, "A Number:", 100
    Close hFile

    ' Now open it back up for reading
    hFile = FreeFile
    Open strFile For Input Access Read As hFile
    Input #hFile, varData(1), varData(2), varData(3), _
     varData(4), varData(5)
    Close hFile

    ' Print the data
    For i = 1 To 5
        Debug.Print varData(i)
    Next
End Sub
```

This procedure begins by opening a file for output and writing several values to it. If you stepped through the code, stopping just after the first Close statement, and opened the file, you would see that the contents look like this:

```
"Some Text","A Date:",#1997-01-21#,"A Number:",100
```

The procedure then opens the file again for read access, uses Input # to read the data into five Variant variables, stored as an array, and prints them to the Immediate window.

NOTE When using Input #, the number of variables must match the number of data elements in the file.

Print #   Finally, there's the Print # statement. You may recognize the statement from the Print method of the Debug object. In fact, the two statements work in much the same manner. Print # writes a series of values to a file open in output or append mode. Unlike Write #, however, Print # does not format the data with quotes or number signs. Furthermore, Print # separates each value with tabs, not commas. If you were to substitute Print # for Write # in the previous example, the output file would look like this:

```
Some Text     A Date:     1/21/97    A Number:     100
```

Since there are no commas, you could not use Input # to read the file. You would need to use Input or Line Input instead.

The Print # statement is normally used with just one piece of data, commonly a line of text. Listing 12.15 contains a simple procedure to add line numbers to a text file. It opens one file in input mode and another, new file in output mode. It then loops through the input file, reads each line, and writes the line number and original text to the output file using Print #.

Listing 12.15: Use Print # to Add Lines Numbers to a Text File

```
Sub dhAddLineNumbers(strFileIn As String, strFileOut As String)
    Dim hFileIn As Long
    Dim hFileOut As Long
    Dim strInput As String
    Dim i As Integer

    ' Open first file for input
    hFileIn = FreeFile
    Open strFileIn For Input Access Read As hFileIn

    ' Open the second file for output
    hFileOut = FreeFile
    Open strFileOut For Output Access Write As hFileOut

    ' Read each line from the input file, add a line
    ' number and write it to the output file
    Do Until EOF(hFileIn)
        i = i + 1
        Line Input #hFileIn, strInput
        Print #hFileOut, i & ":", strInput
    Loop

    ' Close the files
```

```
        Close hFileIn
        Close hFileOut
End Sub
```

> **WARNING** When opening two or more files simultaneously, always call FreeFile for the second file handle after opening the first file. Otherwise, both file handles will be the same (since you haven't used the first handle, it's still free), and an error will occur when you try to open the second file.

Random Access

Although not often used in today's world of Automation-enabled database engines like Microsoft Jet, VBA's random-access file functions can still be used to produce database-like behavior with very little overhead. The functions work by manipulating "records" in the form of user-defined datatypes. When you open a file for random access, you pass the size of the record to the Open statement. All subsequent read and write operations then move data to and from variables of a given user-defined type in memory. Furthermore, these functions, Get and Put, transparently handle the task of overwriting existing records in the middle of a file.

To illustrate this functionality, assume the following user-defined datatype:

```
Type dhEmployee
    ID As Integer
    FirstName As String * 10
    LastName As String * 10
    Department As Integer
    HireDate As Date
    Salary As Currency
End Type
```

This represents a fictitious employee record. Note the fixed-length String variables. You must use fixed-length strings to prevent the record-oriented nature of this process from breaking down. This is due to the fact that you must tell VBA what the record size is when you open it. Errors will occur if the record is of variable size.

Listing 12.16 shows two functions designed to read and write data in this format to and from a file. Each function uses the same Open statement:

```
Open strFile For Random Access Read Write _
    As hFile Len = Len(empIn)
```

Note that the file is opened in random mode and that the record length (determined by applying the Len function to the record variable) is passed to the Open statement.

Listing 12.16: Read and Write to a Random-Access File

```
Function dhReadEmp(strFile As String, _
 emp As dhEmployee) As Boolean

    Dim hFile As Long
    Dim empIn As dhEmployee

    ' Open file for random access
    hFile = FreeFile
    Open strFile For Random Access Read Write _
     As hFile Len = Len(empIn)

    ' Try to find the employee in existing records
    Do Until EOF(hFile)

        ' Read in the record
        Get hFile, , empIn

        ' Check IDs
        If empIn.ID = emp.ID Then
            emp = empIn
            dhReadEmp = True
            Exit Do
        End If
    Loop

    Close hFile
End Function

Function dhSaveEmp(strFile As String, _
 empToSave As dhEmployee) As Boolean

    Dim hFile As Long
    Dim empIn As dhEmployee
    Dim lngRec As Long

    ' Open the file for random access
    hFile = FreeFile
    Open strFile For Random Access Read Write _
     As hFile Len = Len(empIn)
```

```
      ' Try to find the employee in existing records
      Do Until EOF(hFile)
          lngRec = lngRec + 1

          ' Read in the record
          Get hFile, lngRec, empIn

          ' Check IDs
          If empIn.ID = empToSave.ID Then

              ' Write the new data and get out
              Put hFile, lngRec, empToSave
              GoTo ExitHere
          End If
      Loop

      ' Record doesn't exist so write at end
      Put hFile, , empToSave

ExitHere:
      dhSaveEmp = True
      Close hFile
End Function
```

Each function loops through the contents of the file, loading existing data into a record variable, empIn. In the case of dhReadEmp, the function is not concerned with the record number per se. If the record is found, the function returns it to the calling procedure. dhSaveEmp, on the other hand, uses a variable to track the record number (lngRec). If an existing record is found, the procedure replaces it with the new record simply by specifying the record number in the Put statement. That's one reason this mode of data access is so powerful. You can read or write to *any* record in the file based on its number!

NOTE **A procedure that demonstrates this functionality, dhTestRandom, is included in the sample code but not printed here.**

Of course, it would be difficult to convince anyone that what we've just described constitutes a database. After all, to find a given record, our procedures loop through every record in the file! But by using complex data structures such as linked lists and embedded pointers, you could create an extremely sophisticated database system using these functions. Why you would want to, given the availability of component-based technologies, is another question.

The Windows API: Where the Real Power Is

As good as the built-in VBA functions are, they don't do everything you might need to do in an application. For instance, what if you need to find out how much disk space is free or change the volume label of a disk? You'll need to use the Windows API to accomplish these tasks. This section examines a few of the many API functions that relate to disks and files.

Comparing API Functions with VBA Functions

Before looking at specific functions, let's compare the VBA functions we've already discussed with their Windows API equivalents. You'll see many similarities. After all, when you call a VBA function, VBA is making the associated API calls on your behalf.

Table 12.4 lists the VBA disk and file functions, along with their comparable Windows API counterparts. Where the functionality provided by the Windows API functions differs from the VBA functions, it is noted in the right-hand column. Since the Windows API is a more complex interface than VBA, if there is no appreciable benefit to using an API function, we don't cover it in this chapter.

TABLE 12.4 Comparing VBA and Windows API Disk and File Functions

VBA Function(s)	Comparable API Function(s)	How API Functions Differ
ChDir, ChDrive	SetCurrentDirectory	No added functionality
CurDir	GetCurrentDirectory	No added functionality
Dir	FindFirstFile, FindNextFile, FindClose	Require more function calls but yield more information about each file
FileCopy	CopyFile	Allows you to prevent overwriting an existing file
FileDateTime	GetFileTime	Much more complex, but gives you access to all three file times (creation, access, and last-written)

TABLE 12.4   Comparing VBA and Windows API Disk and File Functions (continued)

VBA Function(s)	Comparable API Function(s)	How API Functions Differ
FileLen	GetFileSize	Works with really huge files (greater than 2GB)
GetAttr	GetFileAttributes	No added functionality
Kill	DeleteFile	No added functionality
MkDir, RmDir	CreateDirectory	
CreateDirectoryEx		
RemoveDirectory	Support for NT security attributes	
Name	MoveFile	No added functionality
SetAttr	SetFileAttributes	No added functionality
Open, Input, Print, Write, Close	CreateFile, ReadFile, WriteFile, CloseHandle	This is like comparing apples and oranges. You must use the Create-File API function to obtain file handles, but in general, using the VBA functions for file I/O is simpler

In addition to the API calls that duplicate built-in functionality, there is a whole host of others than offer capabilities not found in VBA. Table 12.5 lists the ones mentioned in this chapter. There are certainly others, but most are too esoteric or too complex to warrant coverage here.

TABLE 12.5   Windows API Functions with No VBA Equivalent

Function(s)	Description
CompareFileTime	Compares the file time of two files
FindFirstChange Notification, FindNext-ChangeNotification, FindCloseChangeNotification	Instruct Windows to notify your application when a file or directory changes
GetBinaryType	Determines whether a file is an executable and if it is, the type

TABLE 12.5   Windows API Functions with No VBA Equivalent (continued)

Function(s)	Description
GetDiskFreeSpace space	Retrieves information about a disk drive, including available disk
GetDriveType	Determines what type a drive is (fixed, removable, network, CD-ROM, or RAM disk)
GetFileInformationByHandle	Retrieves detailed file information in a single function call
GetFullPathName	Retrieves the full path name for a file, given a partial path
GetLogicalDrives, GetLogicalDriveStrings	Retrieve the logical drives for the computer either as a bitmask or as a null-delimited string
GetShortPathName	Retrieves the short (8.3) file name associated with a given long file name
GetTempFileName	Computes a temporary file name based on a directory name, prefix characters, and, optionally, a unique integer
GetTempPath	Retrieves the directory designated to hold temporary files
GetVolumeInformation	Retrieves information about the file system and specified volume
SearchPath	Searches for a file, given a search path or the default system paths
SetFileTime	Changes the times associated with a given file
SetVolumeLabel	Sets the volume label for a drive

Getting Disk Information

VBA has a number of functions that deal with files but very few that deal with disks. For example, there is no way to determine the disk space available on a given drive or the number and type of drives installed in your computer. Fortunately, the Windows API comes to the rescue with a myriad of functions to accomplish these tasks as well as many others. All the code for this section is contained in the basDiskInfo module of the sample Excel workbook and the DISKINFO.BAS file.

How Many Drives Do You Have?

To find out how many drives you have, the best place to start is with two functions that determine the number of drives installed in your computer, including both physical drives and network connections. The two functions are GetLogical-Drives and GetLogicalDriveStrings. Which one you use will depend on what type of data you're dealing with.

GetLogicalDrives is a simple function call that returns drive information packed into a single long integer. Each bit represents a drive letter (the first bit for drive A, the second for drive B, and so on), with 1 indicating that the drive is installed. The declaration for GetLogicalDrives is

```
Declare Function GetLogicalDrives Lib "kernel32" () As Long
```

It's pretty simple. What little complexity there is comes in deciphering the bits. Listing 12.17 shows a procedure, dhGetDrivesByNum, that takes the result of calling GetLogicalDrives and performs a bitwise comparison on the first 26 bits. If it finds a drive, the procedure adds the drive number to a VBA collection passed as an argument.

> **TIP**
>
> VBA Collection objects are extremely useful in situations like this. In fact, it's a good idea to consider a collection wherever you're thinking of using an array.

Listing 12.17: Fetch Logical Drives by Number

```
Function dhGetDrivesByNum(colDrives As Collection) _
 As Integer

    Dim lngDrives As Long
    Dim intDrive As Integer

    ' Reset the collection
    Set colDrives = New Collection

    ' Get the logical drives
    lngDrives = GetLogicalDrives()

    ' Do a bitwise compare on the first 26 bits
    For intDrive = 0 To 25
```

```
        If (lngDrives And (2 ^ intDrive)) <> 0 Then
            colDrives.Add intDrive, Chr(65 + intDrive)
        End If
    Next

    ' Return the number of drives found
    dhGetDrivesByNum = colDrives.Count

End Function
```

Using GetLogicalDriveStrings presents a different type of complexity, although not daunting by any stretch of the imagination. GetLogicalDriveStrings returns drive letters in a single string buffer. Each drive letter is separated by a null character (ASCII code 0), with the entire string terminated by two Nulls. (This is often referred to as a *double null-terminated* string.) Listing 12.18 shows the counterpart to dhGetDrivesByNum, a procedure called dhGetDrivesByString. After allocating a buffer and calling GetLogicalDriveStrings, dhGetDrivesByString parses the buffer, looking for null characters. Like dhGetDrivesByNum, it also adds these drive letters to a VBA collection passed to the function.

Listing 12.18: Fetch Logical Drives, This Time by Letter

```
Function dhGetDrivesByString(colDrives As Collection) _
 As Integer

    Dim strBuffer As String
    Dim lngBytes As Long
    Dim intPos As Integer
    Dim intPos2 As Integer
    Dim strDrive As String

    ' Reset the collection
    Set colDrives = New Collection

    ' Set up a buffer
    strBuffer = Space(255)

    ' Get the logical drive string
    lngBytes = GetLogicalDriveStrings( _
     Len(strBuffer), strBuffer)

    ' Parse the drive string by looking
    ' for the null delimiter
    intPos2 = 1
    intPos = InStr(intPos2, strBuffer, vbNullChar)
```

```
        Do Until intPos = 0 Or intPos > lngBytes

            ' Parse out the drive letter
            strDrive = mid(strBuffer, intPos2, intPos - intPos2)

            ' Add it to the collection
            colDrives.Add strDrive, strDrive

            ' Find the next drive letter
            intPos2 = intPos + 1
            intPos = InStr(intPos2, strBuffer, Chr(0))
        Loop

        ' Return the number of drives found
        dhGetDrivesByString = colDrives.Count

End Function
```

Listing 12.19 shows a sample procedure that tests each method. You can run this code from the Immediate window. Figure 12.2 shows the results.

Listing 12.19: Test the Methods for Retrieving Logical Drives

```
Sub dhPrintDrives()
    Dim colDrives As New Collection
    Dim varDrive As Variant

    ' First by number
    Debug.Print "Drives found: " & _
      dhGetDrivesByNum(colDrives)
    For Each varDrive In colDrives
        Debug.Print varDrive,
    Next

    Debug.Print

    ' Then by letter
    Debug.Print "Drives found: " & _
      dhGetDrivesByString(colDrives)
    For Each varDrive In colDrives
        Debug.Print varDrive,
    Next
End Sub
```

FIGURE 12.2

Logical drive information

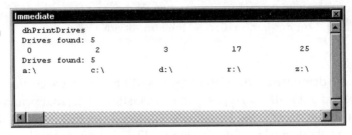

What Kind of Drives Are They?

Once you've determined which drives are on your system, you can call another Windows API function, GetDriveType, to find out what kind of drive each one is. GetDriveType's declaration is as follows:

```
Declare Function GetDriveType Lib "kernel32" _
 Alias "GetDriveTypeA" (ByVal nDrive As String) As Long
```

GetDriveType accepts a string representing the root directory of a drive (including the colon and backslash and like those produced by dhGetDrivesByString) and returns a code indicating what type of drive it is. It can be any one of the values listed in Table 12.6.

TABLE 12.6   Drive Type Constants for GetDriveType

Value	Constant	Description
0	DRIVE_UNKNOWN	Drive does not exist or type cannot be determined
1	DRIVE_NOROOT	String passed was not the root directory
2	DRIVE_REMOVABLE	Removable media
3	DRIVE_FIXED	Fixed disk
4	DRIVE_REMOTE	Network drive
5	DRIVE_CDROM	CD-ROM
6	DRIVE_RAMDISK	RAM disk

> **TIP**   If you pass the vbNullString constant as the drive letter, GetDriveType returns information on the current drive.

To demonstrate the GetDriveType API function, we created a sample procedure called dhPrintDriveTypes (shown in Listing 12.20) that prints the type of each installed drive to the Immediate window. Note that it uses dhGetDrivesByString to generate the list of drives. Figure 12.3 illustrates sample output.

Listing 12.20: Print the Type of Each Installed Drive

```
Sub dhPrintDriveTypes()
    Dim colDrives As New Collection
    Dim varDrive As Variant
    Dim lngType As Long

    ' Get drive letters
    If dhGetDrivesByString(colDrives) > 0 Then
        For Each varDrive In colDrives
            ' Print drive letter
            Debug.Print varDrive,

            ' Print drive type
            lngType = GetDriveType(CStr(varDrive))
            Select Case lngType
                Case DRIVE_UNKNOWN
                    Debug.Print "Unknown"
                Case DRIVE_NOROOT
                    Debug.Print "Unknown"
                Case DRIVE_REMOVABLE
                    Debug.Print "Removable Media"
                Case DRIVE_FIXED
                    Debug.Print "Fixed Disk"
                Case DRIVE_REMOTE
                    Debug.Print "Network Drive"
                Case DRIVE_CDROM
                    Debug.Print "CD-ROM"
                Case DRIVE_RAMDISK
                    Debug.Print "RAM Disk"
            End Select
        Next
    End If
End Sub
```

FIGURE 12.3

Printing drive types

> **NOTE** Strings passed to GetDriveType must represent the root directory; otherwise, the function will be unable to determine the drive type.

How Much Space Is Left?

Perhaps the most common question VBA developers want to ask concerning disk drives is, "How much disk space is available?" Answering this question was extremely difficult under 16-bit versions of BASIC because it involved making DOS interrupt calls—not an easy task from VBA. The Win32 API, however, added a simple function to retrieve this information, GetDiskFreeSpace. In fact, this function can tell you much more about a disk than how much space is available. The declaration for GetDiskFreeSpace is

```
Declare Function GetDiskFreeSpace Lib "kernel32" _
 Alias "GetDiskFreeSpaceA" _
 (ByVal lpRootPathName As String, _
 lpSectorsPerCluster As Long, _
 lpBytesPerSector As Long, _
 lpNumberOfFreeClusters As Long, _
 lpTotalNumberOfClusters As Long) As Long
```

As you can see, even though it's a single function call, Microsoft hasn't given away the amount of available disk space for free—you have to compute it based on the information returned to you by the function. As with GetDriveType, you pass a string representing the root directory of a drive. You also pass four long integers that GetDiskFreeSpace fills in with drive information (number of sectors per cluster, number of bytes per sector, free clusters, and total clusters). From there, it's a simple mathematical exercise to compute the free disk space in bytes.

TIP

If you pass the vbNullString constant as the drive letter, GetDiskFree-Space returns information on the current drive.

We've boiled this down to two useful functions, dhFreeDiskSpace and dhTotalDiskSpace, shown in Listing 12.21. This listing also shows a test procedure, dhPrintDiskSpace, that demonstrates how to call the two functions. Figure 12.4 shows sample output.

FIGURE 12.4

Printing disk space for installed drives

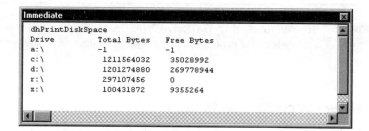

NOTE

If the GetDiskFreeSpace function fails (returns False) both dhFree-DiskSpace and dhTotalDiskSpace return −1.

Listing 12.21: Functions For Determining Total and Free Disk Space

```
Function dhTotalDiskSpace(Optional strDrive As _
  String = vbNullString) As Long

    Dim lngSectorsPerCluster As Long
    Dim lngBytesPerSector As Long
    Dim lngNumberOfFreeClusters As Long
    Dim lngTotalNumberOfClusters As Long

    ' Call GetDiskFreeSpace
    If CBool(GetDiskFreeSpace(strDrive, _
      lngSectorsPerCluster, _
      lngBytesPerSector, _
      lngNumberOfFreeClusters, _
      lngTotalNumberOfClusters)) Then
```

```
                    ' If successful compute total disk space
                    dhTotalDiskSpace = _
                     lngSectorsPerCluster * _
                     lngBytesPerSector * _
                     lngTotalNumberOfClusters
             Else
                    dhTotalDiskSpace = -1
             End If
      End Function

      Function dhFreeDiskSpace(Optional strDrive As _
        String = vbNullString) As Long

             Dim lngSectorsPerCluster As Long
             Dim lngBytesPerSector As Long
             Dim lngNumberOfFreeClusters As Long
             Dim lngTotalNumberOfClusters As Long

             ' Call GetDiskFreeSpace
             If CBool(GetDiskFreeSpace(strDrive, _
               lngSectorsPerCluster, _
               lngBytesPerSector, _
               lngNumberOfFreeClusters, _
               lngTotalNumberOfClusters)) Then

                    ' If successful compute free disk space
                    dhFreeDiskSpace = _
                     lngSectorsPerCluster * _
                     lngBytesPerSector * _
                     lngNumberOfFreeClusters
             Else
                    dhFreeDiskSpace = -1
             End If
      End Function

      Sub dhPrintDiskSpace()
             Dim colDrives As New Collection
             Dim varDrive As Variant

             ' Get drive letters
             If dhGetDrivesByString(colDrives) > 0 Then

                    ' Print header
                    Debug.Print "Drive", "Total Bytes", "Free Bytes"

                    ' Print drive space for all drives
                    For Each varDrive In colDrives
```

```
        Debug.Print varDrive, _
            dhTotalDiskSpace(CStr(varDrive)), _
            dhFreeDiskSpace(CStr(varDrive))

    Next
  End If
End Sub
```

What about Drive Labels?

The last disk-related API functions covered in this chapter concern a disk's volume label. You know that 11-character string you can set when you format a disk? Using the VBA Dir function, you can retrieve a disk's volume label, but you can't set it. With the Windows API functions GetVolumeInformation and SetVolumeLabel, you can do that and more.

In addition to the volume label, GetVolumeInformation returns information on the volume's serial number, the maximum file name length, and the name of the installed file system. The declaration for GetVolumeInformation is

```
Declare Function GetVolumeInformation Lib "kernel32" _
 Alias "GetVolumeInformationA" _
 (ByVal lpRootPathName As String, _
 ByVal lpVolumeNameBuffer As String, _
 ByVal nVolumeNameSize As Long, _
 lpVolumeSerialNumber As Long, _
 lpMaximumComponentLength As Long, _
 lpFileSystemFlags As Long, _
 ByVal lpFileSystemNameBuffer As String, _
 ByVal nFileSystemNameSize As Long) As Long
```

We created a procedure that accepts a drive's root directory and prints information about the volume to the Immediate window. Since the function call is straightforward, and to save space, we decided not to include the code listing here. You can find the procedure, called dhPrintVolInfo, in the basDiskInfo module in the sample Excel workbook or DISKFILE.BAS.

GetVolumeInformation's counterpart, SetVolumeLabel, is a simple function with a single purpose: to set the volume label of a disk drive. Its declaration is

```
Declare Function SetVolumeLabel Lib "kernel32" _
 Alias "SetVolumeLabelA" (ByVal lpRootPathName As String, _
 ByVal lpVolumeName As String) As Long
```

As with SetVolumeLabel's cousins, you pass a string containing the root directory of a drive as the first argument. The second argument is the string containing the new volume label. If you wish, you can remove the volume label completely. Due to a bug in Windows 95, however, there are two ways to do this. Under Windows NT, the function works as designed. You pass a null pointer (vbNullString) to the function to delete the volume label. Under Windows 95, this doesn't work. Instead you must pass an empty string (""). If SetVolumeLabel is successful in changing the volume label, it returns True; otherwise it returns False.

Fun with Paths

One of the most common (and most tedious) tasks a VBA programmer must perform is manipulating file paths. Whether you're deriving the full path from a partial path, parsing paths, or determining the short form of a path, you'll undoubtedly devote more than a few moments to dealing with these issues during your programming career. All the code for this section is contained in the basPathFun module of the sample Excel workbook and the PATHFUN.BAS file.

Parsing Paths

Often you'll need to break a complete file path into its components. Typically, this means separating the file name from the path. You may also want to treat the file extension as a separate component. At the extreme end, breaking a path into individual directories is sometimes desirable. We've written two VBA functions to aid you in this process.

> **NOTE** These and other functions in this chapter use string functions introduced in Chapter 1. For more information on how they work, see that chapter.

The first VBA function, shown in Listing 12.22, is dhParsePath, which takes a complete file path and separates it into path and file name components. Note that it accepts variables for the resulting components by reference and modifies them. An optional argument, varExt, represents a variable for the file extension. If this is passed to dhParsePath, the function strips the file extension from the name and places it in the variable. If this argument isn't passed, dhParsePath includes the extension with the file name. You can test this function by calling the dhTest-ParsePath procedure, which is explained in the section "A Path-Parsing Example" a little later in this chapter.

Listing 12.22: A Function That Breaks Apart File Paths

```
Sub dhParsePath(ByVal strFullPath As String, _
 ByRef strPath As String, ByRef strFile As String, _
 Optional ByRef varExt As Variant)

    Dim lngPos As Long

    ' If varExt was passed, get the file extension
    If Not IsMissing(varExt) Then
        lngPos = dhRInstr(strFullPath, ".")
        If lngPos > 0 Then
            varExt = mid(strFullPath, lngPos + 1)
        Else
            varExt = ""
        End If
    Else
        varExt = ""
    End If

    ' Now get the file name, removing the extension
    ' if necessary
    lngPos = dhRInstr(strFullPath, "\")
    If lngPos > 0 Then
        strFile = mid(strFullPath, lngPos + 1, _
         Len(strFullPath) - lngPos - Len(varExt))
        If Len(varExt) Then
            strFile = Left(strFile, Len(strFile) - 1)
        End If
        strPath = Left(strFullPath, lngPos - 1)
    End If
End Sub
```

A more complex function is shown in Listing 12.23. The dhGetPathParts function breaks a complete path into numerous components, based on each subdirectory in the path. You call it by passing a path and a VBA Collection object. The function places the components, which include the drive letter, each subdirectory, and the file name, into the collection. We use this function in other procedures in the sample code contained on the CD-ROM .

Listing 12.23: Decompose a Path into Atomic Components

```
Function dhGetPathParts(strPath As String, _
 colParts As Collection) As Long
```

```
Dim intPos As Integer
Dim intFound As Integer
Dim strFound As String

intPos = 1
Do
    ' Search for the first backslash
    intFound = InStr(intPos, strPath, "\")

    ' If found, add the text between it and the
    ' preceding backslash to the collection
    If intFound > 0 Then
        strFound = mid(strPath, intPos, intFound - intPos)
        colParts.Add strFound
        intPos = intFound + 1
    Else
        ' There are no more backslashes so just
        ' add the rest of the string
        colParts.Add mid(strPath, intPos)
    End If
Loop While intFound > 0

' Return the number of parts
dhGetPathParts = colParts.Count
End Function
```

Retrieving Complete and Short Path Names

The Windows API also offers several functions that deal with paths. Some, like GetTempPath, are discussed in other sections of this chapter because they relate to other topics. Two that can't be categorized with other functions are GetFull-PathName and GetShortPath name. They are declared as:

```
Declare Function GetFullPathName Lib "kernel32" _
 Alias "GetFullPathNameA" _
 (ByVal lpFileName As String, ByVal nBufferLength As Long, _
 ByVal lpBuffer As String, ByVal lpFilePart As String) As Long

Declare Function GetShortPathName Lib "kernel32" _
 Alias "GetShortPathNameA" _
 (ByVal lpszLongPath As String, _
 ByVal lpszShortPath As String, _
 ByVal cchBuffer As Long) As Long
```

The sole purpose of GetFullPathName is to create a fully qualified path from a given partial path and file name, based on the current directory. This means that if you simply pass a file name, GetFullPathName will append the path of the current directory to it. If you pass a relative path, such as "..\..\SOMEFILE.TXT", GetFullPathName will resolve the relative path to the current directory and return the result. We've written a VBA wrapper for the GetFullPath function called dhFullPath, shown in Listing 12.24.

Listing 12.24: The dhFullPath Function Resolves Relative Paths and File Names

```
Function dhFullPath(strPath As String) As String
    Dim strBuffer As String
    Dim strFilePart As String
    Dim lngBytes As Long

    ' Set up the buffer
    strBuffer = Space(MAX_PATH)

    ' Call GetFullPathName
    lngBytes = GetFullPathName(strPath, Len(strBuffer), _
     strBuffer, strFilePart)

    ' If successful, parse the buffer
    If lngBytes > 0 Then
        dhFullPath = Left(strBuffer, lngBytes)
    End If
End Function
```

To test this function, try running the following code from the Immediate window:

```
?dhFullPath(Dir("*.*"))
```

The Dir statement returns the first file in the current directory. dhFullPath then computes the complete path. Be careful when using this function, however, since GetFullPathName doesn't verify that the resulting file name is valid or that the file actually exists. For instance, the following statement retrieves the first file in the directory above the current one and appends it to the current directory name:

```
?dhFullPath(Dir("..\*.*"))
```

Even though the file exists, the path is invalid.

GetShortPathName is useful if you need to work with file names in their old 8.3 form. For example, perhaps your application needs to exchange files with another system that doesn't support long file names (such as Windows 3.x). GetShort-PathName accepts a long file name and returns its associated short name. Again, we've provided a simple wrapper function you can call, dhShortPath, shown in Listing 12.25.

Listing 12.25: dhShortPath Returns a File's 8.3 File Name

```
Function dhShortPath(strPath As String) As String
    Dim strBuffer As String
    Dim lngBytes As Long

    ' Set up a buffer
    strBuffer = Space(MAX_PATH)

    ' Call GetShortPathName
    lngBytes = GetShortPathName(strPath, strBuffer, _
     Len(strBuffer))

    ' If succcessful parse the buffer
    If lngBytes > 0 Then
        dhShortPath = Left(strBuffer, lngBytes)
    End If
End Function
```

A Path-Parsing Example

Listing 12.26 shows a procedure that demonstrates the functions we've just discussed. It begins by retrieving the first file in the current directory. It then calls the other functions to compute the full path, the short path, and the path parts. Some sample output is shown in Figure 12.5.

Listing 12.26: A Procedure to Demonstrate Path Parsing

```
Sub dhTestParsePath()
    Dim strCurrFile As String
    Dim strFullPath As String
    Dim strShortPath As String
    Dim strPath As String
    Dim strFile As String
    Dim varExt As Variant
    Dim lngParts As Long
    Dim colParts As New Collection
```

```
Dim varPart As Variant

' Get first file from current directory
strCurrFile = Dir("*.*")

' Get the full path name
strFullPath = dhFullPath(strCurrFile)

' Get the short path name
strShortPath = dhShortPath(strFullPath)

' Parse the path into its parts
Call dhParsePath(strFullPath, strPath, strFile, varExt)

' Decompose the entire path
lngParts = dhGetPathParts(strFullPath, colParts)

' Print the information
Debug.Print "File:", strCurrFile
Debug.Print "Full path:", strFullPath
Debug.Print "Short path:", strShortPath
Debug.Print "Path:", strPath
Debug.Print "Filename:", strFile
Debug.Print "Extension:", varExt
Debug.Print "Path parts:", lngParts
lngParts = 2
For Each varPart In colParts
    Debug.Print Space(lngParts) & varPart
    lngParts = lngParts + 2
Next
End Sub
```

FIGURE 12.5

Result of parsing a
file path

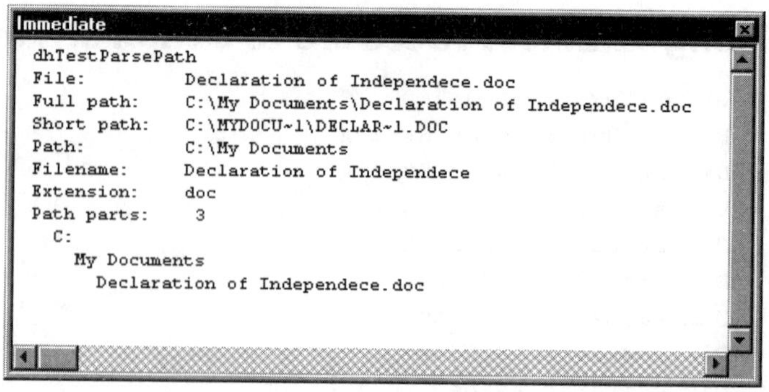

A Hardcore Replacement for Dir

If the VBA Dir function does not offer all the power you need, consider using the underlying Windows API functions that Dir is based on: FindFirstFile, FindNext-File, and FindClose. Individually, these three functions emulate the functionality of various forms of the VBA Dir function. FindFirstFile initiates a directory search and returns the first matching file name, just as Dir does when you pass a file specification. FindNextFile locates the next matching file, and FindClose terminates a search. Calling Dir again with a new file specification performs this last step implicitly.

These functions go even further than Dir, however. In addition to matching file names, these functions return additional information, such as creation date, size, and short (8.3) file name. Declarations for the functions are shown here:

```
' Functions for searching for files in a given directory
Declare Function FindFirstFile Lib "kernel32" _
 Alias "FindFirstFileA" (ByVal lpFileName As String, _
 lpFindFileData As WIN32_FIND_DATA) As Long

Declare Function FindNextFile Lib "kernel32" _
 Alias "FindNextFileA" (ByVal hFindFile As Long, _
 lpFindFileData As WIN32_FIND_DATA) As Long

Declare Function FindClose Lib "kernel32" _
 (ByVal hFindFile As Long) As Long
```

NOTE   These functions don't actually "find" files in the sense that they search your hard disk. For that you'll have to write custom VBA code. If you simply need to find a file given a certain search path, see the discussion of the SearchPath API function in the section "Searching For Files" later in this chapter.

All the code for this section is contained in the basFindFunctions module of the sample Excel workbook and the FINDFUNC.BAS file.

Calling the "Find" Functions

You call FindFirstFile with a file specification, using the same rules as when passing a file specification to Dir: you can pass a complete or partial path, including wildcards or UNC server names. You also pass a pointer to a WIN32_FIND_DATA structure. FindFirstFile fills in the members of this structure with information on the matching file. The definition of the structure is as follows:

```
Type WIN32_FIND_DATA
    lngFileAttributes As Long              ' File attributes
    ftCreationTime As FILETIME             ' Creation time
    ftLastAccessTime As FILETIME           ' Last access time
    ftLastWriteTime As FILETIME            ' Last modified time
    lngFileSizeHigh As Long                ' Size (high word)
    lngFileSizeLow As Long                 ' Size (low word)
    lngReserved0 As Long                   ' reserved
    lngReserved1 As Long                   ' reserved
    strFileName As String * MAX_PATH       ' File name
    strAlternate As String * 14            ' 8.3 name
End Type
```

NOTE   MAX_PATH is defined as 260, the maximum path size for Windows.

As you can see from the type definition, you can gather quite a bit of information from a single function call. (For more information on the FILETIME structure, see the section "Windows API Dates and Times" later in this chapter.)

If FindFirstFile locates a file matching the passed specification, it fills in the WIN32_FIND_DATA structure and returns a handle to the find operation. You use this handle in subsequent calls to FindNextFile. When you no longer want to continue searching, call FindClose, passing the handle of the find operation you want to abandon.

If FindFirstFile fails, it returns –1. You can then inspect the LastDLLError property of VBA's Err object for the error code returned by the DLL function. FindNextFile simply returns True if the next find operation was successful and False if it wasn't.

With this information in hand, you can build a simple function that lists the files in a given directory. Listing 12.27 shows the dhFindFiles procedure, which does just that. It begins by calling FindFirstFile with a path passed as an argument. If this is successful, the procedure then calls FindNextFile inside a Do...Loop, continuing until FindNextFile returns False.

Listing 12.27: List Files in a Given Directory Using API Functions

```
Sub dhFindFiles(strPath As String)
    Dim fd As WIN32_FIND_DATA
    Dim hFind As Long

    ' Find the first file
    hFind = FindFirstFile(strPath, fd)

    ' If successful...
    If hFind > 0 Then
        Do
            ' Print file information
            With fd
                Debug.Print dhTrimNull(.strFileName), _
                    .lngFileSizeLow & " bytes", _
                    dhBuildAttrString(.lngFileAttributes)
            End With

        ' Find the next file and continue as long
        ' as there are files to be found
        Loop While CBool(FindNextFile(hFind, fd))

        ' Terminate the find operation
        Call FindClose(hFind)
    End If
End Sub
```

Since the file name members in WIN32_FIND_DATA are fixed-length strings, the procedure must parse the results, looking for a terminating null character.

To test this procedure, try calling it from the Immediate window. Figure 12.6 shows what the output might look like.

A New and Improved Dir

Having all this extra information at your disposal creates some interesting possibilities. We've used these API functions to create a replacement for the VBA Dir function. Why have we done this? One drawback to the VBA Dir function is that, while it lets you include files with certain attributes in the search, it does not allow you to limit the search based on a set of attributes. Our replacement, dhDir, does.

FIGURE 12.6

File information pro-
duced by calling
dhFindFiles

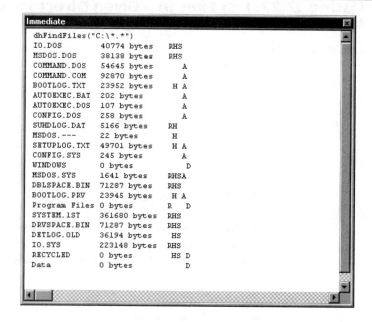

FIGURE 12.6

File information pro-
duced by calling
dhFindFiles

Listing 12.28 shows the dhDir function, along with a helper function, dhFind-
ByAttr. We've structured dhDir so you can call it just as you would the VBA Dir
function. Specifically, you call it with a path name to begin a search and then call
it with no arguments to continue retrieving matching file names. Unlike Dir, however, our function executes an exclusive search when you provide an attribute
value. You can override this behavior, and thus revert to the same functionality
Dir provides, by passing False as the optional third argument.

Listing 12.28: Our Replacement for the VBA Dir Function

```
Function dhDir(Optional ByVal strPath As String = "", _
 Optional lngAttributes As Long = vbNormal, _
 Optional fExclusive As Boolean = True) As String

    Dim fd As WIN32_FIND_DATA
    Static hFind As Long
    Static lngAttr As Long
    Static fEx As Boolean

    ' If no path was passed, try to find the next file
    If strPath = "" Then
```

```
        If hFind > 0 Then
            If CBool(FindNextFile(hFind, fd)) Then
                dhDir = dhFindByAttr(hFind, fd, lngAttr, fEx)
            End If
        End If

    ' Otherwise, start a new search
    Else
        ' Close the last find if there was one
        If hFind > 0 Then
            Call FindClose(hFind)
        End If

        ' Store the attributes and exclusive settings
        lngAttr = lngAttributes
        fEx = fExclusive

        ' If the path ends in a backslash, assume
        ' all files and append "*.*"
        If Right(strPath, 1) = "\" Then
            strPath = strPath & "*.*"
        End If

        ' Find the first file
        hFind = FindFirstFile(strPath, fd)
        If hFind > 0 Then
            dhDir = dhFindByAttr(hFind, fd, lngAttr, fEx)
        End If
    End If
End Function

Function dhFindByAttr(hFind As Long, _
 fd As WIN32_FIND_DATA, lngAttr As Long, _
 fExclusive As Boolean) As String

    Dim fOK As Boolean

    ' Continue looking for files until one
    ' matches the given attributes exactly
    ' (if fExclusive is True) or just contains
    ' them (if fExclusive is False)
    Do
        If fExclusive Then
            fOK = fd.lngFileAttributes = lngAttr
        Else
```

```
            fOK = (fd.lngFileAttributes And lngAttr) = lngAttr
        End If

        If fOK Then
            dhFindByAttr = dhTrimNull(fd.strFileName)
            Exit Do
        End If
    Loop While FindNextFile(hFind, fd)
End Function
```

Our function works by first calling FindFirstFile to begin a new search (but only if you pass a file specification in the first argument). The dhFindByAttr function checks the file's attributes against the requested set and, if no match is found, uses FindNextFile to return the next file name. This continues until a match is found or no more files matching the original specification exist. Static variables in dhDir are used to store parameter values between function calls.

Figure 12.7 shows an example of calling dhDir to search for all files in the root directory that have the read-only, system, and hidden attributes set. The first call to dhDir establishes the search parameters. Subsequent calls return other files with these exact three attributes.

FIGURE 12.7

Calling dhDir to perform an exclusive directory search

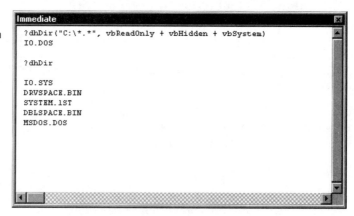

```
Immediate                                                    ☒
?dhDir("C:\*.*", vbReadOnly + vbHidden + vbSystem)
IO.DOS

?dhDir

IO.SYS
DRVSPACE.BIN
SYSTEM.1ST
DBLSPACE.BIN
MSDOS.DOS
```

Figure 12.8 shows a similar directory search, but this time the search is not exclusive. It returns all files that have the three attributes set, regardless of whether they have any others set. As a result, the MSDOS.SYS file, which has all three attributes plus the archive attribute, is included in this search.

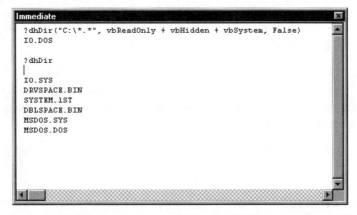

FIGURE 12.8

Calling dhDir to perform an inclusive directory search

Exploiting the True Power of FindFirstFile

At this point you might be wondering why we went to all this trouble for what you might describe as a minimum gain in functionality over Dir. First of all, dhDir does serve a purpose. How often have you wanted to retrieve a list of *only* subdirectories without having to weed out normal files? Second, the true power of these functions lies in the additional information you get as part of the function call. We exploit this power when we present our object model for files in the section "An Object Model for Directories and Files" later in this chapter.

Windows Notification Functions

Have you ever needed to know when the contents of a file or directory have changed? For example, suppose you're writing a "drop-box" application that monitors a network directory for incoming files. Wouldn't it be nice if Windows could tell your application when a file arrives? Well, it can, if you use the file notification functions discussed in this section. All the code for this section is contained in the basNotification module of the sample Excel workbook and the NOTIFY.BAS file.

How Change Notifications Work

The functions FindFirstChangeNotification, FindNextChangeNotification, and FindCloseChangeNotification are similar to the Find functions just described, except that instead of returning results right away, they establish *change handles* that you pass to the operating system. Each change handle denotes a particular state change, such as a directory being renamed. When the event occurs, Windows notifies your application. You can then continue monitoring the directory or cancel the change handle.

You may have noticed this effect when using Windows Explorer. If you leave a directory window open and use another application to copy a file to that directory, Explorer shows the new file immediately; you don't have to manually refresh the window contents.

You can choose to monitor one or more conditions using a bitmask of values from Table 12.7.

T A B L E   1 2 . 7   Values for Monitoring Conditions

Constant	Description
FILE_NOTIFY_CHANGE_FILE_NAME	File creations, deletions, and name changes
FILE_NOTIFY_CHANGE_DIR_NAME	Directory creations, deletions, and name changes
FILE_NOTIFY_CHANGE_ATTRIBUTES	File or directory attribute changes
FILE_NOTIFY_CHANGE_SIZE	File size changes
FILE_NOTIFY_CHANGE_LAST_WRITE	Changes to a file's last write time
FILE_NOTIFY_CHANGE_SECURITY	File security descriptor changes (Windows NT only)

Setting Up a Change Notification

You establish a change notification using the FindFirstChangeNotification function. Its declaration is as follows:

```
Declare Function FindFirstChangeNotification Lib "kernel32" _
 Alias "FindFirstChangeNotificationA" _
 (ByVal lpPathName As String, ByVal bWatchSubtree As Long, _
 ByVal dwNotifyFilter As Long) As Long
```

The lpPathName argument is the name of a directory you want to monitor. If you want to monitor any subdirectories as well, pass 1 as the second argument. The third argument is a combination of values from Table 12.7.

If successful, FindFirstChangeNotification returns a change handle. (If it fails, it returns –1). You pass this change handle to another Windows API function, WaitForSingleObject:

```
Declare Function WaitForSingleObject Lib "kernel32" _
 (ByVal hHandle As Long, ByVal dwMilliseconds As Long) _
 As Long
```

WaitForSingleObject is a generic function designed to work with a number of Windows notification handles. When you call the function, it does not return until one of the following two things happens:

- The event associated with the change handle occurs.

- The number of milliseconds passed as the second argument elapses.

TIP If you want to wait indefinitely, pass &HFFFF as the second argument.

This brings up the downside of using these functions: your VBA procedure waits until the event occurs, effectively halting your application. Therefore, these functions are of limited use in single-threaded environments like the current version of VBA (although if VBA ever becomes multithreaded, these functions will be extremely useful). Nonetheless, in some circumstances, like the drop-box scenario mentioned at the beginning of this section, you may not mind this behavior.

What to Do When a Notification Occurs

When WaitForSingleObject returns, the result indicates whether the event has occurred (WAIT_OBJECT_0) or the timeout period has elapsed (WAIT_TIME-OUT). Based on this value, you can take appropriate action. In our drop-box scenario, for example, a return value of WAIT_OBJECT_0 would be your cue to scan the directory for the new file and begin the file-manipulation process.

Then, if you want to continue waiting for another change, call FindNextChange-Notification, passing the change handle obtained earlier from FindFirstChange-Notification. FindNextChangeNotification returns True if Windows is ready to resume monitoring the directory for changes. Then you call WaitForSingleObject again, and the process repeats itself. When you no longer want to monitor changes, call FindCloseChangeNotification.

Using Change Notifications

For the reasons described earlier in in this discussion, these functions are difficult to demonstrate using VBA. Nonetheless, we've put together a little "game" that demonstrates how to use the functions. You can think of it as a computerized version of the arcade game featuring little gophers that pop up from random holes. The object of that game is to whack each gopher with a rubber mallet before it disappears back into its den. Listing 12.29 shows the heart of our gopher-whacking game, the dhFunWithNotify procedure.

Listing 12.29: Test Notification Functions and Have Fun Too

```
Sub dhFunWithNotify(strPath As String, ByVal lngTimeout As Long)
    Dim colPaths As New Collection
    Dim strFile As String
    Dim hChange As Long
    Dim lngStatus As Long
    Dim lngFlags As Long
    Dim fKeepGoing As Boolean
    Dim lngScore As Long
    Dim lngTotalScore As Long

    Const dhcBaseScore = 100000

    ' Build a list of subdirectories beneath strPath
    Debug.Print "Building directory list..."
    If dhGetSubdirectories(strPath, colPaths) = 0 Then
        Debug.Print "Could not build subdirectory list!"
        Exit Sub
    End If

    ' Set up flags
    lngFlags = FILE_NOTIFY_CHANGE_FILE_NAME

    ' Create the first file
    Debug.Print "Here we go!!!"
    strFile = dhCreateTempFile(dhGetRandomFile(colPaths), _
     "~DH")
    If strFile = "" Then
        Debug.Print "Error creating first file!"
        Exit Sub
    End If
```

```
' Create first change notification
hChange = FindFirstChangeNotification(strPath, _
 1, lngFlags)

' Make sure it was successful
If hChange > 0 Then

    ' Loop until timeout has occurred,
    ' the notification function fails,
    ' or our timeout reaches zero
    Do

        ' Print the relative file name
        Debug.Print "You have " & lngTimeout / 1000 & _
         " seconds to delete:"
        Debug.Print "..\" & mid(strFile, Len(strPath) + 2)

        ' Wait for the change to happen
        lngStatus = WaitForSingleObject(hChange, _
         lngTimeout)

        ' What happened?
        Select Case lngStatus
            Case WAIT_OBJECT_0
                ' A change happened! Check to see if
                ' the right file was deleted
                If Dir(strFile) = "" Then

                    ' File is gone! Compute score
                    lngScore = CLng((dhcBaseScore * _
                     colPaths.Count) / lngTimeout)
                    lngTotalScore = lngTotalScore + _
                     lngScore
                    Debug.Print "Good job! Score " & _
                     lngScore & " points"

                    ' Create next temp file
                    strFile = dhCreateTempFile( _
                     dhGetRandomFile(colPaths), "~DH")
                    fKeepGoing = CBool(Len(strFile))

                    ' If successful...
                    If fKeepGoing Then

                        ' Call FindNextChangeNotification
                        ' once to clear change handle
```

```
                    Call FindNextChangeNotification( _
                    hChange)

                    ' Call it again to establish the
                    ' next change event
                    fKeepGoing = CBool( _
                    FindNextChangeNotification( _
                    hChange))

                    ' Reduce timeout and wait again
                    lngTimeout = lngTimeout - 500
                Else
                    Debug.Print "Error creating file!"
                End If
            Else
                ' The file's still there!
                Debug.Print _
                 "Oh, no! You got the wrong file!"
                fKeepGoing = False
            End If
        Case WAIT_TIMEOUT
            ' The wait timed out!
            Debug.Print "Time's up! Timeout = " & _
             lngTimeout & " ms"
            fKeepGoing = False

        Case WAIT_FAILED
            ' This is bad, the wait didn't work
            Debug.Print "Wait failed!"
            fKeepGoing = False
        End Select

    Loop While fKeepGoing And (lngTimeout > 0)

    ' Close the change notification
    Call FindCloseChangeNotification(hChange)

    ' Print exit message
    Debug.Print "Total score: " & lngTotalScore
    Debug.Print "Thanks for playing"
    End If
End Sub
```

You start the game by calling dhFunWithNotify, passing a directory name and a timeout value in milliseconds. dhFunWithNotify then builds a list of all the subdirectories beneath the given directory and creates a zero-byte file in one of them. The object of the game is to find the file using Windows Explorer and delete it before time runs out. If you're successful, dhFunWithNotify creates a new file for you to find. To make things a bit more challenging, dhFunWithNotify also reduces the timeout value by 500 milliseconds (one half second) each time you successfully find the file! Your score is based on the number of subdirectories and how fast you can delete the file. See how long you can continue finding and deleting files before the timeout elapses. The more subdirectories you specify, the more challenging the game becomes.

> **TIP**
>
> To get the best results, position the VBA Immediate window so you can see it while working in Explorer.

While the example is whimsical, it does point out how you can use the notification functions. The procedure calls FindFirstChangeNotification to establish the initial change handle, passing the original directory name. Note that it also passes 1 as the second argument. Passing the number 1 forces the function to include subdirectories in the change notification. The other item worth noting is that FindNextChangeNotification is called twice. This is necessary because the process requesting the change notification is also causing a change event (in this case, each time a new file is created). Calling FindNextChangeNotification the first time clears the notification for the newly created file. Calling it a second time sets up a new notification.

You can find the helper functions dhFunWithNotify uses here in the basNotification module of the sample Excel workbook or the NOTIFY.BAS file.

> **TIP**
>
> If you find yourself playing this wonderfully exciting game as often as we do, you'll accumulate a number of zero-byte files on your hard disk. To get rid of them, use the Windows Find dialog to search for all files that begin with "~DH".

Monitoring Multiple Changes

You can also monitor more than one change event simultaneously—for example, to monitor changes to two completely separate directory trees. To do this, you create an *array* of change handles, calling FindFirstNotificationHandle once for each condition. You then call another API function, WaitForMultipleObjects, passing the first element of the array and the total number of handles in the array. You can also specify whether WaitForMultipleObjects should wait for *all* the events to happen or any *one* of them. In the latter case, when an event occurs, the return value from WaitForMultipleObjects will be WAIT_OBJECT_0 plus a number indicating which event it was. If you wish, you can then call FindNextNotification-Handle just as in our example.

> **NOTE** We included the declaration for WaitForMultipleObjects in the sample code but did not create an example of how to use it. You should, however, be able to deduce this from the function declaration.

Searching for Files

Another common task many applications must perform is searching for a particular file. Simple searches in a known directory can be accomplished easily using Dir or dhDir. Sometimes, however, you don't know where to look for a file. You can write custom VBA procedures that utilize API functions to help you find files, and they can be simple or complex, depending on your needs. All the code for this section is contained in the basSearch module of the sample Excel workbook and the FSEARCH.BAS file.

Using the SearchPath API Function

The Windows API offers a simple solution in the form of the SearchPath function. SearchPath is designed to search for files in a series of directories. The declaration for SearchPath is shown here:

```
Declare Function SearchPath Lib "kernel32" _
  Alias "SearchPathA" (ByVal lpPath As String, _
  ByVal lpFileName As String, ByVal lpExtension As String, _
  ByVal nBufferLength As Long, ByVal lpBuffer As String, _
  ByVal lpFilePart As String) As Long
```

Which directories SearchPath looks in is controlled by the first argument, lpPath. If you pass a null pointer (using the vbNullString constant), SearchPath looks in the following directories, in order:

1. The directory from which your application loaded

2. The application's current directory

3. Under Windows 95, the Windows system directory. Under Windows NT, the 32-bit Windows system directory

4. Under Windows NT only, the 16-bit Windows system directory

5. The Windows directory

6. The directories listed in the PATH environment variable

You can override this behavior by passing a value in the lpPath argument. The value takes the form of a DOS PATH statement, with individual directories separated by semicolons. For example:

```
C:\MYDATA;C:\MYAPPS;D:\SOME OTHER FILES;C:\BACKUPS
```

You pass the file name you're looking for in the lpFileName argument. If the file name doesn't contain a file extension, you can pass one in the lpExtension argument, and SearchPath will append it to the results for you. Listing 12.30 shows the dhSearch function. We wrapped the SearchPath function inside this function so you could call it easily. Just pass a file name and, optionally, a search path, and the function will return the full path to the file, if found. Figure 12.9 shows an example of calling the function.

Listing 12.30: dhSearch Looks for Files in Particular Directories

```
Function dhSearch(strFile As String, _
 Optional strPath As String = vbNullString) As String

    Dim strBuffer As String
    Dim lngBytes As Long
    Dim strFilePart As String

    ' Create a buffer
    strBuffer = Space(MAX_PATH)

    ' Call search path
    lngBytes = SearchPath(strPath, strFile, vbNullString, _
     Len(strBuffer), strBuffer, strFilePart)
```

713

```
        ' If successful, parse out the file name
        If lngBytes > 0 Then
            dhSearch = Left(strBuffer, lngBytes)
        End If
End Function
```

FIGURE 12.9

Calling the dhSearch
function

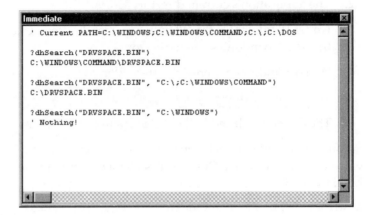

Recursive Searches with VBA

SearchPath is a convenient and powerful function, but what if you need to search
your entire hard disk? Unfortunately, there is no API function that will do that
(we dearly wish there were), but you can write your own VBA function to do it.
The key is to create a function that can be called recursively.

The dhFindAllFiles Function   We've created such a function for you,
dhFindAllFiles, as shown in Listing 12.31. It may seem complex, but that's mostly
because we added a few bells and whistles that aren't completely necessary but
that make it much more fun.

Listing 12.31: Use the dhFindAllFiles Function to Search Your Entire Hard Disk

```
Function dhFindAllFiles(strSpec As String, _
 ByVal strPath As String, colFound As Collection, _
 Optional lngAttr As Long = -1, _
 Optional fRecursive As Boolean = True, _
 Optional objCallback As Object) As Long
```

```
Dim strFile As String
Dim colSubDir As New Collection
Dim varDir As Variant

' Make sure strPath ends in a backslash
If Right(strPath, 1) <> "\" Then
    strPath = strPath & "\"
End If

' If the callback object was supplied
' call its Searching method
If Not objCallback Is Nothing Then
    objCallback.Searching strPath
End If

' Find all files in the directory--if no
' attributes were specified use a non-exclusive
' search for all files, otherwise use a
' restrictive search for the attributes
If lngAttr = -1 Then
    strFile = dhDir(strPath & strSpec, , False)
Else
    strFile = dhDir(strPath & strSpec, lngAttr)
End If

Do Until strFile = ""

    ' Add file to collection if attributes match
    ' (special case directories "." and "..")
    If ((GetAttr(strPath & strFile) And lngAttr) > 0) _
     And (strFile <> ".") And (strFile <> "..") Then
        colFound.Add strPath & strFile
    End If

    ' If the callback object was supplied
    ' call its Found method
    If Not objCallback Is Nothing Then
        objCallback.Found strPath, strFile
    End If

    ' Get the next file
    strFile = dhDir
Loop
```

```
' If the recursive flag is set build a list
' of all the subdirectories
If fRecursive Then

    strFile = dhDir(strPath, vbDirectory)
    Do Until strFile = ""
        ' Ignore "." and ".."
        If strFile <> "." And strFile <> ".." Then

            ' Add each to the directory collection
            colSubDir.Add strPath & strFile
        End If
        strFile = dhDir
    Loop

    ' Now recurse through each subdirectory
    For Each varDir In colSubDir
        dhFindAllFiles strSpec, varDir, colFound, _
        lngAttr, fRecursive, objCallback
    Next
End If

    ' Return the number of found files
    dhFindAllFiles = colFound.Count
End Function
```

Basically, the function works like this:

1. Given a file specification (such as *.TXT) and a starting directory, it scans the directory for all files matching the specification.

2. It adds each file name it finds to a VBA Collection object supplied by the calling procedure.

3. After finding all the files in the directory, it scans the directory a second time, looking for subdirectories.

4. It adds each subdirectory to an internal Collection object.

5. It iterates through each subdirectory in the Collection object and calls itself recursively, passing the subdirectory as a new starting point.

dhFindAllFiles passes the same collection of found files down the call chain into deeper and deeper subdirectory levels. When all the subdirectories have been scanned, the collection contains a complete list of files matching the original specification.

Testing dhFindAllFiles   To demonstrate this function, we've provided a procedure called dhPrintFoundFiles, shown in Listing 12.32. dhPrintFoundFiles accepts a file specification and path and passes them directly to dhFindAllFiles. It also performs the other required task: it declares a new VBA Collection object and passes it to dhFindAllFiles along with the other information. Figure 12.10 shows you how to call dhPrintFoundFiles and what the output might look like.

Listing 12.32: This Procedure Tests dhFindAllFiles

```
Sub dhPrintFoundFiles(strSpec As String, strPath As String)

    Dim colFound As New Collection
    Dim lngFound As Long
    Dim varFound As Variant

    ' Test the file find logic
    Debug.Print "Starting search..."

    ' Call dhFindAllFiles
    lngFound = dhFindAllFiles(strSpec, strPath, colFound)

    ' Print the results
    Debug.Print "Done. Found: " & lngFound

    ' With the collection of file names
    ' you can do something with them
    Debug.Print
    Debug.Print "What we found:"
    Debug.Print "================"

    For Each varFound In colFound
        Debug.Print varFound
    Next
End Sub
```

Once you have the collection of found files, you can use them to drive another process. We simply print them to the Immediate window using a For Each loop, but you could use them in other file operations (copying, deleting, and so on).

FIGURE 12.10

Performing a file search using dhPrintFoundFiles

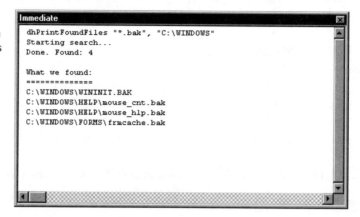

```
Immediate                                                    [×]
  dhPrintFoundFiles "*.bak", "C:\WINDOWS"
  Starting search...
  Done. Found: 4

  What we found:
  ==============
  C:\WINDOWS\WININIT.BAK
  C:\WINDOWS\HELP\mouse_cnt.bak
  C:\WINDOWS\HELP\mouse_hlp.bak
  C:\WINDOWS\FORMS\frmcache.bak
```

Embellishments to dhFindAllFiles   We dressed up the basic functionality in dhFindAllFiles in three ways. First, we added an optional argument to limit the search to files with a given set of attributes. By default, this argument, lngAttr, is set to –1. This instructs the dhDir functions to find all files matching the specification. You can override this by passing your own set of attributes. In this case, dhDir performs a restrictive search, finding only those files that have the given attributes.

Second, we provided an option (fRecursive) to control the recursive function calls. Setting this option to False forces dhFindAllFiles to search only the original starting directory.

The third embellishment we added is a provision for a callback object (objCallback). A *callback object* is a pointer to a VBA class that implements a set of required methods, Searching and Found. As each new subdirectory is searched, dhFindAllFiles calls the Searching method, passing the subdirectory name. Furthermore, when dhFindAllFiles finds a file, it calls the Found method, passing the path and file name. Since the search process may take a long time (especially if you're searching your whole hard disk), you may want to provide your users with feedback on the progress. If you've ever used the Windows 95 or Windows NT Find dialog, you know it displays, in the status bar, the directory currently being searched. It also adds each file to a list as it is found. You can implement similar functionality using a callback object of your own.

To demonstrate how this works, we created a very simple callback object class called FileFindCallback, shown in Listing 12.33. It implements the required methods, Found and Searching. The Found method prints the found file names to the Immediate window.

Listing 12.33: A Simple Callback Class

```
Public Sub Found(Path As String, File As String)
    ' This gets called each time a
    ' matching file is found
    Debug.Print Path & File
End Sub

Public Sub Searching(Path As String)
    ' This gets called each time a new
    ' directory is searched
End Sub
```

NOTE The callback object passed to dhFindAllFiles is declared using the Object datatype instead of a specific datatype such as FileFindCallback. We did this so you could pass a pointer to any object that implemented the required methods.

Listing 12.34 shows a modified version of the dhPrintFoundFiles procedure called dhPrintFoundFilesWithFeedback. It declares a new instance of the FileFindCallback class and passes it to dhFindAllFiles. As each matching file name is found, it is printed to the Immediate window. Try this out yourself by calling dhPrintFoundFilesWithFeedback from the Immediate window.

Listing 12.34: dhPrintFoundFilesWithFeedback Uses a Callback Object

```
Sub dhPrintFoundFilesWithFeedback(strSpec As String, _
 strPath As String)

    Dim colFound As New Collection
    Dim lngFound As Long
    Dim objCallback As New FileFindCallback

    ' Test the file find logic
    Debug.Print "Starting search..."

    ' Call dhFindAllFiles, passing a callback
    ' object--the callback object will print
```

```
    ' the file names to the Immediate window
    ' as they are found
    lngFound = dhFindAllFiles(strSpec, strPath, _
     colFound, , , objCallback)

    ' Print the results
    Debug.Print "Done. Found: " & lngFound
End Sub
```

These embellishments are just the beginning. The Windows Find dialog, for instance, lets you customize the search by specifying file sizes, dates, and even the text the files contain. If you feel like a challenge, you can extend the dhFind-AllFiles function using the other file functions mentioned in this chapter.

Procuring Temporary File Names

Many applications use temporary files to store intermediate results while processing data. All the major Microsoft applications use them for various reasons. If your application needs to use temporary files, there are two API functions you should use to choose a file name and path. GetTempPath returns the directory designated to hold temporary files. The directory returned will be one of those listed below, evaluated in the order listed:

1. The directory specified by the TMP environmental variable

2. The directory specified by the TEMP environmental variable

3. The current directory if neither TMP nor TEMP is defined

GetTempFileName creates a temporary file name, given a path, a prefix string, and, optionally, a unique integer. If you pass a nonzero value as the integer, GetTempFileName converts it to hexadecimal and concatenates it with the path and prefix. In this case, the function does not test to see whether the file already exists. If you pass a 0, GetTempFileName chooses a number based on the system clock. It continues to choose numbers until it can construct a file name that does not already exist.

All the code for this section is contained in the basTempFiles module of the sample Excel workbook and the TEMPFILE.BAS file.

The declaration for each function is shown here:

```
Declare Function GetTempPath Lib "kernel32" _
 Alias "GetTempPathA" (ByVal nBufferLength As Long, _
 ByVal lpBuffer As String) As Long
```

```
Declare Function GetTempFileName Lib "kernel32" _
 Alias "GetTempFileNameA" (ByVal lpszPath As String, _
 ByVal lpPrefixString As String, ByVal wUnique As Long, _
 ByVal lpTempFileName As String) As Long
```

Using these two functions together, you can create a single VBA function that returns a unique temporary file name. We've done this for you in the form of the dhTempFileName function shown in Listing 12.35. Note that the function accepts an optional argument for the file prefix. If you omit this argument, the string "~DH" is used.

Listing 12.35: dhTempFileName Computes a Unique Temporary File Name

```
Function dhTempFileName( _
 Optional strPrefix As String = "~DH") As String

    Dim strPath As String
    Dim strBuffer As String
    Dim lngBytes As Long

    ' Set up a buffer
    strBuffer = Space(MAX_PATH)

    ' Call GetTempPath
    lngBytes = GetTempPath(Len(strBuffer), strBuffer)

    ' If successful extract the path
    If lngBytes > 0 Then
        strPath = Left(strBuffer, lngBytes)

        ' Reset the buffer and call GetTempFileName
        strBuffer = Space(MAX_PATH)
        lngBytes = GetTempFileName(strPath, _
         strPrefix, 0, strBuffer)

        ' If successful extract the file name
        If lngBytes > 0 Then
            dhTempFileName = Left(strBuffer, lngBytes)
        End If
    End If
End Function
```

Note that GetTempFileName actually creates the temporary file. If you don't use the file, be sure to delete it using the VBA Kill function.

Getting a (Windows) Handle on Files

The discussion of the VBA file I/O functions earlier in this chapter introduced the concept of file handles. To work with a file using some of the Windows API functions, you must also get a handle to it. These handles are not equivalent, however. You cannot use a file handle derived from the VBA FreeFile function with Windows API functions.

All the code for this section is contained in the basFileHandles module of the sample Excel workbook and the HANDLES.BAS file.

Using the CreateFile Function

You obtain file handles by calling the CreateFile function. CreateFile has a myriad of uses in addition to opening and creating files. We could spend an entire chapter, and then some, fully explaining all the things you can use CreateFile for. For our purposes, however, we'll stick to opening a file for read-only access.

CreateFiles is declared as follows:

```
Declare Function CreateFile Lib "kernel32" _
 Alias "CreateFileA" _
 (ByVal lpFileName As String, _
 ByVal dwDesiredAccess As Long, _
 ByVal dwShareMode As Long, _
 lpSecurityAttributes As Any, _
 ByVal dwCreationDisposition As Long, _
 ByVal dwFlagsAndAttributes As Long, _
 ByVal hTemplateFile As Long) As Long
```

> **NOTE**
> The lpSecurityAttributes parameter, declared As Any in our example, is normally a pointer to a SECURITY_ATTRIBUTES structure. These structures are used to set and retrieve Windows NT security descriptor information. Operating system security is a complex topic in its own right and beyond the scope of this book. In all our examples, we pass null pointers to functions that accept security attributes.

Table 12.8 lists the many arguments to CreateFile, along with the allowable constants, where applicable. The meanings of the constants should be self-explanatory. For more information on CreateFile and its arguments, consult the Win32 Software Development Kit documentation.

TABLE 12.8   Arguments to CreateFile

Argument	Description	Allowable Values
lpFileName	Path to the file or directory to open	Any valid, fully qualified file path
dwDesiredAccess	Desired file access (bitmask)	GENERIC_READ, GENERIC_WRITE,
dwShareMode	File-sharing mode (bitmask)	FILE_SHARE_READ, FILE_SHARE_WRITE
lpSecurityAttributes	Windows NT security information	Pointer to SECURITY_ATTRIBUTES structure
dwCreationDisposition	Defines what action to take if file does (or does not) exist	CREATE_NEW, CREATE_ALWAYS, OPEN_EXISTING, OPEN_ALWAYS, TRUNCATE_EXISTING
dwFlagsAndAttributes	File attributes (bitmask)	FILE_ATTRIBUTE_ARCHIVE, FILE_ATTRIBUTE_COMPRESSED, FILE_ATTRIBUTE_NORMAL, FILE_ATTRIBUTE_HIDDEN, FILE_ATTRIBUTE_READONLY, FILE_ATTRIBUTE_SYSTEM, FILE_FLAG_WRITE_THROUGH, FILE_FLAG_OVERLAPPED, FILE_FLAG_NO_BUFFERING, FILE_FLAG_RANDOM_ACCESS, FILE_FLAG_SEQUENTIAL_SCAN, FILE_FLAG_DELETE_ON_CLOSE, FILE_FLAG_BACKUP_SEMANTICS, FILE_FLAG_POSIX_SEMANTICS
hTemplateFile	Defines the file to use as a template for attributes	File handle. Invalid under Windows 95 and ignored in our examples

If you look carefully at the arguments and constants shown in Table 12.8, you should see a similarity between them and the options for the VBA Open statement. This is no coincidence; the capabilities are comparable.

A Quick and Dirty Wrapper

Since most of our examples involve opening a file for simple read-only access, we wrote a wrapper function for CreateFile called dhQuickOpenFile. Shown in

Listing 12.36, it accepts a file name and an optional access mode (GENERIC_ READ is the default) and returns the result of calling CreateFile. If CreateFile is successful in opening the file, the result is a handle to the open file. If an error occurs, CreateFile returns –1. Any procedure calling dhQuickOpenFile should check for this value.

> **TIP**
>
> Many Windows API functions, including CreateFile, return error codes via the GetLastError API function. You can use the LastDLLError property of VBA's Err object to determine this error code after a failed API call.

Listing 12.36: dhQuickOpenFile, a Wrapper Function for CreateFile

```
Function dhQuickOpenFile(strFile As String, _
 Optional lngMode As Long = GENERIC_READ) As Long

    ' Call CreateFile to open the file in
    ' read-only, shared mode unless the user
    ' has passed a different access method--
    ' return the resulting file handle
    dhQuickOpenFile = CreateFile(strFile, lngMode, _
     FILE_SHARE_READ Or FILE_SHARE_WRITE, _
     ByVal 0&, OPEN_EXISTING, _
     FILE_ATTRIBUTE_NORMAL Or _
     FILE_FLAG_RANDOM_ACCESS, 0&)

End Function
```

A Simple Example

To demonstrate dhQuickOpenFile (and thus CreateFile), the procedure in Listing 12.37 opens a given file and prints the file's size (using the GetFileSize API function) to the Immediate window.

Listing 12.37: Print a File's Size the API Way

```
Sub dhPrintSizeAPI(strFile As String)
    Dim hFile As Long
    Dim lngSizeLower As Long
    Dim lngSizeUpper As Long
```

```
        ' Open the file and get the handle
        hFile = dhQuickOpenFile(strFile)

        ' If successful, print the size--
        ' if not, print the DLL error code
        If hFile > 0 Then

            ' Get the file size
            lngSizeLower = GetFileSize(hFile, lngSizeUpper)

            ' Print the results
            Debug.Print lngSizeLower & " bytes"

            ' Close the file
            Call CloseHandle(hFile)
        Else
            Debug.Print "Error calling CreateFile: " & _
             Err.LastDllError
        End If
End Sub
```

You'll notice that, just like our VBA function examples, the procedure closes the file after it's finished using it. In this case, it calls the CloseHandle API function. (CloseHandle is a function used to close various Kernel object handles.)

Getting File Information Quickly

Now that you understand what Windows file handles are and how to get them, you're ready for a little gem of an API function called GetFileInformationBy-Handle. In a single function call, you can retrieve almost everything you ever wanted to know about a file. The information returned is similar to what you get using the Find functions described earlier in this chapter, but you use an open file handle instead of performing a directory scan.

GetFileInformationByHandle uses a user-defined datatype to hold the information. The declaration for this type, BY_HANDLE_FILE_INFORMATION, is as follows:

```
Type BY_HANDLE_FILE_INFORMATION
    lngFileAttributes As Long        ' File attributes
    ftCreationTime As FILETIME       ' Creation time
    ftLastAccessTime As FILETIME     ' Last access time
    ftLastWriteTime As FILETIME      ' Last write time
    lngVolumeSerialNumber As Long    ' Serial number
```

```
        lngFileSizeHigh As Long        ' File size high-order word
        lngFileSizeLow As Long         ' File size low-order word
        lngNumberOfLinks As Long       ' Links to file (1 for FAT)
        lngFileIndexHigh As Long       ' Unique ID high-order word
        lngFileIndexLow As Long        ' Unique ID low-order word
    End Type
```

GetFileInformationByHandle accepts a file handle and pointer to an instance of this structure and returns True or False, indicating success or failure. For an explanantion of the FILETIME members, see the next section.

Windows API Dates and Times

Before going any further in discussing Windows API file and disk functions, we need to spend some time discussing date and time issues because a number of tasks (like setting the creation date of a file) require expressing time values in a way the Windows API understands. Specifically, the API uses two time formats, system time and file time, neither of which is directly compatible with VBA. These formats are discussed in the following sections.

All the code for this discussion is contained in the basDatesAndTimes module of the sample Excel workbook and the DATETIME.BAS file.

System Time

System time is the format used internally by Windows 95 and Windows NT. Functions that deal in system time express it using a user-defined datatype called, appropriately, SYSTEMTIME. The datatype is structured as follows:

```
Type SYSTEMTIME
    intYear As Integer
    intMonth As Integer
    intDayOfWeek As Integer
    intDay As Integer
    intHour As Integer
    intMinute As Integer
    intSecond As Integer
    intMilliseconds As Integer
End Type
```

As you can see, each date and time element is represented by a separate integer value. Using this format, you can represent any date from January 1, 32768 B.C. to

December 31, 32767. This date range is wide enough for most applications, except perhaps archeological or paleontological programs.

We've provided two procedures for converting between VBA and system time values. Listing 12.38 shows these functions, dhSysTimeToVBATime and dhVBA-TimeToSysTime.

Listing 12.38: Convert between VBA and System Time Formats

```
Function dhSysTimeToVBATime(stSysTime As SYSTEMTIME) As Date
    ' Consrtuct a VBA date/time value using the
    ' DateSerial and TimeSerial functions
    With stSysTime
        dhSysTimeToVBATime = _
        DateSerial(.intYear, .intMonth, .intDay) + _
        TimeSerial(.intHour, .intMinute, .intSecond)
    End With
End Function

Sub dhVBATimeToSysTime(datTime As Date, stSysTime As SYSTEMTIME)
    ' Fill in the structure with date and time parts
    With stSysTime
        .intMonth = Month(datTime)
        .intDay = Day(datTime)
        .intYear = Year(datTime)

        .intHour = Hour(datTime)
        .intMinute = Minute(datTime)
        .intSecond = Second(datTime)
    End With
End Sub
```

When working with system time data, keep in mind that Windows tracks time internally using *coordinated universal time* (UTC). Coordinated universal time is loosely defined as the current time of day in Greenwich, England, and is sometimes called Greenwich Mean Time (GMT). You can retrieve the current system time by calling the GetSystemTime API function. Most functions that utilize the SYSTEMTIME datatype assume the time being passed is in UTC format.

Local time is the current time of day where you are; that is, in the time zone specified on your system. If you want to know the current local time, call the GetLocalTime API function. While there is no direct way to convert between the two time scales, you can retrieve time zone information by calling the GetTimeZoneInformation function. The information returned (via another user-defined type called TIME_ZONE_INFORMATION) contains, among other things, the time zone *bias*—the difference between local time and coordinated universal time.

File Time

The other type of time format you'll come across in disk and file functions, *file time*, is used to set and retrieve the three time values associated with files and directories. 32-bit Windows operating systems track the time a file was created, the time it was last accessed, and the time it was last modified.

Like system times, file times use a user-defined type. Called FILETIME, it's structured as follows:

```
Type FILETIME
    lngLowDateTime As Long
    lngHighDateTime As Long
End Type
```

The contents of a FILETIME structure are not quite as obvious as those of SYSTEMTIME. The two long integers that make up FILETIME represent a 64-bit number containing (and we're not making this up) the number of 100-nanosecond intervals since January 1, 1601!

Fortunately, you rarely have to work with FILETIME data in its raw format. The Windows API contains functions that convert from file time to system time and back. Using these functions, we were able to create the VBA time conversion functions shown in Listing 12.39.

Listing 12.39: Functions for Converting between File Time and VBA Time

```
Function dhFileTimeToVBATime(ftFileTime As FILETIME, _
 Optional fLocal As Boolean = True) As Date

    Dim stSystem As SYSTEMTIME
    Dim ftLocalFileTime As FILETIME

    ' If the user wants local time, convert the file
    ' time to local file time
    If fLocal Then
```

```
          Call FileTimeToLocalFileTime(ftFileTime, ftLocalFileTime)
          ftFileTime = ftLocalFileTime
    End If

    ' Convert the file time to system time then
    ' call our own function to convert to VBA time
    If CBool(FileTimeToSystemTime(ftFileTime, stSystem)) Then
        dhFileTimeToVBATime = dhSysTimeToVBATime(stSystem)
    End If
End Function

Sub dhVBATimeToFileTime(datTime As Date, ftTime As FILETIME, _
 Optional fLocal As Boolean = True)

    Dim stSystem As SYSTEMTIME
    Dim ftSystem As FILETIME

    ' Call our function to convert the VBA time to
    ' system time
    Call dhVBATimeToSysTime(datTime, stSystem)

    ' Convert the system time to file time
    If CBool(SystemTimeToFileTime(stSystem, ftTime)) Then

        ' If the VBA time was local time, convert the
        ' local file time to system file time
        If fLocal Then
            Call LocalFileTimeToFileTime(ftTime, ftSystem)
            ftTime = ftSystem
        End If
    End If
End Sub
```

Note that each function accepts a flag value, fLocal, as an optional argument. If this is set to True (the default), the VBA time value is treated as local time. If fLocal is False, it's treated as system, or UTC, time.

Working with File Times

With the discussion of time formats out of the way, let's take a look at API functions that deal in file dates and times. A common requirement for some applications is to be able to set the creation time of a file. You may have noticed that when you install an application from a company like Microsoft, all the files have the same creation date and time. As mentioned earlier in this discussion, the file system actually tracks three time values for each file. Using Windows API functions, you can set and retrieve all of them. This section shows you how this is done and how to compare the times of two files quickly and easily.

Getting and Setting File Times

The functions that enable you to get and set file times are GetFileTime and SetFileTime. The declarations for these functions are as follows. (Note that each accepts a file handle as the first argument.)

```
Declare Function GetFileTime Lib "kernel32" _
 (ByVal hFile As Long, lpCreationTime As FILETIME, _
 lpLastAccessTime As FILETIME, _
 lpLastWriteTime As FILETIME) As Long

Declare Function SetFileTime Lib "kernel32" _
 (ByVal hFile As Long, lpCreationTime As FILETIME, _
 lpLastAccessTime As FILETIME, _
 lpLastWriteTime As FILETIME) As Long
```

Since the FILETIME format can be tricky to work with, we've come up with several wrapper functions you can use to set or retrieve file times. These functions open the file (using dhQuickOpenFile) and handle the conversion between time formats. Listing 12.40 shows the first two, dhGetFileTimes and dhSetFileTimes. Each uses a custom structure, dhtypFileTimes, not shown in Listing 12.40. We created this structure, which groups three VBA Date variables, to make it convenient to work with all three file time values at once.

Listing 12.40: Two Functions for Retrieving or Setting All Three File Times

```
Function dhGetFileTimes(strFile As String, _
 dftTimes As dhtypFileTimes) As Boolean

    Dim ftCreate As FILETIME
    Dim ftAccess As FILETIME
    Dim ftWrite As FILETIME
    Dim hFile As Long
    Dim lngRet As Long

    ' Open the file
    hFile = dhQuickOpenFile(strFile)
    If hFile > 0 Then
```

```
        ' Call GetFileTime to fetch time information
        ' into the local FILETIME structures
        If CBool(GetFileTime(hFile, ftCreate, _
         ftAccess, ftWrite)) Then

            ' If successful, convert the values to
            ' VBA Date format and return them in
            ' the passed dhtypFileTimes structure
            With dftTimes
                .datCreated = FileTimeToVBATime(ftCreate)
                .datAccessed = FileTimeToVBATime(ftAccess)
                .datModified = FileTimeToVBATime(ftWrite)
            End With

            ' Return success
            dhGetFileTimes = True
        End If

        ' Close the file
        Call CloseHandle(hFile)
    End If
End Function

Function dhSetFileTimes(strFile As String, _
 dftTimes As dhtypFileTimes) As Boolean

    Dim ftCreated As FILETIME
    Dim ftAccessed As FILETIME
    Dim ftModified As FILETIME
    Dim hFile As Long

    ' Open the file for write access
    hFile = dhQuickOpenFile(strFile, GENERIC_WRITE)

    ' If successful then...
    If hFile > 0 Then

        ' Convert the passed time to a FILETIME
        With dftTimes
            Call VBATimeToFileTime(.datCreated, ftCreated)
            Call VBATimeToFileTime(.datAccessed, ftAccessed)
            Call VBATimeToFileTime(.datModified, ftModified)
        End With

        ' Set the times
        If CBool(SetFileTime(hFile, ftCreated, _
         ftAccessed, ftModified)) Then
```

```
                    ' Return success
                    dhSetFileTimes = True
                End If

                ' Close the file
                Call CloseHandle(hFile)
            End If
    End Function
```

As an example, suppose you wanted to set the creation, last access, and last write times of a file to midnight, January 1, 1997. You could use code like this:

```
Dim dft As dhtypFileTimes

With dft
    .datCreated = #1/1/97 12:00:00 AM#
    .datCreated = #1/1/97 12:00:00 AM#
    .datCreated = #1/1/97 12:00:00 AM#
End With

Call dhSetFileTimes("C:\SOMEFILE.EXE", dft)
```

WARNING   If you use dhSetFileTimes to change a file time value, be sure not to leave any of the structure elements blank. Doing so will set the file time to 0 or, expressed as a VBA date, Saturday, December 30, 1899!

Both functions require you to declare a dhtypFileTimes variable and pass it as the second argument. If you want to retrieve or modify only a single file time, you can use two other VBA functions we've provided, dhGetFileTimesEx and dhSetFileTimesEx. Instead of a user-defined datatype, these functions accept an integer specifying which time or times you're interested in. In the case of dhGetFileTimesEx, this is a single number indicating *one* of the time values. dhSetFileTimesEx, on the other hand, accepts a bitmask of numbers and changes *one or more* time values to the supplied time. Both functions have reasonable defaults for these arguments, so you don't have to supply a value if you don't want to. The following code illustrates how you might call these functions:

```
' Get the last modified time for WIN.INI
Debug.Print dhGetFileTimesEx("C:\WINDOWS\WIN.INI")
```

```
' Get the last accessed time for WIN.INI
Debug.Print dhGetFileTimesEx("C:\WINDOWS\WIN.INI", _
 dhcFileTimeAccessed)

' Set the last modified and last accessed time for WIN.INI
' to right now
Debug.Print dhSetFileTimesEx("C:\WINDOWS\WIN.INI", Now)

' Set the created time for WIN.INI to yesterday
Debug.Print dhSetFileTimesEx("C:\WINDOWS\WIN.INI", Now - 1, _
 dhcFileTimeCreated)
```

> **NOTE**
>
> Since dhGetFileTimesEx and dhSetFileTimesEx are basically modified versions of dhGetFileTimes and dhSetFileTimes, we haven't included their code here. You can find it, along with the constant definitions, in the sample files for this chapter.

Comparing File Times

In addition to simply retrieving the time values associated with a file, you'll sometimes need to compare them against those of another file. You might do this, for example, to determine whether a file on a desktop computer and another on a laptop are the same. While you could retrieve the times for both files using the functions described above, there is also a simple Windows API call you can use, CompareFileTime:

```
Declare Function CompareFileTime Lib "kernel32" _
 (lpFileTime1 As FILETIME, lpFileTime2 As FILETIME) As Long
```

CompareFileTime accepts pointers to two FILETIME structures and returns a result indicating the difference, if any, between them. It returns –1 if the first file time is less than the second, 1 if it's greater, and 0 if the two are equal. Listing 12.41 shows a function that uses CompareFileTime to compute the difference between the time values for two files. To use it, pass the path to both files, along with the time you want to check. Note that it returns the same values as CompareFileTime except in the event of an error (perhaps due to an invalid file name), in which case it returns –2.

Listing 12.41: Use the Windows API to Compare File Times

```
Function dhCompareFileTime(strFile1 As String, _
 strFile2 As String, Optional intTime As _
 Integer = dhcFileTimeModified) As Long

    Dim ftCreate1 As FILETIME
    Dim ftAccess1 As FILETIME
    Dim ftWrite1 As FILETIME
    Dim hFile1 As Long
    Dim ftCreate2 As FILETIME
    Dim ftAccess2 As FILETIME
    Dim ftWrite2 As FILETIME
    Dim hFile2 As Long

    ' Set a return value in case things go wrong
    dhCompareFileTime = -2

    ' Open the first file
    hFile1 = dhQuickOpenFile(strFile1)
    If hFile1 > 0 Then

        ' Open the second file
        hFile2 = dhQuickOpenFile(strFile2)
        If hFile2 > 0 Then

            ' Get the file times
            If CBool(GetFileTime(hFile1, ftCreate1, _
             ftAccess1, ftWrite1)) Then
                If CBool(GetFileTime(hFile2, ftCreate2, _
                 ftAccess2, ftWrite2)) Then

                    ' Call CompareFileTime for the
                    ' requested time and return the result
                    Select Case intTime
                        Case dhcFileTimeCreated
                            dhCompareFileTime = _
                             CompareFileTime(ftCreate1, _
                             ftCreate2)
                        Case dhcFileTimeAccessed
                            dhCompareFileTime = _
```

```
                        CompareFileTime(ftAccess1, _
                            ftAccess2)
                    Case dhcFileTimeModified
                        dhCompareFileTime = _
                            CompareFileTime(ftWrite1, ftWrite2)
                End Select
            End If
        End If

        ' Close the second file
        Call CloseHandle(hFile2)
    End If

    ' Close the first file
    Call CloseHandle(hFile1)
    End If
End Function
```

NOTE   For more information on comparing and manipulating dates and times using VBA, see Chapter 2.

Using the Windows Common Dialogs

While not directly related to manipulating files, learning to use the Windows common file dialogs can come in handy in many applications. If you've ever needed to build a dialog for file selection, you know what a pain this can be. You need to provide a way for users to browse files and directories, filter the selections, and enter a file name directly. The Windows common dialogs provide all this and more, and they are relatively easy to use. This section explains how to open and use the Open and Save As dialogs, which are merely variations of the same form. Figure 12.11 shows the Open dialog.

All the code for this section is contained in the basCommonDialog module of the sample Excel workbook and the COMMDLG.BAS file.

FIGURE 12.11

The Windows common
Open File dialog

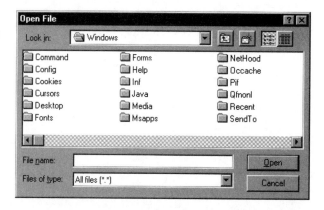

The OPENFILENAME Structure

The functionality of both dialogs revolves around a complex user-defined structure called OPENFILENAME. Listing 12.42 shows its declaration, along with
those of the two API functions that utilize it, GetOpenFileName and GetSave-
FileName. Comments in the code listing briefly describe the structure's member
variables. Some of the more important ones are discussed in the remainder of this
section.

Listing 12.42: Required Declarations for Using Windows Common File Dialogs

```
Type OPENFILENAME
      lngStructSize As Long            ' Size of structure
      hwndOwner As Long                ' Owner window handle
      hInstance As Long                ' Template instance handle
      strFilter As String              ' Filter string
      strCustomFilter As String        ' Selected filter string
      intMaxCustFilter As Long         ' Len(strCustomFilter)
      intFilterIndex As Long           ' Index of filter string
      strFile As String                ' Selected file name & path
      intMaxFile As Long               ' Len(strFile)
      strFileTitle As String           ' Selected file name
      intMaxFileTitle As Long          ' Len(strFileTitle)
      strInitialDir As String          ' Directory name
      strTitle As String               ' Dialog title
      lngFlags As Long                 ' Dialog flags
```

```
         intFileOffset As Integer          ' Offset of file name
         intFileExtension As Integer       ' Offset of file extension
         strDefExt As String               ' Default file extension
         lngCustData As Long               ' Custom data for hook
         lngfnHook As Long                 ' LP to hook function
         strTemplateName As String         ' Dialog template name
End Type

Declare Function GetOpenFileName Lib "comdlg32.dll" _
  Alias "GetOpenFileNameA" (ofn As OPENFILENAME) As Boolean

Declare Function GetSaveFileName Lib "comdlg32.dll" _
  Alias "GetSaveFileNameA" (ofn As OPENFILENAME) As Boolean
```

As you can see from the listing, the functions themselves are quite simple, accepting a pointer to the structure and returning a True or False to indicate success or failure. (True means that a user has selected a file; False means the user canceled the dialog or an error occurred.) To open a dialog, you declare an instance of the OPENFILENAME type, populate its member variables, and call one of the functions. When the function returns, you inspect the contents of the structure to determine the user's choices.

Using OPENFILENAME

Despite the fact that OPENFILENAME is a complex structure, you rarely if ever need to use all the member variables. Some of the more important ones are listed here:

Variable	Description
hwndOwner	Handle of the window that owns the dialog. Failure to set this properly can result in a "orphaned" dialog
strFilter	String used to filter file names. Made up of null-delimited pairs of values, one representing a description ("Text Files") and the other a file specification ("*.txt")
intFilterIndex	Indicates which filter pair should be used when the dialog opens
strFile	Initial file name. Will be used to store the file name the user selects

Variable	Description
strInitialDir	Initial directory used when the dialog opens
strTitle	Dialog title
lngFlags	Bitmask of values from Table 12.9 that control dialog behavior

Perhaps the most important variable is lngFlags, because it determines how the dialog operates and what validation, if any, it performs.

The contents of lngFlags are derived from the list of constants in Table 12.9. The next section, which presents a wrapper function for the API, explains some of the more important ones.

NOTE We've purposely omitted several of the constants that can't be used or are redundant in VBA. We've also included three custom flags that are convenient and often-used combinations of others.

TABLE 12.9 OPENFILENAME Flags

Constant	Used for	Description
OFN_ALLOWMULTISELECT	Open	Allows users to select multiple files. The results are returned as the directory followed by the 8.3 file names, all separated by spaces
OFN_CREATEPROMPT	Open	If the user types a nonexistent file name, the dialog prompts the user to create the file
OFN_EXPLORER	Both	Forces Windows Explorer–style dialogs (unnecessary in most circumstances)
OFN_EXTENSIONDIFFERENT	Both	Specifies that the user typed an extension that differs from the strDefExt member
OFN_FILEMUSTEXIST	Both	Forces the user to select or type the name of an existing file (must be combined with OFN_PATHMUSTEXIST)
OFN_HIDEREADONLY	Both	Hides the Read Only check box

TABLE 12.9   OPENFILENAME Flags (continued)

Constant	Used for	Description
OFN_NOCHANGEDIR	Both	Restores the current directory to its original value if the user changed the directory while searching for files
OFN_NODEREFERENCELINKS	Both	If set, the dialog returns the actual name of a Windows 95 shortcut rather than the file it references
OFN_NOREADONLYRETURN	Both	Specifies that the returned file does not have the Read Only check box checked and is not in a write-protected directory
OFN_NOTESTFILECREATE	Save As	Dialog does not verify that you can create the file after the dialog returns
OFN_NOVALIDATE	Both	Dialog does not verify that the file name entered is valid
OFN_OVERWRITEPROMPT	Save As	Warns the user that the selected file already exists
OFN_PATHMUSTEXIST	Both	Forces the user to select or type the name of an existing directory
OFN_READONLY	Open	Checks the Read Only text box when the dialog opens and returns its state when the dialog closes
OFN_SHAREAWARE	Both	Ignores sharing violations
dfOFN_OPENEXISTING	Open	Combination of OFN_PATHMUSTEXIST, OFN_FILEMUSTEXIST, and OFN_HIDEREADONLY
dfOFN_SAVENEW	Save As	Combination of OFN_PATHMUSTEXIST, OFN_OVERWRITEPROMPT, and OFN_HIDEREADONLY
dfOFN_SAVENEWPATH	Save As	Combination of OFN_OVERWRITEPROMPT and OFN_HIDEREADONLY

> **NOTE**
> Some of these flags (like OFN_READONLY) are set by the dialog when it closes. This allows you to find out what options the user chose in addition to the file name.

Calling the Functions the Easy Way

As already mentioned, you trigger the dialog by instantiating and populating an OPENFILENAME structure and passing it to one of the API functions. Since this can often be a tedious programming task, we've encapsulated it in a VBA function, dhFileDialog, which is shown in Listing 12.43. dhFileDialog accepts arguments that map directly to the member variables in OPENFILENAME. To make it convenient to call the function, however, we made all the arguments optional. In fact, the hardest part about understanding how the function works is deciphering the declaration!

Listing 12.43: The dhFileDialog Function

```
Function dhFileDialog( _
 Optional strInitDir As String, _
 Optional strFilter As String = _
  "All files (*.*)" & vbNullChar & "*.*" & _
  vbNullChar & vbNullChar, _
 Optional intFilterIndex As Integer = 1, _
 Optional strDefaultExt As String, _
 Optional strFileName As String, _
 Optional strDialogTitle As String = "Open File", _
 Optional hwnd As Long = -1, _
 Optional fOpenFile As Boolean = True, _
 Optional ByRef lngFlags As Long = _
  dhOFN_OPENEXISTING) As Variant

    Dim ofn As OPENFILENAME
    Dim strFileTitle As String
    Dim fResult As Boolean

    ' Fill in some of the missing arguments
    If strInitDir = "" Then
        strInitDir = CurDir
    End If
    If hwnd = -1 Then
```

```
        hwnd = GetActiveWindow()
End If

' Set up the return buffers
strFileName = strFileName & String(255 - Len(strFileName), 0)
strFileTitle = String(255, 0)

' Fill in the OPENFILENAME structure members
With ofn
    .lngStructSize = Len(ofn)
    .hwndOwner = hwnd
    .strFilter = strFilter
    .intFilterIndex = intFilterIndex
    .strFile = strFileName
    .intMaxFile = Len(strFileName)
    .strFileTitle = strFileTitle
    .intMaxFileTitle = Len(strFileTitle)
    .strTitle = strDialogTitle
    .lngFlags = lngFlags
    .strDefExt = strDefaultExt
    .strInitialDir = strInitDir
    .hInstance = 0
    .strCustomFilter = String(255, 0)
    .intMaxCustFilter = 255
    .lngfnHook = 0
End With

' Call the right function
If fOpenFile Then
    fResult = GetOpenFileName(ofn)
Else
    fResult = GetSaveFileName(ofn)
End If

' If successful, return the file name,
' otherwise return Null
If fResult Then
    ' Return any flags to the calling procedure
    lngFlags = ofn.lngFlags

    ' Return the result
    dhFileDialog = dhTrimNull(ofn.strFile)
Else
    dhFileDialog = Null
```

```
        End If
End Function
```

Most of the arguments (such as strInitDir) are pretty much self-explanatory. You pass values you want sent on to the API functions. Nonetheless, a few arguments warrant additional explanation.

The strFilter argument supplies the dialog's file-filtering mechanism. Note that the argument defaults to showing all files. If you want to override the default, you need to construct a new filter string. For example, consider the following string formula:

```
strNewFilter = "Word Documents" & vbNullChar & "*.doc" & _
  vbNullChar & "Text Files" & vbNullChar & "*.txt" & _
  vbNullChar & "All Files" & vbNullChar & "*.*" & _
  vbNullChar & vbNulLChar
```

It creates a string with three separate filter conditions; one for Word documents, one for text files, and one for all files. Note that the string stored in strNewFilter is made up of description and file specification substrings. Each of these substrings is separated by a null character (using the vbNullChar constant), and each pair is separated from the next by another Null. Finally, the entire string is terminated by two Nulls.

The lngFlags argument passes flag values to the dialog functions. We've provided some reasonable defaults for the Open dialog. If you want to call the Save dialog or simply want to override the default, you'll need to pass a bitmask of values in this argument.

Finally, the fOpenFile argument determines which dialog to display. Passing True (the default) opens the Open dialog, while passing False opens the Save As dialog. Listing 12.44 shows several examples of using the function. The use of named arguments makes it easy to customize the function call.

Listing 12.44: Different Ways of Calling dhFileDialog

```
Sub dhTestDialog()
    ' Open a file in the current directory
    Debug.Print dhFileDialog()

    ' Open multiple files in the Windows directory
    Debug.Print dhFileDialog(strInitDir:="C:\WINDOWS", _
      lngFlags:=dhOFN_OPENEXISTING Or OFN_ALLOWMULTISELECT _
      Or OFN_EXPLORER)
```

```
      ' Save a file as a text file
      Debug.Print dhFileDialog(strFilter:="Text Files" & _
        vbNullChar & "*.txt" & vbNullChar & vbNullChar, _
        strDialogTitle:="Save As", lngFlags:=dhOFN_SAVENEW, _
        fOpenFile:=False)
  End Sub
```

An Object Model for Directories and Files

Since you've been reading this book, it should be clear that we are extremely fond of VBA class modules. Who wouldn't be? Once they've been developed and debugged, they become truly robust, reusable components. Furthermore, the objects created from class modules insulate the developer using them from the complexities of their inner workings. To round out the discussion of disk and file manipulation functions, this section presents yet another object model, this one representing directories and files. Due to space limitations, we can't cover the entire object model in depth. Instead, we highlight significant features and advantages that the classes offer over traditional procedures. Additionally, due to time constraints, the object model is far from complete. As in prior chapters, however, we hope you can see the benefits encapsulation brings to what can be complex tasks.

NOTE If you've read Chapter 10, you should see similarities between the object model presented here and the one discussed in that chapter.

Using the Classes

The few classes that make up our object model are relatively simple. This is due primarily to the hierarchical nature of the file system. In fact, we need only four VBA class modules to represent this system:

- The File class represents a single disk file and features properties you might expect, such as Name, Attributes, and Size.

- The Files class implements a collection of File objects and includes a Refresh method that reads a directory of files from disk.

- The Directory class represents a directory and contains collections of files and subdirectories.

- The Directories class implements a collection of Directory objects and includes a Refresh method that reads subdirectories from disk.

You use the classes by declaring a new instance of the Directory class and setting its Name property to a valid directory name. For example:

```
Dim objDir As New Directory
objDir.Name = "C:\WINDOWS\TEMP"
```

Populating Subdirectories

Setting the Name property for the first time causes the class to call the Refresh method of its Files and Subdirectories collections. You can see this in the Property Let procedure shown in Listing 12.45. Also shown is what happens if the property value is changed. In this case, the procedure renames the directory.

Listing 12.45: Changing a Directory Name Has Numerous Implications

```
Property Let Name(ByVal strName As String)
    On Error GoTo HandleError

    Dim fFirstTime As Boolean
    Dim strOldName As String
    Dim strOldPath As String

    ' Is this the first time?
    If mstrName = "" Then
        fFirstTime = True
    End If

    ' If it is the first time, refresh the collections
    If fFirstTime Then
        ' Store the new name
        mstrName = strName
```

```
            ' Refresh files and directories
            mobjFiles.Refresh
            mobjDirectories.Refresh
        Else

            ' If not we will rename the direcory
            ' so make sure it still exists
            If Exists() Then

                ' Store the current name and path
                strOldName = mstrName
                strOldPath = FullPath()

                ' Change error handler
                On Error GoTo RenameError

                ' Store the new name
                mstrName = strName

                ' Rename the directory
                Name strOldPath As FullPath()
            Else
                ' Otherwise, remove it from the parent
                ' directory if it has one
                If Not mobjParent Is Nothing Then
                    mobjParent.Subdirectories.Remove mstrID
                End If
            End If
        End If

ExitHere:
    Exit Property
RenameError:
    ' Reset old name
    mstrName = strOldName
HandleError:
    Err.Raise Err.Number + vbObjectError, _
        "Directory::Name (Let)", Err.Description
End Property
```

As each new subdirectory is added by the Refresh and Add methods (not shown here), its name is set for the first time, thus triggering a refresh of its subdirectories. This recursive directory scanning happens until all subdirectories beneath the current one have been added.

> **WARNING** The more subdirectories that exist under a given directory, the longer it takes for the code to execute. If you use the Directory class, make its scope as narrow as possible.

Creating New Directories

As much as possible, we wanted this object model to be a "live" representation of the file system. If VBA were a true multithreaded environment, we could have used the notification API functions presented in the section "Windows Notification Functions" earlier in this chapter to make our classes respond dynamically to changes. Since that's not possible, we settled for the next best thing. As you modify objects and properties in our object model, it makes appropriate changes to the file system. One example of this behavior is in the creation of subdirectories. When you call the Add method of a Directory object's Subdirectories collection, the procedure creates a new subdirectory on your disk. Listing 12.46 lists the code for the Add method.

> **NOTE** This behavior can be suppressed by passing True as the second, optional argument to Add. The Refresh method uses this technique when adding existing subdirectories to the collection.

Listing 12.46: Adding a Directory to the Collection Also Creates One on Your Disk

```
Public Function Add(Name As String, _
 Optional fExisting As Boolean = False) As Directory

    ' Create new Directory instance
    Dim objDirectory As New Directory

    ' Set the new Directory's Parent property
    ' to point to the collection's Parent
    Set objDirectory.Parent = mobjParent

    ' If this is not an existing directory, create one
    If Not fExisting Then
```

```
      MkDir dhFixPath(mobjParent.FullPath) & Name
  End If

  ' Set the requisite Name property--this, in turn,
  ' will add all of its subdirectories
  objDirectory.Name = Name

  ' Add new instance to the collection,
  ' using its ID as the unique key
  mcolDirectories.Add objDirectory, objDirectory.ID

  ' Set the return Directory to reference the new object
  Set Add = objDirectory
End Function
```

Copying Directories

Building an object model around file functions lets you overcome many of the limitations of procedural programming. For example, copying an entire directory tree involves recursively iterating the files in a subdirectory, a task made difficult by the limitations of the Dir function—each new directory scan resets Dir's internal directory pointer. One option for overcoming this limitation would be to use the Find functions mentioned in the section "A Hardcore Replacement for Dir" earlier in this chapter to create multiple find handles, one for each subdirectory in the tree.

Our object model makes this tedious task unnecessary, however, thanks to the inherent multiple-instancing capability of VBA class modules. Since each Directory object has independent collections of files and subdirectories, it need only call methods of those classes recursively to copy an entire directory structure. Listings 12.47 and 12.48 show the Copy method of the File and Directory classes, respectively. You can see how the Directory class recursively calls its own Copy method.

Listing 12.47: Copy Method of the File Class

```
Public Function Copy(Path As String, _
 Optional Overwrite As Boolean = True) As Boolean

    ' Call the CopyFile API function and return the result
    Copy = CBool(CopyFile(FullPath(), Path, Abs(Not Overwrite)))
End Function
```

Listing 12.48: Copy Method of the Directory Class

```
Public Function Copy(ByVal Path As String, _
 Optional CopyFiles As Boolean = True) As Boolean

    Dim lngCount As Long

    ' Fix up the path
    Path = dhFixPath(Path)

    ' If requested, copy the files
    If CopyFiles Then
        With mobjFiles
            For lngCount = 1 To .Count
                With .Item(lngCount)
                    If Not .Copy(Path & .Name) Then
                        GoTo ExitHere
                    End If
                End With
            Next
        End With
    End If

    ' Now copy the subdirectories
    With mobjDirectories
        For lngCount = 1 To .Count
            With .Item(lngCount)
                ' Create the directory
                If Not CBool(CreateDirectory(Path & .Name, 0&)) _
                 Then
                    GoTo ExitHere
                End If
                ' Copy the files
                If Not .Copy(Path & .Name, CopyFiles) Then
                    GoTo ExitHere
                End If
            End With
        Next
    End With

    ' Set return value
    Copy = True
ExitHere:
End Function
```

Both methods call Windows API functions (CopyFile and Create-Directory) because, unlike their VBA counterparts, they return values indicating success or failure.

To demonstrate how easy it is to copy a directory tree, we've created a simple procedure called dhCopyTree (shown in Listing 12.49). You call the function with source and target paths, and with just three lines of code, the source tree is replicated in the target directory!

Listing 12.49: Copy an Entire Directory Tree

```
Function dhCopyTree(strFrom As String, strTo As String) _
 As Boolean
    Dim objDir As New Directory

    ' Set up Directory object
    objDir.Name = strFrom

    ' Copy away!
    dhCopyTree = objDir.Copy(strTo)
End Function
```

Extending the Object Model

You could certainly spend a great deal of time extending the object model we've provided. You could, for instance, add callback object support for methods that take a long time to execute. We also purposely did not implement every single property procedure you would likely need (such as ones for modifying individual attributes). Our object model was designed to reinforce the object-oriented design considerations we've presented thoughout the rest of the book.

Summary

This chapter has presented a lot of information regarding disk and file manipulation using VBA. Specifically, we covered the following topics:

- How to use VBA file and directory information functions such as Dir, GetAttr, FileLen, and FileDateTime

- How to copy, move, create, and delete files and directories

- How to create and modify files using VBA file I/O functions

- How to search for files on your hard disk

- How to manipulate path names and temporary files

- Using Windows API functions to retrieve file and disk information such as the volume label, disk types, and free space

- How to set and retrieve file dates and times

- How to force Windows to inform you when the contents of a directory have changed

- Using a VBA class module–based system for easing file and directory management

In addition to supplying you with "out of the box" functions you can use in your applications, we tried to help you understand how you can utilize both VBA and Windows API functions to get the most out of the file system.

CHAPTER
THIRTEEN

13

Adding Multimedia to Your Applications

- Understanding Windows multimedia services

- Playing WAV files

- Controlling your CD player

- Exploring digital video with AVI files

To wrap up this book on VBA development, we decided to include a chapter on multimedia. Why, you might ask? After all, it's such an immense subject that entire books have been written about it. We couldn't possibly explain everything you need to know to write complete multimedia titles. Fortunately, that's not what we wanted to do. Our intent was to provide you with a few simple tricks you can use to enhance your application. Even the most serious developers have, from time to time, wanted to play sound files or video clips in their applications. In this chapter, you'll learn a few very easy techniques to make this happen. The chapter begins with a discussion of the multimedia capabilities of Windows 95 and Windows NT 4.0. It then takes a look at individual topics that range from playing sound files to running video clips in a window. By the end of this chapter, you should have a basic understanding of how Windows handles multimedia, as well as a grab bag of useful VBA functions to add to your applications.

Table 13.1 lists the sample files included on the CD-ROM for this chapter.

TABLE 13.1   Sample Files

File Name	Description
MMEDIA.XLS	Excel 97 file with sample functions
MMEDIA.MDB	Access 97 database with sample functions
FRMVIDEO.FRM	VBA user form for AVI example
CLASSEX.BAS	Code for class modules
CSTRING.BAS	Code for MCI command string example
MCICONST.BAS	MCI constant declarations
MCIFUNCS.BAS	MCI functions
MCITYPES.BAS	MCI type declarations
REGISTRY.BAS	Registry functions from Chapter 10
SIMPLE.BAS	Simple multimedia examples
UTILITY.BAS	Utility functions

TABLE 13.1   Sample Files (continued)

File Name	Description
CDPLAY.CLS	CDPlayer class module
VIDPLAY.CLS	VideoPlayer class module
WAVEPLAY.CLS	WavePlayer class module
VBABOOK.WAV	Sample WAV file
GO.WAV	Sample WAV file
NORTH.WAV	Sample WAV file
EAST.WAV	Sample WAV file
SOUTH.WAV	Sample WAV file
WEST.WAV	Sample WAV file
WAVE.DLL	Resource-only DLL containing embedded WAV files
WAVE.RC	Resource script for WAVE.DLL
WAVE.MAK	Make file for WAVE.DLL

NOTE

To test our sample code you will, of course, need a multimedia-capable computer. You'll also need, at a minimum, a sound card and CD player to test our samples.

An Introduction to Windows Multimedia

Before exploring the various techniques for manipulating multimedia elements, let's take a look at the foundation on which they are based: the

Windows multimedia subsystems. While the examples in this chapter are just the tip of the iceberg as far as multimedia is concerned, this section gives you an overview of the many multimedia capabilities Windows offers.

Multimedia Services and MCI

Multimedia capability is a relative new feature of Windows. Microsoft first introduced real multimedia support as an add-on to Windows 3.x called the Multimedia Extensions. These were additional DLLs that implemented functions for playing digital sound and video as well as MIDI (Musical Instrument Digital Interface) files. With the advent of Windows 95, Microsoft integrated these functions directly into the operating system. Even though they still exist as separate DLLs apart from the traditional Windows API triad of User, Kernel, and GDI, you can now be assured that the functions are available on any machine running Windows 95 or Windows NT 4.0. (This does not mean, however, that you can count on the presence of multimedia hardware necessary to make them work!)

The multimedia support in the current versions of Windows has matured into a robust environment with support for numerous and varied hardware devices, such as digital audio and laser disc players, audio compact discs, overlay video (aka "TV-in-a-window"), and animation. Much of this is coordinated through the Media Control Interface (MCI). MCI defines a function interface to control different multimedia devices. Even though the features of the devices themselves vary greatly, they all share a more or less common set of abilities. For example, all must open some sort of multimedia data (referred to as a *media object* in this chapter), be it a sound file or an audio compact disc track. All have the ability to play the data as well as manipulate the current position (rewind, fast forward, and so on). This section reviews the capabilities of several multimedia devices. Later sections in this chapter demonstrate how to control them using MCI commands.

> **NOTE**
>
> MCI is considered a *high-level* multimedia interface because the devices themselves handle most of the work of manipulating media objects. Windows also has a host of *low-level* multimedia functions that give you a fine degree of control over multimedia data. Since it's unlikely that you'll choose VBA to build an application such as, say, a speech recognition system, we decided to stick with the high-level functions in this chapter.

Waveform Audio

Waveform audio is the correct term for the ever-popular WAV file format so familiar to Windows users. You create waveform audio using a sound card capable of taking analog input from a microphone and converting it to a digital signal. Waveform audio is the most common way of providing sound effects for applications, because of its ability to duplicate sounds exactly, with a high degree of clarity. You can affect the level of quality by controlling the following input parameters:

- **Sample rate:** The number of digital "snapshots" taken each second (often denoted by the term *hertz*, abbreviated Hz). The more samples you take, the better the quality. You can choose one of three distinct values: 11025 Hz (radio or voice quality), 22050 Hz (medium quality), or 44100 Hz (CD quality).

- **Bits per sample:** Determines how accurate each sample is. The more data per sample you store, the better the quality. You can store either 8 or 16 bits per sample.

- **Channels:** Refers to whether you record in stereophonic (2 channels) or monophonic (1 channel).

The downside to waveform audio is the amount of storage space required for sound data. For example, 60 seconds of CD-quality, 16-bit stereo sound require 10,584,000 bytes of storage! (That's 60 x 44100 x (16 / 8) x 2.) Fortunately, you rarely need this level of clarity. Due to the mediocre quality of many sound cards, plus the inefficiency of the human ear, 11025 Hz, 8-bit monophonic sounds are usually adequate for sound effects and voice prompts.

Compact Disc Audio

If you really need CD-quality audio, you should use CD audio tracks. MCI offers simple functions for playing CD audio, and the storage requirements are zero because the media are on a compact disc. The one problem with CD audio, however, is the difficulty of producing it. Unless you purchase the right to use existing content, you'll have to create your own. This is a time-consuming process requiring considerable artistic talent.

MIDI Audio

MIDI audio offers a compromise between waveform audio and CD audio. MIDI (which stands for Musical Instrument Digital Interface) is the format understood by electronic synthesizers. Most sound cards include an FM synthesizer chip capable of producing music from MIDI commands. Unlike waveform audio, which stores an exact replica of recorded sound, MIDI audio is stored as "songs" made up of information regarding musical instruments, notes, pitch, duration, and so on. For this reason, the storage requirements are quite low. For example, Windows 95 ships with a MIDI-encoded version of Johann Sebastian Bach's Brandenburg Concerto No. 3. Despite the fact that the concerto is over six minutes long, the song file is only about 140K in size.

There are, however, three drawbacks to MIDI files. First, since the songs don't store actual sounds but instead define musical instruments, it's up to the sound card to supply the actual sound, so the output will vary from one sound card to the next. The second problem is that unless you have a specially designed sound card, the CPU must process the musical information, adding to the overall system load. Third, sound cards that use FM synthesizers to produce the output can only *approximate* the true sound of an instrument by modulating the frequency of a carrier wave. Newer sound cards that store digital samples of actual instruments (so-called *wave table* sound cards) reproduce the intended music much more accurately, but they are still more expensive and less prevalent than FM synthesizer-based cards. For these reasons, MIDI songs are normally used as background music for games where instrumental fidelity is not essential.

Digital Video

One of the best features of Windows 95 and Windows NT 4.0 is their ability to process digital video. You probably know this feature better as AVI files. Microsoft shipped software called Video for Windows that allowed you to view AVI files under Windows 3.x. In fact, Video for Windows defined the AVI file format, which is the most popular format around today. With Windows 95 and NT 4.0, digital video is now an integral part of the multimedia subsystem.

NOTE   **Other digital video formats include Apple QuickTime, MPEG, and DVI (Digital Video Interactive).**

Digital video files are created using special hardware that converts the analog signal from a television tuner or VCR into digital images. The quality of the image can vary greatly depending on the size of the image, the speed of playback (measured in frames per second), and the compression algorithms used.

Compression is used, for example, so that not every pixel an image comprises need be updated if it doesn't change from frame to frame. A variety of compression algorithms offer different levels of speed and size reduction.

In addition to using analog-to-digital converter hardware, you can create AVI files with software products such as Microsoft Camcorder (which ships as part of Office 97). These products produce computer-generated frames based on screen capture or other means and are particularly useful for creating demos or instructional videos for software programs.

Like digital audio, digital video suffers the problem of media size. Even a short video clip recorded at small frame size can take up 500K or more of disk space. To further complicate matters, to view an AVI file you must have the same *codec* (*co*mpression/*dec*ompression software) used to create the file on your computer. While most computers have numerous codecs installed, allowing them to play back most videos, there is a chance for incompatibility. You can see which ones you have using the Control Panel Multimedia applet, shown in Figure 13.1.

FIGURE 13.1

Viewing audio and video codecs in the Control Panel

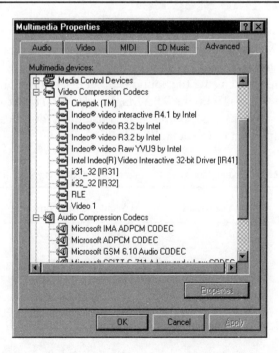

One-Step Multimedia

Unless you're writing a complete multimedia title, your multimedia needs are probably quite simple. You may, for example, just want to generate a simple sound or play a certain WAV file. This section explains how to do this using single VBA statements.

Beeping Away

If all you want to do is generate a simple, obvious noise, nothing beats the VBA Beep statement. This single statement generates a sound regardless of the presence of multimedia hardware. If no hardware is installed, the result is just a "beep" from the computer's speaker. If, on the other hand, a sound card is installed, VBA plays the default system sound. (For more information on system sounds, see the section "Playing System Event Sounds" later in this chapter.)

MessageBeep: One Step Better

If the default system sound doesn't tickle your fancy, you can resort to the Windows API MessageBeep function. MessageBeep plays one of five predefined sounds associated with a message box icon. These sounds are based on the system sounds you define using the Sounds applet in Control Panel. You can use the same constants you use with the VBA MsgBox function or those defined by the Windows API. Table 13.2 lists both sets of constants. (You can also pass the value &HFFFFFFFF to produce the default sound.)

TABLE 13.2 VBA and Windows API Constants for Producing System Sounds

Value	VBA Constant	Windows API Constant
0	none	MB_OK
16	vbCritical	MB_ICONHAND or MB_ICONSTOP
32	vbQuestion	MB_ICONQUESTION
48	vbExclamation	MB_ICONEXCLAMATION
64	vbInformation	MB_ICONASTERISK or MB_ICONINFORMATION

MessageBeep is a simple function that accepts one of the constants listed in Table 13.2 and produces that sound. If no sound card is installed, the function simply produces a beep from the computer speaker.

If your development tool doesn't already play a system sound when it displays a message box, you can use the MessageBeep and MsgBox functions together to do this. The dhMsgBeep function shown in Listing 13.1 provides an example.

Listing 13.1: Make a Message Box Make Noise

```
Function dhMsgBeep(strMsg As String, _
 Optional lngType As Long = 0, _
 Optional strCaption As String = "") As Long

    Dim lngSound As Long

    ' Get sound type
    lngSound = lngType And &HF0

    ' Play sound
    Call MessageBeep(lngSound)

    ' Show message box
    If strCaption = "" Then
        dhMsgBeep = MsgBox(strMsg, lngType)
    Else
        dhMsgBeep = MsgBox(strMsg, lngType, strCaption)
    End If
End Function
```

Playing Waveform Audio with PlaySound

For the ultimate in one-step multimedia, you can use the PlaySound API function. This simple function lets you play any arbitrary waveform audio file, including system sounds and waveform data contained in executable files. The declaration of the PlaySound function is as follows:

```
Declare Function PlaySound Lib "winmm.dll" _
 Alias "PlaySoundA" (ByVal lpszSoundName As String, _
 ByVal hMod As Long, ByVal uFlags As Long) As Long
```

As you can see, PlaySound accepts only three arguments: the name of a sound, the handle to a loaded module (more on that in a moment), and a set of flags. The function is nonetheless highly versatile. Table 13.3 lists the flags you can pass to the function.

TABLE 13.3 PlaySound Flag Constants

PlaySound Flag	Description
SND_SYNC	Plays the sound synchronously (the default)
SND_ASYNC	Plays the sound asynchronously
SND_NODEFAULT	If the specified sound is invalid, PlaySound does not play the default sound
SND_LOOP	Loops the sound until the next call to PlaySound
SND_NOSTOP	Does not stop the sound currently playing
SND_NOWAIT	Doesn't wait if the sound driver is busy
SND_MEMORY	The lpszSoundName argument is a pointer to a sound in memory
SND_ALIAS	Sound is a system sound name
SND_ALIAS_ID	Sound is a system sound identifier
SND_FILENAME	Sound is a file name
SND_RESOURCE	Sound is a resource name

Regardless of the other flags you choose to pass to the function, you should pass one of the following: SND_FILENAME, SND_ALIAS, or SND_MEMORY. These flags tell PlaySound how to interpret the lpszSoundName argument—as a file name, a system event name, or a memory address. The following sections discuss each of these methods.

NOTE If you don't pass one of these flags, PlaySound tries to determine the meaning of the lpszSoundName argument on its own. It's usually better, however, to do this yourself.

NOTE   The hMod argument is used only to play embedded resources with the SND_MEMORY flag and must be set to 0 otherwise.

Playing WAV Files

The most obvious use for PlaySound is to play arbitrary WAV files. You pass the path to the wave file and a set of flags. The most common flags, along with SND_FILENAME, are SND_SYNC and SND_ASYNC. Passing the SND_SYNC flag forces PlaySound to play the entire file before returning control to your application. Conversely, the SND_ASYNC flag tells PlaySound to cue the sound, begin playback, and return immediately. Suppose, for example, you wanted to play a WAV file containing instructions on how to use your application while a user was using it. You could use a statement like this:

```
Call PlaySound("C:\MYAPP\SOUNDS\HOWTO.WAV", 0&, _
 SND_ANSYC Or SND_FILENAME)
```

This would play the sound asynchronously, allowing the user to interact with your application while the sound was playing.

TIP   When using PlaySound to play WAV files, you usually don't need to include the SND_FILENAME flag. Under almost all circumstances, PlaySound will correctly determine that the first argument is the name of a file. Furthermore, if you don't specify a path, PlaySound will look for the file using the same search rules followed by the SearchPath function described in Chapter 12.

If PlaySound cannot play the requested sound, perhaps because the file name you passed does not exist, it plays the default Windows sound (the familiar electronic "ding"). If you don't want to hear this sound, pass the SND_NODEFAULT flag. The function's return value will tell you whether the sound was played successfully, as the following code illustrates:

```
If Not CBool(PlaySound("MYSOUND.WAV", 0&, SND_NODEFAULT)) Then
    ' Something went wrong!
End If
```

NOTE If you don't include the SND_NODEFAULT flag and PlaySound can't play the requested sound, it plays the default sound *and* returns a value of 1, indicating success!

If you want to repeat a sound continuously, pass the SND_LOOP flag. PlaySound will continue to call the sound over and over until you call the function again. You can call it with another sound or an empty string to stop the current sound from looping. For instance, suppose you wanted to create the illusion of a barking dog for a theft-deterrent system. You might use code like this:

```
' Make the dog bark
Call PlaySound("BARK.WAV", 0&, SND_FILENAME Or SND_LOOP)

' Okay, that's enough!
Call PlaySound("", 0&, SND_NODEFAULT)
```

Playing System Event Sounds

The PlaySound function also provides an easy way to play Windows system event sounds. The discussion of the MessageBeep function earlier in this chapter explained a few of the system sounds. Other system sounds include system start and stop, window minimize and maximize, and the infamous critical stop. (That's the event associated with an IPF.) You can change the sounds associated with various events using the Sounds applet in the Control Panel, which is shown in Figure 13.2.

Playing Stock System Sounds   To play a system sound using PlaySound, you must specify its name along with the SND_ALIAS flag. For example:

```
Call PlaySound("AppGPFault", 0&, SND_ALIAS Or SND_NODEFAULT)
```

Table 13.4 lists the system sounds recognized by the PlaySound function, as well as the descriptions shown in the Sounds applet. Note that the two are different. The system sound names are fixed and are mapped to the descriptive text shown in the Sounds applet by Registry settings. You can find the mappings in the HKEY_CURRENT_USER\AppEvents\EventLabels key.

FIGURE 13.2

You can change
system sounds using
the Sounds applet
in the Control Panel

TABLE 13.4   System Sounds You Can Play Using PlaySound

System Sound Name	Default Description in Control Panel
.Default	Default sound
AppGPFault	Program error
Close	Close program
EmptyRecycleBin	Empty Recycle Bin
MailBeep	New Mail Notification
Maximize	Maximize
MenuCommand	Menu command
MenuPopup	Menu popup

TABLE 13.4 System Sounds You Can Play Using PlaySound (continued)

System Sound Name	Default Description in Control Panel
Minimize	Minimize
Open	Open program
RestoreDown	Restore down
RestoreUp	Restore up
SystemAsterisk	Asterisk
SystemExclamation	Exclamation
SystemExit	Exit Windows
SystemHand	Critical Stop
SystemQuestion	Question
SystemStart	Start Windows

Playing Application Event Sounds   In addition to the system sounds listed in Table 13.4, other applications may add event sounds that can also be customized using the Sounds applet. Unfortunately, you can't play these sounds directly using PlaySound and the SND_ALIAS flag. To play application-specific sounds, you must first look in the Registry to locate the sound entry, read the name of the WAV file, and then call PlaySound.

All event sounds, including the system sounds, are stored in the HKEY_CURRENT_USER\AppEvents\Schemes\Apps key. Windows system sounds are stored in a subkey called ".Default" (note the leading period). Other applications may add additional subkeys with their own event sounds. Beneath every subkey are other subkeys for each event, and beneath those are subkeys representing the default sound associated with the event, the sound that is currently assigned, and the sounds associated with any sound schemes you may have installed. Figure 13.3 shows the Registry Editor open to a portion of this wild Registry branch.

FIGURE 13.3

Registry entries for event
sounds

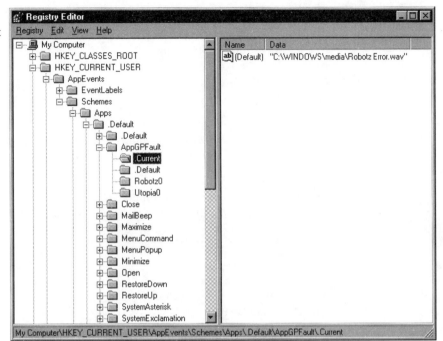

To make retrieving the name of the sound file associated with an application event easier, we created a function called dhGetEventSound. This function uses the Registry functions explained in Chapter 10 to retrieve the sound associated with any event, be it system or application specific. Listing 13.2 shows the dhGetEventSound function.

NOTE For those of you keeping score at home, the dhGetEventSound function was adapted from the dhReadWallpaper procedure described in the section "Working with Registry Values" in Chapter 10.

Listing 13.2: Retrieve Any Event Sound from the Registry

```
Function dhGetEventSound( _
  Optional strApp As String = ".Default", _
```

```
Optional strEvent As String = ".Default", _
Optional strScheme As String = ".Current") As String

   Dim hKeySound As Long
   Dim strKeySound As String
   Dim lngResult As Long
   Dim strBuffer As String
   Dim cb As Long

   ' Build the key name
   strKeySound = "AppEvents\Schemes\Apps\" & _
    strApp & "\" & strEvent & "\" & strScheme

   ' Open the sound key
   lngResult = RegOpenKeyEx(dhcHKeyCurrentUser, _
    strKeySound, 0&, dhcKeyAllAccess, hKeySound)

   ' Make sure the call succeeded
   If lngResult = dhcSuccess Then

       ' Create the buffer
       strBuffer = Space(255)
       cb = Len(strBuffer)

       ' Read the default value
       lngResult = RegQueryValueEx(hKeySound, "", _
        0&, dhcRegSz, ByVal strBuffer, cb)

       ' Check return value
       If lngResult = dhcSuccess Then

           ' Return the value
           dhGetEventSound = Left(strBuffer, cb)
       End If

       ' Close the sound key
       lngResult = RegCloseKey(hKeySound)
   End If
End Function
```

As you can see from the function declaration, dhGetEventSound accepts three optional arguments representing the application name, event name, and sound scheme. We've supplied default values that, if you call the function with no arguments, cause dhGetEventSound to return the default system sound. You can override these defaults with settings of your own. For example, the following code plays the WAV file associated with starting Quicken 6.0. (Naturally, you must have installed Quicken for this to work.)

```
Dim strFile As String

' Get the name of the WAV file
strFile = dhGetEventSound("Quicken", "Open Program")

' Play the WAV file if successful
If strFile <> "" Then
    Call PlaySound(strFile, 0&, SND_FILENAME Or SND_NODEFAULT)
End If
```

TIP Unless you want to play a sound associated with a sound scheme other than the current one, leave the third argument blank.

Playing Embedded Sounds

The last use for PlaySound is to play sounds that are embedded within an EXE or DLL file. Executable files (we'll consider DLLs executable files for the purpose of this discussion) usually contain numerous embedded objects, known generically as *resources*. Common resources include icons, bitmaps, menus, string tables, and dialog box definitions. Application developers embed resources because doing so reduces the number of additional files that must be distributed with the application. Furthermore, it's difficult, although by no means impossible, to extract embedded resources from an executable. Embedding a resource, therefore, is a convenient way to protect intellectual property.

Creating Embedded WAV Files If you plan on using numerous WAV files in your application, you may want to consider embedding them in a DLL, even though it may not contain any program code. Developers commonly create *resource-only* DLLs for this purpose. Creating a resource-DLL requires only two steps:

1. Compile individual WAV files (or other resources) into a resource file using a *resource compiler* such as RC.EXE, which ships with Microsoft Visual C++.

2. Link the resource file into a DLL using a linker such as LINK.EXE, which also comes with Microsoft Visual C++.

Accomplishing the first step requires that you create a resource script. A *resource script* tells the resource compiler what files to include and how to identify them in the resource file. Listing 13.3 shows the contents of WAVE.RC, a sample resource script we've provided for this chapter.

Listing 13.3: A Sample Resource Script

```
//////////////////////////////////////////////////////////////
//
// Resource script for creating embedded WAV files
//
// Make sure each WAVE resource is assigned a unique number!
//
//////////////////////////////////////////////////////////////

101 WAVE DISCARDABLE "GO.WAV"

201 WAVE DISCARDABLE "NORTH.WAV"
202 WAVE DISCARDABLE "EAST.WAV"
203 WAVE DISCARDABLE "SOUTH.WAV"
204 WAVE DISCARDABLE "WEST.WAV"

// End RC file
```

Each line in the script file (except those beginning with //, which are comments) identifies a resource. For each line you must include

- A unique number or name (without quotes) identifying the resource

- The type of resource (WAVE, in this case)

- The keyword DISCARDABLE (which tells Windows it can dynamically load and unload the resource)

- The path to the resource

NOTE
If the files are not located in the same directory as the RC file, you need to include the path. Furthermore, since RC.EXE conforms to the same rules as a C compiler, you must double all path separators (for example, "C:\\WAVE\\GO.WAV").

You compile the resource script into a resource file by running RC.EXE from the command line. For example,

```
RC WAVE.RC
```

results in a resource file with the same name as the resource script and an .RES file extension.

At this point you need to link the resource file into a DLL. Since this is a resource-only DLL, requiring no other object files, you can use a command line like the following (assuming you're using Microsoft's LINK.EXE linker):

```
LINK /out:WAVE.DLL /dll /machine:i386 /noentry wave.res
```

Each part of the command line has a specific meaning:

- /out:*outputfile* defines the output file.

- /dll informs LINK.EXE to produce a DLL.

- /machine:*machinetype* defines the binary executable format.

- /noentry informs LINK.EXE that there is no entry point (that is, this is a resource-only DLL).

- The remaining entries are the input files separated by spaces.

> **TIP**
>
> You can also use a make file instead of specifying all the options on the command line. Use the syntax "LINK @*makefile*", where *makefile* is the name of the make file. We've included a make file, WAVE.MAK, with the sample code.

Playing an Embedded WAV File   Once you've compiled a series of WAV files into a DLL, you can use PlaySound to play one. It's not quite that simple, however, because you have to load the resource into memory first. That involves loading the DLL, finding the resource, loading the resource, and calling Play-Sound with the SND_MEMORY flag. Don't despair, though; we've created a wrapper function, dhPlayResource, that takes care of all these tasks for you. It's shown in Listing 13.4.

> **TIP**
>
> If you're using Visual Basic as your development tool, you can use VB's LoadResource function to obtain a memory pointer to the resource in place of the library- and resource-loading code in Listing 13.4.

Listing 13.4: The dhPlayResource Function Plays an Embedded WAV File

```
Function dhPlayResource(strLibrary As String, _
 varResource As Variant, Optional lngFlags As Long = 0) _
 As Boolean

    Dim hMod As Long
    Dim hRes As Long
    Dim lngRes As Long
    Dim fOk As Boolean

    ' Load the library as a data file
    hMod = LoadLibraryEx(strLibrary, 0&, _
     LOAD_LIBRARY_AS_DATAFILE)
    If hMod <> 0 Then

        ' If the resource is a number add the "#",
        ' otherwise just use it
        If IsNumeric(varResource) Then
            varResource = "#" & varResource
        End If

        ' Find the WAVE resource in the library
        lngRes = FindResource(hMod, CStr(varResource), "WAVE")
        If lngRes <> 0 Then
            ' Load the resource
            hRes = LoadResource(hMod, lngRes)
            If hRes <> 0 Then
                ' Lock the resource and play it
                If CBool(LockResource(hRes)) Then
                    dhPlayResource = CBool(PlayResSound( _
                        hRes, 0&, SND_MEMORY Or lngFlags))
                End If
                ' Free the resource
                Call FreeResource(hRes)
            End If
        End If

        ' Free the library
        Call FreeLibrary(hMod)
    End If
End Function
```

Since a discussion of loading resources from an executable file goes beyond the scope of this book, you'll have to deduce how the function works on your own. (Do notice, however, that the call to PlaySound includes the SND_MEMORY flag.) You can try out the function by calling it with WAVE.DLL, the sample DLL provided with this chapter. It contains the five WAV files referenced in the WAVE.RC file. To play these sounds, try executing the following code:

```
?dhPlayResource("WAVE.DLL", 101), dhPlayResource("WAVE.DLL", 201)
```

NOTE Because you must supply a pointer to the resource in memory as a long integer, we created a second declaration for PlaySound, called PlayResSound, which defines the first argument as Long.

TIP If you're using Visual Basic *and* you have compiled WAVE resources into your executable file, you can use a much more convenient form of PlaySound. Simply pass the instance handle of your VB application as the second argument in addition to the resource name and the SND_RESOURCE flag—for example: PlaySound("WAVENAME", App.hInstance, SND_RESOURCE).

WARNING Whatever you do, don't call the dhPlayResource function with the SND_ASYNC flag! This will cause the library to be unloaded before the sound is finished playing, resulting in a very nasty IPF.

Understanding the Media Control Interface

The Media Control Interface component of Windows' multimedia services is an extremely powerful mechanism for controlling multimedia devices. Using just a few (three!) functions, it can play audio CDs, record digital audio, control VCRs... You get the idea. Furthermore, it offers two ways of controlling devices: a command string–based approach and a command message–based approach. This section looks at MCI in detail, including both interfaces.

Due to space limitations, we couldn't provide a complete listing of MCI commands and their options. If the examples in this book aren't enough for you to accomplish your tasks, consult additional resources such as the Microsoft Developer Network (MSDN) library CD-ROM. You can also find MSDN online at http://www.microsoft.com/msdn/sdk.

Working with MCI Devices

MCI was designed from the start to support a number of different multimedia devices. Each device is assigned a unique device type that can be expressed as a text description or a number. You use these designations in MCI functions. Table 13.5 provides a summary of the device types, along with their identifiers.

TABLE 13.5   Multimedia Device Types and MCI Designations

Device	Device Type Constant	Device Type String
Compact disc audio	MCI_DEVTYPE_CD_AUDIO	cdaudio
Digital video in a window	MCI_DEVTYPE_DIGITAL_VIDEO	digitalvideo or avivideo
Digital-audio tape player	MCI_DEVTYPE_DAT	dat
Image scanner	MCI_DEVTYPE_SCANNER	scanner
MIDI sequencer	MCI_DEVTYPE_SEQUENCER	sequencer
Other MCI devices	MCI_DEVTYPE_OTHER	other
Overlay video (analog)	MCI_DEVTYPE_OVERLAY	overlay or avivideo
Video-cassette recorder or player	MCI_DEVTYPE_VCR	vcr
Videodisc player	MCI_DEVTYPE_VIDEODISC	videodisc
Waveform audio	MCI_DEVTYPE_WAVEFORM_AUDIO	waveaudio

Simple versus Complex Device Types

As far as MCI is concerned, there are two broad classes of multimedia devices: simple and complex. Simple devices are those that are more or less inseparable from the media they handle. For example, audio CD players are simple devices because they can handle only one media object at a time (the compact disc), and the media is either available for playing or it isn't. Complex devices, on the other hand, can create, save, load, and unload media objects dynamically. Windows' waveform audio driver is an example of a complex device. You can use it to create and save new WAV files or to load and play existing ones.

Determining Which Devices Are Installed

Device information is stored in the system Registry in the HKEY_LOCAL_ MACHINE\System\CurrentControlSet\control\MediaResources\mci key. Figure 13.4 shows REGEDIT open to this branch. You can use the Registry functions explained in Chapter 10 to retrieve this information.

FIGURE 13.4

Viewing installed MCI devices in the Registry

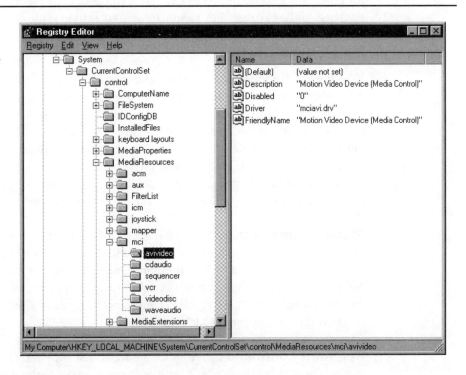

Note the Disabled value for the Registry key shown in Figure 13.4. While there may be a number of MCI devices listed, those that aren't actually installed in the computer will have a Disabled setting of 1.

Working with Devices

Regardless of which type of device you decide to use, working with devices follows the same overall pattern. You begin by *opening* the device. This tells MCI what device you intend to use and prepares it for subsequent commands. If the device is available (which may not be the case—a device could be in use by another process), MCI assigns the device a unique *device ID* that your application uses to control the device.

Once you've opened a device, you use it by sending various commands, using one of the two supported interfaces. The following sections describe the interfaces in detail.

Finally, when you're finished using a device, you *close* it. Closing a device releases any memory allocated by MCI for the session. It also makes the device available for other applications or processes. This is important for media types such as compact disc audio because they cannot be shared among multiple applications.

MCI Commands

Whether you decide to use the command string interface or the command message interface, you control devices using a fixed set of commands. These commands are represented by both strings and numeric constants for use with the different interfaces. While all devices must support a core set of commands, some commands apply only to certain device types. MCI categorizes commands in one of four ways: system, required, basic, and extended. The next few sections explain each category and summarize the commands that make it up. Later sections give examples of using these commands to play CD audio, waveform audio, and digital video devices.

System Commands   *System commands,* of which there are only two, are handled directly by MCI rather than by individual devices. The MCI_BREAK command (also represented by the command string "break") sets a *break key* for an MCI device. You press the break key to interrupt device actions, such as playing and recording. The MCI_SYSINFO command (command string "sysinfo") requests information about MCI devices.

Required Commands   All MCI devices must support a set of *required commands.* These commands, along with a standard set of options, represent the common capabilities of all MCI devices. Table 13.6 summarizes the MCI required commands. (This and other tables in this section list the command message constant as well as the command string and description.)

TABLE 13.6 MCI Required Commands

Command Message Constant	Command String	Description
MCI_GETDEVCAPS	capability	Obtains device capabilities (for example, whether the device can record media objects)
MCI_CLOSE	close	Closes the device
MCI_INFO	info	Obtains textual device information
MCI_OPEN	open	Opens the device and, optionally, a media object
MCI_STATUS	status	Obtains status information (for example, whether the device is currently playing)

Basic Commands As you can see from Table 13.6, required commands supply only the minimum functionality needed to initialize, query, and close a device. To control a device for a useful purpose, you must call one of the *basic commands* shown in Table 13.7. Most, but not all, devices implement these commands. If you need to know whether a device supports a particular command before calling it, you can use the MCI_GETDEVCAPS command listed in Table 13.6. Most of the examples later in this chapter focus on these commands.

TABLE 13.7 MCI Basic Commands

Command Message Constant	Command String	Description
MCI_LOAD	load	Loads a media object from a file
MCI_PAUSE	pause	Pauses playback or recording
MCI_PLAY	play	Starts playback
MCI_RECORD	record	Starts recording
MCI_RESUME	resume	Resumes paused playback or recording
MCI_SAVE	save	Saves media object to disk

TABLE 13.7 MCI Basic Commands (continued)

Command Message Constant	Command String	Description
MCI_SEEK	seek	Positions current playback or recording position
MCI_SET	set	Sets various operating parameters
MCI_STATUS	status	Obtains status information (Note that this is also a required command.)
MCI_STOP	stop	Stops playback

Extended Commands A few devices, such as digital video and videodisc players, support *extended commands*. These tend to be the most complex of the lot, designed to enable features specific to a particular device. Table 13.8 summarizes these commands, along with the devices they apply to.

TABLE 13.8 MCI Extended Commands

Command Message Constant	Command String	Description	Applies to
MCI_CONFIGURE	configure	Displays a configuration dialog	digitalvideo
MCI_CUE	cue	Cues a file for playback	digitalvideo, waveaudio
MCI_DELETE	delete	Deletes a portion of a media object	waveaudio
MCI_ESCAPE	escape	Sends escape codes to a device	videodisc
MCI_FREEZE	freeze	Freezes video signal acquisition	overlay
MCI_PUT	put	Defines source, destination, and frame windows	digitalvideo, overlay
MCI_REALIZE	realize	Realizes a device's palette into a device context	digitalvideo
MCI_SETAUDIO	setaudio	Sets audio parameters	digitalvideo

TABLE 13.8   MCI Extended Commands (continued)

Command Message Constant	Command String	Description	Applies to
MCI_SETVIDEO	setvideo	Sets video parameters	digitalvideo
MCI_SIGNAL	signal	Identifies a specific position within a signal	digitalvideo
MCI_SPIN	spin	Starts or stops disc spinning	videodisc
MCI_STEP	step	Steps through playback frame by frame	digitalvideo, videodisc
MCI_UNFREEZE	unfreeze	Enables video signal acquisition	overlay
MCI_UPDATE	update	Repaints the current frame	digitalvideo
MCI_WHERE	where	Defines source, destination, or frame areas	digitalvideo, overlay
MCI_WINDOW	window	Controls the display window	digitalvideo, overlay

The MCI Command String Interface

The MCI command string interface was designed to allow control of multimedia devices using simple string-based commands. Originally aimed at programming languages that could not easily handle complex data structures, it has been mostly supplanted by the more powerful and flexible command message interface described in the next section. Nonetheless, we cover this interface here both for completeness and because, for simple tasks, it's easier to implement than command messages.

The mciSendString Function

All the command string capabilities are accessed with a single function, mciSendString. Its declaration is as follows:

```
Declare Function mciSendString _
 Lib "winmm.dll" Alias "mciSendStringA" _
 (ByVal lpstrCommand As String, _
```

```
ByVal lpstrReturnString As String, _
ByVal uReturnLength As Long, _
ByVal hwndCallback As Long) As Long
```

As you can see, mciSendString accepts four arguments that dictate the command carried out by the device. It returns 0 on success and a nonzero error code on failure. The error codes are the same as those used by the command message interface. (For more information, see the section "MCI Errors" later in this chapter.)

Of the four arguments, you'll be primarily interested in only the first two. These two arguments allow you to send commands and receive results from MCI. The third argument, uReturnLength, is merely an indicator of the size of the data returned. The final argument, hwndCallback, is the handle of the window that you want to receive status messages from MCI. Since you can't create callback functions directly using VBA, it's of little use.

Constructing Command Strings

You instruct MCI to take action by passing a command string in the lpstrCommand argument. Constructing command strings is probably the second most tedious part of working with the command string interface. (Parsing return information is the first!) The more complex the action you want to take, the more tedious it is. Command strings use a standard verb-object-modifier syntax:

command mediatype | filename | alias [options]

All command strings begin with a predefined MCI command. It's followed by the media type descriptor string, a registered multimedia file name, or an *alias* (which is just a unique string). Specifying an alias when you open a device makes it easier to refer back to the device in subsequent commands. Following the device or alias are any options a particular command requires.

Listing 13.5 shows a simple procedure that plays a MIDI file. You can see that command strings are constructed by concatenating the file name to MCI commands and that an alias is used to refer back to the open device.

NOTE　For all our examples involving MCI, you should step through the code one line at a time. Otherwise, the device will be closed before you have a chance to see or hear the results.

Listing 13.5: Play a MIDI File Using the MCI Command String Interface

```
Sub dhPlayMIDIFile(strFile As String)
    Dim strCommand As String
    Dim strRet As String
    Dim lngBytes As Long
    Dim lngRet As Long

    ' Open the file (must have a .MID or .RMI extension)
    strCommand = "open " & strFile & " alias seq"
    strRet = Space(255)
    lngRet = mciSendString(strCommand, strRet, lngBytes, 0&)

    ' If successful, start playback
    If lngRet = 0 Then
        strCommand = "play seq"
        strRet = Space(255)
        lngRet = mciSendString(strCommand, strRet, lngBytes, 0&)
    End If

    ' Close the device
    strCommand = "close seq"
    strRet = Space(255)
    lngRet = mciSendString(strCommand, strRet, lngBytes, 0&)
End Sub
```

NOTE   If the file name passed in an MCI command string contains spaces, you must enclose the file name in double quotation marks.

In this example, no information is returned by MCI, so allocating space for a buffer in the strRet variable is unnecessary. For those commands that do return information (such as the "where" command), you should allocate the buffer prior to calling mciSendString and inspect its contents afterward. This section has considered the command string interface as a simple method of playing multimedia elements. For information on retrieving information using the command message interface, see the section "MCI Information Functions" later in this chapter.

The MCI Command Message Interface

The MCI command message interface is a simple but powerful mechanism for controlling multimedia devices. Like the command string interface, its purpose is to allow you to send commands to devices. Rather than using text strings, however, the command message interface uses integer commands and structures to specify options.

The mciSendCommand Function

You use the command message interface by calling the mciSendCommand function, which is declared as follows:

```
Declare Function mciSendCommand _
 Lib "winmm.dll" Alias "mciSendCommandA" _
 (ByVal wDeviceID As Long, ByVal uMessage As Long, _
 ByVal dwParam1 As Long, dwParam2 As Any) As Long
```

You pass four pieces of information in the function's arguments:

- The device ID of an open device. This can be 0 for devices not yet opened or MCI_ALL_DEVICE_ID to send a message to all open devices

- The message expressed as a numeric constant

- A bitmask of flags associated with the message

- A pointer to a structure containing details concerning the message

Like its counterpart mciSendString, mciSendCommand returns 0 on success or an MCI error code on failure. The beauty of mciSendCommand is that it works with a variety of devices through its ability to accept different datatypes as the fourth argument.

General Message Flags

The third argument to mciSendCommand is a combination of flags that fine-tune the behavior of the command. Most of the flag values are associated with certain commands and the data structures they use. (See the next section, "Message Information Structures.") There are two flags, however, you can use with all commands: MCI_WAIT and MCI_NOTIFY.

The MCI_WAIT flag instructs MCI to wait until the command has been carried out. Depending on the device, this may take a considerable amount of time. Audio CD devices, for example, must spin up in response to an MCI_OPEN command. Loading a large WAV file into a waveform audio device can also be time consuming. Omitting this flag causes the mciSendCommand function to return immediately, but use this option with care—if you attempt to carry out another, dependent action before the first action completes (playing a WAV file before it's finished loading, for instance), the command may fail.

If you choose not to use the MCI_WAIT flag, you can determine the status of a device by issuing the MCI_STATUS command. (See the section "MCI Information Functions" a little later in this chapter for more information.)

The MCI_NOTIFY flag instructs MCI to notify your application when the command completes. Specifically, it sends an MM_MCINOTIFY message to a window that you designate. If you are using a development tool capable of intercepting window messages, you can use this flag to detect, for instance, when MCI has finished loading a file.

Message Information Structures

MCI defines numerous datatypes that you use in conjunction with different commands. We've included the declarations for these types in the basMCITypes module of the sample Excel workbook. Since there are so many, the ones used in this chapter are explained in the sections describing our sample code.

In general, each command message has an associated structure. For example, the MCI_OPEN command uses the MCI_OPEN_PARMS structure:

```
Type MCI_OPEN_PARMS
    lngCallback As Long
    lngDeviceID As Long
    strDeviceType As String
    strElementName As String
    strAlias As String
End Type
```

NOTE

Every structure designed to work with MCI commands has a lngCallback member. You use this to specify the handle of a window that will receive an MM_MCINOTIFY message when the command finishes. Of course, this feature is useful only if you're using a development tool that can hook into a window's message queue or you have an ActiveX control that can do so.

The MCI message interface does not require you to use every member variable of a structure. Instead, you fill in the values you need and pass a bitmask of flags to mciSendCommand that indicate which elements are used. For example, if you were opening a waveform audio device and set the strElementName member to the name of a WAV file, you would also need to pass the MCI_OPEN_ELEMENT flag as part of the call to mciSendCommand. If you pass a flag but don't fill in the member variable with a valid value, an error occurs.

Additionally, some devices may use more complex structures for certain commands. For example, overlay video devices use the MCI_OVLY_OPEN_PARMS structure with the MCI_OPEN command instead of MCI_OPEN_PARMS. These structures let you supply additional information that is unique to the device.

MCI Errors

If an error occurs during a call to mciSendCommand, the result is a nonzero error code. MCI has conveniently provided a function called mciGetErrorString that returns a description for a given error code. You should always check the result of calling mciSendCommand and, if it's greater than 0, call mciGetErrorString to retrieve the text. We've written a wrapper function called dhMCIError to enable you to do this. Listing 13.6 shows the function, along with the declaration for mciGetErrorString.

Listing 13.6: A Function for Retrieving MCI Error Descriptions

```
Declare Function mciGetErrorString _
 Lib "winmm.dll" Alias "mciGetErrorStringA" _
 (ByVal dwError As Long, ByVal lpstrBuffer As String, _
 ByVal uLength As Long) As Long

Function dhMCIError(ByVal lngErr As Long, _
 Optional varTag As Variant) As String

    Dim strBuffer As String
    Dim lngPos As Long
    Dim lngRet As Long

    If lngErr <> 0 Then
        ' Set up a buffer
        strBuffer = Space(1024)

        Call mciGetErrorString(lngErr, strBuffer, _
         Len(strBuffer))
```

```
        ' Trim string
        lngPos = InStr(strBuffer, vbNullChar)
        If lngPos > 0 Then
            strBuffer = Left(strBuffer, lngPos - 1)

            ' Get tag?
            lngPos = InStr(strBuffer, " ")
            If Not IsMissing(varTag) And lngPos > 0 Then
                varTag = Left(strBuffer, lngPos - 1)
            End If

            ' Return result
            dhMCIError = Mid(strBuffer, lngPos + 1)
        End If
    End If
End Function
```

You can pass an optional Variant argument to the function. All MCI error messages begin with the string "MMSYSTEM*xxx* ", where *xxx* is the error code. dhMCIError normally strips this encoded error string from the text it returns. If you supply a variable as the varTag argument, however, dhMCIError places the prefix text in it.

MCI Time Formats

MCI expresses time intervals for devices using a number of different formats. Retrieving the current position and controlling playback depend on your understanding of these formats. Table 13.9 lists the numeric constant and description of each format.

TABLE 13.9 MCI Time Formats

Time Format Constant	Description
MCI_FORMAT_BYTES	Bytes (in pulse code modulated [PCM] format files)
MCI_FORMAT_MILLISECONDS	Milliseconds
MCI_FORMAT_MSF	Minute/second/frame
MCI_FORMAT_SAMPLES	Samples
MCI_FORMAT_SMPTE_24	SMPTE, 24 frame

TABLE 13.9 MCI Time Formats (continued)

Time Format Constant	Description
MCI_FORMAT_SMPTE_25	SMPTE, 25 frame
MCI_FORMAT_SMPTE_30	SMPTE, 30 frame
MCI_FORMAT_SMPTE_30DROP	SMPTE, 30 frame drop
MCI_FORMAT_TMSF	Track/minute/second/frame
MCI_SEQ_FORMAT_SONGPTR	MIDI song pointer

Not all time formats are appropriate for all device types. In general, you'll use TMSF format for compact disc audio, milliseconds, or samples for waveform audio, and the SMPTE (Society of Motion Picture and Television Engineers) formats for all video devices.

Regardless of the format, MCI stores time information in a long integer. For TMSF, MSF, and SMPTE types, each byte represents a distinct unit of time. Table 13.10 lists these formats and the information packed into each byte.

TABLE 13.10 Data Storage for Different Time Formats

Byte Position	TMSF	MSF	SMPTE
High-order word/high-order byte	Frames	Unused	Frames
High-order word/low-order byte	Seconds	Frames	Seconds
Low-order word/high-order byte	Minutes	Seconds	Minutes
Low-order word/low-order byte	Tracks	Minutes	Hours

To make it easy to convert from MCI to VBA time formats, we created the function shown in Listing 13.7. You call it with the value and format of an MCI time interval. The result is a VBA Date variable. Listing 13.7 also shows the user-defined datatypes we created to make splitting a long integer into its component bytes easier.

Listing 13.7: Convert between MCI and VBA Time Formats

```
Type dhDoubleWordByByte
    LowWordLowByte As Byte
    LowWordHighByte As Byte
    HighWordLowByte As Byte
    HighWordHighByte As Byte
End Type

Type dhDoubleWordLong
    DoubleWord As Long
End Type

Function dhMCITimeToVBATime(lngTime As Long, _
 lngTimeFormat As Long) As Date

    Dim dwb As dhDoubleWordByByte
    Dim dwl As dhDoubleWordLong
    Dim datResult As Date

    ' Break up long into four bytes using LSet
    dwl.DoubleWord = lngTime
    LSet dwb = dwl

    ' Use the busted-up bytes
    With dwb
        ' Which time format?
        Select Case lngTimeFormat
            ' frames (assume 30/sec)
            Case MCI_FORMAT_FRAMES
                datResult = TimeSerial(0, _
                0, lngTime / 30)
            ' minute/second/frame
            Case MCI_FORMAT_MSF
                datResult = TimeSerial(0, _
                .LowWordLowByte, _
                .LowWordHighByte)
            ' track/minute/second/frame
            Case MCI_FORMAT_TMSF
                datResult = TimeSerial(0, _
                .LowWordHighByte, _
                .HighWordLowByte)
            ' Society of Motion Picture Engineers
```

```
            ' (hour/minute/second/frame)
            Case MCI_FORMAT_SMPTE_24, _
             MCI_FORMAT_SMPTE_25, _
             MCI_FORMAT_SMPTE_30, _
             MCI_FORMAT_SMPTE_30DROP, _
             MCI_FORMAT_HMS
                datResult = TimeSerial( _
                 .LowWordLowByte, _
                 .LowWordHighByte, _
                 .HighWordLowByte)
            ' Milliseconds
            Case MCI_FORMAT_MILLISECONDS
                datResult = lngTime / 86400000
        End Select
    End With

    ' Set the return value
    dhMCITimeToVBATime = datResult
End Function
```

MCI Information Functions

In addition to specific examples of controlling multimedia devices, there are two commands you can use to obtain information about a device. We've encapsulated these commands, MCI_STATUS and MCI_INFO, in two wrapper functions.

MCI_STATUS   You use the MCI_STATUS command to obtain status information regarding a device. For example, you can determine whether a CD audio device is ready to play. We've written a wrapper function for this command, dhMCIStatus, which is shown in Listing 13.8.

Listing 13.8: A Wrapper Function for the MCI_STATUS Command

```
Function dhMCIStatus(lngDevID As Long, lngItem As Long, _
 Optional lngAddlFlags As Long = 0, _
 Optional bytTrack As Byte = 0) As Long

    Dim mst As MCI_STATUS_PARMS
    Dim lngRet As Long

    ' Make sure device ID is valid
    If lngDevID Then
```

```
        ' Set values of MCI_STATUS_ITEM structure
        With mst
            .lngItem = lngItem
            .lngTrack = bytTrack

            ' Call mciSendCommand
            lngRet = mciSendCommand(lngDevID, MCI_STATUS, _
            MCI_STATUS_ITEM Or lngAddlFlags, mst)

            ' If successful, return lngReturn
            ' member of MCI_STATUS_ITEM structure
            If lngRet = 0 Then
                dhMCIStatus = .lngReturn
            End If
        End With
    End If
End Function
```

dhMCIStatus accepts a device ID and a status item number. A complete list of status items is shown in Table 13.11. You can also pass an optional bitmask of additional flags that dhMCIStatus merges with the required flag (MCI_STATUS_ITEM) before passing it to mciSendCommand. Finally, for status information that applies to a particular media track, you can pass the track number.

NOTE For track-dependent information, you must pass the MCI_TRACK flag in the lngAddlFlags argument in addition to the track number.

TABLE 13.11 MCI_STATUS_ITEM Types

Status Item Constant	Description
MCI_STATUS_LENGTH	Length of a particular media object or track
MCI_STATUS_POSITION	Current position (in the current time format)
MCI_STATUS_NUMBER_OF_TRACKS	Number of tracks for the current audio compact disc
MCI_STATUS_MODE	Current device mode (stopped, playing, and so on)

TABLE 13.11 MCI_STATUS_ITEM Types (continued)

Status Item Constant	Description
MCI_STATUS_MEDIA_PRESENT	Returns 1 if CD audio media is present
MCI_STATUS_TIME_FORMAT	Current time format
MCI_STATUS_READY	Returns 1 if the device is ready to play/record
MCI_STATUS_CURRENT_TRACK	The CD audio track currently playing
MCI_WAVE_STATUS_BLOCKALIGN	Waveform audio block alignment
MCI_WAVE_STATUS_FORMATTAG	Waveform audio format tag (for example, "PCM" for pulse code modulation)
MCI_WAVE_STATUS_CHANNELS	Waveform audio channels (1 = mono, 2 = stereo)
MCI_WAVE_STATUS_SAMPLESPERSEC	Waveform audio sample rate in Hertz (11025, 22050, or 44100)
MCI_WAVE_STATUS_AVGBYTESPERSEC	Average storage size for 1 second of waveform audio
MCI_WAVE_STATUS_BITSPERSAMPLE	Waveform audio bits per sample (8 or 16)
MCI_WAVE_STATUS_LEVEL	Waveform audio record level
MCI_SEQ_STATUS_TEMPO	MIDI sequencer tempo
MCI_SEQ_STATUS_PORT	MIDI sequencer port
MCI_SEQ_STATUS_OFFSET	MIDI sequencer SMPTE offset
MCI_SEQ_STATUS_DIVTYPE	MIDI sequencer file division type

To determine whether a CD audio device is ready to play, you would use a statement like this:

```
fReady = CBool(dhMCIStatus(lngDeviceID, MCI_STATUS_READY))
```

You can use the MCI_STATUS command to return the current operating mode of a device. Calling dhMCIStatus with the MCI_STATUS_MODE constant results in one of the constant values listed in Table 13.12. For example, you can determine whether a device such as a CD audio player is currently playing by using code like this:

```
fIsPlaying = (dhMCIStatus(lngDeviceID, MCI_STATUS_MODE) = _
 MCI_MODE_PLAY)
```

TABLE 13.12 Device Modes

Device Mode Constant	Description
MCI_MODE_NOT_READY	Device is not ready to play or record
MCI_MODE_STOP	Device is currently stopped
MCI_MODE_PLAY	Device is currently playing
MCI_MODE_RECORD	Device is currently recording
MCI_MODE_SEEK	Device is currently seeking (moving to new position)
MCI_MODE_PAUSE	Device is currently paused
MCI_MODE_OPEN	Device door is open

MCI_INFO You use the MCI_INFO command to obtain textual information for a device. For example, you can determine the unique media ID assigned to audio compact discs. We've written a wrapper function for the MCI_INFO command called dhMCIInfo, shown in Listing 13.9.

Listing 13.9: A Wrapper Function for the MCI_INFO Command

```
Function dhMCIInfo(lngDevID As Long, lngInfo As Long) As String
    Dim min As MCI_INFO_PARMS
    Dim lngRet As Long

    If lngDevID Then
        With min
            ' Set up buffer
            .strReturn = Space(255)
```

```
            .lngRetSize = Len(.strReturn)
            lngRet = mciSendCommand(lngDevID, MCI_INFO, _
             lngInfo, min)

            ' If successful, return portion of
            ' strReturn buffer
            If lngRet = 0 Then
                dhMCIInfo = Left(.strReturn, _
                 InStr(.strReturn, vbNullChar) - 1)
            End If
        End With
    End If
End Function
```

You call dhMCIInfo with a device ID and one of the item constants listed in Table 13.13. To return the media ID for a compact disc, therefore, you would use code like this:

```
strMediaID = dhMCIInfo(lngDeviceID, MCI_INFO_MEDIA_IDENTITY)
```

TABLE 13.13 MCI_INFO Types

Information Item Constant	Description
MCI_INFO_PRODUCT	Description of the device hardware
MCI_INFO_FILE	Media file name
MCI_INFO_MEDIA_UPC	Media UPC (Universal Product Code)
MCI_INFO_MEDIA_IDENTITY	Unique media identifier
MCI_INFO_NAME	Name of the current track or MIDI sequence
MCI_INFO_COPYRIGHT	Media copyright information

NOTE Not all information items apply to all devices and media types. If you request an inappropriate item, the result is an empty string.

Putting MCI to Work

To demonstrate the power of the Media Control Interface, we've constructed several working examples that do such things as playing audio CDs and recording waveform audio. We've implemented all of these as class modules to make them easy to integrate into your applications. The next several sections use the samples to explain the basic elements of MCI's command message interface.

Playing Audio CDs

One of the simplest applications of MCI is playing audio compact discs. It's simple because all you really have to do is open the CD audio device and start playback. We've added a few additional features to our class module, however, such as the ability to retrieve track times and play individual tracks. You'll find all the sample code in the CDPlayer class module. Table 13.14 provides a complete listing of its properties and methods.

TABLE 13.14 CDPlayer Class Properties and Methods

Member Type	Name	Description
Properties	Frame	Current track position in frames
	IsReady	Returns True if the device is ready to play
	IsPlaying	Returns True if the device is playing
	MediaID	Compact disc media identifier
	Minute	Current track position in minutes
	Mode	Current device mode
	Second	Current track position in seconds
	Time	Current track position as a VBA Date value
	Track	Current track
	Tracks	Number of tracks

TABLE 13.14 CDPlayer Class Properties and Methods (continued)

Member Type	Name	Description
	TrackTime	Track length for a given track
Methods	Pause	Pauses playback
	Play	Starts playback at current position or plays a given track
	Position	Positions the device to a given track, minute, and second
	StopPlaying	Stops playback

Opening a Device

To open any device, you send the MCI_OPEN command, specifying the device type you want to open. This information is contained in an instance of the MCI_OPEN_PARMS datatype:

```
Type MCI_OPEN_PARMS
    lngCallback As Long
    lngDeviceID As Long
    strDeviceType As String
    strElementName As String
    strAlias As String
End Type
```

At a minimum, you must specify the device type in the strDeviceType member. You can optionally supply the name of a media object (such as a WAV file) in the strElementName member. If you want to assign an alias to the open device, pass it in the strAlias member.

Since an audio compact disc device is a simple device, you needn't supply an element name. Our CDPlayer class opens the device in a procedure called OpenDevice. Listing 13.10 shows the portion of the procedure that calls mciSendCommand.

Listing 13.10: Open an Audio Compact Disc Device

```
Dim lngRet As Long
Dim mop As MCI_OPEN_PARMS
```

```
' If we're already open then close
If mlngDevID Then
    Call CloseDevice
End If

' Set device type
mop.strDeviceType = "cdaudio"

' Open the device
lngRet = mciSendCommand(0&, MCI_OPEN, MCI_OPEN_TYPE, mop)
If lngRet = 0 Then
    ' Store the device id
    mlngDevID = mop.lngDeviceID
Else
    Err.Raise lngRet, "CDPlayer::OpenDevice", _
    dhMCIError(lngRet)
End If
```

Note the device type, "cdaudio". This informs MCI of the device to open. The flag in the function call, MCI_OPEN_TYPE, instructs MCI to look at the strDevice-Type member of the MCI_OPEN_PARMS structure.

If the function call is successful, the procedure stores the contents of the lngDeviceID member in a class-level variable, mlngDevID. We use this in subsequent calls to identify the device.

Getting Track Information

After opening the device, OpenDevice retrieves information on the number and length of tracks on the compact disc. Listing 13.11 shows the code that accomplishes this.

Listing 13.11: Retrieve Compact Disk Track Information

```
' Get number of tracks
lngRet = dhMCIStatus(mlngDevID, _
 MCI_STATUS_NUMBER_OF_TRACKS)
If lngRet > 0 Then

    ' Get track times (note: these
    ' will be in MSF time format)
    Set mcolTracks = New Collection
    For bytTrack = 1 To lngRet

        ' Get time for one track
        lngRet = dhMCIStatus(mlngDevID, _
```

```
            MCI_STATUS_LENGTH, MCI_TRACK, bytTrack)

            ' Add track time to collection
            mcolTracks.Add lngRet, "Track" & bytTrack
        Next
    End If
```

The procedure uses the dhMCIStatus function described in the section "MCI Information Functions" earlier in this chapter) to obtain the number of tracks. It then calls the function again, once for each track, to retrieve the length of each track in MSF time format. To make it easy to retrieve this information later, the procedure adds the data to a class-level VBA Collection object, mcolTracks.

Setting the Time Format

Once the track information has been collected, the procedure sets the time format of the device to TMSF (tracks/minutes/seconds/frames). It does this so it will be easy to play an individual track. If the procedure didn't change the format, all commands to play a portion of the compact disc would have to be expressed in MSF format. A single function call using the MCI_SET command changes the time format:

```
msp.lngTimeFormat = MCI_FORMAT_TMSF
lngRet = mciSendCommand(mlngDevID, MCI_SET, _
 MCI_SET_TIME_FORMAT, msp)
```

Note that setting the lngTimeFormat member of an MCI_SET_PARMS structure specifies the new time format.

Starting Playback

The Play method is a good example of using the MCI_PLAY command. You can use MCI_PLAY to start playback at a particular point in a media object or at the current position. Listing 13.12 shows CDPlayer's Play method as well as the MCI_PLAY_PARMS declaration.

Listing 13.12: Play a CD Audio Track

```
Type MCI_PLAY_PARMS
    lngCallback As Long
    lngFrom As Long
    lngTo As Long
End Type
```

```
Public Sub Play(Optional Track As Byte = 0)
    Dim mpp As MCI_PLAY_PARMS
    Dim lngRet As Long

    If mlngDevID Then

        ' If no track was supplied play from
        ' the current position
        If Track = 0 Then
            lngRet = mciSendCommand(mlngDevID, _
            MCI_PLAY, 0&, 0&)

        ' Otherwise, set begin and end tracks
        ' and play just that track
        Else
            mpp.lngFrom = Track
            mpp.lngTo = Track + 1
            lngRet = mciSendCommand(mlngDevID, MCI_PLAY, _
            MCI_FROM Or MCI_TO, mpp)
        End If

        If lngRet <> 0 Then
            Err.Raise lngRet, "CDPlayer::Play", _
            dhMCIError(lngRet)
        End If
    End If
End Sub
```

You'll notice that Play accepts an optional track number. If this is omitted, Play simply starts playback at the current position by calling the MCI_PLAY command with no additional flags and a null pointer in place of the MCI_PLAY_PARMS structure. On the other hand, if a track number is supplied, it sets the lngFrom and lngTo members of the structure and calls MCI_PLAY with the MCI_FROM and MCI_TO flags.

> **NOTE** Even though the lngFrom and lngTo members of the MCI_PLAY_PARMS structure should be expressed using the TMSF time format, that's not important in this case. Since in TMFS format, the track number is stored in the low-order byte of the low-order word, you can just set the value of these members to the track number directly.

Changing Playback Position

On most devices, you can change the current playback or recording position by issuing the MCI_SEEK command. You use the MCI_SEEK_PARMS structure, setting its lngTo member variable to the new position, expressed in the device's current time format. Listing 13.13 shows the Position method that accomplishes this task for the CDPlayer class, along with the definition of the MCI_SEEK_PARMS structure.

Listing 13.13: Change the Playback Position with the MCI_SEEK Command

```
Type MCI_SEEK_PARMS
    lngCallback As Long
    lngTo As Long
End Type

Public Sub Position( _
 Optional Track As Byte = 0, _
 Optional Minute As Byte = 0, _
 Optional Second As Byte = 0)

    Dim dwb As dhDoubleWordByByte
    Dim dwl As dhDoubleWordLong
    Dim msk As MCI_SEEK_PARMS
    Dim lngRet As Long
    Dim fWasPlaying As Boolean

    If mlngDevID Then
        ' If the disc is playing, pause it
        If IsPlaying Then
            Me.Pause
            fWasPlaying = True
        End If

        ' If no track was supplied then assume
        ' the current one
        If Track = 0 Then
            Track = Me.Track
        End If

        ' Construct position in TMSF format
        With dwb
            .LowWordLowByte = Track
```

```
            .LowWordHighByte = Minute
            .HighWordLowByte = Second
        End With
        LSet dwl = dwb

        ' Set time and call MCI_SEEK
        msk.lngTo = dwl.DoubleWord
        lngRet = mciSendCommand(mlngDevID, _
         MCI_SEEK, MCI_TO, msk)

        If lngRet = 0 Then
            ' If cd was playing when this was
            ' called, resume playing
            If fWasPlaying Then
                Me.Play
            End If
        Else
            Err.Raise lngRet, "CDPlayer::Position", _
             dhMCIError(lngRet)
        End If
    End If
End Sub
```

The Position method accepts track, minute, and second values as optional arguments, assuming the current track if none was supplied. It creates a TMSF time value from these arguments using the user-defined datatypes explained in the section "MCI Time Formats" earlier in this chapter. After checking to see whether the disc is currently playing and pausing it if it is, the Position method issues the MCI_SEEK command, passing the MCI_TO flag and a pointer to the MCI_SEEK_PARMS structure. If the call to mciSendCommand was successful, the method restarts the CD if necessary by calling the Play method.

NOTE The IsPlaying property referenced in Listing 13.13 is implemented using the dhMCIStatus function explained in the section "MCI Information Functions" earlier in this chapter.

Pausing and Stopping Playback

The last general topic in this section is pausing and stopping playback. While we use CD audio as an example, you can apply these techniques to most MCI devices. Listing 13.14 shows the Pause and StopPlaying methods. Note that all they do is issue the appropriate MCI command (MCI_PAUSE or MCI_STOP).

Listing 13.14: Pause and Stop Playback

```
Public Sub Pause()
    Dim lngRet As Long

    If mlngDevID Then
        ' Pause playback by issuing the MCI_PAUSE command
        lngRet = mciSendCommand(mlngDevID, MCI_PAUSE, 0&, 0&)
        If lngRet <> 0 Then
            Err.Raise lngRet, "CDPlayer::Pause", _
              dhMCIError(lngRet)
        End If
    End If
End Sub

Public Sub StopPlaying()
    Dim lngRet As Long

    If mlngDevID Then
        ' Stop playback by issuing the MCI_STOP command
        lngRet = mciSendCommand(mlngDevID, MCI_STOP, 0&, 0&)
        If lngRet <> 0 Then
            Err.Raise lngRet, "CDPlayer::StopPlaying", _
              dhMCIError(lngRet)
        End If
    End If
End Sub
```

An Example

We've created a simple procedure to show off our CDPlayer class. Shown in Listing 13.15, this procedure prints information about the currently loaded compact disc, starts playback, pauses playback, and moves to different tracks and locations.

Listing 13.15: Play Around with an Audio Compact Disc

```
Sub dhTestCD()
    Dim cd As CDPlayer
    Dim bytTrack As Byte
```

```vba
    ' Create a new instance
    Set cd = New CDPlayer
    With cd

        ' Make sure the device is ready
        If .IsReady Then

            ' Print CD and track information
            Debug.Print "Media ID: " & .MediaID
            Debug.Print .Tracks & " tracks"
            Debug.Print "=========="
            For bytTrack = 1 To .Tracks
                Debug.Print "Track " & bytTrack & ": " & _
                  Format(.TrackTime(bytTrack), "nn:ss")
            Next

            ' Start playback
            .Play

            ' Print the current position
            Debug.Print .Track & " " & .Minute & _
              ":" & Format(.Second, "00")

            ' Move to second track
            .Position Track:=2

            ' Pause playback
            .Pause

            ' Skip ahead to the 1-minute mark
            .Position Minute:=1

            ' Restart playback
            .Play

            ' Stop playback
            .StopPlaying
        End If
    End With

    ' Terminate instance
    Set cd = Nothing
End Sub
```

Figure 13.5 shows the VBA Immediate window with the results of running dhTestCD with the *Mission Impossible* compact disc.

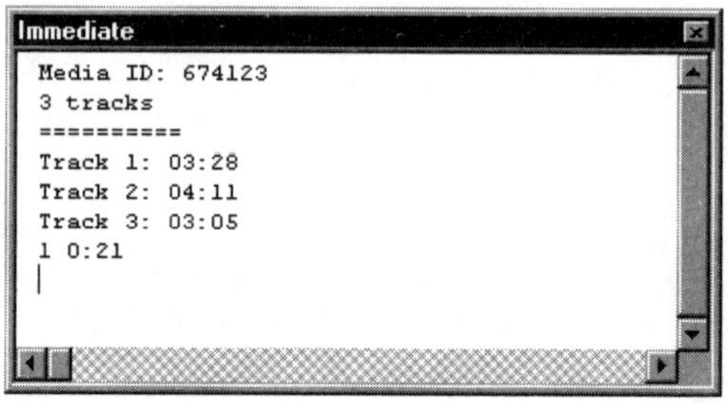

FIGURE 13.5

Playing the *Mission
Impossible* compact disc

```
Immediate                                          ☒
  Media ID: 674123                                 ▲
  3 tracks
  ==========
  Track 1: 03:28
  Track 2: 04:11
  Track 3: 03:05
  1 0:21
  |
                                                   ▼
◀ ▯                                              ▶
```

Recording and Playing Waveform Audio

Now let's take a look at another MCI device, waveform audio, better known as
WAV files. Waveform audio devices can be used to record, store, and play digital
audio sounds. We've created a VBA class called WavePlayer that demonstrates
these capabilities. Table 13.15 lists WavePlayer's properties and methods.

TABLE 13.15 WavePlayer Class Properties and Methods

Member Type	Name	Description
Properties	AvgBytesPerSecond	Average storage required for 1 second of audio
	BitsPerSample	Number of bits to use for recording (8 or 16)
	Channels	Number of channels to use for recording (1 or 2)
	Filename	Name of the current WAV file
	FormatTag	Format of recorded media (normally "PCM")
	Length	Length of the sample in milliseconds
	Position	Current playback or record position in number of milliseconds from start of sample
	SampleRate	Sample rate to use for recording (11025, 22050, or 44100)
	Wait	Specifies whether sounds play synchronously or asynchronously

TABLE 13.15 WavePlayer Class Properties and Methods (continued)

Member Type	Name	Description
Methods	Delete	Removes a portion of the current sample
	OpenFile	Opens a WAV file
	Play	Plays the current sample
	Record	Records sound into the current sample
	Reset	Clears the current sample from the device
	Save	Saves the current sample using the current file name
	SaveAs	Saves the current sample using a new file name
	StopRecording	Stops asynchronous recording

Loading Files with Complex Devices

Waveform audio is a *complex* MCI device, which means it operates on a data file instead of a fixed media object like an audio CD. Before you can begin playback on a complex device, you must load or record a sample. You can load a file by specifying a file name when opening a device or by issuing the MCI_LOAD command after the device has been opened.

Waveform audio devices do not support loading a file dynamically. Instead, you must load the file at the same time you open the device. Listing 13.16 shows the private OpenDevice procedure as well as the Open method. Note that all the Open method does is call OpenDevice with a file name.

NOTE We created a separate OpenDevice procedure so we could call it in the Class_Initialize event procedure. This procedure opens the device and prepares it for recording.

Listing 13.16: Open a Waveform Audio File

```
Public Sub OpenFile(WaveFile As String)
    Call OpenDevice(WaveFile)
End Sub

Private Sub OpenDevice(Optional strFile As String = "")
    Dim lngRet As Long
    Dim mwo As MCI_WAVE_OPEN_PARMS

    If mlngDevID Then

        ' Close the device
        Call CloseDevice
    End If

    ' Set member variables
    With mwo
        .strDeviceType = "waveaudio"
        .strElementName = strFile
        .lngBufferSeconds = 10
    End With

    ' Load the requested file
    lngRet = mciSendCommand(mlngDevID, MCI_OPEN, _
     MCI_OPEN_ELEMENT Or MCI_OPEN_TYPE, mwo)
    If lngRet = 0 Then
        mlngDevID = mwo.lngDeviceID
    Else
        Err.Raise lngRet, "WavePlayer::OpenDevice", _
         dhMCIError(lngRet)
    End If
End Sub
```

WavePlayer's OpenDevice procedure, shown in Listing 13.16, differs from the same procedure in the CDPlayer class in three significant ways:

- It uses an MCI_WAVE_OPEN_PARMS structure instead of the standard MCI_OPEN_PARMS. MCI_WAVE_OPEN_PARMS includes an additional member, lngBufferSeconds, which lets you specify the size of the buffer used by the device.

- It passes the name of the file to open in the strElementName member variable.

- It includes the MCI_OPEN_ELEMENT flag in the call to mciSendCommand.

Playing Waveform Audio

Like the CDPlayer class, the WavePlayer class features a Play method. Playing waveform audio is unlike playing CD audio, however, because waveform audio is not broken into tracks. WavePlayer's Play method, therefore, is designed to accept starting and stopping positions in milliseconds rather than a track number. Listing 13.17 shows the code behind the Play method.

Listing 13.17: Play Waveform Audio

```
Public Sub Play(Optional StartTime As Long, _
 Optional StopTime As Long)

    Dim mpp As MCI_PLAY_PARMS
    Dim lngLength As Long
    Dim lngRet As Long

    If mlngDevID Then

        ' Validate inputs
        lngLength = Length()
        If StartTime < 0 Or StartTime > lngLength Then
            StartTime = 0
        End If
        If StopTime <= StartTime Or StopTime > lngLength Then
            StopTime = lngLength
        End If

        ' Play the wave file
        mpp.lngFrom = StartTime
        mpp.lngTo = StopTime
        lngRet = mciSendCommand(mlngDevID, MCI_PLAY, _
         MCI_FROM Or MCI_TO Or mlngWait, mpp)
        If lngRet <> 0 Then
            Err.Raise lngRet, "WavePlayer::Play", _
             dhMCIError(lngRet)
        End If
    End If
End Sub
```

The Play method validates the start and stop values against the length of the current audio sample. If neither argument is supplied, the method plays the entire sample.

Determining the total length of the sample is easy, as the code behind the Length property illustrates:

```
Property Get Length() As Long
    Length = dhMCIStatus(mlngDevID, MCI_STATUS_LENGTH)
End Property
```

> **NOTE** With waveform audio, time is measured in milliseconds, eliminating the need to convert to and from complex time forms such as TMSF.

Recording Waveform Audio

Recording waveform audio is perhaps the most relevant use for the WavePlayer class (since you can play a WAV file simply by calling PlaySound). To record with an MCI device, you issue the MCI_RECORD command, passing a pointer to an instance of the MCI_RECORD_PARMS structure. MCI automatically allocates a buffer for the recorded sound based on settings in the MCI_RECORD_PARMS member variables. You can also start recording without specifying a time interval, and the waveform audio device will record until it receives an MCI_STOP command or you run out of virtual memory.

Listing 13.18 shows the Record method of the WavePlayer class. It accepts three optional arguments: Milliseconds, StartTime, and Overwrite. Milliseconds specifies the length of time for the recording. StartTime represents the point in the current waveform audio file to start recording. The Overwrite argument controls whether the newly recorded sound is inserted into the current file (the default) or replaces existing contents.

Listing 13.18: Record Waveform Audio

```
Type MCI_RECORD_PARMS
    lngCallback As Long
    lngFrom As Long
    lngTo As Long
End Type

Public Sub Record( _
 Optional Milliseconds As Integer = 0, _
 Optional StartTime As Long = -1, _
 Optional Overwrite As Boolean = False)
```

```
Dim mrp As MCI_RECORD_PARMS
Dim lngLength As Long
Dim lngFlags As Long
Dim lngRet As Long

If mlngDevID And Milliseconds >= 0 Then

    ' If StartTime is -1, get current position
    lngLength = Length
    If StartTime < 0 Or StartTime > lngLength Then
        StartTime = Position
    End If

    ' Set flag values
    If Milliseconds > 0 Then
        lngFlags = MCI_FROM Or MCI_TO Or MCI_WAIT
    End If
    If Overwrite Then
        lngFlags = lngFlags Or MCI_RECORD_OVERWRITE
    Else
        lngFlags = lngFlags Or MCI_RECORD_INSERT
    End If

    ' Record for a given number of seconds
    With mrp
        .lngFrom = StartTime
        .lngTo = StartTime + Milliseconds
    End With
    lngRet = mciSendCommand(mlngDevID, MCI_RECORD, _
     lngFlags, mrp)
    If lngRet <> 0 Then
        Err.Raise lngRet, "WavePlayer::Record", _
        dhMCIError(lngRet)
    End If
    End If
End Sub
```

If no start time is specified (or if it exceeds the current size of the file), the start position is set to the current position. The current position is determined by calling dhMCIStatus with the MCI_STATUS_POSITION flag. Our class encapsulates this in the Position property.

The Record method determines the flags to send to mciSendCommand based on the arguments passed to the procedure. If you call Record with a positive value for Milliseconds, the method sets the MCI_FROM, MCI_TO, and

MCI_WAIT flags. If you call the method with no arguments (Milliseconds equals 0), no flags are set. This causes the waveform audio device to start recording and continue until you issue the MCI_STOP command. WavePlayer features a Stop-Recording method that does just this.

> **WARNING** If you issue the MCI_RECORD command with no time interval specified, make sure you don't include the MCI_WAIT flag in the function call.

In either case, the Record method adds either the MCI_RECORD_INSERT or MCI_RECORD_OVERWRITE flag based on the value of the Overwrite argument. This flag controls whether the new sample is inserted into the current file at the specified position or replaces the contents at that position.

Starting and ending positions are determined by the StartTime and Milliseconds arguments. These values are written to the MCI_RECORD_PARMS structure before the call to mciSendCommand.

Setting Input Parameters

Waveform audio devices have a number of configurable parameters that control the quality of input and, subsequently, the quality of output. Our WavePlayer class lets you set and retrieve these values through a series of properties. Table 13.15, presented earlier in this section, listed these properties: AvgBytesPerSecond, BitsPerSample, Channels, and SampleRate. The higher the sample rate, channel, or bits-per-sample setting, the better the quality is. Be aware, however, that as the quality increases, so does the space required to store the sample.

Retrieving these values is accomplished simply by calling the dhMCIStatus function, passing the appropriate status item constant. (See Table 13.11 earlier in this chapter for a list of these constants.) Setting the values, on the other hand, requires issuing the MCI_SET command. Listing 13.19 shows the private Change-Setting procedure, which is called by the Property Let procedures for the properties.

Listing 13.19: Change Waveform Audio Device Input Parameters

```
Private Sub ChangeSetting(lngSetting As Long, lngNewValue _
As Long)
    Dim mws As MCI_WAVE_SET_PARMS
```

```
Dim lngRet As Long

' Make sure device ID is valid
If mlngDevID Then

    ' Use the MCI_WAVE_SET_PARMS structure
    With mws

        ' Get the existing values
        .intFormatTag = Me.FormatTag
        .intBitsPerSample = Me.BitsPerSample
        .intChannels = Me.Channels
        .lngSamplesPerSec = Me.SampleRate

        ' Change the desired setting
        Select Case lngSetting
            Case MCI_WAVE_STATUS_FORMATTAG
                .intFormatTag = lngNewValue
            Case MCI_WAVE_STATUS_CHANNELS
                .intChannels = lngNewValue
            Case MCI_WAVE_STATUS_SAMPLESPERSEC
                .lngSamplesPerSec = lngNewValue
            Case MCI_WAVE_STATUS_BITSPERSAMPLE
                .intBitsPerSample = lngNewValue
        End Select

        ' Compute derived settings
        .lngAvgBytesPerSec = ((.intBitsPerSample / 8) * _
        .intChannels * .lngSamplesPerSec)
        .intBlockAlign = ((.intBitsPerSample / 8) * _
        .intChannels)

        ' Call mciSendCommand
        lngRet = mciSendCommand(mlngDevID, MCI_SET, _
        MCI_WAIT Or MCI_WAVE_SET_FORMATTAG Or _
        MCI_WAVE_SET_BITSPERSAMPLE Or _
        MCI_WAVE_SET_CHANNELS Or _
        MCI_WAVE_SET_SAMPLESPERSEC Or _
        MCI_WAVE_SET_AVGBYTESPERSEC Or _
        MCI_WAVE_SET_BLOCKALIGN, mws)

        If lngRet <> 0 Then
            Err.Raise lngRet, "WavePlayer::ChangeSetting", _
            dhMCIError(lngRet)
        End If
```

```
        End With
    End If
End Sub
```

The procedure works by first retrieving the existing settings into a MCI_WAVE_SET_PARMS structure. It then changes one of those settings based on the value of the lngSetting argument. Two settings, average bytes per second and block alignment, are derived values, so the ChangeSetting procedure computes them based on the new settings. Finally, the procedure issues the MCI_SET command, passing a reference to the MCI_WAVE_SET_PARMS structure and a series of flags representing the various settings.

NOTE While it would appear that you can change settings individually, Microsoft recommends changing all of them at once in the manner we've just described. Failing to do this could result in the waveform audio device falling back into its lowest-quality mode.

Removing Portions of a Waveform Audio File

Unlike most other types of devices, waveform audio devices are capable of deleting portions of the media object they work with. To accomplish this, you issue the MCI_DELETE command with beginning and ending time periods stored in an instance of the MCI_WAVE_DELETE_PARMS structure. Listing 13.20 shows the Delete method of our WavePlayer class. (We omitted the structure declaration because it's identical to the MCI_RECORD_PARMS structure.)

Listing 13.20: Delete a Portion of a Waveform Audio File

```
Public Sub Delete(StartTime As Long, _
  Milliseconds As Long)

    Dim mdp As MCI_WAVE_DELETE_PARMS
    Dim lngLength As Long
    Dim lngRet As Long

    If mlngDevID Then

        ' Validate inputs
        lngLength = Length()
        If StartTime < 0 Or StartTime > lngLength Then
```

```
            StartTime = 0
        End If

        ' Delete the specified portion
        With mdp
            .lngFrom = StartTime
            .lngTo = StartTime + Milliseconds
            If .lngTo > lngLength Then
                .lngTo = lngLength
            End If
        End With
        lngRet = mciSendCommand(mlngDevID, MCI_DELETE, _
         MCI_FROM Or MCI_TO, mdp)
        If lngRet <> 0 Then
            Err.Raise lngRet, "WavePlayer::Delete", _
            dhMCIError(lngRet)
        End If
    End If
End Sub
```

After validating the inputs—the starting point and the length of the sample to delete—the Delete method issues the MCI_DELETE command. If it's successful, a portion of the current file will be completely removed.

Saving a Waveform Audio File

The final bit of waveform audio functionality to look at is saving a recorded or modified file to disk. You do this by issuing the MCI_SAVE command. As you can imagine, there is an associated MCI_SAVE_PARMS structure to go along with the command. We've implemented two methods, SaveAs and Save, to perform this task. Listing 13.21 shows both methods, the private procedure they call to get the job done, and the declaration of the MCI_SAVE_PARMS structure.

Listing 13.21: Save a Waveform Audio File to Disk

```
Type MCI_SAVE_PARMS
    lngCallback As Long
    lpFileName As String
End Type

Public Sub SaveAs(Filename As String)
    If Filename <> "" Then
        Call SaveFile(Filename)
```

```
        End If
End Sub

Public Sub Save()
    Dim strFile As String

    ' Use the current file name
    strFile = Me.Filename
    Call SaveAs(strFile)
End Sub

Private Sub SaveFile(strFile As String)
    Dim lngRet As Long
    Dim msp As MCI_SAVE_PARMS

    If mlngDevID Then

        ' Save the file
        msp.lpFileName = strFile
        lngRet = mciSendCommand(mlngDevID, MCI_SAVE, _
         MCI_SAVE_FILE Or MCI_WAIT, msp)
        If lngRet <> 0 Then
            Err.Raise lngRet, "WavePlayer::Save", _
             dhMCIError(lngRet)
        End If
    End If
End Sub
```

After calling SaveAs for the first time, you can call Save to save the file with the same name. The Save method uses the dhMCIInfo function to obtain the name of the current waveform audio file. If you want to save the file with a different name, just call SaveAs again.

WARNING   When you save a file using the MCI_SAVE command, any existing file is overwritten without warning.

An Example

Our example to demonstrate the WavePlayer class is shown in Listing 13.22. After initializing the class and playing a saved WAV file, the procedure changes the input settings and records 3 seconds of sound. It then plays the sample back, removes the middle 1 second, plays it again, and saves it to disk.

Listing 13.22: Play and Record Waveform Audio

```
Sub dhTestWave()
    Dim wav As WavePlayer

    ' Create new instance
    Set wav = New WavePlayer
    With wav

        ' Open and play a saved WAV file
        .OpenFile "C:\Windows\Media\Chord.wav"
        .Play

        ' Reset the device and record for 3 seconds
        .Reset
        .SampleRate = 22050
        .BitsPerSample = 16
        .Record Milliseconds:=3000

        ' Play the recorded sound
        .Play

        ' Now remove the middle 1 second
        .Delete StartTime:=1000, Milliseconds:=1000

        ' Play it again and then save it
        .Play
        .SaveAs "C:\NEWWAVE.WAV"
    End With

    ' Terminate instance
    Set wav = Nothing
End Sub
```

Putting Digital Video in a Window

Digital video, better known as AVI files, is being used increasingly in multimedia training applications and even as a supplement to standard online help topics. This section shows you how to load an AVI file and play it in any arbitrary window on your desktop. As with the other examples, we created a class (Video-Player) to encapsulate the functionality. Table 13.16 lists VideoPlayer's properties and methods.

TABLE 13.16 VideoPlayer Class Properties and Methods

Member Type	Name	Description
Properties	Caption	Title of display window
	Filename	Name of AVI file
	hWnd	Window handle of display window
	IsPlaying	True if a video clip is playing
	Length	Length of the current clip in milliseconds
	Stretch	True if image is to be stretched to fill the display window
Methods	Center	Centers the image in the display window
	OpenFile	Opens an AVI file
	Play	Plays the current video clip
	StopPlaying	Stops playing the current video clip

NOTE To demonstrate this class, we've included a form (frmVideo) in the sample Excel workbook. If you don't have a copy of Excel 97, you'll need to create a new form in whatever development tool you use.

MCI Video Types

MCI defines two broad categories of video: digital and overlay. Digital video is recorded and saved in a file. Overlay video is based on a direct analog feed and is the basis for those "TV-in-a-window" applications you've no doubt seen advertised. Overlay video requires special hardware in order to operate. Digital video does not.

While MCI defines these two categories and supplies separate commands and structures to manipulate them, they share many characteristics. For example, each must be played in a window, and you can define which portion of that window is used. In describing the techniques required to play digital video, we've "borrowed" some functionality from MCI's overlay video features.

Basic AVI Functionality

There's not much to say about the basic functionality in the VideoPlayer class. You open and close it in much the same manner you do the CDPlayer and Wave-Player classes. You use "avivideo" as the device type and, optionally, the path to an AVI file as the element name. The class implements a number of the same properties and methods as the CDPlayer and WavePlayer classes, such as IsPlaying, Play, and StopPlaying. In fact, the code used to implement these is almost identical. What makes this class unique is how it interacts visually with the system.

Putting Digital Video in a Window

Digital and overlay video must have a window in which to display themselves. You can either specify an existing window or let them create their own. If you choose not to specify a window, the result is the same as though you had simply run an AVI from Explorer. The device creates a window using attributes defined in the Video section of the Multimedia Control Panel applet, shown in Figure 13.6, and the Media Player Options dialog, shown in Figure 13.7.

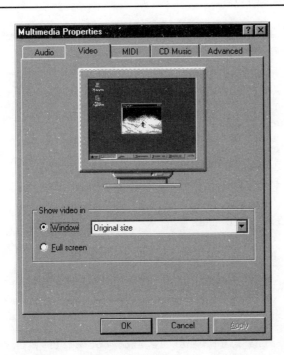

FIGURE 13.7

AVI settings in the
Media Player

Under most circumstances, you'll want to control the playback, restricting it to a certain window and size. To do this you must issue the MCI_WINDOW command after opening the device. You pass, among other things, the handle to the window in which you want playback to happen. We've implemented an hWnd property of the WavePlayer class that accomplishes this. Listing 13.23 shows the Property Let procedure.

Listing 13.23: Setting the hWnd Property Assigns a Window to the Device

```
Property Let hWnd(hWnd As Long)
    Dim mow As MCI_OVLY_WINDOW_PARMS
    Dim lngFlags As Long
    Dim lngRet As Long

    If mlngDevID Then
        ' Set default flags
        lngFlags = MCI_OVLY_WINDOW_HWND

        ' Set stretch flag
        If mfStretch Then
            lngFlags = lngFlags Or _
              MCI_OVLY_WINDOW_ENABLE_STRETCH
        Else
            lngFlags = lngFlags Or _
              MCI_OVLY_WINDOW_DISABLE_STRETCH
        End If

        ' Set the window handle and, optionally, the caption
```

```
        mow.hWnd = hWnd
        If Len(mstrCaption) Then
            mow.strText = mstrCaption
            lngFlags = lngFlags Or _
            MCI_OVLY_WINDOW_TEXT
        End If

        ' Issue the MCI_WINDOW command
        lngRet = mciSendCommand(mlngDevID, MCI_WINDOW, _
         lngFlags, mow)

        ' If successful, store the window handle
        If lngRet = 0 Then
            mHwnd = hWnd
        Else
            mHwnd = 0
            Err.Raise lngRet, "VideoPlayer::hWnd (Let)", _
            dhMCIError(lngRet)
        End If
    End If
End Property
```

The procedure uses an MCI_OVLY_WINDOW_PARMS structure to define the window attributes. The members of this structure let you supply a window handle, a caption, and a display mode (maximized, normal, and so on). Flags passed to the mciSendCommand function validate each of these members. In our example, we maintain a class-level variable, mstrCaption, for a window caption. If the variable is set (non-blank), the procedure adds the MCI_OVLY_WINDOW_TEXT flag to the current set of flags. MCI will in turn change the caption of the specified window.

We also maintain another class variable, mfStretch, which controls whether the video image will be stretched to fill the entire window. If this variable is set to True (via the Stretch property of the class), MCI will stretch the image to completely fill the window's client area. (A window's *client area* is the area inside a window, excluding the window's border and caption.) To further control the size and position, you can issue the MCI_PUT command, described in the next section.

Positioning Playback

If you need to further refine the position of a video clip within the window specified in the MCI_WINDOW command, you issue the MCI_PUT command.

MCI_PUT and its counterpart, MCI_GET, set and retrieve window coordinates for both video source and output elements. To demonstrate how to use these commands, we've implemented a Center method that, when called after you assign a window handle to the video device, centers the output in the window. Listing 13.24 shows the Center method.

Listing 13.24: Center a Video Clip in a Window

```
Public Sub Center()
    Dim morSource As MCI_OVLY_RECT_PARMS
    Dim morDest As MCI_OVLY_RECT_PARMS
    Dim rc As RECT
    Dim lngRet As Long

    ' Make sure we've got something loaded and that
    ' the user has specified a window
    If mlngDevID And Len(AVIFile) > 0 And CBool(mHwnd) Then

        ' Issue the MCI_WHERE command to get the
        ' size of the current AVI file
        lngRet = mciSendCommand(mlngDevID, MCI_WHERE, _
         MCI_OVLY_WHERE_SOURCE, morSource)
        If lngRet = 0 Then

            ' Get the available client area
            If CBool(GetClientRect(mHwnd, rc)) Then

                ' Do the math to center the image
                With rc
                    morDest.rc.Top = (.Bottom - .Top - _
                     morSource.rc.Bottom) / 2
                    morDest.rc.Left = (.Right - .Left - _
                     morSource.rc.Right) / 2
                End With

                ' Issue the MCI_PUT command to place the
                ' output at the computed position in the
                ' destination window
                lngRet = mciSendCommand(mlngDevID, _
                 MCI_PUT, MCI_OVLY_PUT_DESTINATION Or _
                 MCI_OVLY_RECT, morDest)
                If lngRet <> 0 Then
                    Err.Raise lngRet, "VideoPlayer::Center", _
                     dhMCIError(lngRet)
```

```
            End If
        Else
            Err.Raise lngRet, "VideoPlayer::Center", _
            dhMCIError(lngRet)
        End If
    Else
        Err.Raise lngRet, "VideoPlayer::Center", _
        dhMCIError(lngRet)
    End If
    End If
End Sub
```

Both commands rely on two user-defined datatypes. The MCI_OVLY_RECT_ PARMS structure includes the standard callback member, as well as a pointer to the second datatype, RECT. The RECT type is a standard Windows API type used to define the boundaries of a rectangle.

Centering a video clip in a window involves four steps:

1. Determining the size of the source video

2. Determining the size of the window's client area

3. Computing the correct position for the output based on the video and window sizes

4. Setting the destination area to reflect this position

The Center method accomplishes the first step by issuing the MCI_WHERE command. You can use this command to determine the size and position of both the current source video and the output region. The method passes the MCI_ OVLY_WHERE_SOURCE flag, indicating that it wants to know the size of the source video. If the command is successful, the dimensions are stored in the RECT structure within the passed MCI_OVLY_RECT_PARMS variable. The Top and Left member variables will contain the *position* of the video's upper-left corner (initially, these are both 0), and the Bottom and Right members will contain the *height* and *width* of the image, respectively.

NOTE   MCI uses the RECT structure differently from most other Windows API functions. Usually, API functions use the Bottom and Right members to represent the extent of a rectangle relative to the upper-left corner of the client area, not its size.

Determining the size of the target window's client area is easy. The method calls the standard Windows API GetClientRect function to grab the dimensions and place them in the passed RECT structure.

Finally, after performing some simple arithmetic to determine the new position for the video, the Center method issues the MCI_PUT command, passing a pointer to the MCI_OVLY_RECT_PARMS structure containing the new dimensions and the MCI_OVLY_PUT_DESTINATION and MCI_OVLY_RECT flags.

An Example

Our example uses a user form in Excel 97 (shown in Figure 13.8) to display an AVI file. You can use just about any window you can get a handle to, however. Listing 13.25 shows the code behind the form.

FIGURE 13.8

Displaying an AVI file in a window

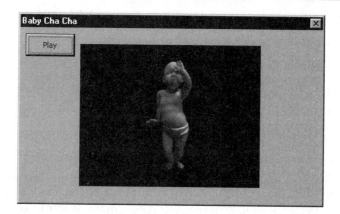

Listing 13.25: Code Required to Use the VideoPlayer Class

```
Option Explicit

' This is required to get a handle to the form
Private Declare Function GetActiveWindow _
  Lib "user32" () As Long

' Private instance of VideoPlayer class
Private vid As VideoPlayer
```

```
Private Sub cmdPlay_Click()
    ' Create a new instance
    Set vid = New VideoPlayer

    ' Open a file
    vid.OpenFile "C:\SOMEVID.AVI"

    ' Set the window and caption
    vid.Caption = "Window Caption"
    vid.hWnd = GetActiveWindow()

    ' Center the video in the window and play it
    vid.Center
    vid.Play
End Sub

Private Sub UserForm_QueryClose(Cancel As Integer, _
CloseMode As Integer)

    ' If video is still playing, stop it
    If vid.IsPlaying Then
        vid.StopPlaying
    End If
End Sub

Private Sub UserForm_Terminate()
    ' Terminate the instance
    Set vid = Nothing
End Sub
```

You can see how the form uses the class to open an AVI file, center it on the screen, and play it. The only other item worth pointing out is the use of the Get-ActiveWindow API function. This function is necessary because VBA user forms do not expose their window handle directly. If you're using a tool like Visual Basic or Access, on the other hand, you can reference this value directly via a form's hWnd property.

Summary

In this chapter, we've presented a few simple techniques for integrating multimedia into your VBA applications. While we could not be as thorough as we would have liked, due to space considerations, we've given you several tools that should add a little life to your programs. We examined the multimedia capabilities of Windows, and the Media Control Interface in particular, as a way of accomplishing the following tasks:

- Playing audio compact disc tracks
- Recording and playing waveform audio
- Displaying digital video in a window

We hope this chapter has also given you the insight to add other multimedia elements to your applications.

APPENDIX
A

The Reddick VBA Naming Conventions

Version 4.0
Greg Reddick
Copyright © 1995–1997 Greg Reddick. All Rights Reserved.
Some of the naming tags, prefixes, and qualifiers in this document are derived from
the Leszynski/Reddick naming conventions, Copyright © 1994 Stan Leszynski and
Greg Reddick.

The purpose of the Reddick VBA (RVBA) naming conventions is to provide a
guideline for naming objects in the Microsoft Visual Basic for Applications (VBA)
language. Having conventions is valuable in any programming project. When you
use them, the name of the object conveys information about the meaning of the
object. These conventions provide a way of standardizing what that meaning is
across the programming industry.

VBA is implemented to interact with a host application—for example,
Microsoft Access, Visual Basic, Microsoft Excel, and Microsoft Project. The RVBA
conventions cover all implementations of the VBA language, regardless of the
host application. Note that some of the tags described in this appendix may not
necessarily have an implementation within some particular host program. The
word *object*, in the context of this document, refers to simple variables, as well as
to objects presented in the interface of the VBA host program.

While I'm the editor of these conventions and in 1992 proposed the original
conventions for Microsoft Access, they are the work of many people, including
Charles Simonyi, who invented the Hungarian conventions on which these are
based; Stan Leszynski, who co-authored several versions of the conventions; and
Paul Litwin, for his contributions and for getting the conventions in front of the
public. Many others, too numerous to mention, have also contributed to the
development of these conventions.

These conventions are intended as a guideline. If you disagree with a particular
part, simply replace that part with what you think works better. However, keep
in mind who will see those changes and place a comment in the header of a module indicating what changes have been made. The conventions are presented
without rationalizations for how they were derived; you may assume that there
are good reasons for the choices that have been made. Send me any questions or
comments about the conventions. (See the addresses at the end of this appendix.)
Suggestions for future versions are welcome.

Changes to the Conventions

These conventions first appeared in print in the charter issue of *Smart Access* in February of 1993. A significantly revised version appeared in the August 1993 issue.

Some of the tags in the version of the conventions presented here have changed from previous versions. Consider all previous tags to be grandfathered into the conventions—you don't need to go back and make changes. For new development work, we leave it up to you to decide whether to use the older tags or the ones suggested here.

An Introduction to Hungarian

The RVBA conventions are based on the Hungarian style, named for the native country of Charles Simonyi, the inventor of this style of naming objects. The objective of Hungarian is to convey information about the object concisely and efficiently. Hungarian takes some getting used to, but once adopted, it quickly becomes second nature. The format of a Hungarian object name is as follows:

[prefixes]tag[BaseName[Suffixes]]

The square brackets indicate optional parts of the object name.

These components have the following meanings:

- **Prefixes:** Modify the tag to indicate additional information. Prefixes are in all lowercase letters. They are usually picked from a standardized list of prefixes, given later in this appendix.

- **Tag:** Short set of characters, usually mnemonic, that indicates the type of the object. The tag is in all lowercase letters. It's usually selected from a standardized list of tags, given later in this appendix.

- **BaseName:** One or more words that indicate what the object represents. The first letter of each word in the base name is capitalized.

- **Suffixes:** Additional information about the meaning of the base name. The first letter of each word in the suffix is capitalized. They are usually picked from a standardized list of suffixes, given later in this appendix.

Notice that the only required part of the object name is the tag. This may seem counterintuitive; you may feel that the base name is the most important part of the object name. However, consider a generic procedure that operates on any form. The fact that the routine operates on a form is the important thing, not what that form represents. Because the routine may operate on forms of many different types, you don't necessarily need a base name. However, if you have more than one object of a type referenced in the routine, you must have a base name on all but one of the object names to differentiate them. Also, unless the routine is generic, the base name conveys information about the variable. In most cases a variable should include a base name.

Tags

You use tags to indicate the datatype of an object, and you construct them using the techniques described in the following sections.

Variable Tags

Use the tags listed in Table A.1 for VBA datatypes. You can also use a specific tag instead of "obj" for any datatype defined by the host application or one of its objects. (See the section "Host Application and Component Extensions to the Conventions" later in this appendix.)

TABLE A.1 Tags for VBA Variables

Tag	Object Type
byt	Byte
f	Boolean
int	Integer
lng	Long
sng	Single
dbl	Double

TABLE A.1 Tags for VBA Variables (continued)

Tag	Object Type
cur	Currency
dtm*	Date
obj	Object
str	String
stf	String (fixed length)
var	Variant

*Prior versions of these naming conventions used the "dat" tag.

Here are several examples:

```
lngCount
intValue
strInput
```

You should explicitly declare all variables, each on a line by itself. Don't use the old type declaration characters, such as %, &, and $. They are extraneous if you use the naming conventions, and there's no character for some of the datatypes, such as Boolean. You should explicitly declare all variables of type Variant, the default, as type Variant. For example:

```
Dim intTotal As Integer
Dim varField As Variant
Dim strName As String
```

Constant Tags

You should indicate generic constants by using the tag "con". If you need to differentiate one class of constants from another, you can invent a class name, such as adh (for *Access Developer's Handbook*), and append the letter *c* to the class—for example, adhcPi. You may want to do this if you have some specific component that has global constants and you want to ensure that they don't conflict with other constants. For example:

```
conPi
adhcError205
```

Tags for User-Defined Types and Classes

User-defined types and user-created class objects are treated the same because user-defined types are really a kind of simple user-defined class. These objects have two components: the class name that defines the structure of the class and a tag that is used for instances of that class. Choose an appropriate name for the class. For example, if you had a user-defined class that described a glyph bitmap created at run time on a form, the class name would be glyph. The tag would be an abbreviation of glyph—perhaps gph. If you had another class that was a collection of these objects, it would use glyphs and gphs, respectively. You can treat a form as a user-defined class with a user interface. For example:

```
gphGlyph
nclName
```

Collection Tags

You treat a collection object with a special tag. You construct the tag using the datatype of the collection followed by the letter "s". For example, if you had a collection of Longs, the tag would be lngs. If it were a collection of user-defined types with the tag gph, the collection would be gphs. Although in theory, a collection can hold objects of different datatypes, in practice, each of the datatypes in the collection is the same. If you do want to use different datatypes in a collection, use the tag objs. For example:

```
intsEntries
erhsHandler
bscsBaseClass
```

Constructing Procedures

VBA procedures require you to name various objects: procedure names, labels, and parameters. These objects are described in the following sections.

Constructing Procedure Names

VBA names event procedures, and you can't change them. You should use the capitalization defined by the system. For user-defined procedure names, capitalize the first letter of each word in the name. For example:

```
cmdOK_Click
GetTitleBarString
PerformInitialization
```

Procedures should always have a scope keyword, Public or Private, when they are declared. For example:

```
Public Function GetTitleBarString() As String
Private Sub PerformInitialization
```

Naming Parameters

You should prefix all parameters in a procedure call with ByVal or ByRef, even though ByRef is optional and redundant. Procedure arguments are named the same as simple variables of the same type, except that arguments passed by reference use the prefix "r". For example:

```
Sub TestValue(ByVal intInput As Integer, _
 ByRef rlngOutput As Long)
Function GetReturnValue(ByVal strKey As String, _
 ByRef rgph As Glyph) As Boolean
```

Prefixes

Prefixes modify an object tag to indicate more information about an object.

Arrays of Objects Prefix

Arrays of an object type use the prefix "a". For example:

```
aintFontSizes
astrNames
```

Index Prefix

You indicate an index into an array with the prefix "i", regardless of the datatype of the index. You may also use the index prefix to index into other enumerated objects, such as a collection of user-defined classes. For example:

```
iaintFontSizes
iastrNames
igphsGlyphCollection
```

Prefixes for Scope and Lifetime

Three levels of scope exist for each variable in VBA: Public, Private, and Local. A variable also has a lifetime of the current procedure or the length of the program. You may optionally use the prefixes in Table A.2 to indicate scope and lifetime.

T A B L E A . 2   Prefixes for Scope and Lifetime

Prefix	Object Type
(none)	Local variable, procedure-level lifetime
s	Local variable, program-level lifetime (static variable)
m	Private (module) variable, program-level lifetime
g	Public (global) variable, program-level lifetime

You also use the "m" and "g" constants with other objects, such as constants, to indicate their scope. For example:

```
intLocalVariable
mintPrivateVariable
gintPublicVariable
mconPi
```

Other Prefixes

Table A.3 lists and describes some other prefixes.

TABLE A.3   Other Commonly Used Prefixes

Prefix	Object Type
c	Count of some object type
h	Handle to a Windows object
r	Parameter passed by reference

Here are some examples:

```
cstrArray
hwndForm
```

Suffixes

Suffixes modify the base name of an object, indicating additional information about a variable. You'll likely create your own suffixes that are specific to your development work. Table A.4 lists some generic VBA suffixes.

TABLE A.4   Commonly Used Suffixes

Suffix	Object Type
Min	The absolute first element in an array or other kind of list
First	The first element to be used in an array or list during the current operation
Last	The last element to be used in an array or list during the current operation
Lim	The upper limit of elements to be used in an array or list. Lim isn't a valid index. Generally, Lim equals Last + 1
Max	The absolutely last element in an array or other kind of list
Cnt	Used with database elements to indicate that the item is a counter. Counter fields are incremented by the system and are numbers of either type Long or type ReplicationId

Here are some examples:

```
iastrNamesMin
iastrNamesMax
iaintFontSizesFirst
igphsGlyphCollectionLast
lngCustomerIdCnt
varOrderIdCnt
```

Host Application and Component Extensions to the Conventions

Each host application for VBA, as well as each component that can be installed, has a set of objects it can use. This section defines tags for the objects in the various host applications and components. Future versions of the conventions will include tags for other VBA hosts and components.

Access 97, Version 8.0 Objects

Table A.5 lists Access object variable tags. Besides being used in code to refer to these object types, these same tags are used to name these kinds of objects in the form and report designers.

TABLE A.5   Access Object Variable Tags

Tag	Object Type
app	Application
bof	BoundObjectFrame
chk	CheckBox
cbo	ComboBox
cmd	CommandButton
ctl	Control

TABLE A.5 Access Object Variable Tags (continued)

Tag	Object Type
ctls	Controls
ocx	CustomControl
dcm	DoCmd
frm	Form
frms	Forms
grl	GroupLevel
hlk	Hyperlink
img	Image
lbl	Label
lin	Line
lst	ListBox
bas (or mdl)	Module
bass (or mdls)	Modules
ole	ObjectFrame
opt	OptionButton
fra	OptionGroup (frame)
pge	Page of Tab Control
pges	Pages (of Tab Control)
brk	PageBreak
pal	PaletteButton
prps	Properties

TABLE A.5   Access Object Variable Tags (continued)

Tag	Object Type
shp	Rectangle (shape)
ref	Reference
refs	References
rpt	Report
rpts	Reports
scr	Screen
sec	Section
sfr	SubForm
srp	SubReport
tab	Tab Control
txt	TextBox
tgl	ToggleButton

Here are some examples:

```
txtName
lblInput
```

For OLE/ActiveX custom controls, you can use the tag OCX, as specified in Table A.5, or more specific object tags if they have been specified for the control.

DAO 3.5 Objects

DAO is the programmatic interface to the Jet database engine shared by Access, VB, and VC++. The tags for DAO 3.5 objects are shown in Table A.6.

TABLE A.6   DAO 3.5 Object Tags

Tag	Object Type
cnx	Connection
cnxs	Connections
cnt	Container
cnts	Containers
db	Database
dbs	Databases
dbe	DBEngine
doc	Document
docs	Documents
err	Error
errs	Errors
fld	Field
flds	Fields
grp	Group
grps	Groups
idx	Index
idxs	Indexes
prm	Parameter
prms	Parameters
prp	Property
prps	Properties

TABLE A.6 DAO 3.5 Object Tags (continued)

Tag	Object Type
qry (or qdf)	QueryDef
qrys (or qdfs)	QueryDefs
rst	Recordset
rsts	Recordsets
rel	Relation
rels	Relations
tbl (or tdf)	TableDef
tbls (or tdfs)	TableDefs
usr	User
usrs	Users
wrk	Workspace
wrks	Workspaces

Here are some examples:

```
rstCustomers
idxPrimaryKey
```

Table A.7 lists the tags used to identify types of objects in a database.

TABLE A.7 Access Database Window Object Tags

Tag	Object Type
cls	Class Module
tbl	Table
qry	Query

TABLE A.7 Access Database Window Object Tags (continued)

Tag	Object Type
frm	Form
rpt	Report
mcr	Macro
bas (or mdl)	Module

If you wish, you can use more exact tags or suffixes to identify the purpose and type of a database object. If you use the suffix, use the tag from Table A.7 to indicate the type. Use either the tag or the suffix found along with the more general tag, but not both. The tags and suffixes are shown in Table A.8.

TABLE A.8 Specific Object Tags and Suffixes for Access Database Window Objects

Tag	Suffix	Object Type
tlkp	Lookup	Table (lookup)
qsel	(none)	Query (select)
qapp	Append	Query (append)
qxtb	XTab	Query (crosstab)
qddl	DDL	Query (DDL)
qdel	Delete	Query (delete)
qflt	Filter	Query (filter)
qlkp	Lookup	Query (lookup)
qmak	MakeTable	Query (make table)
qspt	PassThru	Query (SQL pass-through)
qtot	Totals	Query (totals)

TABLE A.8 Specific Object Tags and Suffixes for Access Database Window Objects (continued)

Tag	Suffix	Object Type
quni	Union	Query (union)
qupd	Update	Query (update)
fdlg	Dlg	Form (dialog)
fmnu	Mnu	Form (menu)
fmsg	Msg	Form (message)
fsfr	SubForm	Form (subform)
rsrp	SubReport	Form (subreport)
mmnu	Mnu	Macro (menu)

Here are some examples:

```
tblValidNamesLookup
tlkpValidNames
fmsgError
mmnuFileMnu
```

When naming objects in a database, don't use spaces. Instead, capitalize the first letter of each word. For example, instead of Quarterly Sales Values Table, use tblQuarterlySalesValues.

There is strong debate over whether fields in a table should have tags. Whether you use them is up to you. However, if you do use them, use the tags from Table A.9.

TABLE A.9 Field Tags (If You Decide to Use Them)

Tag	Object Type
bin	Binary
byt	Byte
guid	Globally unique identifier (GUID) used for replication AutoIncrement fields

TABLE A.9   Field Tags (If You Decide to Use Them) (continued)

Tag	Object Type
lng	Autoincrementing (either sequential or random) Long (used with the suffix Cnt)
cur	Currency
dat	Date/time
dbl	Double
int	Integer
lng	Long
mem	Memo
ole	OLE
sng	Single
str	Text
f	Yes/No

Microsoft Office 8.0 Objects

Table A.10 lists the tags for Microsoft Office 8.0 objects.

TABLE A.10   Microsoft Office 8.0 Object Tags

Tag	Object Type
ast	Assistant
bln	Balloon
chk	BalloonCheckbox
chks	BalloonCheckboxes

TABLE A.10 Microsoft Office 8.0 Object Tags (continued)

Tag	Object Type
lbl	BalloonLabel
lbls	BalloonLabels
cbr	CommandBar
cbrs	CommandBars
cmd	CommandBarButton
cbo	CommandBarComboBox
ctl	CommandBarControl
ctls	CommandBarControls
cbp	CommandBarPopup
dcp	DocumentProperty
dcps	DocumentProperties
sch	FileSearch
ffl	FoundFiles
prt	PropertyTest
prts	PropertyTests

Summary

Using a naming convention requires a considerable initial effort on your part. It also requires that you conform to rules specified by other parties, which is difficult for many programmers. The payoff comes when either you or another programmer has to revisit your code at a later time. Using the conventions makes your code more readable and maintainable.

> **NOTE**
>
> A later version of these conventions that includes updated tags for Visual Basic 5.0 will made be available electronically. This update should be available at several Web sites, including the MCW Technologies site at http://www.mcwtech.com.

Greg Reddick is the president of Gregory Reddick & Associates, a consulting company specializing in software development in Microsoft Access, VB, and C/C++. He worked for four years on the Access development team at Microsoft. He was a coauthor of the *Microsoft Access 95 Developer's Handbook*, published by Sybex. He can be reached at 71501,2564 on CompuServe or 71501.2564@ compuserve.com on the Internet.

APPENDIX
B

Accessing DLLs and the Windows API

- Explaining Dynamic Link Libraries

- Calling DLLs and the Windows API from VBA

- Declaring DLL procedures

- Discovering DLL details

- Converting 16-bit Windows API calls to 32-bit API calls

This appendix discusses one of the most powerful features of VBA: the ability to call Dynamic Link Libraries (DLLs) from VBA procedures. DLLs are primarily written in C or C++, but you can also create them using Pascal and Delphi. Calling a DLL provides a method of performing tasks that standard VBA functions and statements do not permit. For example, VBA has no intrinsic ability to retrieve the amount of free memory available, but you can do it easily with the Windows API.

Even if you are not proficient in C or C++, you can use DLLs someone else has written. Windows itself includes a number of DLLs with hundreds of useful functions. These functions are collectively called the *Windows API. API* is an acronym for "Application Programming Interface," and it is the set of functions Windows programs use to manipulate Windows.

Learning how to call the Windows API, and DLLs in general, allows you to vastly extend your ability to manipulate Windows. This appendix is divided into five main sections:

- The basics of calling a DLL or Windows API call

- Examples of DLL calls

- How to construct a Declare statement to retrieve information from any arbitrary DLL (for more advanced users)

- A closer look at what goes on during DLL calls

- How to convert 16-bit Windows API (from Windows 3.x) into 32-bit Windows API calls (Windows 95 and Windows NT)

Introducing Dynamic Link Libraries

In traditional DOS compiled languages, every application carries around every function it calls, and every application you create includes exactly the same shared code. For example, in standard C used from DOS, you call functions from the C run-time library to read a string from a file, get a character from the keyboard, or get the current time. These functions in the libraries are *statically linked* to the program, which means the code for the functions is included in the executable at the time the executable is created. The problem with this scheme is that if you have 200 programs, all of which write a string to the screen with the printf function, the code for this function is reproduced 200 times on your disk.

Windows uses a different approach: libraries are usually *dynamically linked* to the program. This means that if you have 200 Windows programs, all of which write a string to a window, only one copy of the ExtTextOut code resides on your hard disk. Each program includes only a very small amount of overhead to call this common code. These common routines reside in Dynamic Link Libraries, which normally have the extension .DLL and are stored in the Windows\System directory if more than one program uses them.

Programs that run under Windows call functions the operating system provides. These functions provide facilities to create a window, change its size, read and write Registry entries, manipulate a file, and so on. Windows stores most of these functions in three DLLs: USER32.DLL, GDI32.DLL, and KERNEL32.DLL.

To use a DLL, you need to know the procedures in it and the arguments to each of those procedures. The Windows functions are well documented. To make a call to the Windows API, you just need to understand the documentation for the DLL call. For other DLLs, you'll need to locate and understand the documentation for the DLL. Because traditionally DLLs have been designed to be called from C or C++, the documentation provided is usually stated in terms of calling functions from C or C++. For this reason, you need to develop some skills in translating the terminology from the C perspective into the VBA perspective. This appendix provides most of the tools necessary and tells you where to get the rest of the information you need.

NOTE The Windows API includes more than 1000 functions. Describing them all is beyond the scope of this book (whole books have been written on the subject), but the API calls are documented in several places. We have put a copy of WIN32API.TXT on the CD-ROM that comes with this book. This file includes declarations for all the API functions that Microsoft decided you might want to use from VBA, as well as the definitions of most of the constants and structures used by the API calls. But to find out what the functions mean, you'll need the Win32 documentation. You can find the complete documentation on the Microsoft Developer's Network (Level 1) CD-ROM.

Calling DLL Procedures from VBA

Calling procedures in DLLs is similar to calling procedures in standard VBA. The difference is that the body of the procedure resides in a DLL instead of inside a module. Before calling a function in a DLL, you need to tell VBA where to find it. There are really two kinds of DLLs, and you tell VBA how to call them in two ways:

- By specifying a type library
- By using a Declare statement

Using Type Libraries

The person who creates a DLL may do so in a special way, creating a file called a *type library,* which describes the procedures within the DLL. A type library usually has the extension .OLB or .TLB and is registered with the OLE component of Windows. The setup program that installs the DLL usually creates the proper entries with the Windows Registry to register the type library. If you select Tools ➤ References when an open module has the focus, the dialog shows all the registered type libraries that are available. By placing a check next to the name of your type library, you indicate that everything within the type library is available to VBA.

If you use a type library, there is no need to use Declare statements. The type library includes all the functionality of the Declare statement. In addition, type libraries avoid the difficulties of passing strings to DLLs. (See the section "Passing Strings to a DLL: The Real Story" later in this appendix.) Unfortunately, however, the Windows API doesn't have a type library; you must use Declare statements to call the Windows API.

> **TIP** Several third-party vendors have written type libraries for the Windows API. Check your tools vendors for the available type libraries.

DAO in VBA is an example of a type library. The type library provides all the functionality of DAO to VBA; none of it is really intrinsic to VBA.

NOTE If you are calling a function specified with a type library, you can ignore the information in the rest of this appendix, which deals with calling DLLs through the use of Declare statements. You use functions specified with type libraries just as though they were an intrinsic part of VBA.

Using Declare Statements

A Declare statement is a definition you provide in the declarations section of a module that tells VBA where to find a function and how to call it. (You'll find details on the Declare statement in the section "How to Construct a Declare Statement" later in this appendix.) The important point here is that you need a Declare statement to be able to call a DLL function that is not specified by a type library. Because Microsoft supplies no type library for the Windows API, you need to provide Declare statements for every Windows API call you make.

Fortunately, these statements have already been constructed for you. We've included the WIN32API.TXT file, provided by Microsoft, which has most of the Declare statements you'll need. You'll also need the definition of certain constants and user-defined type declarations. You can also find these definitions in WIN32API.TXT.

TIP Many Microsoft developer products—such as Microsoft Office 97 Developer Edition (previously called the Microsoft Access Developer's Toolkit) and Microsoft Visual Basic—ship with a tool named the API Text Viewer. This tool also provides the Declare statements and other definitions you'll need. It simply searches the WIN32API.TXT and finds the value you've requested. Unfortunately, the user interface on this tool makes it difficult to use; it's faster to use a text editor to find the Declare statement in the WIN32API.TXT file. Quite likely, shareware or freeware tools for providing Declare statements and other definitions will become available as the Win32 API ages, so you may want to look for them on the Internet or other online services.

WARNING   Do not include all of WIN32API.TXT in your application. This large file has at least a thousand declarations within it. The amount of resources it consumes will substantially reduce the performance of your application. Because you will probably use at most several dozen of the declarations in your application, just copy the ones you use into your module.

Here is an example of a Declare statement:

```
Public Declare Function WinHelp Lib "user32" Alias "WinHelpA" _
  (ByVal hwnd As Long, ByVal lpHelpFile As String, _
  ByVal lngCommand As Long, dwData As Any) As Long
```

As mentioned earlier in this section, you place Declare statements in the declarations section of a module. After you specify the Declare statement, you can use the procedure that has been declared just as though it were an intrinsic part of VBA, with a number of important exceptions. The following sections take a look at these exceptions.

WARNING   VBA provides a very safe environment in which to work. The environment is not as safe, however, when you are calling external DLL functions directly. Because you *will* eventually make a mistake attempting to call a Windows API and cause a General Protection (GP) fault, it is important to save your work before running any code that calls a DLL. The first time you attempt to call any given DLL function, or when you make a change to a Declare statement, you must be extra careful because that is when a GP fault will most likely occur. Keep recent backups of your application, just to cover the slight possibility that it becomes corrupted when VBA crashes. DLLs are powerful, but they don't provide the protection from your mistakes that VBA normally gives you.

Passing Arguments to DLLs

You pass arguments to DLLs exactly the same way you pass arguments to any built-in function, with two exceptions, described in the sections "Returning Strings from a DLL" and "Using the Any Datatype" later in this appendix. For example, to find out information about the system on which Windows is running, you call the Windows API function GetSystemMetrics. You retrieve the Declare statement and some constants from WIN32API.TXT and place them in the declarations section of a module. The definitions look like this:

```
Declare Function GetSystemMetrics Lib "user32" _
 (ByVal nIndex As Long) As Long

' GetSystemMetrics() codes
Const SM_CXSCREEN = 0
Const SM_CYSCREEN = 1
Const SM_CXVSCROLL = 2
Const SM_CYHSCROLL = 3
Const SM_CYCAPTION = 4
' etc... There are 75 or so of them.
```

After putting the Declare statement and constant declarations in the declarations section of the module, you can call the GetSystemMetrics function just as though it were part of VBA. For example:

```
lngCyCaption = GetSystemMetrics(SM_CYCAPTION)
```

TIP
For many more examples using the GetSystemMetrics function, see Chapter 9.

Returning Strings from a DLL

Windows has two ways of storing strings, using what C programmers know as BSTR and LPSTR objects. The section "Passing Strings to a DLL: The Real Story" later in this appendix describes the details of how these are stored internally. All the Windows API calls except those dealing with OLE use LPSTRs, not BSTRs. DLLs cannot change the size of an LPSTR string once it has been created. This causes difficulties when you need the DLL to return a value in a string. In fact, DLL functions that deal with LPSTR strings don't actually return strings but instead modify them in memory.

Because a DLL that accepts an LPSTR cannot change the size of a string that's passed to it, the string needs to be big enough to accept the data to be returned before you pass it to the DLL. This means you need to fill the string with enough characters to create a buffer for the DLL to fill in. You normally accomplish this with the Space$ function. The DLL must not write past the end of the string, because that can result in a GP fault. DLL functions that modify strings normally require that you pass another argument that tells how much space has been allocated for the string.

The GetWindowText function is an example of a Windows function that manipulates a string in memory. You pass it a handle to a window, and it returns the text associated with the window into a buffer.

> **NOTE**   A handle is a Long value that uniquely identifies an object to Windows. The first argument to GetWindowText is a handle to a window, also known as an *hwnd* or *hWnd*.

The following is a Declare statement for GetWindowText:

```
Declare Function GetWindowText _
 Lib "user32" Alias "GetWindowTextA" _
 (ByVal hwnd As Long, ByVal lpString As String, _
 ByVal cch As Long) As Long
```

When you call GetWindowText, control passes into the Windows USER32.DLL. The GetWindowText function inside the DLL looks up the handle in Windows' internal data structures and fills in the lpString parameter with the text that is associated with the window. You call GetWindowText as follows. (In this example, hWnd is the window handle of the window from which you want to retrieve the caption.)

```
Dim strReturnedString As String
Dim intRet As Integer

' Allocate enough space for the return value.
strReturnedString = Space$(255)

' Call the GetWindowsText function
intRet = GetWindowText(hwnd, strReturnedString, _
 Len(strReturnedString) + 1)

' Truncate the string to the proper size
strReturnedString = Left$(strReturnedString, intRet)
```

The Space$ function in this example returns a string of 255 spaces followed by a null character. A null character has the ANSI value 0 and is used in LPSTRs to terminate a string. This allows you to use window captions up to 255 characters. In memory, strReturnedString looks like this:

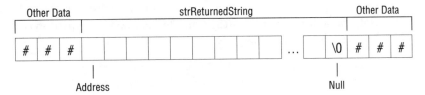

You can see from the illustration that the area in memory corresponding to strReturnedString is identified by an address marking the first byte in the string. You can also see why you don't want to let the DLL function modify too many bytes of memory. Overwriting memory that belongs to other variables or processes will lead to unpredictable results and GP faults.

The code then calls the GetWindowText function. The call has two effects:

- It changes the contents of strReturnedString to be the caption of the window indicated by the hwnd argument, followed by a null character.

- It returns the length of the string placed into strReturnedString, not counting the terminating null character.

After the call, strReturnedString looks like this, in memory:

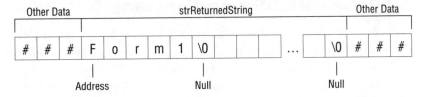

The length of the string hasn't changed, nor has any memory been deallocated— the string is still 255 characters long. Because the DLL cannot make the string shorter, you must, before using strReturnedString, manually truncate the string so that it ends at the character immediately before the null character. Fortunately, the return value of the GetWindowText function tells you exactly how many characters should appear in the final string. You then use the Left$ function to truncate the string. If you passed an invalid value for the hwnd argument, Windows returns a value indicating that the API call failed.

If you call a DLL function that doesn't return a value telling you how many characters are in the returned string, you can search for the null character to determine how long the string should be. The Instr function combined with the Left$ function does the job:

```
strReturnedString = Left$(strReturnedString, _
  Instr(1, strReturnedString, vbNullChar) - 1)
```

WARNING Although the code in the previous fragment works fine when you're sure the returned string contains some actual text, it will fail if the first character of the returned string is a null character—you'll end up trying to retrieve the first −1 characters in the returned string. Many of the modules and classes that work with string API calls in this book include a function named dhTrimNull that accomplishes the same goal more safely.

TIP For many more examples using strings and string functions, see Chapter 1.

Using the vbNullString Constant

The documentation for some API functions indicates that a given parameter can accept either a string or a null value, depending on the circumstances. A Null is a 4-byte value, each byte containing 0, placed directly on the stack. (For a full discussion of what this means, see the section "Understanding Passing By Value and By Reference" later in this appendix.) The main thing you need to know is that to pass a Null, you can use the intrinsic vbNullString constant.

For example, the SetVolumeLabel API function sets the label of a disk. The Declare statement for the function is

```
Declare Function SetVolumeLabel _
  Lib "kernel32" Alias "SetVolumeLabelA" _
  (ByVal lpRootPathName As String, _
  ByVal lpVolumeName As String) As Long
```

These are the two arguments to SetVolumeLabel:

Parameter	Meaning
lpRootPathName	Points to a null-terminated string specifying the root directory of a file system volume. This is the volume the function will label. If this parameter is Null, the root of the current directory is used
lpVolumeName	Points to a string specifying a name for the volume. If this parameter is Null, the function deletes the name of the specified volume

To set the volume label on the C drive to DRIVE_C, you execute the following code:

```
fRet = SetVolumeLabel("C:\", "DRIVE_C")
```

To delete the C drive's volume label using the documented method, you need to pass a Null as the second argument. Normally, VBA wouldn't allow this, because the arguments are declared as Strings. To get around this restriction, VBA supplies the vbNullString constant, a special value designed just for this purpose. To delete the volume label, execute the following code:

```
fRet = SetVolumeLabel("C:\", vbNullString)
```

WARNING Unfortunately, the current shipping version of Windows 95 contains a bug, and the code shown to delete a volume label does not work. (Windows 95 treats vbNullString as an invalid argument, and places random text into the volume label.) It does work as documented in Windows NT. This bug will probably be fixed in a future version of Windows 95. In the meantime, you can work around the bug by setting the label to an empty string ("").

Passing a User-Defined Type to a DLL

Sometimes you need to pass a user-defined type to a DLL. For example, many of the Windows functions that work with coordinates expect you to pass a RECT structure. This structure is a user-defined type, as opposed to one that is supported implicitly by the C or VBA language. To pass the RECT structure, you need to define an equivalent type in VBA. The structure in VBA (extracted from WIN32API.TXT) is

```
Type RECT
    left As Long
    top As Long
    right As Long
    bottom As Long
End Type
```

The declaration of a function that takes a RECT as an argument is as follows:

```
Declare Function GetWindowRect Lib "user32" _
 (ByVal hwnd As Long, lpRect As RECT) As Long
```

A call to GetWindowRect looks like the following. (In this example, the variable hWnd contains the window handle of an existing window.)

```
Dim rct As RECT

If GetWindowRect(hwnd, rct) Then
    With rct
        txtLeft.Value = .left
        txtTop.Value = .top
        txtRight.Value = .right
        txtBottom.Value = .bottom
    End With
End If
```

GetWindowRect returns True if it succeeded in filling in the RECT structure passed in. It then uses the values from the structure to fill in text boxes on a form.

Passing an Array

You can pass individual elements of an array just as you would use any other variable. Sometimes, though, you'll want to pass an entire array to a DLL. You may do this—but only for numeric arrays, not for strings or user-defined ones. (You can pass an array of strings or user-defined types, but only if the DLL understands a special OLE type named SAFEARRAY. Documentation of the specific function will indicate when an array is expected, but almost none of the Windows API calls work with SAFEARRAY structures.) To pass an array, you pass its first element. This, in effect, tells the DLL function the memory address of the first element. Because arrays are always stored in contiguous blocks of memory, the DLL function can deduce the other elements given their size and count. For example, when you call the SetSysColors Windows API function, declared like this:

```
Declare Function SetSysColors Lib "user32" Alias "SetSysColors" _
 (ByVal lngChanges As Long, lngSysColor As Long, _
 lngColorValues As Long) As Long
```

you actually pass two different arrays:

```
Dim alngDisplayElements() As Long
Dim alngRGBValues() As Long
Dim lngCDisplayElements As Long

' Size the arrays for two elements
lngCDisplayElements = 2
ReDim alngDisplayElements(lngCDisplayElements - 1)
ReDim alngRGBValues(lngCDisplayElements - 1)

' Fill the arrays to set two system colors
alngDisplayElements(0) = COLOR_BTNHIGHLIGHT
alngRGBValues(0) = RGB(&HFF, 0, 0)
alngDisplayElements(1) = COLOR_BTNTEXT
alngRGBValues(1) = RGB(0, 0, &HFF)

Call SetSysColors(lngCDisplayElements, _
 alngDisplayElements(0), alngRGBValues(0))
```

NOTE　　**For more information on using the SetSysColors API function, see Chapter 9.**

When passing an array to a DLL function, you must give the function some indication of the size of the array. You do this by passing another argument that gives the size of the array. Without this argument, the DLL can't determine how large the array is and might continue processing beyond the end of the array, in memory. If you pass in a size that is larger than the array that has been allocated, you are telling the DLL that more memory has been allocated than really has been. (In effect, you're lying to the DLL and, like all liars, must suffer the consequences.) When the DLL tries to access the information past the end of the array, it will either find random bytes of data or cause a GP fault, depending on the memory it is trying to access. In other words, be very careful that you pass the correct size in that argument.

How to Construct a Declare Statement

As mentioned earlier in this appendix, if you plan on using only Windows API functions, you won't need to construct Declare statements. Instead, you'll get them from some source, such as WIN32API.TXT. However, at some point you may call a DLL that doesn't have a Declare statement already prepared for it. In this case, you need to construct a Declare statement from scratch. In addition, WIN32API.TXT isn't perfect. Some of the Declare statements don't allow you to call some of the Windows API calls with arguments of certain types. Also, we have found bugs in some of the Declare statements as we have worked with them. These may or may not be fixed in your copy of WIN32API.TXT, so understanding how to construct a Declare statement is a useful skill.

The Declare statement gives VBA six pieces of information about a procedure in an external library:

- The scope of the declaration

- The name of the procedure as you want to call it in your code

- The name and path of the containing DLL

- The name of the procedure as it exists in the DLL

- The number and datatypes of the arguments to the procedure

- If the procedure is a function, the datatype of the return value of the function

Given this information, VBA knows how to locate the function on the hard disk and how to arrange the arguments on the stack so they are acceptable to the DLL. The *stack* is a special segment of memory that programs use for storing temporary information and for communicating between procedures. VBA pushes arguments onto the stack and calls the DLL function, and the DLL manipulates the arguments. Then the DLL places the return value on the stack for VBA to return to your application.

The Declare statement defines the size of the arguments to a DLL function and what the arguments mean. It is *crucial* that the declaration be exactly what the DLL expects. Otherwise, you may be giving the DLL incorrect information, and that may cause the DLL to reference information in an invalid segment of memory. A GP fault results when a program tries to access memory for which it doesn't have read or right privileges. If you receive a GP fault, VBA crashes without giving you a chance to save any changed objects. This is (to understate) what most programmers would call "a bad thing."

Defining the VBA Declare statement is similar to defining any other sub or function, except that there is no body to the procedure. The body of the procedure resides in the DLL. Once you have declared a DLL function, you can call it almost as though the code were part of VBA. Declare statements must appear at the module level in the declarations section. The Declare statement takes one of two forms, depending on whether the DLL function being called returns a value:

> [Public | Private] Declare Sub *subname* Lib *"libname"*
>
> [Alias *"aliasname"*] [([*argumentlist*])]

or

> [Public | Private] Declare Function *functionname*
>
> Lib *"libname"* [Alias *"aliasname"*]
>
> [([*argumentlist*])] [As *type*]

Here is an example of a Declare statement:

```
Private Declare Function FindWindow Lib "user32" _
 Alias "FindWindowA" _
 (ByVal lpClassName As String, _
 ByVal lpWindowName As String) As Long
```

If the function returns no value (that is, it is declared with the return type *void* in the C programming language), you use the Declare Sub format of the Declare statement. If the function returns a value (and almost all of them do), you use the Declare Function format.

Public versus Private

Just as any normal procedure declaration has a scope that determines which other procedures can call it, procedures defined by Declare statements also have a scope. You can call a DLL procedure from code only within the same form or module as the Declare statement if you prefix the Declare statement with the word "Private". You can call a DLL function from any code if the Declare statement is prefixed with the word "Public". Not using either Public or Private is the same as scoping the function with Public. A Declare statement in the declarations section of a class module must have Private scope. A Declare statement in a standard module can have either scope.

> **NOTE**
>
> In this book, to avoid potential naming conflicts and to encapsulate as much of the example code as possible, almost all the DLL declarations have been made Private. If you want to call the same DLL function from multiple modules, you can change the Private keyword to Public and remove extra declarations.

Specifying the Procedure Name

The function or sub name given in the Declare statement is the name that is used when you call it in your code. It must follow the same naming rules as for any VBA procedure name:

- It must begin with a letter.
- The other characters must be in the sets A–Z, a–z, 0–9, or an underscore character.
- It must be unique within the same scope.
- It must be no longer than 255 characters.
- It cannot be a VBA keyword.

If you don't supply an Alias clause, the name of the procedure must match the name of the function in the DLL. (See the section "Specifying the Alias" a little later in this appendix.)

Specifying the Library

The Lib portion of the declaration tells VBA the DLL's name and, potentially, its location on the disk. You must enclose the Lib name in quotes, and it's not case sensitive. If the function you're declaring is in one of the main Windows DLLs, you can omit the .DLL extension. For example, you can use User32, GDI32, or Kernel32 rather than User32.DLL, and so on. VBA appends the .DLL extension to these names for you. For other DLLs, you must include the DLL name.

If you do not include the path on the DLL name, Windows uses this order to search for the DLL:

1. The directory from which the application loaded (For most VBA hosts, that's the directory from which the host is loaded, not the directory where your application is stored.)

2. The current directory

3. Windows NT only: the 32-bit Windows system directory (Windows\System32)

4. The Windows system directory (Windows\System)

5. The Windows directory (Windows)

6. The directories that are listed in the PATH environment variable

This order can cause some confusion. If you put a DLL in the Windows directory but an older version of the DLL exists in the Windows\System directory, the older version will get called. Furthermore, this order has changed from earlier versions of Windows.

Specifying the Alias

You may include an Alias clause when you declare a DLL procedure. The Alias clause of the declaration allows you to map the name of the function from the way it was specified in the DLL to a different name in VBA. There are several reasons why you might use the alias:

- To change an invalid procedure name in the DLL to one VBA allows

- To change the case of the DLL procedure call

- To set the procedure name to a DLL function that is exposed only by ordinal number

- To have a unique procedure name

- To leave off the "A" required by ANSI versions of Windows API calls

These reasons are explained in more detail in the following sections.

TIP

Yes, it's confusing: the Alias clause specifies the real name for the DLL procedure. You'd expect that the text that follows the Alias keyword would specify the alias name for the procedure call, but that's not the way it works. The procedure name that immediately follows the Declare keyword indicates the name you're going to use to call the procedure. The name, in quotes, after the Alias keyword specifies the actual name of the procedure, as it's found in the DLL.

Changing the Procedure Name in the DLL to One VBA Allows

The languages generally used to create DLLs are usually less stringent about procedure names than is VBA. As mentioned earlier in this appendix, VBA function names must consist of alphanumeric or underscore characters and begin with a letter. C function names often begin with an underscore. The function name you specify in the Declare statement must be a valid VBA procedure name, so if the name in the DLL doesn't match the VBA naming rules, you must use an alias. In addition, the name in the DLL might also be a reserved word in VBA, or it might be the name of an existing global variable or function. In these cases, too, you must use an alias.

For example, VBA does not allow function names with a leading underscore. To use the Windows API function _lwrite, then, you might declare the function as:

```
Declare Function lwrite Lib "Kernel32" Alias "_lwrite" _
  (ByVal hFile As Long, ByVal strBuffer As String, _
  ByVal lngBytes As Long) As Long
```

This defines the function name lwrite as the _lwrite function in the Kernel32 Dynamic Link Library.

> **TIP**
>
> Although the _lwrite function still exists in Win32, it is provided only for backward compatibility with 16-bit Windows. You should use the WriteFile function instead if you need this functionality in your applications.

Changing the Case of the DLL Procedure Call

The name of the procedure given in the Declare statement is case sensitive. This means it must exactly match the case of the procedure name in the DLL. If you wish to have the procedure name in your code use a different capitalization than that given in the DLL, you must use an Alias clause. This wasn't true in 16-bit Windows, so if you're converting Declare statements from old code, you need to be aware of this.

Setting the Procedure Name by Ordinal Number

Every function in a DLL is assigned a number, called its *ordinal*. Every function in a DLL *may* expose its name but is not required to do so. When writing a DLL, you choose which procedures within the DLL can be called from code existing outside the DLL; these functions are *exposed*.

To call a function by ordinal, you must know the ordinal number for the function. You can find this information in the documentation for the DLL (if any) or in the DEF file for the DLL. Whichever way you derive the ordinal, you specify *#ordinalnumber* for the alias name—that is, a pound sign followed by the decimal number of the ordinal. For example, the declaration for the _lwrite function presented earlier might be declared as

```
Declare Function lwrite Lib "Kernel32" Alias "#86" _
 (ByVal hFile As Long, ByVal strBuffer As String, _
 ByVal lngBytes As Long) As Long
```

You may declare any function using its ordinal number, but if the name is exported, we recommend you use the name. This is especially important if you do not maintain the DLL. The DLL developer may assume that people will not call a function by ordinal if it is exported by name. Later versions of the DLL may not keep the same ordinal number for the functions in it but will most likely keep the same name.

Having a Unique Procedure Name

Each function declared at the same level of scope in VBA must have a unique name. Normally, this doesn't cause much consternation, because you are not likely to give two different functions the same name or declare the same function twice in your own code. But if you're developing a VBA module that might be included on different systems and that module calls functions in a DLL (including Windows API calls), this issue becomes important.

Suppose your module calls the GetSystemMetrics Windows API call. If you declare the function in the module with Public scope but without an alias, VBA uses the name GetSystemMetrics. If users then decide to use GetSystemMetrics in their own code and declare it as Public, the name in their code conflicts with the name in your module. For this reason, public declarations should always use an alias. Thus, you might declare GetSystemMetrics as

```
Declare Function MYLB_GetSystemMetrics Lib "user32" _
 Alias "GetSytemMetrics" (ByVal lngIndex As Long) As Long
```

When you use the function in the library, you then use MYLB_GetSystem-Metrics as the function name. Doing this enables users to avoid conflicts if they also define GetSystemMetrics.

Leaving Off the "A" Required by ANSI Windows API Calls

You can use the Alias clause to perform any type of procedure renaming that you wish. Because Windows supplies both ANSI and Wide character versions of all the API calls that involve strings (the ANSI versions have a trailing "A" in their names, and the Wide character versions have a trailing "W"), one common use is to rename ANSI Windows API calls to the same name without the trailing "A". The "A" is used in functions such as FindWindowA to indicate that the arguments being passed in are ANSI strings. (You can find a further discussion of ANSI and Unicode functions in the section "Unicode to ANSI and Back" later in this appendix.)

Specifying the Arguments

You pass arguments to a DLL on the stack. The DLL expects those arguments to be placed in a particular order and to have a certain size on the stack. When VBA places arguments on the stack, it looks to the Declare statement for direction. Arguments placed on the stack appear to the DLL as a series of bytes—it knows nothing about their original datatypes. The DLL groups and decodes those bytes to use them in the parameters for the DLL call. If the VBA Declare statement and the DLL don't agree on what those bytes mean, incorrect data appears in the parameters for the DLL call. When the DLL tries to use the parameters, it gets the wrong information. Worse, if your program doesn't place enough data on the stack, the DLL will read data left over from previous use of the stack.

Correctly declaring arguments is the trickiest part of using a DLL from VBA. This subject is discussed in the next main section, "More Advanced Details of Calling DLLs."

TIP Remember, if you've received your Declare statements from some trusted source, there's little chance you'll need to worry about the warnings presented here. If you want to construct declarations yourself, however, this section can make your work much simpler.

Converting C Parameters into VBA Declarations

Most DLLs are written in C or C++. The documentation for DLLs that aren't part of the Windows API is usually in the form of a C header file that provides the type and number of the arguments to the functions in the DLL. Based on the datatype required, you'll need to convert it to an equivalent VBA datatype. Table B.1 shows how to convert various C datatypes to VBA.

TABLE B.1   Conversions between C Datatypes and VBA Datatypes

C Datatype	VBA Datatype
ATOM	ByVal atom As Integer
BOOL	ByVal fValue As Integer
BYTE	ByVal bytValue As Byte
BYTE *	bytValue As Byte
CALLBACK	ByVal lngAddr As Long
char	ByVal bytValue As Byte
char _huge *	ByVal strValue As String
char FAR *	ByVal strValue As String
char NEAR *	ByVal strValue As String
DWORD	ByVal lngValue As Long
FARPROC	ByVal lngAddress As Long
HACCEL	ByVal hAccel As Long
HANDLE	ByVal h As Long
HBITMAP	ByVal hBitmap As Long
HBRUSH	ByVal hBrush As Long
HCURSOR	ByVal hCursor As Long
HDC	ByVal hDC As Long
HDRVR	ByVal hDrvr As Long
HDWP	ByVal hDWP As Long

TABLE B.1 Conversions between C Datatypes and VBA Datatypes (continued)

C Datatype	VBA Datatype
HFILE	ByVal hFile As Integer
HFONT	ByVal hFont As Long
HGDIOBJ	ByVal hGDIObj As Long
HGLOBAL	ByVal hGlobal As Long
HICON	ByVal hIcon As Long
HINSTANCE	ByVal hInstance As Long
HLOCAL	ByVal hLocal As Long
HMENU	ByVal hMenu As Long
HMETAFILE	ByVal hMetafile As Long
HMODULE	ByVal hModule As Long
HPALETTE	ByVal hPalette As Long
HPEN	ByVal hPen As Long
HRGN	ByVal hRgn As Long
HRSRC	ByVal hRsrc As Long
HTASK	ByVal hTask As Long
HWND	ByVal hWnd As Long
int	ByVal intValue As Integer
int FAR *	intValue As Integer
LONG	ByVal lngValue As Long
long	ByVal lngValue As Long
LPARAM	ByVal lngParam As Long

TABLE B.1   Conversions between C Datatypes and VBA Datatypes (continued)

C Datatype	VBA Datatype
LPCSTR	ByVal strValue As String
LPSTR	ByVal strValue As String
LPVOID	varValue As Any
LRESULT	ByVal lngResult As Long
UINT	ByVal intValue As Integer
UINT FAR *	intValue As Integer
void _huge *	bytValue() As Byte
void FAR *	bytValue() As Byte
WORD	ByVal intValue As Integer
WPARAM	ByVal intValue As Integer

More Advanced Details of Calling DLLs

At this point, this appendix has discussed most of the details of calling a DLL. Really understanding what is going on, though, requires a fuller understanding of what happens during a DLL call.

Understanding Passing By Value and By Reference

You can pass an argument on the stack to a DLL in one of two ways: by value or by reference. *By value* means that the caller pushes a copy of the actual passed value onto the stack. *By reference* means that the caller pushes the *address* of what is being passed onto the stack. Unless you tell it otherwise, VBA passes all arguments by reference. On the other hand, most DLLs are written in C, and unless you tell the C compiler otherwise (by passing an address), C passes all arguments by value. The VBA declaration *must* be set up correctly to pass arguments the way the DLL expects them to be passed.

The semantic difference between passing by value and by reference is this:

- When you pass by value, a copy of the value is placed on the stack. Any changes to the value inside the DLL have an effect only on the copy and do not change the value for the calling code.

- When you pass by reference, the address of the original value is placed on the stack. If the DLL makes changes to the value, the calling code will be able to see those changes.

To understand the difference, look at the declaration in C of the function GetFileSize:

```
DWORD GetFileSize
    (
    HANDLE hFile,              // handle of file to get size of
    LPDWORD lpFileSizeHigh,    // address of high-order word
                               // for file size
    );
```

The GetFileSize function takes two arguments:

Parameter	Meaning
hFile	Specifies an open handle of the file for which the size is being returned. The handle must have been created with either GENERIC_READ or GENERIC_WRITE access to the file
lpFileSizeHigh	Points to the variable where the high-order word of the file size is returned. This parameter can be Null if the application does not require the high-order word

The first argument, hFile, is a handle to a file, passed by value. The second, lpFileSizeHigh, is a Long, passed by reference. The function fills in the second argument. Suppose you call this function with the following code:

```
Function dhGetFileSize(ByVal strFile As String) As Long
    Dim hFile As Long
    Dim lngHigh As Long
    Dim curSize As Currency
```

```
hFile = CreateFile(strFile, _
 GENERIC_READ, FILE_SHARE_READ, ByVal 0&, OPEN_EXISTING, _
 0&, 0&)
If Err.LastDllError <> 0 Then
    curSize = GetFileSize(hFile, lngHigh)
    If lngHigh > 0 Then
        curSize = curSize + 2 ^ 32 * lngHigh
    End If
    dhGetFileSize = CLng(curSize)
    Call CloseHandle(hFile)
Else
    dhGetFileSize = -1
End If
End Function
```

At the point where GetFileSize is called, a diagram of the stack looks like this:

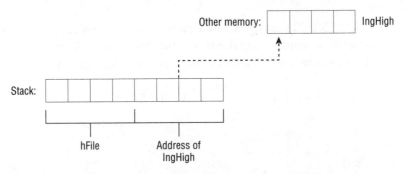

Notice that for hFile, it's the actual value of the variable that you find on the stack (because it's passed *by value*). For lngHigh, the stack contains the address of the variable (because it's passed *by reference*). The important point to remember is that you must always declare the arguments the way the function expects to find them.

Passing Strings to a DLL: The Real Story

As mentioned earlier in this appendix, Windows has two ways of storing strings: using the LPSTR or the BSTR data structure. String parameters to DLL functions must specify which type of string data structure they accept. Internally, VBA uses BSTRs to store strings. If the function accepts an LPSTR as a parameter, the argument must be converted from a BSTR into an LPSTR before being passed in. The vast majority of DLLs that are passed strings expect to be passed LPSTRs, including all the Windows API calls (except OLE calls, which explicitly expect BSTRs).

This means you need some method of converting BSTRs to LPSTRs. To effect this, you should understand how BSTRs and LPSTRs are stored in memory.

An LPSTR is an address of a null-terminated string. A *null-terminated string* is a set of characters followed by a character with the ANSI value 0. An LPSTR is stored in memory like this:

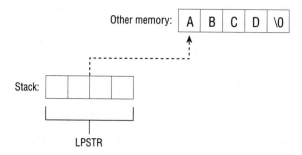

A BSTR is like an LPSTR except that the actual string data is preceded by a 4-byte value representing the size of the string. The address on the stack, however, still points to the first byte in the string. It is stored in memory like this:

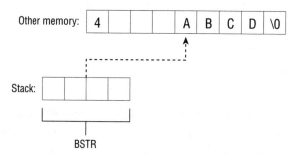

Although these might seem like compatible datatypes, they're not. Unless a DLL function is specifically written to accept a BSTR (and most aren't), you must pass it an LPSTR. How do you tell VBA to pass an LPSTR rather than a BSTR? You declare the argument using the ByVal attribute. Don't worry about VBA placing a string *by value* (that is, all the bytes) on the stack; remember that when it comes to strings, VBA always passes *by reference*. The type of reference (or pointer) it passes, however, differs depending on whether you use ByVal in the declaration. To pass an LPSTR, declare string arguments using ByVal; to pass a BSTR, don't use ByVal. Because almost every Windows API function that accepts strings expects you to pass the string parameters as LPSTRs, almost all Windows API declarations require the ByVal keyword on string parameters.

Using vbNullString: A Closer Look

As shown in the section "Using the vbNullString Constant" earlier in this appendix, you can also pass a Null as the second argument to delete the volume label. How can you pass a null pointer? You cannot pass an empty string, because that would pass a pointer to the empty string. (Remember that strings are passed by reference.) Passing an empty string would result in a stack like this:

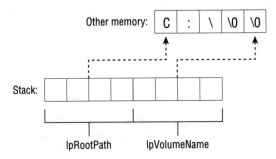

On the other hand, to pass a Null as the second argument, you want the stack to look like this:

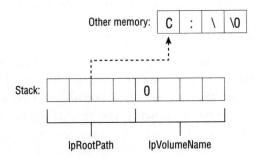

Notice that these two diagrams do not represent the same thing. The first stack passes a pointer to a null character, and the second stack passes a null pointer. How do you pass a null pointer? You pass the vbNullString constant as the second argument. VBA treats the vbNullString constant in a special way. It is a 4-byte-long zero, but no type checking is done on it when it is passed as a string argument. Because the second string argument is declared as being ByVal, passing vbNullString causes a 4-byte-long zero to be placed on the stack. To delete the volume label, you call SetVolumeLabel with:

```
Call SetVolumeLabel("C:\", vbNullString)
```

Unicode to ANSI and Back

The preceding discussion disregards one important subject about passing strings to DLL procedures: VBA stores strings internally as Unicode and converts those strings to ANSI at the time a DLL function call is made. *Unicode* is a character-encoding scheme that uses two bytes to represent each character, allowing representation of 65,536 different characters. The Unicode specification has assigned every character from every major language in the world to one of the Unicode values. ANSI uses only one byte per character and can represent only 256 different characters.

Internally, VBA represents every string in Unicode format. Whenever you make a call to a DLL, VBA intercepts the call if any argument is a string or a user-defined structure that contains a string. VBA creates a temporary buffer, converts the strings from Unicode into ANSI, and places the results in the temporary buffer. Then the pointers are fixed up to point to the converted strings in the temporary buffers. When the function returns, all strings are converted back from ANSI to Unicode before VBA returns control to you.

This conversion from ANSI to Unicode has several implications:

- You must never try to represent binary information within strings if you intend to pass these strings to DLL functions. If the information isn't human readable as ANSI characters, you must pass an array of bytes. That's why VBA introduced the Byte datatype.

- You must call functions that expect ANSI strings. Any Win32 function that has strings as parameters comes in two versions. One ends in the letter "A" and accepts ANSI strings as arguments. The other ends in the letter "W" (for Wide) and accepts Unicode arguments. You must always call the function that ends in the letter "A". Typically, the Declare statement specifies an Alias clause that defines the "A" version to be a generic name without either the "A" or "W". For example, GetWindowText is aliased to be the function GetWindowTextA within the DLL.

- VBA not only translates string arguments passed directly, it translates strings defined in user-defined types.

TIP
If you receive the error message "DLL function not found" when trying to use a DLL function, check to see whether the function uses string arguments. If so, you must specify the ANSI version of the function using an Alias clause.

Using the Any Datatype

Certain API calls require different types of arguments, depending on how they are called. For example, the WinHelp function is defined in the C programming language like this:

```
BOOL WinHelp
    (
    HWND hwnd,            // handle of window requesting Help
    LPCTSTR lpszHelp,     // address of directory-path string
    UINT wCommand,        // type of Help
    DWORD dwData          // additional data
    );
```

The first two arguments are the hWnd of the parent window and the name of the help file. The wCommand argument defines what you want Windows to do with the help file. How the WinHelp function uses the dwData argument depends on which constant you passed in for the wCommand argument. Two possible values for the wCommand argument are described in the following table:

wCommand	dwData	Meaning
HELP_CONTEXT	Unsigned Long Integer containing the context number for the topic	Displays the topic identified by a context number that has been defined in the [MAP] section of the help project file
HELP_PARTIALKEY	Long pointer to a string that contains a keyword for the requested topic	Displays the topic in the keyword list that matches the keyword passed in the dwData parameter, if there is one exact match. If there is more than one match, it displays the Search dialog box with the topics listed in the Go To box. If there is no match, it displays the Search dialog box
		If you just want to bring up the Search dialog box without passing a keyword (the third result), use a long pointer to an empty string

This presents a problem: HELP_CONTEXT wants a Long passed by value on the stack, whereas HELP_PARTIALKEY wants a string passed by reference; the way you call the function determines the datatype of the last argument. How can you declare the function so it allows both choices? The answer is the *Any* datatype. The Any datatype tells VBA that at the time you declare the function, you don't know what the datatype is or how big it is. It defers supplying this information until you call the procedure. This removes compile-time type checking, so all the responsibility for passing reasonable arguments is in your court: you must make sure you actually pass reasonable data to the DLL call. The declaration for this function would be

```
Public Declare Function WinHelp _
 Lib "User32" Alias "WinHelpA" _
 (ByVal hwnd As Long, _
 ByVal lpszHelp As String, _
 ByVal wCommand As Long, _
 dwData As Any) As Long
```

Notice that the datatype for the dwData argument is Any and that it is not declared using ByVal. At the time the function is called, you need to provide VBA with three pieces of information:

- The datatype of the argument

- Whether that datatype should be passed by value or by reference

- The contents of the argument

Notice that you can include ByVal or ByRef in both the Declare statement and the call. Whatever you use in the call overrides what is in the Declare statement.

You can call this function in two ways:

```
lngRet = WinHelp(Me.hwnd, Me.HelpFile, HELP_CONTEXT, ByVal 3&)
lngRet = WinHelp(Me.hwnd, Me.HelpFile, HELP_PARTIALKEY, _
 ByVal "FindThis")
```

The HELP_CONTEXT call to WinHelp passes a "ByVal 3&" in the dwData argument. This provides VBA with the following information:

- The information is to be passed by value.

- Four bytes are to be placed onto the stack.

- The contents of the four bytes should be the value 3.

The ByVal indicates that the argument is passed by value. The ampersand (&) is an indication that the constant is a Long, not an Integer. Without the ampersand, only two bytes would be placed on the stack, whereas the function wants four.

The second example, using the HELP_PARTIALKEY command, provides WinHelp with the following information:

- The information is to be passed by reference.

- The information is a string.

- The string should be converted from a BSTR to an LPSTR.

All strings are passed by reference, and the datatype of the argument is a string constant. The ByVal here performs the conversion between the BSTR and the LPSTR. Because a ByVal wasn't included in the Declare statement for this argument, the ByVal is required in the call statement.

Use the Any datatype carefully; when you use this type, VBA is unable to do type checking at compile time. As an alternative, consider declaring the procedure multiple times using different names and specific datatypes. For example, the following code declares two versions of the WinHelp function, one that accepts a Long value and one that accepts a String value in the dwData argument:

```
Public Declare Function WinHelpContext _
  Lib "User32" Alias "WinHelpA _
  (ByVal hwnd As Long, _
  ByVal lpszHelp As String, _
  ByVal uCommand As Long, _
  ByVal dwData As Long) As Long

Public Declare Function WinHelpPartialKey _
  Lib "User32" Alias "WinHelpA" _
  (ByVal hwnd As Long, _
  ByVal lpszHelp As String, _
  ByVal uCommand As Long, _
  ByVal dwData As String) As Long
```

Using Err.LastDLLError

When you call a Windows API call from Visual Basic, it's always possible that the call will fail. The function indicates this failure by returning some special value, such as 0 or False. When you are using the Windows API from C, you can then call a function named GetLastError to find out why it failed. Unfortunately, calling GetLastError from VBA doesn't report accurate results. The reason is that VBA itself is also doing Windows API calls. By the time you get a chance to call GetLastError, VBA has already messed up the result GetLastError would have reported. To get around this problem, VBA implements the LastDLLError property of the Err object. This property is filled in with the error code of the last DLL call you made. You can use this property instead of calling GetLastError. For example:

```
fRet = SetVolumeLabel("C:\", vbNullString)
If Not fRet Then
    If Err.LastDllError = ERROR_INVALID_PARAMETER then
        MsgBox "Due to a Windows 95 bug, " & _
            "you can't delete the volume label."
    End If
End If
```

Using Callback Functions

A small percentage of the Windows functions require a callback function. A *callback* is a procedure *you* provide for *Windows* to call. Windows calls the callback multiple times, and with each call, Windows passes arguments that reference an object in an internal data structure. For example, a call to the EnumWindows function requires a callback. The callback function is called once for each top-level window currently open and is passed a handle to it, until they have all been enumerated. In the C declaration, the argument in which you indicate the address of the callback has the datatype FARPROC or CALLBACK.

Because VBA cannot intrinsically handle callback functions, there are several ways to handle external functions that require callbacks:

- You can write a DLL that contains a function that can be used for the callback.

- You can use an ActiveX control that already has the callback function written for you. The ActiveX callback procedure will have to generate an event when Windows calls it.

- Visual Basic 5 adds the CallBack keyword to the language, allowing you to effectively pass the address of a VBA procedure to the Windows API. Unfortunately, this technique does not work in VBA 5.0.

User-Defined Types and DWORD Packing

When VBA passes a user-defined type to a DLL, it refuses to allow any particular declaration within the structure to cross a DWORD (4-byte) boundary. Instead, it pads out bytes so that the next definition starts on a DWORD boundary. This means that if you compile your own DLL, you must either provide that padding yourself or use the Struct Member Alignment option the C compiler provides. For example, if you have a structure that looks like this:

```
Type TESTSTRUCT
    intTest As Integer
    bytTest As Byte
    lngTest As Long
End Type
```

the structure in memory is represented like this:

```
intTest
bytTest
One byte of padding to make the lngTest align to a DWORD boundary
lngTest
```

so the structure takes up 8 bytes in memory. If, instead, the structure is arranged like this:

```
Type TESTSTRUCT
    bytTest As Byte
    lngTest As Long
    intTest As Integer
End Type
```

it is padded out to look like this in memory:

```
bytTest
Three bytes of padding
lngTest
intTest
Two bytes of padding
```

and thus it takes up 12 bytes in memory.

If the DLL is compiled with the Struct Member Alignment option, the C compiler provides the appropriate padding to make the structure members line up with the way the structure is passed from VBA. On the other hand, you would be better off arranging the elements within the structure so they are DWORD aligned to begin with.

This implicit padding that VBA provides does not cause a problem with the Windows API, because the API structures have been DWORD aligned, but it can cause a problem if you use other DLLs. If the DLL is not compiled with the Struct Member Alignment option and has elements that cross DWORD boundaries, you cannot pass the bytes in the correct arrangement without doing a very tricky manipulation of the bytes within the structure.

Converting Windows API Calls from 16-Bit Versions of Basic

If you are converting code from a 16-bit Basic host (such as Access 2.0), you'll need to revisit all your Windows API calls; many of them have changed. At a minimum, you'll have to update the Declare statements to refer to 32-bit DLLs and, possibly, adjust those requiring String arguments so that ANSI DLL functions are used. This is a significant amount of work.

Windows API calls come in five classes when ported to Win32:

- Calls that merely have to reference the Win32 libraries instead of the Win16 libraries

- Calls that must be modified to use the ANSI versions of Win32 API functions

- Calls that now have additional functionality under Win32

- Calls that have a new, extended version (such as GetWindowExt, which now has the extended version GetWindowExtEx).

- Calls that are not supported under Win32

Use the following steps as a guideline to make the conversion:

1. Start by finding each of your Declare statements in existing code.

2. Look in the Win32 documentation to determine in which one of the four classes of conversions the call falls.

3. Replace the Declare statement with the new Declare statement (unless the call is no longer supported in Win32).

4. Examine every function call to your Windows API calls. Make sure the arguments match the datatype of the parameters in the Declare statement. A great many of the arguments will need to be changed from Integers to Longs. Make sure these changes propagate throughout your code.

5. Save your application and make a backup copy.

6. Set a breakpoint on each of your API calls. Run your code. When you reach the breakpoint, verify that the arguments are both the correct value and the correct size. Then step through the call.

This is a lot of work, but it is absolutely necessary to get your code to work reliably under Win32.

Table B.2 lists many of the common 16-bit API calls and their replacements in Win32. The table is not exhaustive, but it may help with some of your conversions.

TABLE B.2   Some Windows 3.1 Calls That Need to Be Changed for Windows 95 or Windows NT

Win 16 Call	Replace with
GetAspectRatioFilter	GetAspectRatioFilterEx
GetBitmapDimension	GetBitmapDimensionEx
GetBrushOrg	GetBrushOrgEx
GetClassWord	GetClassLong
GetCurrentPosition	GetCurrentPositionEx
GetPrivateProfileInt	(VBA built-in function GetSetting)
GetPrivateProfileString	(VBA built-in function GetSetting or GetAllSettings)
GetTextExtent	GetTextExtentPoint
GetViewportExt	GetViewportExtEx
GetViewportOrg	GetViewportOrgEx

TABLE B.2   Some Windows 3.1 Calls That Need to Be Changed for Windows 95 or Windows NT (continued)

Win16 Call	Replace with
GetWindowExt	GetWindowExtEx
GetWindowOrg	GetWindowOrgEx
GetWindowWord	GetWindowLong
MoveTo	MoveToEx
OffsetViewportOrg	OffsetViewportOrgEx
OffsetWindowOrg	OffsetWindowOrgEx
ScaleViewportExt	ScaleViewportExtEx
ScaleWindowExt	ScaleWindowExtEx
SetBitmapDimension	SetBitmapDimensionEx
SetClassWord	SetClassLong
SetMetaFileBits	SetMetaFileBitsEx
SetViewportExt	SetViewportExtEx
SetViewportOrg	SetViewportOrgEx
SetWindowExt	SetWindowExtEx
SetWindowOrg	SetWindowdOrgEx
SetWindowWord	SetWindowLong
WritePrivateProfileString	(VBA built-in statement SaveSetting)
AccessResource	(Not available in Win32)
AllocDSToCSAlias	(Not available in Win32)
AllocResource	(Not available in Win32)

TABLE B.2   Some Windows 3.1 Calls That Need to Be Changed for Windows 95 or
Windows NT (continued)

Win16 Call	Replace with
AllocSelector	(Not available in Win32)
Catch	(Not available in Win32)
ChangeSelector	(Not available in Win32)
DefineHandleTable	(Not available in Win32)
FreeProcInstance	(Not available in Win32)
FreeSelector	(Not available in Win32)
GetCodeHandle	(Not available in Win32)
GetCodeInfo	(Not available in Win32)
GetCurrentPDB	(Not available in Win32)
GetEnvironment	(Not available in Win32)
GetFreeSpace	(Not available in Win32)
GetInstanceData	(Not available in Win32)
GetKBCodePage	(Not available in Win32)
GetModuleUsage	(Not available in Win32)
GlobalCompact	(Not available in Win32)
GlobalDOSAlloc	(Not available in Win32)
GlobalDOSFree	(Not available in Win32)
GlobalFix	(Not available in Win32)
GlobalNotify	(Not available in Win32)
GlobalPageLock	(Not available in Win32)

TABLE B.2 Some Windows 3.1 Calls That Need to Be Changed for Windows 95 or Windows NT (continued)

Win 16 Call	Replace with
GlobalUnfix	(Not available in Win32)
GlobalUnwire	(Not available in Win32)
IsGdiObject	(Not available in Win32)
IsTask	(Not available in Win32)
LocalCompact	(Not available in Win32)
LocalShrink	(Not available in Win32)
LockData	(Not available in Win32)
LockSegment	(Not available in Win32)
MakeProcInstance	(Not available in Win32)
NetBIOSCall	(Not available in Win32)
SetEnvironment	(Not available in Win32)
SetResourceHandler	(Not available in Win32)
SetSwapAreaSize	(Not available in Win32)
SwitchStackBack	(Not available in Win32)
SwitchStackTo	(Not available in Win32)
Throw	(Not available in Win32)
UnlockData	(Not available in Win32)
UnlockSegment	(Not available in Win32)
ValidateCodeSegments	(Not available in Win32)
ValidateFreeSpaces	(Not available in Win32)
Yield	(Not available in Win32)

Summary

This appendix has covered the following topics:

- Declaring a DLL procedure from VBA
- Specifying the arguments
- Understanding passing by value and passing by reference
- Converting C parameters into VBA declarations
- Using callback functions
- Returning strings from a DLL
- Understanding the Unicode-to-ANSI issue
- Using the vbNullString constant
- Using the Any datatype
- Passing a user-defined type to a DLL
- Working with user-defined types and DWORD packing
- Passing an array
- Using type libraries
- Using the Windows API
- Converting Windows API calls from 16-bit Basic

The DLL interface allows you to manipulate Windows directly through the Windows API, as well as to call your own DLLs. Combined with a C or C++ compiler and the appropriate knowledge, DLLs allow you to do virtually anything that is possible with Windows. However, even without the use of C or C++, the ability to call the Windows API vastly extends the power of VBA.

Note to the Reader: First level entries are in **bold**. Page numbers in **bold** indicate the principal discussion of a topic or the definition of a term. Page numbers in *italic* indicate illustrations.

NUMBERS AND SYMBOLS

A

B

C

E

I

J

K

O

P

Q

R

T

X

Y

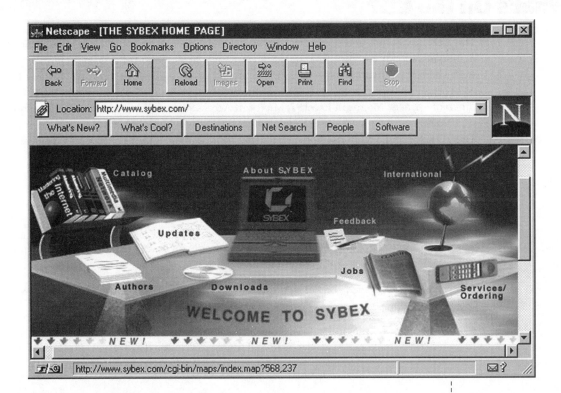

What's On the CD?

This CD is a valuable and necessary companion to the book. It provides a wealth of information in a readily usable format to aid in your VBA development efforts and it works with Microsoft Office 97, Visual Basic 5.0, or any other Visual Basic 5.0 host. We've included every significant example presented in the text, and provided the examples in three different formats: Microsoft Excel 97, Microsoft Access 97, and as individual text files. This way, you'll be able to find a convenient format no matter which VBA host you're using. The CD also includes information on licensing VBA, demonstrations of several VBA hosts, and a beta version of Microsoft's Visual Basic 5.0 Control Creation Edition (VB5CCE).

Here's just a sampling of what you'll find on the CD:

- Many useful functions demonstrating and extending the built-in VBA string, date, and numeric functions

- Class modules providing objects making it simple for you to work with CD players, WAV (sound) files, and AVI (movie) files

- Class modules providing objects that simplify the use of many system information API functions

- Class modules providing objects that allow you to represent the system registry as a hierarchy, making it simple to read and write items in the registry

- Functions and classes making it simple to work with disks and files

- A full running version of Visio Professional 4.5 (limited to 30 days from your first use)

- A demonstration version of Great Plains Software's Dynamics, a full-featured accounting package

- Demonstration versions of four ActiveX controls from VideoSoft, one of the leading producers of compelling add-on tools

For more information about the CD, including installation instructions, see the README.TXT file in the root folder of the CD.

Please note that if you use File Manager, Windows Explorer, or the DOS Copy command to copy the chapter files to your hard disk, the files will be marked as being read-only. You will need to change the file attributes before you can modify the files. To handle this problem in Windows Explorer, follow these steps:

1. Right click on the file or group of files

2. Select Properties from the pop-up menu

3. Clear (uncheck) the Read-only attribute check box

If you use the DOS XCOPY32 command to move the files, the files will not be marked as read-only.